W9-BCB-599

Praise for *Fire and Fortitude*

"This eloquent and powerful narrative is military history written the way it should be. John C. McManus has seamlessly blended the strategic and tactical story with deep analysis of the political context and social composition of armies that embodied the cultures of the nations from which they were formed. During the two years covered by this book, American forces in the Pacific theater transitioned from fighting on a shoestring defensive to the beginning of mighty offensives that would prove irreversible."

—James M. McPherson, Pulitzer Prize–winning author of *Battle Cry of Freedom*

"From the burning waters of Pearl Harbor to the sweltering jungles of Guadalcanal and the icy shores of Alaska's Aleutian Islands, *Fire and Fortitude* is a heart-pounding journey through the tragedies and the triumphs of the Pacific. Historian John C. McManus, armed with an incredible eye for detail and the deft touch of a novelist, has crafted one of the finest epics of World War II."

—James M. Scott, Pulitzer Prize finalist and author of *Target Tokyo* and *Rampage*

"A very fine account of war in the Pacific founded on wide research and excellent judgment."

—Antony Beevor, *New York Times* bestselling author of *D-Day: The Battle for Normandy* and *Ardennes 1944: The Battle of the Bulge*

"John McManus, one of America's great historians, has written a masterpiece. From the red light district in Honolulu just hours before the attack on Pearl Harbor to the nearly forgotten assault on fiercely defended Makin Island, *Fire and Fortitude* is a long-overdue saga of the US Army's punishing fight in the Pacific. McManus brilliantly transports the reader back in time, offering new information and dazzling analysis in this groundbreaking narrative."

—Patrick K. O'Donnell, author of *The Unknowns: The Untold Story of America's Unknown Soldier and WWI's Most Decorated Heroes Who Brought Him Home*

"In this compelling narrative, John McManus does for the US Army in the Pacific what Rick Atkinson did for the Army in Europe: chronicle its growth and transformation from a small, insular, pre-war constabulary into an enormous and efficient fighting machine. In the process he deftly profiles the leaders and captures all of the human drama of the Pacific War."

—Craig L. Symonds, Lincoln Prize–winning author of *World War II at Sea*

"Army ground troops constituted by far the largest element of American military forces arrayed against Japan in the Pacific War, yet their efforts have been overshadowed in the popular American memory by the achievements of the Marines and the Navy. John C. McManus's exhaustively researched and highly readable book goes far to redress the balance. In many ways his treatment of the Army in the war against Japan may well be compared to Rick Atkinson's work on the Army in the European theater."

—Ronald Spector, author of *Eagle Against the Sun: The American War with Japan*

ALSO BY JOHN C. McMANUS

Hell Before Their Very Eyes:
American Soldiers Liberate Concentration Camps in Germany, April 1945

The Dead and Those About to Die:
D-Day: The Big Red One at Omaha Beach

September Hope:
The American Side of a Bridge Too Far

Grunts:
Inside the American Infantry Combat Experience, World War II Through Iraq

American Courage, American Carnage:
The 7th Infantry Regiment's Combat Experience, 1812 Through World War II

The 7th Infantry Regiment:
Combat in the Age of Terror, the Korean War Through the Present

U.S. Military History for Dummies

Alamo in the Ardennes:
The Untold Story of the American Soldiers Who Made the Defense
of Bastogne Possible

The Americans at Normandy:
The Summer of 1944—The American War from the Normandy Beaches
to Falaise

The Americans at D-Day:
The American Experience at the Normandy Invasion

Deadly Sky:
The American Combat Airman in World War II

The Deadly Brotherhood:
The American Combat Soldier in World War II

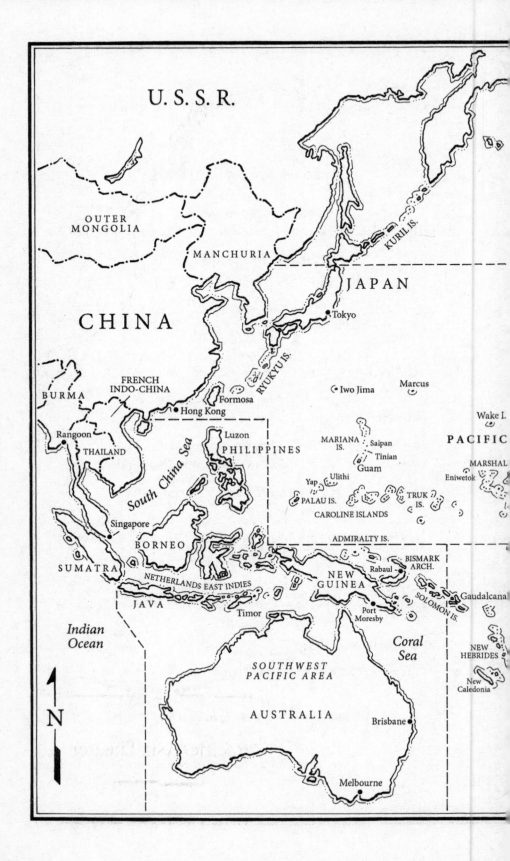

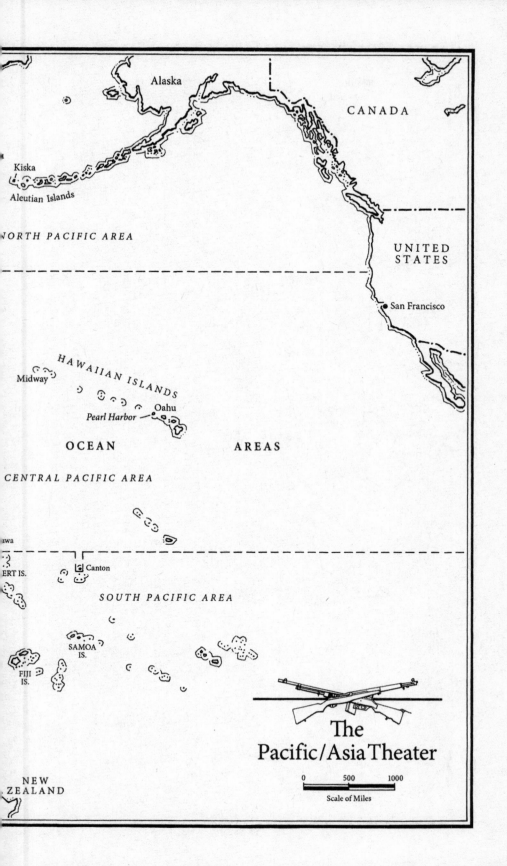

The
Pacific/Asia Theater

Scale of Miles

0   500   1000

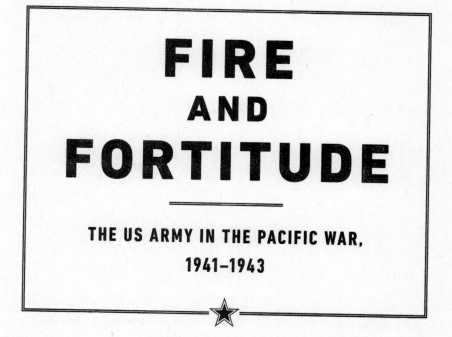

FIRE
AND
FORTITUDE

THE US ARMY IN THE PACIFIC WAR,
1941–1943

JOHN C. McMANUS

CALIBER

CALIBER

An imprint of Penguin Random House LLC
penguinrandomhouse.com

LIBRARY OF CONGRESS CATALOGING-IN-PUBLICATION DATA
Names: McManus, John C., 1965– author.
Title: Fire and fortitude: the US Army in the Pacific War, 1941–1943 / John C. McManus.
Other titles: US Army in the Pacific War, 1941–1943
Description: First edition. | New York, New York: Dutton Caliber, an imprint of Penguin Random House LLC, [2019] | Includes bibliographical references and index.
Identifiers: LCCN 2018037343| ISBN 9780451475046 (hardcover) | ISBN 9780698192768 (ebook)
Subjects: LCSH: World War, 1939-1945—Campaigns—Pacific Area. | United States. Army—History—World War, 1939-1945.
Classification: LCC D767 .M36 2019 | DDC 940.54/26—dc23 LC record available at https://lccn.loc.gov/2018037343

Printed in the United States of America
1   3   5   7   9   10   8   6   4   2

To Nancy, with all my love.

To my incredible parents, Michael and Mary Jane McManus,

and to Ruth and Nelson, who have treated me as their son.

Contents

FIRE
AND
FORTITUDE

Author's Note

Most Pacific theater events and operations took place on the other side of the international date line from North America. Thus, all dates and times in this series are local to the action.

To avoid confusion between morning and afternoon times, this book employs the twenty-four-hour military clock. For instance, 8:00 A.M. is 0800; 2:00 P.M. is 1400, and so on.

In the Japanese and Chinese languages, surnames are listed before given names, e.g., Tōjō Hideki rather than Hideki Tōjō. This is the exact opposite of Western practice. Because this is a work written in the English language, Japanese and Chinese names will be listed in the Western style, except with individuals, like Chiang Kai-shek or Mao Zedong, whose names are widely known in their correct cultural format.

The terms "Jap" and "Nip" are largely viewed today as racist and offensive. During World War II, however, they were used so commonly among Americans, Australians, and Britons—even generals and policy makers—as to take on the status of mundane slang. As such, I will make no attempt to excise the terms from this volume. In no way does this indicate my acceptance or approval of these pejorative words.

Throughout the series the terms "Pacific War" and "Pacific/Asia War" are interchangeable.

All rank designations are current. While many soldiers were promoted several times in the course of the war, I use a person's rank at the appropriate time frame. For instance, Douglas MacArthur began the war as a lieutenant general. In the passages that cover this phase of his life, I refer to him as a lieutenant general. Later, he was promoted to four- and five-star rank. Thus in subsequent chapters, I recognize his new ranks and refer to him appropriately.

The term "native" to describe peoples of Asia, the Pacific Islands, Melanesia, and the like is, in my view, an inappropriate, patronizing, and somewhat dehumanizing legacy of colonialism. After all, one does not refer to someone from France or Poland as a "native," so why would one use the term to describe someone from Burma or Guadalcanal? Thus, this book eschews the term "native" in favor of appropriate local or ethnic designations. The exception, of course, is in quotes from contemporary sources.

There are many versions and dialects of Chinese (Mandarin, Cantonese, etc.). Thus names, places, and terms can have strikingly different English translations, e.g., Chiang Kai-shek versus Jiang Jie-shī. This series employs the most commonly known version of names, places, and terms.

Prologue

T he letters arrived in droves. Most were handwritten, in cursive, on simple, blank stationery. Usually two pages long, the paragraphs were well structured and the spelling generally correct, something of an accomplishment under the circumstances. Blue was the predominant color of the ink, as if only this shade could actually convey the deep emotions of the moment. The letters originated from a dizzying array of American places, prominent and not so prominent: Tererro, New Mexico; Cary, North Carolina; Pocahontas, Illinois; Mountain City, Nevada; Brownsdale, Minnesota; Arco, Georgia; Fort Smith, Arkansas; mixed in with Kansas City, Philadelphia, Chicago, Detroit, and Los Angeles. The varied geography hardly mattered. The commonality of the letter writers' shared experience mattered a lot, probably even more than any of them could grasp at the time. Many of them were middle-aged or older, the graceful loops of motherly handwriting somehow easily distinguishable from the clumsier, blockier writing of the fathers (an odd but readily identifiable distinction between most female and male handwriting that remains no less a mystery today).

The addressee was almost always Major General Paul Mueller, commander of the 81st Infantry Division, whose outfit had just taken Angaur, a tiny limestone island, all of three square miles in size, located in the Palau Islands. Angaur was roughly 5,142 miles from San Francisco, 600 miles from Manila, and, perhaps of most significance, 1,400 miles from Tokyo. It was also 8,017 miles from Philadelphia and 7,233 miles from Pocahontas, Illinois, something the letter writers who came from these places may or may not have known. Regardless, the place was distant, alien, anonymous, and seemingly insignificant. Except that it was not. The sons, brothers, and husbands of those mournful writers all experienced their last moments of life on Angaur. In total, there were 264 of them. Most were buried on the island, in a carefully plotted temporary cemetery, lovingly and respectfully maintained by their comrades. Each grave was marked with a small, inscribed wooden cross. Like a faithful sentinel, a modest chapel loomed over the rows of crosses.

At Mueller's behest, division photographers took snapshots of the grave sites and mailed them to the next of kin. In response, the family members wrote scores of appreciative letters, expressing the full range of human emotion in time of loss. Mrs. Alice Rathburn, lamenting the death of her youngest son, Tommy, wrote that "it was an awful blow but I'm trying to not let it get the best of me. It is awful hard though. I had looked forward to when this war would end and we could be together, for I'm a widow and his homecoming would of [sic] meant so much to me. Now it can never be." Some, like Mary Cann, sister of Lieutenant Joseph Cann, a twenty-seven-year-old artillery officer who was killed by a sniper, found some comfort in religious devotion. "Upheld by our Christian faith," she wrote of her family, "the grief has been mitigated by our belief in his present safety and happiness under our Supreme Commander." Mrs. Marie Heuton, wife of Donald, was disappointed in the paucity of personal effects she received after his death. "Nothing could have made me more blue. All I got was a barracks bag, tie, baseball glove and a few other odds and ends." She wondered, apparently in vain, over the whereabouts of his wallet and personal pictures. The mother of Private First Class (PFC) Leon Vaughn was proud of his courage in carrying out the mission that cost his life. "I can hardly realize it's true. Like all mothers I worshiped my son."

Many others wondered about the last words or the last actions of loved ones. "I would love so much to know if he died conscious of his condition," Mrs. Florence Gose, wrote of her son Kenneth, "please tell how I can find out." Lieutenant Colonel P. M. Hickcox, the division chaplain, obligingly replied that Kenneth had been shot to death while serving as a litter bearer. "The shot was true and Kenneth pitched forward to the ground. Medical aid was summoned but Kenneth did not speak a word. Death was practically instantaneous and there was no evidence that he knew of his condition or suffered at all." Edith Wilson, who had just lost a son killed in Italy, was devastated by the death of her other son, PFC Carl Wilson, on Angaur, though she took solace in the fact that at least she knew where he was buried. "Carl was a grand boy and I just can't hardley [sic] believe they both have been taken from me." Mrs. Anna Clapper was the widow of a World War I veteran. Her son PFC Drexel Clapper was badly wounded on the first day of the invasion and evacuated to a hospital ship, where he died.

His loss nearly took away her will to go on living. "There are no words in my heart that I could write because life seems worthless without my Boy." She proudly affixed a gold star—a universal symbol during the war for the death of a loved one—next to her signature.

Tech Sergeant Tom Bouldin's older sister Adeline, who had practically raised him, could not help but feel anger at the Japanese who had killed him. "I am proud of the fact that he did his bit in helping us to defeat the fiendish Japs—and they will be defeated." Mrs. B. H. Weathers's son John, a young sergeant, had died a hero's death. As he and PFC John White manned a foxhole along their company perimeter one night, a Japanese soldier snuck up and threw a grenade into the hole. "Sgt Weathers reached for it to throw it out, when the grenade exploded and tore his hand off and inflicted deep multiple shrapnel wounds in his side," his commanding officer, Lieutenant Burnie Rye, wrote. Weathers bled to death in the hole. His actions had saved PFC White's life. White was wounded but stayed with the body of his dead sergeant all night until he was evacuated to a hospital the next day. Chaplain Hickcox made a special effort to put Mrs. Weathers in touch with White, and, in a personal letter, the clergyman reassured her that his assistant, a Baptist minister, had officiated her son's funeral at the cemetery. In a memorial address, General Mueller referred to the grave sites as "a place to which our hearts can turn in memory of fallen comrades, and more, perhaps, as an expression to their sorrowing homes that we hold these heroic dead in highest admiration and esteem."[1]

Surely not even one of the more than two hundred men who ended up in that hallowed spot could ever have envisioned, in their happier peacetime days, dying on a remote island called Angaur. The same was of course true for their loved ones and, indeed, for the nation that sent them to fight in such an anonymous locale, a place of tropical shadows, timelessly obscured by its very remoteness. The reverential cultural memory afforded to the Americans who lost their lives at such places as Bunker Hill, Gettysburg, and Normandy would elude the men who reposed beneath those crosses on that Lilliputian island. Indeed, such enduring fame would elude most all Americans who have died in time of war at less iconic places, but especially those who fought World War II in the Pacific. Angaur was just one of the countless many battlefields where Americans fought and died in an existential war against Japan, from Attu to Guadalcanal to Aitape to Morotai to Leyte to Myitkyina to Okinawa and beyond; battles fought over an expanse of ocean, island, and landmass encompassing nearly a third of the earth's surface; battles fought and won by an army better known for its victories in Europe. Cole Kingseed once argued persuasively that five factors contributed to the greater prominence of the Army's war in Europe over the Pacific: the Germany-first strategy that dictated Allied priority of resources and thus the entire course of World War II; the maritime nature of the Pacific struggle, leading historians to a naval-dominated narrative; the cult of personality surrounding General Douglas MacArthur, who, by his own design, absorbed almost all accolades to himself rather than to the soldiers who did the real fighting; unbalanced press coverage by correspondents who found Europe a far easier, and more hospitable, place from which to report than the wilds of the Pacific; and the troubling racial savagery that characterized the war from start to finish. The chaotic and tragic debacles of multiple early Allied defeats have undoubtedly also contributed to this obscurity. After all, Americans never suffered any defeat at the hands of the Germans to equate with the Japanese conquest of the Philippines in 1942. Moreover, the brutal, unfettered manner in which both sides fought the Pacific/Asia War hardly lends itself to a popular good-versus-evil narrative (though unquestionably the United States attempted to adhere to some semblance of humane war-making far more than did its adversary).[2]

Ironically, from the nineteenth century onward, the United States and Japan enjoyed reasonably friendly relations in the early and later stages of their mutual acquaintance. But in between, from the early decades of the twentieth century and culminating with nearly four years of bitter warfare almost unprecedented in its shocking brutality, they engaged in a struggle for the very soul of both nations. It was a multilayered war as much about geopolitics as it was about economics, nationalism, colonialism, and moralism. It was a war that required the full exertion of American manpower, technology, and industrial power, particularly in relation to the mobilization of extraordinarily powerful armed forces. It was a war that saw the time-honored codes of warriors—on both sides—clash with the technological, desperate expedience of modern conflict. The war was characterized by courage, firepower, tenacity, logistics, transportation, medicine, interspecies struggle, race hatred, technology, intelligence, subterfuge, guerrilla nationalism, aviation, sea power, modern propaganda, and especially the terrible enervation of ground combat, arguably the key tipping point in the war's outcome.

And on the American side, the land war was fought primarily by the

Army, though popular memory has focused almost exclusively on the comparatively smaller Marine effort. The Corps made fifteen amphibious combat landings over the course of the entire war. In the spring of 1945, Lieutenant General Robert Eichelberger's 8th Army alone carried out thirty-five amphibious landings over a five-week period in the Philippines. At full strength, and at its largest size ever, the Marine Corps mobilized six combat divisions, comprising about a quarter million troops in theater, all of which were fully dependent on the Navy and the Army for logistical support, since the Corps was designed to function as an expeditionary fighting force, not a self-sustaining military organization. The Army deployed twenty-one infantry and airborne divisions, plus several more regimental combat teams and tank battalions whose manpower equated to three or four more divisions. In addition, the Army handled enormous logistical, transportation, intelligence, medical, and engineering responsibilities (not to mention aviation, a huge topic worthy of its own series but beyond the scope of this one).

By the summer of 1945, 1,804,408 ground soldiers were serving somewhere in the Pacific or Asia. They were part of the third largest land force ever fielded in American history, behind only the European theater armies in World Wars I and II. Though soldiers comprised the main American ground force in the war against Japan, they sometimes felt like junior partners to the more famous Marines. "Out here, mention is seldom seen of the achievements of the Army ground troops," Major General Oscar Griswold, a corps commander, wrote from the South Pacific to a colleague in the fall of 1943, "whereas the Marines are blown up to the skies." To a generation of Americans reared in a mass media culture and for whom the notion of recognition, or credit, for a job well done was of crucial importance, this perception could be corrosive. Paul Fussell, a keenly insightful commentator on World War II American culture, and a combat veteran of the ground war in Europe, opined that for soldiers the ultimate purpose of their dangerous efforts was often the value they ascribed to "the distant, credulous hometown audience for whom one performs by means of letterpress rather than by one's nearby equals who know what the real criteria are. That all-important hometown audience the troops never forgot."

With this ephemeral goal as the measuring stick of worth, the Army often came up short during the war with Japan, and certainly in posterity's view of that war. For some, this led to anger and resentment against Marines as glory hounds with an overactive publicity machine. "The Marines are so hopped up with their publicity—someone has to fight them and I'm the guy," one junior officer huffed in a 1944 letter to his family. Another wrote wearily from Saipan, "Our men are getting awfully tired of reading about the exploits of the marines out here. We have been able on many occasions to identify pictures of 'Marines' in action as being pictures of army troops. The standing joke now is that the Marines' secret weapon is the Army." This anger against a sister service—Marines and soldiers had much more in common than otherwise—was ultimately pointless and counterproductive. The Marine Corps comprised only 5 percent of the US armed forces in World War II and yet Marines suffered 10 percent of all American battle casualties, including more than nineteen thousand fatalities, so the Corps more than earned its vaunted reputation for valor, a fact that most soldiers recognized. If history is to assign something like credit for American ground victory in the Pacific/Asia theater, it properly belongs to both services, with the Army nonetheless playing a significantly larger role. By design, the Army did the vast majority of the planning, the supplying, the transporting, the engineering, the fighting, and the dying to win a war whose end represented a tremendous American triumph as well as a disquieting harbinger with ominous undertones for the American future.[3]

The unglamorous locales, from the jungles of New Guinea, Guadalcanal, and Mindanao to the frozen valleys of Attu, the rocky caves of Biak and Peleliu, the ruined metropolitan blocks of Manila and Cebu City, the grassy hills of Guam and the mind-numbing ridges and peaks of Burma, carried with them a troubling whiff of clairvoyance. "This is the Pacific, WWII, all over again," Stanley "Swede" Larsen, who served in the Second World War with the 25th Infantry Division, wrote from Vietnam in 1965 to one of his former World War II commanders. Now a general, Larsen saw "the same shortages, same malaria problems, personnel headaches, transportation bottlenecks etc. Little . . . could I have guessed exactly 20 years ago that we would go full circle and be back at the same game, in the same part of the world."

Indeed, as Larsen indicated, the battlegrounds of the Pacific, and the war itself, hinted strongly at the patterns of succeeding history, especially for the Army, which, as an institution, shaped much of that history. The fact that the Army bore the brunt of the ground fighting against Japan was by no means a singular occurrence. In fact, it was a true indicator of what was to come. Since World War II, the Army has not only done most of the *ground* fighting—with a strong assist from the Marine Corps—but it has also done the vast majority of America's fighting *altogether*. From Korea to Afghanistan, more than 90 percent of American wartime casualties have been suffered by ground troops, most of whom were Army soldiers and most of whom were killed, wounded, or captured somewhere in Asia. With the exception of brief expeditions in Grenada, Panama, and Somalia, every subsequent war involving Army conventional forces has been fought somewhere on or near the Asian landmass. It is also worth noting that all of this happened at a time when the advent of nuclear weapons (another harbinger unleashed by the Pacific War) and enormous advances in technology were supposed to make the average ground soldier obsolete.[4]

In the Pacific, the Army glimpsed so many more of its future challenges and trends. Examples abound. Soldiers sometimes fought as guerrilla warriors. In many instances, they mobilized local insurgents to fight the Japanese, just as Special Forces would later do in many places around the globe. In this shadow war fought largely in the Philippines and Burma, Americans often had to immerse themselves into exotic cultures, gain the trust of local leaders, and think as a local might, not a Westerner. Similarly, Army soldiers, from New Caledonia to Okinawa, had to learn to develop productive relationships with a dizzying assortment of ethnic groups, tribes, and small countries, not dissimilar to the cross-cultural diplomacy of the Cold War era and the twenty-first century.

Winston Churchill once famously quipped, "There is at least one thing worse than fighting with allies and that is to fight without them." The last time the United States fought a war with no allies was in 1898 against Spain. In the Pacific, the Army fought alongside a variety of partners, most notably Australia, Britain, and China. The Army's relationship with the Australians and the British was at times surprisingly contentious, at least for such culturally similar, long-standing allies. The alliance with Chiang Kai-shek's China stands as perhaps the most flawed and ill-fated in all of American history. The Americans, mainly through the person of Lieutenant General Joseph Stilwell, experienced the enormous frustration of latching themselves to a corrupt, repressive, and maddeningly inefficient regime, one with a voracious appetite for lend-lease support but little inclination to fight the way the Americans wanted them to against the common enemy. For the Army, China would turn into a witch's brew of cultural misunderstandings, byzantine politics, command-inspired backbiting, and willful self-deception (primarily on the part of the American government and general public). It was a frightening foreshadowing of future experiences with many other defective, and corruptive, American alliances, most notably the partnership with South Vietnam.

The challenging conditions of the Pacific War—weather, terrain, poor infrastructure—were nearly unprecedented in American history. With the exception of one cold-weather campaign in the Aleutian Islands, heat was the prevailing pattern. Steamy weather, torrential rain, jungles, coral-ringed beaches, mountains, ridges, deep valleys, lack of roads, harbors, airfields—they all presented enormous challenges, as they would again in such places as Southeast Asia, where the American military would expend enormous resources to build a sustaining infrastructure, and Afghanistan, where the Americans would largely be dependent on perilous roads controlled at times by their veritable enemies and massive friendly airlifts from other bases in the region. Thus, the challenges of engineering, logistics, and transportation for the Army in the Pacific were nearly overwhelming. The vast distances and uncongenial, unfamiliar places practically guaranteed serious issues.

The stressful problem of supplying such a massive effort and fighting a desperate war against a courageous, well-trained foe sorely tested the competence of Army generals. A fascinating coterie of personalities emerged as the lead actors of this enormous human drama: Douglas MacArthur, a military autocrat often driven by his dysfunctional lust for fame and political power; Robert Eichelberger, sensitive and vainglorious but probably the finest commander in the theater, consigned to obscurity by MacArthur's jealous vanity; Walter Krueger, a self-made German immigrant whose brusque, occasionally thoughtless exterior masked a deeply thoughtful personality; Griswold, the calm, clear-eyed corps commander who always seemed to get the toughest, dirtiest missions; Alexander "Sandy" Patch, admired by his men and a consistent winner, the only general to serve as a division and corps commander in one theater and an army commander in another; Stilwell, rough-hewn, constitutionally incapable of dishonesty, brave, adventurous, culturally savvy, yet devoid of diplomatic skills and any semblance of sensitivity to human foibles; division commanders, like Joseph Lawton Collins, Joe Swing, Roscoe Woodruff, Andrew Bruce, and Verne Mudge, who seemed to thrive under the worst of situations, in contrast to Edwin Forrest Harding, Horace Fuller, Ralph Smith, and Albert Burfey Brown, all of whom ended up as tragic figures destroyed by the war's ruthless demands.

The vast majority of these generals, and thousands of other Army leaders at all levels, had to learn how to work closely with the other services, an issue that would become increasingly more important in the decades that followed. Soldiers often fought shoulder to shoulder with the Marine Corps. The Army was heavily dependent upon the Navy for transportation, supplies, and fire support. Indeed, Navy leaders understandably thought of the Pacific as their theater. The Army's commanders largely had to accommodate their naval cousins or risk abject failure. Not quite as challenging, but still problematic, was the job of coordinating with the Army Air Force, nominally part of the same Army but already with one foot out the door to eventual independence. So important was airpower to every aspect of the Pacific War that ground campaigns were often fought primarily to gain control of airfields. Ultimately, though, the Army's generals had to make their aerial and naval colleagues understand that the war could never be won until the enemy was defeated on the ground—a tricky diplomatic task during a time of burgeoning American naval and airpower. Thus, the challenges faced by leaders were immense and the lessons they learned timeless.

The character of the combat itself was eerily prescient of what was to come. While it is true that US wars against Native Americans, Filipino insurgents, and, occasionally, between Americans themselves during the Civil War and Reconstruction were fought with shocking brutality, the Pacific War nonetheless represented a landmark moment in the nature of American conflict. The United States had never experienced a declared war that was fought with so little in the way of established rules and such a dearth of humanity. Ever since, America's opponents have fought with similarly few scruples—quite unapologetically—and no acknowledgment of Western-style rules or restrictions. As did the Japanese, the North Koreans, the Chinese, the Vietcong/North Vietnamese Army, the Baathist Iraqi Army, the Fedayeen Saddam, the Taliban, Al-Qaeda in Iraq all comported themselves with vicious, calculated brutality. In all instances, their abysmal treatment of prisoners bordered on the surreal. The Americans, in turn, attempted to impart their own views of idealistic, legalistic warfare into each conflict but were forced to face their own hypocrisies and moral contradictions. Though this was true of the Pacific War, few Americans thought of it as such at the time, mainly because of the war's overwhelming popularity and the obvious threat posed by Japan. Make no mistake, though. The enormous cost of winning the war, in a spiritual rather than just a material or industrial sense, required Americans to glimpse into this troubling heart of darkness. The Japanese could not be defeated within the same set of rules that the Army had observed while beating the kaiser's Germany (and, for that matter, Hitler's Germany), the imperial Spanish, the Confederacy, Santa Anna's Mexico, and even imperial Britain. The clash with Japan was certainly ideological, as it had been with some of these other opponents. But it was also cultural, as it would be, at least in part, with future antagonists.

American material and technological superiority unquestionably aided Allied victory against Japan, so much so that it has sometimes led to a wrongheaded conventional wisdom that such economic superiority made the victory inevitable, or at least was the deciding factor in the war. "In the end it was superior American industrial power and organizational ability which had succeeded," one of the Pacific War's ablest chroniclers explained in an influential summation. But, in reality, victory demanded far more from the American nation than prodigious production. It required fighting at its most elemental and unforgiving level, fighting of a sort that is incomprehensible to those who haven't experienced it—a kill-or-be-killed mentality reflecting the will to destroy an opponent, strip him to his very core, bludgeon him into a supine state of total vulnerability. American soldiers were willing to fight this way, in some of the most inhospitable places on earth and for years on end. The American public at home was willing to support this kind of conflict, in spite of the immense cost, human and otherwise, to prosecute the war to its ultimate finish of near unconditional Japanese surrender.[5]

The true determining factor in this conflict's outcome, as with nearly all wars, was human will. In the Pacific, the Americans would be determined to fight to the finish with all weapons at their disposal, while observing only the rules that led to survival and victory. This has not been true in the decades since. Surely, the United States enjoyed even greater material advantages over the communists in Korea and Vietnam, the Baathists in the Middle East, the insurgents of the twenty-first century. Why, then, was there no inevitable American victory in any of these wars? Why did the United States settle for a compromise peace in Korea and Desert Storm, outright defeat in Vietnam, and an unsatisfying stalemate in the self-consciously misnamed Global War on Terrorism? True, World War II was a declared war fought for total-war objectives. But it was costlier than all these other conflicts by a considerable factor. The answer was that the American people were willing to do whatever was required to defeat Japan. The soldiers who fought on their behalf were equally willing to fight in whatever manner was necessary, to win what many of them perceived as an almost exterminationist war of survival (the lone and notable exception was the American refusal to employ chemical weapons, though this was due more to fear of in-kind retaliation than any moral restraint). Herein began for Americans the notion of "gloves off" style, culturally charged warfare with all its inherent distasteful by-products. In retrospect, then, the Pacific War sowed the seeds of a modern American tendency toward moral ambiguities, bitter self-recrimination, and controversy in the waging of war.

The war foretold a fundamental shift in American economic interests and geopolitics, away from Europe and toward Asia and the Pacific, one that has endured ever since. It was the first time the United States ever sent combat troops specifically to fight on the Asian landmass against an Asian enemy and the first time America ever committed itself to massive military and economic aid to an Asian ally. When Japan, for its own perceived existential interests, sought to upset a shaky balance of power on the Asian continent (and thus the influence of Western powers in a divided China), as well as a sclerotic Western colonial edifice throughout Asia and the Pacific, the United States saw this as a mortal threat. Thus began a longstanding American commitment to this balance of power in Asia, not just during World War II but also throughout the Cold War and beyond—a commitment that was undoubtedly a factor leading to American involvement in the Korean and Vietnam Wars. Indeed, one could argue that it was anything but irrelevant to subsequent American wars.

The Pacific War unleashed powerful nationalistic, ethnic, and ideological forces that the United States could not begin to control. It led to postcolonial wars from Malaya to Indonesia to Vietnam to the Philippines. It unleashed ethnically conscious, nonwhite nationalist movements that forced Americans to confront their own racial inequalities. It led to representative government for a former adversary and repressive government for a former ally, an outcome few could have predicted in 1941. The tremors of these tectonic shifts have dictated most all the succeeding history in the region, a kaleidoscope of occurrences that have deeply affected American diplomacy and economic interests for many decades, from the Chinese Civil War to the Indonesian and Malaysian nightclub bombings.

And as history continues its relentless forward march, the realities of the Pacific War grow increasingly distant, buried underneath endless layers of myth, distortion, emotional insulation, and well-meaning—but trite—hero-worship. "The real war will never get in the books," Walt Whitman once wrote of the Civil War. The same could be said of World War II. Beneath our comfortable cultural veneer of the greatest generation fighting the good war, the real story of the Pacific/Asia War awaits telling, the dirty war, the merciless war, the Army's war.

PART ONE

ONSLAUGHT

1

Stunned

The place seemed inherently peaceful, idyllic, a tropical paradise far removed from a world busily consuming itself with the flames of war. Hawaii was an attractive spot, offering a laid-back lifestyle of beach excursions, sports, and nightclubs. By the standards of mid-twentieth-century America, it was an odd place, a nominally postimperial territory nonetheless controlled by a central government located on a distant continent, many thousands of miles to the east. The ethnic composition was like nowhere else under the domain of the American government. The original islanders, generally Polynesian in origin, coexisted alongside an Asian/Pacific stew of Koreans, Chinese, Filipinos, and Japanese, the largest single ethnic group. Whites were the most dominant group, at least in terms of wealth and influence. Almost all of them had originated from the United States, but by 1941, many could trace deep roots in the islands, dating back to the previous century. By comparison, most all of the soldiers assigned to the Hawaiian Department were newcomers, temporary tourists within the span of the territory's history. The same was true for their comrades in the other services, most prominent of which was of course the Navy, whose Pacific fleet had moved, by order of President Franklin Roosevelt, from San Diego to Pearl Harbor on the island of Oahu in 1940. The push for empire and world influence had brought Americans to Hawaiian shores over a half century earlier. However questionable this had been in a moral sense, it had resulted in the happy strategic by-product of an American-controlled island chain closer geographically—and ethnically—to Tokyo than Washington.

Since the fleet's relocation to Pearl Harbor, and as war with Japan grew from possibility to probability, the military presence in Hawaii grew. This was especially true on Oahu, the most heavily populated island and, as such, the critical mass of all American defenses. The Army had elements

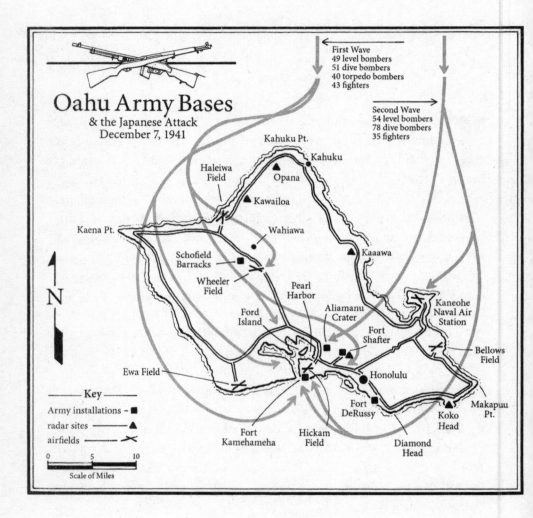

Oahu Army Bases
& the Japanese Attack
December 7, 1941

First Wave
49 level bombers
51 dive bombers
40 torpedo bombers
43 fighters

Second Wave
54 level bombers
78 dive bombers
35 fighters

Kahuku Pt.

Kahuku

Haleiwa Field

Opana

Kawailoa

Kaena Pt.

Wahiawa

Schofield Barracks

Kaaawa

Wheeler Field

Pearl Harbor

Ford Island

Aliamanu Crater

Kaneohe Naval Air Station

Fort Shafter

Bellows Field

Ewa Field

Honolulu

Makapuu Pt.

Fort DeRussy

Koko Head

Fort Kamehameha

Hickam Field

Diamond Head

N

Key
Army installations – ■
radar sites ▲
airfields ✕

0   5   10
Scale of Miles

of two understrength infantry divisions, the 24th and the 25th, on Oahu. They were based at Schofield Barracks, a scenic post located about twelve miles north of Pearl Harbor. The Coast Artillery Corps, the defensive bulwark of the old Army, manned a series of small forts near Pearl Harbor and along coastal areas of the island, highlighted by Fort Shafter between Pearl to the west and Honolulu to the east. Army Air Corps fields also dotted the island, most notably Hickam Field, at the eastern edge of Pearl and Wheeler Field adjacent to Schofield Barracks.

By the middle of 1941, the forty-three thousand soldiers of the Army's Hawaiian Department (both ground and air forces) were under the command of Lieutenant General Walter Short. About twenty-five thousand of those soldiers defended Oahu. The Army also maintained substantial medical facilities at Hickam Field, Schofield Station Hospital, and Tripler General Hospital on the western side of Honolulu. "Here in Hawaii we all live in a citadel or gigantically fortified island," Short told a Honolulu paper in April 1941. The general's mission was to use his air- and ground power to protect the fleet and to guard against an amphibious invasion. Personally, he believed that ethnic Japanese locals—almost three-quarters of whom were actually US citizens—posed the greatest threat to his command, either through sabotage or an outright uprising.

Many of the soldiers were Regular Army volunteers, professionals for whom the service offered a stable refuge from a troubled economy. Peacetime draftees, levied during the federal government's belated preparations for war in 1940 and 1941, fleshed out the ranks. It was an Army with one boot firmly anchored in the early twentieth century, equipped with World War I–era uniforms and weapons, rigidly stratified, both insular and intimate, at the same time professional and rustic. Soldiers took basic training when they reached their assigned units, rather than before, as became customary during the war and ever since. Promotions came slowly; sergeants ruled like lords; officers were often distant figures, like a higher social group in an immutable caste system; Saturday morning inspections were like a military Sabbath; custom was sacrosanct, regulations unquestioned. "There were professional privates," recalled Robert Greenwood, a Coast Artilleryman at Hickam Field. "There were fellows that had been in the Army fifteen or twenty years. I can remember there were guys from World War One." The Army was their home. He knew one man who had served in every rank from private to first sergeant, getting busted several times for binge drinking. "He'd give you twenty-seven days out of the month of outstanding soldiering and then he'd go off on a three-day lost weekend."

Privates made only twenty-one dollars a month. A soldier's reputation was his most valuable currency. Those whom the sergeants and corporals labeled as rebellious or lazy were often assigned to the worst details, such as cutting down thorny bushes or scrubbing garbage cans or policing up cigarette butts. If the noncommissioned officers (NCOs) thought of a soldier as a reliable man, then he often avoided such undesirable chores. Private Martin Rodgers, a Coast Artilleryman at Fort Shafter, later referred to the service as "a nasty army . . . a rough army. It was somewhat like the Roman Legion." Marriages were rare for low-ranking enlisted soldiers. Everyone, even the NCOs, lived in the barracks. It was an old-world army, later made famous in the novel and movie *From Here to Eternity*, and it was an army that would soon be swept away by expansion and modernism in the war that was coming.[1]

For the troops, duty on Oahu was equal parts tourist excursion, summer camp, and boot camp—strict discipline somehow mixed together with an easy tropical lifestyle. Duty days started with reveille, followed by calisthenics and training. "You used to do all of your gun drills in the morning primarily," Greenwood said, "in the afternoon you had details." Everyone—especially infantrymen—occasionally trained in "the field" which usually meant hiking and camping somewhere among Oahu's many hills and mountains. "In some of the areas where we went on hikes, the mud was like . . . glue, so your foot would sink in there," one soldier remembered. It was not uncommon for a soldier to lose his boot as he attempted to extract his foot from the mud. Food on post was plentiful and nutritious, typically with eggs for breakfast, meat and potatoes for other meals. Social life revolved around gambling, sports, and drinking. Dice and card games were common, especially on payday, when all too many down-on-their-luck soldiers frittered away their meager wages in marathon sessions. Anyone who cheated was ostracized or harshly disciplined by sergeants, who would encircle the offender and take turns elbowing or tackling him until they felt that the lesson had sunk in.

Athletics were deeply embedded in Army tradition. The most popular sports were baseball, basketball, football, and boxing. Commanders saw useful parallels between the inherent competitive physicality of sports and the job of soldiering. Prevailing wisdom held that being associated with a

good unit athletic team, or an individual boxing champion, could be helpful for an officer's promotion prospects. Thus, good athletes often received
special privileges. "You didn't go to the field when your unit would go out,"
Corporal Kenneth Nine of the 27th Infantry Regiment said. "You'd stay
behind and play your sport. I took up boxing, track, baseball, and basketball." Typically, during the company formation after lunch, first sergeants
told the athletes to form one group while everyone else formed another.
The jocks then spent their afternoon practicing or playing games. The
other soldiers were put to work cleaning barracks or cutting grass, among
many other onerous chores. Companies competed against other companies, regiments against other regiments, Army against Navy, and so on.
The winners earned bragging rights, and sometimes substantial wagering
money, for their respective unit or service.[2]

On post, entertainment consisted of movies, USO shows, and music.
Beautiful beaches and an incredible array of bars and fleshpots offered
plenty of diversion for anyone who managed to obtain a weekend pass to
leave post. For young soldiers who lived an austere life in an all-male environment, the opportunity to experience the nightlife—inevitably referred
to in the slang of the time as getting "screwed, stewed, and tattooed"—
usually proved irresistible. Hotel and Canal Streets in Honolulu earned a
reputation as an interracial red-light district. The women reflected the diverse ethnic character of the island. Whites—haoles in local lingo—were
decidedly in the minority. On any given weekend night, lines of servicemen could be seen queued up at the various houses of prostitution. During
occasional lulls in business, the ladies themselves would take turns plying
for new customers with a unique—and ironic in light of later events—
proposition: "Come on in and fuck the Japs! Two dollars!" Military and
civil authorities enforced cleanliness and organization to this Hawaiian
version of the world's oldest profession. The women were given frequent
physicals; most were registered with the police. "You didn't get any venereal disease by going to those places," Greenwood claimed, "because when
you went there, even if you just went in to listen to the jukebox, you had to
take a prophylactic preventative before you left." Copious numbers of military policemen lurked nearby, making sure that soldiers complied with
these instructions.

Nearby streets featured pinball game rooms, tattoo parlors, dance halls,
and restaurants with names like Bunny Ranch and Lousy Lui's. Nightclubs

catered to soldiers with cheap booze and big band music, generating over-flow weekend crowds. Sailors queued in meandering white lines; soldiers waited in khaki clumps sprinkled among enclaves of Marines decked out in forest green and, occasionally, servicemen dressed in civilian slacks and Hawaiian shirts. "You'd have to line up outside, and they would issue you two small tickets, just like . . . door passes," Corporal Nine said. "You'd line up there until the waitress or bouncer would lead you in. You could either get two bottles of beer or two mixed drinks. When you finished those up, you'd go somewhere else." Soldiers wandered from watering hole to watering hole, becoming drunk as the evening progressed.

One of the most popular haunts was the Black Cat Café, where off-duty servicemen flocked to have their picture taken with a Hawaiian hula girl in a special photo gallery. The Black Cat offered slot machines and cheap food. A hot dog cost ten cents, a hamburger fifteen cents, and a full turkey dinner could be had for fifty cents. The Armed Services YMCA was located conveniently across the street, and rooms were cheap enough for low-ranking enlisted men to afford a weekend stay. The Royal Hawaiian and Moana hotels at the Waikiki beach were more expensive but still attracted plenty of soldiers for high-quality orchestra music and integrated dancing. Elsewhere, racial tension sometimes festered between the predominantly white servicemen and locals of Asian descent. "There are plenty of 'gooks,'" Private Harold Kennedy wrote to his mother in the fall of 1941. "Japs, Hawaiians, Chinks and half caste mixed foreigners. The soldiers don't like them and they reciprocate in kind. They have knifed several men here when they ventured into their part of town." Military police from the Army and the Navy patrolled the night spots relentlessly, separating racist hotheads, breaking up the inevitable beery fights, apprehending the occasional obnoxious and screaming lout or thief or angler, in general keeping order as best they could, a thankless and unpopular job.

Officers naturally had even more social options, including parties in polite local society and officers' clubs on the various posts. Lieutenant William Moore, a young, married artillery officer in the 24th Infantry Division, rarely even ventured into Honolulu. "We ate at the club almost every night. On weekends and Wednesday nights . . . they had dinner and dancing." He also had a personal automobile, which afforded him the opportunity to tour the island, taking in the sights. "We visited the communities along the coastline . . . along the north half of the island . . . and particularly we admired the flowers and vegetation that existed." On the dating scene, officers enjoyed the easiest access to available women, white or otherwise. Pamela Bradbury, a civilian dietitian who worked at the Schofield Barracks station hospital, juggled a full social calendar, dating many officers in her off-duty hours. "Your date always brought you . . . a flower lei. We all dressed up. We wore evening clothes, even to the boxing matches or the theater or whatever, and the fellows wore their white coats."[3]

Although the military bases on Oahu had endured multiple alerts as war with Japan loomed in the fall of 1941, the evening of December 6 was like any other Saturday night on the island. Bars and restaurants were as crowded as ever. Barracks, gun positions, and ships were thinly manned as thousands of soldiers and sailors enjoyed liberty at the usual dizzying array of night spots from Honolulu to Pearl City. Admiral Husband Kimmel, ill-fated commander of the Pacific Fleet, had a standing invitation for champagne and small talk at the Japanese consulate. He politely declined in favor of a dinner party hosted by the commander of his cruiser battle force, Rear Admiral Herbert Leary, and his wife at the Halekulani hotel. As was customary for the mild-mannered Kimmel, he nursed one drink and was home, in bed, by 2200. After cocktails at a colonel's home, General Short, his wife, and several members of his staff attended "Ann Etzler's Cabaret," an annual charity dinner and dance at the Schofield Barracks officers' club. As the Shorts drove home with another couple, they passed Pearl Harbor, where the resplendent fleet was bathed in lights. "What a target that would make," General Short remarked with eerie prescience. At the Royal Hawaiian hotel, couples danced to up-tempo orchestra music and, between sets, rested over dinner. Pamela Bradbury danced the evening away with her date, a young personnel officer from Wheeler Field. To Bradbury, the Royal Hawaiian was "the loveliest spot on the island," a place where she could feel special and savor the rich local social life. At midnight, the dancing stopped and the band played the national anthem.

Lieutenant Monica Conter, a young nurse stationed at the thirty-bed Hickam Field hospital, had a date with her future husband, Lieutenant Bernard "Barney" Benning. They had planned to go to a party at the Pearl Harbor officers' club, but initially found it too crowded with naval officers on liberty, so instead they took a walk down to the harbor. "It was the most beautiful sight I've ever seen," she said, "all the battleships and the lights with the reflection on the water. We were just overwhelmed. I'll never forget it." There were nearly one hundred warships moored around the scenic harbor, a mute emblem of American maritime might. When Conter and

Benning noticed launches taking large groups of Navy men back to their ships, they returned to the club, found it less crowded, and settled in for a night of drinking and socializing. "We were the last ones to leave that night. They had started putting chairs around to secure the bar," only hours before Conter was scheduled for hospital duty at 0700. As she and Barney parted, they made plans for another date on Sunday, swimming, a movie, and barbecued spare ribs. Private Greenwood, the Coast Artilleryman, went to the beach and then hit the bustling Honolulu bars. He ran into a Navy buddy with whom he downed several drinks. "It was getting late, and we'd been up really doing the town." The sailor was due back aboard his ship. Greenwood decided to accompany him back to Pearl Harbor and then look for another friend at nearby Hickam Field. But Greenwood could not find his other buddy. Loaded with alcohol and tiring, he found "a bunk of somebody who was out on pass and I sacked out." In the meantime, as the orchestra played "The Star-Spangled Banner" at the Royal Hawaiian hotel, Lieutenant Commander Edwin Layton, the Pacific Fleet's intelligence officer, stood at attention alongside everyone else. Having absorbed weeks of disquieting reports about Japan's belligerent intentions and the probable imminence of war, he felt a wild urge to yell "Wake up, America!" Instead, he stood still and kept quiet.[4]

★

The Japanese strike on Pearl Harbor targeted American airpower and sea power. The ground soldiers just happened to be in the way. The purpose was to cripple the United States Pacific Fleet and American aviation in order to give Japan a free hand to conquer sources of raw materials in the Pacific and, to a lesser extent, on the Asian mainland. Along the way, the Japanese hoped to demolish the British and Dutch imperial empires and achieve such an obvious degree of economic parity with the United States that the Americans would choose to sue for peace. All of this was predicated on the expectation of a short war, since a longer struggle was not to Japan's advantage. Many of the Army and Navy officers who had come to dominate Japan's government believed that, in the unhappy event of a protracted war, Japan's superior fighting spirit, *Yamato-damashii*, would surely negate America's material advantages. They were correct that human will tends to determine the winner of wars, but they failed to take into account that their American adversaries could be capable of matching them in that regard, while greatly exceeding them in logistical, industrial, engineering, and technological output.

Pearl Harbor was to be the centerpiece of a series of attacks, launched over six thousand miles of ocean, island, and continent, from British Malaya to the Philippines to the South Pacific to Hawaii. Japanese naval aviation, the finest in the world as of 1941, was the tool the Japanese war planners employed to inflict what they hoped would be deadly damage to the American fleet. The mastermind of the surprise aerial attack was Isoroku Yamamoto, commander in chief of the Japanese Combined Fleet. A thoughtful, passionate internationalist and advocate of airpower, Yamamoto had been deeply impressed with a devastating carrier-borne raid launched by the Royal Navy against the anchored Italian fleet at Taranto in 1940. British planes had achieved complete surprise, heavily damaging three battleships. In an ominous portent for Yamamoto's concept, the Italians were able to recover all three ships from the shallow harbor waters and effect repairs. Admiral Yamamoto believed Japan's more potent carrier force could inflict even more damage on the US fleet. Having spent many years in the United States, he knew his adversary well. By most accounts, he actually liked Americans and opposed going to war with them. In effect, he was like a man in a barroom who has no wish to fight a burly opponent but, feeling he has no choice, decides that he must launch a surprise haymaker to have any hope of prevailing. In late November, as negotiations between the Japanese and American governments reached a final stage— and with the realization among power brokers on both sides that war was now almost unavoidable—a powerful fleet left the Kuril Islands and sailed stealthily east, its whereabouts and intentions largely unknown to the Americans. This strike force, under the command of Vice Admiral Chuichi Nagumo, boasted six carriers, two battleships, and a powerful blend of destroyers and cruisers. For the raid, Nagumo planned to launch 360 torpedo bombers, dive bombers, and fighters in two waves. Their job was to inflict massive damage on ships, planes, and airfields. Submarines functioned as a reconnaissance screen for Nagumo's fleet. They were also to launch five small subs—about forty-five feet long, nicknamed "midget" submarines by the Americans—to lie in wait at the mouth of Pearl Harbor, where they were to torpedo any ships that attempted to flee the air attacks.

By the early-morning hours of December 7, the fleet lay 230 nautical miles northwest of Oahu, ready for action. Reconnaissance planes sallied forth first, before sunrise, at about 0600. Their job was to scout Pearl Harbor and its environs to make sure the enemy fleet was still in place. A few minutes later, they were followed by the first wave, consisting of torpedo bombers (armed with specially fitted torpedoes that could run in the shallow Pearl waters), and dive and level bombers and fighters. The second wave, consisting exclusively of bombers and fighters, took off at 0700.

As the lead planes flew south, the sun began to peak over the eastern horizon. On Oahu rays of regenerative sunlight illuminated the sandy beaches and calm waters. Honolulu tended to be very quiet on Sunday mornings, "like a small New England town," in the view of one resident, and this day was no different. At the Waikiki beach, the Pacific lapped so gently on the moist sand that surfers abandoned any hope of finding waves big enough to ride to shore. There were few clouds in the sky. Mount Tantalus was clearly visible beyond the city skyline. Streets were nearly empty. It was all routine, seemingly like any other Hawaiian Sunday, the pleasant, sleepy residue of peacetime in an exotic place.

Most Americans, whether civilian or military, were asleep. Among those who were awake, there was no sense of impending danger, and yet there were some ominous warnings. A destroyer, the USS *Ward*, sank a midget sub at 0645 when it brazenly attempted to follow another American ship into the harbor. It took nearly half an hour for the coded communication report of the sinking to reach the duty officer at 14th Naval District Headquarters, the appropriate next level of command. Rear Admiral Claude Bloch, commandant of the district, dispatched another destroyer to the scene and dutifully informed Kimmel's staff. Because of telephone exchange issues, the admiral did not receive the message until just before the bombing began. So as a result of communication snags, the Japanese got away with an egregious error that could have compromised their entire operation.

Nor was this the only fortune that favored the attackers on that Sunday morning. The Army operated a half-dozen rudimentary mobile radar stations on the island, one of which was functioning at Opana, just inland from the north coast, over two hundred feet above sea level. Under orders from General Short, the sets normally operated from 0400 to 0700, the hours the general considered most likely for a carrier-borne attack or amphibious invasion. At 0702, the two operators, Privates Joseph Lockard and George Elliott, saw a large, luminous blip on their screen, indicating a substantial flight of well over fifty aircraft. Soon multiple blips showed up. For seven minutes, the two privates puzzled over what they were seeing before finally agreeing to call the aircraft warning information center at Fort Shafter, where most everyone had ended the duty shift. The officer in charge, a twenty-eight-year-old fighter pilot, Lieutenant Kermit Tyler, had almost no training or experience at the job. "I had no idea what my duties were," he later said. Lockard told the lieutenant that the blips represented the biggest sightings he had ever seen. He did not, though, tell Tyler that the sighting contained more than fifty planes. Tyler never imagined that the blips could represent enemy aircraft. Instead, he interpreted the information through the lens of his own preconceptions. He knew that the fleet's carriers were not in harbor—a more fortunate circumstance than he could possibly have imagined at that moment—so he assumed the planes were probably from the Navy. Then he thought of something else. As he had driven in his car earlier that morning to the information center, he had turned on the radio and heard Hawaiian music. From a previous conversation with a bomber pilot, he knew that when radio stations played music all night, it meant that a flight of B-17s was due from the mainland (the music functioned as a navigational aid for the bombers). Tyler figured the blips must be the B-17s. In a phrase that would become infamous, but one that the laid-back Tyler apparently used a lot, he told Lockard, "Well, don't worry about it."

Placated, but still curious, Lockard and Elliott continued to monitor the blips until 0739, when they became obscured by surrounding mountains. The incident represented a fiasco in wrong assumptions and poor preparation and coordination. One cannot help but wonder how many lives would have been saved if Lieutenant Tyler had not turned on his car radio or if he had not spoken with the bomber pilot. If Lockard had told Tyler the large number of planes he saw on his screen, even the inexperienced lieutenant would have known something was up, because that number would have represented most of the Army Air Corps' fleet of B-17s. "As I think back on it, because of my personality, I was probably the wrong person at the wrong place that morning," Tyler reflected decades later. Moreover, there was no real provision for the Army and the Navy to communicate what they had seen to each other and coordinate accordingly. Both had received major warnings of what was to come, and yet they could hardly communicate effectively with their own people, much less anyone in the other service.[5]

The by-product of this parochialism—indeed amateurism—was that the Japanese strike force achieved complete operational surprise. "Pearl Harbor was still asleep in the morning mist," recalled Lieutenant

Commander Kenju Nakaya, who led the first formation of planes. "It was calm and serene inside the harbor, not even a trace of smoke from the ships at Oahu. The orderly groups of barracks, the wriggling white line of automobile road climbing up to the mountaintop, fine objectives of attack in all directions." Commander Mitsuo Fuchida, in the lead of the level bombers, took in the splendor of dozens of ships moored around the harbor, some in double rows, and thought, "What a majestic sight! Almost unbelievable!"

Around the quiet harbor, Honolulu church bells could be heard tolling, summoning the faithful to their services. The gonging of the distant bells was only slightly muffled by a gentle breeze and the lapping of the water. Aboard the ships, crewmen prepared to raise the Stars and Stripes, and play the national anthem, a typical morning routine. Suddenly the jarring, almost incongruous droning of airplane engines infused the area as the Japanese planes began their well-planned assault. In that instant, the world changed. At Forts Weaver and Kamehameha, a pair of small Army Coast Artillery installations that guarded the entrance to Pearl Harbor and adjacent Hickam Field, only a smattering of soldiers were on duty. Confused, not knowing what was going on, they craned their necks and watched the strange planes approach and buzz past on their way to savaging the ships. In a few seconds, the harbor was alive with explosions, fire, and smoke. One by one, torpedoes and bombs mauled the ships moored along battleship row, most famously the USS *Arizona*, which was fatally hit and sunk in mere moments, with hundreds of crewmen trapped belowdecks, where they drowned or suffocated, never even knowing what was happening. Other enemy planes bombed and strafed Hickam Field, where planes were lined up wing tip to wing tip—as a precaution against sabotage—on runways and in hangars. Private Greenwood, who had found a bunk at Hickam to sleep off a hangover, had just roused himself to get coffee at the mess hall when he saw the planes. He figured they must be part of a Navy exercise. Then he saw one of the planes drop a bomb. "That jerk!" he thought. "They're supposed to be dropping dummies."

Japanese bombs scored a direct hit on the Hale Makai Barracks, where men were just starting to line up for breakfast. In seconds, thirty-five men were killed and many others wounded, including one who was lacerated by the jagged edges of a shattered mayonnaise jar. The Japanese aviators continued bombing and strafing adjacent buildings, hangars, and runways against almost no antiaircraft opposition. In several instances, soldiers who were scrambling frantically to man guns or haul ammunition were cut down by strafing enemy aircraft.

At a nearby house that functioned as officers' quarters, Major Stephen Kallis, executive officer of a Coast Artillery regiment, was sleeping off the effects of the Saturday-night party at the Pearl Harbor Navy club when the thumping of explosions awakened him. With each explosion, the house shook. He hastily donned his uniform and stepped outside to see what was going on. As he did so, he saw a silver-and-blue plane cruise past at about five hundred feet. "I could see the red ball of Japan on the fuselage, just behind the cockpit. I looked out to sea and saw what seemed to be dozens of planes coming in at extremely low altitudes." Explosions continued to reverberate from the direction of Hickam Field. As the reality of the Japanese attack sunk home to him, he took off for the unit barracks to roust his men. Along the way, he was strafed by a Japanese fighter, "sparks bouncing the pavement near [his] feet." When he arrived at the barracks, half-dressed soldiers were lined up, receiving ammunition from the first sergeant (mostly for .30- and .50-caliber machine guns). Kallis and the sergeant organized a hasty unit movement to Battery Hasbrouck, near the entrance to Pearl Harbor. From there, Kallis figured he would be in good position to shoot at Japanese planes and repel potential enemy paratroopers. At Hasbrouck, the major looked back in the direction of Pearl and saw an immense pall of smoke rising from the decimated ships. "Hickam Barracks was also burning, and five or six planes . . . were blazing fiercely, sending up huge clouds of pitch-black smoke. A large hangar ballooned up and exploded as I watched. Everywhere, Jap planes dived and zoomed. The din was unimaginable."

From Hasbrouck, they fired their machine guns and a few Springfield rifles at any Japanese planes that came into range. They watched as a B-17— undoubtedly from the flight that Lieutenant Tyler had been expecting— attempted to land at Hickam, only to be chased away by enemy fighters. Throughout that terrible morning, the surprised B-17 crewmen who had flown all night from the West Coast found themselves attempting to land in the middle of raids at various airfields. Somehow eight of them landed at Hickam and three at other fields. In the channel that led out of the harbor, angry-looking destroyers, guns blazing, roared toward the open sea. Periodically, they disappeared inside the water spouts of near misses but relentlessly pressed on. Everyone in Kallis's outfit except the first sergeant was new to combat. The major circulated around, hoping to calm the nerves of the young soldiers and his own as well. Faces were pale with fright. Major Kallis felt a lump in his stomach, "a very unpleasant feeling that someone is tying knots in your intestines." He suspected many of the men did too, but they kept fighting. They scored a few hits on enemy aircraft but did not see any go down. At times, they flew so low and so close that one gunner felt that if he threw a baseball at them, he "could probably hit them, if [he] could throw high enough." Kallis believed that his men damaged two enemy planes.[6]

At Fort Kamehameha, soldiers of the 55th Coast Artillery Regiment set up machine guns on a tennis court and blazed away at the buzzing attackers. A Zero fighter plane flown by Petty Officer First Class Takashi Hirano was soon hit, careened out of control, struck a tree and then a wall, and skidded to a surreal stop. "The pilot was dead," Colonel William McCarthy said, "stuffed in the tree, but the plane was on the ground." The engine and propeller ricocheted around an ordnance shop and plowed into several men who were standing outside. "One man was completely decapitated. Another man apparently had been hit by the props, because his legs and arms and head were off, lying right on the grass." By one post-battle estimate, the ill-prepared antiaircraft batteries accounted for just four enemy planes, felled mostly by machine gun and automatic rifle fire.

At Hickam, confused and frightened soldiers scurried around, attempting to fight back. One officer emerged from a gutter where he had taken cover from the bouncing bullets of strafing planes and roared, "Disperse those planes!" For most of the aircraft, it was much too late. Even as some of them burned, courageous crewmen jumped onto the wings, disconnected the engines, and hauled them to comparative safety. One of the pilots, nude except for a flapping bathrobe, rushed out of his quarters, shook his fist at a strafing Zero fighter plane, and shouted, "I *knew* the little sons of bitches would do it on a Sunday! I *knew* it!" Another pilot, Lieutenant Vernon Reeves, saw a plane with its wing nearly touching the ground, zip past his window and shoot at the officers' club. Reeves could not help but feel professional admiration for the skill of whomever was at the controls. Typical of many Americans in 1941, he could not imagine such skill could be possible for anyone other than a white man, arguably an attitude that had led to the Japanese achieving such complete surprise. "He must be a German," Reeves said to one of his buddies. Private Greenwood, dazed and in shock, rushed randomly along the buildings, fighting fires with shirts and blankets. He saw soldiers shoot the locks off ammo storage lockers, everywhere a common occurrence during the attack. In peacetime, all ammo had to be meticulously accounted for and, typically, only charge of quarters sergeants or commanding officers carried keys to the storage lockers. In the chaos of the moment, no one cared for such niceties anymore. Greenwood took a Springfield rifle and a cartridge belt off a wounded man. He dove to the ground, shouldered the rifle and began snapping off shots at strafing enemy planes. A ricocheting bullet barely missed him. The Japanese planes were so close that he could see the faces of the pilots, another common phenomenon that day. Several times Greenwood tried to line up a target and snap off an accurate shot, with little effect, but it allowed him to vent his rage at all the death and destruction around him. "I'd have thrown rocks at them. I'd have done anything. I'd have tried to bite the damn plane or kick it."

One low-flying plane squeezed off several rounds that burst a water main. Gobs of water spewed forth with such force that a truck was knocked on its side. More bombers appeared overhead and unleashed a torrent of ordnance, touching off explosions along the runways and hangars. More American planes were wrecked. The runways were pocked with gaping holes. Any US plane that attempted to take off was immediately attacked by multiple enemy aircraft. Many of the Japanese pilots had strict orders to keep American planes from taking off and interfering with the vital task of bombing and torpedoing the US fleet. Perched atop a pole next to the Hale Makai Barracks, an American flag was now tattered but still flew defiantly as clouds of smoke gushed past. Yesterday's adversaries became today's allies. When the field's stockade came under attack, the inmates were released and immediately rushed to help a lone sergeant man a machine gun and fire repeated bursts at the Japanese. A bomb scored a direct hit on the Snake Ranch, a brand-new base beer garden. A first sergeant from a truck company dashed angrily after the offending plane, shook his fist, and shouted, "You dirty SOBs! You've bombed the most important building on the post!" Elsewhere, a private who was rushing to a machine-gun position found himself targeted and pinned down by a strafing aircraft. Instead of trying to outrun the strafer, he ducked into a latrine, hugged a toilet bowl for cover, and lived to relate the tale of this ignominious close call to his buddies.

In his office at Hickam, Lieutenant Colonel Jimmy Mollison, chief of staff of the Hawaiian Air Force, called Colonel Walter Phillips, Short's chief of staff at Fort Shafter, to report news of the raid. Phillips could not see Pearl from Shafter, but he had heard explosions and was puzzled as to what they might be. Even so, he was dubious when Mollison told him the extent of the enemy attack. "You're out of your mind, Jimmy. What's the matter, are you drunk? Wake up!"

Exasperated, Mollison held the phone out so that Phillips could hear the thumping of explosions and the chatter of machine guns. "I can hear it," Phillips conceded. "I'll send over a liaison officer." Mollison found the promise less than comforting, especially an instant later when the ceiling of his office collapsed.

When Colonel Phillips informed General Short of the attack, the general ordered him to put all troops on full alert and prepare for the possibility of an amphibious invasion. "I didn't know how serious the attack might develop," he later testified to an inquiry board, "if they would take a chance like that, they might even take a chance on a landing of troops." As yet, though, he had no true comprehension of the disaster that was unfolding. An officer who had come from Pearl told him, "I just saw two battleships sunk."

Short stared back skeptically, "That's ridiculous," he retorted, and then walked away.[7]

★

At nearly the same time, dive bombers and fighters pounced on Wheeler Field, where dozens of P-40 and P-36 fighter planes aircraft were lined up under armed guard in neat rows on the concrete runway adjacent to their hangars. Ironically, the base's commander, Colonel William Flood, had recently ordered the building of one hundred dirt bunkers that would have provided the planes some shelter from the bombs and bullets. Owing to Short's order to use all measures to prevent sabotage, Flood had reluctantly parked them in the open. Ammo had even been removed from the fighters and stored in the hangars. The colonel was reading his morning newspaper when he heard the low-flying planes and their ordnance. He ran outside and saw the Japanese "bombing and strafing the base, the planes, the officers' quarters, and even the golf course. I could see some of the Japanese pilots lean out and smile as they zoomed by . . . hell, I could even see the gold in their teeth."

Orange flames gushed skyward as planes exploded; they were parked so close together that one fire led to another in a chain reaction. Oily black smoke belched from the roasting hulks. The window glass of hangars and machine shops shattered and flew in all directions. The shards bounced on the tarmac with an odd sound akin to pebbles on stone. The corrugated iron roof of one hangar twisted into knots and collapsed in a deformed mass. The post exchange was demolished as was a nearby barracks. Half the base's planes were destroyed, including thirty of the relatively new P-40s. Thirty-seven men were dead, fifty-three wounded, and six missing. Some of the dead looked like they were merely taking cover; only when their buddies patted them on the back or turned them over did they realize they were staring into the blank, half-opened eyes of corpses.

For the Japanese aviators, Schofield Barracks, located adjacent to devastated Wheeler Field, was merely a low-priority target of opportunity. By any measure, Schofield was a thing of beauty. Five quadrangles of sturdy, cream-colored three-story barracks sprawled along neatly maintained parade fields whose lush green grass was always kept appropriately low cut. Here and there, palm trees dotted the area. One infantry battalion of four companies occupied each barracks building. "They were open-bay barracks," Corporal Nine said, "the beds went down through the bay." Beyond the barracks, officers' homes were laid out in army-straight lines. Typically, each house dated to the early twentieth century and featured three bedrooms, a kitchen, a dining room, and a bathroom. Many of the senior officers lived in more substantial houses at Wahiawa, a couple miles off post.

Major General Maxwell Murray, commander of the 25th Infantry Division, was sitting in his home when he heard the buzzing of a low-flying plane. Annoyed at what he figured must be some hotshot pilot showing off, he grabbed a pen to write down the plane's serial number. He reached his front door in time to see the plane disgorge a bomb over Wheeler Field. The explosion from this bomb and others, along with the tattering of strafing, began to reverberate around the area. Inside a nearby house in Wahiawa, Lieutenant Colonel Aubrey "Red" Newman, intelligence officer of the 24th Infantry Division, was reading a newspaper in bed, his black cat asleep at his feet. To his professional ears, the thumping explosions and chattering of machine-gun fire were unmistakable sounds. "I jumped from bed, scattering cat and bedclothes, and headed for the porch. From there I could see Wheeler Field, and the flaming destruction of the surprise attack." Clad in bathrobes and pajamas, military family members poured out of their Wahiawa homes and stood in their backyards, staring in horror at the strafing planes. Eunice Yeo, wife of an artillery officer, had been watching her five-year-old son sweep their fireplace to prepare for the imminent arrival of Santa Claus when she heard the planes and rushed outside to have a look.

"I saw a plane swooping toward us, and I saw the orange rising sun insignia on the wing and the Japanese pilot looking down at us." Her heart seemed to skip several beats as she realized exactly what was happening.

In the barracks at Schofield, most men were either asleep, eating breakfast, or preparing to eat. James Jones, one day to become a legendary novelist but on this day a company clerk, was in the mess hall enjoying an extra pint of milk with a plate of eggs and pancakes when he heard the thumping. "They doing some blasting?" an older soldier asked almost unintelligibly through a mouthful of pancakes. Jones had no idea. Corporal Nine, sitting in the bay of his company barracks, assumed, like thousands of others that morning, that the other services were doing some sort of special training. "Well, there's the damned Air Force and Navy on maneuvers again," he said wearily. Private Hollis Peacock, a young infantryman on his way to breakfast, heard the screaming of a diving plane and worried that the pilot had lost control. "He had better pull out, or he won't make it," Hollis said to the men around him. In the next instant they heard a wham and the barracks shook. They scrambled to a nearby window and immediately understood that they were under attack. Others who ran outside to have a look were still not so certain. As one group stood and studied the swooping aircraft, an NCO nodded knowingly and said, "Yeah, there they are. The Marines are camouflaging their planes again. We're having another sham battle."

Once the terrible truth had sunk in, soldiers scrambled hurriedly to get weapons and fight back. Helmets askew, they clomped down staircases and boiled out of the buildings, onto the quadrangles. Bugles had served as the melodious intercom of the barracks, sounding everything from reveille to chow to formation. Now disheveled buglers desperately sounded the alert. Soldiers set up machine guns on rooftops or propped them over walls. Browning automatic riflemen (BAR) squeezed off bursts. Other riflemen popped away ineffectually. A few soldiers even fired pistols. Some of the ammo dated back to 1918 and could be more hazardous to the shooter than the target. By and large, the attackers had little to fear from the small-arms fire. In one notable exception, a pair of BAR men emptied several clips into an overflying aircraft and saw it crash and burn on the other side of their building. The flames were so intense that the two men could not get close to the plane. From a distance, they saw the dead Japanese crewmen, "just all crushed down in the cockpit."

The semiorganized chaos produced incidents both absurd and hair-raising. One supply sergeant refused to release any ammunition or weapons unless he received proper receipts. Another was physically forced by the men to open up. As a young lieutenant supervised, a machine-gun team set up in the quadrangle. Then he hollered, "Don't shoot, or they'll shoot back!" Another overzealous machine gunner did not share the lieutenant's compunctions. The gunner leaned on his trigger and kept firing, even when the gun's tripod accidentally folded up. Bullets flew in every direction, shattering a clock over the guard mount station but fortunately missing his fellow soldiers. Other gunners had no time to set up water-cooled heavy machine guns properly. In several instances, they hastily propped the receiver over their arms and blazed away, an improvisation that left them with third-degree burns on their wrists and biceps. At one quadrangle, a swashbuckling Japanese fighter pilot strafed the parade ground at tree top height, chewing up an even line of muddy divots. Apparently fearing no return fire, he banked his plane, grinned, and waved at a gaping group of American soldiers who were huddled along a wall. "A white silk scarf streamed out behind his neck, and he wore a white ribbon around his helmet just above the goggles, with a red spot in the center of his forehead," one of the soldiers remembered. The headband was a *hachimaki*, traditionally worn by samurai warriors as they headed into battle. The 24th Division operations officer (G3) grabbed an M1 Garand rifle and stared down a strafing aircraft. The plane flew low and slow, right at him. The officer was an expert shooter with the bolt-action Springfield rifle, but he had never even held the semiautomatic Garand in his hands. He had no idea how to load it (a unique process that required using one's thumb to push an eight-round clip into the rifle's breech and then extracting that thumb before the bolt slammed shut). As the unschooled staff officer struggled to load the clip, the Japanese plane flew right overhead, almost close enough to touch, and then out of range. "My chance to be a hero and I didn't know how to load that damned rifle!" he later lamented.[8]

Aside from pockmarked walls, bomb craters, and wounded pride, the damage to Schofield was minimal. Communication nodes were largely intact. General Short's alert order reached the appropriate Army commands, setting in motion prewar plans to guard against a potential invasion. By 0900, soldiers of the two infantry divisions were already loading aboard trucks that took them southward to prepared positions along the coast.

Though there were occasional strafing scares, the leading units actually reached the south coast quickly, even while the second wave of Japanese planes was attacking Pearl and its environs. "We could see the planes, fire, smoke and hear the explosions," Private Peacock recalled. The troops spent the day manning pillboxes they had built on south Oahu beaches during maneuvers several weeks earlier. They set up machine guns, dug foxholes, filled sandbags, cleared fields of fire, cleaned ammo, and waited tensely for an invasion that never came. For some, these pillboxes brought back pleasant memories because, during the maneuvers and construction, they had used them for illicit liaisons with local girls.

★

General Short had taken to his battle command post, located at the Aliamanu Crater, three miles west of Fort Shafter, inside a deep underground ordnance storage tunnel. Signalmen labored to keep the command post switchboard and telephone wires in operation. Deeply worried about an invasion, Short paced and conversed calmly but urgently with staff officers. Lieutenant Samuel Bradlyn, a young signals officer, had never been this close to the general. Bradlyn had thought of high-ranking men as Olympian figures. Instead, he was surprised to see that Short was just as prone to such human frailties as indecision or confusion as anyone else. Short called Joseph Poindexter, the territorial governor, and urged him to declare martial law. This would give the Army the power to suspend the writ of habeas corpus, implement military courts, censor media reports, enforce a blackout (or curfew), close schools, and even halt liquor sales. The understandably reluctant governor temporized until he could consult with the White House. President Roosevelt, still reeling from the grim reports of the surprise attack, assured him that martial law was appropriate and necessary. Before the day was out, Governor Poindexter signed the proclamation, and it was to remain in place for the entire war. Webley Edwards, a popular local broadcaster on radio station KGMB, took to the airwaves and advised the population, "Keep calm, everybody. Oahu is under attack. This is no joke. It's the real McCoy." Even with such definite information, some island residents were either ignorant of the attack or remained skeptical of such reports as a hoax akin to Orson Welles's famous 1938 "The War of the Worlds" broadcast about a notional Martian invasion.

General Short ordered the evacuation of Army dependents, a plan he had worked out many weeks earlier. Buses and car pools were to transport everyone temporarily to the University of Hawaii (where the football team had just beaten Willamette the day before), local schools, and the YWCA. Eventually, the family members were to move in with host families in safe areas of the island or, more commonly, they would simply go back to the mainland. Loud speaker-laden cars began to circulate up and down the streets of the various posts, roaring evacuation instructions. Soldiers knocked on doors. Near Schofield, Eunice Yeo was preparing baby formula for her infant daughter when a frightened soldier appeared at her door. "Ma'am, the Japanese have attacked. Dress in your warmest clothes and report to the nearest barracks." Others received similar instructions. Ruth Lawson had seen her husband, a infantry captain, scramble to headquarters at the first signs of the attack. This left her alone in their one-story stucco home with her mother and daughter. Lawson was still in her night-gown, pondering what to do next. The sound of Japanese planes making power dives made her wonder if they were specifically targeting her house. In her words: "My stomach must have dropped to my toes and my heart catapulted to my throat." When she heard a knock at her door, she half wondered whether it might be a Japanese soldier. Instead, it was a young GI who jumped into her home to dodge a strafing plane. When he regained his composure, he told Lawson, "If you get dressed, I'll get you to a safer place." In one surreal instance, a Chinese-American soldier knocked at the door of a major's family. Unschooled in the differences among Asian ethnic groups, and terrified that he might be a Japanese masquerading as an American, they refused to unlock their door. He was forced to shout evacuation instructions through the door. A few blocks away, military policemen told Bess Tittle and her neighbors to report to the nearest barracks building. In the early moments of the attack, her husband, Lieutenant Norm Tittle, a radar officer, had hopped into his car and told her, "Take care of the baby," in reference to their three-month-old son. As Bess and a friend hurriedly gathered formula, bottles, and sterilizers for the baby, "the back door flew open and there stood two young GIs with tommy guns pointed right at us." The two surprised women screamed. The soldiers sheepishly lowered their guns and helped them find the proper building. The haste proved to be a classic Army instance of hurry up and wait. The vast majority of the family members spent the day inside nearby barracks or mess halls. They waited in frightened, ignorant bewilderment for buses to arrive from Honolulu. Most were not evacuated until well into the evening, only to endure a stressful, tortuous three-hour journey to Honolulu along crowded roads darkened by the blackout. The Red Cross provided them with welcome food, medical supplies, and blankets.[9]

All over the island, rumors spread like a virus. Panicked reports circulated of Japanese parachute and glider landings seemingly everywhere. The paratroopers had the rising-sun emblem sewn on the backs of their uniforms or over their left-breast pocket. In one instance, a soldier investigated one such "landing," only to find a kite in a tree. Colonel Newman, intelligence officer of the 24th Division, received at least six such allegedly confirmed-airborne-landing reports. "This did not make sense. From what base could they have come?" In each instance, when he checked the reports, he quickly found them to be groundless. When the field telephones went out of service at one infantry command post, nearly every soldier assumed that the wires had been cut by Japanese saboteurs. In truth, a soldier who had needed some wire had cut a piece for himself and had inadvertently severed the lines.

Japanese spies had supposedly driven milk trucks to Pearl Harbor and Hickam, where they delivered cans of milk equipped with homing devices that guided their planes to targets. The milk-truck drivers were said to have zipped up and down the Hickam flight line, knocking the tails off planes. The side of one truck dropped down, revealing machine gunners who sprayed the flight line. In another variation of the milk-truck rumor, Japanese soldiers were said to have set up a roadblock by disguising their armored vehicle as an innocuous truck. The Japanese population had risen up as a "fifth column" to aid their erstwhile countrymen. They had surrounded Oahu with white sampans as a guidepost to the aviators. They had cut arrows into their cane fields, pointing in the direction of Pearl. Stories circulated of individual Japanese who had bought drinks for servicemen the night before in hopes of rendering them drunk and ineffective for the next day's surprise attack. Erroneous reports of mysterious fleets, naval bombardments, and amphibious troop landings were rife. In one typical instance, Colonel Newman received a report from an artillery observation post of an enemy submarine. The observers called in artillery fire on the "sub" and the shells supposedly sank it, as evidenced by swimmers in the water. In reality, as Colonel Newman soon deduced, the sub was actually a porpoise and the swimmers were other porpoises, "understandably excited about artillery shells falling around them." Perhaps the most annoying rumor was that Japanese agents had poisoned the island's water supply.

Major Kallis, the antiaircraft officer at Fort Kamehameha, and his troops worked up a powerful thirst while trying to ward off the aerial attacks. He noticed a hydrant nearby but, because of the poison-water reports, he was reluctant to let anyone drink from it. He sent some men in a truck to the unit mess hall to retrieve cold milk. "When they arrived, the kitchen blew up in their faces. No food, no drink, and a lot of battery-fund[ed] property smashed to fragments. All of this fanned the flames of our fury." A cold-hearted colonel at the Hickam dispensary attempted to test the safety of the water on the unit's mascot dog. As if wise to the scheme, the dog refused to drink a drop. "The mental and emotional shock resulting from a sudden and unexpected attack is often far more devastating in effect than the physical damage justifies," Newman later wrote sagely.

Indeed, all of these wild tales were the natural by-product of the over-imagination that occurs when an enemy achieves complete surprise—if they can do this, then they must be capable of practically anything! At times, this mind-set nearly led to fear-filled reprisals. A Coast Artillery unit apprehended a man whom they believed was a Japanese spy. The suspect apparently understood no English. Frustrated with their inability to communicate with the man, soldiers prodded him menacingly with bayonets. "On every side was a soldier with a bayonet pressed against his ribs," Lieutenant Colonel Herbert Blackwell related in a letter to his wife. "From the expression on the faces of these soldiers, I could see that they would have liked to have used the bayonets more violently. They were exercising extreme self-control." A shuttle bus carrying soldiers from Honolulu to Schofield Barracks was stopped by a military policeman. When the MP noticed that the driver was Japanese, he immediately ordered him off the bus and arrested him. "This guy hadn't done anything," a soldier on the bus recalled. "He was just driving the bus!" In a more troubling incident, a group of sailors encountered five ethnic Japanese civilians on a small road north of Pearl Harbor. One of the sailors insisted on shooting them all. At first his comrades agreed. The civilians stood fearfully, not saying a word. Several uneasy moments passed before one of the sailors said quietly, "We are not beasts. These people had nothing to do with the attack." The sailor's rational statement immediately defused the tension. The sailors went on their way. The civilians breathed a huge sigh of relief. In fact, as Hawaiians of Japanese descent realized the magnitude of Japan's attack, some began to worry about the possibility of bloody reprisals. Wild rumors spread among them that the Army was planning to round up and kill all Japanese in Hawaii. Later in the day, the rumor was amended. The Army would kill all the men but leave the women to starve.[10]

★

In the midst of such tall tales, there was the brutal reality of a mass-casualty event. With distressing rapidity, hospitals all over the area were inundated with the wounded and the dying. The thirty-bed Hickam Field station hospital was so new that it was still not even fully equipped. Within a few moments, the small crew of doctors and nurses had to transition from a peacetime mode of individual surgical care into a combat clearing station, dealing with more casualties than the staff could handle, even with assistance from the wives of servicemen who offered to help and were put to work making dressings by the hundreds. Most of the casualties had been hit in the Hickam attacks. Many of the wounded were coated not just in blood but with the dust and detritus of wrecked buildings. The hospital's electricity went out and stayed out. "All of these patients were coming in," recalled Lieutenant Conter, who had partied the previous evening with her future husband. "We were putting them out on the porch. There were some who were killed, and we were putting them in the backyard behind the hospital." Lieutenant Joseph Pomerance, a physician, remembered the hospital veranda as "just covered with wounded or dying men. You could see them with the top of their skulls blown off and still breathing . . . and their brains exposed. You could see their guts all hanging out or their legs blown off." One of the other doctors gave them morphine shots to dull their pain until they died. A soldier approached Conter and asked her to help his sergeant. She took one look and realized he was already dead. "Oh, he can't go," the soldier moaned, "he's too great a guy." Tourniquets were in short supply. As one doctor recorded in a post-battle report, the medics improvised with "belts, gas masks, cords, pistol-holder cords, and muslin strips." One of the patients apparently knew that tourniquets could be dangerous if they were tied too tight. He told a passing nurse, "Let it bleed every few minutes." By and large, the wounded were suffering from fragment and bullet wounds and, according to one report, "such secondary missiles as pieces of macadam [road], stones, brick and mortar, and steel." Nurses worked hurriedly to sterilize syringes and clean wounds, but they were often so overwhelmed that they frequently gave unsterilized injections. In spite of this, there were no recorded instances of infection.

Casualties from the Wheeler bombings poured into the stately stucco-and-tile station hospital at Schofield Barracks. Surgeons immediately implemented a priority system of treatment (often referred to as triage). "This constituted a problem of the greatest importance," one physician reported a few months later, "because the proper selection of patients who were to go to the operating room immediately and those that might be permitted to wait had a great bearing on the excellence of the treatment . . . and upon the mortality and morbidity which followed treatment." Priority went to head injuries, sucking chest wounds, perforated abdominal wounds, and amputees. Compound fractures and soft-tissue wounds were secondary, followed by ambulatory fragmentation injuries. The few patients who were already occupying beds in what had been a sleepy hospital yielded them to the newly wounded. A baby had been born the night before. Nurses made sure the newborn received proper milk and oxygen and kept her out of the way. Wounded men arrived on stretchers hauled by heavily burdened bearers. In some cases, the bearers laid them on the floor. In others, they put them on empty beds. "They were all young, good-looking kids," Lieutenant Ada Olsson, a nurse, recalled. Nurses took down their names, found them a bed or a spot on the floor, and filled out medical charts for them. Many were victims of horrifying wounds. To Lieutenant Rhoda Ziesler, another nurse, they "looked so ghastly, most of them in shock, yet conscious. I never saw nor hope to see again such casualties." One luckless nurse drew the surreal job of attempting to match discarded arms and hands with the stumps of traumatic amputees. At times doctors had to operate on patients who were still in shock. More commonly, they received plasma transfusions to stabilize their vital signs before surgery.[11]

The Army's Tripler General Hospital, located at Fort Shafter, was the leading military medical facility in the area. Named for a pioneering Civil War medical officer, Tripler was a sprawling two-story installation with wide verandas that served as wards. Throughout the day, ambulances, trucks, and any other road-worthy conveyance shuttled wounded men to Tripler, where they received top-notch surgical and postoperative care. The high-quality treatment stemmed partially from good preparation and partially from good luck. Colonel Edgar King, the Hawaiian Department surgeon, had established a medical preparedness committee in conjunction with the Honolulu County Medical Society. Together they had organized surgical teams and trained them to deal with an emergency medical situation. By sheer chance, Dr. John Moorhead, a distinguished trauma surgeon from New York City who had served on the front lines in World War I, happened to be in Honolulu to give a series of lectures at a medical conference. He had taken pains to make sure that military doctors attended his talks. Fortuitously, on Friday night he had given a well-received lecture on the treatment of wounds to an audience of about three hundred physicians, half of whom were military.

On Sunday morning, he was in the auditorium at the Mabel Smyth Memorial Building in Honolulu, preparing to begin a lecture about burns, when everyone heard the bursting of shells outside. He said the explosions reminded him of Château-Thierry, and as it was Sunday, he quipped, " 'Be ye also ready, for in the hour that ye know not; the Son of Man cometh.' " As if on cue, a local doctor rushed into the auditorium with news of the attack and the urgent need for surgeons at Tripler. Moorhead and a group of civilian doctors thus augmented the hospital's complement of available medical personnel, a real lifesaver on this day.

The previous summer, Honolulu authorities had established a major disaster council to prepare for emergencies. The council launched a makeshift ambulance service. This accounted for the availability of the many diverse vehicles that dumped off the wounded, the dying, and the dead. The drivers and their helpers had scoured every scene of disaster, erring on the side of transporting anyone who seemed to have even a remote chance of living. "You'd go through the barracks," Medic Leon Sell explained many years later to an interviewer, "and you'd find them laying in bed. Maybe they had no head or maybe part of their torso was missing. You'd find them scattered all over the barracks. You didn't know what belonged to who or who belonged to what. So you'd kind of have to sift through." The body parts of the living and dead were often mixed as the medics unloaded the vehicles. Doctors performed numerous amputations on stretcher-bound men.

The dying expired fast, well before they could make it to surgery. In a matter of minutes, a newly opened recreation building turned makeshift morgue was filled to capacity, so fast, in the recollection of one nurse, "that there weren't enough corpsmen to take the dead there. We just piled one on top of the other on carriers in the hallway." A few times, they even removed a corpse from a bloody bed and placed a wounded man in the bed without changing the sheets. One mortally wounded man gazed at a nurse, said, "Kiss the boys goodbye," and died. Another with a gaping hole in his chest took a swig of water from a glass offered by his nurse. He smiled kindly, said "thank you," and expired on the spot. Already the morgue building permeated with the stench of the dead (and would for several more days). Identification of the deceased was at times a problem, though some were wearing dog tags.

The wounded lay waiting along the verandas, most of which had been hastily cleared of previous patients who promptly vacated their beds and did what they could to help. The notable exception was two men in traction, whom Lieutenant Revella Guest, their nurse, had to watch "like a hawk . . . because they were going to cut themselves out . . . and go to war." All day long, the wounded were triaged and treated—a conveyor belt of human suffering, surgery, and reclamation. To Lieutenant Mary Slaughter, a young nurse, the injured men were "the most awful sight my eyes ever beheld. Arms, legs, hands, faces, insides and outsides, gone. We were busy giving heart stimulants, morphine, blood, glucose, redressing the severe bleeding, watching them die, and all the time not a peep out of a blessed soul. Blood, gore . . . it was terrible. They kept coming in from surgery, from first aid, from the field, no moans, no cries, no sound." Lieutenant Elizabeth Elmer, a surgical nurse, remembered "arms and legs just shot off—a terrible mass of tissues, bones, blood." She spent most of the day cleaning debris from open wounds and pouring sulfanilamide powder into each wound to prevent infection. The grisly job left her covered in blood.

There was an insatiable demand for blood plasma. Dr. Forrest Pinkerton hurried to a local company where the council had stored it in substantial quantities. He stowed the plasma in the trunk of his car, distributed it among several hospitals, and then got on the radio asking for more blood donors. Hundreds of volunteers converged on medical facilities, including Tripler, in such numbers that medics ran out of containers and resorted to using sterilized Coca-Cola bottles. Military wives, daughters, civilian employees from Fort Shafter, and other local women converged on Tripler, offering to help. Most were put to work buying candy, pencils, and other gifts for the patients. Some of the wounded men recognized local prostitutes among these volunteers and mentioned this to Lieutenant Elmer. By and large, no one cared (a victory for commonsense humanism over pointless moralism). With a chuckle, Elmer's supervisor told her, "Well, the boys spent enough money on them. Now it's their turn to spend some money on the boys." One of the prostitutes went to work cleaning the Coke bottles and tubes for blood donors. The doctor who supervised the blood donation effort eventually came to think of her as his most reliable volunteer.

Tripler had three operating rooms. Medics managed to cram seven tables into each room—previously they had contained three—and seldom was a table empty. Surgeons worked nonstop. "The casualties were numerous, varied and severe," Dr. Moorhead wrote. "The embedded foreign bodies were of variable size and depth. The majority of casualties consisted of multiple lacerated wounds and compound comminuted fractures. Loss of limbs, initial or from operation, resulted in only a few postoperative fatalities. Shock and hemorrhage were common, but these were surprisingly well combated by transfusions of blood or liquid plasma." Drawing on his World War I combat-surgery experience, Moorhead knew how to interact with the wounded men. "Son," he told one of them, "you've been through a lot of hell, and you're going into some more. This foot has to come off. But there's been many a good pirate with only one leg!" The distinguished surgeon operated for eleven hours straight. During his first break, Moorhead learned from Tripler's commander that he had wangled him a colonel's commission and recalled him to active duty.

There were few burns among Army casualties. Almost all burn victims from the Pearl Harbor attack were Navy men who were victims of flash burns, or had been badly burned by ship fires or oil fires. Most of the patients who made it to surgeon's tables at Tripler survived. The postoperative mortality rate was fewer than 4 percent. Abdominal wounds were the most serious. In many instances, men incurred belly wounds shortly after eating breakfast. "Hence, in the instance of penetrating wounds of the large and small bowel there was the opportunity for a considerable degree of food and fecal contamination of the peritoneal cavity," one doctor wrote. In a few cases, this proved fatal. Far more common, the surgeons operated successfully and stabilized their patients, regardless of the nature of their wounds. The doctors attributed their success to a number of factors: a well-organized evacuation system, the availability of many trained surgeons, the availability of sufficient blood plasma, clean hospitals, good shock treatment, effective control of infections, and quality aftercare.[12]

★

By midmorning, Japanese aviators of the second wave were on their way back to their carriers. The damage they left in their wake was staggering, though not fatal. Eight battleships, three cruisers, three destroyers, and eight other ships were sunk (though all but three ships, and two-thirds of the battleships, would be salvaged to see action again in the war). A total of 188 American aircraft, including 96 Army Air Corps planes, were destroyed, mostly on the ground. From the Navy, 2,008 were killed and 710 wounded; the Marines had 109 killed and 364 wounded. Some 68 civilians were killed and 35 wounded. Tragically, almost all the civilians were killed or hurt by the exploding shells of American antiaircraft fire, primarily around Honolulu. Army ground forces and the Army Air Corps had 218 killed and 364 wounded. The grim grand total came to 2,403 dead and 1,178 wounded. The Japanese lost twenty-nine planes and fifty-five aviators, mainly among second-wave attackers who braved newly alerted antiaircraft batteries. In addition, the Imperial Japanese Navy lost one regular submarine and five midget subs. Admiral Kimmel and General Short paid the price, whether deservedly or not, for the debacle. Both were soon relieved and retired.

With the second wave safely recovered aboard the carriers, Commander Fuchida strongly urged Admiral Nagumo to launch a third strike. In spite of the tremendous damage he and the other aviators had inflicted on the Americans, Fuchida knew that valuable targets such as Pearl's submarine fleet, oil-storage tanks, repair yards, and maintenance facilities remained unscathed. The Pacific Fleet's three major carriers also remained at large. Concerned by the unknown whereabouts of those carriers, as well as the possibility of retaliatory strikes from land-based aircraft, Nagumo decided to withdraw, a fateful decision, one that allowed the Japanese to get away like phantoms in the night but one that left the Pacific Fleet a foundation on which to regroup. The preservation of the oil-storage facilities (or "tank farm," as it was known) preserved mobility for the American fleet. The submarine fleet, though obsolescent, formed the kernel of a force that would eventually come to cripple the Imperial Navy's freedom of movement. The absence of the carriers from the harbor was another break for the Americans. Most ominously for the Japanese, the Pearl Harbor attack was a strategic failure. Rather than stun the Americans into submission, it had the opposite effect of rallying the country to pursue ultimate victory.

All of these permutations were for a later day, though. As the sun set on December 7, Oahu was a traumatized, nervous wreck. The American military installations, aroused now into wartime mode, were really more of a danger to themselves than the escaped enemy. All night long, jumpy antiaircraft crewmen and sentries spewed forth fidgety, irresponsible bursts of fire at any perceived threat. Ground units shot at ground units. In one instance, two infantry outfits exchanged fire across a gully, a masochistic battle that ended only when one soldier was lightly wounded and yelled in profanity so vivid and uniquely American that the other outfit realized they were not up against the Japanese. In several places, "attacking" mules and deer were shot by nervous sentries. One commanding officer foolishly lit up a cigarette and was almost killed by his own men. At the 24th Infantry Division garbage dump, soldiers used hoses to douse burning refuse and thus comply with new blackout restrictions. Someone confused the smell of damp, smoldering garbage with the odor of poison gas. A false gas alert subsequently spread like proverbial wildfire through the division. At the submarine base, a sentry fired so consistently at his relief that he ended up on duty all night.

Meanwhile, the Pearl Harbor area and Oahu coastline lit up with antiaircraft fire as tracer rounds stabbed into the air. The eerie glow of fires bathed the harbor and Wheeler Field, "almost like daylight," in the recollection of one soldier. "Some gunner would test his gun by firing a burst into the air, and every gun within earshot would do the same," said Major Kallis, the Coast Artillery officer. To him, the area seemed "full of Roman candles." Each time the shooting started, more rumors would spread of follow-up Japanese attacks, thus creating even more hysteria. "We'd settle down, and another gun would go off," recalled Lieutenant Elmer, the Tripler nurse. Each time she and the others assumed that the Japanese had returned for another raid or perhaps an actual invasion. "It went on like that most of the night." Wounded men, recovering from the shock of serious injuries and invasive surgery, felt helpless and frightened. Lieutenant Slaughter went from bed to bed, comforting them, calming them as best she could. One teenaged patient with a throat wound begged her to stay with him until he fell asleep, "and before he went to sleep [he] asked me to kiss him good night." The stress manifested itself in loose bowels. One after the other, nurses rushed to the latrine. "Your insides quiver when you're scared," Lieutenant Olsson said, "and you have to go to the bathroom all the time." The sound of flushing toilets could be heard for hours on end.

Ironically, Major Kallis's most frightening moment of the day happened not during the Japanese attack but when his duties required him to walk several hundred yards to check on the batteries in the midst of "invisible troops with very itchy trigger fingers." In the most tragic, and foolish, friendly fire incident, gunners at Pearl shot down four Navy carrier planes that had been searching for the Japanese fleet and were subsequently attempting to land at the naval air station on Ford Island. One plane crashed into a local tavern; another at Wheeler Field. At least two pilots were killed. "I doubt if there was ever a night of so much sweat and so little danger," commented Lieutenant Colonel Newman, the intelligence officer. As much as anything else, all this dangerous profligacy of fire was the product of wild rumors and poor leadership—the former responsible for creating hysteria, the latter for not putting a stop to it.[13]

★

Seldom in history does one day unleash tectonic tremors that reverberate for many decades, but December 7 was such a day. In its immediate aftermath, too, the effect was profound. In Washington, Congress and the president rushed to declare war on Japan, with only one dissenting vote. The overwhelming support for war proved an indication of the country's deadliest weapon—a unified sense of purpose to defeat Japan (and the other Axis powers). In Chungking, Chiang received the news in the middle of the night. Elated at the prospect of expanding his cooperative alliance with the United States, he immediately dictated a letter for Roosevelt, pledging a renewed commitment to their "common battle." In Tokyo, Shigeru Nakamura, a well-known broadcaster, read Emperor Hirohito's rescript declaring war on the Western powers. Hideki Tōjō, the army general and prime minster who headed up Japan's military-dominated government, followed with a speech. "Our adversaries, boasting rich natural resources, aim at the domination of the world . . . ," he asserted. "The rise or fall of our empire and the prosperity or ruin of East Asia literally depend upon the outcome of the war." Later in the day, the government shared some details of the Pearl Harbor attack. People responded to these momentous announcements with solemn patriotism. Crowds descended on the imperial palace. Heads of households wore formal kimonos adorned with family crests. At the palace gate, they spread their arms and bowed formally. Others clapped their hands and shouted "Banzai!" Throughout the city, bands played martial music. In restaurants, diners dropped chopsticks and forks, and stood with bowed heads. Some sobbed excitedly; others sensed the grave momentousness of the occasion and shed tears of emotion. On one building, someone hung a banner that read, "Bury them! America and Britain are our Enemy!" A crowd of middle-aged men, clad in Western-style business suits, carried a banner that read, "One Hundred Million Bullets of Fire!" a reference to the full population and fighting spirit of Japan. At the Yasukuni Shrine—Japan's version of Arlington National

Cemetery—elderly men, many of whom were undoubtedly veterans of previous wars, bowed and prayed. Schoolchildren gathered in groups and trekked to the emperor's palace to demonstrate their devotion to a monarch whom each one of them had been taught was a god on earth. Sei Ito, a thoughtful novelist, expressed the feelings of many Japanese when he scrawled in his diary that evening, "Our fate is that we are not able to think of ourselves as a first-class people unless we fight the white first-class people of the world."

Those who would soon shape the war as important battle captains, and those who would be shaped by it as fighting soldiers, received the news with the same surprise and foreboding wariness as anyone else. In the bedroom of his Manila Hotel penthouse suite, Lieutenant General MacArthur, commander of Filipino-American forces in the Philippines, was awakened from a deep sleep by the insistent ringing of his phone. Upon hearing the terrible news from Major General Richard Sutherland, his chief of staff, a puzzled MacArthur exclaimed, "Pearl Harbor? It should be our strongest position." Somehow, MacArthur formed the impression that the Japanese had suffered a serious defeat. Major General Stilwell, fated to become the most influential American in China, arguably for the entire twentieth century, was serving as a corps commander at the Presidio in California. On that Sunday morning, he and his wife, Winifred, were hosting a brunch for Stilwell's officers at the couple's seaside Carmel home. As the group munched on sandwiches and sipped coffee, they heard the terrible news over a radio that was playing in the background. Stilwell stared out at the Pacific Ocean, as if straining to see the Japanese fleet, and said presciently, "By God, they'll rue this day for generations to come. There's no power on earth like the aroused people of the United States. And the Japs will be destroyed by that power." Later, with characteristically curt skepticism, he documented in his diary a sampling of the overwrought, panicky reports his headquarters soon received. "Jap fleet 20 min. south ... 10 min out. Rumors begin ... Japs going to bomb Bremerton." On the east coast, Major General Eichelberger was sitting at a desk in his superintendent's quarters at West Point, catching up on the Sunday newspapers and administrative work, half listening to the radio, when he heard breathless reports of the Pearl Harbor attacks. As a West Pointer, Eichelberger saw the superintendency as a dream job. But with a war on now, he resolved to request a combat command from General George Marshall, the Army's chief of staff and one of his mentors.

At Nichols Field, a fighter base on the main Philippine island of Luzon, PFC Blair Robinett, an engineer soldier, was sleeping off a hangover when a buddy woke him up and told him that the Japanese had bombed Pearl Harbor. "You crazy stupid ass," an unbelieving Robinett replied, "get away from me. Nobody's at war." Elsewhere on Luzon, Sergeant Forrest Knox and several other soldiers of the 192nd Tank Battalion were planning to pull a gag on a buddy at breakfast. But when the announcement came, breakfast was canceled, a momentary inconvenience that would eventually prove horribly prescient. At the time, though, they were just angry that their prank was foiled. "We were furious with the Japs for ruining the best gag we ever thought up," he later said. At Fort Lewis, Washington, the National Guardsmen and draftees of F Company, 163rd Infantry Regiment were lounging in their barracks, passing a lazy Sunday, after many months of training and maneuvers. Some were reading or writing. Others were counting the days left in their compulsory military service. Still others were nursing hangovers, resolving never to take a drink again. In the corner of the barracks, a lone radio reported the depressing news. A sad realization settled over the men—no one was getting out of the Army any time soon. "The natural reaction, of course, was thoughts of home," one of them recalled, "that of mother, sister, and that girl patiently awaiting your return." Back on Oahu, Lieutenant Slaughter, for the moment much more intimately acquainted than those homesick soldiers with the full human disaster of the war's sudden onset, sat at a breakfast table, fighting off the exhaustion that came from twenty-two straight hours of surgical duty. She ate quietly while involuntary tears streamed down her cheeks. "Those boys—I could not get them off my mind." Thousands of miles away, an anonymous Japanese infantry soldier who would someday meet his death in the South Pacific heard the big news and, out of deep Pan-Asian idealism, confided to his diary. "JAPAN-AMERICA war! It looks as though the hardships we have borne until now will be rewarded. The object of this war is to secure the lands for the various people on this earth. The independence of each country will be respected. A union of the various countries in the Far East is planned and with its combined strength the Far East will be freed of the white man's aggression."[14]

And thus the war began. . . .

2

Hostages to Fortune

N o one could really control the Philippines' archipelago of seventy-one hundred islands. Ninety-four percent of the land area was confined to eleven of these islands. Even so, geography practically guaranteed diversity. The cluster of islands were multilingual (more than sixty-five dialects), multicultural, and multiethnic, so much so that the main issue for any inhabitant hoping to travel or do business from island to island was to figure out how to communicate. Sprinkled among the island clusters that comprised the Philippines were the ethnic descendants of Asia and the western Pacific alike. Located fewer than one thousand miles from the Chinese coast, the islands were an irresistible destination for invaders of every stripe—Hindu Malayan empire builders, Southeast Asians, Muslims, Japanese, and, most prominent, Spaniards who brought with them Western concepts of law, religion, trade, and commerce. Indeed, Spain gave this place its very name as well as more than four hundred years of imperial oversight.

Like the Hawaiian Islands, the Philippines were an unlikely landing spot for Americans. And yet during a brief war with Spain in 1898, the United States destroyed Spanish naval power in the archipelago and made common cause with Filipino nationalists to end the Spanish imperial presence. Upon war's end, President William McKinley found himself with several unpalatable options: return the Philippines to Spain; sell them to another imperial power; support Filipino independence, knowing full well that the archipelago could hardly govern itself, much less fend off imperial predators such as Germany and France; or he could support American annexation of the islands. He swallowed hard and decided on the last option. "There was nothing left to do but take them all, and educate the Filipinos, and uplift and civilize them," he later told an interviewer, using unavowed paternalistic phraseology that many in his time would have considered humane.

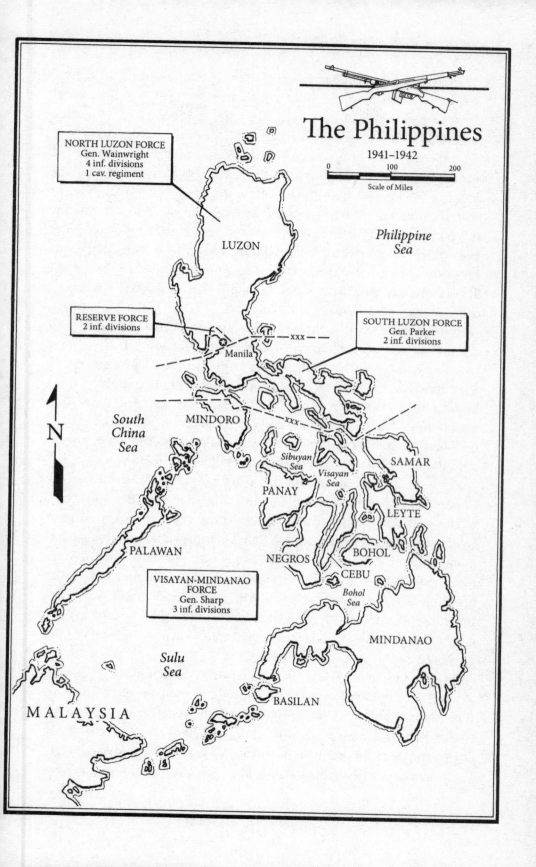

The Philippines

1941–1942

NORTH LUZON FORCE
Gen. Wainwright
4 inf. divisions
1 cav. regiment

RESERVE FORCE
2 inf. divisions

SOUTH LUZON FORCE
Gen. Parker
2 inf. divisions

VISAYAN-MINDANAO
FORCE
Gen. Sharp
3 inf. divisions

0   100   200

Scale of Miles

LUZON

*Philippine
Sea*

Manila

*South
China
Sea*

N

MINDORO

*Sibuyan
Sea*

*Visayan
Sea*

SAMAR

PANAY

LEYTE

PALAWAN

NEGROS

BOHOL

CEBU

*Bohol
Sea*

MINDANAO

*Sulu
Sea*

MALAYSIA

BASILAN

The decision proved to be one of the most fateful in American history. Not only did it deepen the American commitment to the multinational open-door balance of power arrangement in China, but it also committed the United States to the cultivation and defense of the archipelago, a vexing, expensive, and nearly impossible mission. In the perceptive view of one contemporary analyst, the commitment to the Philippines made the Americans "hostages to fortune." In the near term, roughly from 1898–1902, the decision led to a bitter, atrocity-laced, but successful, counterinsurgent war against Filipino nationalists, some of whom had stood shoulder to shoulder with American soldiers during the war with Spain. In the longer term, nominal ownership of the Philippines committed the United States to maintaining the status quo in the Western Pacific, thus setting a collision course with expansionist Japan.

By the mid-1930s, after three decades of governing the Philippines as a colonial territory, this obligation was growing wearisome, from a moral and economic standpoint, to the American government. Many Americans who understood all too well their own country's anti-colonial origins found the idea of an imperial empire repugnant. The expense of governing, maintaining, and fortifying the archipelago was also unpopular during desperate economic times, when the vast majority of Americans saw no need for internationalist overseas responsibilities. So in March 1934, Congress passed the Tydings–McDuffie Act, designed to transition the country to eventual independence in 1946. The Philippines became a commonwealth, with a national assembly, a president, a constitution, and plans to create autonomous armed forces. The Americans pledged to abandon many military installations in 1946, though the question of naval bases remained nebulous. Regardless of future intentions, the geopolitical reality of the moment mandated continued American dominance of the Philippines. The commonwealth was a "nation" in name only. It could not really govern the archipelago, and it could not begin to defend itself against the possibility of Japanese encroachment.[1]

Manuel Quezon, the new Filipino president, understood all of this, so, to a great extent, he welcomed the continued American presence. The same was true for the majority of his seventeen million countrymen and women. Quezon was the son of a Spanish soldier who had settled on Luzon, the largest and most important of the islands. Young Quezon had once fought the Americans as a guerrilla warrior, serving as a key aide for Emilio Aguinaldo, the charismatic Filipino nationalist whom the Americans captured in 1901 and who shortly thereafter swore loyalty to the United States.

Quezon and the Roosevelt administration planned to build up an independent Filipino military force capable of defending the country when independence became a reality. For this, both parties were ill prepared. The American military presence in the Philippines had seldom amounted to little more than about ten thousand troops, half of whom were Philippine Scouts, locals who served as US soldiers. In 1935, Quezon turned to an old friend, General MacArthur, the current Army chief of staff, to help him build a national military force. What initially appeared to be an odd, albeit unique, sunset posting for the Army's number one soldier instead became a summons to the stage for the central figure of the American war against Japan. In the Army's long history, MacArthur is the only chief of staff whose most significant and notable service occurred *after* leaving the top post. MacArthur's ties to the Philippines were deep and abiding. His father, Arthur MacArthur Jr., had been a Civil War Medal of Honor recipient and prominent general who had served, from 1898 to 1901, as a key commander of American military forces in the Philippines. Quezon himself had once surrendered personally to Arthur MacArthur's troops.

Since graduating from West Point in 1903, Douglas had served multiple tours in the archipelago. In 1904, during his first deployment to the Philippines as a mapping engineer, Lieutenant MacArthur had first met and befriended a young Quezon, who was fresh out of law school at the University of Santo Tomas, in Manila. Douglas's affection for the country and its people was sincere. "The Philippines charmed me," he later wrote. "The languorous laze that seemed to glamorize even the most routine chores of life, the fun-loving men, the moonbeam delicacy of its lovely women, fastened me with a grip that has never relaxed."

MacArthur's egomaniacal affection for himself was even more pronounced than his love for the Philippines. He routinely referred to himself in the third person, especially when recounting stories to friends or aides. In social situations he was, in the recollection of one observer, "a captivating, spellbinding talker," prone to monopolizing a conversation, sometimes for hours on end. When peers clustered together at cocktail parties or other social gatherings and focused their attention upon anything other than MacArthur, he often affected aloofness, hovering on the edges, staring into the distance as if pondering some elusive profundity (a common pose in photos of him).

Pompous, bombastic, and vainglorious, MacArthur came to the commonwealth with a partially deserved reputation for intellectual agility and personal bravery. At West Point, he earned the prestigious honor of first captain of the corps of cadets. The story later circulated in some circles that MacArthur had recorded the highest ever grade point average at the Point. As was so common with MacArthur, there was merely a kernel of truth buried beneath hagiographic layers of myth. His West Point academic career had indeed been distinguished, but there was no real way to compare grades achieved in different eras. In World War I, he had served in a series of jobs, including as a brigade commander and division chief of staff, with the 42nd Division. He began the war as a major and ended it as a brigadier general with multiple decorations for valor and a reputation for lead-from-the-front bravery. There was no way, though, to validate the widespread claim of his adherents that he was the most decorated, courageous officer in the American Expeditionary Forces.

Though MacArthur seldom thought of himself in such terms, he was the ultimate Army insider. As the son of a respected general, he enjoyed a built-in network of patrons and an intuitive understanding of how to advance. He was anything but obscure. Decision-makers either knew him personally or knew of him, especially after his distinguished World War I service. Mary, his mother, devoted her life to the furtherance of his career. She was widowed in 1912 when Arthur collapsed and died while making a speech at a veterans' reunion. Eleven years later she suffered another terrible blow when Douglas's elder brother Arthur III, a rising naval officer, died of a burst appendix. For Mary, little could penetrate the gloom of loss besides her Douglas, on whom she had doted for years (even living in a nearby hotel during his cadet years). She wrote obsequious, beseeching letters on his behalf to Army leaders, most notably John Pershing, the former commander of the American Expeditionary Forces, who had once served as a junior officer under Douglas's father. After the war Pershing became chief of staff. "My hope and ambition in life is to live long enough to see this son made a General Officer, and I feel I am placing my entire life, as it were, in your hand for consideration," she lobbied in one such letter to Pershing, hoping to persuade him to place Douglas on a list of permanent generals. Another time, she begged Pershing to use his powers as chief of staff to promote her son. "I am presuming on a long and loyal friendship for you—to open my heart in this appeal for my Boy. You are so powerful in all Army matters, that you could give him promotion by the stroke of your pen! *You* have never failed me yet—and somehow I know you will not in this request." MacArthur received this promotion and several others, all the way, in 1930, to the chief of staff job, an achievement his father had yearned for but never attained.

MacArthur compiled a mixed record during his tenure in the top job. On the upside, he skillfully served two administrations, one Republican, one Democrat, and he fought hard for military preparedness. On the downside, in 1932 he had presided over the Army's disgraceful suppression of the so-called Bonus Marchers, a large group of World War I veterans who were hard hit by the Depression and who marched on Washington in hopes of early collection of government bonuses. Claiming that there was "incipient revolution in the air," MacArthur used armed troops to disperse and eject these destitute veterans, most of whom wanted little more than what the government owed them.

MacArthur's behavior in his personal life also left much to be desired. Newly divorced after a miserable marriage to socialite Louise Cromwell, he had struck up a relationship with a sixteen-year-old girl in the Philippines immediately before becoming chief of staff. The fifty-year-old MacArthur secretly arranged for the girl, Isabel Rosario Cooper, to come to Washington, where he put her up in a Georgetown apartment and engaged in a kind of sugar-daddy relationship with her. In a later era, MacArthur's egregiously inappropriate relationship most likely would have seen him put on trial for child molestation and then stripped of his commission and his job as an afterthought. But the relationship never became public. When columnist Drew Pearson found out about Isabel from MacArthur's ex-wife, Louise, he blackmailed MacArthur with the information in exchange for MacArthur's pledge to drop a pending libel suit against the controversial columnist for a piece he had written excoriating the general's supposed dictatorial actions during the Bonus March fiasco. From a more modern viewpoint, MacArthur was very lucky. Had he lived in the television or social media age of intrusive mass media, he could well have been undone and disgraced, living out the rest of his days as a mercurial and fascinating but scorned man.[2]

Instead, he ended up in the Philippines, drawing a handsome salary of eighteen thousand dollars a year plus fifteen thousand dollars per year in allowances from the commonwealth alongside his Army pay, since he remained on active duty, though no longer with a chief of staff's four stars. He took his ailing mother with him, along with a small staff that included a particularly competent and dependable aide, Major Dwight Eisenhower, who had already served under MacArthur for almost three years. In December 1935, shortly after MacArthur and his entourage arrived in the Philippines, his mother died. In Eisenhower's recollection, her passing "affected the general's spirits for many months." When MacArthur next visited the United States two years later—the last time he would see his home country for nearly a decade and a half—he arranged for his mother to be interred at Arlington National Cemetery alongside his father. While in the United States, Douglas also remarried. He had met thirty-seven-year-old Jean Faircloth, a Tennessee heiress, aboard ship on his way to the islands in 1935. Short, petite, bright, socially adept and kindhearted, Jean was enamored of soldiers. Like MacArthur's mother, she traced her lineage to Confederate war heroes (one of Jean's grandfathers had actually fought against MacArthur's father at Missionary Ridge). For nearly two years, as MacArthur undertook his duties in Manila, the two engaged in a comfortable, caring courtship. They were nearly inseparable, lifelong soul mates in the truest meaning of the phrase. Jean gave birth to their only child, Arthur IV, in 1938. The family lived in a six-room, air-conditioned penthouse suite atop the new Manila Hotel.

With characteristic breezy optimism, MacArthur set about the gargantuan task of establishing a viable armed force. Quezon once asked him, "General, do you think that the Philippines, once independent, can defend itself?" MacArthur responded firmly, "I don't *think* they can. I *know* they can." The assurance had no basis in reality. MacArthur envisioned a Swiss-style defense force with a small regular army augmented by a large ready reserve of trained men. Quezon's fledgling government could not hope to mobilize such an armed force that might be capable of defending such a diffuse array of islands. For one thing, the commonwealth did not have the money. For another, it did not have the capability to care for them properly while in service, much less arm and equip them to modern standards. Some members of the national assembly deeply objected to the idea of building up an army at the expense of infrastructure, domestic programs, and the personal liberty of individuals. Conscription did not go well.

Trainees were often illiterate, with no idea of basic sanitation and no real motivation to subject themselves to military discipline. Outside of the Scouts, there were few professional soldiers among the population. Officers and NCOs were scarce. More than anything else, language proved to be an almost insurmountable barrier. It was not unusual for men in one company to speak at least six different dialects, each of which was unintelligible to the other, a military Tower of Babel that guaranteed frustration and inertia.

All of these issues stemmed from one problem: President Quezon was attempting to implement the first indigenous central authority in the history of the archipelago, and he had nothing like the necessary political cohesion and economic development necessary for the creation of such a modern nation state. In that sense, national defense was just one vexing problem among many dozens.

Quezon conferred the rank of field marshal on MacArthur—probably at the latter's behest—a new level of empty pomposity even for such a genius of self-aggrandizement. At a promotion ceremony that might have made Hermann Göring blush, MacArthur wore a specially designed black-and-white sharkskin uniform and accepted a gold field marshal's baton from Quezon. The field marshal soon had to admit to himself that the commonwealth government was in no position to support his defense plans. Increasingly he turned to the American government for help, pleading mainly for weapons and equipment, something of a tough sell to a country that was still in the throes of the Depression. As yet, there was little popular support for rejuvenating the American armed forces, and naturally less so for the Philippines. Defense budgets were still parsimonious; the Army and the Navy were already stretched reed-thin and had little to spare from their own sparse inventories. An impatient Quezon began to push the Roosevelt administration for early independence in 1939. The Filipino president began playing a double game of sorts; he traveled to Tokyo, urged the Japanese to respect Filipino sovereignty and probably offered neutrality in return. Quezon's actions had a chilling effect on his influence in Washington and made MacArthur's task that much more difficult. After all, why invest scarce resources in a country that was soon to receive its independence, whether in 1939 or 1946?

Echoes of past differences also had an effect. Some American policy makers wondered whether it was wise to put weapons into the hands of potentially rebellious Filipinos who might just decide to turn them on Americans. Nor was official Washington universally enamored of MacArthur's mission. Frank Murphy, the newly retired high commissioner of the Philippines, maintained that MacArthur's plans were a threat to liberty in the Philippines. He urged Roosevelt to end MacArthur's mission and bring him home.

Under these circumstances, MacArthur did well to get anything for his nascent army. He was ably assisted by Eisenhower, who, in 1938, traveled home and made the official rounds, lobbying on behalf of his chief. "I have encountered nothing but the most sympathetic attitude toward your task and your plans," he assured MacArthur in a detailed letter on the meetings. The War Department sent World War I–era artillery pieces, trench mortars, machine guns, Browning automatic rifles, and bolt-action Enfield rifles. Unfortunately, some of the ammunition for these weapons was in poor shape and would only degrade under tropical conditions in the Philippines.

There was less sympathy in Washington for allowing MacArthur to continue double-dipping as both a field marshal in the employ of an ostensibly foreign government and an active-duty officer. Probably at President Roosevelt's behest, General Malin Craig, the new Army chief of staff, informed MacArthur that he would be recalled from Manila at the end of 1937 and assigned new duties. The obvious countermove from the field marshal was to retire and remain in the islands. In a warm, albeit disingenuous letter, he notified General Craig of this decision. "My Philippine work is practically accomplished and I am very anxious indeed to return to my ancestral home in Milwaukee, Wisconsin. There are many cultural matters that all my life, I have been anxious to explore." MacArthur also alluded to nonexistent personal health issues and downplayed the likelihood of war. "The United States will not become involved in war in my day. The magnificent leadership of President Roosevelt practically assures against such a calamity."

Milwaukee need not have gotten its hopes up for the return of the great man. He had no intention of leaving the Philippines. He stayed on indefinitely as Quezon's military adviser, drawing a $36,000-a-year salary, laboring at the same thankless (some might say hopeless) task. Over time, Quezon distanced himself from MacArthur and even mused openly to Francis Sayre Sr., the new American high commissioner, about the possibility of dismissing him. The president publicly repudiated MacArthur's security plans and cut defense funding. Once, when the field marshal tried to see Quezon, the president's secretary Jorge Vargas told him the president was too busy. "Jorge," MacArthur responded, "some day your boss is going to want to see me more than I want to see him."

Eisenhower became cognizant of the divide, especially when the president seemed to seek him out and confide in him rather than MacArthur. By 1939, Eisenhower was fed up with the whole mess. He badly wanted a command of his own. For years he had functioned as MacArthur's personal man Friday, a role in life that ultimately did not suit his own personal ambitions and capabilities. He insisted on reassignment back to the United States. Both MacArthur and Quezon attempted to dissuade him, the latter allegedly with an offer of a lucrative contract, but Ike refused. Self-centered as always, MacArthur was hardly the type of commander to foster or encourage the ambitions of his aides. He seldom pushed hard for their advancement, preferring instead that they choose to spend their careers serving him. He saw Eisenhower's exodus as an act of disloyalty and never really forgave him. The Filipino armed forces, after nearly five years of intensive labor by MacArthur and his staff, were nowhere near a state of readiness. "We had to content ourselves with an attempt to produce a military adequate to deal with domestic revolt and to provide at least a passive type of defense around the perimeter of the Islands to slow up the advance of any aggressor until some friendly nation, presumably the United States, came to their aid," Ike later wrote.[3]

Only in 1941, as war with Japan grew imminent, did this situation begin to change, though the Filipino armed forces were never truly prepared for war. In the months before Pearl Harbor, the War Department belatedly and hurriedly began to build up Filipino-American military forces in the archipelago. The key moment of this too-little-too-late mobilization was July 26, when President Roosevelt recalled MacArthur to active duty as commander of the US Army Forces of the Far East (USAFFE) which, in spite of the grand-sounding name, primarily encompassed the Philippines. Commonwealth forces were to be absorbed into the US Army. MacArthur's return to active duty created something of an awkward command situation with Major General George Grunert, an amiable, respected cavalryman who headed the Philippine Department and thus presided over all US Army troops on the islands. MacArthur wrote to the War Department and urged Grunert's immediate recall. Secretary of War Henry Stimson and General George Marshall, who had succeeded Craig as chief of staff, both agreed, as did President Roosevelt. Effective immediately, MacArthur took control of all military forces in the Philippines. This seemingly innocuous decision set the course for MacArthur's rise to martial stardom, not to mention Grunert's consignment to obscurity.[4]

One of the new commander's main tasks was to mobilize the commonwealth armed forces into active duty. Ten reserve divisions—existing mostly on paper—were called into service throughout the fall. The authorized strength of each division was seventy-five soldiers. Added to this was the 1st Regular Division, smaller support units and the constabulary, a police-like force of local troops trained primarily for internal security. The job of putting flesh on bones was gargantuan. Harried American officers had to prepare campsites and training areas and arrange for the soldiers to be fed, equipped, and trained. A cadre of forty American officers and twenty American NCOs or Philippine Scouts served as the skeleton around which each division was formed. Weapons, ammo, and infrastructure were all substandard. "The men had no individual entrenching tools," Major Malcolm Fortier, an adviser to the 41st Infantry Division, later wrote. Uniforms were shabby. Leather footgear was ill-suited for the wide tendencies of local feet, causing such bad blisters that, according to Fortier, "many men went bare foot rather than wear them." Radios and field phones were antiquated. Vehicles were scarce, as were proper medical supplies. Even the 1st Regular Division, theoretically composed of professional soldiers, was barely provisioned. "It was inadequately equipped with leftovers if there were any," Captain Alfredo Santos, one of the officers, wrote. "It had no organic artillery. It went to war without any steel helmets. It had mortars but no mortar shells. It had .50 Cal MG ammunition but had no MG's for these ammunitions." Only after the war began did the unit begin to receive anything like the necessary supplies. Another typical outfit, the 92nd Infantry Regiment, never did. They were clothed in short pants, short-sleeved shirts, tennis shoes, and coconut-palm-frond helmets. They carried only light canvas packs and Enfield rifles.

Language and cultural problems persisted even for units composed of men from the same region. "They spoke eleven different dialects," Colonel Glen Townsend, commander of the 11th Infantry Regiment, 11th Infantry Division, later said. "Christian and Pagan had little liking for each other. Although all the enlisted personnel had taken the prescribed five and a half months [of] training, they were proficient only in close-order drill and saluting. The officers, being mainly political appointees, had less training than the men they were supposed to lead." One of his machine-gun companies proved to be a near total loss because the troops could not begin to communicate with one another. Townsend's officers resorted to using sign language and diagrams. This reduced training, in the estimation of one captain to "demonstration, application, and supervision." In another unit, the language gap also bordered on the ridiculous. American officers gave instructions in English to Filipino officers who then translated to their sergeants in Tagalog, who, in turn, translated the Tagalog instructions into a local dialect. In the estimation of one officer, the Filipino soldiers were "undisciplined, untrained, and unequipped."

Most of the men were in decent physical condition, though they were small and did not have quite as much endurance as a typical American soldier. A substantial number of the local men were eager to serve, especially when properly treated by their American and Filipino trainers. By and large, Americans and Filipinos got along very well. Even so, too many of the Americans, all of whom were white, viewed Filipinos as racial inferiors. When a constabulary sergeant politely attempted to corral an unruly drunk American woman at a Manila bar, she slapped him and screamed, "We Americans are the ruling race here. You Filipinos are dirt." The Army & Navy Club in Manila refused to serve nonwhites. Even mestizos, the light-skinned, mixed-race descendants of Spaniards, were not welcome. Lieutenant Lloyd Goad, a young physician, found this out firsthand one night when he and a friend brought their mestizo dates to the club. When the women visited the bathroom, the club manager took them aside and explained the rules. "No Filipinos or mestizos permitted. Anglos and Spanish okay." The following morning, Goad even found in his mailbox a written reminder of the club's racist rules.

To combat and forestall such ignorant attitudes, Brigadier General Edward "Ned" King, a genteel Georgian and commander at Fort Stotsenburg on Luzon, felt compelled to tell newly arrived officers, "There is no such thing as racial superiority." King stressed that any American who expected to be obeyed by his Filipino subordinates must first demonstrate true leadership. In his opinion, the Filipino soldier was "proud and sensitive and many of his reactions have their root in real or fancied racial slights . . . throughout history he has demonstrated personal bravery of individual fighting ability, even against superior arms and disciplined force." King wisely urged his young leaders not to judge local soldiers by American customs or standards, but through the lens of their own culture. They especially needed to follow up with their men to make sure they followed orders because Filipino troops tended to say, "Yes, sir" and then do nothing, a potential court-martial offense in the US Army, but nothing more than a cultural propensity within the comparatively laid-back lifestyle of the islands. In this sense, the role of these American professional soldiers foreshadowed the Special Forces mission of the postwar era. The Filipino soldiers were, in the favorable opinion of Captain Beverly "Ben" Skardon, "lackadaisical but gifted with a remarkable native ingenuity . . . very affectionate and sentimental almost to an extreme. Many would march holding hands or even leave their foxholes to ask permission to visit a friend." At full mobilization, the Philippine armed forces numbered about 120,000 men, plus a token air force.[5]

Mixed units of regulars formed the core of MacArthur's army. The Philippine Division was composed of Scouts and American professional soldiers. Like all World War II army divisions, this one was triangular, with three infantry regiments, the 31st, the 45th, and the 57th, each of which had three battalions. The division also contained engineers, artillery, and other specialists. The 31st Infantry Regiment was all American; Philippine Scouts comprised the majority of manpower in the other two regiments and throughout the rest of the division. Another regular unit was the 26th Cavalry Regiment, a horse-mounted outfit of fiercely proud Scouts led by American officers. Throughout the fall of 1941, the War Department sent whatever US Army reinforcements it could to the Philippines, though MacArthur inexplicably turned down receipt of a National Guard division on the grounds that he did not need it because he already had the Philippine Division and the ten reservist commonwealth divisions. As it was, he received the 200th Coast Artillery Regiment, the 17th Ordnance Battalion, and a provisional tank group composed of the 192nd and 194th Tank Battalions, collectively equipped with 108 M3 Stuart light tanks. The armored units also brought 75-millimeter self-propelled guns with them. The Coast Artillery people added to the antiaircraft, antitank, antiship, and artillery capability of the defense force.

Washington shipped new steel helmets, M1 Garand rifles, machine guns, 37-millimeter antitank guns, medical equipment, fuel, and food to the islands. Aerial strength grew. Between July and December, the air forces morphed from a motley collection of a few planes to a potent defensive weapon. By the eve of the war, MacArthur had 277 aircraft, including 35 modern B-17 bombers and 107 P-40 fighters, just the sort of weapons that could challenge amphibious invaders. Aviation engineers were busily expanding and improving airfields, especially in the area surrounding Manila. At sea, the Philippines were defended by Admiral Thomas Hart's Asiatic Fleet. Hart had one heavy cruiser, one light cruiser, thirteen old destroyers, twenty-nine submarines, some PBY patrol seaplanes, plus a smattering of minesweepers, gunboats, torpedo boats, sub tenders, and the like. Though this was hardly a formidable fleet, especially by later US Navy standards in this war, it did have the capability of inflicting significant damage on an invasion armada. By December, MacArthur's army counted nearly thirty-two thousand American soldiers and almost one hundred thousand Filipino soldiers. In the context of American history, this was a unique force, a colonial army, built almost in the mold of a British imperial army, and yet distinctly more democratic and egalitarian.[6]

The mobilization was basically a race against time. Japanese reconnaissance planes were routinely violating Filipino airspace. American planners hoped and expected that war would not break out until April 1942. But anyone attuned to geopolitical realities in 1941 understood that peace would not last for much longer. "The sparkle went out of Manila in the spring of 1941," said Major General Jonathan Wainwright, soon to be a key commander. "War was coming, and we all knew it." For many years, duty in the Philippines had been a prized assignment for soldiers. The islands offered a low-key, imperial lifestyle. Money went a long way. Most soldiers could afford to hire local domestic help to do their cooking and washing. Filipinos routinely called Americans, even the lowliest private, "Joe" or "Sir." Duty hours were similar to those in Hawaii. Afternoons were usually free, with copious recreational outlets. Social calendars were filled with polo matches, jai alai games, gambling, golf, tennis, swimming, gymnastics, hiking, sightseeing, movies, dining, dances, and boating. Manila nightlife was fast and exciting. Bars teemed with servicemen. Houses of prostitution proliferated. Newly arrived soldiers were warned by wiseacre archipelago veterans to avoid the "benny boys," cross-dressing young men masquerading as female hookers. Off-duty soldiers wandered among the city's pungent open-air markets, where canny merchants loudly haggled with their customers over green bananas, papayas, and unrefrigerated, maggot-addled pork, chicken, beef, snake, monkey, dog, and cat, and where passersby indiscreetly urinated into open gutters. The heat was pervasive. Air-conditioning was nearly unheard of; Americans often showered two or three times a day. Throughout the year, as war approached, military lifestyle became more austere. "Social activities greatly decreased," recalled Lieutenant Madeline Ullom, one of several dozen Army nurses stationed in the Philippines. "Curfews were routine. Alerts were more frequent. Field exercises were longer and more intensive." At the Army & Navy Club, there was still some time for officers to congregate and listen to the annual Army-Navy football game. "The game is broadcast and followed on a big scoreboard," Lieutenant Alexander "Sandy" Nininger, a recent West Point graduate, wrote to his family. "We have cheer leaders, a goat, a mule, bands etc. It was great except that Navy won."

Perhaps the most glaring indicator of war's imminence occurred that spring when the War Department ordered the evacuation of all military family members and dependents. At farewell parties, they were feted with feigned enthusiasm and then, seemingly cloaked in gloomy denial of the terrible days to come, trundled aboard homebound ships. As the ships pulled away, wives and children stood along the railing, tears streaming down their cheeks. From the dock, husbands stared back, "waving with frozen smiles," in Wainwright's recollection, feeling terrible but not wanting to betray any indication of their melancholy. Soon all the families were gone, except for one. MacArthur's wife and son remained. For reasons he never explained (and no one in or out of the Army at the time ever asked him), he did not personally comply with the War Department order. It was not the last time that MacArthur would display a regal tendency to ignore instructions that did not suit him. By disregarding the evacuation order, he brazenly consigned Jean and Arthur to be trapped in the Philippines with him, exposed to the inherent dangers of a war zone. The difficulties they experienced would undoubtedly affect his actions and decisions. Moreover, their presence set a poor example for his command—the rules apparently applied to everyone except for this particular commander. No other American theater commander in World War II had the opportunity to enjoy the presence of his family. Neither his nominal superiors in Washington, nor anyone in the Philippines, seems ever to have addressed this issue with him.[7]

★

Optimism is a wonderful quality if it is grounded in reality. If it is not, then it amounts to nothing more than empty, irresponsible foolhardiness. The American plan in the event of war with Japan recognized the mirthless reality that the Japanese were likely to enjoy local superiority of force in the Philippines. Japanese air, sea, and ground forces were close in proximity and better prepared for war. The US strategy, code-named War Plan Orange, recognized this uncomfortable truth. The Japanese were almost certain to land their troops successfully at any place of their choosing among the thousands of miles of coastline on Luzon and other islands. The key was to stalemate them until help arrived. War Plan Orange (or WPO-3 as it was known by 1941) thus called for Filipino-American forces to hunker down on the highly defensible Bataan peninsula and in coastal forts around Manila Bay where they would deny the Japanese the use of this wonderful harbor. Sustained by prepositioned stocks of food, ammunition, and medical supplies, the defenders were to hold out as best they could until the Navy was able to defeat the Japanese at sea and reinforce the archipelago with fresh troops.

During his years as military adviser, MacArthur came to view Orange as defeatist, so he devised an alternate plan that hinged on repelling the Japanese from the Philippines altogether. His newly constituted Philippine Army, with support from their American friends, was to halt any invasion at the waterline. "My concept . . . was to defeat the enemy on the beaches, where he would be at his weakest in any amphibious landings," he later told an Army historian. Allied air and sea forces would also help ward off the Japanese invaders. Under MacArthur's new plan, the beaches were to be the main arena of decision. Instead of passively allowing the Japanese to establish a foothold in the Philippines, he intended to defeat them at the waterline. Impressed with MacArthur's aggressive optimism, and blithely trusting that, after years on-site, he must know what he was talking about, General Marshall and the War Department approved the abandonment of WPO-3 in favor of MacArthur's defend-the-beaches concept. Exact details were sparse as to how such a nascent army of ill-trained, ill-prepared conscripts was to ward off an enemy who enjoyed the distinct advantages of initiative and mobility of force. Seldom has an American commander of any status prepared a battle plan so inappropriate to his circumstances. At Normandy three years later, Erwin Rommel invested in the same wrongheaded strategy, albeit against a more powerful, better-prepared enemy, but with less coastline to defend and a substantially stronger force at his disposal than MacArthur's Filipino-American army. Given the disaster that the overrated Rommel experienced—even the most hard-pressed Allied invaders at Normandy were held up for only half a day—he would have done well to study MacArthur's flawed plan. During a visit with *Time* magazine journalist Clare Boothe Luce in September 1941, MacArthur explained his thinking with a sports analogy. "Did you ever hear the baseball expression, 'Hit 'em where they ain't'? That's my formula." This was a remarkable phrase to employ because, ironically, it demonstrated the fatal weakness that was to doom the MacArthur plan. The Japanese could just as easily "hit 'em where they ain't," by finding weak spots in his overstretched forces and exploiting them. The paradox seemed completely lost on the USAFFE commander.[8]

To the Japanese, an invasion of the Philippines was a necessary evil. Their experiences with the geographic diversity of the archipelago dated back centuries; they knew full well that the Philippines was a difficult place to control, but they also knew they could not ignore the country. The overarching strategic purpose of their war was to secure raw materials on the Asian mainland and the Malaya-Indonesia basin that was weakly controlled by British and Dutch imperial administrators. Because of the Philippines' proximity to these places, and because it was the gateway to the vast oceanic expanse of the south and central Pacific, it had to be neutralized as an American base. Well over half the Imperial Japanese Army was tied down in China and Manchuria. At the outset of the war, only nine divisions were available for southern—as the Japanese thought of them—operations against the Dutch, British, and Americans. By contrast, more than thirty-five divisions were dealing with the Chinese on the Asian mainland. In the final plans, only two divisions, plus an independent brigade, were available to invade the Philippines. These units were grouped together into the 14th Army under Lieutenant General Masaharu Homma, an amateur playwright and poet who spoke good English and actually opposed war with the United States. He was supported by the Army's 5th Air Group and the Imperial Navy's 3rd Fleet and 11th Air Fleet, collectively a powerful air and sea force.

The Japanese devised an incremental plan to seize the archipelago. Simultaneous air attacks were to destroy or at least neutralize MacArthur's air force. At the same time, expeditionary forces would land in northern Luzon to capture airfields from which the 5th Air Group could support subsequent operations near Manila. With American air strength destroyed or diminished, the bulk of Homma's ground forces would then land at Lingayen Gulf, northwest of Manila, and Lamon Bay, southeast of the capital. From these beachheads they would envelop Manila and the Filipino-American army. "Landing operations will usually be carried out in the face of enemy fire after repulsing attacks from the enemy's army, naval and air forces," Japanese commanders predicted in a final planning document. Soldiers about to embark on the great expedition were imbued by their leaders with a supercharged sense of anti-Western righteousness. "We must think of this next war as one between races," an Army pamphlet urged the troops. "The Occidentals, excepting Germans and Italians, must never be left unpunished, while we are promoting our own rightful ideas." To the peoples of East Asia and the Pacific Islands, European and American imperialists had been like "burglars, we their brothers. At least we are relatives. We Japanese are born in a happy country. Under the august virtue of His Majesty, the Emperor, we have not been exploited a single time by foreigners. This makes the other East Asiatics envious of us. They trust us, respect us, and have hopes of receiving their independence through us." Reading such pamphlets and listening to informal pep talks from their officers, soldiers were encouraged to see themselves as heroic liberators of their ethnic cousins. "We are so moved and inspired that it makes our blood boil and body dance," a machine-gun sergeant confided to his diary. "I feel a spiritual change in me," one young captain enthused.[9]

With this sense of purpose, and in tandem with the Pearl Harbor attack, the Japanese put their Philippines plans into motion. Among their initial targets was Clark Field, located about forty miles northwest of Manila, and home to MacArthur's most important air units, including nineteen B-17 bombers, out of thirty-five total in his aerial fleet. Staging from nearby Formosa (present-day Taiwan), Japan's 11th Air Fleet planes were fueled, armed, and ready to launch by the crack of daylight on December 8. A combination of fog and inaccurate reports of incoming American planes postponed their takeoff. Crewmen stood around for a couple of hours, itching for launch orders, worrying that every minute of delay meant a more aroused American enemy. They could not have known that this delay was fortuitous.

Even several hours after hearing the earth-shattering news of Pearl Harbor, MacArthur's command was still in something of a torpor. Within an hour of finding out that war was on, the general had roused himself from bed, dressed, and gone to his headquarters at Number 1 Calle Victoria, a venerable, rambling wooden building perched atop the west side of Intramuros, the old walled city in downtown Manila, a place where the power of Spanish imperial overseers had once radiated over the beautiful, sparkling waters of the city's bay. MacArthur's headquarters was wedged in among Spanish-built Catholic churches, schools, and the oldest nunnery in the islands. In the confusion of the moment, MacArthur was under the impression that the Japanese had suffered a severe reversal at Pearl, though he had received no official communications informing him as such. On November 27, he had received orders from the War Department urging him to avoid any provocative acts that Japan might use as a justification for war. "If hostilities cannot be avoided," the directive stated, "the United States desires that Japan commit the first overt act." He was, though, fully empowered to conduct appropriate aerial and sea reconnaissance missions around the archipelago and to take whatever steps he deemed necessary to protect his command. MacArthur seemed to interpret this as an order not to take offensive action of any kind. President Quezon even later claimed, with no real evidence, that the general clung to the hope that the Japanese would respect Filipino neutrality and bypass the islands. It is hard to believe that, after spending six years in the Philippines building up an army, MacArthur could have entertained any such illusions. "My orders were explicit not to initiate hostilities against the Japanese," he later explained. The Philippines had a "somewhat indeterminate international position in many minds, especially the Filipinos and their government. While I personally had not the slightest doubt we would be attacked, great local hope existed that this would not be the case." MacArthur was, in essence, saying he sat tight in order to placate the wishes of Quezon.

Regardless, there is little doubt that the general's transition into a wartime mentality was not swift. To a great extent, MacArthur's apparent confusion over the nature of the crisis led to a fiasco of miscommunication, mixed intentions, and poorly coordinated actions with Lieutenant General Lewis Brereton, who had taken command of MacArthur's Far East Air Force in November. Brereton had actually graduated from the Naval Academy in 1911 but he subsequently resigned to accept a commission in the Army's Coast Artillery Corps. But Louie, as he was generally called, was drawn to aviation. He became one of the Army's first pilots and served several months as a combat squadron and wing commander during World

War I. As a pioneering aviator, Brereton helped to establish the Army Air Corps. As a senior leader, he was competent but uninspiring, a canny insider who cultivated friends in key places and led more through his ability to navigate military bureaucracy than any predilection for inspiring subordinates.

When Brereton found out that the war had begun, his immediate instinct was to plan a B-17 raid on Formosa. He went to Number 1 Calle Victoria and attempted to request permission from MacArthur to launch the mission. Instead, he was waylaid by Major General Sutherland, MacArthur's chief of staff, and denied access to the commander. Relentless and hardworking, Sutherland had joined the staff in 1938 when Lieutenant Colonel Jimmy Ord, a key aide (plus a dear friend and colleague of Eisenhower) had died in a plane crash. Ord's death marked the beginning of the end for Eisenhower in the Philippines and the rise of Sutherland as MacArthur's main confidant and alter ego. Ike's friendship with Ord had made working for MacArthur more bearable. Without Ord, "all the zest was gone," Eisenhower once said, and he resolved to leave the Philippines. Sutherland later bragged that he had supplanted Eisenhower and personally run him out of the archipelago. Whether true or not, the claim itself reveals much about the man. As the Yale-educated son of a US senator from West Virginia, Sutherland was hardly born to soldiering. His father wanted a career in law or business for his son. The elder Sutherland refused to consider arranging an appointment to West Point and insisted on Yale. At Yale, young Dick joined ROTC and, upon graduation, joined a National Guard unit as a private and quickly wangled a commission. In World War I, he saw combat as a company commander. He came to MacArthur from the 15th Infantry Regiment in China. Short and lean with a well-groomed soldierly appearance, Sutherland was brusque and cold. Bright and dedicated, he had little patience for fools or incompetents. One colleague described him as "a secretive, remote person who worked as hard, if not harder, than anybody else." Another characterized him as "a cold machine. No one ever got close to him." Sutherland cared little for anyone's feelings except his superiors', whom he cultivated with near sycophantic devotion. He was a byzantine operator who seemed to regard Army career advancement as a sort of blood sport. Colleagues trusted him only at their peril. Sutherland melded well with MacArthur because of his intellectual brilliance, his secretive devotion, and his bad-cop persona which so contrasted with the general's gentlemanly manner. Whereas MacArthur was usually loath to engage in sharp words or hurt another's feelings, Sutherland had no such compunctions. "Somebody around here has got to be the SOB," he once told a mild-mannered staff officer, "General MacArthur is not going to be, and you certainly aren't going to be, so I guess I'm it."[10]

One way that Sutherland enhanced his own status was by jealously controlling access to MacArthur. So when Brereton showed up at Number 1 Calle Victoria with his request for a Formosa mission, Sutherland's refusal to let him see MacArthur in effect tabled the idea for much of the morning and perpetuated a sense of inertia in the aerial preparations for any imminent Japanese threat. Truth be told, the notion of a Formosa strike did not make good sense. Given the small number of available bombers and fighters, the lack of good information on targets and the powerful Japanese defenses on the island, the raid probably would have met with disaster. In fact, MacArthur and Sutherland correctly felt that it made far more sense to move the B-17s south to Del Monte Field on Mindanao, out of the range of Formosa-based aircraft, but within striking distance of Luzon landing beaches. Both would later maintain that MacArthur had ordered Brereton to redeploy the Clark-based B-17s to Del Monte, to no avail. Brereton had been slow to comply because he felt that Del Monte did not have the capacity to house the entire bomb force, especially because Brereton was expecting any day the arrival there of more B-17s from the 7th Bombardment Group. With the addition of the 7th's bombers, there would be no room for the planes that had been at Clark. As it was, the 7th never made it. Ironically, the unit's B-17s were the aircraft that had become enmeshed in the Pearl Harbor attack. In any case, the upshot of this whole affair was that half the B-17 force remained at Clark and was thus vulnerable to Japanese air attacks.

Brereton did take the precaution of getting these bombers and most of his fighter planes into the air that morning, a commonsense measure, but also a response to numerous reports from radar operators and other observers of enemy planes. The initial Japanese strikes hit Baguio and Tuguegarao in northern Luzon. A few P-40 fighter planes were in the area, but the Japanese bombers unleashed their loads and dashed away before the American pilots could do any damage to them. Closer to midday, bad luck then intervened, though it was the sort of foul fortune that tends to plague only the hapless. After the initial patrols, most of Brereton's planes, including the bombers, had to land to refuel and refit. Fighters from Del Carmen Field, south of Clark, were supposed to cover their refitting comrades, but a dust storm prevented them from taking off. Observer attempts to warn Clark by radio, telegraph, and telephone were all abortive. So because of the Sutherland-sponsored communication and coordination dysfunction in MacArthur's command, Brereton's failure to comply with orders, as well as egregiously poor timing and uncooperative weather, the Japanese arrived over Clark Field at the exact moment when the bulk of the Far East Air Force (FEAF) was on the ground, terribly vulnerable. It was the aviation equivalent of catching an adversary with his pants down and his weapons out of reach. In the recollection of one Japanese aviator, the American planes were "in perfect alignment."

The Japanese pounced on their juicy target with fifty-four twin-engine bombers, organized into two V-formation waves. They flew at twenty-two thousand to twenty-five thousand feet, well above the range of American antiaircraft fire. Gunners of the newly arrived 200th Coast Artillery Regiment were chagrined to realize that their ammunition was too old. The most recent shells had been manufactured in 1932. Aged fuses on the shells were corroded to the point of uselessness. By one estimate, only one out of six of them even exploded. Japanese three-hundred-pound bombs cascaded downward onto the base, wrecking the communications center, maintenance shops, barracks, hangars, and raking stationary planes that were lined up on runways. Tongues of flame swept through the buildings and planes. Oily black smoke disgorged from burning metal and wood. Sticks of bombs exploded on the runways, "like a big giant stepping down the line," in the recollection of one survivor. "The ground beneath us shook," said twenty-one-year-old Private Lester Tenney, whose newly arrived 192nd Tank Battalion was arrayed in defensive positions around the area. "I will always remember the noise of those screeching bombs falling from the sky." The crash of explosions sounded to him like "thousands of large firecrackers going off at the same time. Some were direct hits on our planes, which were standing idle on the tarmac . . . while others exploded all around the airfield, killing or injuring hundreds of men." Staring upward in horror at the one-sided attack, Lieutenant Colonel Ernest Miller, whose 194th Tank Battalion was defending adjacent Fort Stotsenburg, was reminded of "when I had shot ducks lined up on placid waters," back in his native Minnesota. In the wake of the bombers, fighters screamed in at low level, strafing the flaming carcass of what had been a thriving base. Some of the tank crewmen scrambled to the decks of their tanks and fired back at them—mostly ineffectually—with their .30-caliber machine guns. Few of these men had any training or expertise in antiaircraft fire. In the estimation of one gunner, they were lucky to get their bullets within fifty feet of the attackers. "I was firing so much that the empty ammo cases kept building up on the deck," Sergeant Knox said. He hit nothing.

In scenes grotesquely reminiscent of the attack on Hickam Field, crewmen and pilots scrambled to save their planes and take to the skies. Five fighters attempted to take off and were shot down by Japanese fighters. By one estimate, only four American aircraft, all fighters, succeeded in getting airborne. One of them was flown by Lieutenant Randall Keator of the 20th Pursuit Squadron. He and two other aviators, including his squadron commander, Captain Joe Moore, quickly gained altitude. Their intention was to attack the enemy bombers, which, with their bombs disgorged, had turned and headed for home. Instead, Keator and the other two pilots ran into ten Japanese Zero fighters. "We attempted to attack them head on, but they dived underneath and to the side of us and attempted to turn on the third man in our element," Keator wrote. In the melee he got separated from the other two Americans. He made three passes on a group of Zeroes, but they were too high and got away. He turned back for Clark Field and came upon a lone Japanese fighter. "I dived on him from behind and he went down in flames. I don't think he even saw me coming." Keator and the other two men managed to land safely at Clark Field. The damage they beheld was staggering. Buildings were in flames. Smoke obscured much of the area. All of the B-17s and sixteen P-40 fighters were destroyed. The wounded and the dying honeycombed the neatly kept grassy lawns of nearby Sternberg General Hospital. "Many of them were charred and burned beyond recognition," one medic remembered. "Blood as crimson as the hibiscus flowers which bloomed in the yard was scattered everywhere."

A simultaneous complementary raid hit the grass runways of nearby Iba Field. This one-sided Japanese victory accounted for another squadron of sixteen P-40s destroyed, mostly on the ground, as well as the base's radar installation. The human losses at Iba and Clark totaled about eighty men killed and one hundred and fifty wounded. One of the dead was Private Robert Brooks, a light-complexioned African-American draftee who had lied about his age to get into the all-white 192nd Tank Battalion (years later the main parade field at Fort Knox, Kentucky, was named for him to honor his status as the first African American tanker killed in World War II). Japanese losses totaled seven planes. Within half a day of the war's commencement, the Americans had already lost the air battle of the Philippines, an aviation disaster without parallel in the country's history. The destruction of the FEAF further compromised the security of Admiral Hart's already overmatched Asiatic Fleet. The combination of Japanese dominance in the air and at sea meant that they could land troops wherever and whenever they chose.[11]

In the aftermath of the Clark–Iba debacle, a stunned and angry General Henry "Hap" Arnold, head of the Army Air Force in Washington, DC, placed a transoceanic phone call to Brereton, an old friend, and growled, "How in hell could an experienced airman like you get caught with all your planes down?" There really was no way to explain it, and none of the responsible parties were ever held to account for it, as were General Short and Admiral Kimmel, whether fairly or unfairly, for the Pearl Harbor disaster. To aviators, nothing was more humiliating or dishonorable than to lose planes on the ground because of surprise and poor preparation. "If I had been caught with my planes on the ground," Brigadier General Claire Chennault, the American air commander in China, commented, "I could never again have looked my fellow officers squarely in the eye." Brigadier General William Brougher, the American commander of the Philippine Army's 11th Infantry Division, blamed the disaster on the failure of the air commanders to disperse and conceal their vulnerable aircraft properly. To him, this failure stemmed from a lack of professional discipline. "They never did learn to soldier, and they never intended to learn," he raged. "They played at the serious business of preparation for war instead of working at it. Their attitude was one of cockiness, arrogance, discourtesy, lack of discipline, and cooperation. They drank and played excessively, and regarded themselves as superior and privileged people. To hell with them!"

Brereton, Sutherland, and MacArthur were all savvy military operators who knew how to deflect blame without appearing to do so. This disaster occurred undramatically, well beyond the glare of media or public attention. From any fair-minded perspective, all three deserved a share of the blame. Regardless of logistical and basing difficulties, Brereton failed to follow orders and move his B-17s to the relative safe haven of Del Monte. Indeed, Captain Chihaya Takahashi, a staff officer with the 11th Air Fleet, later admitted this was the paramount aerial concern for the Japanese. "[We] feared mostly that . . . the American planes would take refuge in the southern areas, therefore making the campaign very difficult." Sutherland, with typical imperious arrogance, seemed more concerned about controlling access to MacArthur than with facilitating productive action. General MacArthur, as the overall commander, deserved the most opprobrium. He allowed Sutherland to wall him off from the outside world. This led to a disastrous communication gap with Brereton. As a result, MacArthur failed to make sure that his orders to move the B-17s to Del Monte were carried out. The defenders of Clark and Iba Fields paid the initial price for this oversight. Soon the rest of his command would as well.[12]

★

War came to the Philippines with the suddenness of a tornado in the night. As a precaution against air raids, Manila shopkeepers applied adhesive tape to store windows. Lest they be mistaken for the enemy, some posted signs that read "Filipino Store" or "Chinese Store." Sandbag barricades soon proliferated on street corners and in front of private businesses. Civilians created bomb shelters in their homes. Soldiers guarded power plants, bridges, waterworks, and telephone stations. Frantic crowds descended on banks to withdraw money. Tellers could not keep up with the crush of cursing and urgent humanity. Such was the panicked mood at one bank that a pregnant woman was nearly trampled to death. The country's bank commissioner issued a decree limiting withdrawals to two hundred pesos (one hundred dollars) per week. The scarcity of paper currency led to hoarding of coins, making it nearly impossible for merchants to give exact change. Schools closed. People hoarded food. Air-raid sirens wailed at the mere hint of enemy planes. With the eerie howl of the sirens and the attendant rush to bomb shelters, a full night's sleep became a thing of the past. Radio and cable offices were inundated with more outgoing messages than they could ever hope to send. In hopes of escaping bombing, city dwellers fled to the countryside, even as people from rural provinces flocked to urban areas for the same reason. Roads were jammed with vehicles of every type, from trucks to handcarts.

The Philippines National Assembly convened an emergency session and immediately voted to apply two hundred million pesos to national defense. "The zero hour is here," President Quezon announced, "every man or woman must be at his or her post to do the duty assigned to him or her."

The Philippine Constabulary and other soldiers rounded up Japanese nationals for questioning at Bilibid Prison, where Spanish and American imperial authorities had once incarcerated Filipino criminals. Screeners interrogated the Japanese internees. Anyone who could not explain his or her presence in the islands was sent to a holding camp south of Manila. The others were released. Once Italy and Germany declared war on the United States, nationals from those two Axis countries received the same treatment. In a foreshadowing of the angry sectarian divisions that would soon set in among Filipinos over the question of collaboration versus loyalty to the Allied cause, members of the pro-Japanese Ganap Party were rounded up and incarcerated by Quezon's police. The government enforced blackout restrictions at night. In the inky-black darkness, jumpy air-raid wardens and police officers challenged nearly anyone they encountered. "Halt!" they cried in frightened tones. "Advance to be recognized." Often, they fired at anything that seemed threatening. The profligate shooting got so out of hand that MacArthur's headquarters ordered local authorities to turn in all their weapons. In spite of the blackout and the constant air-raid scares, couples still danced each evening in the darkened, air-conditioned cool of the Manila Hotel's dining room.

As in Hawaii, rumors swirled around the archipelago like a malevolent cloud. Once again, in the wake of the Clark–Iba strike, racially patronizing stories circulated that the enemy planes had been crewed, at least partially, by white aviators (presumably wayward German pilots with nothing better to do). Reports spread of poisoned drinking water, Japanese paratrooper landings, and Japanese amphibious invaders at seemingly every beach. The Philippine Army's 21st Infantry Division, defending a portion of Lingayen Gulf, a prime landing spot northwest of Manila, reported "dark shapes" approaching the beaches on the evening of December 10. A battery of 75-millimeter guns opened up, as did soldiers with rifles and machine guns. The shooting was contagious. Eventually the whole area came alive with "a crescent of fire that extended around the southern end of Lingayen Gulf," according to the recollection of one American officer.

The next morning the division commander, Brigadier General Mateo Capinpin, reported to MacArthur's headquarters that he had repelled a Japanese landing. Without attempting to corroborate the story, MacArthur released the news to the media. Wildly inaccurate stories of a Japanese disaster appeared on the front page of the *New York Times*, as well as in Associated Press and United Press International reporting. Eager to chronicle the aftermath of this bloodbath, a Manila-based *Life* magazine photographer rushed to the scene only to find nothing more remarkable than placid waters and soldiers lounging around their weapons. The phantom landing story enjoyed a long enough shelf life to appear in MacArthur's official postwar reports and even his memoirs. In reality, the Japanese had only sent a one-boat reconnaissance team into the area that evening. They dodged the 21st Division shells and bullets while taking note of the unit's positions, information that proved useful for the actual Lingayen landings that took place later in December.

Around Luzon, many observers reported seeing tree-high orange flares that they assumed to be some sort of Japanese signaling system. There were stories of blazing automobiles and specially organized rows of fishing boats pointing to American bases to guide attacking Japanese planes. The most fantastic rumors centered around Japanese fifth columnists. Manila residents reported hearing shortwave radio broadcasts from Japan. Subsequent investigation by Army authorities uncovered no evidence of any shortwave radios. One story held that there were fifteen hundred Japanese soldiers, clad in civilian clothes, scattered about Luzon, just waiting for the word to strike. Supposedly, there were also German soldiers masquerading in American uniforms. The most apocryphal tale involved a Filipino bar owner near Clark who was said to have used a shortwave radio transmitter hidden in a back room of his establishment to tell the Japanese when the B-17s were on the ground. Piggybacking on this story, another explanation for the disaster at Clark soon circulated among the Americans. "Wires to Clark Field were cut by Fifth Columnists," Captain Godfrey "Roly" Ames, a battery commander in the 60th Coast Artillery Regiment on the island of Corregidor, related to his diary a rumor he had recently heard. Unlike many others, Captain Ames dismissed the story as nonsense. "I don't believe it. Radios were working; news broadcasts were on the air; and I know officers from Fort Stotsenburg and Clark Field who *did* know." In another instance, a beautiful girl of Japanese ancestry was said to have been caught by the Navy while conducting espionage. A young naval officer who was in love with her was ordered by a superior to execute her. Without any hesitation, he shot her on the spot. These myriad rumors gave the Japanese too much credit. Postwar interrogations of Japanese officers and investigation of their records found no evidence of any such espionage activities. The Japanese did not have human intelligence assets in the Philippines; nor were they willing to compromise their own military security by sharing with potential agents any details of their plans.[13]

With veritable free rein over Filipino skies, the Japanese launched a new series of air raids to finish off the remnants of the FEAF and clear the way for their initial landings. Enemy aircraft bombed Nichols Field and Cavite Navy Yard, both of which were located in the Manila area. The American opposition at Cavite was so decrepit that nearly every bomb landed within the confines of the base and its docks, touching off massive explosions and fires. "Why don't we fight them?" one sobbing American woman raged as she watched the bombs cascade downward. "Where are our planes?" The sad truth was that the Americans had little or nothing with which to fight back. As noon church bells clanged throughout the city, giant plumes of black smoke rose majestically in the sky, wafting over Manila and the water.

From the vantage point of 1 Calle Victoria, General MacArthur stood hatless, drearily watching the raid. Thin strands of his black hair were combed neatly over his balding head. After he had worked for so many years to prevent just this sort of scenario, the bombing must have been difficult for him to stomach. To MacArthur, Manila was not just a place. It was home. "I knew that he dreaded the possibility that the city would be destroyed," wrote Sidney Huff, one of his trusted aides. Atop the five-story Marsman Building, Admiral Hart also watched in dismay. The raid inflicted five hundred casualties and negated Cavite as a viable base for much of Hart's fleet. Not only were repair shops, docks, and storage buildings destroyed, but two hundred torpedoes were also lost. Even before the war's outbreak, Hart had already withdrawn most of his surface vessels to the Dutch East Indies to serve with the ill-fated American-British-Dutch-Australian (ABDA) command in a vain attempt to stave off the Japanese from seizing these Dutch colonies. The devastating Cavite raid persuaded him that his submarines could no longer operate safely from Manila, so he ordered most of them to sea, where they patrolled individually and ineffectually against the eventual Japanese landings. The failures of these subs removed the last substantial impediment to Japanese amphibious landings. It also made it easier for the Imperial Japanese Navy to implement a loose blockade of the archipelago.

MacArthur and Hart had known each other for a long time. Hart had befriended MacArthur's older brother Arthur back in the 1890s, during their days together at the Naval Academy. The two developed a lifelong friendship. In fact, Hart had served as a pallbearer at Arthur's funeral. Hart knew the MacArthur family so well that he referred to Douglas by his first name. The naval commander was anything but awed by the imperious, larger-than-life personality of his old friend's kid brother. "Douglas knows a lot of things which are just not so," Hart once confided to his diary. "He is a very able and convincing talker—a combination which spells danger." Though Hart respected MacArthur, he paid him little false deference. With a less egotistical personality than MacArthur's, this sort of familiar honesty might have led to a close, positive working relationship. Instead, MacArthur often responded to Hart with toxic condescension. He kept Hart at arm's length, meeting formally with him only on occasion. "Get yourself a real fleet, Tommy, then you will belong," Douglas once told him.

In the wake of the Cavite debacle, MacArthur's estimation of the Asiatic Fleet was now even lower, especially as Hart moved most of his remaining ships out of Philippine waters. The general seemed to have no understanding or appreciation for Hart's unenviable situation. For one thing, his fleet was outgunned by the more powerful Japanese naval forces. For another, the demolition of Brereton's FEAF made every one of Hart's vessels vulnerable to destruction from the air. In spite of MacArthur's long career, this was his first real experience of working closely with the Navy, and he was not impressed with Hart or his service. "Apparently, he was certain that the islands were doomed and made no effort to keep open our lines of supply," MacArthur later wrote. "In addition to his refusal to risk his ships in resisting landings on Luzon, he made no effort to oppose the Japanese blockade." MacArthur formed the opinion that Hart and the Navy had betrayed him. His bitterness over this would complicate his relations with the sea service for the foreseeable future.[14]

★

Even as Japanese planes carried out their missions, General Homma began to land expeditionary forces more than two hundred miles north of Manila at Vigan and Aparri where fifteenth-century Japanese rulers had once established a trading post that earned them a short-lived hegemony over the islands. These modern Japanese descendants were organized into a pair of two thousand soldier detachments (often termed a "*butai*" in Japanese) from the 48th Infantry Division. Dubbed the Kanno and Tanaka Detachments, both were named for their commanders, a common practice in the Imperial Japanese Army. In spite of MacArthur's grand plan to repel the invaders at the waterline, they faced almost no opposition. To defend the entirety of Luzon, the general had divided his army into a pair of corps-size forces. The South Luzon Force, under Brigadier General George Parker, consisted of the Philippine Army's 41st and 51st Divisions, plus some artillery, and was responsible for defending the long, narrow neck of the island south of Manila. Four Philippine divisions, the 11th, the 21st, the 31st, and the 71st formed the core of Major General Wainwright's North Luzon Force. He also had the 26th Cavalry Regiment (Scouts), plus assorted quartermaster and artillery units. MacArthur's reserve consisted of another Philippine Army division, the 91st, plus his best troops, the US Army's Philippine Division, composed of Scouts and American regulars. Major General George Moore's Harbor Defense Force, consisting mainly of Coast Artillery regiments, was arrayed in fortifications in and around Manila Bay, the most notable of which was Corregidor. The Visayan-Mindanao Force, commanded by Brigadier General William Sharp, was comprised of three more Philippine Army divisions and charged with the task of defending the archipelago south of Luzon.

It was a half-trained army, a work in progress existing more on paper than in reality. Even with proper air and naval support, it probably would not have been up to the task of hurling invaders into the sea. Under the present realities, such an expectation was an impossibility. Thus, from the first moment that Japanese troops splashed ashore, MacArthur's beach-defense plan unraveled. Brougher's 11th Division was responsible for defending northern Luzon, a sector "so wide and so large that it should have been defended by at least five divisions," an officer opined in the unit's historical records. The division was spread so thin that Brougher could muster only a company under Lieutenant Alvin Hadley, a young reserve officer, to answer the Aparri landing. Though he was under orders to halt the Japanese at the waterline, he estimated that he was outnumbered by at least a factor of ten to one. He withdrew his men south without posing any resistance. The Japanese quickly improvised beachheads. "Both detachments, in addition to continuing the occupation and maintenance of airfields, would make preparations to advance their main forces," a Japanese after-action report chronicled. Enemy troops began a steady march south along Route 5, directly inland, and Route 3, along the western coast. The story was much the same southeast of Manila, at Legazpi, where the Imperial Army landed twenty-five hundred soldiers from the 33rd Infantry Regiment on December 12. Originating from the Palau Islands, some nine hundred miles to the southeast, this landing force met with no opposition and began moving northward on Route 1, in the direction of Manila. "Have not heard a single rifle shot," one Japanese junior officer recorded in his diary on the day of the landings.

Having retooled the entire American strategic plan for the Philippines, and having deployed his army and its plans around the idea of preventing just these sort of enemy landings, General MacArthur, in the wake of the Legazpi invasion, issued a stunningly ingenuous communiqué. "With the scant forces . . . at my disposal, they could not be employed to defend all the beaches." This in spite of the fact that he had crafted his entire strategy around the notion of beach defense. Now he appeared to be claiming that this was never his actual intention. He continued: "The basic principle of handling my troops is to hold them intact until the enemy has committed himself in force." In a subsequent release, he went on to describe the situation as "well in hand." Actually, it was anything but well in hand. To use his own analogy, the Japanese had "hit 'em where they ain't." The expeditionary invasions demonstrated the Japanese advantages of maneuver and surprise, especially now that they enjoyed control of the air and sea.[15]

With the solidification by the Japanese of new airfields, and their establishment of lodgments north and south of Manila, the initial landings set the stage perfectly for the main invasion at Lingayen Gulf at dawn on December 22. In spite of heavy seas with "waves two meters high," according to an estimate in one Japanese report, the enemy succeeded in landing elements of the 48th Division, plus tanks and artillery pieces, against almost no opposition. The unruly sea made for an unpleasant landing experience— soldiers were wet and exhausted, several landing barges were swamped in the heavy tides, heavy equipment and other supporting matériel could not be landed until the following day. Against a truly prepared and well-equipped enemy, they might have been vulnerable. But not only was the invasion convoy largely unimpeded by US submarine, aircraft, and coastal artillery pieces, the beaches themselves were in no way covered adequately by MacArthur's land forces, immediately demonstrating the folly of his plan to foil the invaders at the waterline. The Japanese enjoyed free rein to consolidate and reinforce a beachhead. Their invasion forces linked up with the Tanaka Detachment coming from the north and immediately began an inexorable southeastward advance toward Manila against what amounted to token resistance from the Philippine Army's 11th, 21st, and 91st Divisions, none of which had the firepower, training, or discipline to halt such a formidable Japanese formation. In their wake, refugees tramped along the roads; others crowded into trucks "loaded with beds and chairs," according to an American reporter who ignorantly assured them, "Our army is fighting them now. Within a short time you will be back in your homes."

General Wainwright, the North Luzon commander, had little at hand to impede the Japanese advance. "My plan was to hit the south-bound Jap spearhead with the best-seasoned men in my command—the 26th Cavalry—and at the same time contain the forces which were landing in the vicinity of Damortis (on the eastern beaches and halfway down Lingayen Gulf)," he later wrote. The commander of the 26th Cavalry Regiment's 850 soldiers was Colonel Clinton Pierce, a stocky, pugnacious Brooklyn native with more than two decades of service in cavalry units. He was a colorful, dynamic leader, an expert horseman who embodied the honor-bound hay-and-manure world of the cavalry. His soldiers represented the hard core of a modern, professional soldier class that had developed in the islands over four decades of American rule. One American officer described them as "second to none. Tough, professional soldiers, they were intensely loyal to the United States and the American officers under whom they served, and they had a fierce pride in their regiment." Some of the NCOs had served with the outfit for more than thirty years. Many of the soldiers were regimental legacies whose fathers had served in the 26th.

Pierce sent a platoon of scout cars to reconnoiter Damortis, a coastal town at the southern flank of the Japanese beachhead. Lieutenant John George, the platoon leader, reported sighting twelve transports and six other warships offshore. According to George, the town itself was under Japanese control. Colonel Pierce was the sort of commander who liked to see conditions for himself. He and Major William Chandler, his operations officer, hopped onto a motorcycle, with Chandler driving and Pierce in the sidecar, and motored to Damortis. Pierce also left orders for the rest of his regiment to join him as soon as possible. They climbed a prominent hill northeast of the town and took in the sight of more naval vessels and sizable numbers of Japanese ground troops. Knowing that his outnumbered regiment could not hope to attack this superior force, he elected to fight a delaying action on this high ground. Troopers arrived at a gallop, dismounted, and set up on the hill and an adjacent ridge. According to one American, the soldiers calmly began "choosing their positions, adjusting their rifle slings, and [proceeded] to pick off Japs as though they were silhouette targets on the rifle range." A pair of Philippine Army companies also added to Pierce's defenses.

The Japanese halted while they attempted to locate Pierce's positions and counterattack with naval and air support. Knowing that the Japanese had tanks ashore, Wainwright got in touch with Brigadier General James Weaver, commander of the Provisional Tank Group, and asked him to deploy the 192nd Tank Battalion in support of Pierce. Some forty-five tanks from this battalion had already been on the move from Fort Stotsenburg since the night before. However, because the ordnance section had failed to deliver fuel to the unit's bivouac area, the battalion now had only enough fuel on hand to muster a platoon. With orders to "hit them at their landing site, and delay their advancement southward," these five M3 Stuart light tanks, under Lieutenant Benjamin Morin took off for Damortis on a narrow paved road. As they approached the town, the road bottlenecked between high ground on the right and swampy rice paddies on the left, limiting the mobility of Morin's vehicles. To make matters worse, they ran head-on into a Japanese force that was well equipped with tanks and 47-millimeter antitank guns. The two sides were so close that Morin, in the lead tank, almost collided with a Japanese tank. As Morin ordered his driver (by placing his foot on the driver's left shoulder) to veer left, a Japanese shell slammed into the front armor of the tank. Morin's M3 careened into the muddy rice paddy. An enemy tank then rammed him, ripping off a tread, immobilizing his M3. The other American tanks desperately began to turn around. "Just as the second tank turned, it was hit by armor-piercing shells," wrote Private Tenney, a crewman aboard one of the tanks. Tenney watched in horror as a Japanese shell tore through the bow gunner's station on an adjacent tank, decapitating the gunner, Private Henry Deckert.

All but Morin's tank managed to escape. The lieutenant and his crew were cornered in the rice paddy. "My immobilized tank . . . continued to take heavy fire and burst into flames." He and the crewmen, Corporal John Cahill, PFC Steve Gados, and PFC Louis Zelis, bailed out. "We were completely at the tender mercy of the Japanese," Morin later quipped. Having fought the first American tank battle of World War II, he and his men became the first American prisoners of war (POWs) in the Philippines. "We were tied up and placed on the decks of . . . four Jap tanks . . . and driven further to the rear." Lieutenant Morin gaped when he saw that the rear area was teaming with transports and arriving troops.

After several hours, when it became obvious to Pierce that he would soon be overwhelmed by a superior force, he gave the word for a phased withdrawal. One by one, each troop (the cavalry term for a company) peeled off and headed south, only to repeat the delaying tactics again at other places. Pierce himself was the last one to withdraw. "Let's get the hell out of here!" he bellowed to Chandler, who was so eager to comply that he "burned dollars' worth of rubber off the tires."

The equine mobility of the 26th made it the perfect delaying and maneuver force. Pierce's horsemen rode from place to place, harassing the Japanese, halting them, and then moving on before the more powerful opponent could inflict fatal damage. "The Japs must have thought the Twenty-Sixth was at least twice its actual size!" one regimental officer exulted. General Wainwright later called it a "true cavalry delaying action, fit to make a man's heart sing."[16]

This impressive retrograde movement revealed a pattern that sometimes repeated itself during the campaign. Japanese ground forces tended to advance cautiously and slowly, especially considering the fact that their comrades controlled the sea and the air. Explanations were numerous. The inhospitable terrain of mountains, jungles, and rice paddies, plus the mediocre road net, made it difficult to move troops rapidly. The forces at General Homma's disposal were limited; he had only two divisions plus accompaniments totaling about forty-three thousand soldiers. At heart, he was a deliberative commander, not a bold one. Though his superiors had earmarked only fifty days for the campaign (so that the troops could then be used elsewhere in the Pacific), he proceeded with little urgency. Because of the difficult terrain and the expeditionary nature of the Japanese ground forces, it was possible for determined American or Filipino units to keep the Japanese off guard.

To complement the Lingayen landings, about seven thousand men from the 16th Division landed on Luzon's east coast, at Lamon Bay, along a narrow isthmus of land located only about forty miles southeast of Manila (at the same time the enemy also landed soldiers at Davao in Mindanao, the southernmost major island in the archipelago). As elsewhere, the Allied plan at Lamon was to defend the coastline with poorly armed and trained Philippine Army units, the 51st Division and the 1st Regular Division. These troops were spread wafer-thin throughout the area. In one typical disposition, forty miles of undefended coastline separated two infantry battalions from the 1st Regular Division. The Filipino soldiers still had no steel helmets. Some mortar crews had their tubes but no ammo. Some machine gunners had the opposite problem, ammo but no guns. Quite a few soldiers had never fired a weapon in their lives. Officers were fortunate to know the names of their men, much less their capabilities. There were no beach fortifications of any kind. Nor was there any artillery in place to defend the east coast. When landing barges began disgorging Japanese troops during the early-morning hours of December 24, the results were predictable. Though some of the Philippine forces fought stubbornly, they were unable to prevent the Japanese from securing a beachhead. Only at Mauban, where the Imperial Army's 2nd Battalion, 20th Infantry Regiment happened to run right into a battalion from the 1st Regular Division, did the Japanese experience anything like threatening resistance at the coast. "Fighting tooth and nail against tremendous odds, the men stuck to their posts until 0700 hours when enemy naval planes strafed and bombed our position with out mercy," Captain Santos, a battalion commander in the division, later wrote. "Hand to hand fighting on the beaches was the order of the day." If true, this was sobering information when one considers the realities inherent in such fighting—the desperation of personal struggles to the death, the use of bayonets, rifle butts, fists, and even teeth to kill another man at intimate distance. Regardless, in the end it was not enough. The Japanese began a relentless inland advance and eventually linked up with the Kimura Detachment, which had landed at Legazpi over a week earlier.

In Manila, MacArthur, newly restored to his four-star rank, radioed word to the War Department of the new enemy landings. At Lingayen alone, he estimated Japanese strength at "80,000 to 100,000 men of four to six divisions. I have available on Luzon about 40,000 men in units partially equipped." The dramatic overestimate of enemy strength and substantial underestimate of his own available forces would have warmed the heart of George McClellan, whose wildly inflated assessments of Confederate strength during the Civil War became legendary. Indeed, MacArthur himself was a knowledgeable student of the war (and a product of it, since his father was a Union war hero and his mother the sibling of Confederate soldiers), so McClellan's foibles could not have escaped his attention. In any event, the irony of his own misestimate seems never to have sunk in with MacArthur, and it helped form the self-serving myth—liberally stoked by the general—that he was heavily outnumbered in the Philippines. The implication of the myth was that MacArthur faced nearly impossible odds and that he did not receive proper reinforcements and resupply from Washington. Even in his memoirs, written more than two decades later, when the actual Japanese order of battle was well-known, MacArthur clung to his Alamo-like mythology. He claimed the presence of six enemy divisions, an army "twice my own strength on Luzon."

In the wake of the Lingayen-Lamon landings, MacArthur realized that his plan to turn back the invaders at the coast had failed. The Japanese had now established two formidable pincers on either side of Manila, both moving toward the capital and both in good position to destroy the North and South Luzon forces piece by piece. The wrongheaded MacArthur plan, as events were now unfolding, was leading straight to disaster. Brigadier General Clifford Bluemel, commander of the Philippine Army's 31st Division, had never liked the idea of junking WPO-3. With his division facing the possibility of being cut off in central Luzon, he was even less enamored of MacArthur's strategic planning. "Now that was a plan that had been worked on for over twenty-five years," he said in reference to WPO-3, "as far as I could see, there wasn't anything to replace it with except his pledge, 'We will meet them at the beaches.' Any man who'll . . . say what MacArthur did, I'll say he doesn't know his tactics." Bluemel saw this as an "inability to command. To discard a plan like that, I thought it was a terrible thing."

To his credit, MacArthur recognized this and adjusted to reality rather than stubbornly clinging to his crumbling plan. In his December 22 radiogram to the War Department, he reported his intention to go back to WPO-3. He now planned to fight a "delaying action on successive lines through the central Luzon plain to final positions on Bataan to cover Corregidor." Rather than see Manila laid waste as an urban battleground, he would declare it an open city, end the blackout, and evacuate all military forces. The next day, his headquarters communicated official word to all subordinate commands that "WPO-3 is in effect." Basically, Wainwright's North Luzon units were supposed to hold the Japanese long enough for Parker's South Luzon troops to withdraw into Bataan. Wainwright would then follow in kind.[17]

As Allied soldiers cleared out of Manila, fear and confusion swept through the population. At one restaurant, a diner asked another what "open city" meant. The other replied correctly, "It is what they did in Paris before the government fled and the Germans came in." Some Filipinos were reluctant to take their chances with an army that they knew had behaved with little but cruel barbarity in China. Crowds of evacuees, some of whom had come to the city when the war began, now took to the roads. The exodus turned every avenue of egress "black with people striving to reach their native villages before the murderous armies overwhelmed them," in the recollection of American war correspondent Clark Lee. Trains were so crowded that people clung to the roofs of boxcars. In a complete reversal of previous policy, police went street to street, commanding residents to remove blackout curtains, even going so far as threatening to arrest anyone who did not comply. Shopkeepers ignored the Christmas season and closed. At one storefront, a man dressed in a Santa Claus costume piled sandbags rather than Christmas items. Dewey Boulevard, once a thriving artery, was soon devoid of vehicle traffic. Nightclubs and hotels were quiet. Multicolored beach umbrellas that had once shaded customers from the tropical sun were now strewn randomly on empty lawns.

In the recollection of Major Carlos Romulo, a Filipino newspaper editor who had been called into service at MacArthur's headquarters, these previously pleasant places "all looked like funeral parlors." Sunken ships clogged the harbor "like tombstones." Near Cavite, the stench of death still permeated the air along with the smoke of fires that still had not completely abated. Uncollected garbage lay piled up on sidewalks. Engineers and rear guard troops destroyed anything that might be useful to the Japanese. Railroad cars were dynamited, tracks torn apart; bridges were blown up as were aircraft hangars and other military buildings. Small yachts in Manila Bay were set afire. Dramatic pyrotechnics eventuated from the demolition of Manila's fuel supplies. At nearly the same moment, soldiers exploded charges, igniting fuel storage facilities at Fort McKinley to the southeast, Nichols Field to the south, and Pandacan in the heart of the city. The explosions "shook every building in the city," American war correspondent Charles Van Landingham wrote in the *Saturday Evening Post*. "Columns of heavy black smoke rose more than a mile into the still night air, licked by great sheets of flame, sweeping upward with a roar that made normal conversation impossible." The roaring flames devoured several warehouses adjacent to the Pandacan tanks. Ten million gallons of fuel gushed in unruly rivers toward the bay. The largest stream flowed into the Pasig River, Manila's main water artery. "We introduced crude oil and chemicals into the gasoline," MacArthur's deputy chief of staff, Brigadier General Richard Marshall, later said. As a result of this combustible mix, flames danced atop the stream of gasoline, touching off fires along the banks of the river.

To Van Landingham, it was "a funeral pyre worthy of the passing of a great lady—the Manila I loved."

The Japanese did not recognize Manila's status as an open, noncombatant city. They continued to launch air raids on the docks and downtown area, adding tragic loss of life to the destruction of buildings and infrastructure. The lifting of the blackout only made it easier for Japanese aviators to find their targets. Major Romulo witnessed the remnants of one family of seven who had made their home aboard a houseboat on the Pasig. The boat itself had been shattered by a Japanese bomb. The water around the wreck was "purple with blood. Only the father and mother and two of the boys were left. They kept diving into the river in a desperate attempt to find a trace of the other three children. Police were forcibly restraining the mother. She knelt there, wailing in her dripping clothes, while the father and two boys kept diving—diving." To these survivors and many thousands of others around Manila and elsewhere, the orgy of fire, destruction, upheaval, and uncertainty seemed, in the estimation of one observer, "like the end of the world."[18]

Having implemented WPO-3, MacArthur knew he had no choice but to evacuate his headquarters from vulnerable Number 1 Calle Victoria to Corregidor, the fortified, tadpole-shaped island that guarded the entrance to Manila Bay. At 1100 on December 24, he informed his staff of the evacuation order. Marshall and a few others remained behind to oversee the evacuation efforts and the rerouting of supplies to Bataan (they would not leave for another week). In a courtyard outside the building, soldiers burned sensitive papers and loaded trucks with baggage and food. President Quezon, his family, other members of the Filipino government plus American High Commissioner Sayre and his family all boarded a small ship that transported them to Corregidor. At nearly the same time, General Homma landed in the wake of his victorious troops at Lingayen and established his headquarters in the coastal town of Bauang, where Moro pirates had once launched raids against Spanish imperial settlements.

Admiral Hart and Lieutenant General Brereton both left the Philippines altogether. Before Brereton left, he finally got his meeting with MacArthur. Vain and self-involved even under these circumstances, MacArthur said to Brereton, "I hope you will tell the people outside what we have done and protect my reputation as a fighter."

Brereton replied, "General, your reputation will never need any protecting."

At dusk on Christmas Eve, MacArthur emerged from his office and shook hands with Major Romulo, one of the stay-behinds. "I'll be back, Carlos!" He glanced at his four-star flag and summoned PFC Paul Rogers, his stenographer. "Rogers, cut off that flag for me." Rogers could not find a knife or scissors, so he undid the thongs, rolled up the flag, and handed it to the general. With Sutherland on his heels, MacArthur left and got into a limousine that took him to the pier where crewmen were loading dozens of big boxes full of American currency (recovered from local banks) and Filipino government gold reserves aboard the *Don Esteban*. At the Manila Hotel, Huff, a former naval officer and trusted aide who had recently been called to Army active duty by MacArthur and awarded lieutenant colonel rank, gathered the general's family for the move. Here was the sad consequence of MacArthur's failure to evacuate his wife and child months earlier with the other military dependents. For nearly three weeks since the onset of the war, his family had endured life in a city that was under a steady series of air raids. Now the family would soon be subjected to much worse on one of the war's most battered islands. Jean had little time to pack anything but a few clothes and necessities for Arthur; his nanny, Ah Cheu; and herself. Huff arranged for a light truck to take them to the pier. A Filipino driver waited patiently downstairs. Just as Jean finished packing, she noticed a small glass case full of MacArthur's medals and his field marshal's baton. She wrapped the case and baton in a towel and placed them in her suitcase. Huff carried the baggage to the truck. When he came back, Jean was taking one last look at their lovely home. She saw a bronze vase given decades earlier to General Arthur MacArthur by Japan's Emperor Meiji Mutsuhito, grandfather of Hirohito. Jean picked up the vase and placed it carefully on a table in the reception area, near the front door. "Maybe when the Japanese see it, they will respect our home," she said, grinning hopefully. She took her toddler son by the hand, "Ready to go to Corregidor, Arthur?"

Under cover of darkness on this saddest of Christmas Eves, the *Don Esteban*—fully loaded now with financial and human cargo—ferried the general's party thirty miles across the bay, to Corregidor. "Behind us Manila was burning, a spectacular display of sound and light," Rogers later wrote. "Fire and smoke illuminated our departure, and exploding munition dumps added to the sound." A small group of young officers sang a few Christmas carols. Colonel Lewis Beebe could not help but think of his family many thousands of miles away in Minnesota. "I recalled so vividly the snow clad hills, the decorations on the streets, the lighted candles and wreathes [sic] in the windows of the homes, Christmas trees being decorated, happy families opening presents around a glowing fireplace." The memories unleashed in him such a powerful wave of nostalgia and longing that he had to suppress them or risk giving into complete melancholy. The beautiful songs petered out, replaced only by brooding silence and the churning of the ship's engines.[19]

MacArthur's decision to re-embrace WPO-3 came with enough time to allow the army to get away to Bataan and avoid defeat in detail around Luzon. But he could not escape the logistical consequences of the ill-considered prewar strategic audible he had called in favor of beach defense. The Orange concept provided for the storage of mass quantities of food, medical supplies, ammunition, and other vital items to hold out on Bataan and Corregidor for up to a year. When MacArthur reoriented the archipelago's defenses in favor of coastal defense, the logistical tail, by necessity, had to follow. Supplies were now scattered all over Luzon instead of waiting in place on Bataan. The job of moving all this matériel from the docks of Manila and elsewhere around the island—and all in the midst of a chaotic withdrawal from a pursuing enemy—was nearly impossible. In the confusion, large amounts of ammunition, fresh meat, canned rations, and vegetables were left behind. The Manila railroad was completely out of service because crews had fled in the face of Japanese bombing raids. By Christmas Day, not even one locomotive was in operation. Trucks were scarce. Colonel Michael Quinn, a quartermaster officer, had leased one thousand vehicles from local auto dealers, few of which even had cabs or windshields. At most, he could muster about twenty operational vehicles per division. Brigadier General Charles Drake, the USAFFE quartermaster, had anticipated all these issues. He had conducted a prewar study of the logistics involved in a potential withdrawal to Bataan. By his calculations, even with adequate transportation, it would take two weeks to move six months' worth of supplies for an army of forty-three thousand soldiers, which was about half the number that eventually ended up making it to Bataan. After the onset of war, each time Drake requested permission to begin stocking the peninsula, MacArthur turned him down.

Local politics made the crisis even worse. The Army had purchased huge quantities of rice and sugar. There were ten million tons of rice at Cabanatuan alone. President Quezon ordered that none of these foodstuffs be moved out of the provinces where they were stored. "This was to assure the civilian population of these staple foods," Drake stated in a comprehensive report. As a result, "not one grain of the rice at Cabanatuan was touched," according to Lieutenant Colonel Miller. When American officers attempted to confiscate thousands of cases of canned food and clothing from Manila warehouses owned by Japanese firms, Quezon prohibited this as well. In both instances, MacArthur declined to overrule the Filipino president, even going so far as threatening to court-martial anyone who violated the integrity of the Japanese warehouses. Thus, as a direct consequence of the general's decisions, huge amounts of life-sustaining food were left behind. In one terrible instance, a desperate mob of civilians, concerned that the Army was making off with the last of local food, looted a shipment at a Manila dock. They converged on the cargo, "like flies on a dunghill," in the unkind recollection of one observer. People made off with numerous bags of flour and parcels of canned cherries. Even when matériel remained nominally under Army control, there was no guarantee it would get to where it was needed. Most vehicles were not equipped with blackout lights. Soldiers improvised by slathering coats of opaque paint on headlights and covering them with blue cellophane. Others simply drove with their headlights off, leading to numerous accidents and injuries. In a few cases, Filipino drivers absconded with truckloads of food, gear, and medical supplies, much of which later showed up on the black market in prisoner-of-war camps.

By the time the dust settled, MacArthur's logisticians calculated that the food stocks on Bataan were nowhere near sufficient enough to support the Army for any appreciable length of time. Concealed in well-scattered dumps were thirty days' worth of prepackaged rations, fifty days of canned meats and fish, forty days of canned milk, thirty days of flour, thirty days of canned beans and tomatoes, and twenty days of rice. There were negligible amounts of sugar, lard, and coffee. Such staples as fresh meat, potatoes, and cereal were practically nonexistent. The natural solution was to look to the adjacent sea for sustenance. General Drake established a fishery at the village of Lamao. Working at night, Filipino fishermen caught some twelve thousand pounds of fresh fish per day until Japanese air attacks and friendly fire on the boats by jumpy Philippine Constabulary troops made the job too dangerous. Drake also established an abattoir under the supervision of the Veterinary Corps. Between thirty and forty animals were slaughtered per day, accounting for about thirty thousand pounds of meat, enough to provide each soldier with about six ounces of meat every other day. In all, the Army slaughtered 3,880 carabao, 87 mules, 200 cattle, 100 pigs, and 326 horses, the beloved mounts of the 26th Cavalry (the destruction of which comprised the ultimate trauma for a cavalryman). It all amounted only to a pittance. "It looked like a lot of food to the casual observer," Colonel Beebe, the supply officer, later wrote, "but when one has 100,000 people to feed, the daily issues are appalling."

Had MacArthur maintained the original Orange plan, his forces would have been significantly better provisioned, perhaps not to full capacity but certainly enough to sustain his men with adequate nutrition for many months. Moreover, he could have improved their situation by interceding with Quezon, perhaps negotiating with the president to release some of the Cabanatuan rice as well as the food stored in Japanese-owned warehouses. General MacArthur's star-crossed strategic decisions and lack of action thus consigned his army to a steady degradation from malnutrition and undercut any possibility, however remote, that his command could hold out long enough to foil the Japanese conquest of Luzon.[20]

3

Doomed

As early-morning mist dissipated on New Year's Day, the sun peeked over the eastern horizon. The Imperial Japanese Army was on the verge of entering Manila. To the northwest, the few roads leading into Bataan were clogged with the vehicles and humanity of a half-disciplined retreating army. The narrow lanes were covered with "Army trucks, Pambusco buses, and civilian automobiles," in the recollection of one private. The limited number of vehicles available to the Army all seemed to be packed into this narrow corner of Luzon. Because of the haphazard, last-minute nature of the withdrawal, some trucks that might have carried badly needed supplies were instead empty. Along the shoulders of the road, civilians and soldiers walked southward in crowded, sweaty clusters, everyone bound for Bataan. For the troops, unit integrity was nearly impossible to maintain. In some instances, units were strung out for miles, the men wandering in leaderless confusion, knowing only that they must keep walking south. As they trudged along, they kept scanning the skies, intently on the lookout for strafing Japanese planes. At any indication of an air raid, soldiers scattered away from the road or abandoned their vehicles. Some of the Filipino soldiers, having fled, never came back. Their abandoned vehicles added to the traffic snarl. In one instance, Sergeant William Matson, an American half-track crewman, saw a truck-load of local soldiers hop off their vehicle and run away, never to return. Matson stole their truck and discovered it was loaded with flour, ammunition, and gasoline. He drove it all the way to his unit bivouac, where he and his buddies turned the flour into fresh-baked bread. "We were the envy of other outfits."

At Calumpit, several miles to the northeast, American engineers had prepared the modern steel girder bridges for demolition by dynamite. A pair of three-hundred-foot spans, one for rail traffic and the other for automobiles, stretched over the Pampanga River. To a great extent, the key to buying time for the Army to conduct its final withdrawal into the Bataan peninsula was to blow these bridges before the Japanese could capture them and put themselves in a position to cut off or destroy many of the troops streaming into Bataan. With control of the skies, the Japanese were in an ideal position to bomb the bridges by air. Incredibly, Colonel Monjiro Akiyama, the air officer of Homma's 14th Army, viewed the Calumpit bridges as unimportant, so he earmarked his available aircraft for other missions. General Wainwright's North Luzon Force had spent more than a week conducting a harried, phased withdrawal. One of his most potent weapons, the 194th Tank Battalion, guarded the bridges. His engineer, Colonel Harry Skerry, was under orders to destroy the spans once the last Filipino-American troops crossed to the Allied-held side of the river. Wainwright, Skerry, and several other officers had spent a long night at the bridge site, watching as troops and tanks from the South Luzon Force materialized like ghosts out of the darkness. Each time these groups approached Calumpit, tension rippled through Wainwright and the other soldiers until they could tell that the strangers were not Japanese. Each time the troops retreated, mostly in silence, to the other side of the Pampanga.

At 0500, as dawn shadows danced across the river, Wainwright made sure that all friendly troops were on the correct (west) side of the river and then ordered Skerry to blow the charges. But Skerry knew that a platoon-size group of Filipino Scouts from the 14th Engineers under Major Narciso Manzano was still operating on the other side of the river. Skerry asked the general to wait another hour and Wainwright agreed. Skerry spent that time checking the charges. He had supervised the placement of three tons of dynamite on the rail bridge and four on the road bridge. After a little more than an hour, with no sign of Manzano's people, Wainwright and the others heard the distant sounds of rifle fire somewhere to the east. He raised a pair of binoculars to his eyes and saw Japanese soldiers in the distance. There was no more time. "Skerry, we cannot wait any longer," he said. "Blow it now."

With a nod, Colonel Skerry and his troops went to work. Moments later a pair of tremendous explosions erupted with a deafening roar. Metal girders twisted almost pretzel-like, in seeming agony. Both spans shook and then collapsed into the river, a diligent past feat of civil engineering

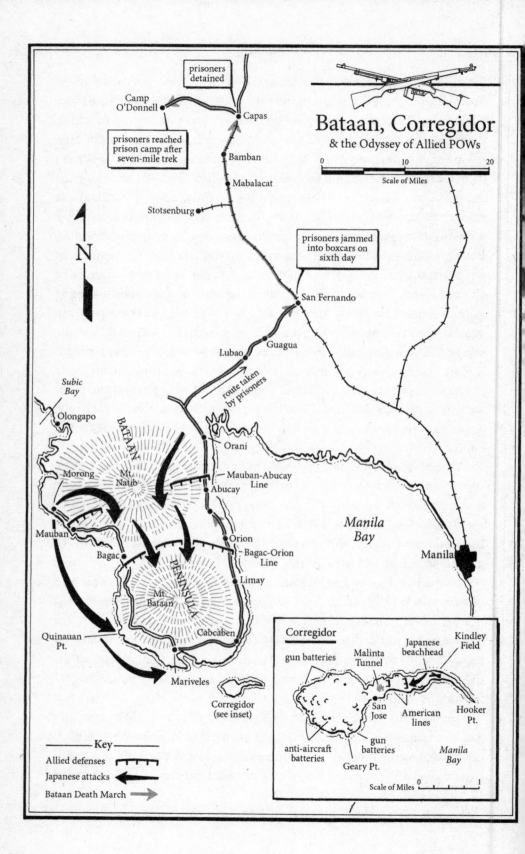

prisoners
detained

Camp
O'Donnell

Capas

prisoners reached
prison camp after
seven-mile trek

Bamban

Mabalacat

Stotsenburg

Bataan, Corregidor
& the Odyssey of Allied POWs

0   10   20
Scale of Miles

prisoners jammed
into boxcars on
sixth day

San Fernando

N

Lubao   Guagua

*Subic
Bay*

route taken
by prisoners

Olongapo

BATAAN

Orani

Morong

Mt.
Natib

Mauban-Abucay
Line

Abucay

*Manila
Bay*

Mauban

Orion

Bagac

PENINSULA

Bagac-Orion
Line

Limay

Mt.
Bataan

Manila

Quinauan
Pt.

Cabcaben

Mariveles

Corregidor
(see inset)

Corregidor

gun batteries

Malinta
Tunnel

Japanese
beachhead

Kindley
Field

San Jose

American
lines

Hooker
Pt.

anti-aircraft
batteries

gun
batteries

*Manila
Bay*

Geary Pt.

Scale of Miles   0   1

Key

Allied defenses

Japanese attacks

Bataan Death March

destroyed in a matter of seconds. "It's too bad we had to destroy such costly and important structures," Wainwright muttered. True, but it had to be done. In total, Allied engineers wrecked 180 bridges on Luzon, of which Calumpit was the most important. With such restricted mobility, the Japanese had little chance to thwart the Allied retreat to Bataan.[1]

By early January, when the figurative debris had settled, some eighty thousand soldiers and twenty-five thousand civilians had managed to withdraw to the peninsula. MacArthur saw the successful withdrawal as a brilliant masterstroke. "I have always regarded it as . . . not only [the] most vital decision of the Philippine campaign but in its corollary consequences one of the most decisive of the war," he wrote in a postwar questionnaire sent to him by an Army historian. He also made sure to include unattributed statements from Japanese commanders who apparently saw the retreat as a "great strategic move." In a separate postwar report, MacArthur related more confirmation from Japanese officers of his "brilliant move." One staff officer even commented, "The Japanese had never planned for or expected a withdrawal to Bataan." If this was true, then they had been astonishingly ignorant of War Plan Orange, the American strategic intention in the Philippines for decades. From a more objective point of view, the withdrawal represented a reasonably successful salvage effort, not any sort of tour de force—any action that led to the unnecessary extinction by starvation and disease of an army could never be considered a positive thing. The retreat succeeded for several reasons: the skill of field commanders such as Wainwright, the small size and relative immobility of the Japanese opposition, and the inability of Homma to discern MacArthur's intentions until it was too late.

Meanwhile, the Allied troops on Bataan were largely exhausted and hungry, though their ordeal was just beginning. Because of the tight food situation, and the likelihood that, with the Japanese in control of the sea and the air, any resupply from the outside would be problematic at the least (though MacArthur's headquarters would attempt to commission blockade runners), General Drake recommended that the Army go on half rations. This amounted to about two thousand calories per day for each soldier, about half the necessary requirements for full nutrition, especially now that men were often engaged in the grinding physical labor of digging defensive positions. Typically, the ration amounted to a canteen cup full of rice, twice a day, perhaps augmented by a few ounces of carabao meat, corned beef, or salmon, to go with an occasional small can of condensed milk, an ounce of dried fruit or raisins, a couple ounces of flour, and a little coffee. Often the carabao meat was so freshly killed that it still had hair on it.

MacArthur reorganized his army into a new corps-level-command structure. I Corps, under Wainwright, now defended the western half of Bataan, from Mauban on the coast to Mount Natib, a 4,222-foot peak that dominated the central spine of the peninsula. Parker's II Corps defended from Natib to the east coast at Mabatang. From coast to coast, Bataan was anywhere between twenty-five and thirty miles wide. The terrain was good for defenders, mostly jungles, hills, and mountains, with a liberal sprinkling of swamps, sugarcane fields, and narrow trails. Coastal roads served as the only decent transit points for vehicles and large formations of troops. Commanders implemented a layered defense with an outpost line, a main line, and a reserve line, usually to a depth of two miles. In I Corps, the Philippine Army's 1st Regular Division manned the forward positions, backed up primarily by the Philippine Army's 31st Division and the 26th Cavalry. In II Corps Parker placed the 41st and 51st Divisions of the Philippine Army on the front line. The USAFFE's most important remaining asset, the US Army's Philippine Division, acted as a ready reserve. Wherever possible, double aprons of barbed wire were strung. In front of the barbed wire, soldiers sowed modified mines, consisting of a stick or two of dynamite connected to an electric cap inside a box. Troops cut down brush to clear fields of fire for machine guns. The roads were adorned with tank barriers "made of heavy logs, 12 to 14 inches, embedded in the ground at various heights and angles," according to one officer. Along the roads, the men dug deep tank traps. Probably the most potent weapon was the artillery. Parker alone had 130 guns and howitzers of various calibers, from 75- to 155-millimeter pieces. Wainwright's batteries were even augmented by dismounted naval guns.

These defensive positions were fairly formidable but hardly comfortable. During the heat of the day, brightly colored coral snakes sometimes slithered into foxholes and trench lines, probably in an attempt to escape the sun. Anyone who removed his shoes learned to examine them carefully before putting them back on, lest he find one of those snakes inside. Clouds of mosquitoes ascended from the swamps and ditches to feast on the soldiers' flesh. Few men had mosquito nets or repellent.[2]

With Manila in their hands and the remnants of Filipino-American forces now penned into Bataan and Corregidor, the Japanese believed the end of the campaign was imminent. In the bigger picture, their operations in Burma, Southeast Asia, Indonesia, Hong Kong, Malaya, and the South Pacific were going so well that the Japanese high command wanted to keep up the momentum while the Allies remained so badly off guard. In early January, Homma's superiors ordered him to release his best fighting outfit, the 48th Division, plus most of the 5th Air Group for use in the conquest of Java. The removal of these powerful formations meant that the Japanese were now even more outnumbered in the Philippines (so much for MacArthur's preposterous claims of facing vastly superior numbers). The Imperial Army's 16th Division was still broken up into small detachments consolidating control of Manila and its environs. The division had 120 men killed and another 240 wounded, relatively light casualties by later Japanese standards. The 16th probably needed at least a week for the full outfit to reorganize and get into position to attack the Allied forces on Bataan. Homma also had the newly arrived 65th Brigade, a half-trained, poorly equipped detachment of seventy-five hundred infantry reservists who were supposed to function as an occupation force. He and his staff badly underestimated the remaining strength of their adversaries—twenty-five thousand soldiers on Bataan and maybe another fifteen thousand on Corregidor. With little concrete data about them, the Japanese blithely estimated their condition and morale as poor. Though the 65th was hardly a prepared fighting force—the commander described it as "absolutely unfit for combat"—Homma figured it was nonetheless suited to take the lead for what appeared to be nothing more than a mopping-up operation. "It is difficult to perceive any good qualities in general in the enemy," a 65th Brigade officer wrote.

At the end of the first week of January, Homma ordered the whole brigade—reinforced now to a strength of about thirteen thousand men, plus arriving elements of the 16th Division—to launch enveloping attacks along the axes of both coastal roads. Fierce combat ensued, especially near the once quaint roadside town of Abucay. The brunt of the Japanese assault hit at the juncture of the 41st Division and the 57th Infantry Regiment. The latter was a superb, well-armed regiment of Scouts from the Philippine Division. In the eerie darkness, aided by artillery and mortar fire, the Japanese attacked. "Screaming 'Banzai,' in a frenzied fashion, the leading men hurled themselves on the barbed wire and made bridges of their bodies over which the remainder passed," Captain John Olson, the regimental adjutant, later wrote. The wire almost became invisible under the weight of dead bodies. "They were piled so high our machine guns didn't have any more field of fire," PFC Wilburn Snyder said. "We killed them with pistols as they came over. It was horrible. They came with these shrill cries. You killed them or you didn't stop them." To Captain Ernest Brown, a company commander, the stunted sugarcane field in front of his unit's defensive line seemed to "vomit Japanese in great numbers, screaming, howling, yelling 'Banzai' as they charged. They continued to come, threw themselves against our wire, and the waves behind them leaped on their comrades up and over. It seemed they were acrobats in the manner they crossed the moon lit stretch of ground between the cane field and our position." In some cases, enemy soldiers jumped onto the box mines, blowing themselves up to create craters in which others took cover. Artillery shells shrieked in and exploded, sending hot fragments in every direction, blowing some of the Japanese infantrymen to bits. Lieutenant Colonel Philip Fry, commander of the 3rd Battalion, 57th Infantry later said the artillery fire was the "sweetest music I have ever heard." Seventy-five-millimeter batteries from the Scouts' 24th Field Artillery Battalion fired from ranges of three hundred yards or less, so close that the gun shields were dented by Japanese bullets. The infantry Scouts added devastating sheets of machine-gun and rifle fire to the roiling mass of running and jumping enemy soldiers. An American artillery shell scored a direct hit on the 65th's artillery headquarters and, according to the unit's after-action report, "in an instant the greater part of the staff was wiped out."

On and on it went as the two sides bludgeoned each other. In a seven-day period, the Japanese launched more than ten separate assaults, the Americans several counterattacks of their own. During the worst of the fighting, General MacArthur contemplated having to abandon Bataan and even ordered the movement of food to Corregidor, worsening the already acute hunger on the peninsula. He also drew up plans for the possibility of evacuating the Philippine Division to Corregidor.

Allied outpost holes were frequently overrun; captured Scouts were often executed on the spot, their remains lying inert with "hands . . . tied behind their backs . . . gagged and face down," according to Captain Brown. These grim discoveries only added to the considerable fighting spirit of the Scouts, earning the admiration of nearly every American who served with them. "I have never seen, nor do I ever expect to see, any better or braver soldiers," one American colonel wrote. "They were truly an inspiration." The Japanese took to driving herds of carabao to trip mines ahead of their assault troops. Imperial Army soldiers beat drums, howled war cries, and shot off firecrackers in hopes of simulating rifle fire, to little avail. "The firepower of a battalion armed with modern weapons plus the Gerand [sic] rifle is beyond my descriptive powers," Fry wrote to his wife, Venice. "It is a mystery to me how anyone can come through it alive, but they do!" He correctly deduced that the Japanese had not expected "serious opposition, therefore [they] had not expected a highly organized position." This hubris cost them many lives. In the recollection of one American, the barbed wire was "covered with dead bodies, many of which were officers." One of the dead men was the platoon leader of Sergeant Nakamura, a thirty-year-old machine gunner. "I recalled my brotherly association with him since the organization of our unit," he related sadly to his diary. "It is terrible to have to lose a man. I am downhearted. Everyone became silent after the death of our leader."[3]

Wayward attackers and deliberate infiltrators were soon operating in substantial numbers behind the Filipino-American lines. During daylight hours, they sniped at the Scouts relentlessly, inflicting few casualties but restricting mobility and keeping nerves on edge. The best of these stalwart shooters demonstrated a disturbing ability to single out American officers and Filipino sergeants. The snipers were enough of a problem that commanders began to assemble handpicked teams to hunt and kill them. Twenty-three-year-old Lieutenant Alexander "Sandy" Nininger Jr. led one such team. Young Nininger had just graduated seventy-eighth in his class from West Point the previous June. He had hoped to branch engineer, but his class standing was a bit too low. So infantry was his second choice. He requested duty in the Philippines and arrived in November 1941.

Nininger had taken an unconventional path to a soldier's life. His father, Alexander Sr., was a theater owner and former actor who had moved the family with some frequency throughout the Deep South, before settling in Fort Lauderdale, Florida. Sandy was a sickly child who had difficulty dealing with the hot, humid Florida climate, so the family spent some time in the fresh air and mountains around West Point. The boy saw cadets parading on the plain and apparently was bitten forever by the soldier bug. As he grew to maturity, his health improved and he became a good high school athlete with a lean physicality. His parents split when he was four, and his father quickly remarried. By the time he fulfilled his dream of attending the academy, he was five foot ten, 160 pounds of muscle, a freckle-faced kid with sandy-blond hair and piercing hazel eyes.

He remained very close to his father. Easygoing by nature, he was devoutly religious and introspective, a lover of art, poetry, classical music, and languages. During his cadet years, he wrote thoughtful, descriptive letters to his family. "My generation that should carry such high ideals is faced with a future of burden, despair, disillusionment, a future that we feel holds bottomless pits, that may cease abruptly for any one of us at any time," he wrote presciently to his father and stepmother in a cadet letter after the outbreak of war in Europe. As a devout Christian Scientist, Nininger did not embrace violence, so he often struggled to reconcile his religious side with his military calling. "You carry on the Church, and I'll defend it," he once told a friend who was entering the ministry. "We are going to need each other." Before he left for the Philippines, his stepmother had asked him about the contrast. He responded with idealism. "Mother, get this straight, I love my country, my home, my family, my friends, and I am willing to sacrifice for them and the cause of right." Alexander Sr., a combat veteran himself, urged him to keep this sense of commitment, but not at the expense of losing his humanity. "We are very proud of you my son. In a war such as this the emotions of hatred often get the best of many ranks. But they must be made to realize that a war of aggression such as this was thrust upon a great multitude of people, and made them our enemies against their will and judgement. They too love their homes and families." Something nagged at Sandy, though. Like any young officer, he wondered if he had the courage to do his job in combat, especially since he was not a natural fighter. More than this, he sensed that he would not live a long life. Before going to the Philippines, he told a girlfriend, "in the most matter-of-fact way," as she recalled it, that he would not return.

As Nininger led the anti-sniper team, such premonitions and ruminations probably seemed a world away. Around his neck he wore a black crucifix that his father had given him. The cross had special meaning for the family. A Catholic priest had given it to Sandy's father years earlier when he had played a priest in a Vancouver stage production. Ever since then, the elder Nininger had worn it until passing it on to his son when he embarked for the archipelago. Lieutenant Nininger and his men soon clashed with Japanese soldiers who were hidden in trees and foxholes. He led multiple expeditions against these enemy salients, inflicting damage and forcing the Japanese to retreat. In one instance, he found an enemy soldier in a tree and shot him. The man's body fell in a heap not far from Nininger's feet. The young lieutenant stood up, either in surprise or exaltation, and yelled. This probably alerted his location to a Japanese rifleman, who shot him in the thigh. With a bandage around his leg, he continued to fight. He armed himself with grenades, an M1 Garand rifle, and either a Browning automatic rifle or perhaps a Thompson submachine gun (contemporary accounts claim he had a Japanese submachine gun, but this is highly unlikely, since they were probably not available yet). He prowled from foxhole to foxhole, pitching grenades and spraying deadly fire into any Japanese soldiers he encountered. He seemed so intent on his efforts that he soon outpaced his men and fought as a lone wolf. "Some say he seemed to go berserk at the time," a family member wrote many years later.

Nininger repeatedly fought with the Japanese at virtual spitting range, where danger was obviously the greatest. He took a rifle slug to the shoulder. A medic treated his wound and attempted to keep him under cover in a shell hole. Lieutenant Nininger refused to stay. He resumed his advance, was soon wounded a third time, but kept going, even though he had to know his chances of survival were not good. The percentages finally caught up to him. After hurling grenades into several foxholes, killing or wounding their occupants, he came under fire from an enemy machine gun. Captain Brown, watching from a distance, saw him turn and begin running at the gun. As Nininger hurled a grenade at the gun position, he "caught a burst of fire full in the face." The young lieutenant was probably dead before he hit the ground. The grenade exploded, killing the two gun crewmen and an officer. In his wake, other Scouts pressed the attack, forced the Japanese to retreat, and recovered Nininger's body. He was buried in the cemetery of a small Catholic church near Abucay. A Protestant chaplain conducted a small, subdued service. Captain Fred Yeager, Nininger's company commander, gently removed the crucifix from his neck. Yeager would carry the religious symbol with him through many months of combat and years of captivity until finally returning it to Nininger's father after the war. Surprisingly, despite the lieutenant's burial in the church cemetery, his remains have never been found.

No one ever really knew for certain how many Japanese soldiers Lieutenant Nininger killed or wounded (unfounded rumors claimed the number was in the dozens). What is certain is that he played a major role in snuffing out sniper resistance in the 57th's rear areas and thus skyrocketed morale at a grim time. "His action acted like a tonic on the men around him and added greatly to the success of our counterattack," his regimental commander, Lieutenant Colonel George Clarke, told the family in a wartime letter. Another officer remembered that Nininger's exploits "electrified the whole command and gave new hope and determination to the forces on Bataan." At Clarke's recommendation, Nininger received the Medal of Honor, the first American in World War II to be awarded the nation's highest military decoration.[4]

Unfortunately, not all the leadership at Abucay was as inspiring as Nininger's. Clarke, a World War I veteran, was probably past his prime. Enemy aircraft terrified him, almost to the point of complete debilitation. He was convinced that modern planes had made survival in battle for foot soldiers nearly impossible. "Any time one could be seen, he tended to throw himself into a hole to escape the sight of it," recalled Major Harold K. Johnson, his operations officer. Clarke would force everyone else to take cover for fear that they would give away their position. "This got to be pretty ridiculous." The colonel was such a defeatist that, since the onset of the war, he had repeatedly told Johnson and his staff that surrender was the best option since "we didn't have a chance of withstanding a Japanese attack and . . . we would all be slaughtered." Clarke had even written to several friends with specific instructions as to what items they should send him in prison camp. He also seemed to resent courageous actions on the part of his men. One day Clarke remonstrated Captain Elbridge Fendall, his Service Company commander, and another officer for riding on a motorcycle in the daytime, defying attacks from enemy planes. "[He] came running out and wanted to know what in Hell we were doing there in daylight. He told us to get off the road in daylight, and though we tried to show him it was important that we talk to him, he wouldn't listen to us and ordered us away."

The fearful colonel placed his command post in a dugout and rarely left. To run the regiment, he relied heavily on Johnson, a man of extraordinary competence and character. The thirty-year-old Johnson was a North Dakotan who descended from the Scandinavian roots of the upper Midwest. He had graduated from West Point in 1933. Nicknamed "Johnny" in the Army, he struggled between his duty to serve Clarke properly and his obligation to keep the regiment functioning. This was hard to do, especially because the commander's lethargy was contagious. "Every time I left him," Johnson said, "his head would poke up by the time I got five or ten yards away. He would say, 'Johnny, come back. I've got to talk with you.' By the time I got back, his comment would be, 'I don't think you should be away from the phone.' Once you spend some time like that, it's very easy to spend more time."

Johnson almost felt like a babysitter to his commander and a partner in his "dugoutitis." He relied heavily on Captain Frank Anders, the regimental intelligence officer, to be his eyes and ears. The colonel's ineffectiveness created a power vacuum of sorts, and Johnson found himself assuming virtual command. "[He] had to run the regiment, and he did," one of the battalion commanders later said. The situation was not sustainable, especially when Clarke took to lying against the dugout wall and hiding under a blanket. Even the sound of friendly artillery fire spooked him, to the point where he ordered the batteries to cease fire lest the enemy respond in kind. He had clearly reached his end point. In Johnson's estimation, he was "pretty much a broken man because he was the victim of his fears" and "incapable of knowing or caring about what transpired." Lieutenant Colonel Fry described Clarke as "completely shot and a sick man."

During a visit to the 57th command post, General Sutherland found out about this toxic situation and immediately arranged, in tandem with General Parker, for Clarke's relief. He was removed and evacuated from the Philippines on the next outgoing submarine. Colonel Arnold Funk took over the regiment and relocated the command post from the dugout to the Abucay church. "It is utterly impossible to describe the relief I felt when [he] appeared on the scene," Johnson related to his diary. Funk served for a week before being promoted to brigadier general and assigned to a different job. Fry, who drove himself relentlessly, moved up to regimental command for several days until he suffered a stroke and had to be hospitalized (for a time his right side was paralyzed, but he did recover). By the end of January, Lieutenant Colonel Edmund "Ted" Lilly had settled in as the 57th's well-respected, and final, commander.[5]

Though the Japanese attacks at Abucay and elsewhere were costly and largely ineffective, they did force the Allied army into a fighting withdrawal about five miles south to a new defensive line spanning from Bagac on the west coast to Orion on the east coast. Whereas earlier in the campaign, Homma had not moved his forces with particular alacrity, he now grew overly bold. Hoping to finish off his adversaries, he renewed his

attacks on the I Corps sector along the west coast and ordered three separate amphibious landings, totaling about two battalions, in southern
Bataan, several miles behind the Allied lines. Scratch forces of planeless
airmen and shipless sailors, plus a few Marines, guarded these rear areas.
They were hardly a formidable force.

By and large, though, the landings were amateurish, poorly coordinated, and aimless. Troops landed on the wrong beaches and wandered
about in abject confusion. American patrol torpedo (PT) boats sank at
least two transports. Communication between the soldiers and their air
and naval support was nonexistent. The troops went ashore with nowhere
near enough food, ammunition, and medical supplies to operate for any
length of time behind enemy lines. Resupply efforts were almost wholly
ineffective. Even before embarking on this junket, some of the men had
sensed that they were courting disaster. "I know this is a suicide unit and
have made up my mind to die," one of them scribbled in his diary.

Had these units landed as one concentrated, properly supported and
coordinated force, they might well have posed a serious threat to the ability
of the Bataan forces to continue operating. Instead, they amounted to net-
tlesome boils that needed lancing. To be sure, though, the threat they
posed was serious enough that Wainwright was forced to divert substantial
forces from the 45th and 57th Infantry Regiments (Philippine Scouts), plus
tank support, collectively some of his best formations, to deal with them.
Some of Corregidor's powerful batteries also pounded the enemy units.
General MacArthur, in a surprising echo to his failed coastal defense concept, apparently believed that his paltry rear-defense forces should have
prevented the landings altogether. "Get the Jap before he lands," he wrote
in a February 1 memo to all units. "Ten minutes of accurate fire placed on
the Jap just prior to, and during the period of attempted landing may save
three or four days time necessary to hunt him in the brush and the woods."

With their backs to the sea, the Japanese were soon penned into perimeters on several fingerlike peninsulas in southern Bataan. Here they demonstrated what would become a long-standing pattern in the Pacific
War—a preference to die rather than surrender. In these battles of the
"Points," as the Allies called them, the Japanese fought fiercely and held out
for a couple of weeks. A few dozen were evacuated by sea; most died in
place, hungry, depleted, and defiant. "We have been without water since
this morning," one of them wrote in his diary. "Our food consists of dry

bread, crackers and dried cereals. The direct sun makes us sweat. We are terribly thirsty. Men are getting weak." A doctor, sensing that death was near, felt compelled to write down a final testament of his intentions. "I have made up my mind. I will not have a disgraceful ending. I went back to my patients and told them it is better and more honorable to die with a pistol shot . . . than to be captured."

Some took shelter in coastal caves and held out as long as they could. Small teams of dynamite-wielding Americans went cave to cave, blasting these holdouts. Some of the enemy soldiers jumped off cliffs into the sea and either tried to swim to safety or drown themselves. In one instance, a cornered Japanese soldier swam to a reef while an American NCO waded out and attempted to persuade him to surrender. "Come on in, son," he said. "You're okay. Come on in." With no apparent hesitation, the man lunged off the reef, into the surf, and drowned himself. A few bedraggled Japanese did surrender, and they were generally well treated.

Hundreds of badly swollen Japanese bodies were strewn around the ravines, the jungles, and the beaches where the fighting had been the fierc-est. "It was a regular slaughter house," Major Johnson wrote. "Dead Japa-nese filled every foxhole [sic]. On the shore bloated bodies of men who attempted to escape by swimming floated in." The 1st and 2nd Battalions of the Imperial Army's 20th Infantry were annihilated. The Japanese prob-ably lost at least fifteen hundred men. Japanese custom called for the ashes of the fallen to be shipped home to their families. But in the vast majority of cases, the remains of these men simply rotted in place. The half-starving Filipino-Americans did not have the wherewithal or the energy to give them a proper burial. The cost of eliminating the Japanese landings was significant: one battalion from the 45th Infantry lost more than half its strength; a company from the 57th was down to forty men. Their dead and wounded were dedicated professional soldiers who could not be replaced.

To the north, closer to Wainwright's main line of resistance near Bagac, heavy Japanese attacks pressured the Allied line. The enemy push breached the line in several spots but failed to collapse Allied resistance. Groups of infiltrating and advancing Japanese soldiers became isolated in several small perimeters that the Allies dubbed the "Tuol Pockets." The Japanese attempted to resupply the pockets by air, but their drops were inaccurate. Food and medical supplies often fell into grateful American and Filipino hands. From January 26 to February 16, Philippine Army soldiers and US

Army tankers fought to snuff out enemy resistance. Aided by thick jungle, the Japanese held out with nearly hysterical desperation. Artillery and mortars pounded the pockets, though not as effectively as they might have. The Allies had very little ammunition for their 81-millimeter mortar tubes, so they used antiquated 3-inch Stokes ammunition left over from World War I. Duds were the rule rather than the exception. "Live rounds to duds never exceeded a proportion of one to five," sniffed one unit after action report. The task of eliminating the pockets was akin to subduing a wildcat in a gunny sack. According to General Wainwright, who was often at or near the front lines, "it was a savage ferreting job. We had to go up and practically breathe in the faces of the dug-in Japs." Tanks lined up tread to tread, "maybe ten feet or less between vehicles," according to one crewman, and rolled forward, blasting away at any suitable targets. Their ammunition expenditure was so profligate that hard-pressed logisticians threatened to cut off their resupply. Igorot tribesmen, hailing from the mountainous regions of Luzon, rode atop buttoned-up tanks, guiding drivers in the direction of Japanese foxholes by pounding with clubs on the right or left side of the turret. Junior officers also rode on tanks, from which they rained grenades on Japanese positions.

Casualties among supporting Browning automatic riflemen were so high that, according to Captain Archie McMaster, "men felt damned" when chosen to carry that weapon. In one of these attacks, Lieutenant Willibald Bianchi, a 45th Infantry staff officer and graduate of the South Dakota State University ROTC program, volunteered to function as a rifleman. Hit multiple times by enemy machine-gun bullets, he discarded his rifle, fought back with a pistol, and destroyed an enemy machine-gun nest with a grenade. Two more bullets slammed into his chest. Though he had trouble walking, he managed to climb atop the turret of a tank and fire its machine gun at another enemy machine-gun nest, which poured heavy fire in return. He kept blazing away until the tank was hit by a 37-millimeter shell. He was knocked unconscious and thrown from the tank. With their hair on fire, the crew bailed out. The badly wounded lieutenant was carried away on a stretcher. He survived and received the second Medal of Honor awarded in World War II.

Reports filtered in from civilians and soldiers who escaped captivity that the Japanese were in poor shape, thirsty, low on medicine and food, "so hungry they were killing horses for food," according to one account. The Japanese made desperate attempts to break out of the pockets. In one mass assault, they overran a platoon of Filipino soldiers, killing eighteen of twenty-nine men in their foxholes. They made it about six hundred yards before succumbing to an Allied counterattack. For the Japanese, only death beckoned, not escape. When Philippine Army soldiers ran out of conventional grenades, they took to placing dynamite charges, nails, and match fuses inside shoots of bamboo. The fuses were erratic, so much so that the Japanese often threw the bamboo grenades back. Still, enough of the homemade explosives did damage to make them worthwhile. "Day by day the area held by the enemy was reduced in size," according to an 11th Infantry Regiment after-action report. In the recollection of one Filipino officer, the Japanese "stubbornly contested every foot of the ground." The fighting raged at handshake range. Allied soldiers leapfrogged from fox-hole to foxhole, pouring small-arms fire and grenades into them. Most of the time, the Japanese stayed in their holes and died in them. In some spots, the fire was so intense that it chewed the bark and foliage off trees; some were even sawed in half. Captain McMaster took a squad-size patrol to hunt down one particularly stubborn group of Japanese. His Scouts quickly killed three enemy soldiers, but their officer was alive and unhurt. Wielding an ornamental sword, he charged. Private Mario de la Cruz calmly shot him twice in the forehead, once in the cheekbone and once in the mouth. Between explosions of 75- and 155-millimeter artillery shells, Japanese soldiers could be heard crying. Some of the Filipino soldiers also reached the breaking point. In one unit alone, doctors recorded forty cases of self-inflicted wounds.

In the end, there was no formal surrender, only the elimination of all remaining resistance (a harbinger for later stages of the Pacific War). In the pockets, the Japanese lost the equivalent of another battalion. The dead tended to be packed together, reflecting the shrinking nature of their perimeters as the battle reached its final stage. To Lieutenant John Wright, it was "impossible to . . . describe that sight; words just won't paint the real picture." In the tropical heat, the stench of their decomposing bodies was overwhelming, to the point where Captain McMaster's company had to "fall back until we could advance beyond them. Blue bottle flies sent out an unbelievably strange noise." Another officer remembered that "maggots and blood filled the trickle of the Tuol River." Dead bodies in foxholes were pa-pered over with a few spades of dirt. Most of the rest simply rotted in place.[6]

★

Dismayed by the failure of these attacks and the terrible losses he had suffered, Homma decided to halt offensive operations. For every man he had lost in combat, another was down with dysentery, malaria, or beriberi. His timetable was blown. He withdrew his army a few miles north, to good defensible ground, and, knowing time was on his side, resolved to let starvation and disease weaken the Filipino-American army. But he also knew that the only honorable way to defeat them and end the campaign was in battle. So, with tremendous reluctance, he appealed to his superiors for reinforcements, thus losing face with them. According to Homma's staff officers, he wept as he composed the message.

MacArthur's situation was obviously worse. He knew full well that his army was dying a slow logistical death. From his headquarters on Corregidor, he repeatedly appealed to General Marshall and the War Department for help in the form of troops, ships, planes, and supplies. The hard-pressed USAFFE commander could not understand why the power brokers in Washington did not do more to send help. He was an ardent opponent of the administration's Europe-first policy, which he not only considered wrongheaded but also borderline disastrous. To MacArthur it made no sense to earmark scarce resources to Britain and the Soviet Union while American troops in the Philippines faced the very real imminence of extinction. He especially resented the fact that the Soviets refused to join the war against Japan. He called for the pooling of ABDA forces for a counteroffensive in the Philippines and an effort to push the Japanese out of Indonesia and Malaya, a plan at variance with reality. His rancor occasionally boiled over in his communications with Washington. "The temper of the Filipinos is one of almost violent resentment against the United States," he admonished Marshall in one cable. "Every one of them expected help, and when it has not been forthcoming, they believe they have been betrayed in favor of others. In spite of the great prestige that I enjoy with them, I have had to exert every effort . . . to keep them to continue a seemingly hopeless battle." MacArthur warned that without proper support, they would collapse altogether. In one thinly veiled attempt to emphasize the seriousness of his situation, MacArthur radioed Washington that, in the event of his death, Sutherland was to be his successor. Eisenhower, in his new capacity as chief of the War Plans Division, read the message and cuttingly commented to his diary: "He still likes his boot lickers."

The relationship between MacArthur and Marshall was always one of wary correctness. They did not trust each other and never really would. To some extent this was a legacy of the past. The two had met before World War I and since then had not been particularly fond of each other. Unlike all of Marshall's other commanders, MacArthur had once served in the top job. The two generals were the same age, and yet Marshall had once been far junior to MacArthur. Indeed, it was said in Army circles that as chief of staff, MacArthur had assigned then Colonel Marshall to a dead-end job with an Illinois National Guard unit in hopes of killing his career. Marshall was not the type to hold a grudge, though. Like a pilot attempting to keep a valuable but dangerously quirky airplane under control, Marshall labored assiduously to appease MacArthur while still keeping him in his subordinate place. "Arms and equipment were so short that General Marshall was practically desperate," Eisenhower later wrote. During the early months of 1942, as the situation in the Philippines grew progressively worse, Marshall alternately reproved, placated, and reassured MacArthur, often promising more than the government could deliver.

After carefully studying the situation, Eisenhower had already briefed Marshall that the necessary reinforcements to save the Philippines could never arrive before the current garrison's collapse. Still, Ike knew the political temper of the Philippines well enough to understand that the United States must be perceived locally as doing all it could to rescue the situation. "They may excuse failure, but they will not excuse abandonment," he said of the Filipino people. A ten-million-dollar plan to commission ships in Australia to run supplies through the blockade resulted in little more than an ineffectual trickle. For the time being, there was little else the government could do. Yet Marshall at times irresponsibly hinted that significant help was on the way. "Every day of time you gain is vital to the concentration of overwhelming power for our purpose," he assured MacArthur in one cable after outlining efforts to send him a powerful air force. MacArthur promptly converted these mere hints into a full-blown declaration of salvation for his troops. "Help is on the way from the United States," he told them in a message that was read by commanders to soldiers in every unit. "Thousands of troops and hundreds of planes are being dispatched. The exact time of arrival is unknown as they will have to fight their way through. It is imperative that our troops hold until these reinforcements arrive."

Regardless of the mixed signals he had received from Washington, he should have known better than to make such misleading and reckless claims. "I think that [they] had an adverse effect," Captain Cecil Forinash of the 45th Infantry Regiment (Scouts) later opined. The rescue message was an early indication of MacArthur's tendency toward alternate reality in his public pronunciations. The communiqués released by his headquarters—now in defeat and even later in victory—were sometimes at such divergence from reality as to presage the infamous five o'clock follies of the Vietnam era. One crowning example was a claim by MacArthur's headquarters that General Homma, because of his failure to destroy Filipino-American forces on Bataan and Corregidor, had committed suicide by ritual hari-kari. "His suicide took place in my old apartment, which he occupied in the Manila Hotel," General MacArthur claimed. In private, he quipped, "I hope he didn't mess up my bathroom." Supposedly, Homma's funeral was conducted in Manila with the emperor's representatives present and the general's ashes subsequently flown home to Japan. There was not a shred of truth in such assertions.

The communiqués also revealed an excruciatingly self-centered, almost megalomaniacal, side to MacArthur. Seldom was anyone else ever mentioned; credit for success was rarely shared with any other individual or command. "He was . . . the only commander I recall who used the heading bearing his own name for official messages and communiqués," Eisenhower later said. Of 142 communiqués dispatched by USAFFE headquarters during this period, 109 mentioned only MacArthur. As Sutherland verified years later, the general carefully checked all press releases and even wrote many himself, "always with an eye on their effect on the MacArthur legend." A New Year's Day press release perhaps illustrated, more than any other, this tendency to mix nonsense and self-generated hagiography. "General MacArthur narrowly escaped serious injury in a recent bombing raid in Bataan Province when a large bomb exploded less than ten feet away from him." During the raid a pair of unnamed but faithful aides had apparently shielded him with their bodies, an unmistakable attempt at Secret Service imagery. In truth, the general had not yet been to Bataan. Nor was it possible to remain unscathed from a bomb exploding at such close range.[7]

Such communiqués promoted the idea that he was personally at the front, alongside the combat troops, leading them in battle (a laurel more properly afforded to Wainwright). In truth, General MacArthur made only one documented visit to Bataan, on January 10, when he spent the entire day visiting both I and II Corps. Otherwise he remained at Corregidor, hardly out of danger but certainly not serving on the front line. While he might well have inspired the hungry, disease-ridden Bataan defenders with more personal appearances, there was nothing wrong or dishonorable about running his command from the comparative safety of Corregidor. But his unnecessary self-aggrandizement, irresponsible pronunciations, and exaggerations left him open to distorted characterizations on the part of some of the more disillusioned and cynical among the Bataan garrison. Given the hype, many of the soldiers—amounting to a substantial minority—could not help but wonder why, as the weeks of privation continued unabated, the great unseen general was seemingly so powerless to improve their circumstances. They soon dubbed him with the inaccurate, unfair nickname "Dugout Doug," a moniker that proved to be a favorite among MacArthur detractors for the rest of his life. Major Dean Sherry, serving as an adviser to the Philippine Constabulary, was shocked to hear widespread ridicule of the USAFFE commander. "There was no attempt to conceal their utmost contempt for him. I heard of no senior officer who did anything in an attempt to change that attitude of the troops." A sardonic, disrespectful ditty began to circulate among the Bataan men, many of whom incorrectly imagined that the Corregidor garrison was safely tucked away in bunkers, feasting away on food meant for I and II Corps soldiers. Sung to the "Battle Hymn of the Republic," the new tune was called "USAFFE Cry of Freedom":

> Dugout Doug MacArthur lies a shaking on the Rock,
> safe from all the bombers and from any sudden shock.
> Dugout Doug is eating of the best food on Bataan,
> and his troops go starving on.
> Dugout Doug's not timid; he's just cautious, not afraid.
> He's protecting carefully the stars that Franklin made.
> Four-star generals are rare as good food on Bataan,
> and his troops go starving on.

Actually the general was not eating well at all. In two and a half months on the island, he lost twenty-five pounds. Though the Corregidor soldiers did eat somewhat better than their comrades on Bataan, the typical daily ration consisted mainly of tinned salmon and rice. From December 29 onward, Corregidor came under occasional air raids and shellfire from the Manila side of the bay, the combination of which wrecked the main barracks and most other aboveground structures. In the 1920s Army engineers had blasted dozens of lateral subterranean tunnels through the solid rock of Malinta Hill. The bombproof laterals were concrete reinforced, with electric lights, fans that circulated fresh air, and even a double-track railway that ran along the main entry tunnel. Malinta Tunnel, as the troops called it, offered safe, albeit claustrophobic, shelter from enemy bombs. Though MacArthur situated his headquarters in the tunnels and personally worked there each day, he insisted on spending his nights and much of his other time aboveground. At first he and his family lived in the home of Major General Moore, commander of all coastal defense fortifications. When Moore's house was destroyed by a bombing raid, MacArthur moved to a small gray bungalow about a quarter mile from the Malinta Tunnel entrance. When the bombing or shelling started, Jean and Ah Cheu would grab Arthur and take off in a car for Malinta, on the island's main road. The routine took a toll on her. "Corregidor was the longest part of the war for me," she later said. In addition to her natural grace and decency as a person, she was often courageous. One day, as bombs rained down, she halted her car to pick up Clark Lee, a war correspondent. "By stopping, she had spent the precious couple of minutes that might have meant the difference between her being killed on the road, and reaching a place of safety," he noted appreciatively.

The general was no less courageous. On multiple occasions, he refused to take cover during raids or shelling. He thought of himself as a man of destiny of the sort that enemy ordnance could not derail. Under fire, Lieutenant Colonel Huff and his other staff members found it nearly impossible to get him to take cover. One day MacArthur was in the Malinta Tunnel when Japanese planes began disgorging bombs. He sauntered out of the tunnel into the open and, with his hands in his pockets and a pipe jutting from his jaw, looked skyward as if studying the attackers.

"General, you really ought to keep under cover," Huff urged him.

"There isn't a Japanese bomb or bullet made that has my name on it and there won't be," MacArthur replied.

Frequently, he circulated around the island visiting the Coast Artilleryman who comprised much of the garrison and whose batteries were deployed at defensible points near the coastal areas. He strode purposefully from position to position, ornamental walking cane in hand (he later abandoned the cane when he discovered that many soldiers believed he needed it to support himself). In one instance, as MacArthur was inspecting a battery from the 59th Coast Artillery Regiment, a bombing raid commenced. Sergeant William Sanchez urged him to cease the inspection and take cover, but he refused. "Son, if you let the enemy dictate the war, the war is lost," he told Sanchez. "Besides, you're with me. There isn't a bullet or bomb or shell that's going to harm me. And as long as you're with me, you're safe." Captain "Roly"Ames, a battery commander in the 60th Coast Artillery Regiment was standing alongside MacArthur during another raid. As the Japanese planes approached, Ames yearned to take cover. The general stood still watching the attackers through binoculars, "never taking the field glasses from his eyes." Bombs exploded uncomfortably close, but MacArthur did not move an inch. Figuring that if the old man could take it, he could, too, Captain Ames gritted his teeth and stayed in place. "The general (Mac) was out today," he wrote in his journal later that night. "The men appreciated that." On another occasion, during a heavy mortar and artillery bombardment, soldiers began running for the shelter of the Malinta Tunnel. "But General MacArthur just stood out there in the open, giving orders and directing men with calmness and confidence," in the recollection of Lieutenant Wright. "He seemed to be utterly oblivious to fear of the incoming mortar rounds. He was especially unconcerned for his own safety and set an example for us junior officers." Because of the general's confidence and courage, Wright and many other soldiers on Corregidor held him in awe. "I almost worshipped General MacArthur," Wright said. "I never heard anyone on Corregidor downgrade General MacArthur's courage."[8]

MacArthur's bravery belied the inner turmoil he faced with his little family in daily danger and his army in an impossible situation. Arthur turned four years old during the Corregidor siege. As a present, a tailor fashioned a military overseas cap for him. The boy ran up and down the tunnel singing "Battle Hymn of the Republic," an ironic choice given the very different connotations of the tune to many on Bataan. He insisted on being called "Sergeant" because he had noticed that sergeants often drove vehicles. While he seemed not to understand the danger of the bombing, his mother and father constantly worried for his safety. It was not unusual for Jean to spirit Arthur to the tunnel three or four times a night in reaction to bomb scares. Jean's affable, engaging personality made her well suited to visit the growing number of wounded men in the tunnel hospital. She became a regular at their bedsides. She and Ah Cheu constantly had to shield Arthur from seeing the worst of the combat wounds. Though Arthur seemed to adjust well to the adverse environment, it was hardly ideal to have a four-year-old child in the middle of a combat zone, much less the theater commander's wife. If, as seemed likely, resistance eventually collapsed on Bataan and the Japanese overran Corregidor, what would happen to MacArthur's family? Would they die alongside the general? Would they surrender to the Japanese? Should MacArthur evacuate Jean, Arthur, and Ah Cheu before this happened? Should he allow himself to be captured or should he commit suicide? These unsettling questions must have weighed heavily on him. No modern American military commander of similar rank had ever dealt with such a dilemma. Even Robert E. Lee, one of the most hard pressed commanders in American history, knew that his wife Mary was safe at home and would be well treated if she ever did come under enemy control. MacArthur, who had created this terrible situation for himself, enjoyed no such reassurances.

To make matters worse, a submarine slipped into Corregidor harbor one night and evacuated President Quezon, High Commissioner Sayre, and their families, creating pressure from Washington for MacArthur to save his own family. Quezon was suffering terribly from a worsening case of tuberculosis. His heavy, wet coughs could be heard night and day throughout the Malinta laterals. Brokenhearted, deeply disappointed at what he considered to be America's failure to live up to its pledge to defend his country, he made a desperate proposal to Roosevelt for early independence. Perhaps with independence, he could declare the archipelago neutral, end the fighting, and negotiate the withdrawal of American and Japanese forces. But this was pure fantasy. Neither Washington nor Tokyo would ever agree to such a proposal (though MacArthur initially provided a lukewarm endorsement). So the sad, ailing president instead acceded to evacuation to the United States. Jean, in the meantime, insisted on staying with her husband.[9]

In essence, the dilemma was then foisted upon the Roosevelt administration. The initial phase of the war had brought little besides bad news to the American people. Knowing how important public opinion was to the prosecution of war in a representative republic, the president was constantly concerned with sustaining morale. In this sense, the preposterously optimistic claims of MacArthur's communiques dovetailed nicely with

Roosevelt's efforts. Stoked by the administration, MacArthur had become a national hero, a powerful symbol of defiant American resistance. The general's almost mystic self-promotion had morphed into a politically potent cult of personality. From New York to North Carolina, new parents were naming their baby boys Douglas MacArthur. Streets were renamed after him as were city parks, buildings, and even dams. The town of MacArthur, North Carolina, received a new post office on the strength of its name alone. A Democratic senator wrote to the president urging him to rename Corregidor to MacArthur Island. State legislatures, governors, and hundreds of politicians fell all over themselves to prepare resolutions honoring MacArthur. Newspaper headlines routinely referred to him as "The Lion of Luzon." The Congress designated June 13 as national "Douglas MacArthur Day," to commemorate the storied day forty-three years earlier when the great man had entered West Point. Nationwide, the general received scores of honorary memberships in clubs and societies and a Doctor of Laws degree from the University of Wisconsin. A Native American tribe adopted him as a formal member. The National Father's Day Committee chose him as Number One Father for 1942. Enterprising merchants sold MacArthur lapel buttons. Hero-worshipping authors wrote books with titles like *MacArthur the Magnificent* and *General Douglas MacArthur: Fighter for Freedom*.

Newspaper editorialists rushed to join the adulation of MacArthur. "He is one of the greatest fighting generals of this or any other war," the *Philadelphia Record* gushed. "This is the kind of history which your children will tell your grandchildren, which will go down in the schoolbooks alongside Valley Forge, Yorktown, Gettysburg and Chateau Thierry." The *Baltimore Sun* described him as "something of a military genius with the capacity to foresee contingents and take the best use of resources at his disposal. He has some conception of that high romance which lifts the soldier's calling to a level where on occasion Ethereal lights play upon it." A home-front-radio military commentator assured his listeners that MacArthur's decision to withdraw to Bataan was "one of the truly great pieces of strategy in this war. . . . [It] required imagination, insight and strong character." Whether out of ignorance or obfuscation, the commentator failed to mention MacArthur's summary rejection of WPO-3.

In an ironic twist, the rabidly anti-Roosevelt Republican press outdid the administration in lionizing the great general. Since his chief-of-staff days, he had always been cozy with Republicans. Now he emerged as a right-wing darling, a potential presidential contender for 1944 (instead of torpedoing such talk, he would someday seize upon it and begin plans for a presidential run even as he commanded military forces). The pro-MacArthur frenzy morphed into a push by politicians of both parties to bring him home and put him in charge of all US armed forces, either in a newly created military position or as secretary of war. "Place him at the very top," Wendell Willkie, who had run unsuccessfully against Roosevelt in 1940, urged the president during a February speech. "Keep bureaucratic and political hands off him. Give him the responsibility and the power of coordinating all the armed forces of the nation to their most effective use."

There was never any possibility that this would happen. For one thing, the Navy would never have yielded authority to MacArthur any more than the Army would have subordinated itself to any naval officer. For another, Admiral Ernest King, chief of naval operations, detested MacArthur. Moreover, Roosevelt wanted no part of MacArthur in such a role. He was more useful to the president—and less dangerous politically—as a distant hero, rather than an influential policy maker.

The MacArthur adoration movement did lead to a major decision, though, and one that still has no equivalent in American military history. It convinced Roosevelt that losing MacArthur and his family to the Japanese, either as prisoners or fatalities, would inflict major damage to the people's morale. So, on February 22, the president formally ordered MacArthur out of the Philippines. The general temporized for a couple of days before replying. He later professed to contemplating "resigning my commission and joining the Bataan force as a simple volunteer." He never mentioned what would happen to Arthur and Jean if he had opted for such a draconian course of action. In truth, the statement was pure MacArthur hyperbole. Certainly he cared deeply for the troops whom Roosevelt was ordering him to abandon. But for a general with a long history of defying orders that he did not like, he proved more than willing to obey this one, just on his own time and in his own way. He asked for a delay until he felt the right political and moral moment had arrived for him to leave. Roosevelt and Marshall readily agreed.

The presidential order for a general to forsake his troops in the field had no precedent before or since in American military history. By ordering it, Roosevelt was in part bowing to public sentiment, but he also believed it was the right thing to do for the greater purpose of winning the war. So in that sense, there was some justification for the order, though it was un-doubtedly cold-blooded and at variance with all American military com-mand ethics. The administration's decision to confer the Medal of Honor upon MacArthur was another matter altogether. The stateside MacArthur hysteria had created a congressional movement to award the medal to the general. The idea, though, originated primarily with Sutherland and Mar-shall. Probably in hopes of building up MacArthur's hero reputation as an even greater justification for saving him, and forestalling inevitable Japa-nese propaganda that would portray MacArthur as a coward for leaving his men, Roosevelt agreed to the nomination. Roosevelt had known the general for a long time. Their relationship was less than an honest one. In face-to-face dealings or correspondence, they exuded flowery respect. In private, they expressed little besides byzantine personal distrust and abject contempt for each other. The president had little enthusiasm for awarding the medal to MacArthur. But, as he later admitted to a confidant, he had simply yielded to congressional and public opinion. The citation, written mostly by Marshall, was a model of deception. It lauded MacArthur "for gallantry and intrepidity above and beyond the call of duty in action against invading Japanese forces, and for the heroic conduct of defensive and offensive operations on the Bataan Peninsula," a place he had visited once, while seeing no action. For a man of Marshall's integrity, it was an uncharacteristically dishonest moment, perhaps his worst as chief of staff. From any fair-minded viewpoint, the decoration was incredibly inappro-priate and overtly political, if not downright appalling. It equated MacAr-thur's actions with the likes of Nininger and Bianchi, thus cheapening the immense value of the nation's highest military decoration, one reserved only for the most courageous and the most self-sacrificing of soldiers. The award said nothing good about the administration that would confer it, nor the officer who would accept it.[10]

The infamy did not end with an undeserved Medal of Honor. On Janu-ary 3, President Quezon had signed Executive Order #1, a directive to pay MacArthur and several of his key staff officers substantial bonus money from the Philippines treasury. MacArthur was to receive $500,000, Suther-land $75,000, Richard Marshall $45,000, and Sidney Huff $20,000. Osten-sibly the payment was for services these men had rendered during their advisory capacity to the Philippines armed forces. However, the money also covered time they had spent on active duty in the US Army, and this was expressly against regulations. As with so many aspects of MacArthur, there was little precedent before or since for this situation. Basically, he was preparing to take money from a foreign government, albeit one that was still subordinated to the United States, and all while wearing the uniform of his country. Beyond the illegality outlined in Army regulations, this was stunningly unethical. Any officer with a sense of propriety and morality would have refused such an offer out of hand. MacArthur chose to accept it. The others did the same.

Quezon's motives for the payment have never been clear. Perhaps he hoped to influence MacArthur and his staff members to push Washington as hard as they could for assistance to the archipelago. Or maybe he hoped to obligate them for some sort of personal loyalty to him. Regardless, the money was to be transferred in mid-February from the government's account in the Chase Manhattan Bank to the personal accounts of each man. The $500,000 (more than $7.6 million in today's dollars) did not seem to be enough for MacArthur. As PFC Rogers, the stenographer, typed up the necessary paperwork late on the evening of February 13, he heard the general comment to Sutherland that the payments hardly covered the income they had lost while serving the military mission. MacArthur's comment was mystifying. Did he mean he could have made more money on active duty in the US Army? Certainly not. Private industry? Perhaps. An inveterate record keeper, Rogers seemed to sense the controversial nature of the documents he was typing. When he was alone that night, he noted the transactions but downgraded the payment amounts. "It was not cleverly done but it satisfied my sense of propriety," he said many years later. On the evening he typed the paperwork, his only personal reaction in the diary was to exclaim, "God! I would like to be a general." Because the financial transactions had to be cleared through the War Department, the Roosevelt administration had to approve the payments. The matter came to the personal attention of Secretary of War Stimson and Roosevelt. For reasons known only to them, they declined to stop the payments. MacArthur and the others got their money. The American people knew nothing about it. If they had, perhaps the coast-to-coast hero-worship of their idol would have abated. One of the few who did know was Eisenhower, and he did not approve. A few months later, when Quezon reached the United States, he met privately with Eisenhower and offered him a bonus of his own. Ike politely declined. The MacArthur bonus payments remained secret until nearly four decades later.[11]

On March 12, MacArthur and his entourage prepared to leave Corregidor and take flight to Australia. The general decided to escape by PT boat and B-17 bomber rather than by submarine, as most everyone expected. Under cover of darkness, MacArthur, his family, Ah Cheu, and seventeen carefully and secretly selected members of his staff gathered in prearranged groups and clambered aboard a fleet of four PT boats commanded by Lieutenant John Bulkeley. The group included Sutherland, Marshall, and Huff. The only enlisted man was Rogers. As MacArthur prepared to board his boat, he shook hands with someone at the dock and said, "I shall return," a phrase he would reprise much more famously once he reached Australia. The odyssey to the island continent was a grueling five-day affair. The PT boats managed to sideslip blockading Japanese warships, with many nervous close calls, and then deposit their thoroughly seasick passengers at Del Monte, on American-controlled Mindanao. They spent four days waiting for suitable B-17s to ferry them to Australia. Not until the morning of March 17 did they make it to northern Australia. Probably as a justification for his exodus, MacArthur professed the belief that a powerful avenging army was waiting for him in Australia. This force of planes, troops, and transports would "enable me almost at once to return at the head of an effective rescue operation," he later wrote. Only when he reached Australia, so the story went, did he find out the terrible truth that there were no available forces to rescue the Philippines. It is hard to believe that someone of MacArthur's considerable intelligence actually believed this. After all, if such powerful military forces were waiting in Australia, how had they gotten there, and why had they not already come to the rescue or at least attempted to do so? No one would have understood the obvious answers to these questions better than MacArthur. Somewhere within him, he must have known the unhappy truth. The Filipino-American army was doomed, and he would not share the fate of his luckless soldiers. He had escaped. The guilt over his salvation and the desire to assuage it would consume him and animate his actions for the rest of the war.[12]

★

Like MacArthur, Wainwright was born to soldiering and deeply affected by his family's martial past. Wainwright's grandfather was a naval officer who was killed in the Civil War. His father was a prominent, West Point–trained cavalry officer who had died in 1902 while serving in the

Philippines. Jonathan inherited the love of military life from his forebears. He graduated from West Point in 1906 as first captain of the corps of cadets. Like his father, he found himself especially drawn to the cavalry, where he served for most of his career before achieving high command in 1941. Wainwright's lean, lanky physique earned him the nickname Skinny, surely one of the most appropriate monikers in the entire Army. All of his peers and superiors called him Skinny. Only MacArthur addressed him as Jonathan.

Throughout the Army, Wainwright had a well-deserved reputation as a down-to-earth field soldier who loved being with troops and horses, and not always in that order. He was also a heavy drinker. It was said that, in the span of a field march, he could polish off an entire tumbler of liquor and remain firmly atop his mount, with no visible signs of inebriation. As was true with Ulysses S. Grant, Wainwright's subordinates worried that his drinking might one day overtake him, but their concerns never dampened their great devotion to him. Wainwright's intelligence, his tremendous bravery in combat, and his innate decency as a person engendered respect and affection for him among his men. "He had great physical courage and was quick on decisions," one of his soldiers later said of him. "He was a lion of a man." Colonel Milton Hill, his inspector general, recalled at least one instance during the fighting on Bataan when Wainwright shouldered a rifle and fought side by side with his soldiers. To Hill, "his ability as a military leader . . . was so outstanding as to be apparent to everyone." During the Battle of the Points, Wainwright came upon a Japanese prisoner who was under guard at a command post. The prisoner's hands were tied with wire behind his back. To Wainwright, the enemy soldier looked forlorn and uncomfortable. He ordered his men to untie him and give him a cigarette, a precious commodity on Bataan. The small kindness of the general's actions made a deep impression on Major Harold Johnson. He and the other men viewed Wainwright as "a warm and concerned commander."

When MacArthur left for Australia, Wainwright inherited control of the Philippines battle. The initial command arrangement was odd and unworkable, undoubtedly a by-product of MacArthur's fantasy of immediately leading a powerful relief force back to the Philippines. Before embarking on his exodus, he had told Wainwright, "I'll come back as soon as I can with as much as I can." From Australia, MacArthur attempted to maintain control of the USAFFE, something he neglected to mention to

Marshall. When the chief of staff discovered MacArthur's machinations, he moved quickly to put a stop to this dysfunctional and unsustainable arrangement. He promoted to Wainwright to lieutenant general and designated him commander of the newly created US Forces in the Philippines (USFIP) command. Major General Ned King was elevated to command of the Bataan forces, with I and II Corps under his control. Major General Sharp, newly promoted, remained in command of all other Allied forces south of Luzon, a comparatively quiet sector.[13]

Though Wainwright was determined to fight on as best he could, he fully understood the hopelessness of his situation. All over Bataan and to a lesser extent on Corregidor, starvation and disease lurked like a malevolent stalker. If all politics is local, so indeed is all hunger. The archipelago contained plenty of food, just nowhere near enough on Bataan and Corregidor. For Wainwright, one of the saddest moments was when he realized that the terrible time had come for the proud troopers of the 26th Cavalry to turn in their own horses for slaughter. Fodder had run out. The horses were losing weight. They had to be butchered while they could still provide some meat for the soldiers. "Captain, you will begin killing the horses at once," Wainwright, with tears in his eyes, sadly ordered the regiment's quartermaster. The goodbyes were heartrending. Hard-bitten cavalrymen wept openly and hugged the necks of their faithful steeds. The victims included Joseph Conrad, a one-time ribbon-winning mount with a beautiful coat whom Wainwright had ridden many times and loved like an old friend. Even while facing starvation, the troopers of the 26th refused to eat horse meat. Some 250 horses were killed and eaten by the Army. The death of these horses marked the end of the US Army's horse cavalry, something that would have been unthinkable to nineteenth-century soldiers. The 26th and other units were also forced to kill their pack mules, many of whom were regarded fondly by the troops as fellow soldiers. Even so, one soldier remembered the mule meat as "tasty, succulent, and tender."

Day by day, hunger degraded the energy and efficiency of the army. Vitamin-deprived soldiers experienced night blindness. Patrolling troops were more interested in foraging for food than in gathering information about the Japanese. Men consumed anything they could get their hands on, in hopes of augmenting their meager portions of rice, which, in the view of most, tasted like wallpaper paste. One junior officer remembered eating "edible plants, roots, snails, snakes, wild chickens, bananas, wild pigs and anything else." Captain Fendall, whose job as Service Company commander of the 57th Infantry entailed finding any way he could to provision the soldiers, sent out hunting parties. The hunters would set up a machine gun, then fan out, beat the bushes in hopes of driving animals in the direction of the gun. They used coconuts as bait to trap monkeys. At various times Fendall's hunting parties "brought in a monkey, an iguana, and a wild pig. The monkey was a little on the gristly side." The monkey carcasses reminded Private Michael Campbell of "a naked human child. It was such a traumatic experience that I had to force myself to eat." Resourceful Scouts of the 45th Infantry found a tree whose young leaves could be cooked and eaten. "Tastes sour and resembles the ararosip [seaweed]," one Filipino sergeant commented in his diary.

As always, front-line troops suffered the worst privations. Fuel shortages and Japanese air raids made it difficult for quartermasters to truck supplies forward along Bataan's few workable roads. Truckloads of food were hijacked by soldiers or civilians in rear areas before they could make it forward. One driver was discovered to have hoarded one thousand cans of tomatoes, evaporated milk, and juice. Even military policemen whose mission was to prevent such pilferage helped themselves at times to boxes of rations. Some units padded their strength reports in hopes of rating more food allocations from supply officers. Others squirreled away crates of food in barbed-wire-enclosed dumps that were guarded round the clock. The chaotic nature of the logistical lifeline made for an uneven distribution of food supplies. "Some units got corn beef, others none," Colonel Richard Mallonee wrote. "Some had corned beef hash in lieu of fish. Some got eight ounces of rice, others 3.7. Some got flour in place of bread, some hard tack." Even when small quantities of meat did reach front-line troops, it had sometimes spoiled in the tropical heat or become inundated with maggots. At the end of March, meat became even more scarce when a Japanese bomb scored a direct hit on Corregidor's refrigeration plant. About 250 quarters of fresh carabao meat spoiled before it could be distributed on Bataan. General Wainwright ordered an increase in the Bataan garrison's rice ration at the expense of Corregidor, but this hardly put a dent in the hunger problem.

By April, the average soldier was eating only about one thousand calories per day, "hardly enough to sustain life, let alone fighting men," in the estimation of Captain Everett Mead, the supply officer for the 31st Infantry Regiment. "Hunger was a nagging thing that never went away," Sergeant

Knox, a tank crewman, later said. Soldiers no longer had the energy to carry out their myriad duties. Some had lost as much as twenty-five pounds. According to Colonel Mallonee, the parsimonious amounts of food, spread out into two small meals per day, were "grossly inadequate to maintain physical fitness or maintain the strength necessary to go at high speed twenty hours a day, digging trenches, manhandling trucks, carrying artillery ammunition on your shoulders for several kilometers on jungle trails." In the memory of another American, the soldiers "looked like the walking dead." Few had the energy to improve their fortifications or even clean their weapons.

The near manic hunger for tobacco made the misery even worse for the Army's large population of smokers. Among these men, the yearning for a smoke was, in the estimation of one Filipino sergeant, "second to food." Some units were down to one cigarette a day per man. "Soldiers will pounce upon any discarded cigarette stub for a single puff," Brigadier General Hugh "Pat" Casey, the theater engineer, wrote after an inspection of the front line. Because, in his estimation, there was no difference between "the physical needs of smokers [in] front and rear echelon units," he strongly recommended the establishment of an equitable distribution system for cigarettes. So powerful was the yearning for tobacco among the addicted that they took to trawling along the ground in search of cigarette butts and improvising their own smokes by stripping leaves from local trees. "Some use Samac-subusub [sic] and albutra leaves," Sergeant R. Miguel, a Filipino Scout chronicled in his diary. In hopes of feeding his own habit, he took to smoking these leaves. "[It] does not taste very good . . . but what can I do?" From Casey on down, no one seems to have pondered the obvious, and infinitely healthier, solution to the problem—quitting.

Disease—malnutrition's close cousin—was now ravaging the army. Malaria, dysentery, and beriberi were rife. Stocks of quinine and other anti-malarial drugs had dwindled from scarce to near nothingness. Few men had mosquito nets. The starvation diet further lowered their resistance to disease. Anyone who slept for any length of time awoke to painfully swollen, almost unresponsive, limbs and joints, an early indication of beriberi. Almost everyone was afflicted with some health problem. Wainwright's commanders estimated that between 75 and 80 percent of their troops were incapacitated either by disease, wounds, or the energy-sapping effects of malnutrition. "Malaria and dysentery were taking a heavy toll," Lieutenant Eugene Conrad of the 31st Infantry Regiment wrote. "There was hardly a man that did not have one or the other. Everyone grew weaker day by day." Even the 31st, Wainwright's best combat unit, was reduced to about 40 or 50 percent efficiency. Poor sanitation, bad water, and the starvation diet—not to mention the stress of the situation—led to a near epidemic of diarrhea. Listless soldiers found themselves afflicted with stabbing abdominal pains and urgent calls to defecate at all hours of the day. "We were weak, we had no food or medicine, we had fever, and we had the runs," one man later said. "We were in pretty bad shape." Sanitary conditions bordered on the abysmal, especially in half-trained Philippine Army units. Swarms of flies inundated kitchens and front-line positions to feed on dead flesh, feces, and spoiled food. In the opinion of Lieutenant Colonel Walter Waterous, a highly experienced physician, the insect problem was "beyond comprehension." Another soldier estimated that the flies were "almost, but not quite, as great a nuisance as the dive bombers." In the recollection of Lieutenant Clara Mueller, a young nurse, the flies "were on dressings, on food . . . thick, large green ones. With one swat, quite a number could be killed." Latrines consisted mainly of straddle trenches. Often soldiers simply did their business anywhere and everywhere. This was particularly true of untrained Filipino troops who had no schooling about proper field sanitation. "To scramble out of a foxhole at night and run for the platoon latrine in the inky jungle darkness with dysentery or diarrhea dogging at his heels required a lot more training and field discipline than the average Filipino was granted the time to acquire," wrote Colonel Skerry, the engineer. "As a result, the main line of resistance of our battle position . . . could almost be located by the odor."[14]

During the Army's retreat to Bataan, medics had established a pair of hospitals in the southern part of the peninsula. General Hospital Number 1 was initially located in a collection of modest wooden buildings at Camp Limay before moving southwest several miles to a half-built engineer campsite during the late-January Abucay fighting. General Hospital Number 2 was an open-air facility located under jungle canopy about a mile west of Cabcaben, near the southern tip of Bataan. Both were located near rivers that provided fresh water for their many sanitary needs. General Hospital Number 1 was designed for combat surgery and General Hospital Number 2 for convalescence. But, in practice, as the army deteriorated, both hospitals were inundated with patients of every type and description. Though they were theoretically supposed to handle about one thousand patients apiece, they were both treating two and three times that number by the end of March, with hundreds more pouring in, to the point where medical administrators could no longer keep accurate admission records (plus another four thousand patients were being treated in smaller field hospitals closer to the lines).

Patients arrived by ambulance or by bus or on litters carried by exhausted comrades, or often they just staggered in on foot. At General Hospital Number 1, the staff improvised and built triple-tier bunks that were packed into narrow wards inside modest engineer buildings and under the corrugated metal roofs of partially finished structures. Patients at General Hospital Number 2 were splayed onto cots that were spread out among the bamboo thistle and jungle foliage. Orderlies were often forced to kill snakes that clustered underneath the patient cots. Fortunately, rain at this time of year was unusual, but summer promised to bring the monsoon season. No one was quite sure how the patients could be sheltered from the torrential rains if the campaign lasted into June or July. The dry weather led to clouds of dust, much of which settled over the patients, the operating tables and the food. "The trees and bushes are covered with dust," Supply Sergeant Thomas Houston told his diary. "The air is filled with dust. We eat, breathe, and work in dust." Surgeons operated inside makeshift tents. Sewage consisted of a fly-swarmed open-pit latrine. Eventually engineers built box latrines, which at least offered some privacy. When patients died, orderlies quietly hauled their bodies to an adjacent area where harried graves-registration soldiers lumped them together in mass burials. "We tried not to hear the scraping of the spades or the thud of earth thrown on earth, but we couldn't get away from it," one nurse later wrote. In a replication of prewar imperialism, Filipino refugees and Chinese transplants were hired to do much of the cooking, cleaning, and laundry housekeeping tasks. Rats were a constant problem, especially at night, when they roamed the area in search of food. Often they could be heard skittering around the floor of the patient wards or the staff's crude living quarters, even on their cots. No matter how exhausted the medics were, they learned to check for rats before getting into bed.

At these crude medical facilities, a mixed force of doctors, nurses, orderlies, and Filipino civilians worked around the clock to save lives, all under blackout conditions. Power was provided by spotty generators. Combat casualties flooded into the surgical wards. Captain Alfred Weinstein, a surgeon from Atlanta, remembered the "zzz-zzz-zzz of a saw as it cut through bone, the rasp of a file as the freshly cut end, dripping red marrow, was ground smooth; the plop of an amputated leg dropping into a bucket, the grind of a rounded burr drill eating its way through a skull, the tap, tap, tap of a mallet on a chisel gouging out a shell fragment deeply imbedded in bone, the hiss of the sterilizer blowing off steam, the soft patter of nurses' feet scurrying back and forth, the snip of scissors cutting through muscle, the swish of the mop on the floor cleaning up blood, the strangling, gasping, irregular respiration of soldiers with chest wounds ... the shuffle of feet as weary surgeons and nurses shifted their weight from one leg to another." Colonel Irvin Alexander, a patient for several weeks in the open wards of General Hospital Number 2, spent much time listening to the quiet babble of Filipino patients, plaintively begging for water and access to a urinal. "Soft voices speaking various dialects could be heard calling hospital corps men at all hours of the day and night."

Food was slightly more plentiful than at the front, though still nowhere near enough to meet nutritional needs. Patients were fed twice a day, mainly salmon or sardines with some rice or thin sandwiches, or runny oatmeal gruel washed down with a little tea. Almost every patient had some sort of skin infection, usually ringworm or scabies. Surgeons who operated on bowels and abdomens routinely found live worms. Patients with acute diarrhea had to make at least fifty latrine visits per day, often with the assistance of a medic. Admissions for malaria, assorted fevers, dysentery, and other diseases was running in the hundreds per day. In one night shift alone, Lieutenant Colonel Waterous received between seventy-five and one hundred acute malaria cases. "On various men's backs and arms ... I counted and killed 64 Anopheles mosquitoes. All these men subsequently developed malaria." He could do little besides dole out tiny amounts of quinine, try to keep them hydrated and hope for the best. With just a hint of hyperbole, he later opined that this was "the most chaotic malaria situation which probibly [sic] ever existed."

An army that was succumbing to logistical strangulation had neither the means nor the energy to deal with swarms of malaria-causing anopheles mosquitoes. Undernourished doctors and nurses were anything but impervious to the disease. Lieutenant Ethel "Sally" Blaine was so feverish from malaria that she had trouble standing, but she had a bed placed in the middle of her duty ward and directed the actions of other staff members. When Lieutenant Lucy Wilson found herself close to fainting during operations, she wedged her arm into a space next to the operating table and stayed on her feet. Surgeons were at times so sick that they worried they might do more harm than good to their patients. Like many other doctors, Captain John Bumgarner's case of malaria was at times "almost incapacitating. My chills, my aches, and my febrile episodes were totally unpredictable."

Though women had formed the critical mass of the Army Nurse Corps since the early twentieth century, they had never been immersed in this sort of combat and privation. The idea of women experiencing such peril and stress was repugnant to World War II–era Americans of both genders. However, for the eighty-three American nurses on Bataan, there was now no other choice. Though they did not carry weapons or fight, they faced the same dangers and hardships as their male fellow soldiers. Both hospitals were marked with white or red crosses. Even so, General Hospital Number 1 was bombed twice—whether intentionally is still a matter of debate—with loss of life, though not among the nurses. Clad in khaki Army Air Force coveralls or khaki trousers and shirts, the nurses performed with competence and courage. In the estimation of Colonel Wibb Cooper, the ranking medical officer in the theater, they did "excellent and heroic work. In general their morale was on a par with the officers, their bravery was exemplary and an impression of fear was rarely manifested." The nurses changed bloody, pus-filled dressings, administered medicine, kept records, washed filthy patients, assisted in operations, enforced whatever cleanliness standards they could, and in general raised the morale of the wounded and the sick.

The women lived in crude burlap tents. In some cases, they took shelter in abandoned buses. As a concession to feminine privacy, special bathing areas were cordoned off with canvas shelter halves. As they washed, the women sang or told jokes. "Our washing and daily bath was all taken care of in the creek," Lieutenant Mueller said of her group's bathing spot. "We sat on a boulder and went to it. Crawfish nibbled on our toes. Occasionally our soap slipped out of our hands and went down the creek and me after it. When bombers came over while we were bathing and anti aircraft let loose, we scrambled out quickly." The water also offered a small refuge from the trauma and seriousness of their surroundings. "On my break, feeling somewhat solemn, I went down to the creek, sat on a rock, put my feet in the water to cool off, and wrote my mother a letter," Lieutenant Leona Gastinger recalled of one such instance. Almost involuntarily, she sobbed for several moments. Feeling much better, she cleaned up and returned to her grisly work.

Gastinger and the others cared for distressingly large numbers of maimed and sick men. With infections rife, and sanitary conditions less than ideal, the gas-gangrene ward became an especially horrible place. "The putrid odor, the ugly exposed wounds, the monstrous limbs where the infection had not yet been cut out, the agonized moans of 'Take it off, please take it off,' made it a place to avoid when one could," Lieutenant Juanita Redmond wrote. With limited supplies of medicine, doctors took to performing radical debridements, sometimes cutting to the bone, sloughing away necrotic tissue, swabbing the open wound with peroxide, and then exposing it to fresh air and sunlight as a means of killing bacteria. The process was remarkably effective. In a way that was hard to quantify but no less real, the presence of the women seemed to bring out the best in the wounded and sick soldiers, as if they were trying to show their masculinity by putting on the best face for their nurses. In one typical instance, a quadruple amputee smiled at Lieutenant Hattie Brantley and exclaimed, "What's a nice girl like you doing in a situation like this?" Captain Bumgarner, a surgeon, was filled with admiration for the competence and resilience of the nurses. "One of the most remarkable things coming out of our experience in Bataan was the presence and performance of the army nurses. In retrospect I believe that they were the greatest morale boost present in that unhappy little area of jungle. I was continually amazed that anyone living and working under such primitive conditions could remain as calm, pleasant, efficient, and impeccably neat and clean as those remarkable nurses. I believe that their presence in the wards around the sprawling hospital meant more to the patients than any other single thing."[15]

Like Bumgarner, the Japanese also understood the intangible importance of morale. From the air, they began dropping propaganda leaflets, urging the troops to capitulate with such entreaties as "Don't wait to die," and "What Are You Fighting For?" One handbill portrayed a mouthwatering array of food and liquor, including a Thanksgiving turkey and a chocolate cake. Another leaflet asked the soldiers why they should fight to the death while their commander (obviously MacArthur) had abandoned them. In the evenings, the Japanese used a Manila radio station to broadcast American music, playing a mournful tune called "I'm Waiting for Ships That Never Come In" over and over. "[It] does not help our morale any," Captain Achille Tisdelle, General King's aide-de-camp, recorded in his diary. "The men joke happily but underneath they are disquieted." The uneasiness and resentment over their abandonment, manifested themselves in a sardonic poem, "The Battling Bastards of Bataan," written by Frank Hewlett, a United Press correspondent.

No mama, no papa, no Uncle Sam,
No aunts, no uncles, no cousins, no nieces,
No pills, no planes, no artillery pieces,
And nobody gives a damn.

Considering the seriousness of the situation, the Army's psyche remained remarkably stable. "Just like anything else, attitude is so important," one soldier asserted. Some stalwarts held out hope that MacArthur's exodus meant that he would soon return at the head of a powerful rescue force. Most everyone else understood that such notions were fanciful. Barring some miracle, death or captivity beckoned. "At last I have found what I have searched for all my life—a cause and a job in which I can lose myself completely and to which I can give every ounce of my strength and my mind," Lieutenant Henry Lee of the Philippine Division wrote in a letter to his family, one that was widely reprinted in American newspapers. "I have mentally and spiritually conquered my fear of death." On Corregidor, the soldiers of Battery C, 60th Coast Artillery Regiment, even published a small newspaper called the *Morrison Hill Gazette*. The title was derived from the battery's position on the northern coast of the island. Boasting the "latest and bestest news," and edited by "J. Wellington Whatshisname" (actually the editor was Staff Sergeant Bernard Hopkins), the paper reported communiqué-oriented news from the various fighting fronts around the world. The jocular motto of the paper was "Bless be he who bloweth his own horn, for his'n shall be blowed!" Hopkins shared the latest gossip, cartoons, lost and found notices, rumors, and the odd editorial. One cartoon featured a brawny, slingshot-wielding American corporal chasing an egregiously caricatured, bucktoothed, bespectacled Japanese soldier. "Don't shoot, me friend of Americans," the Japanese soldier wailed. An accompanying editorial railed against whining complainers. "NOW EVERYBODY EXPECTS THAT SORT OF STUFF FROM A BABY, because being a baby and squalling and wetting things up sort of go together. But when they grow older and get past a recruiting officer and continue to squall and be a baby and wet things up—well, good Coast Artillerymen have a name for them and IT AIN'T COMPLIMENTARY!!" Another sharply worded editorial offered to send complainers to the front lines on Bataan, for a reality check. "Maybe after 3 days of laying in the dense jungle, without removing their clothes, with only boiled unsweetened rice to eat," they would understand that conditions on Corregidor could be much, much worse.

During the retreat from Manila, a small group of communications specialists had transported radio equipment from the city into the Malinta Tunnel and rendered it operable. Soon they used the equipment to broadcast what they called "The Voice of Freedom." Inspired by what they had read and heard about underground radio transmitters in German-occupied Europe, "The Voice of Freedom" staff trumpeted defiant, propaganda-laced broadcasts urging soldiers to fight on and Filipino civilians to remain true to the Allied cause. The announcers created the impression that they were transmitting straight from the front lines on Bataan (the Japanese never seemed to know the truth of their whereabouts). They hinted strongly, and irresponsibly, that help was on the way. "It makes good listening," Sergeant Houston commented to his diary. "We are heartened to hear that the Asiatic fleet is giving a Japanese fleet hell." It was doing no such thing, of course, but Houston and thousands of other soldiers still liked to hear of distant victories.

One of the main voices on the daily broadcasts was Major Romulo, the former Manila newspapermen. He related tales of soldier exploits, such as Lieutenant Bianchi's, and he assured Japanese soldiers that their cause was anything but just. "We have fought you, soldiers of Japan, and we want to tell you, people of Japan who were left behind, that we will fight you to the end!" He even sent personal messages to his family, from whom he was estranged because of the war, and urged them to "be of good cheer in your silent houses. Sleep quietly through the night of defeat. We will come back sooner than you think."[16]

★

In spite of the daily barrage of such defiant, reassuring broadcasts, the night of defeat could not be forestalled any longer. While the Bataan garrison withered on the proverbial vine, their Japanese enemies had now grown stronger in spite of serious disease and hunger problems of their own. In February, when General Homma had reluctantly ordered a halt to offensive operations, 14th Army had been down to about three thousand effectives on the front lines. At least one thousand more soldiers had been evacuated to Japan because of serious wounds or disease. The supply situation was such that soldiers were on half rations, subsisting on parsimonious quantities of rice, augmented by small bits of fish or meat. Medicine was in short supply. More than fifteen thousand soldiers were debilitated by disease, primarily malaria. The portrait of neglect, privation and deteriorated health was remarkably similar to that of the Filipino-American army. There was one key difference, though. With enough time and effort, the Japanese could rehabilitate their army with reinforcements and proper supplies. This cost Homma face with his superiors, but victory mattered much more than his personal status.

By the end of March, 14th Army had received elements of two new divisions, the 4th and the 21st. There were new artillery units, engineers, signals outfits, medics, quartermasters, and an infusion of new planes and crewmen organized into the 22nd Air Brigade. Replacements had infused the ranks of the 16th Division and the 65th Brigade and tank units were in place. Homma's army was thus rejuvenated while Wainwright's was at the end of its endurance. On April 3—Good Friday—when Homma launched a new offensive, the results were predictable. Though the fighting was ferocious, the Filipino-American soldiers had little chance of staving off the Japanese offensive. By one estimate, the command was at 25 percent efficiency, meaning that three-quarters of the soldiers were either totally incapacitated or nearly so.

Enemy air and artillery bombardment had been intensifying for several weeks. Now it was nearly overwhelming. Captain Tisdelle, in his diary, spoke of a "sky black with planes." Sergeant Miguel, the Scout, and another habitual diarist, similarly recorded "heavy bombing all over our front line." Machine-gun posts and foxholes were obliterated. Telephone lines were wrecked. General Hospital Number 1 was hit by several bombs, killing at least fifty people. Any moving vehicle risked getting strafed and roasted by marauding Japanese aircraft. "We lost every gun, every truck, and every piece of equipment that we had," said Private Leon Beck, a member of the 31st Infantry Regiment Antitank Company, said. Incendiary bombs touched off smoke-belching fires in the dry-season brush. The 41st Division and other Philippine Army units disintegrated into chaotic, retreating mobs of soldiers. "A great many of the men had discarded their rifles[,] and Filipino officers, dressed in fatigue clothes, the same as their men, would not identify themselves," wrote Brigadier General Bluemel, a division commander whose herculean efforts to rally men, organize counterattacks, and stabilize the situation, earned him the Distinguished Service Cross. Cryptic reports of enemy tanks only added to the stampede.

Within hours of the initial attacks, the Japanese had breached the lines and begun a relentless southward advance. General King repeatedly counterattacked and inflicted substantial casualties especially by utilizing whatever artillery he had left. In one typical instance, a newly arrived Japanese soldier was hit by shell fragments within minutes of entering combat. As he tended to his wound and looked around, he saw "men without arms and legs and with stomachs ripped open. I was dumbfounded! It was tragic and gruesome, and I could not even look at them." The Japanese push was relentless, even reckless. "Japanese infantry charged our position in such large numbers that they literally used their dead and dying soldiers as stepping-stones," Private Tenney, the tank crewman, later wrote.

But regardless of the damage inflicted on the attackers, there was no way that men on the verge of incapacitation from hunger and disease could hope to hold off such an onslaught. "Our Philippine Army, Scouts and the one regiment of Americans [the 31st Infantry] were to [sic] far gone from starvation, fatigue and disease to do much," Lieutenant Colonel Fry later wrote. When General King ordered the 31st Infantry to plug a major gap in the line, a significant number of the troops had trouble just staying on their feet, much less carrying out an attack. "What we were going to counterattack with, I have no earthly idea," one of the men later quipped. Lieutenant Conrad, a company commander, attempted to organize his troops but found that many "were so sick and weak with malaria and dysentery that they were unable to even start the march." In some cases, feverish soldiers who, in the recollection of another officer "could hardly walk," and yet tried to stagger to their feet rather than be left behind. Philippine Army units ceased to exist. A bus full of wounded soldiers took a direct from a Japanese bomb, setting the vehicle afire and killing many who were too debilitated to escape. Roads were jammed with vehicles, military stragglers, and civilian refugees, a panicked mob with little focus but to escape, even though there was really nowhere to hide anymore. "There are women, children, men old and young, some are sick and several are wounded by Bullets or bomb shrapnels," Sergeant Miguel recorded in his diary. "They look pale & sickly." At General Hospital Number 2, an overwhelmed doctor took stock of the situation and said if the fighting continued, the garrison would face "the worst massacre in history. We have over seven thousand patients now. There are no front lines; we haven't anything to fight with."

From his musty tunnel on Corregidor, General Wainwright cabled the War Department: "Fresh Japanese troops are continuing their forward drive in Bataan with great vigor. A heavy attack on our position is now in progress." Brigadier General Funk, King's chief of staff, visited Skinny and relayed a message that the Bataan forces now had little choice but to surrender. But Wainwright had already received no-surrender orders from both Roosevelt and MacArthur. "General, you go back and tell General King that he will not surrender," Wainwright replied. "Tell him he will attack. Those are my orders."

"General, you know, of course, what the situation is over there," Funk cautioned. "You know what the outcome will be."

"I do," Wainwright said, but his orders stood.

Though Wainwright remained adamant about continued resistance on Bataan, he understood that defeat on the peninsula was imminent. He issued orders for the evacuation to Corregidor of the nurses and the 45th Infantry Regiment (Scouts). The nurses were successfully spirited away under great stress and danger on the evening of April 8. The situation was too chaotic for the whole 45th to make it onto the barges that were earmarked to get them to Corregidor. Individuals from this unit and others did evacuate—mainly by swimming the three miles from the Bataan peninsula to Corregidor—but most remained behind.

From Australia, MacArthur chimed in with the kind of counterattack order that would have made even the notorious World War I château generals shake their heads in embarrassment. He ordered both of King's corps to attack, "with full tank strength and maximum artillery concentration," seize Japanese bases on the eastern coast of Bataan, and unhinge the entire enemy position. "If successful the supplies seized at this base might well rectify the situation." If not, the men could simply fight as guerrillas. If MacArthur honestly thought such an order had any chance of success, the historian must wonder why the general did not issue it several weeks before, when he was still in the Philippines and the army had not yet deteriorated into a nightmarish state of starvation and sickness. In Bluemel's hard-bitten view, the order reflected a person "totally ignorant of the situation and the condition of the troops on Bataan."[17]

This and the no-surrender order were the equivalent of commanding a paralyzed man to run a relay race. No one knew this better than Ned King. By the evening of April 8, he understood he had two choices: surrender or face total destruction. Before the Vietnam War, Americans liked to tell themselves that they had never lost a war. Southerners like King knew this was untrue. He was the grandson and nephew of Confederate officers. Ironically born on the Fourth of July, 1884, and steeped in the Lost Cause myth of the Old South, though never embracing its poisonous, self-serving racism, King could now relate to the terrible predicament his forebears had faced. Like them, he cared for his soldiers and he saw no purpose in their extinction. Environment, nationality, and culture matter a great deal in the outlook of a commander. Had he been a Japanese officer, honor would have demanded such extinction. To King's way of thinking, honor demanded instead their preservation, provided there was no hope of rescue and no means of continued resistance (and there was hope of neither).

In spite of Wainwright's orders, King knew he must reluctantly issue a surrender order. That evening of April 8, he broke the news to his staff, all of whom concurred with the decision. "There was not a dry eye present," Colonel James Collier, his operations officer, later said. To shield the staff and General Wainwright from possible repercussions, he took sole responsibility for the decision. "It is the end of my career," King declared. He had served since 1908, earning reputation as a reliable, extraordinarily competent artillery officer who treated everyone with unfailing courtesy. "His courageous leadership was at all times inspiring," one of his officers later wrote. King fully expected to be court-martialed someday for disobeying orders, and he wanted to make sure that no one else would face the same opprobrium. Two of his staff officers, Colonel Everett Williams and Major Marshall Hurt, volunteered for the dangerous job of going to the Japanese lines, under a white flag of truce, to facilitate a meeting between King and his opponents. The two succeeded in arranging for a meeting the next day at Lamao.

Meanwhile, the general ordered the destruction of anything that might be useful to the Japanese, including weapons, ammunition, and military equipment. He made sure to gas up and preserve a fleet of over one thousand trucks and other vehicles to transport his weakened men to prison camps once they had surrendered. All night long, Bataan rocked with explosions and fires as units destroyed ordnance, mainly by setting TNT charges or simply shooting at it. The air reeked of smoke and gunpowder. The nighttime sky was weirdly alit with the glows of raging fires. Fragments whizzed menacingly everywhere; tracer rounds zigzagged through the darkness. "I have never heard such terrific explosions before," Captain Tisdelle told his diary. "Our CP [command post] is being rained with shell fragments and shells splash in the air." One of the main ammo dumps was located adjacent to General Hospital Number 1. The detonations were so dangerous that the hospital staff engaged in the laborious task of moving the patients to a safer spot. The explosion at the Navy's main dump, in a quarry near Mariveles, blew up with such force that it created a landslide that killed several people. As if attuned to the human Götterdämmerung unfolding on the peninsula, nature chimed in with a pair of unsettling earthquakes in the course of that apocalyptic evening. "Even the earth is shaken by our decision," one of King's officers muttered.[18]

At daybreak on April 9, the same day that Robert E. Lee had surrendered to Ulysses S. Grant at Appomattox seventy-seven years earlier, King said a quick prayer and set out in a jeep for Lamao, with several staff members in tow. As a nineteen-year-old descendant of Confederate officers, King had once served on a cannon crew that fired a final salute at the funeral of General John B. Gordon, a legendary Civil War commander and former governor of the state. On this sad morning in 1942, as King's group drove to Lamao, the famous words of Lee kept running through King's mind. "Then there is nothing left to do but to go and see General Grant, and I would rather die a thousand deaths."

King would find his enemy much less chivalrous than had Lee. When King and his party reached the Japanese lines (after being strafed several times by enemy aircraft), they had difficulty making the local Japanese commander, Major General Kameichiro Nagano, understand who they were and why they had come. The party waited for some time in the sun, standing erect, as several hundred Japanese soldiers stared silently and curiously at them. King had donned his last clean, undamaged khaki uniform, but after taking cover in ditches several times from the strafing planes, the general looked, in Captain Tisdelle's estimation, like he "had not washed since the war began." In the tropical heat, the mustachioed King's thinning reddish-gray hair was plastered against his middle-aged head. General Homma refused to meet with King. Instead, he sent his operations officer, Colonel Motoo Nakayama, who at last pulled up in a shiny Cadillac. The little party of enemies met outside, adjacent to the local agricultural station office. They sat in austere wooden chairs opposite a tiny table of the sort that might serve a two-person party at a café. Nakayama and an English-speaking Japanese captain sat on one side. On the other side, King sat with his legs crossed, head held high, between Tisdelle and two other staffers who flanked him. "I never saw him look more like a soldier than in this hour of defeat," Tisdelle wrote. Japanese soldiers hovered around, snapping photos of the event.

Nakayama refused to salute King or even meet eyes with him. He was under the impression or the hope (as was Homma we might suppose) that he was meeting with Wainwright, who would be in a position to surrender all Allied forces in the Philippines. Instead, Nakayama found himself dealing only with the commander of the Luzon force, a confusing and substantial letdown. For several moments, King and Nakayama bickered back and forth through the interpreter as King made the Japanese officer understand that he controlled only the forces on Bataan and had no power to summon Wainwright or influence his actions in any way. "For what purpose have you come?" Nakayama asked. King explained that he had come to avert further bloodshed and negotiate an armistice while he dispersed surrender orders to the units under his command and worked with the Japanese to facilitate their transition into captivity. King mentioned the vehicles he had gathered to carry his men to a prison location of Japanese choosing. Nakayama was in no mood to discuss such specifics. "You will surrender unconditionally," he demanded in an eerie echo of Grant, not at Appomattox but earlier in the Civil War. King asked several times if his men would be properly treated as prisoners of war. Nakayama refused to answer. "I want you to tell me how these men . . . will be treated," the Georgian pressed. An exasperated Nakayama barked something at the interpreter, who, according to the Americans, spoke English with a bizarre Prussian accent. The interpreter turned to King and bellowed, "The Japanese are not barbarians!"[19]

★

Word of the surrender gradually spread among the Filipino-American troops. A few felt betrayed. Most were too exhausted and hungry to dissent. The luckiest and most intrepid among King's men melted away and began a long struggle as guerrilla warriors (something the Imperial Japanese Army had anticipated and rightly feared, since its commanders knew that controlling the whole archipelago was an impossibility). The vast majority of the Allied soldiers, more than seventy-five thousand, now found themselves in the custody of the Japanese, who were seriously unprepared for the responsibility of caring for so many captives. Homma's staff still had no idea of the actual size of King's force. At most, they thought that there were forty thousand to forty-five thousand Filipino-American soldiers on Bataan, a serious underestimate. Incredibly, the Japanese also had no idea how badly their new prisoners were suffering from disease and malnutrition. They simply assumed that the Americans and Filipinos were in similar physical condition to their own soldiers, capable of hiking a couple dozen miles per day. Though General King, in the course of his contentious conversation with Colonel Nakayama, had clearly outlined the desperate condition of his soldiers, the Japanese officer had either failed to grasp this message or simply did not care. Since King knew his men were in no condition to walk any substantial distances, he had emphasized the availability of American vehicles to move the troops to their prison camp. This made no impression on Nakayama. He and other Japanese leaders never made any provision to use the trucks for this purpose. Nor, upon returning to 14th Army headquarters, did the colonel raise any alarms for General Homma about the condition of King's soldiers.

To be sure, Homma's staff had planned for the care and feeding of Bataan prisoners, though they had expected resistance to go deeper into April, and their preparations were not complete as of King's surrender. With Corregidor still unconquered, and Manila Bay thus useless to the Japanese, and under great pressure from Tokyo to wrap up the Philippines campaign, Homma's main preoccupation now was to take Corregidor. He could not afford the luxury of keeping Allied prisoners in southern Bataan. For one thing, they would be in the middle of a battle; for another they might compromise his operational security. The prisoners had to be moved out of Bataan, as quickly as possible. General Homma made the terrible mistake of failing to designate one commander for this mission. Instead, he divided the responsibility between two of his staff officers, setting the stage for disorganization and chaos. Colonel Toshimitsu Takatsu, his administration and supply officer, was to gather all the prisoners and get them to Balanga, a small city on the east coast, about halfway up the peninsula. From there, Major General Yoshikata Kawane, the 14th Army's transportation officer, was charged with the task of moving them from Balanga to a permanent camp in central Luzon. In all, the prisoners would have to cover, on average, about seventy miles from southern Bataan to San Fernando, where trains could take them twenty-five more miles to a railhead at Capas, located about nine miles by foot from an old Philippine Army depot, Camp O'Donnell, that would now become a temporary prison facility.

The 14th Army was hardly a vehicle-rich organization. Nearly all military vehicles were needed for the supply and movement of friendly troops. So most of the POWs would have to move on foot, standard practice in the Imperial Japanese Army. Takatsu and Kawane planned for rest areas, feeding points, and even a hospital along the route. None of these preparations were complete at the time of the surrender. The 14th Army's supply situation was not particularly good, either. Food was basic but not copious. Medicine was in short supply. The malaria rate among Japanese soldiers had skyrocketed as their army advanced deeper into the mosquito-infested areas of southern Bataan. With combat soldiers in short supply, most of those men earmarked for the job of shepherding prisoners were transportation troops. Needless to say, they had no training in the proper treatment of POWs or the logistics of moving them from place to place. In sum, the Japanese were unprepared captors in nearly every way, especially in terms of logistics and medical care, much less knowledge about the nature and number of their new prisoners.

Nor were the Japanese particularly enthusiastic captors. From the high command down to the humblest soldier, surrender was largely viewed as dishonorable and unthinkable, a cowardly act that brought humiliating shame to family members. Japanese representatives had signed the 1929 Geneva Convention provisions for the proper treatment of POWs. But their government had never ratified it, mainly out of concern that full ratification would provide an excuse for Japanese servicemen to consider the act of surrender legal and honorable. A soldier's handbook circulated among Homma's troops warned them that "plundering, being beguiled by women, or intentionally killing non-resisting people is absolutely against the good name and moral code of Japan. Control yourself so as not to spoil your reverence to the Emperor, his soldiers and his Army." It was up to Japanese officers and NCOs to translate this high-minded rhetoric into everyday reality. Far too many not only had no interest in doing so, but also they actively disdained such ethics.

All of these factors, in addition to brutal tropical heat and Bataan's poor infrastructure, laid the foundation for a tragedy of epic proportions. Over the course of about three weeks, ragged groups of Allied soldiers were marched up and out of Bataan, often in cavalry-like agony. At the time and for the next several years they referred to their odyssey as the "March of Death," though history has settled on the moniker "Bataan Death March." The Death March was not an organized, calculated atrocity, in the manner of the gas chambers at Auschwitz or the cold-blooded executions in Katyn Forest. Instead, it was the product of chaos, poor planning, command confusion, inertia, disorganization, and dismissive cruelty. If the Filipino-American soldiers had been in good physical condition, most could have withstood the heat, the long hikes, and the inadequate amounts of food, water, and medical care. But for soldiers on the verge of starvation and decrepitude from disease, such treatment was more than they could endure.

The march did not consist of a long, organized column. It was comprised of many groups, large and small, in various places, moving to and fro, often under differing treatment, even among individuals much less groups. The experience was governed primarily by randomness. Some soldiers (especially those of higher rank like King) did ride part or all the way to San Fernando or O'Donnell. Many other senior officers, including generals, walked most of the route; often the Japanese told the Americans that they were dissolving all distinctions of rank. Some prisoners were treated fairly well by their guards, who gave them decent amounts of food and allowed them access to water. When Japanese tankers overran General Hospital Number 1, they allowed the staff and the patients to remain in place and even assisted them whenever they could. Most everyone who was fortunate enough to be at this hospital avoided the march altogether.

In sharp contrast to the situation at General Hospital Number 1, the Japanese troops who took General Hospital Number 2 cut food rations and proceeded to loot the place with impunity. The Japanese then placed artillery units adjacent to the hospital from which they proceeded to bombard Corregidor. American gunners on the island tried to avoid hitting their own people here and elsewhere (this friendly fire was a source of tremendous concern to Wainwright), but scores were killed or wounded by fire from the Corregidor batteries. At General Hospital Number 2, Japanese soldiers prompted thousands of Filipino patients and caregivers to leave by hinting that they were free to go home. But the Japanese had made no provision for repatriating these men. Most of the patients were in rotten condition, malnourished, feverish from malaria, doubled over with dysentery. Some were even amputees whose wounds had not healed. Instead of going home under proper supervision, they simply melted into the larger streams of mistreated humanity trudging north on Bataan's dusty, unpaved roads, where an untold number died.

For far too many of the Allied soldiers moving north on those roads, death and misery stalked them minute by minute for days on end. The paucity of food and medical care could, to generous historical minds, be chalked up to Homma's dysfunctional command arrangements and the 14th Army's tenuous supply situation. The ubiquitous cruelty of many Japanese guards and their propensity toward mindless violence was another matter altogether. When Filipino civilians, sometimes at risk to themselves, tried to give food and water to the prisoners, Japanese guards usually put a stop to this, sometimes by bayoneting and clubbing the offenders. Often, they deliberately withheld access to water or medical care. Dehydration was universal. Possession of a canteen could mean the difference between life and death. Thirst-crazed men who had not been trained in proper water discipline drank from polluted, muddy puddles, which only weakened them more with parasites, dysentery, and other ailments. When sick, exhausted prisoners who fell out of their columns or had any trouble keeping up, the usual response from the guards was slapping, kicking, beating, and stabbing rather than first aid or some thoughtful form of coercion. "No one was permitted to lag behind, or to stop for rest," a postwar Army provost marshal report stated. "Whoever fell by the wayside or was observed trying to get food from the natives [Filipinos], or to secure drinking water anywhere, was either clubbed, bayoneted or shot outright."

This barbarous treatment accounted for much of the suffering and death among the prisoners. The language barrier was such that seldom could guards communicate in any meaningful way with their captives, beyond brute force or indifference. "The Jap orders were if one did not march, one was usually shot in the head," General Bluemel grimly summarized in a postwar statement. He personally witnessed three such summary executions of Filipino soldiers. Prisoners tried to stick together and urge one another to keep going just a little bit farther, maybe just to the next stopping point, but when a man staggered or fell behind, there was usually little his buddies could do to save him. There were also moments of petty brutality and humiliation. One Japanese soldier approached Private Tenney, the former tank crewman, and gestured for a cigarette. Tenney, a nonsmoker, told him he did not have any. "He smiled and then a second later hit me in the face with the butt of his gun. Blood spurted from my nose and then from a deep gash in my cheekbone. He laughed and said something that made all his buddies laugh too." One of Tenney's friends offered a cigarette to the soldier. He took the whole pack. Then he and his comrades repaid the American by beating him senseless with rifle butts and bamboo poles.

Looting and thievery were common. Most of the prisoners were relieved of watches, rings, money, wallets, and any other item of perceived value. Anyone caught in possession of Japanese items risked summary execution on the spot. Soldiers discovered imperial yen notes on one American captain. A Japanese officer forced him to his knees, pulled a sword from his scabbard, and, with terrifying alacrity, decapitated him. The victim's head bounced crazily for several yards, almost bumping into a nearby group of horrified prisoners. His torso pitched forward, twitching violently, gushing red arterial blood onto the dusty ground.

Japanese soldiers riding in trucks alongside the columns of prisoners sometimes clubbed men with poles or rifle butts. One truckload of soldiers threw a rope around an unsuspecting prisoner's neck and dragged him in the rocky dust for about a hundred yards until he managed to wriggle himself free. Bleeding profusely, the angry American raged, "You bastards! I'll live to pee on your graves!" Elsewhere, a Japanese officer on horseback galloped past exhausted prisoners, swinging a sharpened samurai sword to and fro, apparently in hopes of goring or cutting the head off a captive.[20]

Sunning-out treatments were common. The prisoners were packed together in an open area, under the broiling sun, sometimes for hours at a time, often within sight of artesian water wells. The guards meted out severe punishment to anyone who made a move for the wells. "There were several men shot and many were beaten unmercifully for trying to get a little water," one American soldier testified in a postwar witness statement. "I, personally, saw one American soldier shot because he was sick and unable to keep up." He also saw an ill major, who had been terribly mistreated, commit suicide by jumping off a bridge. Another soldier testified to seeing Japanese soldiers order locals to bury sick men alive, a fairly common occurrence during the march. "One of the soldiers had sufficient vitality to move slightly and was aware of what was happening to him. He cried piteously, and twice crawled from the grave after being covered. After his second emergence, the irrated [sic] Jap ordered a civilian member of the digging party to hit the soldier over the head with his shovel. He was then replaced in the grave and caused no further trouble." In another instance, a group of guards hung a Filipino soldier to a tree by his thumbs and slowly bayoneted him to death.

In general, the Japanese dished out the worst treatment to the Filipinos, belying the anticolonial, Pan-Asian war rhetoric of the soldier's handbook. The worst example was the mass execution, mainly by stabbing, of about four hundred officers and NCOs from the Philippine Army's 91st Division and a few other units. "They . . . made us sit on the ground," recalled Captain Pedro Felix, one of the few survivors. The condemned sat together with their hands bound behind their backs. "Just before executing us, the

Jap soldiers . . . stuck . . . cigarettes into our mouths and lighted them for us. But on a given signal by the Jap officer in charge, they started bayoneting and beheading us." Carried out near the Pantingan River by soldiers of the 65th Brigade, the massacre was the closest thing to a premeditated atrocity during the Death March.

Far more common, the Filipino soldiers were brutalized on an individual basis. "I saw Filipinos on their knees with their hands up in a form of surrender or supplication . . . pleading with guards for their lives, and then saw the guard lunge at them with the bayonet, and then the man fall over [dead]," Lieutenant Colonel Harold K. Johnson of the 57th Infantry Regiment (Scouts) said decades later. Promoted just before the surrender, the thoughtful Johnson learned much during the Death March about the fickleness of fortune and human nature. "You never knew if you were going to get a bayonet or a ride to the next stop." While the terrible circumstances had brought out the worst in some people—theft of food, canteens, and clothing was rampant—Johnson was the opposite. As the march unfolded, he found himself becoming more philosophical with a deeper belief in God. He of course wanted to survive, mostly for the chance to reunite with his wife, Dorothy, someday. He thought of her constantly, but there was more on his mind as well. Johnson had always been imbued with a strong upper-Midwestern sense of honor. West Point had only solidified this personal code. Now, in captivity, this blend of ethics and faith seemed to hold the key to not only his survival but also, and perhaps even more important, to that of many of his fellow soldiers. "God was close and very real in those hours," he later said.

Johnson came to believe that the Japanese guards were so quick to brutalize others because they were routinely subjected to the same treatment. "Physical beating was just one form of discipline . . . and it was the way they treated their own troops." Corporal punishment was indeed standard practice in the Imperial Japanese Army and in many other walks of civilian life, such as schools. On several occasions during the march, American soldiers witnessed individual Japanese soldiers in passing columns fall down and lay still, overcome with exhaustion. Sergeants kicked and berated them, sometimes with blows to the face. "I have personally seen [Japanese soldiers] beaten unconscious," one American prisoner later said. Sergeant Arthur Thomas saw one such enemy soldier fall to the ground and lie prostrate. With no hesitation, one of his comrades took his pack and kept walking. Another soldier kicked and beat him, almost as if testing whether he was faking some sort of infirmity. When it was clear he was not, a medic finally materialized and "gave him some sort of shot and, in a little while, he got up and staggered away, supported by other Japanese soldiers." Like child abuse, the cycle of violence tended to repeat itself as those who had been mistreated transferred their anger by doing the same to others. For far too many soldiers, beatings and sadism grotesquely equated to proper discipline and respect for authority.

Obviously none of this excused atrocity-laden behavior, but it did provide the kernel of an explanation as to why soldiers who had been arbitrarily beaten by their own countrymen would have little compunction about thrashing dehumanized enemy soldiers whom they had been indoctrinated to believe were a mortal threat to Japan. Many of the Japanese soldiers seethed with an especially vitriolic anger for the Filipinos, whom they had initially believed they were liberating only to see them fight alongside the Americans to kill or wound many treasured comrades. In a typical instance, wounded Japanese soldiers urged the guards of a group of Filipino POWs to slaughter them on the spot. "Kill every last one of them! Don't let them eat!" Just as filth spawns disease, the world of war, especially this one, could generate this kind of nightmarish disregard for humanity, mercy, and common decency, when otherwise normal, considerate individuals behaved with terrifying levels of cruelty and immorality. Such was the situation during the march. It is hard to imagine that many of the Japanese perpetrators embarked upon military service in the Philippines intending to behave with such disgraceful criminality, and this makes the actions of these ordinary men all the more disquieting. Though Homma clearly did not order these atrocities and later claimed no firsthand knowledge of them, he would nonetheless be held responsible for them by his enemies in a postwar trial and would pay with his life.

Allied prisoners learned quickly not to resist or even express any verbal dissent lest they subject themselves to the special sadistic attention of guards. In one rare exception, Captain Alvin Poweleit, a doctor and former semipro boxer, interceded against a guard who was severely beating an enlisted man. Poweleit landed a terrific blow to the enemy soldier's jaw that knocked him down. Before he could recover, Poweleit leaped on him, snapped his neck, and ditched his body in a bamboo thicket. Fortunately for Poweleit and the other man, no other Japanese guards were close enough to witness what happened. The two Allied soldiers hurried away before they could notice.

Sanitation was nonexistent. Dysentery-ridden marchers were routinely forced to sit or sleep in or near their own excremental filth or that of others who had preceded them. "Human waste is scattered around which makes everybody very discomfort," Sergeant Miguel, the Filipino Scout, managed to jot down hurriedly in his diary during the terrible odyssey. At Lubao, a key stopping point, the Japanese often herded hundreds of diarrhea-stricken men into a mid-size sheet-iron warehouse owned by the National Rice and Corn Corporation. There they would spend an evening packed together in brutal heat, with no latrine. The filthiness and deprivation was nearly unimaginable. "Very few went outside to deficate [sic]," one American survivor recounted. "I personally had seven bowel movements that night and there were other men worse than myself."

Dead bodies soon lined the terrible route all the way from Mariveles to Capas. A few unfortunates who died on the road were run over by vehicles and smashed so flat that, in the recollection of one soldier, "I thought it was loose clothing." Most of the dying crawled to nearby ditches or the jungle to spend their last moments before they expired. "Human corpses lined the road on either side from Mariveles to San Fernando," one survivor vividly recalled. Most of the bodies were inundated with maggots and flies. In some instances, they were picked over by birds or animals of prey. The stench of death hung over the eastern side of the peninsula, like a gloomy veil. "[They] smell very, very bad," Sergeant Miguel told his secret diary, which he kept hidden during the march.

For the majority, who somehow managed to keep going, survival was simply a matter of "shuffling along through powder thin dust that was often four to six inches deep," wrote Captain Olson, the adjutant of the 57th Infantry. "Prisoners and guards soon had their sweat-soaked bodies covered with a thick coat of tan that gave a uniformity of appearance to both groups. Some men screamed at their tormentors that they were sick, wounded or too exhausted to go on. The reaction was swift and decisive. A fierce jab with a bayonet into the chest or a bullet in the head . . . and the body was pushed into a ditch or the bushes by the side of the road. The message quickly sank into the aching heads of the others in the column. Keep going no matter how hard it is to put one foot in front of the other! He who cannot move will soon be unable to move forever more!" The dust was so thick it was nearly suffocating. "We breathed it, tasted it, swallowed it," Colonel Mallonee later wrote. "The horrible, scorching heat of that tropical sun is something I will remember for the rest of my life."

Those who made it to San Fernando were packed aboard overcrowded boxcars for a suffocating journey to Capas, anywhere from three to five hours away. The temperature in the cars was well above one hundred degrees. Men had almost no room to move, much less sit or lie down. To Corporal Hubert Gater, the journey was "almost indescribable. Men fainting with no place to fall. Those with dysentery had no control of themselves. As the car swayed, the urine, the sweat, and the vomit rolled three inches deep back and forth around and in our shoes." Some did not survive. When the trains reached Capas, the living hauled their remains off the boxcars and stacked them by the tracks. The survivors staggered the final nine miles to O'Donnell, their Death March journey at last ended. Lieutenant Lee, who had written an upbeat letter to his family only two months earlier, now took to the solace of writing poetry to remember those who had not made it through the march:

So now you are dead. The easy words contain
No sense of loss, no sorrow, no despair.
Thus hunger, thirst, fatigue combine to drain
All feeling from our hearts. The endless glare,
The brutal heat, anesthetize the mind.
I cannot mourn you now. I lift my load,
The suffering column moves on. I leave behind
Only another corpse beside the road.

By the early part of May, when the infamous march finally petered out, some six hundred American and five thousand to ten thousand Filipino soldiers had lost their lives. About ninety-three hundred Americans and fifty thousand Filipinos had somehow managed to survive and make it to O'Donnell. For them, the Death March was over physically—mentally and emotionally it would never really cease—but a new nightmare of hellish captivity was only beginning.[21]

★

During the height of the Death March, it was possible for soldiers on Corregidor to peer through field glasses and catch glimpses of the marchers, spread into ragged columns, long and short, plodding steadily, wearily north, tramping up clouds of dust. As the viewer shifted his binoculars to and fro, he could just make out individuals here and there through the mists of suffocating dust. Though spared the horrors of the march, the defenders of Corregidor and the other fortified islands in Manila Bay knew that their own final hour was now at hand. The intensity of Japanese aerial and artillery bombardment had increased substantially, especially now that they controlled the Bataan peninsula. Hidden artillery pieces along the coast now pummeled Corregidor at point-blank range. In all, the Japanese unleashed more than three hundred air raids and many hundreds of thousands of artillery shells—including sixteen thousand on one particularly violent day—at the besieged defenders of the Rock. With the possible exception of Malta in the Mediterranean, no other island had been pummeled so badly up to this stage in World War II. General Wainwright even received a warm note of encouragement from Lieutenant General Sir William Dobbie, the governor of battered Malta. Certainly no Americans had withstood such a bone-jattering besiegement bombardment since the Civil War. Nor would they again until Khe Sanh in 1968. Corregidor's garrison had swollen to about thirteen thousand military personnel plus a few thousand civilians who either lived on the island or had taken refuge there from the fighting elsewhere. Wainwright estimated that about two thousand soldiers, many of whom were nearly incapacitated by exhaustion and disease, had escaped from Bataan.

Much of the garrison consisted of administrative and headquarters specialists, many of whom spent their days working in the laterals of the Malinta Hill Tunnel complex. Some of them rarely emerged from their subterranean world. "Everyone who doesn't need to be elsewhere was in a tunnel," Captain Ames recalled. The skin of these "tunnel rats" soon grew sallow from lack of sun exposure. In addition to the Coast Artillery units, the only combat troops on the island were Colonel Samuel Howard's fifteen hundred leathernecks of the 4th Marine Regiment, a unit that had been moved in August 1941 from Shanghai to the Philippines. The Marines were augmented by shipless sailors, Philippine Army soldiers, Scouts, and American Bataan escapees from the Philippine Division. The infantry Marines and their new ad hoc colleagues were deployed to defend the likely landing beaches at the narrow neck of the tadpole shaped island. By the nature of their jobs, these men and the Coast Artillery soldiers were exposed to the worst dangers of the bombardment. The tunnels were usually inaccessible to them for any substantial stretches of time—unless they were wounded—and this generated some resentment of those who lived and worked there. The combat troops sardonically offered to create a special decoration for them—the Distinguished Tunnel Service medal—and they suggested special medical treatment for any of them who might experience shelter shock (rather than shell shock).

Round the clock, but especially during daylight hours, little Corregidor echoed with the explosions of bombs and shells. Japanese artillerymen hurled projectiles from both the Bataan and Manila sides of the bay, a far deadlier threat than the air attacks. "One day's shelling did more damage than all the bombing put together," Major Stephen Mellnick, a Coast Artillery officer, later wrote. The suffocating enemy ordnance altered the topography of a once-quaint place. "Once small depressions were filled with landslides," an army report chronicled. "Hills and hammocks became depressions. Paved roads disintegrated into dust. The few level areas became cratered upheavals. Even the beaches . . . changed shape." It became almost impossible for any vehicle to move, especially during the day. Rocky rubble and muddy shoreline collapsed onto picturesque beaches where the children of soldiers had once played. The mile-long Topside Barracks, once an emblem of America's professional army in the archipelago, was now reduced to little more than a dilapidated, wrecked shell of masonry. The Topside parade ground, where generations of American soldiers had drilled in perfect cadence, was now a kill zone, pockmarked with craters. The same was true of a nearby golf course. Trolley tracks that had once transported military families and civilian employees around the island were torn into shambles. Wooden homes and administrative buildings were long gone. The water-supply system was damaged. External telephone and power lines were largely destroyed as were many guns and mortars of the Coast Artillery units. A bomb scored a direct hit on one unit's kitchen, destroying a carefully prepared gelatin dessert, a real morale buster because the men had chipped in several days' worth of scarce fruit rations to make the treat. "It was almost impossible to move about except at a crawl . . . without bringing down a barrage of artillery fire," said the diary of Battery C, 60th Coast Artillery Regiment. The explosions denuded much of the thick jungle foliage that used to shade some of the island. Brush fires burned fiercely. The smoke from these fires was sometimes so thick that it provided the defenders welcome concealment from the prying eyes of Japanese artillery observers and an enemy observation balloon. This was the exception, though. The troops spent most of the day inside bunkers, specially dug tunnels, and foxholes. To avoid exposing themselves, they waited until darkness to haul water, eat their sparse meals, and carry supplies. But vitamin A deficiency in their diet made it increasingly difficult for them to see at night. In an effort to alleviate this problem, one battery commander resorted to giving his men a mixed cocktail of cod liver oil and boric acid that he had scrounged from the Malinta Hill Tunnel hospital.[22]

Amid the constant cascade of fire, casualties began to pile up, especially among the batteries. A 240-millimeter shell scored a direct hit on a generator used by one battery in the 60th Coast Artillery Regiment. Fire swept in every direction, burning four men to death and wounding four others. "The deaths and injuries that day was a distinct shock to all of us," Lieutenant Colonel Elvin Barr, the regiment's executive officer, told his diary. "The men had lost some of their good friends, many of them just couldn't believe it. The morale of the men started downward. Had they been able to fight back, they would have felt better, but now frequent shellings added to their helpless misery and even our big guns could do little in reply." On one afternoon alone, Japanese gunners showered the southern part of the island with more than thirty-six hundred rounds. The heaviest part of the bombardment hit Batteries Geary and Crockett, located just south of what used to be the golf course. One shell touched off sixteen hundred powder charges at Battery Geary, detonating a titanic explosion that shook the entire island, so much so that some in the tunnels thought an earthquake had hit. "We rattled in our tiny refuges like seeds in a gourd," one officer later wrote.

Debris flew in every direction. Thirteen-ton mortars flew through the air like toys. One of them catapulted 150 yards and landed facedown on the golf course. "There was a tremendous roar like a thunder clap," wrote Private Campbell, a 31st Infantry Regiment soldier who had escaped Bataan to serve now at Battery Geary. "The sky grew dark with falling debris, the ground shook and I was rattled in my hole like a peanut shaken by a monkey." He heard a shrieking noise and saw a huge slab of concrete flying through the air, right at him. He flattened himself at the bottom of his foxhole. "The block of concrete landed across my hole with a great thud that shook me violently; the impact filled the hole with a thick cloud of dust and I began coughing and vomiting." Campbell was shaken but unwounded. Others were not so fortunate. Battery Geary was reduced to nothing more than a smoking crater. Campbell climbed out his hole to behold a horrifying scene. "Dead men were all around; flesh, clothing, wood, cement, equipment and gun parts were blasted into a mess. Maimed soldiers were crawling about, dazed and crying." Dozens were killed, wounded, or missing. Four men were trapped within the battery's concrete fortifications. Engineers spent the entire night working to drill through the concrete to set them free. They succeeded in making a big enough hole to pass food and water to the men. By morning the hole was big enough to evacuate the four to the Malinta hospital. One died; the other three survived.

The area around Malinta Hill was hardly impervious to the shelling. In the evenings, the "tunnel rats" liked to stand just outside the entrance to the complex, singing, enjoying some fresh air and smoking cigarettes. One night, as several dozen of them congregated, an artillery shell screamed in and exploded among them. The carnage was horrible. Pieces of people were stuck in the tall iron gate that served as the Malinta entrance. Stretcher bearers scrambled to the scene, groping around in the darkness, recovering anyone who looked alive and spiriting them inside the tunnels. Doctors and nurses worked frantically to save anyone they could. Lieutenant Mueller, the nurse, remembered seeing "arms torn off . . . legs just hanging on." Another nurse, Lieutenant Helen Cassiani was staring open-mouthed at the gate when a severed head rolled past her feet. Suppressing the urge to vomit, she turned away in disgust. All night long the doctors and nurses worked on the wounded and the dying. They gave injections, administered anesthesia, stitched up gaping wounds, removed fragments, and attempted to keep the wounded from going into shock. "Legs and arms had been wrenched off," Lieutenant Redmond wrote. "There were jagged flesh wounds; pieces of exploded shrapnel stuck in ugly wounds; deaths from shock mounted no matter how frantically we worked over the victims." Doctors were so inundated with major surgeries that they assigned operations on the more lightly wounded to the nurses. Lieutenant Redmond performed a toe amputation and was chagrined to see the amputated toe drop perfectly into the open hand of an arm that had already been amputated from someone else. The stress of such a mass-casualty event was beyond imagination. "Something cracks inside you," she said, "You can't ever be quite the same again." Fourteen men were killed and another seventy wounded.

Comprising one thousand beds, many of which were stacked two or three high, the hospital occupied thirteen laterals near the north entrance to the complex. Though conditions were hardly ideal, they were much better than the hospitals on Bataan. There were latrines with flush toilets, cold-water showers, electricity (as long as the power plant was not bombed out), and running water. The kitchen consisted of three electric stoves. At times the power generators failed, forcing the medics to rely on flashlights. "If you ever wanted to feel what the darkness of the Egyptian pyramids must have been like," Lieutenant Brantley later said, "then you should have been in Malinta Tunnel when the lights went out."

Though the hospital was impervious to the bombardment, the staff and patients could not completely escape its effects. At all hours, they heard the whumping of explosions, some close enough to knock cabinets over or beds askew. With each explosion, concrete chips and dust scattered to and fro, prompting many to worry that the tunnels would collapse, burying everyone alive or crushing them to death. "The vibration of that bombing was horrible," Lieutenant Edith Shacklette said, "and it would make your head ache." Migraines were common, as was hearing loss. The air was dank and moist, with an unhealthy odor. Patients lay clustered in bunks that lined the lateral walls. Their moans and groans melded with the distant sounds of explosions. The helplessness bred claustrophobia in many. "It made you want to weep to see them in there," said General Wainwright, who visited them often, "trapped, while the place shook from the bombing and shelling outside." Decades later, visitors to these dank laterals swore they could hear the ghostly whispers and gasps of the wounded, still pleading for help.

The staff worked twelve- and sixteen-hour days. The nurses who escaped from Bataan were melded with those already on duty. The women slept in a private lateral of their own. Combat fatigue cases were unusual (the same had been true on Bataan) probably because most everyone understood that, with nowhere to escape, there was a clear existential purpose to all fighting. One of the few exceptions was an artilleryman who had been talking to a friend during a shelling, leaned over to pick something up, and rose just in time to see the remains of his friend's head whiz past him. After this experience, he grew hysterical to the point of insanity. The medics could do little except try to keep him comfortable. Disease was nowhere near as big of a problem as at Bataan. Men who had escaped the peninsula accounted for most all cases of dysentery. The vast majority of the patients were victims of concussion and wounds from "bomb and shell fragments with no small arms bullet wounds," according to Colonel Cooper, the USFIP surgeon. "There was a high proportion of killed outright to the total casualties."[23]

General Wainwright had taken over MacArthur's tunnel quarters consisting of a pair of seven-by-nine-foot rooms in Lateral 10. Ventilation was bad. Someone had painted the ceiling white, brightening an otherwise dark space. The general's days began at 0600, when he rose from his simple cot, dressed, and made the rounds of Malinta and other parts of Corregidor to inspect "the damage wrought since I slept." He divided his days between doing paperwork in his tunnel headquarters and roaming around, taking the pulse of his command. He was easygoing, an engaging and almost startlingly honest talker with anyone regardless of rank, a gloomy and yet oddly inspirational figure for the men and women of the besieged garrison. When a field-grade officer smartly saluted him one day and congratulated him on his promotion to three-star rank, he casually saluted back and said, "Hell of a sop for my having to end my career by surrendering." Wainwright ate the same ascetical meals of fish and rice as everyone else, the exception being a midday bowl of soup he often consumed for lunch. His leanness gave him a rooster-like appearance. His face was perpetually drawn. Fatigue and total dedication to duty seemed somehow to emanate in equal measures from his sad countenance. Because day after day he regularly exposed himself to the perpetual Japanese bombardment, he experienced several close calls. One afternoon as he prepared to inspect an artillery battery, he paused for a few moments to light a cigar. A shell exploded several feet away, right where he would have been had he not stopped to light up his cigar. "My head suddenly felt as if someone had rammed a red-hot pipe through one ear and out the other." He was not hit, but the explosion burst his left eardrum and permanently damaged the hearing in his right ear. For several hours, all noises, even explosions, sounded muffled to him. His hearing improved, but it was never quite the same again.

By late April, Wainwright knew he was in the same situation as King had been just three weeks earlier. Wainwright, in spite of his no-surrender order to King, did not blame the Georgian for what he had done. "He was faced with a terrible situation and he made a brave and determined decision," Wainwright later wrote. The end at Corregidor was clearly imminent, and Wainwright was readying for it. Though the valorous competence of the nurses was inspirational to the men, many, including Wainwright, felt an underlying uneasiness about their presence. When the end came, how would the Japanese treat them? In captivity the men could no longer protect the nurses, a horrifying, emasculating scenario to a generation of American males who firmly believed that an essential part of manhood was to protect womanhood from physical harm and sexual defilement.

In hopes of getting some of the nurses out of Corregidor before the inevitable capitulation, Wainwright requested that General MacArthur send his only two Navy PBY seaplanes from Australia to the Rock. MacArthur acceded. The two planes managed to make it to a fueling point on an American-controlled portion of Mindanao and then, under cover of darkness, they landed on the waters adjacent to Corregidor. Together the two aircraft were capable of evacuating about fifty people. MacArthur had requested the evacuation of a few select officers, including an intelligence specialist and cryptographers. Wainwright chose some of the others. "Believe me, it was a hard list to make up," he said. "It is not an easy thing to be a judge of whether a man or woman will go free or stay in hell." He chose only those "who were in no physical condition to take captivity." He designated Colonel Cooper, the surgeon, and Captain Maude Davison, the highly respected head nurse, to decide which of her nurses would go. The basis of their decision-making was obscure at the time and has remained so ever since. Davison once claimed that she merely picked names out of a hat, but no one else ever corroborated this. Most likely, she chose on the same basis as Wainwright, in favor of those who were in poor physical or emotional condition. Even so, not all the twenty evacuees were in particularly bad shape. Some were thought of as the most beautiful women in the outfit. The nebulous nature of the selection process led to substantial resentment among some of the stay-behinds for the attractive evacuees (in a few instances, the bitterness lasted for many decades). The anger only increased when forty-seven-year-old Lieutenant Josephine "Josie" Nesbit and a couple of other "deserving" women were chosen but declined to go. Unfounded rumors spread that the good-looking evacuees were picked because of relationships with officers on MacArthur's staff. Much of the rancor focused on Lieutenant Redmond, who was an auburn-haired beauty and seemed to be in anything but poor condition. "As far as I'm concerned, Redmond was on [that list] because of her connections," Lieutenant Cassiani later sniped. "Politics works no matter where you are and what the circumstances." Lieutenant Redmond had been through a lot of trauma on Bataan and Corregidor. Like everyone on the list, she was riven with ambivalence. The idea of abandoning patients and comrades was repugnant. And yet the allure of getting out was nearly irresistible. "I did not know what to think, nor how I felt," she wrote. "I wanted to go, and I didn't want to go. Probably I would never see the other nurses again, and I wanted to stay with them and face whatever was to come; we had faced so much together, I felt like a deserter." As an officer, she felt it was her duty to obey orders.

Late in the evening on April 29, Emperor Hirohito's birthday, Wainwright himself escorted the chosen ones to a dock, where they boarded boats to ferry them out to the planes. He helped several onto the boats and bade them goodbye. Lieutenant Redmond, one of the last to leave, put her arms around and gave him a kiss. "Thank you, General," she said.

As Wainwright and several others watched anxiously, the planes taxied and took to the air so quickly that Japanese antiaircraft batteries at Cavite could not mobilize to shoot at them. Both planes made it to Lake Lanao on Mindanao, where they hid for a day and then attempted to take off the following night. The plane carrying Redmond took off and made it to Australia, where she and the others did the best they could to decompress. "They were . . . nervous, exhausted, pacing the floor, unable to settle down," Captain N. B. Sauve, an intelligence officer who met them, later wrote. The fuselage of the other plane was torn open by a rock during takeoff, severely damaging the plane. The crew and a Navy salvage unit worked to effect repairs while the passengers hid inland at an old hotel. By the time the repairs were done, the crew could no longer make contact with the passengers, so they had to leave them behind. All of them, including ten nurses and Wainwright's former intelligence officer, were later captured by the Japanese. A third group of chosen evacuees was trundled aboard a submarine, the USS *Spearfish* on May 3. Eleven Army nurses, one Navy nurse, and a Navy wife were part of this group. The sub stayed submerged for twenty-two uncomfortable hours but made it to the safety of Australia. "The submariners were so good to us," said Lieutenant Wilson, who was so ravaged by dysentery that she was down to seventy pounds. "They gave us some of their clothing as we had lost everything we owned." Many of the courageous escapees hoped to go back to the Philippines after a brief recuperation, but obviously this was impossible.[24]

Even as General Wainwright prepared for the coming moment of doom, General Homma put the finishing touches on a plan to invade Corregidor. With Bataan under control, he had redeployed some of his army to expand operations on Mindanao, Panay, and Cebu in the southern part of the archipelago. It had taken him nearly a month to assemble the necessary boats, barges, artillery, equipment, air support, and soldiers to invade Corregidor. For the main assault, he tapped the 4th Division, supported by the 7th Tank Regiment and artillery pieces from the 16th Division. After a heavy preinvasion bombardment, two thousand troops were to land at the extreme tip of the island, between North Point and Cavalry Point on the evening of May 5.

As the sun set and darkness blanketed Corregidor, the pounding of the barrage intensified noticeably. Hundreds of shells pummeled the landing beaches, the battery areas, and the environs of Malinta Hill. Many battery searchlights were destroyed, communications decimated. The constant shelling guaranteed that the beach defenders could not be reinforced. Some artillery pieces and machine guns were destroyed, but many remained in service. In his tiny room inside Lateral 10 of the Malinta tunnels, even hearing-impaired Wainwright noticed the differing nature of the menacing explosions. He looked at Brigadier General Beebe, his chief of staff, and said, "I don't like the sound of that, Lew. This sounds to me just like artillery preparation before an attack."

At about 2200, under a moonless black sky, the landing boats set off from Cabcaben, on the Bataan coast, and soon approached the beaches. The landing craft ranged in size; some held 30 men, others as many as 170. Nervous assault troops softly sang a haunting melody called "Prayer in the Dawn." Unruly currents swept the boats too far to the east, away from the designated landing beaches. The schedule was blown. Units got mixed up. Looking down on the mini armada, one Marine whispered to another, "How many of 'em you reckon there are?" His buddy replied, "A lot more than there are of us."

The remaining searchlights came to life and zeroed in on the boats. Soon a devastating stream of artillery, mortar, and machine-gun and rifle fire lanced through the vulnerable craft. "The light artillery fired point-blank at the approaching vessels," an Army report vividly chronicled, "causing a sickening slaughter among its occupants. Direct hits blew the craft out of the water." Several boats sank. Men were flung into the water, where they drowned. Others were cut to pieces before they could get ashore. Japanese artillery soon knocked out the searchlights, but this hardly mattered. In the eerie half-light of flares, tracer rounds and explosions, the Americans could see hundreds of enemy soldiers staggering and struggling in the water and on the beach. Many who made it ashore were glopped with a residue of oil from the combination of their own wrecked craft and other vessels that had previously sunk in these narrow waters. Terror-stricken, they lunged for the cover of small rocky cliffs that over-looked the narrow beach (maybe ten yards or so). Some claimed they were Filipinos and begged for the Allies to cease fire. The Marines and their colleagues kept up a merciless wave of fire on the exposed attackers. Mortar rounds exploded with incredible accuracy. Devastating stitches of fire from .30- and .50-caliber machine guns tore "their thighs and ripped their hips to pieces," one Japanese survivor later testified. At one machine gun, Corporal Joseph Johnson, a transplanted 31st Infantry Regiment soldier, glimpsed them as "targets, small, fleeting, darting in the shadows." Rows of these men went down like ten pins at a bowling alley. In the memory of one Marine, it was "like shooting ducks in a barrel. The Japanese would run up and down the beach and each time there would be less men in the charges." Some plunged back into the water and took shelter behind boulders. All around them, wrecked craft and dead soldiers floated aimlessly and eerily. One American commander counted twenty-two sunken or heavily damaged boats. In a few instances, dozens of enemy bodies, still wearing their orange life vests, were packed inside the boats. Sharks circled the water in a frenzy, feeding on the flesh of the dead.

As a last recourse, some of the Japanese soldiers on the beach played dead. "Not even a finger moved, not a muscle twitched during those long, dreadful hours of waiting," one of them later recalled. A tank rumbled ashore and was immediately showered with grenades. The tank was un-scathed but several nearby soldiers were killed instantly. Young officers, like Lieutenant Machizuki, gathered survivors and led them on desperate charges over the soaked cliffs, point-blank at the machine gunners and riflemen. "Bullets whistled around me, splashing into the water. A soldier beside me gasped, 'His Imperial Majesty,' and that was the last of him. If it had not been for the fact that it was the dark hour before the dawn, pitch black, I doubt if any of us would be alive today to tell the story." By one estimate, over half the attackers were killed. One group of sixteen Marines and Scouts accounted for three hundred enemy dead. Between one-half and one-third of the boats were sunk or destroyed. When General Homma, at his headquarters on Bataan, received fragmentary reports of the slaughter, despair consumed him. "My God, I have failed miserably," he thought. According to his information, he had only twenty-one boats left, which meant that it would take many hours before he could send more troops to Corregidor. Wainwright was equally in crisis. He spent the night in the tunnels alternating between the Marine command post and that of General Moore, the coastal-defense-fortifications commander. Allied losses were terrible, between six hundred and eight hundred dead and one thousand wounded. There were no stretcher bearers to move the wounded to the tunnel hospital. Many of those who tried to hobble their way to Malinta were killed. Frustrated requests from the defenders for reinforcement, ammunition resupply, and fire support poured in to Wainwright. But there was little to nothing that Skinny could do.

Through raw courage, luck, and the inability of the Filipino-Americans to reinforce their beleaguered coastal defenders, the Japanese managed to envelop and overrun some of the leading positions and establish a shaky beachhead. In the confusion of the night, hand-to-hand fighting was not uncommon. Corporal Edwin Franklin, addled by the nearby explosion of a Japanese grenade, engaged in a stabbing match with an enemy soldier. "I ain't going this fucking way!" he thought to himself. Though he was slashed in the chest, he plunged his bayonet into the other man's vitals, snuffing out his life. All night long and in the early hours of daylight on May 6, the fighting raged like this until the battered Japanese survivors, plus a trio of tanks, managed to push across the narrow neck of the island and begin a relentless westward advance, almost to within sight of Malinta Hill. Moore stripped the remaining Coast Artillery batteries of crewmen to set up a final defensive line between the Japanese and the tunnel complex, a move tantamount to a physician's last attempt to save a dying patient. Coast Artillery as a branch died in front of Malinta Hill that day, never to be revived again in the modern Army.[25]

Meanwhile, General Wainwright paced up and down one of the laterals, deep in thought. Etched on his lean, drawn face was the exhaustion of a sleepless night, the responsibility of high command, and the stress of months of combat. He knew he had to decide if he could squeeze any more resistance out of the garrison or bow to the inevitable and surrender. Every minute he temporized could mean the death or maiming of untold numbers of his men, and Homma's, too. He went through a mental checklist: "Shaken troops, beach defenses literally pulverized, assault boat barriers wrecked, concrete machine-gun nests reduced to powder, the great majority of seacoast guns as well as fire control instruments destroyed; forty-six of the forty-eight beach defense 75-mm guns knocked out, communications gone, movement of troops all but impossible because of the continued shelling."

It all meant that he must surrender immediately. It was true that he had inflicted staggering damage on the invaders. But every minute his forces grew weaker; he could not sustain this resistance. Eventually, the Japanese could reinforce their landings and, at their leisure, annihilate his people. At 1015 he ordered Beebe to broadcast on "The Voice of Freedom" a previously prepared surrender statement. Fifteen minutes later, Beebe stepped to the microphone and forced the repugnant words from his mouth. "Message for General Homma . . . or the present commander in chief of the Imperial Japanese Forces on Luzon. For military reasons which General Wainwright considers sufficient, and to put a stop to further sacrifice of human life, the commanding general will surrender to your Excellency today the . . . fortified islands at the entrance to Manila Bay." Orders circulated to destroy all weapons and equipment that might be valuable to the Japanese.

Wainwright composed a final message to President Roosevelt. "With broken heart and head bowed in sadness but not in shame I report to Your Excellency that today I must arrange terms for the surrender of the fortified islands of Manila Bay. There is a limit to human endurance and that limit has long since been past. Without prospect of relief I feel it is my duty to my country and to my gallant troops to end this useless effusion of blood and human sacrifice." To MacArthur, he cabled, "We have done our full duty for you and for our country. We are sad but unashamed." In Lateral 12, Technician Fifth Grade (Tech 5) Irving Strobing, a signals clerk, tapped out the last coded messages from Corregidor to the outside world. "The jig's up. Everyone is bawling like a baby. My love to all. God bless you and keep you."

★

Unlike King, Wainwright got a face-to-face meeting with Homma. The two commanders and many of their staff officers met on Bataan, at a house about a mile north of Cabcaben. The meeting did not go well for much the same reason that King's session with Colonel Nakayama had been so stormy—disagreement over who and what the Americans wished to surrender. Homma wanted Wainwright to surrender all Allied forces in the Philippines, including General Sharp's troops in the central and southern part of the archipelago. Wainwright tried to argue that he controlled only the Manila Bay forces. Homma abruptly left the meeting, refusing to formally cease hostilities until Wainwright surrendered everything. Skinny knew his garrison was now at the mercy of the Japanese. Most of their weapons were destroyed. They were hungry and exhausted. Their supply situation was hopeless. At least two thousand had already surrendered in the course of the day on May 6. He could not risk any serious resumption of combat since this would lead to a humanitarian disaster. So he bent to Homma's will and composed a message ordering Sharp to surrender. At Japanese insistence, he even broadcast the message from a Manila radio station. When Wainwright returned to Corregidor, his exhausted troops, now under Japanese guard, struggled to their feet, came to attention, and saluted him. Such was their respect for a man they had come to revere. Tears poured down Skinny's cheeks. "I feel I have taken a dreadful step," was all he could say. Like King before him, Wainwright was convinced he would someday be court-martialed or perhaps just reviled back home.

Many of Sharp's men on Mindanao and elsewhere in the Visayas refused to comply and simply continued the war as guerrillas. But Sharp believed that if he did not abide by the surrender order, the Japanese would execute the eleven thousand men and women of the Corregidor garrison whom they had captured. Indeed, the Japanese did keep them on the island for several weeks as virtual hostages, though they never overtly threatened to execute them. Sharp and the majority of his commanders surrendered by the end of May. MacArthur was deeply angered by this, and he blamed Wainwright. When MacArthur heard about Skinny's order to surrender all forces in the Philippines, he fired off a cable to General Marshall. "I believe Wainwright has temporarily become unbalanced and his condition renders him susceptible of enemy use." MacArthur clearly had little notion of the dreadful, unresolvable dilemma that Wainwright had faced, much less the terrible privation of the captivity he and his soldiers now faced. After all, MacArthur had gotten out of the Philippines before having to make the same sort of painful, soul-racking decisions. It was far easier to sit in judgment from the safety and comfort of Australia. MacArthur's anger developed into a grudge that lasted several years. "I ordered them to keep on fighting, and Skinny ordered them to surrender," MacArthur later said of the Visayas forces. "It was not a very creditable thing." In the summer of 1942, when Marshall asked MacArthur to recommend Wainwright for the Medal of Honor, the general not only refused but did all he could to kill the nomination. Freshly decorated with his own questionable Medal of Honor, MacArthur argued, apparently with a straight face, that if an unworthy Wainwright got the award, it would represent an injustice to other USFIP soldiers who were truly deserving. "Poor

Wainwright!" a sympathetic Eisenhower wrote in his diary. "He did the fighting in the Philippine Islands, another got such glory as the public could find in the operation."[26]

As MacArthur undoubtedly sensed, the ignominy of all these capitulations was profound. It was the first and only time a Marine regiment ever surrendered, and it was the largest surrender of American military personnel since the Civil War. The formal surrenders represented the last capitulation of any sizable force in the history of the American armed forces. In a military sense, Corregidor was the only time the Japanese engaged in a beach assault against substantial American resistance, and this was fortunate, for they did not do well (the same had been true months earlier at the Points on Bataan). The Imperial Army and Navy coordinated poorly. Soldiers were ill prepared for amphibious warfare. Planning was unimaginative. Had the Japanese faced a better-provisioned, healthier enemy at Corregidor, they would surely have failed. For any Japanese commander who cared to notice, the tenacious Allied resistance served as an ominous indicator that fighting spirit would not be unique to the Japanese side in this war. The challenges inherent in the brief amphibious battle presaged many of the difficulties the Americans would someday encounter when the war turned and they began to launch invasions. Corregidor especially demonstrated the vulnerability of troops on an open beach and the imperviousness of well-prepared fortifications to all but the most suffocating bombardment.

From Bataan to Mindanao, the surrenders represented the tragic final result of years of poor decisions and inadequate preparation. Temporizing about the status of Filipino independence and the US position in the Far East, the American government had failed to provide for a proper defense of the archipelago, at least until it was too late. Compounding these errors, Roosevelt and Quezon had invested their hope for Filipino security in a general whose strategic vision was, at best, based on overweening optimism and, at worst, in conflict with reality. More than one hundred thousand Allied soldiers, including more than twenty thousand Americans, paid for this faulty strategic reasoning with their freedom, and many with their very lives. To add proverbial insult to injury, the American president rewarded this general with the salvation of evacuation, high-command responsibility, and the nation's highest medal for valor. It was not a particularly uplifting chapter in the long military history of the United States.

At the time and ever since, commentators and historians have described the campaign as leading to the "fall of the Philippines," a description of dubious accuracy. To be sure, the Japanese established military and some level of political control over key portions of the archipelago. They had indeed conquered the islands, but only in the same way the Germans had conquered Yugoslavia in 1941. As with Hitler's legions in the Balkans, the Japanese could never, and would never, truly control the archipelago. With China absorbing much of Japan's ground-combat power, the empire would never have enough troops to keep the Philippines in line. Just as the Germans found themselves enmeshed in a fierce guerrilla struggle to maintain any semblance of control in multicultural, multilingual Yugoslavia, the Japanese within months began to experience the same difficulties throughout many of the similarly heterogeneous islands. Honeycombed as they were with jungles, mountains, barrios, and villages, in addition to a major capital city, the Philippines would prove to be fertile ground for insurgent warfare. Moreover, if the day ever arrived when the Americans mobilized the military forces and the political will to return to the Philippines, then Japanese power would be in question even more. In that sense, the events of that tragic spring of 1942 were really a prologue, not an epilogue.

4

Allies of a Kind

China was not really a nation so much as it was a civilization, one of the world's oldest. For thousands of years, it was a place of powerful emperors and technological and philosophical innovation, with the Chinese themselves the dominant Asian ethnic group. If all history was truly a progression, then this venerable civilization would have been far ahead of comparatively fuzzy-cheeked America by the 1940s. Instead, in the penetrating words of one US Army report, the country was "caught in mid-passage between semi-feudalism and modern statehood." The nineteenth-century history of the country had been dominated by the so-called open door, a term that alluded to the presence and encroachment of foreign imperial powers, most notably Britain and France but eventually the United States and Japan as well, that carved out economic centers of gravity for themselves, often at the expense of Chinese sovereignty. The open door (often referred to by the Chinese as the century of humiliation) was based on the notion of a balance of power among the participants, all the better for collective security and peace, since no nation was truly dominant. If there was equilibrium among the imperial powers, there was hardly much of the same for the Chinese people. The most infamous example of the open door's unequal nature was the 1842 Treaty of Nanjing, when the British, out of determination to trade opium in China, gained control of Hong Kong, along with access to all Chinese ports. The long-term result was drug addiction for millions of Chinese and the steady decline of Chinese emperors, who seemed powerless to compete with the West financially, technologically, and militarily. An inevitable countervailing push for nationalistic modernity among rising Chinese industrial, professional, and venture-market classes culminated in the 1911 collapse of the Manchu dynasty in favor of an unstable republic. The revolution did anything but quell the domestic political turmoil. Two main contenders for long-term power emerged, the Communists under Mao Zedong and the

Kuomintang, or Nationalist Party, under General Chiang, a diminutive, cerebral, calculating military man and Christian who sported a shaved head and wore false teeth. Chiang and the Nationalists preferred modernization, a vaguely pro-Western postimperial foreign policy and transition to representative government, though the party itself and its leadership were actually totalitarian in nature. The Kuomintang controlled the Chinese government but not necessarily the country. The Communists operated as a veritable shadow government, particularly in the northern and western portions of China, where they were influential.

China's internal divisions worked to Japan's advantage, especially as the island nation's industrial and military power grew in the early decades of the twentieth century. Expansion-minded militarists, particularly in the Imperial Army, saw China as the best place to acquire the resources so necessary for Japan's continued growth and long-term parity with the resource-rich United States and the British Empire. What began as adventurism morphed into national policy. As a legacy to the partial Japanese victory in the 1904–1905 Russo-Japanese War, the Kwantung Army had remained in the Chinese province of Manchuria to police the South Manchuria Railway Company, which the Japanese had established on land won from the Russians. The Kwantung Army was dominated by expansionists, and it operated more or less autonomously of the Japanese government. In 1931 soldiers of this army seized Manchuria and set up a puppet government, all without permission from Tokyo. This in turn led to more unauthorized Japanese encroachments in north China and tremendous tension between Chiang's government and the Japanese government in Tokyo.

As a result of this tension, an otherwise minor, random altercation between Japanese and Chinese troops in July 1937 at the Marco Polo Bridge ten miles outside of Beijing eventually boiled over into full-blown war between the two Asian powers. Chiang felt that if he backed down he would lose all of northern China to Japanese control, and possibly his governing power in whatever remained of his country. When he sent troops to the area where the incident had taken place, the Tokyo government decided that they must respond in kind to protect their troops and other Japanese nationals in China. Japanese leaders were also tantalized by the prospect of controlling all of northern China. Thus, by late summer, China and Japan had plunged into a massive undeclared war that would forever alter both countries. In terms of tactics, operational capability, political cohesiveness, firepower, airpower, and technological power, the Chinese were no match for the Japanese. The Imperial Army overran almost all of eastern China, the coastal seaports, Shanghai, and the Nationalist capital of Nanjing, where they engaged in a protracted looting, raping, and killing spree that had few, if any, parallels in modern history. As the war spread, millions of Chinese were killed or displaced. The Chiang government fled to the ramshackle provincial river town of Chungking in western China. The Communists joined in the fight alongside their countrymen in a supposed front of national unity. In reality, though, both the Communists and the Nationalists still largely viewed the other as the main enemy. Cooperation was minimal. Mutual hostility was common.

In China, the Imperial Japanese Army's expansionists now had their long-sought war of conquest, but closure had eluded them by the end of 1941. As long as the Nationalists and Communists remained intact, so, too, did China. The war in China had of course led to a deterioration in relations between Japan and the United States. The Americans wanted what they had always wanted in relation to China—a balance of power. Moreover, decades of involvement in the country by American missionaries, journalists, businessmen, and other opinion shapers had created a protective sense of proprietorship for China among some American policy makers, what one analyst aptly called "a compound of guilt, guardianship and illusion." Japan was clearly seeking to supplant the old open door with a new power structure. The Americans saw this as unacceptable on every level, from the moral to the geopolitical. Since neither country was willing to back away from their differing visions for China—and really Asia as a whole—the conflict grew irreconcilable. Much to their chagrin, the Japanese belatedly realized that war with China meant a larger conflict with the Americans and their European friends. So when the Japanese attacked the imperial European powers and the United States in December 1941, they basically opted to embark upon two wars of expansion, one on the Asian continent, to satisfy the Imperial Army's adventurists, and one in the Pacific Ocean, to satisfy the Imperial Navy's expansionists. In essence, Tōjō's government thus elected to fight a monumental two-front war, strikingly similar, and every bit as self-defeating, as what Hitler had done in Europe.[1]

★

In response to a summons from the War Department, fifty-eight-year-old Major General Stilwell left his West Coast corps command, and his beloved family, and arrived in Washington by Christmas Eve 1941. Wiry and lean, modest in height, Stilwell had already spent nearly four decades in the Army since graduating from West Point in 1904. Though he had little command experience, he had served in a dizzying array of posts, from World War I staff duty in France to military attaché responsibilities in China. Wrinkles on his forehead and around his dark blue eyes hinted at his advancing years, as did the salt-and-pepper color of his close-cropped hair, which he wore in a high-and-tight style unusual for his time. Stilwell could see nothing without his glasses. Proximity to an ammo-dump explosion during World War I cost him most of the vision in his left eye, so much so that he could barely distinguish the outline of his own fingers at anything more than three feet. His right eye required a strong corrective lens, and it tired easily under the strain of providing Stilwell most of his visual access to the world. In the Army, he had a reputation for absolute integrity in actions and speech, to the point where he seldom held back his occasionally venomous thoughts, earning the wary nickname "Vinegar Joe." In equal measure, he had no patience for hyperbole, phoniness, or pretense. "At times he was caustic, sarcastic, critical, harsh, uncompromising and unyielding," Brigadier General Thomas Hearn, his wartime chief of staff opined, "at others, he was kindly, understanding, patient, sympathetic, generous, almost fatherly."

He was a complex man, an energetic mixture of intellect, courage, and withering judgment. Driven almost madly to succeed, he nonetheless could not bear to compromise any principle in support of a personal goal or mission objective. "He had a simple, almost child-like faith in what he considered to be *right*," explained Frank Dorn, one of his closest aides, who revered him. "Though he recognized all the shades of gray in life and conduct, he was firm in his belief that right was shining white and wrong was blackest black." Liberal in his human sentiments, he was politically conservative. Deeply loyal to subordinates and friends alike, he could not understand treachery in others. He rejected the dogma of organized religion even as he embraced a personal relationship with God. "In a number of ways I consider Uncle Joe one of the finest men I ever knew," Colonel David Barrett, another longtime subordinate, opined, "but in a few respects I rate him as unbelievably small. His integrity was beyond question, although the same could not always be said of his judgment. He could be unbelievably kind and considerate, and yet he could be capable of actions that savored of cruelty, to say nothing of pettyness [sic] and narrow[-]mindedness."

Opinionated and strong-willed, he nursed hatreds, some of which were self-defeating, such as his disdain for the British, and some of which were pointless and bizarre, like his contempt for the Army's cavalry branch. "The Cavalry does have some use, you can always eat the horses," he once quipped, with characteristic insensitivity, to a subordinate (one can only imagine how Wainwright would have reacted to such a comment!). Stilwell held the world and those around him to his own lofty standards, setting himself up for constant frustration. He developed the habit of blowing off steam from these frustrations in caustic diary entries and honest letters to his wife, Winifred, with whom he shared a deep, loving bond. "It would be bad to let the family down," he once wrote to her during the war, "so I'm expecting everybody to pull hard for the old deck hand." Though his duties took him away from home for long stretches of time, he shared an equally warm relationship with his five children, around whom he always seemed to be at ease. He laughed, played, and nurtured them intellectually. When his youngest son and daughter came home in tears one day after a bad scolding from a teacher, he promptly withdrew them from the school and taught them at home for a year. "Stilwell family life was remarkable," Barrett wrote, "for example their constant study of worthwhile things and activities such as art, history and language, particularly Chinese, and so on. They used to have . . . seminars for which the Stilwell children would prepare and present papers." Stilwell had a facility for languages, ranking near the top of his class in French and Spanish during his third class year at West Point. As a young officer he taught Spanish at the academy. In China, he became a fluent speaker and writer of the language. Tellingly, his personal motto was a Latin phrase meaning "Don't let the bastards get you down."

By the time Stilwell arrived in Washington, the Arcadia Conference, the first of several wartime meetings between Prime Minister Churchill and President Roosevelt, was in full swing. The two leaders affirmed their commitment to the Germany-first policy, accelerated lend-lease for both Britain and the USSR, and the establishment of the short-lived, ineffective ABDA command in the Pacific. The two allies consummated a tentative agreement to launch an invasion, code-named Torch, somewhere in Vichy French–controlled Africa in 1942. To shape grand strategy, issue orders, and organize their mutual efforts, Churchill and Roosevelt agreed to establish the Combined Chiefs of Staff, populated by the top military leaders from both countries, an unprecedented close cooperation between two sovereign nations. Washington itself was in a state of semiorganized chaos, of the sort that suffuses the manic early stages of a momentous task. The frenzied mood was anything but impressive to the no-nonsense Stilwell. "My impression of Washington is a rush of clerks in and out of doors . . . doors always swinging, people with papers rushing after other people with papers, groups in corners whispering in huddles . . . buzzers ringing, telephones ringing, rooms crowded, with clerks all banging away at typewriters," he wrote to his wife one evening from his room at the venerable Hay-Adams hotel, just a few blocks from the White House. He yearned to bring order to the madness.

So did General Marshall, whose relationship with Stilwell went back to the First World War. The two liked and respected each other. If the businesslike Marshall could be said to have had any friends in the Army, certainly Stilwell was among them. "General Marshall's admiration of General Stilwell was based entirely upon the latter's toughness and effectiveness as a leader in both training and combat," Frank McCarthy, a member of Marshall's staff, later wrote. Their relationship had especially solidified a decade and a half before World War II, when Marshall served as assistant commandant of the Infantry School at Fort Benning and had handpicked Stilwell to head up the tactical section. Marshall was deeply impressed with Stilwell's energy and intelligence. In one of Stilwell's efficiency reports, Marshall judged him "qualified for any command in peace and war . . . modesty and unassuming methods have prevented this officer from being widely known as one of the exceptionally brilliant and cultured men in the army." Marshall's memory for military talent has become a thing of legend to historians of the era and certainly with justification. But as chief of staff, Marshall did not just rely on past impressions to make vital command selections for global warfare. He commissioned, for instance, a survey of general officers asking them to rank the Army's corps commanders. They judged Stilwell to be number one. These results only confirmed Marshall's previous estimate of his great abilities, so he tapped him for command of the North Africa invasion, the plum assignment of the moment. It was probably merciful that Stilwell had no idea what the future actually held for him. Emerging from the meeting with Marshall, an ebullient Stilwell told Dorn, his aide-de-camp, "It's North Africa for us." The general put together a staff and began intensive planning. In an ironic twist of history, he was ably assisted in these efforts by Brigadier General Eisenhower, the current War Plans Division chief of operations and the man who actually would command Torch as the first step of his rise to historical immortality.[2]

At the same time that Stilwell prepared for North Africa, the Arcadia conferees wrestled with the issue of how to deal with Chiang's China. Under the near-crippling weight of waging global warfare, as well as the limited means currently at their disposal, their choices were limited. American and British leaders were rightly concerned with serious problems in Europe and the Pacific. If the Soviet Union collapsed, an unassailable Germany would dominate an empire from the Pyrenees to the Urals and the fjords of Norway to the sands of North Africa and maybe the whole Middle East. German submarines were on a rampage in the Atlantic, sinking hundreds of thousands of tons of vital shipping. If this continued, Britain's lifeline to its colonies and North America could be severed, bringing the country to its knees and marginalizing the United States. Japan was on the verge of conquering British-controlled Malaya, the Dutch East Indies (Indonesia), the Philippines, and large swaths of the South Pacific. A Japanese invasion of Australia appeared to be a real possibility. Using Thailand (Siam) as a base, the Japanese had pushed into the British colony of Burma and were in the process of outfighting and outmaneuvering a British colonial army.

In this planetary context, China appeared to be something of an afterthought, especially to the British, who were far more concerned about checking Hitler and preserving their own empire than aiding Chiang, whom they patronizingly saw as little more than a backward Oriental despot. By contrast, the Americans saw China as vital for two main reasons. First, in spite of the serious internal problems that plagued the country, the fact was that the Chinese were tying down a substantial portion of Japan's ground and air forces. The Japanese continued to spend an inordinate amount of blood and treasure to control a vast stretch of territory in China, regardless of how militarily ineffectual their opponents might or might not be. Every Japanese soldier in China was not available to fight the Allies elsewhere. Since the Americans already understood that, among the Western powers, they would do the vast majority of the fighting against Japan, especially at sea and in island operations, the Chinese role was no small matter to them. Second, China might well become an ideal base from which American bombers could strike Japan; under certain conditions, an American amphibious invasion force might well use China as a sally base. Hovering under the surface of these grand strategic permutations was a queasy anxiety that Chiang, if not properly supported, might negotiate some sort of peace agreement with the Japanese. The result of such a deal would be the same as a Chinese military defeat. Hundreds of thousands of Japanese soldiers would be freed up for action elsewhere, at least as long as Japan had the shipping to support and transport them. Third, the Roosevelt administration, reflecting years of American open-door idealism, hoped that a revitalized, democratic, cohesive, pro-American China would form the bulwark of a peaceful postwar Asian order. As such, the goal of keeping China in the war and tying down the Japanese in Asia was important to Roosevelt (just as keeping the Soviet Union engaged against Germany was vital in Europe). Even so, the hard-pressed Americans could offer few tangibles to their Chinese allies. There was no possibility of the American government sending substantial ground combat forces, nor would there ever be. Besides airpower and engineering know-how, the Americans could offer little besides logistical support and at this only a pittance by comparison with the prodigious largesse earmarked for Britain, the Soviet Union, and other European theater allies.

Since the previous summer, the Roosevelt administration had been sending lend-lease material to Chiang, via a circuitous route that stretched from Rangoon and along crude roads in Burma to Kunming in southwestern China. The aid was administered by Brigadier General John Magruder and a small staff termed the American Military Mission in China. Though tenuous and now under threat as a result of the Japanese invasion of Burma, the road was China's only supply link to the outside world. Chiang wanted more lend-lease—his voracious appetite for American material support would never abate in the years ahead—and closer cooperation among the Allies. In an effort to accommodate these wishes, and afford China at least ephemeral status as an equal in the Allied grand alliance, Roosevelt directed that a high-ranking American officer be sent to Chungking to work closely with Chiang, the Generalissimo. Chiang welcomed the idea. The president hoped the appointment of this officer would buck up Chinese morale and communicate the seriousness of his intentions to Chiang. In effect this meant symbolism over substance, a bad harbinger for future relations. To the Chinese, the Americans seemed to talk out of both side of their mouths. They paid lip service to China's importance as an equal partner in the alliance, but were not willing enough to back up those words with priority of action. To a great extent, this impression would bedevil relations for the rest of the war.

Chiang had ample reason to be skeptical of American resolve because

he had appealed to the United States for help since the beginning of his war
with Japan. As Chiang saw it, by opposing the Japanese, he was fighting
not just for his country's sovereignty but also for American interests in
China. He believed that the Americans should have been fighting alongside him since 1937. (In the midst of the Depression and widespread opposition to involvement in any foreign wars, the American public would
never have tolerated this.) He had felt isolated and abandoned, not just by
the Americans but also by the world as a whole. The League of Nations had
done little to combat Japanese aggression besides mutter ineffectual words.
For better than four years, his country had fought alone against the Japanese onslaught, losing huge swaths of territory. By one estimate, Chinese
military fatalities already numbered more than one million, including
many of Chiang's best, most committed soldiers; civilian deaths from starvation, dislocation, floods, privation, atrocities, disease, combat, and other
causes numbered many millions more. Plus, the communists still loomed
as a major domestic competitor for power. It was only right, then, that the
Americans provide him all the help they could.

In hopes of persuading the Generalissimo that they were doing this, but
with few other specific dictates, Roosevelt and Secretary of War Stimson
chose Lieutenant General Hugh Drum to go to China. Drum was a long-
serving officer of lofty reputation who had functioned as General Pershing's chief of staff during World War I and was the current commander of
the 1st Army in New York. In 1939, when Roosevelt had chosen Marshall
as chief of staff, he had passed over Drum but, in a conversation typical of
the president's charming but duplicitous personality, indicated to Drum
that he would receive an important command in any future war. To Drum
this meant Europe and a position equivalent to Pershing's in the Great
War. When Marshall and Stimson told him he was bound instead for
China, he had difficulty hiding his disappointment, especially as the
vagueness of his duties, the confusing chain of command, and the lack of
coordinating policies between Chinese and American leaders became apparent to him. Drum basically studied, questioned, and talked his way out
of the job. He never openly declined the post, but Marshall came to believe
that Drum thought it was too minor of a job for a man of his stature, so the
chief of staff and Stimson instead fixed their gaze on Stilwell. The choice
was logical because Stilwell had served many years in China, spoke and
wrote the language, understood the culture, and greatly sympathized with

the people, if not necessarily their leaders. Stilwell much preferred to command Torch, but he loyally acceded to the wishes of his superiors, famously answering, "I'll go where I'm sent," in reply to the question of whether he would do the job. The lives of three senior officers, and of course untold millions of other people in China and elsewhere, were thus shaped by this quixotic series of Washington events. Drum served another year before retiring to the minor notoriety of having a midsize Army post in upstate New York named after him. Stilwell was promoted to lieutenant general, went to China to supplant Magruder, and soon found himself enmeshed in many of the problems Drum had foreseen. Eisenhower eventually got command of Torch and became, arguably, the most famous general in modern American history.[3]

After an arduous stop-and-start journey of twenty thousand miles and twenty-three days that took Stilwell and his staff by plane from South America to Egypt and India, they finally arrived in Chungking on March 5. Curious crowds and dignitaries greeted them. A band struggled through the Chinese and American national anthems. As the target of several Japanese bombing raids, the Nationalist capital was hardly an attractive place. To Dorn, the city was like a "bedraggled buzzard on a promontory between the Yangtze and Kialing [Jialing] rivers, its crumbling cliffs buttressed by high stone walls, its bombed-out fire-blackened buildings reeking acridly of wet ashes." Workers cleared rubble and erected makeshift, rickety new buildings of which the prominent color seemed to be gray or muddy brown. To evade enemy bombs, people had carved out bomb shelters in caves overlooking the rivers. Chungking's population was swollen with refugees and ruined business owners, who had seen their assets destroyed in the fighting or appropriated by the warring armies. The city stank of rotting food and human waste. With little access to sanitary facilities, some of the residents squatted and relieved themselves anywhere they could. Much of the population was afflicted with tuberculosis. Owing to the Chinese tendency to spit anywhere and everywhere, "the streets were literally covered with bloody sputum," in the recollection of Lieutenant Ray Chesley, an American medical officer. Stilwell and six members of his staff were billeted in a comfortable multistory home belonging to T. V. Soong, Chiang's powerful and wealthy brother-in-law. Stilwell's expansive bedroom led to a terrace overlooking the Jialing River.

Stilwell's orders read, "Your mission is to increase the effectiveness of

United States assistance to the Chinese government for the prosecution of the war and to assist in improving the combat efficiency of the Chinese Army." The directive was short on specifics. Stilwell was to wear many hats. He was commander of all American forces in China, Burma, and India, tiny though they were. He was Chiang's chief of staff and the ranking American military representative to the Nationalist government. He was also to oversee the lend-lease effort. Technically, he was a theater commander similar in status to Eisenhower in Europe and MacArthur in the Southwest Pacific. In truth, his powers were vague, mainly because there was nothing like the unity of purpose—and thus command—of these other theaters. The governments he served were united only in their antipathy to the Japanese. Otherwise they worked at cross-purposes. "The British and Americans wished to give the impression that China was a serious ally without actually putting much effort into the relationship, while Chiang overestimated what he was worth to the Western Allies," Rana Mitter, a leading historian of China in World War II, wrote sagely.

In a deeper sense, China was in the midst of a three-way civil war every bit as much as a foreign invasion. In addition to the Nationalists and the Communists, Wang Ching-wei, whose credentials as a Chinese Nationalist were, in the view of some, almost on par with those of Chiang or Mao, presided over a pro-Japanese government in the occupied portions of the country. History has tended to brand Wang a puppet in the manner of Vidkun Quisling in Norway or Pierre Laval in France, but this was not so apparent at the time. All three groups controlled large armies of varying quality and discipline. From that broader viewpoint, with Chiang the Americans were dealing with just one of three Chinese power centers, though certainly the most important one. His Kuomintang Party was really, in the view of one knowledgeable American analyst, "a group of competing factions, not yet welded into national unity. Chiang Kai-shek manipulated a precarious balance in an effort to incorporate into his totalitarian party the following diverse groups: war lords, dissident units in his own armies, provincial cliques, the Communists, and even some of the Japanese-controlled puppets." Chiang's agenda was long-term control of China, not short-term operations against the Japanese. The tactical quality of his army mattered much less than the viability of his political coalition. To him, the Americans represented a source of weapons and sustenance, along with international political legitimacy for his regime.

The Americans, for the larger purpose of tying down Japanese troops and solidifying a truly sovereign, pro-Western China, saw their purpose in the theater as building up Chiang's armies in the American image and enlisting their help to fight the Japanese.

With decades of imperial exploitation in their mutual past, the Chinese, and Chiang in particular, were understandably contemptuous of the British. "I despise them, but I also respect them," the Generalissimo once confided to his diary. He wanted no part of any unified command with them, nor was he even enthusiastic about the idea of Nationalist troops serving alongside them. In 1940, the British had briefly yielded to Japanese demands to close the vital Burma road, cutting China off. Even though they opened the road up again within a few months, Chiang had neither forgotten nor forgiven the British for this. He was determined that the war would result in the end of British imperial influence in China.

Though nominally concerned with Japanese expansion in Asia, the British really cared for only one agenda in this theater—the preservation of their empire in Burma and India. The latter country of four hundred million people, many of whom were impoverished and illiterate, was in an extremely restive state. At the outbreak of the war, the British government had committed India to the Allied cause without consulting any Indian leaders (about 2.5 million Indians would serve in the British armed forces during the war). Mahatma Gandhi, an anti-British, pro-independence leader of transcendent spirituality, believed that India should withdraw from the empire and the war. By 1942 his "Quit India" movement of non-violent civil disobedience was threatening to overthrow British imperial control. Other powerful Indian leaders, like Jawaharlal Nehru, a pro-Allied nationalist who also favored independence, joined the Quit India movement. Chiang enraged Churchill by traveling to India in February 1942 and meeting with both Indian leaders, conferring a distinctly non-Western, Pan-Asian legitimacy upon them. The Generalissimo was playing a double game. He sympathized with the goal of Indian independence but wanted to maintain the British presence in India until Japan was defeated. He believed that supporting Indian nationalists was the best way to stabilize the uneasy domestic situation in the subcontinent and keep India in the Allied column. "The British may not understand this, but I believe it may be of advantage to Britain," he told his diary.[4]

★

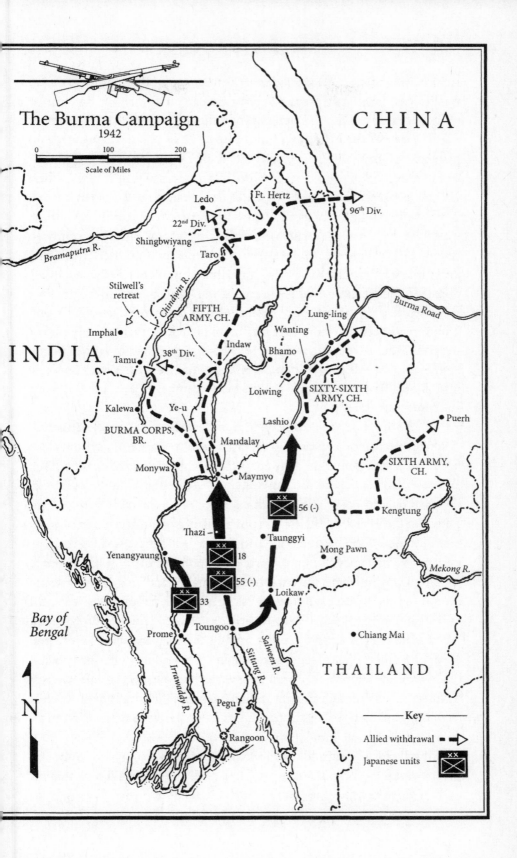

The Burma Campaign
1942

0   100   200
Scale of Miles

CHINA

Ft. Hertz
Ledo
22nd Div.
Shingbwiyang
Taro
96th Div.
Bramaputra R.
Lung-ling
Burma Road
Stilwell's
retreat
FIFTH
ARMY, CH.
Wanting
Imphal
Chindwin R.
Indaw
Bhamo
INDIA
Tamu
38th Div.
Loiwing
SIXTY-SIXTH
ARMY, CH.
Kalewa
Ye-u
Lashio
Puerh
BURMA CORPS,
BR.
Mandalay
SIXTH ARMY,
CH.
Monywa
Maymyo
Kengtung

Thazi
56 (-)
Taunggyi
Mong Pawn
Mekong R.
Yenangyaung
18
33
55 (-)
Loikaw
Bay of
Bengal
Prome
Toungoo
Salween R.
Chiang Mai

N

THAILAND

Irrawady R.
Sittang R.
Pegu
Rangoon

Key
Allied withdrawal
Japanese units

In the spring of 1942, the headache of the moment for these Allies of a kind was Burma, where two Japanese divisions and an air brigade had knifed into the country, taken the vital port of Rangoon on March 6, and were in the process of dismantling an ill-motivated British colonial army made up primarily of locals and Indians. Knowing that if the Japanese seized control of Burma they would sever China's last terrestrial link to its Allies, Chiang in January had offered to send troops to help the British in Burma. But out of colonial pride and for fear that once in Burma the Chinese would never leave, the British had initially turned him down only to change their mind as the Burma crisis grew more profound. In late February, Chiang had sent two armies—the 5th and the 6th, totaling about six divisions, plus reserves into northern Burma—and agreed, in face-to-face meetings, to give Stilwell operational control of these units. "In all fairness, it must have been a severe strain on him to put a foreigner in command of regular Chinese troops in action," Stilwell wrote. "It had never been done before, and he was trying it on short acquaintance with a man he knew little about." The two men had first met in December 1938, but they did not yet know each other well.

When Stilwell got to Burma on March 12, he found a terrible situation. "No plan, no reconnaissance, no security, no intelligence, no prisoners . . . left flank wide open at the Salween [River]," he related to his diary. The Japanese had reinforced their invasion forces. Using Rangoon as a base, they had pushed north and were threatening to cut off and destroy Allied units. On the Allied side, there was no semblance of unified action or command. Cooperation between the British and the Chinese was nearly nonexistent. Burma itself was in the process of political disintegration. Some 126 languages and dialects were spoken among the dizzying array of ethnic groups that populated the country. "Ardent young nationalists, resentful of British domination, had been eagerly receptive to Japanese propaganda which stressed the need for unity among the Asiatic races," wrote one American officer. To consolidate their control over Burma, the British had made it an Indian province and, in essence, had outsourced imperialism by fostering a dominant class of Indian overseers, hundreds of thousands of whom were uprooted by the fighting and vulnerable to reprisals from an angry, aroused local population.

Stilwell quickly realized his command authority was in name only. The British certainly did not answer to him. With the dire military situation and the Burmese social upheaval, they were focused primarily on salvaging the remnants of their army and using it to defend the eastern frontier of India. "My position is impossible from the start," Field Marshal Sir Harold Alexander, the British military commander, told Stilwell in one meeting, irritating Vinegar Joe's Anglophobic tendencies. "The snooty bastard," he fumed in his diary. "I said I was not exactly on a bed of roses either. *That* had not occurred to him. Looked me over as if I had just crawled out from under a rock." Nor, in spite of Chiang's promises, did Chinese commanders pay much heed to his orders. As a military man, the Generalissimo soon understood that the chances of stopping the Japanese offensive were minimal at best. Some of his most reliable soldiers, many of whom had been trained and equipped by German advisers during the 1930s, were serving in the two armies in Burma. Losing them would weaken his regime politically and perhaps compromise his ability to defend China's southwestern borders.

Stilwell envisioned a bold counteroffensive to maintain control of the road from Mandalay in central Burma to the Chinese border, a tall order under the circumstances. He measured nearly all Chinese and British officers by his estimate of their aggressiveness and willingness to fight. Under different circumstances, this would have been logical, but in the dysfunctional maw of this colonial, geostrategic meltdown, the willingness to attack or stay in place and fight to the end often served little purpose. Rather than see Chinese troops squandered for nothing, Chiang on several occasions undercut Stilwell by surreptitiously issuing countermanding or contradictory orders to Chinese commanders. The result was more command chaos. "There were too many cooks stirring the rice-pots," one American officer quipped. Stilwell and his American staff spent most of their time in Burma careening from crisis to crisis, ineffectually attempting to turn the situation around, with little success. It was an unprecedented role for an Army general. He commanded almost no Americans and only nominally the foreign soldiers who were supposed to be under his charge. There was a whiff of pointlessness about Stilwell's actions, like a man trying to capture the ocean in a bottle. His results-oriented temperament was anything but suited to these dog-chasing-tail experiences and the frustration set in. "Good God. What are we fighting for?" he wondered in one diary entry after he heard that the retreating British were destroying Burmese oil wells.

Stilwell saw Chiang's actions as duplicitous meddling. Chiang saw them as necessary steps to save his two valuable armies from total destruction.

He already regarded Stilwell as overly aggressive, all too willing to risk the soldiers of another nation for no great purpose. In one telling exchange, he told Stilwell that the 5th and 6th Armies must not under any circumstances be defeated, and Stilwell reacted with stupefied incredulity. "I told him to send someone who could guarantee that because I couldn't," the American related to his diary. "In war we'd have to do our best and take what came." For Stilwell, war meant risking soldiers in tactical operations against the enemy, with no certain outcome. To Chiang, operations were pointless in the absence of a strategic advantage regardless of tactical victory or defeat. On another occasion, Chiang radioed Stilwell and ordered him to provide one watermelon for every four Chinese soldiers in the field, an absolute impossibility—it was the rough equivalent of passing out dinner mints to passengers on the *Titanic*. "Watermelons!" an exasperated Stilwell blurted when he read the order. "With the whole goddamn place falling apart." Though minor, the incident had significant consequences because it solidified Stilwell's growing opinion of Chiang as a tampering, small-minded despot, out of touch with the realities of modern warfare.[5]

By May the abortive Burma campaign was coming to a catastrophic end. Refugees and the shattered remnants of Allied units fled west along poor roads and through heavy jungles. "The retreat was sheer misery," Lieutenant General William Slim, the extraordinarily able British commander of the Burma Corps, wrote in his memoirs, "Ploughing their way up slopes, over a track inches deep in slippery mud, soaked to the skin, rotten with fever, ill-fed, and shivering as the air grew cooler, the troops went on, hour after hour, day after day. All of them, British, Indian, Gurkha, were gaunt and ragged as scarecrows." The goal for these troops and everyone else was to make it over the mountain ranges that curtained western Burma and get into India or to make it north over similarly high ground to China. Very few, if any, Burmese could be found among these retreating souls. Nearly one million soldiers and civilians were on the move, amid terrible conditions, natural and otherwise. The heat and humidity were intense. Potable water and food were scarce, medical care almost nonexistent. In a sure sign of accelerated devolution, canteens became as valuable as gold, typewriters as worthless as junk. Burmese society disintegrated into vengeful anarchy. A social order based largely on exploitation and stratification now collapsed entirely, as locals sniffed the demise of the British lion. Many Burmese hated the British colonial presence, especially the Indians who had descended on their country and benefited so richly as imperial middlemen. Locals were hardly any friendlier to the Chinese, whom they viewed as menacing northern neighbors. Retreating Chinese soldiers were sniped at and occasionally attacked openly by irate Burmese. The Chinese responded by shooting at any Burmese whom they considered a threat and stealing whatever they wanted from the villages. Many of the troops were on the verge of starvation. In the present-tense account of one survivor: "The soldiers are all in rags and look very gaunt. Everyone is carrying a bag of rice, a water-can, a diesel tin, and in the other hand, a walking stick."

Indian refugees who happened upon the wrong village were apprehended by tribesmen and decapitated on the spot. Japanese aerial bombings and widespread arson accounted for hundreds of fires from the large city of Mandalay northward, in the wake of the fleeing armies and refugees. Torch-wielding mobs set fire to buildings and property. Amid the crackling flames were forlorn signs urging locals to join the Auxiliary Fire Service. Billowing smoke could be seen for miles in any direction, "in the jungles, by the side of the road, in the towns . . . masses of huge orange flame, great crackling blazes that ate their way unopposed and unhindered through the ramshackle wooden structures of Burma," one observer recalled. Mandalay itself burned for weeks. Animals fed on the bloated corpses of the dead. Knife-wielding Burmese sabotaged the main railroad over which many of the refugees might have been evacuated. The attackers opened switches, wrecked signal boxes, and tore up rails and freight cars.

Burmese nationalist leaders led an open revolt and called for attacks on Indo-British troops. Policemen threw away their badges and made common cause with deserting Burmese colonial soldiers against their former masters or the refugees. When members of a British tank crew unwarily dismounted from their vehicle to rest, they were attacked and killed, their bodies mutilated and left to rot. Their horrified comrades responded by killing all the inhabitants of a nearby village and destroying their homes. Some local nationalists functioned as guides for Japanese units, or simply fought alongside them as auxiliaries. A vivid sign of the spreading rebellion was the proliferation of tattooing, typified by large blue or red swatches on the torso. Men gathered in Buddhist temples and plotted uprisings. Chinese troops took to shooting Buddhist priests on sight. In retaliation, the priests helped advancing Japanese troops hunt down the fleeing Chinese soldiers. Desperate for sustenance, the Chinese sometimes looted anything of value from Kachin villages in northern Burma, thus mistreating one of the few

Burmese ethnic groups that was loyal to the British. Untold numbers of uprooted Kachins died from disease and starvation. Their shabby treatment only exacerbated tension between Chiang's forces and the British.

Planes from the China National Aviation Corporation, the Royal Air Force, and the US Army Air Force attempted to sustain the fleeing Chinese troops by air-dropping supplies to them. Conditions presented an even bigger problem than Japanese planes. Torrential rains, low clouds, and the steep ridges, mountains, and jungles of northern Burma made the resupply drops extremely difficult. Aviators filled burlap bags with rice or salt and placed them in the doorways of C-47 transport aircraft. "All we had to do was to fly through the monsoon rains of Burma, dodge the mountains, and find the places to drop the food to the waiting Chinese," Colonel Robert Scott, an American pilot, sarcastically explained. "Then, dodging the jungle trees, we'd go down as low as we dared and shove the bags out the door." The drops were well executed and helpful, but nowhere near adequate to meet the needs of so many thousands of retreating soldiers. Some units lost all integrity as individuals or groups simply fended for themselves. More common, the Chinese divisions (usually numbering no more than about eight thousand men) remained intact but were diminished as hundreds or thousands fell by the wayside from combat, hunger, disorientation, disease, or local attacks. "The condition of the Army troops is pitiful," Colonel Haydon Boatner, one of Stilwell's staff officers, reported to his superiors. "They are completely demoralized, disorganized and marching in small bands. They are carrying out worthless equipment . . . though exhausted. The sickness of the Chinese is due to malaria, dysentery and exhaustion."

As always in war, some of the worst suffering was reserved for the noncombatants, especially Indian refugees. Swarms of landlords, merchants, lenders, midlevel officials, Eurasians, women, children, and the elderly crowded the roads and trails, kicking up powdery clouds of dust that followed their columns like a malevolent apparition. Jack Belden, an American correspondent with long experience covering Asia, remembered the refugees as a "misery ridden lot. Fire had spread disease and pestilence . . . and a cholera epidemic had started." He saw cholera victims collapse and die. "Still others, too sick, weary, or frightened to go on, sat among the smoking debris, many with a dying and uncomprehending look in their eyes." Dorn encountered one group and was nearly speechless at their condition. "Men crawled in the dirt with cracked and broken bowls in their

outstretched hands. Families too degraded to be ashamed of their naked-
ness whimpered for food and water. Infants sucked at limp, dried breasts
as their famished, hollow-eyed mothers stared at them in despair. Abandoned children snarled over a few grains of rice. The stench of rot and
death and misery was everywhere." Deaths probably numbered in the hundreds of thousands. By one estimate, more than eight hundred thousand
perished; the exact number still remains obscure. "The whitened bones
that lay under arching ferns and at the bottoms of treacherous ravines were
never counted," Dorn later wrote. Some who made it to India were so debilitated by their ordeal that physically they were never the same again.
"The physical condition of the refugees upon emerging from the jungles
was simply God-awful," Boatner remembered. "No other word describes
it. They were emaciated, sick . . . mostly with malaria, dysentery, some mite
or scrub typhus . . . and infested with jungle sores."[6]

Stilwell himself became a refugee. Unlike almost all the others, his odyssey was by choice. As the fighting front collapsed, members of his staff
urged him to hop a plane to New Delhi, where he could reform his headquarters and regain command of the big picture. Mindful of how defeats
in Asia, the Philippines, and elsewhere were eroding Western prestige
among the Chinese and other Asian allies, he refused to turn tail and escape so easily. "I will tell you why," he explained. "If I run out now that will
be one more defeat, one more surrender. I could not command the Chinese
again." Using poor physical or mental condition as the main yardstick for
selection, he and Dorn prepared a list of headquarters personnel who
would be evacuated by air. Stilwell held back those whom he thought of as
the toughest, the most valuable or the most resourceful. As the list neared
completion, Stilwell, with his characteristic cigarette holder sticking at a
jaunty angle out of his mouth, looked at Dorn and said, "I guess you'll want
to fly out, too."

Shocked and indignant at what he considered an insult, Dorn sput-
tered, "Me? What makes you think . . . ?"

Stilwell guffawed. "Come on. Where's your sense of humor? Can't you
take a joke anymore? You'll stay."

The chosen ones were flown out without incident. Led by Colonel Caleb
Haynes and the aforementioned Colonel Scott of the Assam-Burma-China
Ferry Command, the aviators then came back for Stilwell. The two pilots
had direct orders from General Arnold to fly Vinegar Joe back to India. In
a tea planter's house near Shwebo (about fifty miles north of Mandalay)

where Stilwell's advance headquarters was still in place, Haynes reported their intentions to the general. Sitting at a desk, wearing a World War I–era campaign hat, Stilwell fixed his nearsighted gaze on Colonel Haynes and politely refused. Stunned, the pilot told him they had spotted advancing Japanese units only twenty miles away. Still, the old man remained resolute in his Private Ryan–like intention to eschew evacuation. As the nominal commander of the 5th and 6th Armies, he believed that flying to India equated to abandoning his soldiers. He intended to go north to the key crossroads town of Myitkyina (pronounced "Mitchinar"), where he believed the bulk of the Chinese troops were in the process of retreating. At Myitkyina he intended to do whatever he could to help them get out of Burma. Shocked and undoubtedly muttering to himself about the mental state of this crazy old infantryman, the pilot departed.

Stilwell surely made the decision with the best of intentions. But when he and his group set out northward in a vehicle convoy bound for Myitkyina, they soon found out that, owing to railroad outages, impassable roads, and Japanese advances, there was no way of making it to the town. Every mile they moved north brought them closer to pointless mortal danger. Stilwell decided that the group must abandon its vehicles and head on foot due west for India. So ironically, instead of linking up with the Chinese evacuees and helping to save them, he was, in effect, now forced to abandon them. "Chinese control very weak," he radioed General Marshall. "Believe collapse near." Stilwell informed Chiang nothing of his intentions, a significant oversight and one which the Chinese leader thought of as tantamount to insubordination, especially since Stilwell was leaving Burma without the Generalissimo's orders.

If the general had left with Haynes and Scott, perhaps he could have subsequently aided aerial supply drops, or coordinated, from the vantage point of a higher headquarters, a more orderly retreat. In a pinch, he might even have found a way to get from India into northern Burma, where he presumably would have affected the situation in some positive fashion. Instead, he and a diverse group of more than one hundred Americans, British, Chinese, Burmese laborers and female nurses, Indians, and the war correspondent Jack Belden embarked on a courageous but strategically pointless 140-mile exodus across some of the toughest terrain in Asia. Hoping to avoid the streams of refugees and stay well ahead of the Japanese, General Stilwell chose to employ little-used, crude dirt roads and trails through difficult jungle terrain, across multiple rivers, and over forested mountains to Imphal, an east Indian border town. "We were ordered to throw away everything we could not carry and bed rolls were cut down to a ground-sheet, blanket and mosquito bar," one of the Americans remembered. A small column of mules helped carry food and medical supplies. Everyone was subjected to extreme heat, heavy monsoon rains, steep mountain paths and ridges, raging streams, and the many challenges posed by moving through thick jungle.

Stilwell's goal was to cover fourteen miles per day, necessitating a brisk pace that the trekkers soon dubbed the "Stilwell Stride." He permitted an average of ten minutes' rest for every hour on the move. He personally led most of the way, outpacing nearly all the younger men, several of whom were nearly incapacitated by the heat and privation. On the first day alone, thirty-nine-year-old Major Frank Merrill was overcome with heat exhaustion and the beginnings of a heart condition that would only get worse and make him poorly suited to serve in this theater. "He was unconscious for almost three hours," Colonel Robert Williams, the ranking medical officer, said. "Cold, clammy skin, pulseless for long periods." Merrill and several other debilitated American officers had to be dragged on air mattresses by other members of the group until they could get up and walk again. Stilwell was angry and embarrassed by the poor physical condition of these men. "Damn it, Williams, you and I can stand it," he fumed one day to the doctor, who, like the general, was also in his fifties. "We're both older than any of them. Why can't they take it?" In his diary that evening, Stilwell commented, "Damn poor show of physique." On another occasion, the general was disgusted to find out that one of his American officers had disregarded his order to get rid of all nonessentials and had selfishly overloaded a mule with his mattress, personal effects, dress uniforms, suits, and even a dinner jacket. Stilwell severely reprimanded the officer and delighted in kicking all of his contraband into a stream. The general in his diary wrote of the offender: "[He] is a slob."

As if determined to make up for the perceived sins of these men, he drove himself relentlessly and never faltered. Day after day, he led the column, a wiry, diminutive example of single-minded determination. "Obstinately scrutinizing his watch and counting out 105 steps to the minute, the bow-legged general slogged steadily onward . . . and the long column of men and girls stretched out in single file behind him as far as the eye could see," Belden, an old friend of Stilwell's, later wrote. The odyssey lasted from May 7 to 20. The group subsisted largely on rice, corned beef, porridge, and tea. A food drop by the Royal Air Force and trade with local tribes also helped sustain them. "The hardship of the march can be easily imagined," Major Felix Nowakowski wrote. "I personally dropped from 160 pounds to 130 pounds."

Because of the discipline that Stilwell imposed on the group and his daily example of personal leadership, everyone made it to safety. Though the general demonstrated a remarkable physical constitution during the trek, the ordeal took a definite toll on him. He lost twenty pounds; his hands trembled; his skin was yellow with jaundice, and his weak eyes looked almost like empty sockets. It would be weeks before he gained back the weight and recuperated physically, if indeed he ever really did.

The adventurous nature of the walkout, and the centrality of Stilwell as the dominant individual, appealed to the American public's lust for a movie-style hero. Press coverage of the journey and Stilwell's actions was universally positive, especially in the influential Time Life empire controlled by the pro-Chinese publisher Henry Luce. In one article, *Life* referred to the trek as "one of the war's most heroic stories." Belden, in a *Time* article, described the general as "iron-haired, grim, skeleton-thin . . . with a tommy gun on his shoulder." Stilwell was solidified in the public mind as an indomitable hero, not quite on par with MacArthur but lionized all the same. Unassuming and results-oriented as ever, Stilwell himself was surprised at the adulation he received simply for escaping from a disastrous situation. In a famously frank exchange with correspondents he told them, "There is no such thing as a glorious retreat. I claim we got a hell of a beating. We got run out of Burma, and it's humiliating as hell." He advocated regrouping and taking the country back as soon as possible to reopen the landward supply route to China, a goal that would animate his actions for the rest of his time in theater.

In the media and elsewhere, there seemed to be little reflection on the overall purpose and necessity of the walkout. In truth, it had been avoidable altogether and it accomplished little except for the successful exodus of Stilwell's group. Stilwell could have, and probably should have, arranged for everyone to be evacuated by air. He exposed more than one hundred people, and himself, to unnecessary, life-threatening hardship. During the journey, he was largely out of communication with the outside world, an unacceptable circumstance for an ostensible theater commander. To be sure, during the walkout he demonstrated ethical, inspirational, and fair leadership, plus the willingness to lead by example, all of which were reflections of his personal character. But the odyssey, by its very unnecessary nature, also demonstrated his impulsiveness and a disturbing lack of bigger-picture vision.

The Chinese view of Stilwell's actions was dramatically different from that of the American media, General Marshall and Secretary Stimson, all of whom lauded the general for indomitable heroism. Chiang believed that Vinegar Joe had abandoned his Chinese soldiers, and as the Generalissimo noted in his diary, the American "lacked the virtue and vision of a commander. One doesn't expect this of one's military adviser. Could it be that because of the battle, his nerves have given way?" The irony of this was that Stilwell thought his actions represented the opposite of abandonment. He had stayed behind in Burma out of sensitivity to this very concern. But Chiang could not know this, and the two men never communicated about it in such a way as to clear up any misunderstanding. So the Chinese leader remained outraged at this perceived desertion. He was also astounded that Stilwell left Burma without orders and with no direct communication, even as Stilwell found time to keep General Marshall appraised of his plans. "Stilwell deserted our troops," the Generalissimo wrote bluntly to himself. The residual anger over this perception, and the Burma campaign as a whole, eroded his trust in Stilwell. The general, for his part, blamed the debacle on British ineffectiveness, the disunity of the Allied command, and especially the duplicitous fecklessness of Chiang and many of his commanders. Already contemptuous of the Generalissimo, he certainly did not trust him. The relationship between these two important leaders had thus declined from one of chary cooperation to toxic distrust. Both felt double-crossed by the other.[7]

★

Still fighting off the effects of jaundice and fatigue, Stilwell met with Chiang and his English-speaking, politically formidable wife, Mei-ling Soong, in Chungking on June 4. The Chiangs greeted him cordially and invited him to spend the weekend at Yellow Mountain, a retreat home they owned a few miles outside of town. Stilwell politely declined. Chiang, still miffed at Stilwell's lack of communication during the Burma campaign, asked him if he received the messages he had sent. Stilwell muttered some excuse that the communications were too garbled but offered no other explanation for his conduct (which Chiang viewed as disrespectful and insubordinate). Eschewing the Chinese preference for courteous evasion

of unpleasant truths, Stilwell immediately launched into a frank discourse
on the poor state of the Chinese Army. Even the 5th and 6th Armies, supposedly some of Chiang's best soldiers, had not performed particularly
well in Burma. "I gave them the full story, pulling no punches, naming
names," Stilwell later wrote. "No one else dares to tell him the truth, so it's
up to me all the more."

The realities were stark. Some three hundred divisions were spread
thinly throughout the country. On average, each was 40 percent under
strength. Officers enriched themselves by appropriating food and money
meant for their men. Soldiers who had little access to medical care were
wracked with cholera, dysentery, malaria, and other diseases. Some were
on the verge of starvation. Too often they stole food from the population,
a tendency that hardly endeared the Nationalist Army to the people.
Some of the troops engaged in black-market trade with the Japanese. The
conscription system was arbitrary and unfair. According to an estimate
prepared for Stilwell by Dorn, only 56 percent of recruits ever made it
from induction centers to their units. The rest either deserted or died
from starvation, disease, or neglect. Not surprisingly, morale in many
outfits was poor. "The lowly Chinese soldier doesn't want to be in the
army," one American adviser wrote in a frank report. "Isn't interested in
learning to be a soldier[,] for he wants the solitude of his rice patties [sic]
and his village, and will do only what he absolutely must and no more.
He doesn't hate the Japanese any more than he hates the Americans or the
British or the French. It is my opinion that the Chinese Army today is an
inefficient, uninterested, incapable and selfish mob which has no national
interest at heart whatever and does not desire to fight for its people or its
country."

Stilwell urged Chiang to relieve, or even shoot if necessary, several corrupt, incompetent generals who had performed poorly in Burma. Stilwell
presented the Chiangs with a carefully organized memo calling for sweeping reform of the Nationalist forces. The army was too large, too spread
out, with too many hollow, understrength, poorly equipped, poorly led
units of dubious loyalty and utility. Chiang did not really command an
army so much as a military quilt. Reliable units and commanders were in
too short supply. Some senior commanders were nothing more than glorified warlords who maintained local control but could not really be trusted
by anyone. Others were loyal enough to Chiang but they were corrupt,
petty dictators who stole from their troops and local civilians and consum-

mated informal truce agreements with nearby Japanese commanders. These venal lords absorbed precious resources and human capital, for no greater good. Like a gardener pruning rosebushes, Stilwell called for a dramatic consolidation of the army into a smaller, better-equipped, -trained and -led force of far more potency. He envisioned a lean force of about one hundred reliable divisions. In his opinion, the time had come to weed out the corrupt, the traitorous, the physically unfit, the cowardly, the disloyal, and the lazy. "A few dependable, well-equipped, well-supported divisions would be worth far more than double the number of the present average," he wrote. "Rewards for gallant conduct should be made promptly. Punishment must be prompt and ruthless, no matter what the rank of the offender. The situation looks dark, but it can be saved by a vigorous and immediate overhaul of the entire organization. The Army will be smaller, but it will be far more efficient and easier to supply and handle." Stilwell strongly believed that the Chinese soldier, if properly led, trained, and equipped, could fight as well as any soldier in the world. These reforms could make that happen. He also called for Chiang to name one overall military commander, protected from outside interference, accountable only to the Generalissimo. The general had enough tact not to advance his own name for the position, though the implication was obvious. Mei-ling Soong glanced at the memo and remarked, "That's what the German advisers [in the 1930s] told him."

The Chiangs' recognition of this continuity did not necessarily mean they could, or would, do anything to make the necessary changes. Stilwell's proposal represented the ideal Western culture solution to the problems at hand. But in 1940s China, as he must have known deep down, since he was an expert on the people and the culture, there was little chance that his sensible reforms could become reality. Even if Chiang had been willing to overlook the implicit insult (and potential loss of face) of having a foreigner hector him so openly about the failures of his army, he had to place political considerations before military reforms. For good reason, Luce's *Life* magazine once referred to him as "the shrewdest politician in China." With the Japanese in control of China's most highly developed infrastructure, its great seaports, much of its industrial capability and arable farmland, and with the Communists looming as a menacing rival for long-term influence in the country, and with his own power so shaky in too much of Nationalist-occupied China, and with allies of dubious reliability and from whom, after the loss of Burma, he was now cut off, Chiang was in a difficult position. The reforms that Stilwell envisioned might well produce rivals for power among the best of the generals or even an idealistic groundswell for a more representative government among the troops and anyone else they might influence. Under these circumstances, the Nationalist Party could implode, leaving a power vacuum for the Communists or Wang or the Japanese to fill. In this context, political reliability meant more than competence or willingness to fight the Japanese in tactical battles. Chiang knew as a soldier that this situation was hardly ideal, but it was a necessity under the circumstances. Even if, as Stilwell claimed, his formations were indeed weak and hollow, and too often controlled by knaves, they at least provided a presence for the regime, and this mattered more to the Generalissimo than having a smaller, better-quality army whose reach throughout the country might not be as comprehensive.

While Stilwell was certainly more concerned for the welfare of the average Chinese soldier than Chiang, the American was even more focused on the mutual objective of defeating Japan. To him the Communists were only a tangential consideration within that larger goal. If Japan was defeated, then Wang and the other collaborators would cease to be a factor. For Chiang, the situation was far more complicated, a zero-sum game to see who could outlast whom. Moreover, he had already suffered millions of casualties at the hands of the Japanese, fighting them more or less all alone. And yet somehow, in spite of terrible adversity and obvious flaws, he and his government had survived. From that point of view, his strategic concept had worked so far—avoiding total defeat to Japan could be tantamount to victory, provided the Nationalists emerged as China's long-term rulers. So he felt he must preserve his strength. This meant stasis on the issue of reform and, in a military sense, the continuation of defensive warfare. It also meant that American lend-lease supplies were vital since the influx of weaponry, food, capital, hardware, vehicles, and other equipment might well strengthen his armies for the long haul. The Americans, by contrast, wanted these goodies put to immediate use by Chinese armies in battle against the Japanese. The tension over these conflicting agendas would never abate.[8]

Later in June, at another meeting with Chiang, Stilwell realized that his memo would have no effect (in fact this would be one of many such memoranda that the Generalissimo essentially ignored). Mei-ling Soong told Stilwell, "Heads cannot be lopped off, otherwise nothing would be left." Years later, she asserted that Stilwell did not understand the crucial differences between the American and Chinese armies. The US Army, she claimed, was mechanized and held together by machinery and organization. "The Chinese Army, on the other hand, is held together largely on the concept of personal loyalty. When Stilwell inveighed against the factor of personal loyalty he was striking at the very thing upon which the morale of the Chinese Army depended." She seemed not to understand, or admit, that Stilwell was all in favor of personal loyalty provided it was based on honesty, accountability, and professionalism, instead of corrupt, counterproductive bargaining, and patronage. In any case, at the meeting, Chiang sidestepped Stilwell's recommendations and spoke philosophically. "There is a secret for the direction of Chinese troops unlike the direction of foreign troops. I am well aware that our senior officers do not possess enough education and sufficient capacity for work. Knowing their limited capacity I plan ahead for them. We have been carrying on the war of resistance for five years in such conditions. If you are with me closely for a few months, you will understand the psychology of the Chinese officers, and I will tell you more about their peculiarities."

Stilwell was not the sort to adapt to cultural realities and develop a more nuanced approach to fulfilling his plans. In a way, this was surprising. No one in the US Army knew more about China, its people, its heritage, its culture, and its political realities than Stilwell. He spoke the language with true mastery. No other American officer of similar rank could have conversed with Chiang so efficiently in his native tongue. Stilwell loved China. He wanted nothing but the best for it. And yet he could not bring himself to abide Chiang and his ways (and really the regime as a whole). Perhaps his black-and-white outlook made him loath to subordinate himself and take orders from someone he did not respect. He grew angrier, more intractable, and more resentful. In one letter to his wife, Win, he described Chiang as "a stubborn, ignorant, prejudiced, conceited despot who never hears the truth except from me and finds it hard to believe."

Before going to China he had already privately begun referring to Chiang by the derisive nickname Peanut, and he hardly refrained from using it during his time in China. Many members of the household staff that maintained Stilwell's Chungking home were actually informants for Lieutenant General Dai Li's Juntong, a secret police organization so feared in Nationalist China that some equated it to the Gestapo. Li was fanatically loyal to Chiang. The information his informants gathered guaranteed that

Chiang knew all about the Peanut nickname and Stilwell's contempt for him. Dorn claimed that the moniker Peanut originated from a conversation the staff had had with Stilwell during the journey to China. When one staff member compared Chiang's perilous position in China to a "peanut perched on top of a dung heap," Stilwell had replied, "Not a bad description of the old boy." With Stilwell's obvious endorsement, the disrespectful nickname stuck. So, too, did a general attitude of cynical, judgmental contempt among the staff for Chiang and his regime, an attitude Stilwell not only did nothing to quell but also exacerbated with his own outbursts and cynical sarcasm against Chiang. "Have you forgotten he's one of our glorious—repeat glorious—allies?" he once asked Dorn with rhetorical sarcasm dripping from his acid tongue. Like Stilwell, Dorn spoke Chinese and knew the country well. "Chiang Kai-shek failed to live up to any agreements he ever made," Dorn once claimed. He came to detest the Generalissimo, even hinting darkly to his chief during the watermelon fiasco that China would be better off if Chiang were gone.

At the end of June, with the British in headlong retreat from Rommel's armies in North Africa, concern grew among Allied leaders about the possibility that the Axis powers might seize the Suez Canal and much of the Middle East. At the behest of the White House, the War Department informed Stilwell that the bombers and transport aircraft of the 10th Air Force in India (under command of the ubiquitous Lewis Brereton) and the reinforcing heavy bombers that were on the way to Asia would instead be redeployed to North Africa. The planes comprised the majority of Stilwell's air assets, and they were stripped from him at the very time when he badly needed them to carry out a challenging aerial supply effort of China from bases in India. Stilwell was angry and frustrated with the decision. "Now what shall I tell the gissimo?" he raged to his diary in a rare moment of sympathy for Chiang. "We fail in *all* our commitments, and blithely tell him to just carry on, old top." In a later diary entry, he compared "Peanut" and himself to two men stranded on a raft with only a measly sandwich to share between them. He was a theater commander in name only—he controlled few troops, scant resources, and his area was clearly last on the grand strategical priority list.

Predictably, when Stilwell informed Chiang and Mei-ling about the redeployment of the 10th Air Force, they hit the roof. "Every time when the British suffered a defeat, they took away our war equipment or that which had been promised to us," Mei-ling groused. "Such being the case, there is no need for China to continue the war." Chiang asked point-blank about the priorities of the American government. "All I wish to know is whether they don't care about the China Theater of war. For five years [China] has fought not only for herself but also for the Allies. If America and Britain felt the need of maintaining her strength for resistance, they should not continuously pay scant attention to her. The way China is now being treated shows that she is out of the picture altogether." After dropping many ominous hints that China might pursue a settlement with the Japanese, the Chiangs demanded that Stilwell find out a yes or no answer from his government as to whether China was to be an important and necessary theater of war. If not, they intimated that they would explore other options.

Stilwell was in an impossible spot. He was just as peeved about the situation as Chiang. He, too, believed that American and British leaders should place a higher priority on China and send the necessary troops, aircraft, and supplies required to achieve strategic results. He was in the untenable position of explaining policies with which he did not agree to a man he held in low regard, a strong indicator that he possessed very little power to influence decision-makers in Washington and Chungking. In Chinese terms, the removal of the planes indicated a tremendous loss of face for Stilwell, a clear sign that he held little sway with his superiors, and Chiang thought of it as such. The incident represented a significant moment in their difficult relationship. Chiang might have been willing to tolerate the impertinence and impatience of the tempestuous American general if he could produce the kind of results—mainly in the form of lend-lease material and military forces—the Generalissimo wanted. But instead he seemed powerless. Chiang had already looked into getting him replaced, but he realized he was in no position to dictate the firing of a man whom Roosevelt and Marshall had handpicked. Nonetheless, in the months to come, he would make numerous back-channel efforts to have Stilwell recalled. For his part, Stilwell knew that the Chiangs were probably bluffing with their threats of leaving the alliance. If Chiang cut a deal with the Japanese, he would lose all credibility with his party and all resistance-minded Chinese. Such a deal might even lead to the collapse of the Nationalist government. He would destroy his relationship with the United States and forgo desperately needed American aid. But Stilwell knew that the United States could not afford to take the chance that Chiang and his wife might actually make good on their threats.

In the wake of this uncomfortable meeting, Chiang, on June 29, presented Stilwell with a memo called "Three Minimum Requirements for the Maintenance of the China Theater." Dubbed the "Three Demands" by the Americans, it amounted to an ultimatum for much of what Roosevelt had already promised China. Chiang asked for three American divisions to help the Chinese Army restore the road supply route through Burma, five hundred planes in theater, and the monthly aerial transportation of five thousand tons of lend-lease material from airfields in India, over the edges of the Himalayas (called "the Hump" by Americans), to China. Stilwell heartily concurred with the demands. He had actually asked Marshall for one American division; three sounded even better. Roosevelt did not formally reply until October. In a soothing, respectful message, he agreed to the tonnage and even promised an additional one hundred planes but, because of the limited availability of shipping and manpower, he could not provide combat troops. The promises placated Chiang, at least for the moment.[9]

By this time, Stilwell was busily planning a campaign to retake Burma. As long as the Japanese controlled Burma, China was cut off from its allies, dependent upon the perilous vagaries of the inefficient aerial resupply effort over the Himalayas. Stilwell's laser focus was to eject the Japanese from Burma, reopen a road supply route to China and utilize the latter country as a platform for attacking Japan itself, either by air or amphibious invasion. Just as MacArthur was nearly obsessed with the idea of returning to the Philippines, so, too, was Stilwell focused on Burmese redemption. A return to both places certainly made some strategic sense, but for both men, their preoccupation hinted at a deep need to live up to their own personal codes of honor. "He seemed to have an obsession over the disasterous [sic] results of his first campaign in Burma," one confidant later wrote of Stilwell, "[His] all-consuming desire was to redeem the record of his first dismal campaign in Burma by a brilliant second campaign."

To that end, he spent much of his time commuting by air back and forth between Chungking and New Delhi, working with the Chinese and British to plan a counteroffensive whose parameters and code names changed several times. His most ambitious concept, code-named Anakim, called for a three-pronged offensive: the British would recapture Rangoon; an American-trained Chinese force, with British assistance, would advance from Assam in eastern India to Mandalay; on the northern flank a rejuvenated, reequipped, reformed force of some thirty Chinese divisions was to attack out of Yunnan province and eject the Japanese from northern

Burma. The ground forces would be supported by substantial numbers of planes from the Royal Air Force and even several capital ships from the Royal Navy. Stilwell even held out hope that he might actually get the services of an American infantry division to spearhead the drive from Assam.

The planning for the offensive involved a great deal of diplomatic networking and stroking by the usually brusque general. Like potential customers who demonstrate interest in a product but never actually buy, the principal players agreed to his designs and assisted in the planning, though they were loath to follow through with specific, binding commitments. Chiang acceded to Anakim only as long as the British could guarantee Allied control of the air and sea. The British paid lip service to participation, but they expected the Chinese to do most of the fighting and dying. In truth, Churchill had little enthusiasm for operations in Burma, since he saw China's role in the war as tangential and almost insignificant. The cold reality was that Western Allied priorities lay elsewhere. With wide-ranging global commitments, and precedence going to the European theater, neither British nor American leaders had any inclination for providing Stilwell with the kind of reinforcements and strategic priority he would need to pull off Anakim. Moreover, Chiang was lukewarm on the idea for the same reason he was unenthusiastic about reforms and offensive operations. Why lose valuable soldiers in Burma—again—when his main political struggle was in China? Even the prospect of opening up a land supply route from India to his country did not seem to Chiang worth the price he would have to pay to get it.

In the end, Stilwell had to settle for the vague long-range promise from all parties of a more limited offensive to recapture only northern Burma, with no real action planned until well into 1943, if then. Chiang did agree to station troops in India to be trained by Stilwell's American advisers. This force would consist of about nine thousand survivors of the Burma campaign and several thousand more men flown from China to India. The British, after hemming and hawing over concerns that Chinese soldiers in India might join with the Quit India movement, reluctantly agreed to Stilwell's plan to train these men in Ramgarh, at a former prison camp for Italian POWs. For the purpose of carving out a supply route for his campaign, Stilwell ordered work to begin on a road from Ledo, a tiny town in Assam, east to the Burmese border. The Chinese and British agreed to provide some laborers to assist the US Army engineers who, by late 1942, were girding up for the arduous task of building a road through some of

the world's most difficult terrain. Stilwell had no choice but to accommodate these more limited ambitions, the sort that came with lordship of a
strategic backwater.

Nor was this his only forced compromise. In early October Wendell
Willkie, the Republican nominee who had lost the presidential election to
Roosevelt in 1940, visited China on behalf of his former opponent. Blus-
tery, charismatic, and raspy-voiced, Willkie shared Roosevelt's internationalist foreign policy views. Roosevelt had already stamped his war
leadership with a bipartisan imprimatur by appointing notable Republicans Frank Knox and Henry Stimson as his Secretary of the Navy and
Secretary of War respectively. Roosevelt expanded this bipartisan push for
national unity by tapping Willkie to embark upon a forty-nine-day world
tour of Allied nations to gauge their political pulse and build goodwill. At
fifty, Willkie was still, in political terms, a young man. Chiang and Mei-
ling Soong thought he might well succeed Roosevelt as president, so they
were determined to put on the best possible face for him. At the behest of
the regime, Chungking police swept beggars from the streets and closed
shabby-looking shops. In their stead, they strung welcome banners and
signs along the main avenues. From the moment Willkie's plane landed in
Chungking, he was treated like a prince. Schoolchildren lined up for miles
and waved paper Chinese and American flags as Willkie's motorcade
rolled past them. The American delivered a personal letter from Roosevelt
to the Chiangs, expressing friendly comradeship. At Chinese insistence,
Willkie stayed in a guesthouse rather than the American embassy, a tremendous mistake because it hampered his opportunities to access unvar-
nished opinions on the Chinese situation from Ambassador Clarence
Gauss and, for that matter, Stilwell, too.

Specially chosen English-speaking envoys escorted Willkie everywhere
he went. As much as possible, they cocooned him from China's uncomfortable realities and immersed him in the sort of unrelenting political theater
that characterizes totalitarian regimes. "He has to go to lunch, tea, and
dinner every day he is here," Stilwell wrote disapprovingly in his diary.
"They are going to drag him around to see schools and factories and girl
scouts and sewing circles and arsenals and keep him well insulated from
pollution by Americans. The idea is get him so exhausted and keep him so
torpid with food and drink that his faculties will be dulled and he'll be
stuffed with the right doctrines." In one instance, after making a show of
concern for Willkie's safety, the Chinese arranged for him to visit a section

of what they called the front but was actually little more than a peaceful spot where Japanese and Chinese soldiers did business and observed a mutual back-scratching truce. "He mustn't miss it," Stilwell loudly and rudely proclaimed at a cocktail party. "It's where the Japanese and Chinese meet to trade all the goods they need from each other." At the "front," Willkie satisfied his penchant for adventure by peering through a telescope at the muzzles of Japanese guns. Chinese soldiers plied him with Japanese swords and bottles of French wine that had supposedly been captured by Nationalist patrols (even though the items were conspicuously available at local markets). "Willkie is being thoroughly immersed in soft soap, adulation, and flattery," Stilwell wrote with characteristic penetrating disgust.

Willkie seems either not to have seen through the facade or perhaps thought it was for the betterment of the Allied cause if he played along. His subsequent writings, serialized in a series of ten national newspaper articles and a bestselling book called *One World*, presented Chiang's China as a valiant, democratic, hard-fighting ally, the Free China image at its very best. He was especially taken with Mei-ling, with whom he allegedly had a one-night stand, according to Willkie's friend Gardner Cowles Jr., the publisher of *Look* magazine, who stayed in the same house with him. Whether true or not, the rumor of their liaison circulated around gossip-hungry Chungking like an electrical current. Willkie invited Madame Chiang to visit the United States, and she readily accepted. As a graduate of Wellesley College, she had already spent many years in America. Good-looking, articulate, and a person of enormous political savvy, she was the perfect face for the Nationalist government.

This political Kabuki dance might have served as nothing more than a headshaking diversion for the puritanical Stilwell, except for one thing. At one point during Willkie's visit, Claire Chennault, commander of the China Air Task Force, succeeded in catching Willkie's ear and selling him on a strategic concept that was at direct odds with Stilwell's. Newly promoted to brigadier general, Chennault was a courageous, innovative fighter pilot who had led the mercenary American Volunteer Group (or Flying Tigers) before American entry into the war and now commanded a cobbled-together assortment of American medium bombers and fighters that were more than holding their own against Japanese aviators in China. At Willkie's request, Chennault prepared a letter for President Roosevelt, outlining his concept (and not only bypassing his chain of command but the War Department as well). Chennault claimed he could win the war against Japan with only modest reinforcements and priority of supply. "To accomplish the downfall of Japan, I need only this very small American Air Force—105 fighter aircraft of modern design, 30 medium bombers, and in the last phase, some months from now, 12 heavy bombers."

Chennault predicted that this scratch force would destroy Japanese air fleets within six months and then have a free hand to bomb the Imperial Navy and the vulnerable industries of the home islands. The United States Navy could then operate at will, and MacArthur could easily sweep through the Pacific to Japan. "Once the above two objectives are accomplished the complete military subjection of Japan is certain and easy," he wrote with aplomb. The plan was the sort that could be proposed only by a true airpower zealot and one who was stunningly ignorant—almost to a childlike degree—of theater-wide strategy, logistics, naval warfare, Japanese military strength, innovations, and sheer determination. It also revealed a fundamental misunderstanding of the decisive impact of the human factor on the waging of war. A more sophisticated recipient than Willkie would have politely consigned the document to the waste bin where it belonged. But, setting aside the sheer irrationality that a handful of aircraft could somehow win a war that encompassed nearly one-third of the world's surface, the plan seemed to offer an easy, almost bloodless route to victory, and politicians ignored such simple solutions only at their own peril. Willkie dutifully forwarded the document to Roosevelt, who also came to view it sympathetically. So did Chiang, with profound consequences for future events in China.[10]

5

Partners

As a British Commonwealth nation, Australia had been in the war since the beginning. Australian soldiers had fought in such far-flung places as Egypt, Syria, Libya, and Greece. Australian airmen had participated in the Battle of Britain. The Navy had served alongside its British counterpart in the struggle to maintain control of the Mediterranean. And yet all the while, the real threat to Australia's security was brewing much closer to home. Large in area but small in population, with only seven million people, the island nation found itself under serious threat by the stunning, speedy Japanese advance across the Pacific. February 1942 was a particularly difficult month. Some fifteen thousand Australian soldiers were captured when British colonial forces surrendered at Singapore, a devastating blow for a country with such limited manpower. Japanese planes bombed Darwin and other smaller cities along the northern coast of Australia.

The country now found itself in a security situation that was at once unique and vexing. Even as the Japanese expanded their reach southward, to New Guinea, Rabaul, and deep into the Solomon Islands, and thus placed themselves near Australia's northern doorstep, most of the nation's armed forces were deployed on the other side of the world, in no position to defend their country. With the possible exception of neighboring New Zealand, no other nation in World War II faced such an odd and frightening dichotomy. The Australians in 1942 were rather like a besieged homeowner who faces the onslaught of heavily armed prowlers, only to realize that his weapons and bodyguards are located somewhere on the other side of town. When war broke out with Japan—something Australian leaders had worried about for nearly five decades—Prime Minister John Curtin found himself scrambling to defend his island continent. He insisted, over Churchill's vociferous opposition, upon the return of Australian troops from the British forces in North Africa. But this would take time, and even with all the nation's armed forces deployed at home, Australia probably could not hold off any sort of major Japanese air, sea, or land offensive. So the natural place to turn for help was to the Americans. Though they were ill prepared for war and in the process of absorbing terrible defeats in the Philippines and elsewhere, their intrinsic strength was obvious. American war planners had never seriously envisioned the possibility of defending Australia and using it as their main base for a major counteroffensive against the Japanese, but Japanese victories forced this circumstance upon them. Thus began an alliance between two culturally similar and like-minded nations that has remained in place ever since, albeit with plenty of adjustments and disagreements.

As American soldiers began arriving in numbers during the early months of 1942, they were greeted with tremendous enthusiasm by the Australians, many of whom could not hide their immense relief at the soothing presence of the GIs. "The Australian people are quite satisfied that the Americans have come to save them," a Canadian in residence observed. "They have a very high opinion of the American soldiers." Appreciative crowds gathered at piers and station platforms to greet incoming ships and troop trains. Waving and cheering, they studied the newcomers with great curiosity. Often they exchanged souvenirs. Soldiers of the 163rd Infantry Regiment were amazed to see a train station platform packed with people of all ages, roiling and competing for access to the "Yanks," as they almost universally called the Americans. "Especially popular were our American coins of which we traded for the Australian pound, half pound, florin, shilling and sixpence pennies," read the history of the regiment's F Company. "Elderly women unable to come to the station stood waving towels and flags, bringing to us the realization that we were in a land of welcome, all living and fighting for the same cause."

The visitors soon discovered that American cigarettes were a prized commodity, and one they could barter for almost anything. An enthusiastic crowd surprised PFC Allen Douglas and his buddies from the 46th Engineer Construction Battalion as their train began to pull away from a station in Melbourne. To show their own appreciation for the war welcome, Douglas and the other Americans threw cigarettes and other goodies out the window. "People were leaning out of windows and standing in streets cheering and putting up the V for victory sign. It sure made us feel

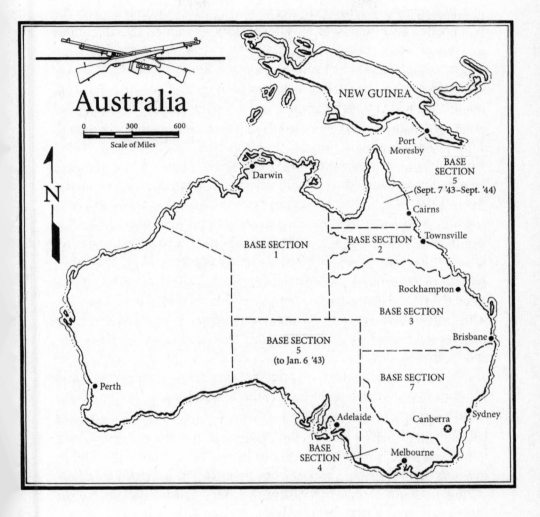

Australia

0   300   600
Scale of Miles

N

NEW GUINEA

Port
Moresby

BASE
SECTION
5
(Sept. 7 '43–Sept. '44)

Darwin

Cairns

Townsville

BASE SECTION
1

BASE SECTION
2

Rockhampton

BASE SECTION
3

Brisbane

BASE SECTION
5
(to Jan. 6 '43)

Perth

BASE SECTION
7

Adelaide

Canberra

Sydney

BASE
SECTION
4

Melbourne

good." In Perth, hero-worshipping boys accosted American soldiers, begging for souvenirs and autographs. On several embarrassing occasions, they asked men for their signature only to discover that they were Australian or British and, in the baldly frank manner of children, they instantly lost all interest. It seemed that everywhere an American soldier went, he was greeted with handshakes, V-for-victory signs, and the ubiquitous greeting of "Hello, Yank!"

The enthusiasm for anything and anyone American extended to war correspondents as well. John Lardner tried to tip his hotel chambermaid, but she refused to accept his gratuity (the American practice of tipping was actually unknown to Australians). "I don't want your money," she said. "You people are here to help us." In Melbourne, William Dunn of CBS News ducked into a doorway to take refuge from a rainstorm one day when he was joined by a middle-aged Australian who "put his arm on my shoulder and started telling me what fine people the American soldiers in Australia were. His one ambition, he said, was to get permission to billet a couple of Yanks in his own home for a while so he could get better acquainted with the American point of view." Reflecting on the encounter, Dunn concluded: "The spirit of welcome and whole hearted hospitality with which the Americans have been greeted here is heartening, to say the least." Australians regularly went out of their way to befriend American soldiers and invite them into their homes for a meal or, as Dunn's experience indicated, shelter.[1]

No one was more welcomed or revered than General MacArthur, who became the very symbol of the US presence as well as the seriousness of the American commitment to defend Australia, even though the general's gaze still seemed to be fixed on the Philippines. "Curtin and Co. more or less offered him the country on a platter when he arrived from the Philippines," a liaison officer in MacArthur's headquarters later said. The Australians even organized a MacArthur Day, during which adoring crowds rallied to cheer his name while effusive messages flooded into his headquarters. In a subsequent opinion poll, Australians named him the most important public figure in the country, well ahead of Curtin.

Upon arriving in the south-coast city of Adelaide, MacArthur met with reporters and famously described his mission as "organizing the American offensive against Japan, a primary object of which is the relief of the Philippines. I came through and I shall return." The implication seemed to be that his presence in Australia was merely temporary until he could go back to the archipelago at the head of a powerful relief expedition. As we have seen, this assertion was based not on reality but on self-justification for his exodus or, more generously, just mere delusion. The media focused on the "I shall return" portion of MacArthur's impromptu briefing, solidifying it as a commitment of sorts (much to the present and future chagrin of Washington grand strategists).

The Australian people seemed to understand far better than MacArthur and the pundits that returning to the Philippines was impossible without first defending Australia. After the press conference, thousands of civilians mobbed MacArthur and his entourage, shouting "Welcome to Australia" and other friendly greetings. When the general reached Melbourne, where he located his headquarters from March to July 1942, a crowd of about six thousand well-wishers gathered on a beautiful, sunny late-summer day to cheer him wildly as he stepped off his train. They were joined by an honor guard of 360 American soldiers from the 43rd Engineers, a passel of high-ranking US and Australian officers, and Curtin's Army Minister Frank Forde. Brigadier General Stephen Chamberlin and other MacArthur staffers had planned every detail of the general's arrival and subsequent movement to his new quarters, at the nearby Menzies hotel. But they could not account for the boisterous exuberance of the crowd. In the recollection of Lieutenant Colonel Huff, "the Australians welcomed him with a kind of frenzy born of their desperate need for hope and encouragement." People crowded around MacArthur, Jean, Arthur, and Ah Cheu—"a cheering and not very orderly crowd of admirers," in Huff's estimation, "and it was a bit frightening." Wielding his cane, MacArthur gave a short talk conveying his high esteem for Australian soldiers and the shared sense of purpose he felt with them. He also could not resist taking some passive-aggressive swipes at his superiors in Washington. "Success in modern war requires something more than courage and a willingness to die: it requires careful preparation. This means the furnishing of sufficient troops and sufficient material to meet the known strength of a potential enemy. No general can make something out of nothing."

Such was the enthusiasm of the crowd that MacArthur and Jean were separated in the melee and actually rode to the Menzies in different vehicles. Australian police and American soldiers cordoned off traffic and attempted to keep the crowd in check. The motorcade rolled between "sidewalks black

with cheering people," according to one witness. Four-star pennants fluttered proudly on MacArthur's Wolseley limousine. As the vehicle glided
past a warehouse complex and negotiated its way several blocks to the hotel,
the friendly Australians smiled and waved at the general. Armed guards
patrolled the hotel entrance and elevator access to the sixth floor, where the
MacArthur family settled. Such was the MacArthur mania down under
that enterprising restaurateurs soon offered a range of dishes to capitalize
on the general's fame. The offerings included the MacArthur salad at the
Hotel Australia in Melbourne and the double-decker MacArthur sandwich,
packed with ham and lamb slathered in mayonnaise, available for order at
most any restaurant.

Friendly and well-mannered as ever, Jean soon became an especially
popular figure among Australians. On one typical occasion, as she and
Huff got into a car after doing some shopping, a group of cheering civilians
gathered around the car. Every bit as bereft of guile and ego as her husband
was imbued with these qualities, she assumed the cheers must be for a
nearby wedding party. "Let's see the bride," she said to Huff.

"There's no wedding," he replied. "It's just your public."

Embarrassed by the adulation and attention, she said, "I'm just shining
in reflected glory." Nonetheless, she smiled and waved at her well-wishers.

In spite of the harrowing escape from the Philippines and the danger
his family had been exposed to, MacArthur never seemed to consider
sending them back to the States. Instead, Jean and Arthur would stay with
him through the entire war. It never seemed to occur to the general, or
perhaps he simply did not care, that everyone who served under him was
forced to endure separation from their families while he enjoyed the company of his. Though Jean undoubtedly provided a likable feminine face for
the American presence in Australia and a soothing supportive partner for
her husband—contributing to the war effort in this sense—some be-
grudged the double standard. "One of the things . . . soldiers most hated
about MacArthur was that we were deprived of our wives and even women
while MacArthur, the minute he got anywhere, sent for his wife," Major
Faubion Bowers, who worked in the Allied Translator and Interpreter Section of his headquarters, later said. "We considered it entirely inappropriate behavior. He was the only general who did that." In spite of the
resentment, no one on the staff or among his superiors in Washington ever
seemed to have broached this issue with him. It remained an appalling
example of double-standard leadership.[2]

By July 1942, there were almost one hundred thousand American troops in Australia and the numbers were still growing (close to one million would pass through or be based in the country during the course of the war). While fears of a Japanese invasion were abating after the Coral Sea and Midway naval victories, the task of rolling back Japanese power in the South Pacific loomed enormous for the new Australian-American partners. MacArthur was by now officially in command of the Southwest Pacific Area (SWPA), a huge expanse that encompassed Australia, New Guinea, New Britain, most of Indonesia, the western portion of the Solomon Islands, and, optimistically, the Philippines. The geography was immense. An Army official historian later wrote of the Australian base as "equivalent to one in South America directing operations against Boston and New York, and planning for an invasion against northwest Canada." Similar to his USAFFE command in the Philippines, the SWPA theater was essentially created for MacArthur with the consent of American and Australian political leaders. MacArthur supplanted Lieutenant General George Brett, an aviator who had previously commanded all American troops in Australia. MacArthur believed that Brett's aviators had failed utterly to provide any sort of support and resupply for the Philippines garrison and, probably unfairly, he focused his frustration almost entirely on General Brett. Given the horrendous circumstances prevalent at the time, MacArthur's judgment was probably too harsh. He even blamed the aviator for the poor state of the B-17s sent to extract him from Mindanao. Once in charge, MacArthur soon got rid of the airman. In a remarkably evenhanded, but cutting, magazine article written soon after the war, Brett opined, "If not entirely fair, his attitude was understandable. The General, a complete egotist, was the center of his own thinking and planning. What he needed must be supplied, no matter the needs of others."

The job of planning and organizing operations and supplying the growing American presence in Australia was enormous. Just as the United Kingdom served as the nexus of the Western Allied effort in Europe, so, too, Australia played the same role, albeit on a smaller scale, during the initial phases of the Pacific War. The US Army set up seven different base sections spread far and wide around the continent among the various Australian states. From these growing bases the sinews of the American war effort proliferated and circulated throughout SWPA. During just one representative month in the spring of 1942, Base Section 4 at Melbourne received and processed 45,461 cases of supplies. Half this cargo sustained the base's operations. The other half was dispersed on twenty-two full rail cars, five water shipments, and five aerial shipments. Another 4,119 gallons of fuel was disseminated, and 14,517 pounds of bread was prepared in the base's bakery. Base Section 7 at Sydney handled such a glut of supplies that the Army had to construct nearly 1.6 million square feet of warehouses and requisition another 742,000 square feet from local buildings just to have enough space in which to store it all.

Unlike its mother country, Australia was not well suited for the role of becoming a major base for so vast an enterprise. "The whole continent of Australia is as undeveloped as the central United States was before the Civil War, or even more so," wrote Brigadier General Chamberlin of MacArthur's staff in a 1942 letter to a colleague. Distances were vast. The transportation networks were underdeveloped. Roads were poorly maintained and sparse, except in or near the cities. The state of Western Australia, physically the largest in the country, had no concrete roads at all. There were, at most, about eleven thousand trucks on hand that were durable enough to survive the poor roads. Transport aircraft were nonexistent. The rainy weather in the Northern Territory and the coastal areas of Queensland made it difficult to truck troops and supplies to Darwin and other hard-pressed spots on Australia's north coast. The gauge width of railroad tracks was not uniform from state to state, making any long-distance travel ponderous. This meant, for instance, that a train carrying freight from Melbourne to Brisbane had to be halted during the journey, the cargo unloaded into new cars suited to ride on tracks of a different width, and then sent on to its final destination. In one telling instance, twenty thousand tons of vital war matériel sat uselessly stalled along sidings between Newcastle and Brisbane. What was more, Australian boxcars were small and could not hold much tonnage, at least by American standards, and the locomotives were slower. Even at full capacity, the journey of moving one American division with its supplies some one thousand miles from Brisbane to Cairns consumed twenty days.

Most of the population was clustered in the cities along the southeastern coast. Port facilities in these urban areas were modern but spread far and wide by geography—the driving distance from Perth on the west coast to Sydney on the east coast was more than twenty-three hundred miles, almost as far as Los Angeles to Baltimore. Melbourne and Sydney were 545 miles apart; Brisbane lay another 570 miles north of Sydney. The loading docks and harbors were dominated by longshoreman unions whose rights and privileges had been hard-earned over decades, but who had now become so powerful that they eroded almost all efficiency in unloading operations. Breaks were common to the point of ludicrousness. Union members did not work in the rain, though they got paid for standing under cover. At most the laborers logged three or four hours of real work per day, a rate that simply could not continue in the context of total war, especially since the military buildup depended so much on the shipping and unloading of the vast sinews of war. When the Americans took matters into their own hands and began unloading ships themselves, the Australian longshoremen reacted with anger and consternation. They had only themselves to blame, though. One study revealed that, on average, Australian professional stevedores unloaded between five and nine tons of cargo per hatch per hour while unschooled American soldiers unloaded twenty-five tons per hatch per hour. Even then ports were clogged with unloaded and unassigned freight to the point where, according to a Base Section 7 report in Sydney, "wharves were actually threatened with collapse because of the mass [of] supplies dumped upon them, and more ships were waiting to unload as soon as space could be cleared."

Because the country was at full military mobilization with nearly 14 percent of its population in uniform, civilian labor was in short supply for the herculean, almost overwhelming, task of building airfields, hangars, barracks, roads, warehouses, and the like. As it was, tens of thousands of Australians did end up working on military construction projects. They helped build more than three hundred airfields of varying quality from temporary grass strips to permanent bases with hangars and modern concrete runways. They played an important role in the building or reconditioning of more than forty-two hundred miles of badly needed road. Even so, there were never anywhere near enough domestic workers to meet the wartime demand. One reason the longshoremen were such a formidable group was that there were so few of them—at most about 12,500 in the whole country. Many of them were, in the estimation of one American, "old, tired, and physically unfit." So acute was the labor shortage that American planners even looked into a scheme to import workers from Indonesia and India, though nothing ever came to fruition.

Pilferage only added to the headaches. "US Army supplies were stolen on ships and wharves, in warehouses and post exchanges, in rail yards, and in motortrucks and railcars," wrote James Masterson in a magisterial official history of Army transportation in SWPA. Consumer items like candy, razor blades, cigarettes, soap, liquor, hand tools, and clothing seemed to disappear with the greatest frequency. In one embarrassing instance, a gang of stevedores became so drunk and belligerent on pilfered liquor that the Army had to pay them to stop unloading the booze. When commanders placed armed guards to oversee the unloading of cargo, civilian stevedores sometimes went on strike. Even when soldiers caught offenders, it was difficult to prosecute them under local law. Better security and oversight kept the problem from growing completely out of control, but Army logisticians learned to budget for an average 3 to 5 percent loss of most any cargo. "They want us to furnish everything including the men to fight the war, and they would like to run the war," Major John Day III, MacArthur's headquarters commandant, wrote of the Australians in an acerbic diary entry.

Given the remote location of the enormous island continent, and the fact that it was largely self-sufficient, the mind-set of Australians tended to be insular. To the high-strung Americans, the local pace of life seemed maddeningly slow. Almost all businesses closed from midday Saturday until Monday morning. Hotel bars often did not stay open after midevening. Road traffic was slow-paced, especially outside of metropolitan Sydney and Melbourne. The tempo of service in restaurants, hotels, milk bars (where ice cream and other dairy products were sold), and department stores was slow by American standards. "Their system, their methods and their line of thought are different from ours," Chamberlin mused. "In many cases measured by our own standards, these methods appear most inefficient. Great patience is necessary. It behooves all of us to know when to give in and when to be firm." To be sure, Americans and Australians shared the commonalities of a Western outlook, the same language, the same religious beliefs, and, at least for white Americans, a common ethnic heritage. In all these respects, Australia was the most similar country to their own that GIs would experience during the war against Japan. Even with such similarities, though, the crucial enterprise of maintaining good relationships required a mutual willingness for diplomacy and understanding. "Most of the time during daylight hours was occupied in receiving calls from local Australians interested in seeking employment, and getting information, or calling in personally," the theater personnel section diary recorded. On one day alone, the personnel soldiers met with the chaplain general of the Australian Army; a representative from the Australian Comforts Fund; a local rabbi; many dozens of private citizens who had homes, offices, or apartments for sale or rent; an Australian state senator hoping to secure employment for his daughter; a local racetrack owner's daughter, who hoped to land a job with the Army's Morale branch; and "a missionary with pointed beard and a load of pamphlets dealing with the morality of soldiers, which he insisted he must distribute personally to the 'boys in our camps.'"[3]

As visitors, the Americans were forced to adjust to life in a foreign country. "The Australians have much in common with us," asserted a pocket guidebook issued to every American soldier. "They're pioneer people; they believe in personal freedom; they love sports; and they're out to lick the Axis all the way. But there are a lot of differences too—their ways of living and thinking on all sorts of things—like tea, central heating, the best way to spend Sunday, or saluting officers and such." After a long sea journey packed aboard troop ships, eating bad food, staving off seasickness and boredom, soldiers were eager to explore their new surroundings, alien though they initially seemed. "At first we all found it exceedingly difficult to become accustomed to the new money, traffic on the wrong side of the street and the difference in speech," wrote the historian of A Company, 163rd Infantry Regiment, 41st Infantry Division. "Everything was new and strange to us," another soldier echoed. This was especially true for the reversal of seasons—in the southern hemisphere winter spans from June to September, summer from December to March, and so on. Some Americans who arrived in the early months of 1942 had just endured their accustomed North American winter only to face the immediate onset of the Australia winter, though the climate around most of the island continent was far milder than in most states back home. The GIs immediately noticed the preponderance of lovingly tended flower gardens in Melbourne and other cities. "Gee, Mom, you would like it here because of the beautiful flowers," many of them wrote in their first letters home. Though the guidebook attempted to educate the troops on Australian history, customs, and phrases, very few Americans knew much about the people or the country. In many instances, when Yanks arrived in Australia, they asked their fellows, "What language is spoken here?"

For people who shared a common language, communication could be surprisingly vexatious. "It was very hard to understand these people and, at first, we wished they would speak english [*sic*], and they wished that we would," PFC Douglas wrote with tongue in cheek. Another soldier joked in a letter to his girlfriend, "You said in your last letter that it was good I was in a country where people spoke the English language. That's what you think!" By any measure, it was incredible that one tongue could be spoken so differently, with such a colorful array of terms and accents. Americans were reasonably used to hearing British accents, but the broader Australian dialect could be especially difficult for them to decode. To American ears, the broad "a" sounded similar to the Cockney inflections of east London (the comparison was best left unsaid, because it would have insulted the hosts). In hospitals, Americans were sometimes given a start by Australian patients who voiced the hope of "going home to-die." Several moments would pass before the Americans realized that the patients were saying "today" not "to die." At a polite tea party in a private home, one American leader was shocked to be asked by the lady of the house, " 'Ave you seen my waist?" Only when the woman added, "She 'asn't been in pictures for a long time," did he realize she was talking about the actress Mae West, not her own waistline. Beyond the usual British-influenced nomenclature—"lift" instead of "elevator," "lorry" for "truck," "chips" rather than "fries," and so forth—American soldiers had to absorb a dizzying array of uniquely local slang terms: a "sheila" was an attractive woman; "shickered" meant drunk; a "cobber" was a good buddy; a "beano" referred to a nice party; a "grafter" was a good worker; "burgoo" was stew; a "face wash" was a washcloth; "fair dinkum" or "dinkum oil" meant the absolute truth; Diggers were Australians; a john was a police officer; bar-stud, or bastard, was a term of affection; a braggart was a skiter.

For their part, the Australians were fascinated with the broad range of American regional accents, everything from fast-talking New Yorkers and New Englanders to flat-toned Midwesterners and the slower, twangy cadence of Southerners. To local ears, the variety could be overwhelming. "I just couldn't quite understand what they were saying," Harriet Oliver, an Australian woman, remarked many years after the war. At Christmastime, one GI seemed to ask a Brisbane businessman for a punch ball. The Australian tracked down the toy for the American, only to discover that he actually wanted a punch bowl for a Christmas party. Just as the Yanks absorbed much of the local slang, Australian soldiers and civilians soon found themselves blurting Americanisms, like "drinking Coke," "stalling a dame," "hitching a ride," "shucks," "cat got your tongue," or "swell." The trappings of American culture, from music to Hollywood to media images to hairstyles, soon proliferated. The Aussies could not help but find themselves immersed in and somewhat overwhelmed by the allure of this powerful mass culture. "The entire keynote of this amazing Army seemed to be enthusiasm," Maureen Meadows, a typist who worked for the Americans, later wrote. "They possessed an 'Oh Boy' attitude towards everything, and it wasn't only beer and blondes or candy and Coca-Cola. Nothing represented a trouble to them. Nothing augured of the impossible."

Since shipping space was at a premium, the Australians agreed to take the lead in feeding the friendly occupation force. By one estimate, Australia in the latter half of 1942 alone provided more than two-thirds of the food consumed by American military forces. From 1942 to 1944, the country produced more than twenty-three millions tons of beef, much of which went into American digestive systems. Milk processing doubled; the canning of vegetables, meats, and dehydrated foods skyrocketed. Australians were struck by the insatiable nature of the GI appetite. "They . . . said we ate like hogs," one soldier recalled. When a pair of American officers made reservations to have a steak dinner for themselves and their dates at a Brisbane restaurant, the hostess replied, "I'm sorry, but we just won't serve steaks to women. They don't eat it all and it's too wasteful." When the hostess found out the women were US Army nurses, presumably with standard American appetites, she then figured nothing would go to waste. "They can have steak," she declared. Indeed, there was even a marked difference in the ration allotments of the two allies. One can of jam could feed twenty Australian soldiers; it took four cans to satisfy a like number of Americans. The standard GI food ration consisted of thirty-nine items; his Australian counterpart required only twenty-four. American and Australian quartermasters compromised by allotting twenty-eight items into the GI diet, including coffee, spaghetti, macaroni, eggs, and rice.

Sanitation standards were notably different. Australia lagged several decades behind the United States in this regard. As a result, Americans were sometimes shocked by what they regarded as unclean habits. Local kitchens were lined with layers of dust and dirt. When food was spilled, Australian cooks generally scooped it up with shovels and threw it right back into a cooking pot. They viewed the American custom of throwing away spillage as inordinately wasteful. Food and garbage were sometimes hauled on the same trucks. Milk was seldom pasteurized; only a small percentage met US Army health codes. Of the two hundred million domestic gallons produced in one year, less than 2 percent was acceptable for consumption under those strictures. One American service command was so concerned about unsanitary conditions and the poor nutritional value of bread prepared in local bakeries that it eventually established its own bakery. The new facility ended up producing twenty-five thousand pounds of bread per day.

The American taste for coffee, fruit juices, cold salads with warm meat, ice cream, cheese, ice water, and fresh vegetables was an entirely new experience for the hosts. The Australian diet was heavy on beef, mutton, bread and butter, washed down with copious amounts of tea. Americans were probably the best-fed soldiers on earth, and yet their penchant for complaining about food was world-class. They soon wrinkled their noses at the ubiquity of mutton and lamb, seemingly served three meals a day with no interlude. "The men were so sick of it, some were vomiting at the smell of it," PFC Douglas claimed. Mutton stew was, in the estimation of another man, "like cold glue . . . with all the delicious appeal of a soggy snowbank." In the recollection of Warrant Officer E. J. Kahn, a typically sardonic mess hall complaint held that "the mutton might not have been so bad if only they'd sheared the sheep more closely before cooking it." Frequently, homesick Americans procured local hot dogs only to discover that they were made from the same hated mutton meat. To the soldiers, it seemed there was nowhere to escape from it. "Mom's famous apple pies were substituted by Mutton billed as Meat Pies," one company history lamented.

The howling about mutton was so pronounced that Michael Stiver, a Sydney-based Office of War Information employee, urged his superiors in Washington to issue warnings to Australia-bound GIs that mutton was the national meat and not to sound off about it. The Australian government responded to American complaints by raising production of other meats, in part by implementing rationing among their own population. Poultry output, tiny by American standards at 240,000 pounds per annum, rose to two million pounds a year. In hopes of satisfying the voracious US appetite for bacon, the Canberra government furnished feed to hog farmers and guaranteed to purchase their animals at a handsome profit. Output rose substantially, peaking at nearly 12 million pounds of bacon, 12 million pounds of ham, and 9.5 million pounds of pork per year. Even then these seemingly staggering numbers were not enough to meet the prodigious American demand.[4]

From Sydney to Melbourne to Brisbane and scores of smaller towns, hungry Americans—eager for an escape from camp and military fare—populated restaurants in large numbers at establishments with names like the Piccadilly Café and the Melbourne Café, the latter of which was confusingly located in Rockhampton rather than its namesake. In conversations, soldiers estimated the size of local cities not by their actual population but the number of restaurants and pubs in a given locale. "Long lines of soldiers remained outside of a restaurant untill [sic] the occupants inside had finished," the historian of Company F, 163rd Infantry wrote of the dining scene in Melbourne. "The waitresses eventually, without asking in many cases what the customer desired, returned with the Yanks['] favorite, ham and eggs—heavy on the eggs." Because of wartime rationing, customers could get only two eggs per meal. Frequently, GIs ate quickly and then moved on to another restaurant to gobble down two more eggs and a bit more ham. Some, like Rogers, the stenographer who had escaped from the Philippines with MacArthur, found quieter spots. Newly promoted to master sergeant at the tender age of twenty-two, he enjoyed several meals at the sedate Scott's Hotel in Melbourne. "An elderly, dignified man served as waiter and instructor." When Rogers was baffled by the complicated blend of flatware, silverware, and a finger bowl at his place setting, the reassuring waiter coached him, "sincerely concerned for my proper education." Rogers enjoyed broth soup, steak, potatoes, and apple pie. For breakfast, he chose from steak and eggs, or broiled kidney and eggs, or lamb chops, muffins, and tea. After the privation of Corregidor, the hearty meals were welcome indeed.

In Brisbane the demand for T-bone steaks increased dramatically as seemingly every soldier ordered one. The only complaint was that Australian chefs seemed unable to prepare them any other way except well done. Elsewhere in the same town, the dining room at the air-conditioned Lennon's Hotel, where MacArthur moved his family in July 1942, was inundated with American customers. The pace of service accelerated greatly. Waitresses quickly learned to fill and refill water glasses. Unfortunately, the presence of the visitors did not do much for the quality of the menu. "The food was only so-so after Lennon's lost its Italian chef toward the start of the war," one American correspondent commented. As with hot dogs, GIs often ordered hamburgers only to find they were made of mutton. Eventually, some enterprising Australian restaurant owners began to make them with real ground beef. Marty's Milk Bar and Cafe in Maryborough featured a hamburger special with egg and bacon. In Sydney, Captain Hyman Samuelson, a white company commander in the predominantly African-American 96th Engineer Battalion, found a greasy-spoon diner where he could order a pair of hamburgers with onions. "It is a small place," he told his diary. "Six stools in a row alongside the counter and four tables." Beef burgers were a decided improvement from the mutton variety, but not quite enough to satisfy discriminating-Yank palates. "The hamburgers still aren't anything to brag about," one soldier wrote in a local newspaper. The American Canteen in Sydney, located on Elizabeth Street just opposite Hyde Park, offered homesick GIs a nice range of American fare, "cooked in the manner in which Americans like it," according to the annual history of the 118th General Hospital. The place soon became "a gathering place for men on passes."

The majority of American soldiers lived and trained in camps away from sizable towns and cities. But for most, it was not difficult to obtain weekend passes or longer furloughs. Crowds of off-duty soldiers became a common sight in most any Australian population center. For the culturally minded, there were museums, zoos, botanical gardens, amusements parks, opera performances, and art galleries. There were plenty of churches for the religiously inclined. Yanks flocked to USO shows, cabarets, band concerts, movies, and in the southeast, picturesque beaches.

Sporting events offered a great outlet, though few American spectators could comprehend the dizzying quandary of rules to otherwise entertaining Australian football matches or the slow-moving, deliberate nature of cricket. Tennis, horse racing, and boxing had some cross-cultural appeal, as did the incomparably great game of baseball, whose heritage in Australia traced back almost sixty years earlier when Albert Spalding had brought a touring team of American major leaguers to the island continent. Ever since, the beautiful game had steadily grown in popularity among the Aussies. Off-duty American soldiers commonly challenged their Digger buddies to friendly ball games, fully expecting to win easily. All too often, they were surprised to face some serious competition. One afternoon, at Melbourne's Royal Park, an Australian team clobbered a US team 12–1 in front of three thousand spectators. On the same day, in Sydney, another local nine defeated its American opposite 14–2. Though the Americans won more often than they lost, especially as the contests became more organized, Australian proficiency at the game was nonetheless impressive. Dunn, the CBS newsman, joked in one broadcast that GIs were starting to wish "they could persuade the War Department to send Hank Greenberg or Bob Feller out to help them handle the competition." Australian newspapers began carrying stories about Major League games and publishing box scores. Beginning with the 1942 World Series, when the Saint Louis Cardinals defeated the New York Yankees in five games, Australian commercial radio stations featured game broadcasts. The American soldiers also played football, and lots of it. In this sport, there was no competition from the locals. The rough-and-tumble organized chaos of the game was incomprehensible to the Australians. To Aussies, the players, decked out in helmets and pads, looked more like paratroopers than athletes. "They'd put the ball down, and one would pick it up and throw it to another," one local journalist wrote, "then all would run a few feet and fall down. Then they'd do it all again." Kickoffs were especially exotic to this particular observer. "One lot would charge at the other as though they were trying to get in a pub door at 5 o'clock."

On Sundays it was often difficult to find anything to do, since movie theaters and most other places of business were, by law, closed. Among the Americans, it was said that Melbourne on a Sunday was just like a New York cemetery except that it was half the size and twice as dead. Soldiers simply wandered the Sunday streets of Australia's cities looking for something, anything, to do, an uneasy situation ripe for trouble. American and Australian military authorities lobbied intensely for revision of the laws, or at the least to make sure that movie theaters were open. Australian clergymen, concerned for traditional piety, were fiercely opposed to any change, as were union leaders who feared the exploitation of workers forced to work on a traditional day of rest. Gradually the religious and labor edifice gave way to the expedience of commerce and leisure as some movie theaters and restaurants opened on Sundays, though never quite enough to quell the throngs of entertainment-hungry soldiers.[5]

★

By far the favorite American pastime was the pursuit of liquor and women. Off-duty soldiers converged on pubs, bars, and nightclubs in locustlike numbers. At times, proprietors defied the law and stayed open past regular closing hours to keep serving the thirsty customers. "Bars were filled to capacity," one soldier later wrote. "The Australians sipping their beer and the Yanks gulping their scotch and beer." The majority of the GIs behaved well and held their liquor appropriately. Indeed, they soon earned a reputation for overly solicitous politeness of the sort that was unusual in Australia (some Diggers said they had never heard "please" and "thank you" so much). With encouragement from local friends, Yanks engraved their names or initials on the ceiling or walls of many pubs.

In time-honored military tradition, though, some men did binge on beer, hard liquor, or wine. Chilled beer was rare in Australia, so the Americans had to learn to drink brew served at room temperature. "I think you got drunk faster on that warm beer," one soldier claimed. Much to the chagrin of many Aussies, particularly clergymen, politicians, and other assorted pillars of the continental community, the sight of pickled soldiers swaying merrily along streets, singing unmelodiously off-key, or passing out in public parks became more common. The combination of young men and alcohol invited mishaps. PFC Douglas and a drunken buddy couldn't find a seat on a base-bound train one night, but they managed to clamber aboard a flatcar carrying fuel drums to a nearby airfield. The train swayed to and fro during the entire journey, nearly pitching them off the flatcar. Douglas's buddy was so intoxicated he would not even try to hang on, forcing Douglas to keep a firm grip on him. "I had to keep grabbing him because he wouldn't hold on. I was frozen, filthy and mad as hell when we got off that train." Alcohol-related misadventures and injuries were chronic. At the Army's Base Section 3 in Brisbane, about one-third of soldiers arrested for infractions were intoxicated. In one rifle company alone, a soldier fell from his hotel bed, hit his head on a china bowl, shattered it, and suffered a deep cut to his cheek; another man jumped a four-foot wall and badly sprained his ankle but did not know it until the following morning when he sobered up; several others wandered drunkenly into rough neighborhoods and were robbed or beaten up; other unwitting drunks were enticed into cabs by cross-dressing men who promptly robbed them.[6]

Whether drunk or sober, most American soldiers could fairly easily distinguish between the sight of men and women. The arrival of love-starved—and sex-obsessed—young Yanks in the hundreds of thousands was a lightning-bolt sexual event for Australian women. Their arrival signaled an odd dichotomy. A traditionally chaste, isolated society was now absorbing newcomers who came from a culture that was steeped in both puritanical and permissive views of sex. In both countries, most hoteliers would not knowingly rent rooms to unmarried couples; the idea of couples living together before marriage was unheard of, at least in polite circles. At the same time, images of bathing beauties and sexually edgy Hollywood storylines dominated American popular culture. The typical GI in Australia seemed far more influenced by permissive, rather than austere, values.

As was the case in Britain and so many other places around the globe during World War II, American soldiers were tremendously appealing to local women. The Americans were well paid. They were generally young, healthy, and well-fed. They had access to candy, cigarettes, chewing gum, and a host of other goodies. They wore nice uniforms, and with their distinctly American ways of speech and comportment, they oozed a sort of exotic, solicitous Hollywood glamour. "All Americans were deemed to be rich and great lovers," one of the soldiers recalled after the war. "This illusion was further created because American manners, of the time, insisted we hold the chair for a lady as she sat down, hold the door for her as she entered, walk on the outside of the sidewalk, 'please and thank you' for everything." The effect on Australian women was almost magical, especially since Australian men did not have a reputation for exhibiting such manners or focusing their attention so intensely on the opposite sex. A common saying of the time held that "Australians are interested in sexual intercourse, not in the least in social intercourse." The Americans were greatly interested in both; for them the latter activity often led to the former. "When they escorted a girl to a function they stayed with her and made her feel she was really something," Margaret Scott, an Aussie, asserted. "Our male took you to a social gathering and left you amongst other women whilst he went to the far end and joined his friends and swilled beer." Another observer noted that the GIs "have the gift of making the girls they escort feel like the finest ladies in the land." In general, the Americans seemed more concerned with chasing girls than were their Digger buddies. One Yank, while discussing wartime rationing in a letter home, concluded pithily, "Just so they don't ration GIRLS, we can get along."

The Americans also had an advantage of proximity. Military-aged Australian men, like their British cousins, were often stationed outside their own country or, if in Australia, away from their women, many of whom were in uniform themselves, worked in war industries, or were otherwise engaged in some contact with the Americans. The Yanks were smitten, almost to the point of obsession, with the sheilas. "Australian girls as a rule are nice looking and are built just right," PFC L. K. Peacock wrote admiringly to a friend. "Very few of them wear stockings. They are very sociable but are easy to offend. They like our cigarettes." In one letter home, Sergeant Paul Kinder gushed, "They go in for tennis, riding and cycling much more than does a Yank, but they like to dance, see American pictures, swim, and converse. They do not go in for bridge etc. as much as American girls, and their tastes and ideas concerning clothes are more conservative. They are nice, and, I believe, healthier than the average American girls."

For all their manners, the Yanks tended to be more forward, more experienced, and less inhibited than the Diggers. Many had little compunction about stealing the girls of their allies. This aggressiveness was especially true for combat troops who were training hard to fight the Japanese and who wondered if they would even live to celebrate another birthday. "I didn't know if I would ever see her again," Sergeant Clarence Jungwirth wrote of his Australian girlfriend. "It looked as if the war was going to drag on for several years, and I really thought I wouldn't survive." Like Jungwirth, many lived for the moment. The sight of soldiers walking hand in hand with their dates, hugging, kissing, and having intimate conversations became all too common in a country where such public displays of affection had previously been taboo. Occasionally, an urban passerby might even spot a Yank and his girlfriend having sex in a park or some other semi-secluded spot. Romances blossomed anywhere and everywhere, from churches to bars to sports venues and cocktail parties. Date-hunting Americans were relentless and ubiquitous, sometimes to the point of overkill. Members of the Women's National Emergency Legion grew so weary of Americans calling their motor pool for dates that they finally told solicitors they would hook them up with a luscious redhead and a brown-eyed beauty. When the Americans showed up, they found a brown-eyed Great Dane and a red Irish setter waiting for them.

Local officials, business owners, and American military authorities tried hard to keep the dating scene under control. House rules at Lennon's Hotel stipulated that no outsiders, especially women, were allowed in after 6:00 P.M. Predictably, a stampede of partygoers made sure to get to the hotel by five forty-five each evening. "There was no rule against leaving the hotel when you wanted," correspondent Lardner explained sagely. Heavily chaperoned dances and parties were common. In one typical instance, soldiers of E Company, 163rd Infantry Regiment hosted an elaborately planned Saturday-evening bash at the mess hall of their camp in Rock-hampton. They arranged with the American and Australian Red Cross to bus in 165 local girls and their "hostesses." To prepare for the big night, soldiers cleared the hall of tables and replaced them with benches where the women could rest between dances. The room was decorated with color-ful paper and red, white, and blue lights. The latrine was thoroughly fumi-gated, vigorously scrubbed, and adorned with quality toilet paper, soap, towels, and a nice mirror. The soldiers sprung for twenty cases of Coke, tea, and coffee, augmented by a nice cold-cut spread with butter, pickles, and tomatoes. On the appointed—and heavily anticipated—evening, the women arrived and mixed with the soldiers for a night of revelry, all under the watchful eyes of chaperones and officers. The unit band played without interruption. "There were red heads, blondes, brunettes and everything a 'Yank' could have wished for," the company historian enthused. "As time went on, the music became sweeter and we danced to our hearts content, every minute bringing us back to the memories of old." At the end of the evening, the women were escorted by the Red Cross hostesses and some lucky soldiers back to their buses. "As they rode away, the lights faded out into the night like a dream."

Besides staying on good terms with chaperones, savvy soldiers learned to ingratiate themselves with the families of local women. Parents were naturally apprehensive about their daughters cavorting with foreigners who might woo them enough to take them away to America or perhaps just use them to satisfy their own desires. One Melbourne father threat-ened to whip his daughter if she dated a Yank. Others commonly told their kids that "nice girls don't go out with Americans." A popular joke said that in China the custom was to throw baby girls to sharks, while in Australia they were allowed to reach the age of eighteen, only to be thrown to the Yanks. When an American actually met parents and other family mem-bers, their fears were usually assuaged. "Mum wasn't very keen on my go-ing out with an 'American' at first," Joan Staines later wrote, "but as soon as she met [him], she liked him."

Often, close relationships developed between GIs and family members, a nice tonic for the homesick Americans. Sergeant Jungwirth even stayed with his girlfriend Valda's aunt while he was on a furlough. Once the mother of Sergeant Frank Kunz's girlfriend Mavis Haddock met him, she practically adopted him as one of her own, inviting him to play tennis and fixing chicken dinners for him. In his recollection, the relationship "was like my family and I can never thank them enough for treating me as such." Master Sergeant Rogers found acceptance from his girlfriend Nancy's Melbourne family when the local paper carried a photograph of MacArthur alongside the men who had escaped from the Philippines. "My picture was included. Nancy and her parents were impressed." The Australian government and American military bureaucracy tried hard to discourage marriages by requiring reams of paperwork, long waiting periods, and approval from many layers of authority. Under the circumstances, though, marriages were inevitable. More than fifteen thousand Australian women wed GIs in the course of the war, usually in quickie ceremonies. A few Australian men even married US Army nurses and other servicewomen. Rogers, who was obviously close to the seat of power and able to manipulate the bureaucracy, ended up marrying Nancy (a union that turned out to be a mistake, since they divorced shortly after the war). One of the most notable marriages involved a key member of MacArthur's staff, Lieutenant Colonel Huff, MacArthur's aide-de-camp, who wedded Keira Tuson, a publicity officer who worked at a Melbourne shopping center.[7]

The massive international dance of the sexes naturally led to some significant problems. Prostitution grew substantially during the war. Australian law offered a confusing duality in relation to this ancient practice. In most states acts of prostitution and brothels themselves were legal, but public solicitation and practice was illegal. The fleshpots of Albert Street in Brisbane, Kings Cross in Sydney, Ford Street in Townsville, and a host of other spots throughout the country beckoned to GIs who had money in their wallets and hormones raging in their systems. "An army is just a group of boys," one GI observed sagely to his diary, "most with sex on the mind." Some of the hookers actually were underage. Australian police and American MPs regularly found thirteen- and fourteen-year-old girls in bed with soldiers. One underage teen was even found with an unnamed full colonel.

Soldiers typically paid between two and ten pounds per encounter. During boom times, women could make as much as one hundred pounds per week. Elite ladies of the evening could make even more. The director general of health in Queensland identified one woman who earned the princely sum of about four thousand pounds in one year. Townsville, in the northeastern part of the country, was especially rough. In contrast with the relatively secure population centers of southern Australia, the city was on a war footing, with trenches, antiaircraft positions, blackout restrictions, and plenty of soldiers, many of whom viewed Townsville as an anything-goes type of place suitable mainly for getting roaring drunk and pursuing a good time before going into ground combat or facing Japanese bombing raids. Local police were not inclined to shut down the brothels that sprung up to service the demand. Soldiers of the 91st Engineer Battalion took frequent breaks from building airfields to patronize a nearby whorehouse. "The place did a tremendous volume of business and proved so satisfactory that such an arrangement might contribute to the efficiency of the fighting forces if made available to all," the unit historian opined. Malicious false rumors soon spread among the population that Women's Auxiliary Australian Air Force (WAAAF) personnel were among the prostitutes. It was said that dozens of pregnant WAAAFs were trundled aboard southbound trains labeled "Return When Empty." The mere existence of such brazen falsehoods said much about the gender mores and tensions of the time.

The demand for sex was such and the town's tropical climate warm enough that professionals frequently plied their trade outdoors, in full view of Australian civilians, leading to shock and dismay. "Things that can be seen around the city of Townsville are more than disgusting," a local member of Parliament wrote disapprovingly. Most common, in Townsville and other places, the liaisons went on discreetly, inside hotels and illicit houses of ill repute, the identity and locations of which were usually known to military and civil authorities. In one typical example, the lobby of Sydney's Australia hotel was nicknamed the "Pit of Passion" during the war. Captain Sauve, a SWPA intelligence officer, even found a way to utilize the popularity of hookers for his own purposes. He employed several women, whom he patronizingly referred to as "little girls," to report to him about any military secrets spilled by their johns in pillow talk. "They would pick up young officers, then later would send in their reports of what the men had told them about military operations." Much to his concern, Sauve found that most of the officers were frighteningly loose-lipped. When General MacArthur found out how Sauve was gathering his information, he "took a dim view," so Sauve put a stop to the practice. "Even so, the desired effect had been achieved," Sauve claimed, "since it was noised about among the young officers that it was unwise to discuss military operations—even in bed."

Some committed greater crimes than blabbing to hookers. With hundreds of thousands of young Americans passing through or living in the country, the laws of probability practically guaranteed that some would run afoul of the law. Soldiers were occasionally involved in corruption and black marketeering, selling tires, fuel, cigarettes, and other items. In some instances they lived on these illegal earnings while they went absent without leave (AWOL) and attempted to blend into Australian society. On one day alone in April 1943, military police sealed off Melbourne and rounded up seventy-five soldiers and Marines who were listed as AWOL by their units. Traffic offenses were common, probably because many of the Americans had difficulty adjusting to driving on the left side of the road. At times this confusion led to tragedy, as in the case of Private Hugh Copeland, who was court-martialed and sentenced to six years hard labor for slamming his truck into a tram, killing four people. Some of the accidents came from speeding and sheer reckless driving. One Australian man recalled seeing American drivers "run women on bicycles off the road into the gutter just for fun." The Army attempted to impose a twenty-five-mile-per hour speed limit on its drivers, but the limit was as hard to enforce for MPs in military life as for civilian police on US roads. There were armed robberies, assaults, bizarre crime sprees involving shakedowns and scams. There were also rapes. As early as May 1942, three cases were already pending. Of fourteen men charged with rape in Queensland during the first year of the US presence, eleven were Americans, one of whom was charged with robbing and raping an eighty-four-year-old Brisbane woman. Sensitive to maintaining good relations with the hosts, the Army made a point of conducting transparent court-martial proceedings and severely punishing the guilty parties with either a life sentence or execution. Though rare, there were some GI murders, too. Private Avelino Fernandez, a thirty-year-old paratrooper, was convicted of beating and kicking Doris Roberts to death in a Brisbane alley during a postcoital rage. The trigger for his frenzy was apparently her request to be paid for the sex. "When she asked me for money, believe me I knocked her down cold," he admitted to Army investigators. "When she got up I knocked her down again. I punched her in the stomach, and I kicked her when she was on the ground. I would do it again. Believe me I was really mad. That dame made me savage." Shortly after his conviction, he was hanged.

The most infamous and frightening case involved a serial killer who preyed on Melbourne women during a sixteen-day whirlwind in May 1942 that set the city deeply on edge. On May 3, the body of Mrs. Ivy Violet McLeod was found in Albert Park; six days later Mrs. Pauline Thompson, wife of a police constable, was found dead on the steps of her apartment; finally the body of Gladys Hosking was found near Camp Pell, the base of the Army's 52nd Signal Battalion. All three women had been strangled to death and their bodies left partially unclothed, though not sexually assaulted. McLeod and Hosking were both forty; Thompson was thirty-one. After an intensive investigation, the homicide squad of the Victoria Police, on the basis of civilian and military witness statements and other damning evidence, apprehended Private Edward Leonski, a twenty-four-year-old member of the 52nd. Leonski was a baby-faced but troubled former grocery clerk from New Jersey who already had a history of problems with drinking and violence toward women. Before the unit shipped out to Australia, he had apparently attempted to strangle a woman, but nothing came of the incident. Once, at Camp Pell, he began to drink heavily and allegedly attempted to rape a woman. Even though he was confined to the stockade for thirty days, no one seems to have considered sending him home or conducting a psychological evaluation. Upon release he embarked on his climactic killing spree, seemingly for pathological reasons he himself could not understand. At one point in May, his unit buddies found him in tears. "Have you ever heard of a werewolf?" he asked one of them. "Ever heard of Dr. Jekyll and Mr. Hyde? I'm like that. I'm two personalities."

Leonski's method was to approach his victim politely in the dark of night, ask for directions, and then attack her. Once in the custody of the Australian police, he admitted to the murders and confessed to three other unsuccessful attempts. When they asked him why he did it, he replied, "I don't know." He later described assaulting Hosking. "She had a lovely voice. I wanted that voice. I grabbed her by the throat. She did not make a sound. She was so soft. I thought, 'I must try to stop that sound.' So I tried to pull her dress over her head. I thought, 'What have I done?' I got her to a fence and pushed her underneath and then climbed over. I pulled her by the armpits and carried her a short distance and fell in the mud. She made funny noises—a sort of gurgling sound."

Due to the horrifying, predatory nature of the crimes, and the major public attention afforded them in media coverage, Prime Minister Curtin came under strong pressure to try Leonski in Australian courts. Instead, he agreed to turn him over to American military authority. A trio of psychiatrists, two American and one Australian, examined Leonski over a thirty-day period and found him sane and fit for trial. According to a staff document from MacArthur's headquarters, "due to scandalous nature of evidence and expected testimony, as well as intense interest displayed by Australian authorities and citizens," the Americans agreed to allow twenty handpicked members of the Australian government and media to witness the proceedings. Newspapers and other media outlets covered the trial in depth. The jury consisted of four colonels, three lieutenant colonels, a major, a captain, and two lieutenants. The presiding judge was Major Hayford Enwall, a former federal judge in Florida. Colonel George Welch, a member of the New York bar, was the prosecutor, and Lieutenant Colonel Spencer Eddy, a judge from New York, defended Leonski. Eddy tried to argue that Leonski's intoxicated state during the crimes mitigated full responsibility, a strategy that fell flat. Leonski was found guilty, and, on November 9, he was executed by hanging at Pentridge Prison (the only foreigner ever put to death in this fashion on Australian soil). His remains were temporarily interred at several cemeteries in Australia before being transported for permanent interment at the Schofield Barracks post cemetery on Oahu.[8]

★

Not surprisingly, given all the sexual activity, illicit and otherwise, the Army soon developed a significant venereal disease problem. In late 1942, 9 percent of the patients admitted to the 118th General Hospital in Sydney were fresh gonorrhea cases. That same year, the reported rate of sexually transmitted diseases was 45.8 per 1,000 soldiers per annum, a high point for the whole war. "An unusually high percentage of these cases were resistant to sulfa drug therapy," Major James Joelson, a urologist in the Melbourne-based 4th General Hospital commented. Only later in the war was penicillin available to treat the afflicted. In the meantime, treatment was restricted to the sulfa drugs and, for more resistant cases, inducement of fever by a specially designed therapy machine. On average, it took the medics thirty days of hospitalization to treat a gonorrhea case and twenty-three days for a syphilis case. In addition to treating combat-wounded, especially as the air war and fighting in New Guinea heated up that year, medics were dealing with the usual range of issues that accompany a large conglomeration of men. Some 201 enlisted men were sent home with dishonorable discharges and twenty-one officers asked to resign for homosexual activity. More seriously, the surgeon reported fifty-four deaths from non-VD diseases and 303 deaths by accident that year. The causes ranged from airplane crashes to traffic accidents to drownings to burns to negligent discharge of firearms to falls to electrocutions and even two unlucky GIs who were killed "by animals." Homicides accounted for four more deaths; suicides, mostly by firearms, for another twenty-four. There were so many fatalities that some quartermasters who had focused their efforts on providing the necessities of living for the big American buildup now had to turn their attention to arranging proper burial for the dead. Eventually they established a US cemetery in each base section, where remains were interred for the duration. With so many afflictions to treat, the theater's chief surgeon looked into saving precious bed space by setting up special hospitals just for venereal disease patients, but there is no evidence that the idea ever caught on. "The problem of venereal disease control in this area is rendered quite difficult due to the distribution of troops over a large area, and in many instances, in small units," he wrote in an annual report.

The medical experts and unit commanders all understood that the best way to deal with venereal disease was through prevention rather than cure. Graphic prevention films, pamphlets, and lectures were common to the point of suffocation. The Army set up prophylactic stations near brothels and anywhere else soldiers and women mixed together. This was in addition to those established by the Australian military. GIs and Aussies alike used each other's stations. On the Australian civil side, government officials, in hopes of encouraging people to seek treatment, attempted to downplay the taboo of promiscuity and dirtiness associated with the disease. In Queensland, they made it known that 80 percent of those who tested positive were actually "quite nice girls who had been indiscreet." The government had the power to force women to take VD tests, receive treatment, and disclose the identity of their partners. Soldiers who contracted the disease could also be compelled to inform their superiors where and from whom they were likely to have gotten it. By late 1944, between 50 and 90 percent of these contacts were identified, apprehended, and treated.

Disease rates declined but the problem never went away, largely because of men visiting the country on brief furloughs. Rates still hovered between seven and thirteen soldiers per one thousand per annum. "Approximately 50% of the new cases reported in this period occurred in men on furlough," a theater-wide investigation reported. The report heaped most of the blame on African-American soldiers for the VD outbreak. "Despite the fact that negroes constituted, on average, only 6% of the total number of men on furlough, they contributed 40% to 60% of the cases among this group," the author wrote. The theater surgeon's report claimed that "although the coloured troops make up approximately 7% of the number of troops in the area, they contributed about 25% of the venereal disease cases reported." In Sydney, African-Americans comprised 15 percent of the American-troop presence but accounted for 61 percent of the cases. Typical of the time, the authors of these reports offered no other context or explanations for these high rates. Influenced by such damning numbers, some American and Australian whites perceived black soldiers as different in their sexual habits, less responsible, less clean, perhaps even more predatory. One Australian politician made a point of complaining to Prime Minister Curtin about the use of local girls "to satisfy the lust of American negroes."[9]

These perceptions and concerns hinted at the larger topic of race, one of the thorniest issues confronting the two allies during the American presence in Australia. Racial inequality was a fundamental precept of both countries. One of the profound absurdities of the Second World War was that these Allied nations, dedicated on paper to the dignity and equality of humanity, and fighting hard against homicidally racist fascist regimes, themselves embraced bigoted and unjust policies of the sort that would have made their social Darwinist enemies stand up and cheer. The US Army was heavily segregated on the basis of race. The vast majority of African-American soldiers served in all-black noncombat units, often under the command of white officers, a practice that represented a military legacy of institutional racial inequality.

The White Australia policy was a prime example of blatant racism among the Aussies. Prevalent since the establishment of the commonwealth in 1901, it was designed to make sure the country remained homogenous and white. Except for dark-skinned Aborigines, who were generally ignored or exploited, Australia was an entirely white country, and some Australians aimed to keep it that way. Initially, Australian government officials hoped that the Americans would not send any African-American soldiers to the continent. When in early 1942 it became clear that this was a vain hope, the Australian government tried at first to prevent the arrival of black soldiers. "We are not prepared to agree to proposal that US troops to be despatched [sic] to Australia should be coloured," the minister of external affairs cabled the Australian embassy in Washington. The realities of global warfare soon dictated otherwise. With Allied resources stretched thin, the Australians were fortunate to receive whatever help the Americans could give them. Trained troops were in short enough supply that the Army could ill afford to exclude African-American soldiers from Australia-bound convoys. Moreover, the Army's own racist segregation policies tended to create an intrinsic demand for black military manpower in Australia. Most African-American soldiers in World War II were assigned to all-black service or labor units, and because such support outfits were badly needed to buttress the huge Allied logistical effort in the Southwest Pacific theater, there was soon an irresistible momentum to the introduction of black troops in Australia. The War Cabinet backpedaled from the government's initial hard-line position and indicated that black soldiers would be welcome at Australian ports as long as they were on the way to somewhere else. This too was untenable. At last, as the first substantial group of African-American troops arrived in Melbourne in late January, the government relented and agreed to make an exception to the White Australia policy as long as the black GIs did not stay permanently and provided "that the USA authorities . . . will have regard to Australian susceptibilities in the numbers they decide to despatch [sic]." In other words, it was okay for black soldiers to come to Australia as long as they remained in the clear minority. This actually dovetailed with the Army's own policies. In the meantime, when the black soldiers arrived at Melbourne, they were subjected to the indignity of initially being denied entry by customs officials while the government sorted out the new policy.

Though not exactly a civil rights crusader, General MacArthur tended to be fair-minded in relation to race. He pledged to take whatever steps he could to incorporate black soldiers smoothly into his command and prevent problems with the hosts. "I will do everything possible to prevent friction or resentment on the part of the Australian government and people at the presence of American colored troops," he wrote to General Marshall. By the end of March there were more than six thousand black soldiers in Australia; at the end of 1942, the number had grown to more than seven thousand. By design, most were assigned to remote areas to build airfields and roads (this was true for the majority of white soldiers as well). Though it was more difficult for black soldiers to get passes for leave in the cities, opportunities were still relatively forthcoming. Apocryphal stories, probably disseminated by white soldiers, spread among the locals that black soldiers had tails. A few Australians who had never encountered a black person actually believed such claptrap. One well-meaning but ignorant Melbourne hostess made sure to put pillows on the chairs of her black guests, in hopes of helping them rest their nonexistent tails. Others stared curiously at the backsides of black soldiers as they walked past them.

Since Australia was almost entirely white, it had no infrastructure to separate the races. Unlike some parts of America, there were no "whites only" and "colored" drinking fountains, restaurants, bars, latrines, and hotels. African-American soldiers could frequent most any local establishment, and surprisingly for a country with a whites-only policy, they encountered few difficulties with the Australians. "It wasn't as big a problem as I thought it would be," recalled Private Charles Gamble, a black soldier. "They didn't resent the blacks. The Australian women didn't resent the blacks." Another soldier commented that "everything was just the opposite to which I expected to find." As with other Americans, the Aussies tended toward friendliness. Black soldiers were often welcomed by locals into dance halls, private homes, pubs, and restaurants.

Most of the racial troubles occurred not with the hosts but among the Americans themselves and usually over the issues that tended to cause violence or tension back home in America—segregation, inequality, and interracial dating. In the Townsville area, when a black unit (probably the 96th Engineers) moved into a camp near PFC Douglas's 46th Engineer Construction Battalion, trouble began immediately. "Every time one went to town they got into a fight. We resented their presence because we had been the only troops around there until then and we had things all our own way. We were big shots until then." On one particularly tense evening, about one hundred black soldiers were involved in a fight with an unrecorded number of white soldiers. White troops, armed with loaded, bayonet-laden rifles, rounded them up. When Captain Samuelson, a white company commander in the 96th, showed up to defuse the situation and retrieve his men, a white corporal pointed a loaded rifle at him. Fortunately no one was hurt. "It is a dirty shame the way white American soldiers treat our boys," Samuelson, a Southerner and civil engineering graduate of Louisiana State University, told his diary shortly after the incident. "The Australians are wonderfully tolerant, but the Americans, especially the Southern boys, are a problem." Though men from both groups were probably responsible for the fight, the town was soon off-limits only to the soldiers of the 96th. In hopes of providing some entertainment for them, Samuelson and other officers organized a movie night at their own camp, with beer for sale. According to him, "it was a horrible flop." There was only enough beer for one bottle per man, and very few soldiers even had enough money to purchase that much beer. The movie was old and unappealing. Plus the sound was on the fritz. "Even those who had money didn't like this kind of recreation," Samuelson wrote sympathetically. "They want to be free, to be with a woman." Samuelson sympathized with and respected his men. "Before I die I must help stamp out this crazy idea that the white man has about his superiority over the colored man," he once told his diary.

In a surprisingly far-sighted pamphlet designed to prepare white officers to lead black troops, the Army urged them to avoid telling racial jokes and referring to their men with such offensive terms as "boy, darky, uncle, nigra," and, the most vile word of all, "nigger." The pamphlet strongly advised using the most socially acceptable terms of the day, "Colored and Negro are the only words which should distinguish colored soldiers from white." But many of the white commanders were not as decent as men like Samuelson. They completely ignored these instructions. Some of these officers were poorly motivated second-raters with little leadership ability who occupied their jobs because the Army bureaucracy tended to prioritize the assignment of higher quality commissioned men to white combat units and shunt the leftovers into black outfits. Worse than this, some of the white officers were avowed racists who had nothing but contempt for their soldiers. "You have to treat these men just like children," one of them told an Army researcher in early 1943. The phrase "treating them 'like children'" in reality meant handling them like second-class citizens at the bottom of the Jim Crow pile. In such situations, the hatred and resentment of the men sometimes boiled over into outright violence. In one especially disturbing incident, several hundred African-American soldiers of the 96th rioted in response to continuous abuse by a pair of hated officers (there were also rumors that an officer had struck a soldier and even stories that one had killed a soldier). The men fired more than seven hundred rounds at officer tents. One targeted captain survived only because he managed to crawl into a nearby ditch and hide until the shooting abated. Nearby Australian infantry units were alerted to set up roadblocks and cordon off the area. Unconfirmed reports claimed that one man was killed and several others seriously injured before the violence ran its course. Throughout the country, black and white military policemen adopted the practice of patrolling together because on their own they might be vulnerable to attack from one group or the other—an ironic case of forced desegregation.

When off-duty black soldiers did get to experience the cities, too often it was not on equal terms. Though Australian bartenders, restaurateurs, hoteliers, shopkeepers, and other business owners usually were inclined to serve everyone without regard to color, the edifice of Jim Crow exclusion and segregation solidified as the American presence grew. Occasionally, when racist white soldiers saw Australians interacting as equals with African-Americans, they would take the Aussies aside for a lecture on the supposed proper place of the races. "Don't encourage the American Negroes in your house," one of them advised, "because give them an inch and they'll take a mile." An Australian soldier who found himself on the receiving end of such an admonition later told his diary, "Evidently slavery is not dead." The disapproval was especially true for Australian women who dated African-American soldiers. In the recollection of one soldier, many white military personnel "took exception to Australian girls walking the streets with Negro escorts, drinking with them in hotel lounges, eating with them in restaurants and even taking them into their homes for dinner."

At times, some especially virulent racists tried to restore their version of order. An ugly incident in Sydney prompted H. B. Chandler, an Australian trade unionist, to apprise MacArthur himself of the circumstances. Chandler conveyed great concerns about "the manner in which coloured American troops are being treated by a certain section of the white American troops and officers." According to Chandler, trouble began when a group of Southern white soldiers decided to hunt down black troops and remove them from the city. "An Army truck with Negroes riding on it was stopped and the troops were ordered out of the truck, they were lined up in public and called all sorts of names. Consequently a fight developed after which the Negroes were gathered into the truck and taken back to their camp." The self-appointed posse enforced a no-go zone for blacks in many of the city's most desirable haunts, including the dance hall at Luna Park and the Hotel Metropole. In a carefully worded reply, MacArthur pled ignorance of the incident and wrote disingenuously, "I wish to assure you . . . that in the American Army, and for that matter, in the American Government, there is absolutely no official discrimination against colored troops." The general ventured the unfounded opinion that the friction probably resulted from "individual deportment and incidents of conduct" rather than race. But he assured Chandler that, even if race had caused the clash, it was only an isolated incident, not an indicator of anything systemic. "You may rest completely assured that so far as I am concerned there is no differentiation whatsoever in the treatment of soldiers. Race and color have no influence."

However true this might have been of MacArthur personally, it was not the case for all too many white soldiers under his command, and he seemed unable, or unwilling, to stop them from discriminating against their black countrymen. A suffocating veil of segregation descended over many of the spots where off-duty soldiers congregated, including American Red Cross servicemen's clubs, Sydney dance halls, such as the Trocadero and Ziegfeld's cabaret nightclub, Townsville hotels, innumerable restaurants, and even the most popular skating rink in Brisbane. Brothels were largely segregated as well. Cathouses for African-Americans were more likely to be raided, shut down by MPs, or remain unsupervised altogether (perhaps this played some role in the higher VD rate among black soldiers). Frequently, black soldiers were invited to dances by locals only to be forcibly disinvited by their white comrades or refused entry by MPs. At times, fights broke out over this rude treatment or when white soldiers tried to force black GIs out of a bar or café. Black officers and war correspondents were routinely excluded from officers' clubs. Separate soldier clubs established for black troops were invariably not as nicely furnished or were located in unappealing areas. Sometimes they were even shut down or neglected altogether by Army authorities.

In all likelihood, the reason this blatantly unfair situation persisted was that it offered the path of least resistance for those in authority. Blacks accounted for only about 7 to 10 percent of the Army's manpower in Australia (and most other overseas theaters). The sobering reality was that most whites, even those who had no particular dislike for blacks or any personal belief in notions of racial superiority, nonetheless favored segregation, if only to avoid friction. A troubling 1943 Army survey revealed that 88 percent of whites favored the practice of placing African-American men in segregated units; 81 percent thought that separate post exchanges (PXs) were a good idea; 85 percent wanted separate service clubs. Among the black respondents, a substantial minority actually agreed, also probably in hopes of avoiding trouble: 38 percent wanted to serve in segregated outfits; 40 percent wanted their own PX, and 48 percent preferred the idea of separate soldier clubs. Given these attitudes, white commanders who were focused on the daunting task of winning a long, bloody war were loath to risk internal strife by rocking the racial boat.[10]

As much or more than race relations, they were concerned with maintaining good relationships with the Australians. By and large, the two peoples got along very well. But as the American presence grew and the wartime months unfolded, there was nonetheless some discord, most commonly in the form of drunken fights between soldiers. Given the combination of alcohol, young men, and war, such fracases were inevitable and probably not an indication of any deep problems. Aussies did, though, resent the higher pay and loftier living standards of the average American soldier. "Our army and its standards of pay, food, clothing and living is playing havoc . . . down here," one American soldier wrote to a friend. "The Australian army is poorly paid, meanly housed and poorly fed and clothed." The perceived wealth of the Yanks fostered an attitude among some Australians that it was okay to scam them, most commonly by overcharging in shops and restaurants, selling them watered-down liquor, or defective souvenirs. A few committed violent crimes against the Americans. There were knifings, assaults, and robberies of every type. One command history commented worriedly on the frequent "ganging up and 'rolling' of lone American soldiers." In Brisbane, a medical corps officer was attacked outside a popular hotel and left for dead with a fractured skull. In Melbourne, when three Australian soldiers attacked a group of Americans, a sympathetic crowd gathered and cheered them on, halting traffic and all police attempts to defuse the altercation. "Onlookers shouted and barracked as though at a football match," a local newspaper reported.

Such occasional crimes and fraud led some Americans to feel bitter about the perceived treachery of the ungrateful locals. "When you go out in a street car, go in a restaurant, or any public place, nobody speaks to Americans," one warrant officer wrote angrily to his family. "We are classed as undesirables. Very few Australians like us, [or] have one good word for us. We are overcharged many times, and nasty remarks are made behind our backs. But let me tell you, if it wouldn't have been for us, there would have been no Australia." In some instances, the two groups seemed to go out of their way to bicker. Some movie theaters played "God Save the King," the anthem of the British empire, before starting the show. At one cinema, some of the Americans took to sitting during the anthem and booing the king. "That led to some pretty good fights between the Aussies and the GIs," one of the Americans later wrote. The brawls would delay the start of the picture anywhere from ten to thirty minutes until order could be restored. Eventually the theater owner established a policy of playing both the British and American anthems before the film. The Diggers stood up for "God Save the King" and then sat down while the Americans stood for "The Star-Spangled Banner."

Without a doubt, the most common point of conflict revolved around women. The tremendous attraction local women felt for Americans naturally led to righteous anger against the Yanks among many Australian men, military or otherwise. "Women are the great cause of hard feelings against us," Sergeant John Montero wrote to a friend. Sad-sack stories of Aussie veterans returning home from North Africa or other combat zones only to find that their girls had abandoned them for an American were so frequent as to become routine. "And when you returned what did you find?" one Australian soldier wrote in a bitter poetic verse. "Just a U.S. guy has left you behind; He's taken your girl—or as he says 'dame.'" Another popular ditty groaned,

> When they send the last Yank home;
> How sorry our women will be;
> Back on six bob a day, the AIF [Australian Imperial Force] pay;
> With no flats or apartments free;
> Once again they'll be alone;
> Women no Aussie will own;
> All they'll have is their clothes;
> And kids who speak through their nose;
> When they send the last Yank home.

The Americans responded with a frequent, taunting chant, "We've got your girls! Got your beer!" A chain of newspapers owned by Sir Keith Murdoch, father of latter-year media magnate Rupert Murdoch, earned a reputation among the Yanks as relentlessly anti-American. *Truth*, a particularly

brassy Melbourne tabloid, often published lurid tales of GI rapes of innocent Australian girls and seduction of married women. On occasion, Australian soldiers vented their frustration over such tales with violence. Small
groups of Diggers roamed around some of the cities, beating up any American soldiers whom they saw dating local girls. In a few instances, they
then turned their scorn on those girls, who, according to one American
officer, "are being insulted and slapped around if they are seen with the
Americans." Spurned Aussie soldiers sometimes picked fights with any GI
in sight, holding their random victims accountable for the crimes of their
countrymen. An American soldier was even shot and killed one morning
as he emerged from the house of a married woman.

The most extreme instance of friction between the Americans and their
hosts happened in the crowded streets of the central business district in
Brisbane on November 26–27, 1942. It began as a simple altercation between an intoxicated American private, his three half-lit Australian soldier
buddies, and an American MP, Private Anthony O'Sullivan. When
O'Sullivan impatiently challenged the private to produce his pass and
threatened him with a baton, the Australians went after the MP. More
Australian soldiers and American MPs were drawn into the melee, and it
soon spread to the street in front of a nearby building housing the American PX canteen. Here the trouble morphed from an anti-MP brawl to an
anti-American riot. For months local resentment had been brewing over
the higher pay and lifestyle of American soldiers. The PX building, generally off-limits to Australians, seemed to symbolize this imbalance. A crowd
of Australians, civilian and military, gathered and began to throw rocks,
bottles, and sticks at the PX building. Someone even hurled a street sign
through the window. Local police and American MPs attempted to
quell the disturbance (there were reports that some Australian MPs removed their armbands and joined in the melee). The Brisbane fire brigade
tried to help but refused a request from the police to turn high-pressure
water hoses on the crowd. According to one American source, the fire hose
"could easily have dispersed the crowd." Alas, it was not to be. In addition
to the attacks on the PX, the nearby American Red Cross canteen was soon
also under siege. Random fights raged on adjacent streets.

At the PX building, American MPs were concerned that the crowd
might overrun them and loot the PX. Several of the MPs, including Private
Norbert Grant, were armed with 12-gauge shotguns. As he attempted to

keep people away from the building, he was waylaid by several Australians who grabbed for the gun. He opened fire. Private Edward Webster, a soldier from an Australian antitank unit, took a full blast in the chest and was killed instantly. Grant fired two more shots, wounding five other Aussie soldiers and two civilians. The tragic and unnecessary death of Webster inflamed an already troubling situation. The details of his demise were distorted by some into evidence of a larger American disregard for Australian lives. Rumors swept through the city of tommy gun-wielding Americans opening fire with impunity at Australian crowds. Stoked by the violence, the confusion, and the rumors, months of Australian resentment against the well-heeled, Lothario-esque Americans boiled over like an unattended teakettle. The next night, vigilante groups of Australian soldiers prowled downtown Brisbane, hunting for Americans, especially MPs and vulnerable, unarmed individuals. Any American who was unfortunate enough to be cornered by them was savagely beaten and kicked. One US officer was walking to a restaurant with his Australian wife when a crowd noticed them and attacked. "There's a bloody Yank! Kill him! Kick his brains out!" some roared in a frenzy. The woman was twice knocked down and the officer beaten. The couple fled to a nearby pharmacy, where the level-headed owner was kind enough to shelter them from the howling mob.

Another crowd gathered at the AMP Insurance building, the location of MacArthur's headquarters, and shouted abuse meant for the general as armed American guards tensely stood fast. Alas, the general was actually in New Guinea at the time. He never witnessed the locals, some of whom must have cheered him months earlier, turn on him, if only for a night. Twenty-one Americans were injured that evening, eleven seriously enough to be hospitalized. Sixteen Australians were wounded over the two nights. Under the circumstances, it was almost miraculous that no one else was killed. If there was anything positive about what became known as the Battle of Brisbane, it was the fact that it seemed to dissolve much of the tension between the two allies. Moreover, US and Australian authorities were determined to make sure such self-defeating events were kept to a minimum (around this time Melbourne also experienced a brawl of lesser intensity). "Cooperation between the Forces has been greatly improved," claimed a report authored several weeks later by the commander of the Army's Base Section 3 in Brisbane.

In the wake of the troubles, Lieutenant General Sir Iven Mackay, the heavily combat-experienced commander of the Australian 2nd Army, made it clear in a thoughtful speech to officers of the Australian 9th Infantry Brigade that interallied fighting was unacceptable and that Yanks and Diggers were natural friends. "Forewarned is forearmed, so we should be able to settle just what to do to prevent the slightest possibility of such disturbances. The fact is that soldiers should behave better than ordinary citizens, and this idea should be impressed upon them by their officers. We must grow tolerant. We must not lose our sense of perspective nor our sense of humor." The vast majority of servicemen, American and Australian, agreed and behaved accordingly. "The Aussies are swell guys and fine soldiers," one American judged in a representative letter home. The prevailing opinion, according to one Digger, was that most problems were caused by "a few loud mouthed idiots on both sides who could not hold their liquor." As the protagonist in an American-produced propaganda film entitled *Australia Is Like This* put it: "We figure the only guys who win a Yank-Aussie row are the Nips." Indeed, the two partners—friends actually—needed each other badly. An arduous job lay ahead for them.[11]

6

Hell

E ven as the Allied war machine slowly, steadily, gained strength, those left behind in the Philippines dealt with the consequences of America's most traumatic initial military defeat. For the vast majority of prisoners who could not escape to become guerrilla warriors, the sickening reality was captivity of the worst and most degrading sort. It is no exaggeration to say that their lot bore substantial equivalence to that of Hitler's concentration camp victims, at least in terms of starvation, neglect, and disease. Not one of these Allied captives was prepared for, or could scarcely have imagined, the ordeal that now befell them.

Throughout April 1942, the survivors of the Death March staggered into an unfinished prison compound, called O'Donnell, that had originally been designed as a prewar training area for the Philippine Army. "Barracks" consisted of nipa palm and thatch roofs over a skeleton of bamboo poles. Rows of bamboo, secured with rattan cord, provided crude sleeping bays. Floors consisted either of dirt or woven mats. The enclosure spanned some 617 acres of treeless rice paddy and grassland. Rusty strands of barbed wire and a few watchtowers ringed the area. Major General Kawane, whose substandard planning had exacerbated the misery of the Death March, had chosen O'Donnell as a POW compound back in March but had done little since to prepare it for the bedraggled, half-starved new occupants. Some of the buildings were in disrepair, with roofs blown all or partially away. At most, the camp might adequately house thirty thousand prisoners. Instead, it would receive at least twice that many.

As the various groups staggered into the compound, they were searched for weapons and valuables by the Japanese guards. "All remaining personal possessions were confiscated," Colonel Mallonee recalled. "Nail files, nail scissors, razors, blades, matches, pen knives, cigarettes and pipe tobacco were confiscated, as were *all* blankets, shelter halves and raincoats." Word spread quickly to discard any items of Japanese origin, such as money, clothing, equipment, or souvenirs. Anyone found with so much as a yen on him risked immediate execution. Filipinos and Americans were rigidly segregated in different sections of the camp. Otherwise there was little organization, at least initially. Almost every unfortunate man who passed through O'Donnell's gates was subjected to a windy, malevolent "welcome" speech from fifty-one-year-old, mustachioed Captain Yoshio Tsuneyoshi, the commandant. A 1915 graduate of the military academy, Tsuneyoshi was a reservist who had been recalled to active service and shunted into this undesirable job because better officers were needed to lead troops in combat. Tsuneyoshi was a third-rater in every way, an office worker in civilian life whose career amounted to very little. On good days he aspired to mediocrity. His military peers were now full colonels; he was still an overage captain. He had neither the preparation nor the competence for the commandant's job. In the estimation of one superior, Tsuneyoshi was not bright, had "no common sense . . . did not handle matters well," and had "no understanding of the prisoners." The fact that the Japanese assigned such a ne'er-do-well to run the camp spoke volumes as to how little they valued proper treatment for prisoners.

Captain Tsuneyoshi took to addressing each group of newly arrived prisoners. He held forth for as long as two hours while his charges stood at attention underneath the broiling hot sun. When men collapsed of heat prostration or dehydration, their comrades were not allowed to assist them until Tsuneyoshi concluded his speech. Clad in a white sport shirt, baggy shorts, and riding boots, the captain strode back and forth in front of the captives, gesturing wildly with his arms, a vaguely ridiculous figure if not for the seriousness of the situation and the privation he was in a position to unleash. A samurai sword swung ominously on his hip. In one instance, he made a point of sitting down to a protracted breakfast of rice and tea as a group of starving prisoners watched, plaintively waiting for him to finish and speak to them. As these actions indicated, he was the sort of man to take out frustrations over his own personal failures on the prisoners who were now helpless to his whims.

The typical Tsuneyoshi speech, relayed to the prisoners through an interpreter, revealed a small-minded man consumed by hatred and one who was indifferent to notions of humanity: American and British domination of Asia and the Pacific was over, he said. Japan would now reign supreme. The empire's victory was inevitable even if it took one hundred years. "You are cowards and should have committed suicide as any Japanese soldier would do when facing capture," he harangued. "I only regret that I cannot destroy you all, but the spirit of Bushido forbids such practice. It is only due to the generosity of the Japanese that you are alive. The slightest violation of orders will result in execution. I have already shot many Filipinos in the last week for disobedience of orders. You are the eternal enemies of Japan. We will fight you and fight you and fight you for one hundred years! You will pay for the way the Japanese have been treated by Americans. We will never be friends with the piggish Americans. You have no rank. You will wear no insignia, and you will salute all Japanese regardless of rank." To Lieutenant Colonel Miller and thousands of other prisoners, the commandant's tirade was interminable. "I wondered if the savage drivel would never end." Captain Olson mentally labeled it the "God-Damn-You Speech." Tsuneyoshi's malice, combined with his trim mustache, earned him the nickname of "Little Adolf" among the prisoners.[1]

The captain's vitriolic orations were really the least of the prisoner's worries, though. Conditions at O'Donnell were horrible. Olson, who after the war became the leading authority on the camp, dubbed this pestilential hellhole the "Andersonville of the Pacific." Though Allied POWs enjoyed better shelter and more space than had the Union captives of the infamous Civil War prison camp, the comparison was hardly inappropriate. "If the Angel of Death ever had a caldron of victims ready for him, it was in O'Donnell," Captain Weinstein, a physician, later wrote. "Amoebic and bacillary dysentery, beri-beri and malaria ravaged the starved, exhausted, beaten men who lacked food, shelter, clothing, medicine and not infrequently the will to live."

Food consisted mostly of steamed, boiled, or milled rice, a gruelish mix called *lugao*. "[It] was spoiled, half rotted, before the cooks got it," Colonel Mallonee wrote. "The result was a smelly, stinky concoction." To another colonel, Michael Quinn, the rice mixture "had the consistency of target paste and tasted like it." Often, the rice was moldy or laced with worms, weevils, and even pebbles and dust. At times, the ricey mess was augmented by tiny bits of vegetables and fish or camotes, a local sweet potato. Salt was scarce to the point of nonexistence. Captain Poweleit, a physician, estimated that the average man received twenty-four ounces of rice in his mess kit. "Only twelve grams of protein was supplied by this rice," he later estimated. Depending on size, each man required about seventy grams of protein per day. Even with three rice meals a day, the protein intake was insufficient, especially for men already on the verge of starvation. At times, prisoners on work details smuggled back into the camp food donated or sold to them by Filipino civilians. When local Red Cross representatives tried to bring in two truckloads of supplies and an entire complement of medical equipment from a Manila hospital, Captain Tsuneyoshi and his guards turned them away. As this indicated, the starvation level rations were the result of Japanese intentions, not any real shortage. Colonel Charles Lawrence, a quartermaster, made several visits with a Japanese officer to a nearby storage facility. "There were about 25,000 bags of rice piled up in the warehouse and on the ground," he wrote, "and ample stocks of other foods within easy reach." These vast supplies included "large quantities of canned meat and milk and meso (a cheese made from soy beans)."

Even more than starvation, dehydration was a major problem, one that was only made worse by the tropical heat. With the exception of a polluted creek and a few low-yield spigots, O'Donnell had almost no intrinsic water supply. As thousands of new prisoners arrived from the Death March and the camp steadily became overcrowded, the problem grew progressively worse. "The securing of water became the prime concern of everyone . . . from General King down to the lowest privates," Olson wrote. Men stood in long lines, sometimes waiting all day under the unrelenting sun, to fill one canteen from the spigots. "Seems like the only people who weren't in line were those who had already gotten their ration," Sergeant Charles Cook recalled. It was not unusual for prisoners to pass out or simply drop dead as they waited in line. The spigots sometimes emitted gushes of water and other times just a trickle. It was purely luck of the draw. Many prisoners waited for hours only to receive little more than droplets when they got their turn at the faucet. "These piteous dehydrated Americans had swollen tongues that they could hardly retract into their mouths, yet they were forced to sit and wait at one of those half inch water pipes and watch Japanese soldiers taking shower baths and then going off and leaving the water running on to the ground," Captain Tisdelle wrote sadly. As they waited their turn, the captives sometimes socialized or traded rumors. But usually the area around the spigots was silent except for "the constant clinking of cans and canteens as the men formed lines to get water," in the recollection of one survivor. Most never forgot the vaguely melancholy sound, so symbolic as it was of O'Donnell's many horrors.

The single canteen of water had to suffice for each prisoner's daily washing and drinking needs. Most of the prisoners were suffering from dysentery, and yet, in the recollection of one man "there was no water to wash off the fecal matter from the men's bodies." Some opportunistic, and unsavory, men took to selling water for as much ten or twenty dollars per canteen. Under the circumstances, dehydration was almost universal. It compounded the debilitating effects of disease and malnutrition. It was misery to experience and not just because of pervasive thirst. "The terrific urge to urinate would come," Lieutenant Colonel Miller later wrote. "Only a bare teaspoon of urine would be forthcoming. The pain accompanying it was almost unbearable." Dehydrated and starving, he went nine days without having a bowel movement. The creek water was so polluted it was only suitable for cooking. One soldier remembered it as "about four inches deep—slimy mud with only a scum of water on the top . . . into which the overflow from the pit latrines seeped. Open pit latrines, full to the top and oozing over the ground, infested with worms, slugs, rats and molding excrement." American officers suspected, probably with good reason, that dead Filipinos were buried close enough to the water to contaminate it even more. Even so, some thirst-crazed Filipino and American prisoners on work details actually drank from the evil mix, in essence killing themselves from a potent brew of microorganisms. Latrines were hardly worthy of the name. "There were a few straddle trenches wholly inadequate because of the tremendous amount of dysentery," a postwar legal brief described. "They overflowed frequently; there was no disinfectant; no screens were provided and flies swarmed from the feces covered hospital to the kitchens and food." When General King, his chaplain Lieutenant Colonel Alfred Oliver, and several other officers protested to Captain Tsuneyoshi about the terrible conditions and lack of necessities, the commandant refused all requests for improvement and upbraided the officers for having the temerity to lodge any such protests. "I hate all Americans and always will hate you," he told a group that included Chaplain Oliver. "The only thing I want to know is when one of you dies. I will then see that you bury each other."[2]

Immersed in such hellish and unsanitary circumstances, death constantly lurked. Americans were dying by the dozens each day, Filipinos in the hundreds. "It became increasingly difficult to find and detail enough men each morning who had the strength to bury those who had died during the night," Colonel Mallonee wrote. Even many decades later, Sergeant Thomas, a captured tanker, shuddered to recall O'Donnell as "a stygian nightmare—rotting bodies stacked everywhere, flies, no water, no tools, no shelter." Flies bred in the millions, if not the billions. "They were so damn thick," PFC Jack Brady recalled. "At night they'd sit on the roofs, and because there were so many of them, whole patches of thatch would fall down. Branches were so thick with flies, they bent right down to the ground. Nowhere, absolutely nowhere, could you get away from those damned flies. They were blue and green, and they were all over the latrines and the food. When you ate, you had to keep waving your hand over the rice to keep the flies from beating you to the chow. Still, sometimes, you'd get flies in your mouth." One man fashioned a makeshift fly swatter out of a piece of bamboo and went hunting. He killed 520 flies in a period of ten minutes. Another man watched as a fly settled on a pile of stinking offal in the latrine, then flew onto a table. When it flew away, it actually left a wet spot on the table. In such squalid circumstances, it was easy to see why disease spread so readily.

With little medicine and no equipment to speak of, medics were powerless to stem the tide of disease and death. "Epidemics of Malaria and Dysentery were rampant," an Army report chronicled. "All members of the camp were suffering from some sort of malnutrition as well. There were no medicines other than a few asperin [sic] tablets, a little tape and a few bandages." The hospital, if such a word was even appropriate, consisted of three crude buildings with wooden flooring and another two that initially featured dirt floors until engineers scrounged some lumber to build crude flooring. There were no beds or blankets. Though almost every prisoner was sick and malnourished, they tried to avoid the hospital like the proverbial plague. The motley hospital buildings, soon dubbed the "House of Horrors" by prisoners, represented nothing more than a place to die. "The hospital served mainly as a place to segregate the more seriously ill from those who were still able to wait upon themselves," Colonel Cooper, the theater surgeon, later wrote. "Many who had a glimpse of conditions that existed around the hospital area preferred to take their chances on the outside rather than run the risk of the added exposure from this concentration of sick." The stench of the hospital area—and really the whole camp—was "indescribable," in the recollection of one soldier. Men took to covering their noses with handkerchiefs or strips of cloth. Nothing helped. The odor of feces, death, and despoilment pervaded in the compound. Inside the bamboo walls of the hospital buildings, the sights were unimaginable. Scores of prisoners lay dying and delirious, awash in their own filth, with dysentery so acute that they were in the throes of uncontrollable diarrhea. "You just continually eliminated feces mixed with blood and mucus," one victim remembered. "It's constant and it gets over everything and everyone."

To make matters worse, the affliction severely diminished the victim's appetite, making recovery more difficult. With every spastic bowel movement, they lost more nutrients and water; obviously only food and liquid could replace those losses. Some of the patients had been hauled into the hospital by medics because they no longer had the strength to make it to the latrine. Some had taken to sleeping alongside the latrine pits and simply leaning over when they had the urge to eliminate. Many of these improvisers were later found dead, covered with flies alongside the sewage of the latrine pits. "I have seen men, not one but 50 or more at a time, lying in their own feces too weak to move and no one to move them," Lieutenant Colonel Chester Johnson later wrote. He himself barely survived a serious case of amoebic dysentery. Some exhausted, diseased prisoners took refuge underneath the crude shacks that served as barracks. Many went to sleep and never woke up. Their comrades were forced to drag the decomposing, maggot-eaten bodies from underneath the barracks for burial outside the camp.[3]

By far the worst part of the hospital was the "Zero Ward," as in those inside had zero chance of survival, at least in the estimation of the medics, who were not in much better shape themselves. For obvious reasons, they also referred to this building as "St. Peter's Ward." Here the level of degradation reached a point of surreal horror. The patients lay in clumps on a feces-covered floor. Most were skeletal, with almost no clothing. They had lost all control of their bodily functions. "I saw white mucous tinged with pink swiped across the buttock of one person who was also out of his mind," Captain McMaster wrote of an unforgettable visit to the Zero Ward. "I saw another patient vomit a deep, green colored liquid. Two men were trying to assist a patient to use a bucket as a toilet, but the patient lacked control and was unable to cooperate." Master Sergeant Fred Gaston, a medic, described the men in the Zero Ward as "nothing but skin and bones, and they had open ulcers on their hips, on their knees, and on their shoulders. These men had no dressings on their wounds, and maggots were eating the open wounds. There were blowflies in this ward by the millions. These men were . . . unable to get off the floor to go to the latrine, and their bowels moved as they lay there. The stench was so unbearable that I couldn't stay." Captain Weinstein attempted to treat the dying men and could never forget the terrible images of their degradation. "Some lay co-matose, flat on their backs, breathing imperceptibly, mouths open, the whites of their eyes rimmed with fat green blowflies. Others were lying on their sides breathing with irregular, rasping, mucous-filled gurgles. They were all gaunt and emaciated, their shaggy hair plastered with feces." By the dozens and then the hundreds they died comatose or delirious, slath-ered in their own filth.

Conditions were even worse in what passed for a hospital in the Filipino compound. One witness remembered "patients . . . almost completely na-ked . . . dying of dysentery and the floor was covered with feces. They were too weak to stand up and walk." A cruel Japanese interpreter delighted in throwing cigarettes on the floor to watch them use their last reserves of energy to scramble through the puddles of noxious human waste to grab them. Sergeant Miguel, the Philippine Scout, was among the afflicted. Over a five-day period, he recorded in his personal diary an average of thirty-five to fifty-five bowel movements per day. "Bad odors (human waste-dead) blooming all over the place," he scribbled tersely. "The toll of deaths is mounting very heavily," as many as 350 per day.

Amid such horrible circumstances, many prisoners lost the will to live. "When a man doesn't want to live," one soldier wrote, "it is pretty easy to die. Many simply gave up and did just that, with nothing more wrong with them than any of the rest of us." Faced with the grimness of this life of horrible deprivation, scores decided they were better off dead and just stopped eating. In Captain McMaster's opinion, they "died of a broken spirit." Often when their companions bade them good night, they re-sponded with a heartfelt goodbye, fully intending to die by morning. In many instances, men force-fed their buddies rather than see them give up. The death toll fell heavily on the young. Almost two-thirds of recorded American deaths at O'Donnell were aged twenty-five or under. "Young men were more easily discouraged, because for the first time they were meeting adversity, while older men had gone through many hard knocks," Lieutenant Colonel David Hardee, a hardened veteran of World War I, explained. "Young bodies were tender and had little surplus; older bodies were tough and had old gristle that furnished fat for the body for weeks. Many of these younger men had not learned the deep lesson of life that happiness is a thing that springs from within." Moreover, those aged twenty-one and under were still growing, so their bodies required more sustenance, a serious obstacle to survival. One evening Captain Olson heard the plaintive, sad voice of a dying teenage soldier calling for his mother. "The hysterical sobs and pleading went on endlessly, rending the hearts who heard the pathetic young man." The older prisoners also drew from greater training on how to avoid ingesting destructive microorganisms in food and water. Plus they had a greater sense of how to conserve energy.

A few prisoners simply lost their minds. One such man was put inside a small shack that served as a psychological ward. "We could see him through the bars, naked, covered all over with feces," Private Zoeth Skinner wrote. "He was completely naked except for shoes. There was at least 4 [inches] of fecal matter on the floor. When fed he would mix part of the fecal matter from the floor and devour the food with much gusto. Some would tease him and he would go into violent fits of rage." Unsubstantiated rumors claimed that other psychological casualties had been put in the shack with him and that he had stomped them to death.

Instead of giving up or losing their sanity, some prisoners went to the other extreme and did anything they could to survive, even at the expense of their comrades. Theft was far too common, as was profiteering of food, water, medicine, clothing, and cigarettes. Those with money could use it to bribe guards or buy illicit food and other items from Filipino civilians. One medic hoarded a precious bottle of quinine and offered to sell tablets to patients who were suffering from acute malaria. Another dragged dysentery-ridden patients out of his ward and dumped them outside, lest he catch anything from them. For those who did not have close friends, an every-man-for-himself kind of anarchy predominated. "I realized it was going to be survival of the fittest," one survivor later said.

Officers tended to have more money and more friends than enlisted men. Not surprisingly, their survival rates were higher. They accounted for about 4 percent of American deaths, though they comprised more than 15 percent of the camp population. Some of them completely abrogated the responsibility of leadership in favor of using their authority to survive. To some extent, this was a result of the initial Japanese order that all prisoners were to be equal with no distinction of rank. But it also stemmed from the desperation of the moment and, in more than a few instances, a failure of leadership. "The standard of officer deteriorated very, very badly," one of them later commented. "There was just a complete disregard . . . for the welfare of anyone." Naturally, enlisted men resented this indifference that came at their expense. "There were a large number of people who objected to this strenuously," PFC Brady said. "They were going to kill the officers responsible." Fortunately, the situation improved as General King and many other officers defied the Japanese and began to reestablish a new chain of command with proper discipline and accountability. In a typical example of the new discipline, they ordered permanent guards posted at the creek to keep soldiers from drinking its fetid water.

Meanwhile, burial details proceeded with the continuous monotony of a factory at full production. All day long, the sad tramp of silent work details could be heard, hauling bodies in blankets hung from poles. One group carried the skinny bodies; another dug the graves. One after the other, they interred the bodies in shallow pits—both group and individual—just outside the camp. "They were nude because their clothes, after being boiled, had been passed on to other prisoners," PFC Andrew Aquila, a frequent member of a burial detail, later said. "We grabbed them by the legs and their flesh would stick to our hands." The water table was so high that the graves could not run deeper than three or four feet (plus the prisoners possessed little energy to dig anything deeper). To keep the bodies from floating in seeping water, the diggers learned to tamp down the remains with bamboo poles until they filled in the pits with dirt. The gravediggers would then pause a few moments, read a prayer, or observe a moment of silence. Captain Albert Fullerton, a graves-registration officer, attempted to organize the grave sites into a proper cemetery and keep a careful record of the burials, a nearly hopeless job under these circumstances. At night, wild dogs frequently dug up and feasted on the unattended remains. Each sunrise brought the terrible sight of those who had died during the night. The work parties would police them up and stack them in a central area for interment. Years later, the survivors used Holocaust-like terminology to describe the dead as stacked like "cordwood" or "firewood." Many of the living could hardly stand to lay eyes on the grisly piles. "I turned my face away from the bodies," Private Tenney noted mournfully. "I just could not look at the gray faces and sunken eyes that still seemed to plead for help."

According to one Army report, 21,684 Filipinos and 1,488 Americans died at O'Donnell over a three-month period from mid-April to mid-July. In his seminal work, Olson estimated American deaths at 1,547, a one-in-six fatality ratio. A postwar Army provost marshal report claimed that more than twenty-six thousand Filipinos died. Probably more than one-third of the local soldiers did not survive O'Donnell. Most of those who lived were released and sent home to their families within a few months. Their treatment reflected Japanese ambivalence about the archipelago and its people. By any measure the Japanese treated their Filipino captives even worse than the Americans, but then they let them go. On one hand, the Japanese were keen to dominate the Filipinos and punish them for allying themselves with the Americans, especially as guerrilla warriors. On the other hand, they hoped to win them over as partners in a new Pan-Japanese alliance.

By the middle of June, American O'Donnell survivors who were in any condition to travel were moved to a more permanent camp at Cabanatuan. Few, if any, were sorry to leave. Perhaps even more than the Death March, O'Donnell set a new and endlessly dismal standard for Japanese amateurism, neglect, indifference, and cruelty. Just as the Confederacy dishonored itself at Andersonville, so, too, the Imperial Japanese Army, hailing from a culture that prized personal dignity and honor, shamed themselves terribly by creating and perpetuating the hellish miasma of O'Donnell. Regretfully, this was not anomaly; it was policy.[4]

★

The Allied soldiers who surrendered at Corregidor were spared the Death March and O'Donnell, but little else. Within a couple of days of General Wainwright's surrender, some eight thousand Americans and five thousand Filipino soldiers and civilians came under Japanese control on the island. Fresh from the bitter fighting that ended the contest for Corregidor, tense, taut-faced Japanese troops rounded them up. "I could see a Japanese squad slowly approaching, led by a lieutenant and a soldier with a flame thrower," Lieutenant Colonel Carl Engelhart, a Japanese-speaking intelligence officer, later wrote of his vantage point from the eastern entrance to the Malinta Tunnel. Before the flamethrower man could unleash a jet of flame, Engelhart hurried out the tunnel and, in fluent Japanese, confirmed the surrender. With the exception of medical personnel, the wounded, the sick, and some senior officers, everyone was congregated a few hundred yards east of Malinta Hill, at a level, concrete-floored outdoor area about the size of two city blocks. This gathering point had once served as a motor pool collection area for the 92nd Coast Artillery Regiment. Everyone called it the 92nd Garage because it was adjacent to the ruins of a building that had once housed unit vehicles. Really, though, it was the equivalent of an open parking lot.

Rigidly segregating the Filipinos from the Americans, the Japanese enclosed the area with makeshift barbed wire fences and packed thousands of men onto this constricted concrete slab. Here they stayed for more than two weeks, sweltering under the relentless sun. Japanese authorities viewed them as captives—or even hostages—to be held in limbo until all Allied soldiers in the archipelago surrendered. The Japanese organized the prisoners into groups of one thousand, under the control of an American colonel, and then subgroups of one hundred, under the supervision of lower-ranking officers. Everyone was given a number, painted on the back of his shirt or trousers. Orders required all prisoners to bow or salute any Japanese soldier from private to field marshal (a common requirement for all prisoners of the Rising Sun and one that would endure through years of captivity). The punishment for failing to greet a Japanese with the proper salutation was usually a beating. In extreme cases, it could lead to execution.

The guards were inveterate thieves. According to one postwar US Army report, they "robbed every prisoner of all his possessions, such as watches, fountain pens, rings, eye glasses, wallets and money." Some Americans resisted only to be beaten severely. One Marine was so infuriated when a guard stole his wallet that he punched him in the face. In response the Japanese soldier drew a sword and decapitated the Marine on the spot. Private Campbell, a rifleman from the Army's 31st Infantry Regiment who had escaped from Bataan to Corregidor only to be captured when the island capitulated, watched in horror as a brusque enemy soldier pulled one of his comrades to his feet. "He had a beautiful gold ring on his left hand. The Jap tried to take it off and could not. He drew his sword and cut off the soldier's finger. He then slipped the ring off the finger dripping with blood!" Another Japanese sliced off the hand and wrist of an American who refused to give up his watch.

Hour upon hour, the prisoners sat clustered together, with little food and water. As at O'Donnell, men spent much of the day standing in long lines, waiting to fill their canteens. Hot, hungry, uncomfortable, packed together, and fearful for the future, tempers often flared. "Starved and thirsty men fly into a rage easily," one officer commented. "Men become like wild animals, except that they add profanity, scurrility, obscenity in their struggle to survive." Unlike at O'Donnell, the Japanese allowed the men to take saltwater baths in the ocean, a welcome opportunity to wash away sweat and grime before returning to the packed compound. "In an effort to secure cover of some kind from the blistering sun, impromptu shelters mushroomed everywhere," wrote Colonel William Braly, who had served as the operations officer of the harbor defenses. "Materials used were corrugated iron, shelter halves, old boards, rags—anything to afford a little shade. Food was on a catch-as-catch-can basis, most groups relying on the pooled resources of the members supplemented by rice brought in occasionally by work parties." Most subsisted on a random mix of rice, canned tomatoes, and sardines. At night, they slept uncomfortably in semi-prone or sitting positions on the hard concrete. Open-pit latrines, some ten feet square and three feet deep, were dug on a hillside above the compound. Some of the noxious contents flowed downward into the sea, exactly in the spot where the prisoners were permitted to bathe. Soon the filth of these pits attracted and bred billions of flies that swarmed the area, especially during daylight hours. Instead of shooing them away, men often had to brush or pick them off their food or their own bodies. In spite of the 92nd Garage's proximity to the sea, with its cleansing breezes, the whole area reeked of excrement and sweat.

The Japanese soon put groups of prisoners to work cleaning up battle damage, loading supplies onto boats and burying the bodies of those who had been killed in battle (along with a few unfortunates who had since died in captivity). The Japanese dead were piled together at the extreme eastern point of Corregidor, near Kindley Field and, as per custom, cremated. In most cases, their ashes and assorted body parts were lovingly preserved by their surviving comrades and sent to their families back in Japan. The work parties usually buried American and Filipino bodies where they lay. The diggers scooped out shallow depressions and with little fanfare, save for the occasional prayer, committed the remains to the rocky earth. Many of the dead had lain for several days in the tropical heat. "The bodies began rotting quickly . . . and drew hordes of flies," Private Campbell later wrote. "The flies soon produced maggots that fed on the rotting flesh. The sight and odor was beyond human limits." In spite of being undernourished, he vomited several times at the gruesome sight and stench of the dead.

Live ordnance still lay practically everywhere. Accidental explosions caused occasional woundings. Men on work parties and their guards learned to tread very carefully wherever heavy fighting had taken place. Though most of the details completed their work without incident, communication was very problematic because few of the Japanese soldiers spoke any English and almost no American understood any Japanese. The difficulty of communication only ratcheted up the natural tension of the moment. Plus, the Japanese were frighteningly tempestuous. Seemingly anything could set them off. One man was beheaded for stealing some canned pineapples. A colonel who collapsed of exhaustion while unloading a barge was beaten into unconsciousness by a Japanese officer. When Colonel Paul Bunker, a burly former West Point all-American football player and classmate of MacArthur's, asked permission to retrieve a blanket and mosquito bar from his old quarters, he was summarily slapped like some sort of wayward child, a profound humiliation for such a long-serving, physically imposing soldier.

Inside the laterals of Malinta Hill, doctors and nurses continued caring for hundreds of wounded and sick men, including some Japanese soldiers who had been wounded in the fighting or since taken sick. Colonel Cooper, the command surgeon, estimated that about half the patients were wounded, 40 percent were down with malaria or other diseases, and 10 percent were hospitalized with psychoneurotic issues. By now the tunnels stank of rot, body odor, mold, disease, and open wounds. The Japanese were stunned at the sight of the female nurses in such a place and did not quite know what to make of them. For months, the American men had worried about what might become of the nurses once under Japanese control. General Wainwright, during his surrender negotiations, succeeded in securing an assurance of correct treatment for them, though no word of this seems to have filtered down to the Imperial Army soldiers who occupied Corregidor. With the exception of one alleged sexual assault, the Japanese troops behaved properly toward the nurses. Enemy commanders restricted access to the tunnels for most of their men and ordered that the American doctors and nurses remain inside for all but about an hour per day. Even so, groups of Japanese officers and other soldiers toured the laterals, seemingly day and night. On one occasion, some of them were about to pull back the sheet that obscured the entrance to the nurse's sleeping quarters. Captain Davison, the fifty-seven-year-old commanding officer of the nurses, stood in the way of the Japanese and cried, "Halt! You cannot come in here until the nurses are dressed." The party waited awkwardly for about ten minutes until everyone was ready. Davison then pulled the sheet back and let them enter. From then on, the nurses slept in their duty clothes, long khaki dresses with Red Cross arm bands. The Japanese seemed to assent. "They didn't know what to do with us, so they allowed us to continue our work in the hospital taking care of our sick and wounded," Lieutenant Ruby Motley recalled. Their curiosity about the nurses was nearly insatiable, though. They photographed a group of them outside the tunnels and assured them they would send copies to General MacArthur to reassure him that his nurses were okay. They interviewed them incessantly, asking them about their favorite sports, their homes, their family backgrounds, and their thoughts on the war. Captain Kazumaro "Buddy" Uno, a Japanese war correspondent and English-speaking alumnus of the University of Utah, was, like many of his countrymen, quite taken with the women. "Some of them were beauties, just like the Hollywood nurses one sees in the movies," he wrote after spending many collegial hours with Colonel Cooper and the nurses. "Despite the terrible strain of their work and the morbid atmosphere of the hospital . . . these girls had managed to keep their lovely appearance—as only American girls know how." Though there was an undercurrent of tension between the nurses and the Japanese, the women generally went about their business without undue interference.

On the evening of May 22, the monsoon season began. Torrential rains swept over Corregidor, inundating the prisoners in the 92nd Garage area. The water was refreshing but too much of a good thing, as it now became impossible to get dry. The contents of the latrines were washed into the compound and the ocean bathing area. Mud and feces coated the whole area. The Japanese, in the meantime, ordered the prisoners to get ready to move. They were herded aboard ships, where they spent an uncomfortable evening packed together with no food or water. The next day, a Sunday, the ships sailed across the harbor, to Manila. The Filipino prisoners were unloaded at a pier and marched to a nearby camp. The American prisoners were deposited into chest-high water. They waded ashore and then coalesced into groups of a thousand men apiece, lined up in columns of four. Alongside the columns, mounted Japanese cavalrymen galloped to and fro. At a command to move out, the prisoners began marching along the spacious, palm-tree-lined vista of Dewey Boulevard, once the crown jewel of the great Chicago architect Daniel Burnham's City Beautiful project to modernize turn-of-the-century Manila and, ever since, the very nerve center of the half-century American presence in the Philippines. On and on the hungry, exhausted, diminished veterans of Corregidor tramped in the midday heat, past the Manila Hotel, where American officers had once spent luxurious R-and-R weekends, the Army and Navy Club, where generations of soldiers and sailors had gathered for friendly recreation, and the military complex where numerous American military commanders had once lived. "The soft tar stuck to our soggy shoes, already full of sand, while the things we carried grew heavier and heavier," Colonel Braly later wrote. The weakest began to discard unnecessary items. Anyone who lagged behind was herded along by lance-wielding cavalrymen who were firm in their orders but at least humane enough to allow the prisoners to stop and help their buddies who staggered or fell.

Along the route, Sunday crowds gaped sadly at the bedraggled prisoners. "Some had uniforms on, some were naked to the waist, all had shoes, some had hats . . . some were empty-handed, some carried bundles, some suitcases," one observer later related to American intelligence sources. Many of the Filipinos wept openly or surreptitiously gave the Americans the V-for-victory sign. "I'll never forget those tears," Lieutenant Colonel Armand Hopkins, executive officer of the 59th Coast Artillery Regiment, reflected with a bit of imperial guilt, "for I wasn't sure we deserved that affection. There were even some who . . . ran out to the ranks, dodging the Jap guards, to give us a drink, or an orange, or a piece of candy." Private Bishop McKendree, another Coast Artilleryman, saw an elderly Filipina with "a handkerchief over her mouth, but I could see the tears running down her cheeks and sheer agony . . . on her face." In one poignant instance, a five-year-old girl standing with her mother recognized her father among the prisoners. "Daddy!" she called out excitedly. Her mother hushed the girl and told her not to greet her dad. "The Japanese will hurt him if you do." The father heard his daughter, glanced at her, choked up a bit, and then had to look away.

The Americans soon referred to their procession as the "gloat march." The purpose of it was patently obvious to everyone. "The Japs wanted to exploit the surrender to the utmost," Hopkins explained, "wiping out all American prestige. This was a way of saying to the populace, 'Here are your proud, haughty Americans, the fine fighting men of the richest country on earth. Look at them now!'" Indeed, humiliation and frustration did burn in the hearts of these men who had once comprised the elite of the archipelago. But otherwise the march backfired on the Japanese. There were no recorded instances of Filipinos jeering or mocking the Americans or demonstrating any other emotion for them besides sympathy. "I could see that the attitude of the people was not the attitude that the Japs had expected," PFC Robert Spielman later jotted in illicit POW notes. "It made a lump in your throat when you realized that the people, WIN OR LOSE, were STILL FOR THE AMERICANS." Like an unspoken referendum, the attitude was apparent to any perceptive person, whether friend or foe. Lieutenant Colonel Hopkins was so impressed by this that he came away with a sense of inner peace—somehow he felt sure now that the United States would win the war, regardless of whether he himself lived to see the victory.[5]

The procession covered seven broiling miles to Bilibid Prison, once home to the archipelago's hardened criminals but now a temporary holding pen for the many thousands of American POWs. In the days that followed, most were moved in groups of five hundred or one thousand to Cabanatuan. At one point during the Manila march, the prisoners had passed the University Club where, unknown to them, General Wainwright stood at an upstairs window sadly watching as the men filed past. "It was a heartbreaking spectacle, this strange review of my troops," he later wrote. Since making his surrender broadcast, the Japanese had held Wainwright, a few other senior officers, and their aides as "captives" at the University Club. Food was adequate and, except for numerous intensive interrogations, the Japanese treated them fairly well, at least by their standards. Brigadier General Beebe, Wainwright's chief of staff, later deemed this period "the best treatment accorded us as prisoners of war." Beebe spent his days reading books from the club's library. Wainwright was saddened to be separated from his men and worried for their welfare. Hearing rumbles of the tragedy unfolding at O'Donnell, he composed a solicitous letter to General Homma begging him to radio President Roosevelt and, in Wainwright's name, request a relief ship with food, medicine, and clothing for the prisoners. Homma never even replied.

On June 9, after the formal surrender of all other Allied forces in the Philippines, the Japanese officially reclassified Wainwright and all the other "captives"—apparently the Japanese had thought of them as collateral or hostages to discourage continued resistance—as prisoners of war, though this did not bring about any improvement in their treatment. All officers of full colonel rank and above, including Beebe and Wainwright, were moved to Tarlac, another bare-bones Philippine Army post, to the north of Manila. Fifteen generals, 106 colonels (or equivalent naval rank), and a handful of enlisted aides were packed together inside a dusty, run-down two-story barracks building. Generals rated cots; most everyone else slept in wooden, double-decker bunks. Few had mattresses, pillows, or blankets. The food was monotonous and barely adequate, mainly rice, plus whatever they could buy. "I discovered that I must learn to eat rice or starve," Beebe commented. "I preferred to eat the rice, although I vowed that no one could make me like it." For Beebe and those who had been held at the University Club in Manila, Tarlac was a step down. For their brother officers who had survived O'Donnell, Tarlac represented some level of improvement. "Rough as it was, with harsh treatment, horrible sanitary conditions, an almost complete absence of medicines, a sort of hit-and-miss schedule of food," Colonel Mallonee wrote, "Tarlac was still a vast improvement over what we had left behind at Hell Hole O'Donnell." It did not last. In August, the Japanese moved them again, this time by ship to Formosa, where they were incarcerated at Karenko, a former Japanese Army barracks now enclosed by barbed wire fencing. From their first meal of wormy, weevil-ridden rice, a terrible sense of foreboding set in. "Thus . . . began the worst period of starvation we were to endure as prisoners of war," Beebe wrote mournfully.[6]

★

One hundred miles north of Manila, at Cabanatuan, where the Japanese had situated three POW enclosures at a former Philippine Army post, conditions were similarly grave, almost a macabre repeat of O'Donnell. Initially, the Japanese maintained the three facilities separately and dubbed them Cabanatuan Numbers 1, 2, and 3. They soon moved about one thousand prisoners to Mindanao, to a work camp called the Davao Penal Colony. In spite of the name, conditions there were less severe. A couple thousand more were shipped miserably aboard packed cargo ships to slave camps in Japan or other places in Japanese-controlled Asia. Within a few months, the Japanese consolidated most all the Cabanatuan prisoners at Camp Number 1. Staff Sergeant Hopkins described the camp as "dreary, desolate . . . acres and acres of low, grassy, swampland, with not a tree in sight, surrounded by barbed wire and Nipponese sentries with fixed bayonets." The population included men captured at Corregidor, survivors of the Death March and O'Donnell, and patients from the two hospitals on Bataan. The prisoners were loosely divided into groups of one thousand, each of which was placed under the command of a lieutenant colonel. The commander and his aides were responsible for producing an accurate count of their men each day, a task so tedious amid the chaos of deaths and hospitalizations that it usually absorbed hours. Most of the prisoners lacked the physical stamina to escape. Even so, enough men got away and linked up with guerrillas to cause the Japanese to implement a new policy.

They delineated groups of ten POWs, known as blood brothers. If anyone from the group escaped, the others would be summarily executed.

Barracks were sturdier and a bit more spacious than those at O'Donnell. Prisoners slept on bays with bamboo mats rather than in beds or cots. Five men crowded into each bay, about 100 to 150 prisoners inside each barracks. Bedbugs were rife. "I found about forty in the corners of my mosquito net this morning," Captain Eugene Forquer noted in his diary one typical day. Food rations, consisting mainly of low-grade rice, hovered near starvation level. One Army report referred to it as a "grossly inadequate diet." Medical care, though better than at O'Donnell, was barebones. Doctors still had little medicine and almost no equipment. Though no one was in particularly good condition, those who had not endured O'Donnell were stunned at the sight of the survivors who merged with them at Cabanatuan. The O'Donnell alumni were so thin, their faces were nearly unrecognizable and they conveyed the appearance of zombies. To Private William Garleb, they looked like "skeletons walking towards you with skin hanging on the bones." Their pallor was grayish yellow, their jaws slack, and their eyes glassy and distant. "It was enough to make you want to lie down and die."

Many actually were on the verge of death. In June alone, 740 died, mainly from dysentery and malaria. By the end of 1942, about two thousand had perished. "Seeing death all around us made us tremble with constant anxiety regarding our own mortality," Private Tenney wrote. Physicians understood, and resented the fact, that nearly all the deaths were preventable. "For me as a doctor the most distressing thought was that they could have been saved, almost without exception, by proper diet and medical care," Captain Bumgarner, a doctor, wrote bitterly. Powerless to stem the tide, the North Carolinian and his fellow medics witnessed the body count grow daily. The experience inspired him to title his postwar memoir *Parade of the Dead*. Everywhere, death and its close cousin hopelessness, lurked like malevolent angels. Inside Cabanatuan's version of the Zero Ward, where conditions were every bit as bad as the ones at O'Donnell, emaciated men expired in a coating of their own execratory and vomitous filth. "They were literally skeletons clothed in skin," the anonymous author of one medical report wrote. The rudimentary hospital was usually overcrowded to the point where doctors were so overwhelmed with patients that they could hardly keep track of them. One physician, Major James

Bruce, recalled only a blur of patients "so ill and crazed with malarial chills, dysentery, and plain hunger that they would go out of the buildings and lie in the grass, where they would defecate and soil themselves."

The end could happen anywhere else, too. Prisoners awoke in the morning to discover baymates dead. When Premier Tōjō decreed that all able-bodied prisoners must work in order to be fed, exhausted men soon began collapsing and dying on work details as they performed hard manual labor. Others died while crawling to the noxious, fly-ridden ditches that initially served as makeshift toilets (eventually American engineers improvised enclosed latrines with a septic-tank system). A few were so weak, they collapsed and drowned in the swampy, maggot-infused maw. Similar to O'Donnell, the young were more likely to die than their elders. According to one source, 85 percent of those who died were under the age of thirty.

One of the dead, emblematic of the otherwise anonymous hundreds and then thousands, was twenty-two-year-old Private Gerald Reeves, formerly a member of the 31st Infantry Regiment's Antitank Company. Several months before Pearl Harbor, he had optimistically written to his mother, "Don't worry about the war because I think we are safe over here." Wracked with sickness and starvation, Reeves was one of many who succumbed to dysentery. Because the Japanese government at this stage had shared no official prisoner lists with neutral intermediaries, the Reeves family, and many thousands of others, had no idea what had become of their loved ones in the Philippines. Only a few months after Reeves's death did the unwitting US government even confirm for Ellen, his mother, that Gerald was a prisoner. Not until the following June did a telegram arrive at her Abilene, Texas, home informing her of Gerald's death. This was all she knew until war's end, when the Army's adjutant general wrote to confirm that Gerald was indeed gone. "The distress you have suffered since you received the sad announcement of his death is most understandable," the letter intoned amid instructions about the life-insurance payments she would soon receive for her son's death in the line of duty. A follow-up letter from an aide to the adjutant general attempted to comfort her: "Anything I can say is scant consolation to you in your grief. It is my fervent hope that later, the knowledge that his courage and sacrifices contributed to the final victory may be of sustaining comfort to you." Such were the sad realities for the Reeves family and many hundreds of others whose loved ones perished at Cabanatuan.[7]

With the life draining away from so many young men, a sense of melancholy cloaked the camp. "Death was easier than life," PFC John Falconer asserted. "It was as easy as letting go of a rope. A lot of people quit hanging on." One highly respected, beloved lieutenant who had demonstrated incredible bravery in combat apparently could not abide the degradation of Cabanatuan captivity. Wracked with dysentery, he resisted all attempts by his fellows to help him survive. Even when they somehow managed to get him extra rice, he refused to eat it. "This fellow just wanted to die," Lieutenant Mark Herbst, a physician, later reflected, "and he did."

On the opposite side of the spectrum, others did anything to survive. An apocryphal story soon circulated that as one brother lay dying of malaria in the Zero Ward, another brother sold stolen quinine for cigarettes. Whether true or not, the story illustrated prisoner perceptions of just how far some were willing to go to live. Initially at Cabanatuan—as at O'Donnell—the degraded officer corps and a murky discipline situation contributed to a dog-eat-dog feel, at least for those who were friendless, separated from comrades who had served in the same unit, or simply without influence. According to one postwar POW study, "it was found that moral integrity could be pretty well judged by inverse ratio to one's state of nutrition." Stealing and black market profiteering were too common. Captain Ames was deeply disturbed by the bad behavior he routinely observed. "It is appalling to what depths civilized American men of good background can sink," he raged to his diary. "Now, stripped of all but the needs of self and faced with manifest danger of death by disease or starvation . . . unheard of and terrible things happened. Men stole food, clothing, cigarettes, everything from each other." West Point–trained, steeped in notions of duty, honor, and country, he was especially disgusted with the behavior of some of his fellow officers. "Many officers stole, lied, argued, fought, befowled [sic] themselves and their surroundings just as much as enlisted men." One prisoner, who had been heavily involved in Manila's underworld even before the war, for a time established his own mini-black-market empire in the camp. He employed a couple of relatively well-fed bodyguards to protect him from reprisals. This was an extreme case, though. In most instances, men made small moral compromises with themselves, justifying their actions to their own conscience as necessary for the greater good of survival. "I'm sure many a man who swiped something carries that guilt with him today," Staff

Sergeant Harold Feiner commented years later. PFC Falconer once scammed an extra bowl of rice, probably at the expense of someone else's ration, and never quite forgave himself for it. "I rationalized my doing it by believing that someone . . . would someday . . . steal my food." Some blamed their excesses on their officers, many of whom comported themselves just as badly. Enlisted men resented them for this, but especially because even well-meaning officers were apparently either unable or unwilling to protect the men from the degrading conditions that led to bad behavior. "For selfish reasons, I desperately wanted to see aggressive leadership from our officers," Private Preston Hubbard later wrote. "I felt that had they made a greater effort, morale among the enlisted men would have been much higher." As in civil life, the absence of acknowledged, accountable authority led to a destructive anarchy that favored the predatory, the aggressive, and the venal, all at the expense of the weak and the high-minded.[8]

As a general rule, there was a direct correlation between the maintenance of proper military discipline and the improvement of camp conditions for everyone. The best officers and NCOs—or at least those who were in good enough physical condition to care—understood this. Nowhere was this more true than at Cabanatuan where the gradual establishment of a chain of command began to stabilize the camp by the late months of 1942. Death rates declined. Work details were organized under supervisory officers and sergeants. Crops were planted and cultivated to augment the prisoner's meager rations. Permanent, covered latrines and an ingenious septic system improved hygiene and slowed the spread of infectious diseases. Medics offered prizes to prisoners for killing flies and rats. One doctor painted catchy hygiene-oriented slogans on wooden signs and displayed them around the compound, similar to roadside billboards back home. In exchange for the prisoner's arduous work, the Japanese agreed to pay wages, in amounts mandated by the Geneva Convention. The agricultural area eventually occupied about thirteen hundred acres. Most of the work parties toiled on this camp farm, cultivating whatever food they could. Prisoners worked from 0600 to 1100, ate a bowl of rice and watery soup for lunch, then resumed their labor from about 1300 to 1800. "This routine went on day after day, without a break, and we were not allowed to talk while in the field, planting, picking, or digging," Private Tenney wrote. Crops included beans, squash, corn, camotes, okra, and eggplant. The Japanese confiscated much of the bounty and ate it themselves, leaving the scrawnier output for the Americans. Anyone who was caught eating vegetables while at work in the fields received a severe beating.

Nothing was more important to the health and welfare of the POWs than the establishment of a camp commissary to procure food, medical supplies, and other valuables from the outside, all of which could mean the difference between life and death for the malnourished prisoners. Without proper supervision and in the wrong hands, the commissary had the potential to become little more than a glorified black-market outlet for anyone with money or other advantages. In this sense, most everyone understood that the commissary-officer position might well be the most powerful and important job in the camp. As such, it called for a competent man of impeccable integrity. "There was only one choice, Johnny Johnson," one prisoner later said. As if by mutual acclamation, Lieutenant Colonel Harold Johnson, formerly of the 57th Infantry Regiment (Scouts), became commissary officer. His colleagues had noticed that the worse things had gotten, the better he seemed to behave. To Johnson, ethics seemed to be a vital part of survival, like oxygen, food, or water for most people. In his view, leadership was not about privileges or glory. It was about selflessness and professionalism. "A foremost consideration of any commander has to be the welfare of the men under him and that he does not abuse his subordinates for personal gain under any circumstances," he once said.

After making it through the Death March, the young West Pointer had barely survived the dreaded Zero Ward at O'Donnell. "I was one of the very few that came out of that place," he later reflected. "I don't know why. I just know that I came out." Restored to some semblance of health, Johnson organized an efficient, fair procurement system. Barracks by barracks, prisoners placed orders for such items as vegetables, meat, tobacco, salt, sugar, and the like. To prevent ordering on credit, the Japanese mandated that each barracks had to put down a deposit to make sure the buyers could pay. "Barracks orders were consolidated by group," Johnson said. "There were four groups at Cabanatuan, including the hospital." He acted as the central purchasing agent for the combination of the four groups, negotiating, under the supervision of camp authorities, deals with outside vendors, both Japanese and Filipino.

To prevent skimming and scamming among the prisoners, he personally supervised distribution to make sure that all orders reached the proper parties. Moreover, he prevailed upon those who had money to contribute to a general fund so that he could purchase food for those who were penniless or sick. As a student of human nature, Johnson grew to understand how to ingratiate himself to the Japanese and, at the same time, outwit them. He made sure to bow and demonstrate proper respect for his captors. Because he was reserved and respectful by nature, this came naturally to him. The Japanese grew to trust him enough that they allowed him to make several trips outside the camp in pursuit of his duties. In addition to his transparent commissary dealings with merchants, he and another officer, Lieutenant Colonel Edward Mack, established clandestine networks with pro-American locals who, at great peril to themselves, worked with Johnson and Mack to donate medicine, clothing, and food to the prisoners. "Huge quantities of [beans], sugar, and in one instance over one hundred pairs of shoes were brought in" to Cabanatuan, Johnson wrote in a postwar letter testifying to the extraordinarily brave efforts of Ramon Amusategui and his wife, Lorenza, who were two of the most important donors. "You have no idea of the gratitude that all the prisoners felt," toward their Filipino benefactors, Johnson told one colleague shortly after the war. The colonel also managed to acquire significant quantities of amebicides to combat dysentery, calamansi syrup to fight scurvy, and sulfanilamide to deal with infections. For all his personal integrity, he had no compunction about deceiving the Japanese. In total, the captors paid their working prisoners about half a million pesos and yet, through deft financial subterfuge, Johnson managed to spend three times that amount of money on commissary items. "My commissary business is booming," he scrawled in a secret diary that he had begun keeping since his arrival at Cabanatuan. "Our pay and the increased number of items available has helped tremendously." He even found a way to acquire games and reading material for his fellow prisoners. He faked invoices and kept sham financial records to keep the Japanese in the dark. "We were audited officially once a month," he said. The Japanese saw only the bogus records. Johnson cultivated trusted paymasters who maintained the real financial records in minute detail and kept them hidden from the enemy.

On Christmas Day, as life stabilized slightly at Cabanatuan, the prisoners received a gift they would never forget. Every man got an eleven-pound Red Cross relief package, each of which contained evaporated milk, biscuits, cheese, cocoa, sardines, margarine, corned beef, chocolate, sugar, powdered orange concentrate, raisins, soup, prunes, instant coffee, cigarettes, pipe tobacco, medicine, vitamin pills, soap, shaving kits, and other toiletries. The packages had arrived in Manila several weeks earlier aboard a pair of international relief ships. The unexpected bounty undoubtedly helped many men survive to see the New Year. Wildly optimistic rumors swirled that high-level American and Japanese leaders were engaging in negotiations to foster prisoner exchanges. Perhaps, many of the prisoners thought, there was hope for a better future after all.[9]

PART TWO

TURNABOUT

7

Possibilities

In the wake of the Japanese naval defeats at Coral Sea and Midway, control of the South Pacific, and one might even say the war itself, now hung in the balance. Both sides aimed to seize the initiative. Both thought in terms of offensives. The Japanese knew that the dream scenario conquests of Midway, Fiji, Samoa, New Caledonia, Australia, and the Hawaiian Islands were beyond their means now. But no matter. With control of the Solomon Islands and the southern coast of New Guinea, they could menace shipping lanes and lines of communication between Australia and the United States and position themselves to batter the northern reaches of the island continent. This could negate or diminish Australia as a base for an American military and logistical buildup and force the locus of the conflict northward to the vast open waters of the Pacific as a contest between blue-water navies, a scenario that might still favor Japan even after the Midway reversal.

The Allies had earned themselves some breathing room from their naval triumphs. They now thought in terms of a counteroffensive designed to wrest control of eastern New Guinea, the Solomons, and Rabaul from the Japanese. In a grand strategical sense, a meeting engagement was brewing between these antagonists. The prize was not really the scrubby islands and jungles over which they would soon fight. In the main, these places were geopolitically worthless, even liabilities to the belligerents. They offered little in the way of resources, infrastructure and political assets to either side. Quite the contrary, actually—the terrain and conditions were some of the worst on the planet. In the same way a boxing ring comprises a convenient forum for a fighter to subdue his opponent, rather than an objective itself, so, too, the value of the South Pacific was as an arena of combat, a happenstance of a place in which to inflict fatal damage on the enemy, a way station to the more valuable locales of the central and northern Pacific, and even Asia itself. To a great extent, success depended on who could get men and matériel to vital objectives first, and this naturally placed a real premium on air- and sea power.

★

On July 2, 1942, after weeks of negotiations between Army and Navy leaders, the American Joint Chiefs issued the "Joint Directive for Offensive Operations in the Southwest Pacific Area." The ambitious directive, though it was backed with few military resources, mandated the seizure of New Guinea, New Britain (including the growing Japanese base at Rabaul), and the Solomon and Santa Cruz Islands. Not surprising, the Army and the Navy could not agree on an overall commander. Instead, Army Chief of Staff General Marshall and Chief of Naval Operations Admiral King compromised. They divided the theater into the Southwest Pacific Area (SWPA) under General MacArthur and the Pacific Ocean Areas (POA) under Admiral Chester Nimitz, commander in chief of the US Pacific Fleet, thus setting the stage for a permanently divided—and rival—American command structure in the Pacific War. Basically, SWPA encompassed the Philippines, the South China Sea, most of Indonesia, Australia, New Guinea, New Britain, New Ireland, and most of the Solomon Islands, with the exception of Guadalcanal, Tulagi, and smaller islands at the southern end of the chain. Nimitz's POA spanned over everything else, a staggering quantity of sea and islands so immense that he subdivided it into the North Pacific Area, the Central Pacific Area, and the South Pacific Area. Nimitz retained direct control of the North and Central Pacific Areas but designated command of the South Pacific Area to Vice Admiral Robert Ghormley. In essence, the directive steered MacArthur's efforts north to New Guinea, somewhere he was already eager to go, on the way to his ultimate objective of the Philippines. The Joint Chiefs also ordered Nimitz's command to take control of the Santa Cruz Islands and southern Solomons, including Tulagi.

Japanese war planners hoped to secure the southern coast of New Guinea, particularly Port Moresby, home to the finest natural harbor in the area and an ideal location for air bases from which to menace Australia and Allied shipping in the Coral Sea. In March, the Japanese, using Rabaul as a sally base, had landed troops at Lae and Salamaua on the northern coast. Foiled subsequently at the Battle of Coral Sea in their attempt to take

Moresby by amphibious invasion, the Japanese decided on an overland campaign to capture it. Hundreds of miles to the southeast, they had by June landed small contingents to build airfields on Tulagi and Guadalcanal. From the latter island, Japanese planes could attack Allied shipping for hundreds of miles in every direction, an existential threat to Australia and any hope of a US-led counteroffensive in the Pacific. The obvious Japanese aim was to establish firm control of land, sea, and air from the south coast of New Guinea to the southern Solomons, "with the objective of isolating Australia by severing the surface communication in the South Pacific between the United States and Australia," one Japanese commander wrote. Once the Allies detected the Japanese presence at Guadalcanal, they planned a shoestring invasion to seize the otherwise insignificant jungle island. Very simply, both sides wanted the same ground in the South Pacific. Only one could have it. The result was a pair of epic battles, one in Papua New Guinea and the other on Guadalcanal and its environs. Though fought by separate American commands, they were really two battles of the same campaign, especially from the Japanese perspective.

As July unfolded, both sides were planning to seize bases at Buna and Gona on the northern coast of Papua New Guinea. At this stage, the Japanese largely enjoyed control of the waters north of New Guinea and they had a ready land force of about eighteen hundred men composed primarily of the 15th Independent Engineer Regiment and elements of the 144th Infantry Regiment. On the evening of July 21–22, these troops landed successfully near Buna and Gona. In the weeks that followed, they were reinforced by 3,000 naval construction troops, 8,000 Imperial Army soldiers, and 450 men of the Imperial Navy's Special Naval Landing Forces, often erroneously called "Marines" by Americans. As yet, the Allies did not possess sufficient air and sea assets to prevent these landings or threaten the enemy beachhead. Known as the South Seas Detachment, the Japanese soldiers had orders to advance south over a crude track known as the Kokoda Trail and take Port Moresby. Within a few days, Japanese engineers had set to work constructing bases near the north coast while the main force began a southerly advance on the Kokoda Trail.

In Brisbane, MacArthur was deeply chagrined by the invasion. For weeks he had anticipated precisely this situation, and yet, in spite of his plans for Buna landings, he had almost felt powerless to act, as if no one else understood the need for rapid action. To him, the successful Japanese

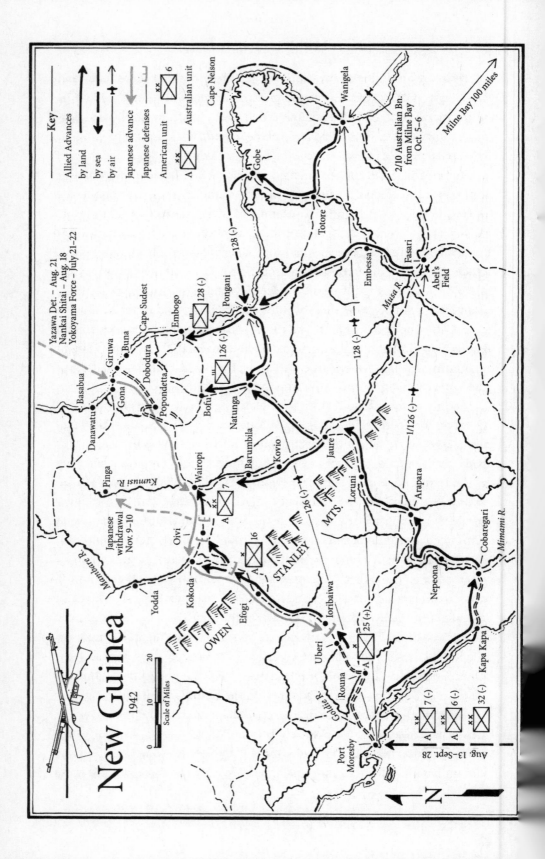

New Guinea
1942

Scale of Miles
0   10   20

Key

Allied Advances
by land
by sea
by air

Japanese advance
Japanese defenses

American unit — Australian unit

Yazawa Det. – Aug. 21
Nankai Shitai – Aug. 18
Yokoyama Force – July 21–22

2/10 Australian Bn.
from Milne Bay
Oct. 5–6

Milne Bay 100 miles

Japanese withdrawal
Nov. 9–10

Aug. 13–Sept. 28

N

Port Moresby
Rouna
Uberi
Ioribaiwa
Efogi
Kokoda
Oivi
Yodda
Wairopi
Pinga
Kumusi R.
Mambare R.
Gona
Basabua
Danawatu
Giruwa
Buna
Dobodura
Cape Sudest
Embogo
Cape Nelson
Wanigela
Gobe
Totore
Embessa
Fasari
Abel's Field
Musa R.
Pongani
Popondetta
Bofu
Natunga
Barumbila
Kovio
Jaure
Loruni
Arapara
Nepeona
Cobaregari
Mimami R.
Kapa Kapa
Golpie R.

OWEN   STANLEY   MTS.

128 (–)
126 (–)
128 (–)
1/126 (–)
128 (–)
126 (–)

A 7
A 16
A 25 (+)
A 7 (–)
A 6 (–)
32 (–)
A 6

invasion, and the strategic reversal it represented, seemed to be the logical result of the Europe-first policy and the ensuing lack of support by the War Department for SWPA. "To make something out of nothing seems to be my military fate in the twilight of my service," he moaned in a letter to an old friend. "I have led one lost cause and am trying desperately not to have it two." Short on troops, shipping, and combat aircraft, he almost felt as if his hands were tied. "My plan of operations to forestall further aggression in New Guinea has been and continues to be seriously affected by the problem of transport and the absence of any assurance of naval help in providing protection for routes of supply," he complained in one long letter to General Marshall. In spite of the challenges, MacArthur did not lack for determination. "We'll defend Australia in New Guinea," he told two of his staff officers in the wake of the Japanese invasion.[1]

Fortunately for the SWPA commander, the task of taking Port Moresby was anything but easy. As the Japanese plunged headlong onto the Kokoda Trail, they had little notion of the terrible adversity presented by the terrain and conditions, much less Allied opposition. The trail was hardly even worthy of the name. By and large, it was a narrow track that wended through nearly one hundred miles of thick jungle, narrow gorges, rope bridges, sharp ridges, steep hills as well as the Owen Stanley mountains and smaller ranges. The tallest peaks spanned from 3,000 to 7,500 feet. Torrential rains were common. Infrastructure was nil, food sources sparse. "Imagine an area of approximately 100 miles long," one Australian officer wrote. "Crumple and fold this into a series of ridges, each rising higher and higher until 7,000 feet is reached, then declining in ridges to 3,000 feet, cover this thickly with jungle, short trees and tall trees tangled with great entwining savage vines, through the oppression of this density cut a little native track 2–3 feet wide, up the ridges, over the spurs, around gorges and down across swiftly flowing happy mountain streams."

The job of negotiating the route would have been a challenge even for experienced hikers in good physical condition. For soldiers who were untrained and unprepared for such conditions, it could be lethal. So ignorant were the Japanese of Kokoda's realities that they brought packhorses who could not hope to survive amid such privation. "Practically all roads in the area of operations were native trails," a Japanese official report explained. "The route over the Owen Stanleys which led across deep gorges and razor-backed ridges was so steep that it was realized that it would have to be completely reconstructed before even packhorses could use it. Transportation of supplies was extremely difficult." Given a bare-bones food requirement of six hundred grams per day per soldier, the bare minimum supply requirement was three daily tons per five thousand soldiers. With resupply by vehicle and animals untenable, everything had to be carried laboriously from the beaches along this tortuous route, a twenty-day expedition just to get to the Owen Stanleys, much less anywhere beyond. Resupply by air was not a feasible option, mainly because the Japanese had few transport aircraft and little established doctrine, a real disadvantage in the face of enemies who were working hard to perfect the particulars of aerial supply and transportation. The Japanese soon hired or impressed Papuan laborers into carrying parties. One commander estimated the minimum need as forty-six hundred carriers just to sustain the advance. The final push for Port Moresby, assuming the South Seas Detachment made it that far, would require thirty-two thousand laborers. This did not even take into account the necessities of arduously evacuating wounded or sick men through such rough country or establishing aid stations to care for them.

The march turned into a sodden nightmare of hunger, disease, misery, and constant danger. Malaria, dysentery, and dengue fever ravaged the ranks, sapping the detachment's combat power. "Our equipment gets wet because of the rain every night, and becomes heavier," one soldier told his diary. "Our bodies smell because of the rain and perspiration. This is the perfume of war." Almost from the beginning, they ran into stubborn opposition from outnumbered Australian militiamen and Papuan infantrymen. Australian national policy required all able-bodied men to serve in the military for home defense, but they could not be compelled to fight overseas. The armed forces were divided into the Citizen Military Forces, known as militia, and the regulars of the Australian Imperial Forces (AIF), the latter of whom were volunteers who could be deployed anywhere. Because Papua New Guinea was technically under the administration of the Australian government, the militia could legally be sent there. The regulars often derided these men as "chocolate soldiers" who would melt away at the first sign of danger. But along the Kokoda Trail, the militiamen, whose average age was eighteen, contested the Japanese advance nearly every step of the way. They were reinforced by soldiers of the AIF's 7th Division. Together they fought a ferocious defensive battle, inflicting casualties on the Japanese while steadily withdrawing south in the direction of Port Moresby. "Worn out by strenuous fighting and exhausting movement, and weakened by lack of food and sleep and shelter, many of them had literally come to a stand still," Lieutenant Colonel Ralph Honner, commander of the 39th Battalion, the main militia unit, later wrote. "Practically every day torrential rains fell all through the afternoon and night, cascading into their cheerless weapon-pits and soaking the clothes they wore—the only ones they had. In these they shivered through the long chill vigil of the lonely nights when they were required to stand awake and alert but still and silent." Often they fought the Japanese at close quarters, in bloody battles to the death, day or night. In the aftermath of these encounters, the bodies of friend and foe frequently lay entwined in death as they could not have been in life. A Japanese newspaper correspondent, witnessing the detritus of one typical battle site, described "men in all postures and conditions showing how desperately they fought and fell."

From July through mid-September, the Australians traded worthless Papuan space for time. Though they were just as ravaged by the jungle, disease, and weather, and just as beset by logistical issues as the Japanese, they knew that, with every forward step, the Japanese grew weaker and ever more distant from their north-coast bases. "Every day I am losing my men," Lieutenant Kogoro Hirano confided to his diary in an experience typical of so many others. "I could not repress tears of bitterness." Staff Sergeant Sadashige Imanishi felt a premonition that he and his comrades had now entered "into something very tough, like we would eat soil in the ground. It was exactly as I expected." Maybe one-third of those who had set out from Buna and Gona were still on their feet. "We are like dead men walking around," Private Jiro Takamura scrawled in his diary.

Through superhuman effort and fighting for nearly every mile, these hardened veterans of the South Seas Detachment made it as far as the Maguli Range, and then to within about twenty-six miles of Port Moresby. From here they could see beautiful ocean waves shimmering tantalizingly in the distance, an incredible sight after endless weeks of suffocating green jungle and mountain. At night, they saw the searchlights of the Seven-Mile Airfield near Port Moresby dance off the tropical clouds. In the daytime, some could make out the peaked roofs and piers of the Allied base. An electrical excitement coursed through the Japanese soldiers. During their terrible march across a forbidding jungle that seemed to some like "treading on some living animal," the thought of Moresby had kept them going. Now here it was before them, seemingly within grasp. Overjoyed, they shed tears, hugged one another tightly, and whooped, "Long live the emperor!" Their objective was so close, they could almost taste it. But eerily reminiscent of the German soldiers who had glimpsed the spires of the Kremlin in Moscow the previous December, the survivors of the South Seas Detachment would get no closer to their prize. Exhausted, on the brink of starvation, diminished in numbers, facing determined, skillful opposition, they had no chance of taking well-defended Port Moresby on their own, with little air support, and no replacements for their considerable losses. Moreover, events elsewhere conspired to sabotage their efforts. When the Americans successfully landed troops from the 1st Marine Division at Guadalcanal on August 7, reinforcements from the Imperial Army's Ichiki and Kawaguchi Detachments that might otherwise have gone to New Guinea instead went to Guadalcanal, an ominous harbinger of the powerful linkage between the two battles for the Japanese.

Even worse, a Japanese invasion of Milne Bay on August 25–26 had failed miserably. Situated on the eastern mouth of Papua, ideally located to control the entire flank of New Guinea from that direction, Milne was an important spot. General MacArthur recognized this. Back in May, he had ordered the establishment of a base there. In this instance, the Allies had seized the initiative, grabbing Milne before the Japanese could get there (and while they were focused on their plan to take Moresby by amphibious invasion, the presage to the Coral Sea battle). Milne Bay was anything but hospitable. Rainfall totaled about two hundred inches per year. The terrain was dominated by swamps, jungles, and mountains. By late August, a battalion of American engineers had managed to carve out an airfield, with two more under construction. The engineers were reinforced by Australian militia and two AIF infantry brigades, including one just returned from service in the Middle East, plus antiaircraft units. The Japanese planned to use Milne to aid their push for Moresby. From Milne, they could stage amphibious forces, supplies, and sally air support. Instead, the Allied garrison of about ten thousand troops decisively defeated the enemy landing force of some two thousand men and several tanks. When the Japanese were sure the invasion had failed, they evacuated thirteen hundred survivors but, in the estimate of US Army official historian Samuel Milner, "virtually none of them in condition to fight." As at Kokoda, the reinforcements that might have augmented the Milne Bay invasion group instead went to Guadalcanal.

In the wake of the Milne Bay disaster and the failure of two major offensives to wipe out the US Marine perimeter around the growing air base at Guadalcanal, the Japanese high command knew there was no longer any chance of taking Moresby by land. The escalating struggle for Guadalcanal now took priority in Japanese strategic planning. Bitter though it may be, the South Seas Detachment would have to turn around and withdraw northward back on the Kokoda Trail, all the way to its bases on the north coast.

Fifty-one-year-old Major General Tomitaro Horii, the South Seas Detachment commander and conqueror of Rabaul, was a man of steely resolve and distant dignity. Stout, gray-haired, the general had embarked upon the expedition mounted atop a splendid white horse who had long since died in the jungle. On the evening of September 24, when he received the withdrawal order from his superior Lieutenant General Haruyoshi Hyakutake, commander of the Imperial Army's 17th Army, he was taken aback to the point of defiance. Sitting cross-legged by candlelight inside his tent, he growled to Lieutenant Colonel Toyonari Tanaka, his chief of staff, "I'm not going back. Not a step. How can we abandon this course after all the blood the men have shed and the hardships they've suffered? I can't give an order like that. I will not retreat an inch. I'd rather disguise myself as a native of these mountains and stay here." A follow-up order from Imperial Headquarters in Tokyo evaporated his defiance, though not his disappointment. The withdrawal was clearly the emperor's will. Horii had no choice but to obey. When Tanaka disseminated the news among the officers, they were devastated. To Lieutenant Hirano, the order "was like a bolt from the blue. It left us momentarily in a daze." He found it "truly regrettable to retreat . . . after pressing so close to Moresby at the cost of enormous sacrifice and casualties." Some commanders urged an all-out assault on Port Moresby. Tanaka, a circumspect and reasonable person, managed to dissuade them, "It would be pointless suicide." Though none of the soldiers could have known that the reversal at Moresby foretold the future pattern of the war, when the Japanese would seldom again advance strategically, at least on land, they did sense that a terrible moment had come. "We never knew how to retreat because we had never done it before," one NCO later said. Before the withdrawal, Horii attempted to soothe the bewildered fury of his men by circulating a laudatory statement among them. "We have waded through knee-deep mud, climbed breathtaking cliffs, uncomplainingly carried heavy weights of guns and ammunition, overcome the shortage of provisions, and thus accomplished a breakthrough of the so-called impregnable Stanley Range. Words cannot describe such hardship. I am truly thankful."

Within a few days, the remnants of the South Seas Detachment began a fighting withdrawal to the north, immersed for weeks in the same terrible battle against the elements, all the while harassed and attacked by the Australians, many of whom were also near the point of total collapse. "Gradually men dropped out utterly exhausted—just couldn't go on," one Australian officer recalled. "It was physically impossible to move. Many were lying down and had been sick." The job of supplying the advance over the tortuous Owen Stanleys was just as difficult for the Australians as it had been for the Japanese. The tail-to-tooth route was daunting. Freight was unloaded at Moresby, transferred to trucks and driven a few miles to a transfer point at Koitaki. From there, the matériel was loaded onto ten jeeps that carried it a few more miles to Owers' Corner, beyond which vehicles could no longer operate. Here the supplies were transferred to the backs of one thousand Papuan carriers (and sixty pack animals that could go only as far as the mountains but not over them) and then hauled all the way to front-line units. At maximum effort, this logistical line could sustain, quite uncomfortably, one brigade-size unit of about thirty-five hundred men.

Even as the Australians lost men to physical depletion, sickness, and combat, they gradually advanced north, nudging Horii's survivors back to the coast. The general himself did not survive the retreat. Within a few dozen miles of the north coast, Horii, Tanaka, and a few others boarded a modified raft and then a canoe in an attempt to ford rain-swollen rivers and link up with the rear bases. They made it to the sea and then tried to paddle down the coast through a heavy rainstorm and get to Gona. The canoe capsized. Tanaka, who could not swim, went down quickly. Horii struggled for a while to get ashore but soon tired. When aides tried to save him, he said, "Don't bother about us older men. Save yourselves. You are young and strong." According to one survivor, his last words were "Tell the troops that Horii died here. Long live the emperor." Something on the order of 14,500 Japanese had participated in the push for Port Moresby. No precise record exists of their losses, but by one reasonable estimate, only about one-third made it back to the north coast. The Australians suffered 1,680 battle casualties, including 625 killed. For every one of these casualties, somewhere between two and three men were lost to disease or physical or mental collapse. No one on either side seems to have calculated the losses, if any, among the Papuan laborers who handled supplies. For the Japanese, the most important casualty of Kokoda was the strategic initiative, at least for the near future in relation to New Guinea. They now had little choice but to hunker down in their perimeters from Gona to Buna and play for time.[2]

★

General MacArthur's headquarters was now in Brisbane, and he had turned the city into his home away from home. With Jean and Arthur, he took up residence in a secluded three-suite apartment at Lennon's, the only air-conditioned hotel in town. A private, heavily guarded elevator allowed MacArthur easy transit into and out of his apartment. The rest of the headquarters personnel—numbering in the hundreds—were crammed into rooms throughout the hotel. The hotel staff installed an awning over the hotel's entrance so the general could make it to his black staff car without fear of intrusion from the elements. The vehicle was adorned with a four-star front license plate and a rear plate that read "USA-1." When he tired of dining on the hotel's kitchen fare, Jean and Ah Cheu began to prepare most of his meals.

SWPA headquarters, generally known as GHQ (general headquarters), was located not far away, inside the nine-story AMP Insurance building, where MacArthur took up station in a spacious eighth-floor office that had once served as the company's boardroom. He worked seven days a week, logging long hours at the office. Each morning, at 0730, he ate breakfast with Jean and Arthur. At 1000, after reading newspapers and reports for a couple of hours, he hopped into his limousine and went to the office, where most staff members had already been working for several hours. At 1400, he went back home for lunch, took a nap until 1600, and then went back to the AMP building. He worked there until midevening, when he finally came home for a late dinner and some family time. When he was home, he doted on Arthur with gifts and affectionate attention. Occasionally he took the boy to the local zoo or read to him. Even more than Sutherland, Jean was MacArthur's confidante. He talked about nearly every aspect of the war with her, probably because he knew he could trust her implicitly. She almost never discussed the war with anyone else. He invariably called her

Jeannie. She referred to him as General or Sir Boss, and rarely ever by his given name.

Faithful to the core, MacArthur was not interested in the local social scene or other women. By contrast, Sutherland, who had a wife and twenty-two-year-old daughter at home, began a torrid affair with Elaine Bessemer-Clark, the wife of a British officer whom the Japanese had captured in Malaya. Elaine was the twenty-eight-year-old socialite daughter of Sir Norman Brookes, an Australian tennis champion whose family had become rich in paper manufacturing and gold mining. Her husband, Captain Reginald Bessemer-Clark, was himself a world-ranked tennis player and the great-grandson of Sir William Bessemer, who had pioneered steel-making technology later made famous by Andrew Carnegie. Rather inconveniently, the young couple had a toddler-age son. Forty-nine-year-old Sutherland was so smitten with Elaine that he arranged for her to work as a receptionist in the headquarters building. Her high-maintenance, blue-blooded sense of entitlement made her unpopular with many of the officers and enlisted soldiers who ran the headquarters. Since she was hardly an obscure figure locally, tongues soon began to wag all over town, and at GHQ, about Sutherland and his new mistress. MacArthur noticed but left his chief of staff's personal life alone.

In Brisbane, the SWPA commander remained a distant and almost mysterious figure to the Australian civilians, some of whom liked to cluster around the hotel entrance and gawk at the general as he made his way to and from his car. He was cordial and polite to anyone who greeted him, but seldom lingered to converse. He had no real hobbies or even distractions other than his family. As hard as MacArthur worked, he was, at this stage, quite distant from the war's terrible realities, an aloof figure, an office general who existed in an orderly, controlled environment (the same was true for Sutherland and most key members of the staff). This undoubtedly led to a profound blind spot about what war-making in the adverse environment of the South Pacific really meant, and this would not serve him well in the months to come.[3]

General MacArthur's immediate strategic goal was to take the Japanese bases at Gona and Buna, and secure Papua New Guinea as soon as possible, lest the enemy achieve success at Guadalcanal and then be in a position to reinforce Papua. In this nightmare scenario, the Japanese could alter the balance of power and once again threaten Milne Bay and perhaps even

Moresby. To eliminate this possibility, and win his first victory of World War II, MacArthur planned for the 7th Division to continue over the Kokoda Trail and capture the Japanese perimeters at Gona and Sanananda. MacArthur now had two US Army National Guard infantry divisions, the 32nd and the 41st, in Australia. He earmarked the 32nd to take Buna. Nicknamed the Red Arrow Division, and with an impressive historical pedigree of World War I combat service, many of the unit's soldiers hailed from Michigan and Wisconsin. Originally the 32nd was slated for service in Europe, until the War Department changed its assignment to SWPA (the change of plan was so haphazard that some of the division's engineers had already boarded ship and set sail for Northern Ireland).

MacArthur planned to move part of the division by sea and air to Pongani, about forty miles east of Buna along the coast. Here they would stage for the offensive to take Buna. At the same time, he wanted to maneuver a battalion-size force by land over the Kapa Kapa Trail—a track of such sparseness that it almost made Kokoda look like an interstate—to push for Wairopi, where they might cut off the retreating Japanese before they could reach the north coast. The plans revealed a commander who was thinking with an unusual mixture of innovation and obliviousness. The Philippine debacle, and the frustrating aftermath of operating on a shoestring in SWPA, had engendered in MacArthur little besides contempt for what he saw as the limited usefulness of the Army Air Force and its leadership. He had indulged his frustration by cashiering Lieutenant General Brett, the air leader in Australia, whom he thought of as disloyal and ineffective. Brett's replacement, Major General George Kenney, assumed his duties on August 4. Diminutive, stocky, and supremely self-confident, the fifty-three-year-old Kenney was a decorated World War I combat aviator and one of the Army Air Force's leading warrior intellectuals.

During their first meeting in MacArthur's office at the AMP building, MacArthur harangued Kenney for an hour about Air Force shortcomings and the supposed disloyalty of its officers. As was his wont, MacArthur paced back and forth while he unloaded his frustrations. His vituperation was so pronounced that, to Kenney, it seemed as if the SWPA commander was saying that the airmen were nothing but "an inefficient rabble of boulevard shock troops whose contribution to the war effort was practically nil." To Kenney's credit, he kept his cool and listened respectfully as MacArthur vented. When MacArthur was finally done, the airman assured the supreme commander that he knew how to run an air force better than anyone else in theater and that, whatever problems the aviation command had right now, he would do everything in his power to fix them and produce the results MacArthur wanted. "As far as the business of loyalty," Kenney later wrote, "I added that . . . there had never been any question of my loyalty to the one I was working for. I would be loyal to him and I would demand of everyone under me that they be loyal too." As Kenney spoke, the expression in MacArthur's eyes changed from anger to shrewd appraisal. When Kenney finished, the general approached with a grin on his face, draped his arm around the little airman, and said, "George, I think we are going to get along together all right." Indeed, it was the beginning of a remarkable and productive relationship. The two men became close colleagues, almost friends. Kenney lived a floor below MacArthur's apartment at Lennon's Hotel. Often the cocksure airman showed up unannounced at the commander's door to discuss a wide array of matters. At times, they conversed deep into the night about future plans and grand strategy.

Though MacArthur unfairly exaggerated the ineffectiveness of Kenney's predecessors, there was no question that Allied air was underachieving. Beyond the MacArthurian hyperbole about disloyalty and incompetence, the SWPA commander was correct that changes were in order. Within a few weeks, Kenney transformed the air contingent into an aggressive, can-do operation. He relieved ineffective commanders, streamlined administration, markedly improved maintenance, living conditions and food, and embraced low-level bombing techniques that would prove to be quite effective against ships. Whereas Brett and, before him, Brereton had lacked the confidence to deal with Sutherland effectively, Kenney proved willing to lock horns with the formidable chief of staff. Shortly before the war, Sutherland had earned a civilian pilot's license and received some training from Air Force colleagues. To him, flying was a sort of relaxation. Ever egotistical, Sutherland figured his mastery of an airplane's controls equated to a larger understanding of modern aerial warfare. Shortly after Kenney assumed command, Sutherland attempted to revise one of the air commander's mission orders, changing plans for bomb tonnage, takeoff times, and other matters. In effect, the chief of staff was trying to make himself the de facto air commander. When an outraged Kenney found out, he immediately confronted Sutherland at his office in the AMP building. Kenney grabbed a sheet of paper and drew a dot on it.

"The blank area represents my knowledge of air matters and the dot symbolizes yours," he said. Kenney further stipulated that, as far as he knew, the theater air commander was named Kenney, not Sutherland. When the chief of staff seemed unmoved, Kenney said flatly, "Let's go in the next room, see General MacArthur, and get this thing straight. I want to find out who is supposed to run this Air Force." Both of them were smart enough to know that MacArthur would reaffirm Kenney's authority. Sutherland backed down. Kenney had made his point.

Kenney also enlightened MacArthur on the game-changing ability of transport aircraft to supply combat troops, move them to and from the battle area, and evacuate wounded men. Nowhere were these ideas more applicable than in forbidding New Guinea, where the unruly climate and the near-total absence of infrastructure made resupply and movement exclusively by land an almost impossible proposition. Whereas the landward journey from south to north coast in Papua took many grueling weeks on foot, an aircraft could cover the same distance in about forty minutes.[4]

General Kenney's success meant that transport aircraft were now available to move troops. From September 16–28, his planes airlifted soldiers of the 32nd Division's 126th and 128th Infantry Regiments from Australia to the Port Moresby area. A few weeks later, they shuttled much of the 128th over the Owen Stanleys to a forward airstrip at Wanigela, where twenty-ton motor launches then transported them by water up the coast to Pongani. The agility with which Kenney and MacArthur pulled this off hinted at a growing Allied aerial proficiency that the Japanese would struggle to match. By moving the troops so effectively into and around New Guinea, MacArthur had embraced an innovative air-ground partnership, one that would only grow in efficiency and strength during the many wartime months to come.

In this light, one cannot escape the belief that MacArthur's plan to move a battalion on the Kapa Kapa Trail over the menacing Owen Stanleys for the long-shot objective of cutting off the retreating Japanese at Wairopi was foolish in the extreme. In normal terrain, with a reasonable climate, perhaps the order would have made some sense. Not in Papua New Guinea, though. "Parts of the island are quite beautiful, but it must be about 95% jungle and mountains," Sergeant Kinder wrote to a friend, shortly after his arrival on the island. "There are no railroads, and the roads would not equal the streets of any small town. There are no stores, and there is nothing to sell, even if there were stores. We wear, and carry, everything we own, and the prevalent method of traveling is by foot over the muddy, rooty, rocky, uphill and downhill, through mud and water, native tracks." The luckless 2nd Battalion, 126th Infantry Regiment received the daunting assignment to advance on the Kapa Kapa Trail, and it was a mission for which they were unprepared. Even their clothing was not ready. They had to dye their fatigues green to help them blend in with the jungle. On the ground, though, the dye soon ran freely and clogged the fabric, exacerbating the intensity of the tropical heat. Though MacArthur had made one visit to Port Moresby by October, he was almost completely ignorant of the conditions these men faced on the trail. From the vantage point of the 32nd Infantry Division's command post outside of Port Moresby, Major General Edwin "Forrest" Harding, the courtly division commander, was deeply troubled by the order. Upon arrival in New Guinea, the general and his staff had already seen how problematic it was to move men and supplies even near the coast, much less in the rougher inland terrain. "The difficulties are almost inconceivable," Major William Hawkins, the division intelligence officer, wrote in his diary. "It means carrying everything on the men's backs for a hundred miles over the roughest country in the world—through mud, heat, rain and insects." He expected "weeks, maybe months of terrific work, under the worst conditions, in pushing men and materials over these razor back ridges, through dense jungle and across streams."

Had MacArthur known of Kapa Kapa's terrible realities, it is difficult to imagine that he would have allowed the 2nd Battalion to proceed on such an ill-conceived wild-goose chase. As Hawkins anticipated, the tribulations they faced were as bad or worse than what the Australians and Japanese dealt with along the Kokoda Trail. "It is ten times worse than you can imagine," First Sergeant Paul Lutjens of E Company scribbled in a small notebook he carried inside his shirt pocket. The heat was suffocating. Rain poured in heavy sheets every afternoon. It was impossible to keep weapons, uniforms, and personal items dry for any substantial length of time. Routinely soaked to the skin, Lieutenant Robert Odell ruefully remembered what an Australian officer had told him a few weeks earlier. "In New Guinea it rains every day for nine months, and then the rainy season sets in!" Exhausted men fell out in droves. "Footing was insecure," Captain Alfred Medendorp who led an advance patrol, later wrote. "Leeches and insects began to be a nuisance. The trail was strewn with cast off articles. Leather toilet sets, soap, socks, towels and extra underwear told a tale of exhaustion and misery. The trail was filled with struggling individuals. Many were lying to one side panting for breath." Thirst-crazed men gulped water from filthy streams and were soon wracked with dysentery. For some, their diarrhea was so uncontrollable that they simply cut a hole in their seat trousers rather than take them off for every spastic bowel movement.

The men were green to the ways of combat. At night they shivered in worried perimeters and shot at anything that moved (fortunately the Japanese were nowhere nearby). During the day, they covered as much ground as they could. "You walk an hour and then rest ten minutes from dawn to dark," Lieutenant Odell, a young platoon leader in F Company, wrote in a fascinating contemporary statement. "You tramp across fields the grass of which reaches high above your head, and cuts your hands every time it touches them; the sun beats down on you unmercifully—you sweat so profusely the salt stings your eyes, and the skin is raw wherever pack or belt touches it. You walk through thick jungle, which until the advent of American troops was seldom if ever seen by another white man. You trip on vines and roots with every step. You sink in mud up to your knees, and sometimes need help extracting yourself. Your clothes—the only ones you carry are what you have on—soon begin to disintegrate from sweat and general wear. You walk through swamps wondering what strange animal you'll see or hear next. You wade mountain streams, some of which reach to your neck and have a current of perhaps 20 m.p.h. You walk, climb, stumble, swim and curse, but always you must keep going. Your lungs seem ready to burst at any minute; your heart goes like a trip-hammer, your knees feel, if indeed they feel at all, like they are certain to collapse at the next step. The mosquitoes . . . bite every inch of skin they can reach. The ants . . . do the same."

Papuan supply carriers taught the Americans how to make fires by rubbing sticks together and how to build makeshift huts by chopping down fauna with machetes. As the column neared the Owen Stanleys, the carriers, most of whom were recruited from coastal areas, gradually melted away. The Americans tended to take this personally—one commander even threatened to place the carriers under armed guard—but they should not have been surprised. Most of the Papuans had no experience in the mountains. They were especially reluctant to climb Mount Suwemalla, or "Ghost Mountain" as they and the Americans called the ten-thousand-feet peak that dominated the Owen Stanleys. Many of the New Guineans believed that Ghost Mountain was haunted, a place to be avoided at all cost, and indeed there was something strange and forbidding about it. "It was the eeriest place I ever saw," Lutjens later said. "The trees were covered with green moss half a foot thick. We would walk along a hog's back, straddling the trail, with a sheer drop of thousands of feet, two feet on either side of us. We kept hearing water running somewhere, but we couldn't find any. We could thrust a stick six feet down through the spongy stuff we were walking on without hitting anything real solid. It was ungodly cold. There wasn't a sign of life. Not a bird. Not a fly. Not a sound. It was the strangest feeling I ever had." For the pittance the Papuan were paid, the laborious nature of their work, the potential dangers of facing the Japanese, and the abstractness of the Allied cause, one could hardly blame them for opting out.

The American troops soon realized they could not hope to carry more than twenty or thirty pounds of gear. They held on to their weapons, ammunition, and food and then threw most everything else away. At designated locations in clearings, C-47s dropped supplies to them. "This was done by placing a stack of the boxes by the open cargo door on the side of the plane," Tech 4 Kenneth Springer explained. "Then the man kicking out the rations would hold on to straps on both sides of the cabin door and kick out the items. The recovery rate of these items was about 70 percent." The drops were well executed, but they barely provided the minimum requirements for the battalion. The food consisted mainly of C rations and far too much bully beef and rice. Many of the soldiers were so revolted by the smell of the bully beef that, when their C rations ran out, they chose not to eat. Men lost as much as twenty, even thirty pounds. The descent out of the mountains proved just as exhausting as the ascent into and over them. "The only thing to be seen while struggling practically straight down one mountainside was the equally steep ascent of another mountain rising a stone's throw away," said Lieutenant Odell. "A succession of four or five of these represented a day's march. I wish I had some record of the amount of sweat that poured off me during this descent alone."

They edged along cliff walls, hung on to vines to maintain their footing. Often it took five or six hours just to cover one mile. The ragged column snaked for two or three miles through the jungle. "Our strength is about gone," First Sergeant Lutjens scrawled in his notebook at one point. "Most of us have dysentery. Boys are falling out and dropping back with the fever.

God, will it never end?" Medics operated as closers, tending to the many soldiers who collapsed or fell by the wayside. "They marched at the tail of the column to care for those suffering from exhaustion, dysentery and other ailments," Lieutenant Colonel Herbert M. Smith later wrote. Smith took over the battalion after the previous commander suffered a heart attack and had to be evacuated back to Moresby. "Many members of the 2nd. Bn. owe their lives to these doctors, because they had marched to the end of their endurance . . . they were ready to call it 'quits' and die." The regimental commander, Colonel Lawrence Quinn was killed in a plane crash as he supervised a resupply drop. Incredibly, though, fatalities and permanent debilitations were minimal during the miserable trek of greater than forty days. In late October, the exhausted battalion reached Jaure and then Wairopi, where they settled down, began patrolling, and experienced their first clashes with Japanese patrols.

Ironically MacArthur by now understood that the idea of cutting off the Japanese retreat to the coast was unrealistic. His realization fully set in when the theater engineer, Brigadier General Hugh "Pat" Casey, persuaded him of the utter futility of building an overland supply road. "Pat, your logic is quite sound," MacArthur told Casey. "We won't build the road." With the idea of the road scrapped, MacArthur fully committed to the notion of airlifting the troops over the Owen Stanleys rather than sending them by land across Papua New Guinea to eliminate the Japanese perimeters. As October ended, two Australian brigades were nearing the Gona-Sanananda area while to the east most of the 32nd Division's 126th and 128th Infantry Regiments were staging around Pongani, Oro Bay, and Natunga, preparing to push for Buna. MacArthur believed that there was no time to lose. He was eager for these forces to press on and snuff out the Japanese-held perimeters before the enemy could reinforce and fortify them. In the bigger picture, he sensed that the success or failure of his offensive to secure Papua might yet depend on the outcome of events at Guadalcanal, where the struggle to control that island now reached a tipping point.[5]

★

The locus of the fighting on Guadalcanal was the airfield. The Americans had invaded the island in August to seize control of this objective and then dubbed it Henderson Field, after Major Lofton Henderson, a Marine

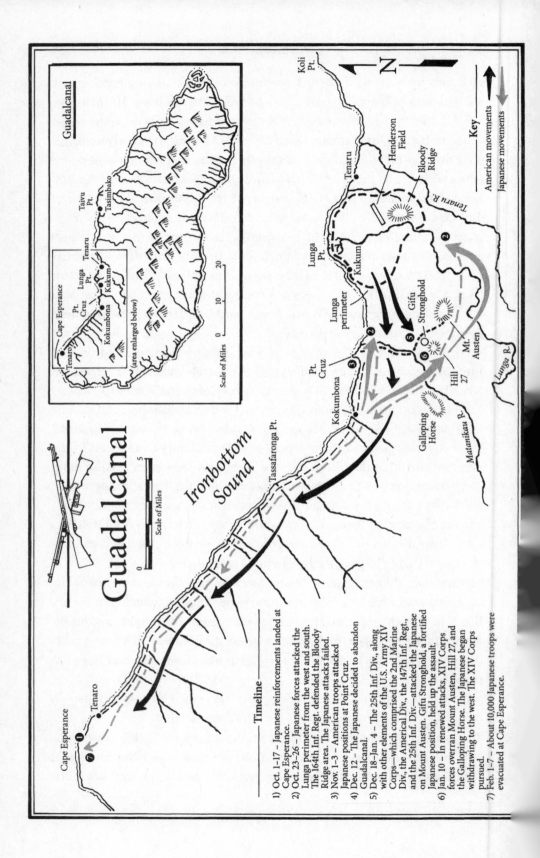

Guadalcanal

Ironbottom Sound

Scale of Miles
0   5

Cape Esperance
Tenaro

Tassafaronga Pt.

Kokumbona

Pt. Cruz

Lunga Pt.
Kukum

Lunga perimeter

Henderson Field

Bloody Ridge

Tenaru

Koli Pt.

Gifu Stronghold

Mt. Austen

Hill 27

Galloping Horse

Matanikau R.

Lunga R.

N

Key
American movements
Japanese movements

Guadalcanal (inset)

Cape Esperance
Tenaro
Pt. Cruz
Lunga Pt.
Kukum
Tenaru
Kokumbona
Taivu Pt.
Tasimbako

(area enlarged below)

Scale of Miles
0   10   20

Timeline

1) Oct. 1–17 – Japanese reinforcements landed at Cape Esperance.

2) Oct. 23–26 – Japanese forces attacked the Lunga perimeter from the west and south. The 164th Inf. Regt. defended the Bloody Ridge area. The Japanese attacks failed.

3) Nov. 1–3 – American troops attacked Japanese positions at Point Cruz.

4) Dec. 12 – The Japanese decided to abandon Guadalcanal.

5) Dec. 18–Jan. 4 – The 25th Inf. Div., along with other elements of the U.S. Army XIV Corps—which comprised the 2nd Marine Div., the Americal Div., the 147th Inf. Regt., and the 25th Inf. Div.—attacked the Japanese on Mount Austen. Gifu Stronghold, a fortified Japanese position, held up the assault.

6) Jan. 10 – In renewed attacks, XIV Corps forces overran Mount Austen, Hill 27, and the Galloping Horse. The Japanese began withdrawing to the west. The XIV Corps pursued.

7) Feb. 1–7 – About 10,000 Japanese troops were evacuated at Cape Esperance.

aviator who was killed in the Battle of Midway. The 1st Marine Division carved out a perimeter around the airfield and its environs. Realizing the vital importance of Henderson Field, the Japanese responded to the American invasion with land, sea, and air forces of their own. Between early August and early October, Guadalcanal escalated into a monumental struggle between the two adversaries, fought in all three dimensions. Japanese land-based planes, hailing primarily from Rabaul and the northern Solomons, attacked US Navy ships and the Marine perimeter. Naval engagements, surface and air, raged for miles in every direction around the island. For much of those two months, the US Navy had difficulty maintaining continuous control of the waters around Guadalcanal, so the undersupplied Marines had to make do with whatever they had. In addition to pounding Henderson by air and sea, the Japanese tried two separate land attacks to capture the airfield. In both instances, they dramatically underestimated the size and strength of the US garrison. The first time, on the evening of August 20–21, about one thousand soldiers from the Imperial Army's 28th Infantry Regiment under Colonel Kiyono Ichiki attempted to overrun the Marine perimeter by assaulting over a narrow sandbar along the coast. The Ichiki Detachment consisted of hardened, close-knit combat soldiers who had known only victory in China. With the sea to their right and Alligator Creek, a swampy lagoon, in front of them, they effectively penned themselves into a kill zone. The Marines slaughtered them in droves and destroyed the Ichiki Detachment as a cohesive fighting unit. Ichiki himself either died in the fighting or committed suicide in the midst of it. "The dead on the beach were so thick that bulldozers were used to bury them," a Marine report chronicled.

Stunned at the potency of American resistance, the Japanese redoubled their efforts to take Guadalcanal. In the weeks that followed the Ichiki Detachment disaster, the Imperial Navy landed more troops from the 4th, 28th, and 124th Infantry Regiments, plus antiaircraft artillery, engineers, mortars, and medics under the command of Major General Kiyotake Kawaguchi. These were soldiers who might well have made a constructive difference in Papua. Instead, they were fed into the Guadalcanal maw. In spite of the disaster at Alligator Creek, Japanese intelligence still dramatically underestimated the number of Americans on the island. Kawaguchi and his officers believed there were about two thousand Marines in the Henderson perimeter. In truth there were at least seven times that many, plus a small force of Marine fighters and fighter bombers that the leather-necks called the Cactus Air Force. From September 12 through 14, Kawa-guchi tried to capture Henderson Field, this time by attempting to take a neck of prominent high ground, known to the Americans as either Edson's Ridge or Bloody Ridge, south of the airfield. Once again, the Marines held firm and inflicted massive losses on the Japanese. "We must have accurate intelligence reports if we are to evaluate the enemy situation correctly!" one Japanese staff officer raged in impotent frustration to his Tokyo superiors.[6]

The harder both sides fought over Guadalcanal, the more important it seemed to become. "Nothing could be done about the New Guinea opera-tion until a victory had been won at Guadalcanal," Major General Shuichi Miyazaki, chief of staff for the Japanese 17th Army, later asserted. By the second week of October, Major General Alexander "Archie" Vandegrift's entire 1st Marine Division was ashore. Almost twenty-three thousand men were covering the hard-pressed perimeter, a sizable force though many were sick with malaria and other tropical diseases. "The early days of Oc-tober found conditions on Guadalcanal still critical," the Army's South Pacific command historian later related. "Japanese naval surface units shelled our installations on shore. Their submarines hunted Allied ship-ping and made difficult the supply and reinforcement of the marines. Their aircraft . . . bombed our positions by day and, if the moon was suitable, by night. We could scramble an average of only 40 fighters and 22 dive or torpedo bombers, based at Henderson Field and a nearby fighter strip." Kawaguchi's failure did not diminish Japanese resolve to take Henderson and win at Guadalcanal. Using destroyers, landing craft, cargo ships, and transport ships, they fed reinforcements from the Imperial Army's 2nd and 38th Divisions onto the island—again these were troops who were diverted from the possibility of serving in Papua—and planned to make another push for the airfield. The reinforcements brought Japanese troop strength to around twenty thousand men. They now planned to pound Henderson by sea and air, in tandem with a ground attack.

Admiral Ghormley, the South Pacific Area commander, worried that the growing Japanese naval and troop strength might eventually prove decisive, especially if the Marines were not reinforced. Major General Mil-lard Harmon, commander of US Army Forces in the South Pacific, shared the concerns of his superior. Harmon recommended an expansion of sur-face naval operations and the reinforcement of the Guadalcanal garrison by an Army infantry regimental combat team as well as construction personnel to expand the operational capability of the airfield. Harmon's command consisted mostly of service troops, engineers, and aviators sprinkled among islands south and east of the Solomons. The primary available ground combat element was 850 miles to the south, at New Caledonia, a Free French colony. These GIs had made a circuitous monthlong ocean journey that had taken them from New York through the Panama Canal to a brief excursion in Australia and thence finally to their ultimate objective in March. Originally known as Task Force 6814, they had since been built from a hodgepodge of National Guard and other formations into a full-strength infantry division. Technically their moniker was the 23rd Infantry Division, but PFC David Fonseca, a signalman, proposed to his superiors that, owing to the division's unique origins, they adopt the name Americal, an amalgam of America and New Caledonia. He found a receptive audience. With the exception of the now defunct Philippine Division, the Americal became the only division-size unit in the Army that was not known by a number. On their left shoulder sleeves, soldiers wore a distinctive blue patch with four white stars that symbolized the Southern Cross, another nod to the unit's origins. The presence of the Americal in New Caledonia solidified Allied control of the colony and forestalled any possibility of a Japanese invasion. For months, the Americal troops trained in the island's tropical heat, hiking myriad rugged hills. "The men got brown and hard and their spirits, though restless, were excellent," said the division's 1942 narrative.

Ghormley possessed only enough shipping and logistical capability to move one regimental combat team to Guadalcanal. Harmon chose the 164th Infantry Regiment, a North Dakota guard unit under Colonel Bryant Moore. The soldiers loaded aboard a pair of transport ships, the USS *Zeilin* and the USS *McCawley*. An escort force of four cruisers, eight destroyers, and three minelayers escorted the convoy safely to Guadalcanal. Throughout the day on October 13, the entire regiment of 2,852 soldiers, plus vehicles, equipment, antitank guns, rations, and other supplies made it safely ashore in spite of two separate Japanese air raids. For weeks, the grizzled, exhausted, hungry Marines had hung on and repelled everything the Japanese could throw at them. Silly rumors—undoubtedly fed by the parochial, self-conscious superiority that nearly all Marines felt toward soldiers—spread around the ranks that Army units were languishing on other islands, living well while the Marines did all the fighting. In the memory of Marine Major Donald Dickson, the stories claimed that soldiers "were all sitting on their fat ducks down there not doing anything, that they were being issued beer, candy, and cigarettes. We didn't have any beer, and we didn't have any candy. Cigarettes were very scarce." The rumor also revealed a common supposition among the Marines, crucial to their service identity and pride, that the Army was always better supplied.

In spite of the rhetoric, the Marines were happy to have some help. For more than two months, they had felt alone, isolated, surrounded. The arrival of the 164th proved that they were actually neither surrounded nor forgotten. To the lean Marines, the newcomers looked chunky and fresh-faced, even though most were actually a few years older. "Their faces were heavy with flesh, their ribs padded, their eyes innocent," observed Private Robert Leckie, a Marine machine gunner. He and his buddies were underweight, filthy, cynical, and their eyes betrayed a combination of numbness and trauma. To the rookies, they were a slightly frightening sight. An Army correspondent described them as "the most vicious, compassionless and thorough destroyers among the fighting men of the world. They have absolutely no mercy; it was knocked out of them the first weeks." In the time-honored tradition of interservice midnight requisitioning, some of the Marines swiped socks, food, soap, and clothing from the 164th's newly landed supplies. "We applauded him as the men of Robin Hood might have sung the praises of Little John upon his return from a light-fingered excursion into Nottingham Town," Leckie wrote of his unit's master thief. Regardless of service, no one seemed to blame the thieves for taking what they needed to function in combat. The burden was on the owner to protect his property. If he did not, then it was fair game. When a soldier in Lieutenant Charles Walker's platoon left his M1 Garand unattended, a Marine stole it and left him an older Springfield bolt-action rifle as compensation. "You greenhorn," an unsympathetic Walker told his soldier. "You're stuck with it! Smarten up!"

The three-sided American perimeter stretched six miles wide and three miles deep. All three regiments of the 1st Marine Division were spread along a defensive line, in a circular formation that stretched from the Matanikau River in the west to Alligator Creek in the east. Vandegrift assigned the 164th responsibility for the eastern flank of the perimeter, the largest sector of all. The 6,600-yard line stretched from the beach all the way to the left flank of the 7th Marine Regiment, south of Henderson Field, adjacent to Edson's Ridge. A Marine defense battalion, engineers, Coast Artillery, and other assorted troops defended the beach. Most of the defensive positions were sandbagged and protected by double aprons of barbed wire. Most faced the sort of thick jungle that blanketed large swaths of Guadalcanal. Significantly, the Marines had forced the Japanese to the west bank of the Matanikau River. This had the effect of limiting Japanese offensive options against the western side of the perimeter, site of the most advantageous terrain along the coast. Instead of relying mainly on a costly river crossing and coastal attack to get to Henderson, the Japanese were forced to consider moving the mass of their forces through thick jungle to conduct a main attack against the Edson's Ridge area. As one more indicator of Guadalcanal's overarching importance to the Japanese, General Hyakutake was now ashore. He located his headquarters in a valley a few miles west of the Matanikau. He fully appreciated the difficulty of his mission to take Henderson Field. He hoped that extensive pounding of the airfield by air, artillery, and sea would ground or destroy the Cactus Air Force. With the American land-based planes out of the picture, Japanese transports would have an easier time landing reinforcements on Guadalcanal and Hyakutake's troops would have more freedom of maneuver all over the island.

The bombardment of Henderson and the adjacent fighter strip thus intensified, particularly on the evening of October 13–14 when a pair of Japanese battleships shelled the airfield and its environs. Over the course of eighty minutes, they fired 918 fourteen-inch rounds. Each high-velocity shell was five feet long and weighed fourteen hundred pounds. Their explosions emitted waves of searing heat and assaulted the eardrums with all the force of intense thunderclaps. According to one Army source, "the explosion of the large shells was at times so violent and continuous that the ground shook like an earthquake." Soldiers and Marines frantically took cover in bunkers, foxholes, ditches, and craters. Lieutenant Walker and several other men were so desperate for shelter that they huddled in a makeshift latrine ditch that offered some overhead cover. "The soft, mushy bottom of the trench and the vile odor told us plenty, but not an objection was heard," he wrote. Terrified men prayed fervently. Some cried uncontrollably. Some soiled themselves. Most never forgot the abject, helpless fear of these terrible moments. "I thought it was the end of the world," one Marine later said. In spite of the tension, the chaplain of the 164th provoked laughter when he concluded a quick prayer and said, "Well, gentlemen, I've done all I can for you."

Runways were cratered. Tall coconut trees were flung into the air. Planes and fuel exploded. Fires lit the night. A Japanese source recorded a scene of "explosions . . . everywhere, and the entire airfield was a sea of flame." Dozens of planes were destroyed or out of commission; forty-one men were killed. Daylight revealed a scene of devastation. In the view of one man, "it looked [like] some god had swept his giant hand" and unleashed wanton destruction. Only forty-two planes could still fly. The handful of B-17 bombers based at Henderson could not operate under such conditions. They took off for Espiritu Santo, several hundred miles to the south in New Caledonia. Lieutenant Walker, soiled by the latrine, got rid of his canvas leggings and washed himself thoroughly in the ocean. As he walked back along the beach, he saw Japanese arms, torsos, and legs sticking out of the sand—the remnants of the Ichiki Detachment.

Japanese air raids inflicted even more damage on Henderson Field. Long-range 150-millimeter artillery pieces, universally called "Pistol Pete" by the Americans, sniped away with intermittent shells, adding to the misery. Subsequent evenings brought more bombardments from enemy cruisers and destroyers, though not as intense as October 13–14. The Americans referred to this nightly pounding as the "Tokyo Express." For nearly a week, Henderson was out of commission, though the grass fighter strip remained in operation for a couple dozen planes. The Cactus Air Force now had only enough fuel on hand for two days of missions. Marines scoured the area and siphoned the tanks of wrecked planes to salvage any fuel they could. C-47s managed to land and replenish their stocks and avert total disaster as Navy Construction Battalions, or Seabees, worked diligently to effect repairs to Henderson Field.[7]

Fortunately for the Americans, Hyakutake was unable to coordinate his ground offensive closely with the air and sea bombardments. It took him almost two weeks, and several postponements, to finalize his plans for the ground assault. Soldiers of the 4th and 124th Infantry Regiments, augmented by light tanks and twenty-five artillery pieces, were to put pressure on the protruding American salient at the Matanikau. Hyakutake placed this force of about three thousand men under the charge of his artillery commander, Major General Tadashi Sumiyoshi. Their mission was to divert American attention and reserves away from Henderson while a maneuver force of fifty-six hundred men, under Lieutenant General Masao Maruyama, commander of the Imperial Army's 2nd Division, was to launch an all-out assault from the south, over Edson's Ridge, and capture Henderson. Appropriately enough, the code word for mission success was "banzai." For this job, Maruyama had almost two full regiments from his division plus trench mortars and light artillery. The Maruyama Force consisted of newly landed troops from the 16th Division and 29th and 230th Infantry Regiments plus Kawaguchi's survivors from the 124th. Maruyama divided his force into two wings. The 29th led the way on the left wing, followed by the 16th in reserve; on the right wing, a battalion from the 124th and two battalions from the 230th were scheduled to lead the attack under the tutelage of Kawaguchi. The plan called for the two wings to crash through Edson's Ridge, roughly where the 7th Marine Regiment sector bordered the 164th Infantry Regiment sector, overrun their leading positions, and seize the field.

Looking deeper into history, we might loosely compare the Maruyama Force's task to that of Stonewall Jackson's flanking attackers at Chancellorsville, though in considerably more challenging conditions against a better-led foe. Much more so than for Jackson's Confederates, the mere job of maneuvering into place required a near superhuman effort from Maruyama's soldiers. With no animals or heavy equipment of any kind, they had to carve out an inland trail with scythes, axes, saws, and machetes through thirty-five miles of thick tropical jungle, and across two rivers, just to put themselves in position to attack the Americans. The march was grueling and the trail so narrow that only a single file of troops could traverse it. Those at the van hacked their way forward. Those at the end often had to wait all day until there was room to move forward. By this time, the men at the vanguard were too exhausted to move. In the apt description of the US Army's official historian, the Maruyama Force "inched along like a worm," and usually in pouring rain. Cooking fires and smoking were prohibited lest the smoke alert the Americans. Soldiers subsisted mainly on unappetizing, uncooked rice balls. Many of the men were feeling the effects of tropical fevers or malaria. Mortars, artillery pieces, and heavy machine guns were moved laboriously by ropes and pulleys. At Hyakutake's insistence, every soldier carried one shell in addition to his regular load of knapsack, personal weapon, ammo, and other equipment. As exhaustion set in, some soldiers discarded the shells and significant amounts of machine-gun ammunition. Many of the guns also had to be abandoned. "After a few days of this, our uniforms were in tatters and we had many open sores constantly irritated by being soaked with sweat," Sergeant Hisakichi Hara of the 230th Infantry recalled. "We trudged at the bottom of an ocean of foliage that denied us the benefit of sunshine."

The jungle was so thick and the trail so dark that many soldiers took to smearing the luminescent carcasses of rotting insects or foliage onto the knapsack of the man to his immediate front to keep from losing sight of him. Only the thought of dying honorably in combat rather than anonymously on the trail kept many of them going. Some, like Captain Jiro Katsumata, a company commander in the 29th Infantry, felt almost too numb to function normally. "I cannot any longer think of anything," he told his diary. He thought of himself as "only a spirit drifting toward an undefined, unknowable world." Sergeant Hara consoled himself by fantasizing about the prospect of capturing enemy rations. "Soon we feast on Yankee food! Roosevelt rations, breakfast biscuits, and coffee." To Lieutenant Kenji Matsumoto, a platoon leader in the 124th Infantry, it seemed as if his men were wasting away before his eyes. "I cannot help from crying when I see the sight of these men marching without food for four and five days and carrying the wounded through the curving and sloping mountain roads. Hiding my tears I encouraged the ones with weak will to march on."

Maps were poor, communications with 7th Army and General Sumiyoshi's diversion force spotty. The Maruyama Force did not make it to within striking distance of Henderson Field until October 23 (and even then many commanders had little idea of their exact location or attacking routes). The Americans were still largely unaware of their presence, though they knew a ground attack was bound to follow the relentless bombardment of Henderson Field. Given all the challenges facing the Japanese, it was hardly surprising that their offensive was poorly coordinated. By late afternoon on the twenty-third, Sumiyoshi was under the impression that the Maruyama Force was ready to go, so he gave the order to attack the Marine salient at the Matanikau late on the afternoon. The push failed, costing the Japanese most of their tanks on Guadalcanal, and alerting the Americans to watch out for an attack elsewhere. After the war, the Japanese commanders all blamed one another for the fiasco.

Meanwhile, everything now depended on the Maruyama Force. "This is the decisive battle between Japan and the United States in which the rise or fall of the Japanese empire will be decided," he told his soldiers in a melodramatic general order. "If we do not succeed in the occupation of these islands, no one should expect to return alive to Japan." Aerial reconnaissance photos provided some good intelligence on the American defenses and the area as a whole, but only senior officers saw the pictures. Back in September, before leading the second Japanese attack, Kawaguchi had compared the Americans to "cornered rats which bite the cat," and implored his soldiers that "the final decision of victory or defeat will lie in spiritual power and not in material strength." The latter view was prevalent among the Japanese, no matter the rank or station. But, having seen his men decimated by American firepower at Edson's Ridge in mid-September, Kawaguchi was more circumspect now. The recon photos of his route of advance revealed an enemy who had heavily fortified the perimeter with well-sited, dug-in machine guns, mortars, and artillery bunkers and trenches, augmented by minefields and barbed wire. "If we attack those strong positions, it will be like throwing eggs against an iron wall," he worriedly told his diary. Rather than attack on this route, he favored maneuvering farther east to probe for a weaker spot on the eastern flank of the American perimeter. He attempted to persuade one of Maruyama's staff officers and then the general himself of this new plan during a brief phone call. Maruyama knew that Kawaguchi's plan would cost more time that he did not have, so he would not hear of it. Kawaguchi refused to relent. "I cannot take responsibility for a frontal attack," he said. Maruyama relieved him and put Colonel Toshinari Shoji, commanding officer of the 230th Infantry, in charge of the right wing, even though Shoji protested that the act of sacking a commander on the eve of battle was "not the way of the samurai." Regardless, the attack would go ahead as planned.[8]

All afternoon on October 24, torrential rain poured down from the gloomy skies above Guadalcanal, making the experience of trudging through the jungle to assembly points even more miserable for troops of the assault companies. The rain had tapered off by nightfall, but the moist, dripping humidity remained. Some men ate a paltry final meal of boiled rice. In the darkness some of them mistakenly mixed mud and pebbles in with their rice. Among the men, the mood of fear was almost palpable. "Is it true that we can eat rich American food if we take the objective?" one young soldier asked Private Ichiro Takizawa. "I hope so," he replied. A frightened corporal who was a university graduate looked at Takizawa and asked, "What do you think of this war? The enemy is human. Why should we kill each other?" Takizawa had no idea what to answer. As his group filed past their regimental commander, Colonel Masajiro Komiya, he noticed Komiya sitting against a tree with arms folded, "like a stone buddha."

The jungle was so dark and bewildering that, in some units, commanders ordered their men to place a hand on the next man's shoulder lest entire squads meander away and get lost. Near midnight, when the attack at last began, it was anything but well orchestrated or even minimally coordinated. Instead of carrying out a carefully prepared plan, the troops simply blundered forward in disorganized clumps. Colonel Shoji's people were so lost that they staggered in behind the 29th Infantry attackers of the left-wing force and played no meaningful role in the battle, thus negating the entire right wing of Maruyama's attack. The heaviest supporting weapons were machine guns. With little training in combined arms coordination— not to mention no supporting artillery or mortar fire—the attackers simply charged headlong at the American lines, most heavily at the section of front that connected the 7th Marine Regiment and the Army's 164th Infantry Regiment.

Some of the assault troops smoked cigarettes, the height of indiscipline and irresponsibility. The cherry-red glow of their cigarettes acted as beacons for the defenders. American machine-gun, rifle, and mortar fire scythed through them. The Americans had put rocks inside ration cans and fixed them to the barbed wire as an alert system. Japanese soldiers brushed against the cans or got hung up on the wire. As Captain Katsumata attempted to crawl quietly over a strand of wire, he saw, to his horror, his men stand up and charge without any instructions from him. Bullets and fragments tore into dozens of them. Mines blew up several more. The captain made it over a strand of barbed wire only to be grazed by machine-gun bullets in his right cheek and right knee. All around, other commanders yelled "*Kogecki!*" the Japanese word for "attack." American artillery and mortar shells screamed in and exploded, lighting up the night and exposing the attackers to horribly accurate fire. The 81-millimeter mortar platoon of M Company, 164th Infantry alone fired twelve hundred shells. H Company added another sixteen hundred rounds. Thirty-seven-millimeter canister fire from the 164th's Antitank Company reaped an especially grim harvest. "In the dim light I could see bodies and more bodies," Lieutenant Walker recalled. "Some were heaped on the barbed wire, which sagged in many places from their weight."

Desperate to escape the heavy fire, the Japanese survivors surged ahead and fought among the forward holes. Grenade duels were common, as were hand-to-hand knife and pistol struggles. The Japanese overran a pair of mortar pits until a Marine counterstroke recaptured the pits and killed off the attackers. To shore up the hard-pressed line, General Vandegrift fed Lieutenant Robert Hall's 3rd Battalion, 164th Infantry from its reserve positions near Henderson Field into the battle, shoring up the hard-pressed line around Edson's Ridge and adding more rifles, machine guns, and mortars to the American mix. Time and again that night, the Japanese tried to overwhelm the US lines, but to no avail.

Following another day of air and sea bombardment (dubbed "Dugout Sunday" by the Americans), the Japanese tried another clumsy, but terrifying, night assault, this time with the 16th Division and the survivors of the 29th Infantry. "The enemy attacked in groups, and as quickly as one group was mowed down another moved up," Lieutenant Walker, whose platoon showered them with mortar shells, later wrote. "For brief, short periods, the din was terrific: antitank guns firing canister . . . two .50 caliber machine guns, many .30 caliber machine guns, 60 and 81 millimeter mortars, and practically all the artillery that could be safely spared." One Marine platoon sergeant, Mitchell Paige, fired a water-cooled .30-caliber machine gun until it was destroyed and then directed the fire of his other section guns and personally led local counterattacks all night long. "Dark shapes crawled across the ground," he said. "Men fought on the ground with bayonets and swords, shouting curses at each other." Indeed, the Japanese commonly called out "Blood for the emperor" as they surged forward. One machine gunner mockingly replied, "Blood for Eleanor!" in a joking reference to Eleanor Roosevelt. More commonly, the Americans yelled, "Tōjō and the emperor eat shit!" For Paige's valor and leadership that evening, he earned the Medal of Honor and a field commission.

In no place did the Japanese succeed in breeching the American defenses for any appreciable length of time. Those who did get behind the American lines were cut off, reduced to wandering around until they were hunted down as quarry by American patrols. Colonel Komiya ended up stranded with one such group, roaming around, searching in vain for any way to get back to their own lines. During his odyssey, the colonel optimistically jotted some notes that he hoped might reach Maruyama's attention. "We carried out our plan regardless of success or failure. The determination of the commanders from the beginning was to die in Guadalcanal if this was unsuccessful. I also have this determination. I am sorry that I lost many troops uselessly. Please forgive me for not being able to apologize to you any more than by death. We must not overlook firepower. I express my sincere apologies." When Komiya knew he was doomed, he destroyed his regimental colors and killed himself. A Marine patrol found the notebook on his body.

The Japanese offensive had been an unmitigated disaster. "It was just as stupid as anything you can imagine," Vandegrift later commented. Though embattled, Henderson Field remained firmly under American control. Japanese soldiers, for all their valor, did not even come within sight of the field. In retrospect, Kawaguchi was right. The attacks were ill-conceived and futile. They established a war long pattern in which Imperial Army commanders squandered the incredible valor of their soldiers for no tangible results. "The Japanese soldiers fight with a sort of fanaticism and never surrender," one Americal platoon leader told a military observer after the battle. "Each attack appears to be the same. They are easily disconcerted by surprise, and if they fail to succeed in what is apparently the only way they know how to fight, they become ineffective." The failed assaults revealed a dangerous lack of offensive imagination among Imperial Army field-grade and senior-level leadership, poor coordination with supporting arms, and a growing, ominous absence of logistical acumen.

The October 25–26 attacks, and the two previous failed attempts for the airfield, were some of the first examples of a foolish tendency on the part of the Japanese (and later in history, several of America's postwar enemies) to attempt human wave assaults into the maelstrom of American firepower. In this instance, the price of failed glory was staggering. Companies K and L of the 164th Infantry buried 975 enemy bodies in front of their positions. Vandegrift's staff estimated Japanese losses at 3,500 dead. The Army put the number at 3,568 casualties of all types, including at least 2,200 fatalities. The bodies of dead Japanese were strewn for thousands of yards in every direction, sometimes in massed groups and sometimes individually, decomposing horribly in the tropical heat. "During the day our burial parties went to work," Lieutenant Colonel Samuel Baglien of the 164th later wrote. The stench of the dead was "quite obnoxious. Flies of every description were beginning to appear." Engineers with bulldozers plowed the bodies like snow, depositing them in communal graves. Sergeant John Stannard of the 164th watched soberly and later commented,

"The carnage of the battlefield was a sight that perhaps only the combat infantryman, who has fought at close quarters, could fully comprehend and look upon without a feeling of horror." By comparison, the American losses were light. The 164th reported twenty-six killed, four missing, and fifty-two wounded. The 7th Marines suffered somewhere around 130 casualties, including thirty dead.

Even as the melancholy Imperial Army survivors retreated along the trail, and in spite of the disastrous failure of the offensive, Japanese leaders were still determined to take Henderson Field. As long as the Americans controlled the airfield, they could menace all Japanese ships and planes within a hundred mile radius of Guadalcanal. Hyakutake arranged for the remainder of the 38th Division to be loaded aboard eleven transport ships and sent to Guadalcanal. In total, the convoy carried ten thousand Imperial Army troops, plus ten thousand tons of supplies and a Naval Landing Force of about two thousand men. The two navies were still fiercely contesting the waters around the island with surface engagements and frequent aerial attacks, land- and carrier-based, as both sides sought to sever the other's waterborne access to Guadalcanal. In fact, the Imperial Navy, on October 26, had sunk the USS *Hornet*, one of the Pacific Fleet's last remaining carriers, while the Henderson Field battle raged.

The struggle for Guadalcanal had boiled down to one immutable fact: the side that controlled the sea and the air would enjoy freedom of reinforcement and resupply and would, as a result, win the battle. On November 14, American planes from Henderson Field heavily bombed the 38th Division convoy, sinking seven transport ships. The four that made it to Guadalcanal were subsequently pummeled by American Coast Artillery batteries and air strikes. The loss of two-thirds of the convoy was a true catastrophe for the Japanese. At most, maybe four thousand soldiers got ashore in condition to fight. At least three thousand were drowned at sea. The rest were rescued from the water by their comrades but were obviously not in much of a position to affect the battle. Units were broken up, commanders dead or diminished, weapons and supplies lost. As a result, Hyakutake did not have the strength for another assault on Henderson and the Japanese lost the initiative (though he and other Japanese leaders were hardly reconciled to the idea of abandoning the goal of taking Henderson).

The destruction of the convoy demonstrated the incredible vulnerability of troops aboard ships—like premium athletes who must brave air travel, their intrinsic strength afforded them no safety in the event of transportation disaster. Because the US Army's entire effort in the Pacific, and other fronts, was dependent upon moving troops, weapons, and matériel safely across oceans, this was of course no small matter. In stark contrast to the Japanese, the Americans succeeded in landing two battalions from the Americal's 182nd Infantry Regiment, plus about 70 percent of its cargo, on November 11, in spite of strong enemy air raids. The opposite results of the Japanese and American convoys signaled a major turning point in the Guadalcanal battle. From here on out, the American grasp of the air and sea grew stronger and the Japanese weaker. Correspondingly, the Americans were in a better position to land the reinforcements that would ultimately decide which side actually secured the island. To be sure, neither side enjoyed anything like naval or aerial supremacy. But the Americans now found themselves on the right side of the probabilities.[9]

★

Just as the Japanese badly underestimated American strength on Guadalcanal, so, too, did Allied intelligence misread the potency of the Japanese defensive perimeters in the Gona-Buna area. For all of MacArthur's drive to succeed, he tended to value sycophantic loyalty above proficiency among his staff members. Perhaps the prime example was Brigadier General Charles Willoughby, his intelligence chief or G2 officer. Born in Germany to a baron father and an American mother, his given name was Karl (or Adolph Charles) Weidenbach. In 1910, at age eighteen, he moved to the United States, became a citizen, and adopted his mother's family name. Thirsting for a military career, he joined the Army as a private, served for a few years, and earned a degree from Gettysburg College and subsequently a commission as an infantry officer. During World War I, he served with the 16th Infantry for a time, but then spent the rest of the war with aviation units. An avid student of military history, extremist right in his personal political views, Willoughby had spent most of his career in staff and instructor positions. As MacArthur's G2, he had merited a spot on one of the PT boats that helped the SWPA commander escape from Corregidor. The group of military refugees who had escaped with MacArthur was now dubbed the "Bataan Gang" by those who had not been in the

Philippines—a rather inaccurate nickname, since few had logged any real time on Bataan.

At six foot three and 220 pounds, Willoughby was physically imposing. Though slightly overweight, he was fastidious in personal appearance and handsome enough to attract frequent attention from women (he actually had a prewar affair with Clare Boothe Luce in Manila). The way he carried himself harkened to an earlier age. "He used to click his heels and bow from the hips, instead of nodding his head," Major Bowers, who worked on the SWPA staff, once said. "He made a big to-do over women. He would kiss ladies' hands." Major General Richard Marshall, the deputy chief of staff who knew him well, once described him as "very correct in his bearing . . . very reserved, dignified, and formal. Sort of a miniature MacArthur." Willoughby's Prussian correctness, the whiff of a German accent, and European pronunciation of such words as "communiqué"—*commi-neek* instead of the more American *communi-kay*—earned him a reputation for stodginess. Behind his back, colleagues and subordinates called him Sir Charles or Baron von Willoughby. But Willoughby had a brooding and volatile side, too. He was given to temper tantrums, especially when he felt that others were infringing on his administrative turf. He sometimes spent hours fulminating over perceived slights from colleagues and superiors. Though bright and intellectually curious, he had a remarkable propensity to be wrong in his analysis of enemy capability and intentions, a distressing characteristic for a high-level intelligence officer. Myopic in his cultural outlook, he also tended to project his own assumptions on those of the enemy he otherwise studied so thoroughly. But he was totally dedicated to MacArthur, to the point of obsequiousness, and with a strong propensity to tell the boss exactly what he wanted to hear. All of this bought him much goodwill from the SWPA commander.

By the middle of November, as MacArthur finalized plans for his two-pronged advance on Gona and Buna, Willoughby painted a picture for him of a beaten, decimated enemy whose defeat was "practically assured." Willoughby estimated that, at most, two thousand depleted, demoralized enemy soldiers were in the area. In his opinion, they were unlikely to be reinforced from Rabaul because the Japanese were redoubling their efforts to take Guadalcanal. The Papua holdouts, many of whom had survived the Kokoda Trail nightmare, were only a rearguard force, awaiting evacuation. He expected that the job of overwhelming them and taking the key coastal objectives would be fairly easy. His opinion strongly influenced MacArthur to the same view. The overconfidence, born of ignorance, filtered from the supreme commander downward. "I am confident that we can take Buna, and that without too much difficulty, unless reinforcements get there before we do," General Harding, the 32nd Infantry Division commander, wrote to a colleague before his division went into battle. Harding was realistic enough to expect some hard fighting, but, like Willoughby, he believed the Japanese were not strong enough to hang on to Buna for any appreciable amount of time. "They have taken some hard knocks, especially from the air, and may not be quite so tough as they were a couple months back." To Sutherland he wrote, "We might find . . . easy pickings with only a shell of sacrifice troops left behind to defend [Buna]."

Unbeknownst to these American generals, the Japanese were anything but reconciled to the idea of giving up their bases on Papua New Guinea's north coast. Willoughby actually underestimated the Japanese garrison by a factor of three. Instead of two thousand dead ends, more than six thousand Japanese manned the perimeters from Gona to Buna, including twenty-two hundred at Buna alone. They were a mix of Imperial Army infantry soldiers, antiaircraft units, Imperial Army engineers, medics, naval construction specialists, and naval landing force infantrymen. Most of the naval troops came from the Sasebo and Yokosuka 5th Special Naval Landing Forces. The army infantrymen were from the 144th and 229th Infantry Regiments. Most of the engineers came from the Imperial Army's 15th Independent Engineers. It was true that some of these men were sick, exhausted Kokoda survivors, but the majority were either fresh reinforcements newly arrived from Rabaul or men who had not participated in the advance over the Owen Stanleys.

What's more, they had turned their coastal perimeters into heavily fortified compounds, honeycombed with superbly camouflaged, log-reinforced bunkers, all of which were actually built aboveground because the area's water table was so close to the surface. "The base of the bunker was a shallow trench, up to 40 feet in length for the larger bunkers, and 6 to 10 feet for the smaller," the Army's official historian wrote. "A framework of columns and beams was set up, the walls were revetted [sic] with coconut logs . . . and a ceiling of two or three courses of such logs laid on top." The Japanese reinforced the logs with hard-packed dirt, sandbags, oil drums, ammo boxes, and even pieces of armor plate. Most of the bunkers

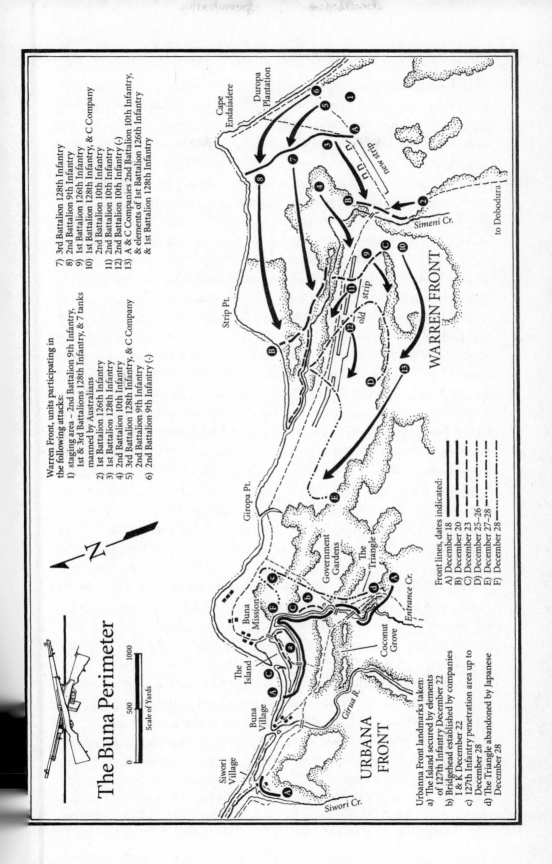

The Buna Perimeter

Scale of Yards
0   500   1000

Warren Front, units participating in the following attacks:

1) staging area – 2nd Battalion 9th Infantry, 1st & 3rd Battalions 128th Infantry, & 7 tanks manned by Australians
2) 1st Battalion 126th Infantry
3) 1st Battalion 128th Infantry
4) 2nd Battalion 10th Infantry
5) 3rd Battalion 128th Infantry, & C Company
6) 2nd Battalion 9th Infantry (-)
7) 3rd Battalion 128th Infantry
8) 2nd Battalion 9th Infantry
9) 1st Battalion 126th Infantry
10) 1st Battalion 128th Infantry, & C Company
11) 2nd Battalion 10th Infantry
12) 2nd Battalion 10th Infantry
13) A & C Companies 2nd Battalion 10th Infantry, & elements of 1st Battalion 126th Infantry & 1st Battalion 128th Infantry

Front lines, dates indicated:
A) December 18
B) December 20
C) December 23
D) December 25–26
E) December 27–28
F) December 28

Urbana Front landmarks taken:
a) The Island secured by elements of 127th Infantry December 22
b) Bridgehead established by companies I & K December 22
c) 127th Infantry penetration area up to December 28
d) The Triangle abandoned by Japanese December 28

WARREN FRONT

URBANA FRONT

Cape Endaiadere
Duropa Plantation
new strip
to Dobodura
Simeni Cr.
Strip Pt.
old strip
Giropa Pt.
Government Gardens
The Triangle
Entrance Cr.
Coconut Grove
Girua R.
Buna Mission
The Island
Buna Village
Siwori Village
Siwori Cr.

were seven to eight feet high, with firing slits for machine guns and rifles. The fortified Buna perimeter was only three and a half miles long and about a mile wide, but it was located on the only traversable land in the area, and it was solidly anchored on both flanks by the sea. Only inundated swampland, jungle, and narrow, confining trails—all of which were covered heavily by the hidden bunkers—approached the perimeter. One Army report later described the swamps as "a stinking jumble of twisted, slime-covered roots and muddy 'soup.'"

Japanese commanders planned to hold on while their comrades defeated the Americans at Guadalcanal. With this accomplished, they would renew the push for Port Moresby. A good indicator of the increased importance they placed on victory in both New Guinea and Guadalcanal was the creation in November of the Truk-based 8th Area Army under Lieutenant General Hitoshi Imamura. Hyakutake's 17th Army was now responsible solely for the Solomons. Control of New Guinea operations went to Lieutenant General Hatazo Adachi's 18th Army. Both of these reinforced armies were now under the direct control of the 8th Area Army.

Neither Willoughby nor anyone else on the Allied side had any real inkling of these realities. In fairness to the SWPA intelligence chief, his sources of information at this stage were limited to aerial photo reconnaissance images, sketchy order-of-battle charts, pieces of Ultra intelligence intercepts (the information gleaned from Japanese communications by Allied codebreakers), and the fragmentary reports of Papuan civilians and Allied patrols. Under these circumstances, he would have done well to present his chief with any semblance of an accurate estimate. But he seemed unable to comprehend the limitations of his own source material and the fact that these very limitations mitigated against any broad conclusions about Japanese strength and intentions. His error was one of overconfidence that bred unfounded conclusions. MacArthur, impatient as ever to secure Papua's north coast, was not inclined to question Willoughby's flawed prognostications.

Under normal circumstances, the Allies would have attempted to take Buna and Gona by an amphibious invasion. But a profusion of coral reefs off the coast made this idea problematic. Plus, at this stage of the war, the Allies did not possess the necessary shipping or landing craft to pull off an invasion. Nor did they have access to much supporting firepower. Owing to the paucity of shipping, in addition to Papua New Guinea's inhospitable terrain and the relatively small size of transport aircraft, they could muster only a few Australian artillery pieces and no tanks. A cocksure Kenney reassured Harding and his commanders that this would not matter. Kenney argued that artillery was useless in the jungle anyway. Planes could provide more effective supporting fire for the troops than the tubes. "The artillery in this theater flies," he quipped.

Harding remained unpersuaded by Kenney's logic. His two infantry regiments, the 126th and 128th, were now in forward positions, within attacking distance of Buna, patrolling, enduring the misery of life in the jungle, waiting for the word to carry out the final assault. He tried to get a pair of Australian twenty-five-pound pieces to them by loading the guns and other ammunition onto a barge, escorted by a motley fleet of supply-laden trawlers. As the convoy attempted to make it to a forward camp near Hariko Point on the coast a few miles east of Buna, Japanese Zeros attacked. The enemy planes could hardly miss such a juicy target. They made several strafing passes and sank the convoy. The twenty-five-pound guns were lost as was a vast quantity of rations, medicine, artillery shells, and other ammunition. Harding swam about a mile to shore, fortunate even to survive. Twenty-four Allied servicemen were killed and another one hundred wounded. At least twenty-eight Papuan civilian laborers and guides were also killed.[10]

The near death of the division commander served as an omen of what was to come, as did the stubborn resistance encountered by the Australians on November 16 when they attempted to move two brigades forward along the Sanananda track in the heart of their sector. "He was well prepared for us, being well dug in with fire lanes cut for his machine-guns," Sergeant G. J. Caling of the Australian 7th Division said of the Japanese. "My platoon ran into a couple of these guns and we had to go to ground." Instead of a rapid advance along the track, the Australians were soon bogged down in a bloody step-by-step struggle.

With the Diggers seemingly halted, MacArthur ordered Harding to lend two battalions from the 126th Infantry, half his force, to assist Major General George Vasey, the 7th Division commander. MacArthur and General Sir Thomas Blamey, the Australian commander of Allied Land Forces in New Guinea, had decided to give priority to the 7th Division attack. Thus, as Harding's offensive began, he had a tenuous supply situation and little in the way of fire support. Moreover, his men were generally in poor physical condition due to the inherent conditions of the jungle, and he had now forfeited half his command to assist a friend. Plus, his troops were in no way trained or prepared for jungle warfare. "Marching, living, and fighting in the jungle requires special training and special equipment," Captain Medendorp later wrote. "[We] had neither."

In spite of all this, a blithely obtuse optimism infused the men as they readied to go forward on November 19. "The impression had been generally prevalent that Buna could be had by walking in and taking over," Colonel H. F. Handy, an Army Ground Forces observer, later wrote. The soldiers were anxious to get to the coast, end the campaign, and get out of New Guinea. In most instances, their commanders had told them that the Japanese were capable of little resistance. If that was true, as most of the men erroneously assumed, then far better to get moving rather than continue sitting around in the jungle, getting preyed upon by mosquitoes and tropical diseases.

The plan was for the 128th Infantry Regiment's 1st and 3rd Battalions to approach Buna from the east, the 1st along the Simemi trail and the 3rd adjacent to the coast, through the Duropa Plantation. Tropical rain cascaded in sheets as the troops move out, but the mood was lighthearted, as if they were embarking on nothing more threatening than a field exercise. "We thought this was going to be a snap," said Sergeant Ernest Gerber, a squad leader. Some soldiers wore steel helmets; others floppy fishing-style caps. Upbeat voices and laughter echoed along the eerie green hollows of the jungle. Some of the men even whistled as they hiked single file on the trails.

When they bumped into the Japanese defensive lines, their world—and the Buna battle—permanently changed. Accurate machine-gun and rifle fire tore through the columns. Every inch of the trails was covered by enemy weapons. In many instances, the Japanese allowed the Americans to advance within spitting distance before tearing them to pieces with stitches of machine-gun fire. The only hope of survival was to hug the ground and perhaps skitter away. "It was dangerous to show even a finger from behind one's own cover, as it would immediately draw a burst of fire," wrote Major David Parker, an engineer observer. "The first opposition from the enemy here was a surprise and shock to our green troops. The enemy positions were amazingly well camouflaged and seemed to have excellent fields of fire. They had been sited to take advantage of any natural alleyways through the jungle. Snipers were everywhere, especially in the trees, and so well camouflaged that it was nearly impossible to discern them. Our troops were pinned down everywhere by extremely ineffective fire. It was impossible to see where the enemy fire was coming from; consequently our own rifle and MG fire was ineffective. It was impossible to cover advance of squads by fire." American grenades and mortars were ineffective because of the terrain and also because it was hard to see the Japanese, whose weapons employed smokeless powder. Plus, in the recollection of Colonel Harry Knight, another Army Ground Forces observer, "sound reverberated so much in the jungle that location of enemy weapons could not be learned . . . unless the guns were very near." The deadly fire seemed to come from all sides, and the jungle was so confining that it was difficult for anyone to know his precise location at any given time. The Japanese were like invisible bogeymen, dealing out death with impunity, a terrible, demoralizing situation. Numerous soldiers told Colonel Knight that they "sure did wish they could see the yellow bastards so they could shoot them." Ever sardonic, the GIs borrowed phraseology from popular science-fiction yarns and began calling them little invisible green men.

When the Americans backtracked and tried to attack through the swamps, rather than on the trails, they met with similar fury. "We found out that was a losing game," Sergeant Gerber recalled. "It was all water, and wherever there was any high land, that's where the Japanese were dug in . . . their pillboxes." The inevitable result of this was tragedy. Bullets splashed into the filthy swamp water, killing and wounding with impunity. Pinned-down men lay miserably in the knee-high water, under an intense tropical sun, praying not to get hit. The overpowering stench of death, jungle decay, moldy swamp water, and gunpowder suffused everything. The stunned battalions halted and took whatever cover they could find. "Foxholes were dug wherever you stopped long enough to dig one," a platoon leader later wrote to a friend. "Water was usually all around you . . . swamp water, brackish and muddy . . . but it's all part of the war."[11]

Day by day in the second half of November, General Harding repeatedly attacked but succeeded only in adding to his casualty list—nearly five hundred by the end of the month, plus a like number down with malaria, dengue fever, or dysentery. In many instances, the bodies of the dead lay decomposing in no-man's-land and could not be recovered. "The stink of rotting bodies . . . was a difficult morale problem to overcome," wrote Major Richard Boerem, executive officer of one battalion. "Most of my time was spent going from one soldier to another in an endeavor to raise

morale." Terrain ruled everything. The thickness of the jungle, the ubiquity of the swamps, the elaborate nature of the Japanese fortifications all
meant that Harding could not mass his forces for any sort of coordinated
attack. Plus he had almost no artillery, and, despite Kenney's claims, close
air support proved largely ineffective. This was small-unit warfare. A
company-size force was large. More commonly squads fought squads.
Gains were measured in yards, not miles. The deadly opposition and cruel
jungle environment worked on the minds of the men. At night many
blazed away at any sound. Front-line positions of the two sides were often
within a stone's throw of each other. For protection from Japanese infiltrators, American soldiers huddled together in foxholes. "You always like
companionship," First Sergeant Lutjens said. "You always like something
you can touch. But even with a guy right there, sometimes it was hard to
get any sleep. You'd wake up in the middle of the night and just lie there,
listening and staring at the black." Thanksgiving came and went. Stalemate
reigned. Buna remained an elusive prize (as did Gona and Sanananda for
the Australians). Harding had once served as a section chief for the Infantry School at Fort Benning. He had edited the *Infantry* magazine. He understood small-unit tactics as well as anyone in the Army, and yet he
seemed unable to find the key to unlock Buna.

This did not escape the attention of his superiors at GHQ. On November 6, MacArthur had temporarily relocated his headquarters to Port
Moresby. He took up residence about a mile west of the main harbor at
Government House, where the Australian governor of Papua had once
lived. The rambling four-bedroom, one-story house offered a nice view of
the sparkling blue bay. A wide screened-in veranda warded off mosquitoes
and fostered a pleasant tropical breeze that somewhat ameliorated the languid heat. Off the veranda, there was a private toilet strictly for the use of
MacArthur and Sutherland. Everyone else used an officer's latrine in an
adjacent building, near the portable houses that provided living space for
the general's staff members. The governor's extensive library of classic volumes, neatly arranged in glass cases, provided leisure reading for anyone
who cared to imbibe. Willoughby stopped to admire the books one afternoon and commented to a stenographer, "Imagine a cultivated, educated
gentleman with these tastes withering away in this wilderness." The home
was staffed by local boys in white kilts that functioned as a tropical uniform of sorts. Outside, they maintained, in the recollection of one reporter,

"a riotous tropical garden of frangipanni and hibiscus and flametrees." A constabulary guard force of barefooted local infantrymen, outfitted in khaki kilts with military belts and bandoliers of ammunition for their rifles, kept watch night and day. The supreme commander himself was said to prowl the grounds in a silk dressing gown adorned with a black dragon on the back. Upon arrival, he was so certain of a quick victory at Buna that he had told Sutherland, "Well, Dick, I won't get a haircut until this is all over and we're back home [in Australia]."

Even two weeks later, after the failed initial attacks, he remained optimistic enough to issue a fantastical communiqué. "Our ground forces have rapidly closed in now and pinned the enemy down on the narrow coastal strip from Buna to Gona. We are fighting on the outskirts of both places." The next day he ordered an astounded Harding, "Take Buna today at all costs." To no avail. Still the place remained in Japanese hands and the supreme commander's hair kept growing, unchecked. Unconfirmed reports, some originating from Blamey, circulated at Government House of 32nd Division soldiers refusing to fight, chucking their weapons, and skulking in rear areas. With every passing day, and every dispiriting story, MacArthur's patience with Harding grew thinner. "Harding is in bad," Kenney, newly promoted to lieutenant general, jotted in his diary on November 27. "Sutherland would like to have his job. Stories of actions and even cowardice of our troops not good. Officers don't know their job of leadership. Commanders too far to the rear. We are bringing back a lot of sick and shell shocked boys . . . but not really many wounded."

MacArthur's communiqués dishonestly implied that he was at the Buna front, personally directing the fighting. This was an absolute sham. MacArthur had not yet visited Buna, nor would he ever, and this deprived him of any true grasp of the 32nd Division's situation. Instead, he was merely a dislocated bystander, almost totally at the mercy of secondhand reports. When Blamey shared cryptic stories of the 32nd's issues and delicately implied that his confidence in American soldiers was low, MacArthur had little choice but to take him at face value. It was a humiliating, bitter moment for the supreme commander, not just because of national pride but because he himself had foolishly—and undiplomatically—spewed much venom about Australian shortcomings during the Kokoda Trail fighting. His communiqués seldom mentioned the Australians, an egregious insult to the country that, at this stage, was still shouldering the majority of the South Pacific war effort. Back in Australia, he had allowed many of his officers, in private and public conversations, to run down the fighting acumen of their allies. In pillow talk with their Australian girl-friends, some Philippines escapees bragged of their own bravery and ridiculed the Diggers for their supposed lack of fighting timbre at such battlegrounds as Singapore and Kokoda. In return, the Aussies were only too happy to point out American failures, especially now that the Yanks were bogged down alongside them in Papua. With little history of cooperation, and still unsure of the other's proficiency as fighters, they naturally began pointing fingers at each other over the problems in New Guinea, a state of affairs that did no one but the Japanese any good, and one that cried out for strong, unifying leadership.

On November 27, instead of hopping aboard one of Kenney's transport planes to fly over to Buna and judge the condition of the 32nd for himself, he sent two officers from his operations section, Colonel Robert McBride and Lieutenant Colonel David Larr, to investigate. After a two-day visit, they painted a troubling, and reasonably accurate, picture of inertia and poor leadership. But Larr was probably not the best choice for the job because he and Colonel John Mott, formerly the 32nd Division's chief of staff, whom Harding had designated to command half his divisional front, hated each other "with considerable fervor," in Harding's recollection. The division commander thought of Larr as "a typical theoretical staff officer who knew nothing of the kind of battle we had on our hands. Nor did he spend enough time in the battle area to come up with a trustworthy report." Though this was undoubtedly a fair point, the two staff officers also conversed with War Department observers who actually had been on the ground for several weeks, gathering information to prepare extensive reports for Washington. One of the observers, Colonel Knight, reported that "our troops did not have the will and determination to go forward in spite of casualties and close with and kill the enemy." He felt that the men were too dependent on supporting weaponry, "reluctant to believe that it was their duty to personally go forward and kill the Japs themselves." Another observer, this one from SWPA, contended that "the [32nd] Division as a whole lacks discipline and . . . the will to perform. The men as a whole have to be pulled and kicked along rather than led."

When MacArthur heard all this, he resolved to make changes. He sensed correctly that there were indeed problems, leadership and otherwise, at Buna and that he must take action. Other than this realization, though, he understood almost nothing of Buna's realities. Willoughby's poor intelligence estimates remained at the foundation of his outlook. So, in MacArthur's mind, the opposition at Buna was feeble. Therefore the lack of results must stem solely from bad leadership on the ground and poor soldier material. Since he had no firsthand conception of the Buna terrain and conditions, nor the immense challenge for poorly conditioned troops of assaulting, with little supporting fire, a maze of mutually supporting bunkers, his mentality was distorted.

It was certainly true that progress was slow. The salient question was *why*. MacArthur remained too distant from the scene to know. Resentful soldiers began calling MacArthur's Port Moresby headquarters "the Ivory Tower." Lieutenant Odell and his men "unanimously condemned higher headquarters for wholly inadequate recognition of the Buna situation, especially with regard to intelligence, and in a lesser degree, supply." Lieutenant Colonel Herbert A. Smith, a battalion commander, later criticized officers who "never themselves got close enough to see the conditions under which the front line troops were fighting." Not only were the soldiers "green and untried," but they were dealing with "a situation entirely foreign to anything they had ever encountered before. Many had fever, dysentery and 'jungle rot.' All had been living on short rations. Most important, we had no suitable weapons with which to knock out the Jap pillboxes." To knock out these bunkers, the troops had only "rifles, hand grenades and human courage. Men had to crawl on their bellies as close as possible to the Jap pillboxes, and then make a sudden rush in the hope of getting close enough to push hand grenades thru the firing slots. Many more failed than succeeded."

Again, rather than traveling to Buna to find this out for himself, MacArthur sent Sutherland on November 30 for one more fact-finding mission. The chief of staff flew to Dobodura, an American-controlled airstrip and site of the 32nd's forward command post, located on a grassy plain about seven miles south of Buna. When Sutherland arrived, Harding was in the midst of an animated argument with Lieutenant General Edmund "Ned" Herring, the Australian commander of the Advance New Guinea Force, the Allied front-line ground forces, and Harding's nominal superior. The two men sat on ammo boxes just a few feet apart and conversed intently. They respected each other, but failure had frayed their working relationship. Harding still resented the loss of the 126th to the Australians. His third infantry regiment, the 127th, was now at Port Moresby, in reserve, and Harding wanted them moved up to the Buna front immediately. But Herring would not assent. He thought Harding already had adequate reserves, and he doubted that it would be possible to keep a new regiment properly supplied. "I explained somewhat heatedly that we had *no* reserves, and I argued to the best of my ability for additional troops," Harding recorded in his diary. Exasperated, the American division commander later wrote to an Army official historian. "Herring's headquarters and Blamey's never had any more than the haziest idea of what was going on in my sector."

Herring excused himself shortly after Sutherland arrived. Though the arrogant chief of staff was largely disliked throughout the Army, he and Harding were good friends who had known each other for years. The two sat down for a quick lunch. Hoping to draw on that friendship and engage in a trusting, down-to-earth conversation, Harding related his difficult situation and prevailed upon Sutherland to give him the 127th. But Sutherland was in anything but an accommodating mood. "His answer was that the problem of supplying the troops was taxing the transport facilities of the Air Corps to the utmost, and that no more troops could be brought in until reserve supplies had been built up at Dobodura," Harding told his diary. The chief of staff pressed his old friend to focus instead on replacing ineffective commanders. The gentlemanly Harding was a fine professional soldier, but he was loyal and patient almost to a fault. He defended his senior officers and expressed reluctance to make any changes. Harding's loyalty to officers whom Sutherland thought of as incompetent was seemingly a last straw of sorts for Sutherland. Knowing MacArthur's growing dissatisfaction with Harding, Sutherland apparently decided his friend was not worth saving. In the World War II Army, such crystallizing moments could make or break careers, sever or strengthen decades-old friendships. "I considered him one with whom I could be perfectly frank who would be the same with me," Harding later wrote sadly. "I was but he wasn't." Shortly after lunch, Sutherland flew back to Port Moresby. He immediately met with MacArthur and recommended his old friend's relief from command of the 32nd Division. Change was coming at Buna.[12]

Soldiers from the 25th Infantry Division move to Oahu's south coast in the wake of the surprise Pearl Harbor attack. While the Japanese primarily targeted American sea and air power, the ground troops came under attack at numerous bases. By the evening of December 7, they found themselves on full alert for an invasion that never came.
US ARMY

American soldiers in the Philippines, circa 1942. Men like these formed the foundation of a colonial-style army unique in American history. Roughly three quarters of the force was composed of Filipinos.
US ARMY

An American gun crew, probably from the Philippine Division, on Bataan. Though rudimentary by later American standards, the artillery inflicted serious casualties on the Japanese during the Philippines campaign.
US ARMY

The deceivingly innocuous beginning of the infamous Bataan Death March. Here, under the watchful eyes of Japanese guards, American and Filipino captives sort out their belongings before embarking on the march. About 600 Americans and between 5,000 and 10,000 Filipinos died from privation, atrocities, exhaustion, disease, and starvation during the hellish movement. For the survivors, the horrors of captivity awaited.
US ARMY

Major General Jonathan Wainwright (left) and General Douglas MacArthur confer during the latter's only documented visit to Bataan. A salty, courageous, and hard-drinking cavalryman, Wainwright was left with the hopeless task of trying to hang on in the Philippines after MacArthur evacuated to Australia with much of his staff.
NATIONAL ARCHIVES

Outside the Malinta Tunnel, Corregidor, on May 6, 1942, where thousands of Americans and Filipinos surrendered. Though they did not endure the hell of the Bataan Death March, they faced many hard months and years of captivity. About a third did not survive.
US ARMY

An Army nurse inoculates a newly arrived American soldier in Australia. About one million Americans were either stationed in or passed through the country in the course of the war. Their presence had a dramatic impact on every aspect of local life and helped solidify an alliance that continues to this day.
US ARMY

Generalissimo Chiang Kai-shek (left); his wife, Soong Mei-ling; and Lieutenant General Joseph Stilwell share an uncharacteristic moment of levity. Arguably the most influential American in China in the twentieth century, the caustic, upright Stilwell chafed at the inefficiency and corruption he saw in Chiang's government. The tension between Stilwell and Chinese leaders reflected the differing agendas of the United States and China, allies of a kind, rather than through true mutual interest.
NATIONAL ARCHIVES

Conditions at Buna were horrendous. Mere existence was a challenge in the pestilential swamps, jungles, and mud. Sickness and disease, especially malaria, took a major toll on the ranks of the 32nd Infantry Division.
NATIONAL ARCHIVES

The strain of combat, Buna. Here, exhausted troops from the 127th Infantry Regiment, 32nd Infantry Division prepare to attack part of the Triangle, home to a powerful nest of fiercely defended bunkers.
NATIONAL ARCHIVES

At Buna, wounded men await evacuation. Casualty rates from death, wounding, and disease hovered around 100 percent. Wounded men were carried laboriously through the jungle to portable surgical hospitals or for immediate evacuation to Port Moresby by Allied aviators. Though the Papuans did not participate in front-line fighting, they played a vital role as litter bearers, scouts, and supply carriers.
US ARMY (LEFT)
NATIONAL ARCHIVES (BELOW)

The strain of the Buna campaign shows on the faces of an undernourished Brigadier General Albert Waldron (middle, with open shirt and cigarette) and the men around him. Waldron eventually assumed command of the shattered 32nd Infantry Division.
NATIONAL ARCHIVES

One of about 13,000 Japanese soldiers who lost their lives in the struggle for Buna and its environs. Racked with disease and hunger, almost all chose to fight to the death rather than surrender.

Lieutenant General Robert Eichelberger (standing in foreground in a light-colored uniform) with members of his staff at the front in Buna. Ordered by MacArthur to take Buna or not come back alive, Eichelberger infused the Allied front with a new sense of purpose, winning America's first ground victory of World War II. Overly sensitive to slights but friendly and highly intelligent, he would become arguably the finest American ground commander in theater.

The terrain on Guadalcanal, an island covered with razorback ridges and thick jungle. For the troops, the mere process of hiking, patrolling, or attacking a few hundred yards could be exhausting.

US ARMY

The challenge of operating tanks in the Guadalcanal jungle were endless. Though armor would play a vital role in the Pacific War, terrain like this far too often did limit the mobility and usefulness of tanks.

HOOVER INSTITUTION ARCHIVES

Treating the wounded on Guadalcanal. In many instances, it took days to evacuate a wounded man out of the jungle maw.

Major General Alexander "Sandy" Patch (sitting at right) with a pair of colleagues in New Caledonia. Originally commander of the Americal Division, Patch at Guadalcanal became commander of XIV Corps, with Marine and Army units under his control. Born and bred to soldiering, Patch looked down upon profanity and detested arrogance in an officer. In the midst of masterminding the final American victory at Guadalcanal, he wrote emotional, soul-searching letters to his wife, Julia. After Guadalcanal, he was transferred to the European theater to command the 7th Army, becoming the only general to command a corps in one theater and an army in another.
NATIONAL ARCHIVES

Major General J. Lawton Collins, commander of the 25th Infantry Division (foreground, with watch, holding a rifle). Nicknamed "Lightning Joe," Collins proved himself to be an unusually ambitious and energetic commander at Guadalcanal and New Georgia. At the end of 1943, he was transferred to the European theater to take command of VII Corps, whose assault units invaded Utah Beach on D-Day.
NATIONAL ARCHIVES

Some of the very few Japanese prisoners on Guadalcanal. Although almost 11,000 Japanese soldiers were successfully evacuated by the Imperial Japanese Navy at the end of the campaign, most fought to the death or succumbed to starvation or disease. Only about 1,000 became prisoners.
HOOVER INSTITUTION ARCHIVES

The Pacific War had a major cultural side. Patronizingly dubbed "natives" by Americans, islanders from all over the South Pacific played a significant role in the Allied War Effort, especially as hired laborers. The best American commanders learned to work well with locals and respect their culture.
US ARMY

Major General John Hester (with glasses and map), commander of the 43rd Infantry Division at New Georgia. Because of serious combat fatigue problems within the division, as well as his own infirmity and the costly nature of the campaign, he was eventually eased out of command responsibility by his superiors.

NATIONAL ARCHIVES

Major General Oscar Griswold (front row, extreme left), who succeeded Patch as commander of XIV Corps and extracted a hard-won American victory at New Georgia. Modest and self-effacing, Griswold soon earned a reputation as a reliable commander who could take on the dirtiest jobs and get results.

NATIONAL ARCHIVES

The challenges of waging war over a huge expanse of ocean, continent, and islands were endless. The Army was largely dependent upon the Navy for transportation and some supply. Literally every conceivable item, such as these fuel barrels, had to be shipped and processed.
NATIONAL ARCHIVES

Wherever the Americans went, they brought their logistical largesse. Engineers and quartermasters converted huge swaths of jungle, coastline, and harbor into mini American cities. They also processed, organized, and moved hundreds of thousands of tons of matériel.
NATIONAL ARCHIVES

At Attu, in Alaska's Aleutian Islands, the 7th Infantry Division fought the only cold-weather battle in the war against Japan. Because of inadequate planning, soldiers were not equipped well enough for the island's harsh conditions. Hundreds suffered from frozen feet and other cold-weather maladies.
NATIONAL ARCHIVES

Seventh Division artillerymen drag their piece through Attu's enervating muskeg, a spongy, marshy bog of decomposed sediment, lichen, and moss, a black muck that proliferated much of the island. The muskeg, combined with snowy ridges and fog, made any advance difficult, much less the ferocity of Japanese resistance.
NATIONAL ARCHIVES

American soldiers of the 7th Division land at Attu's ominously named Massacre Bay. In over two weeks of heavy fighting, the division suffered 25 percent casualties, the highest rate in relation to Japanese losses of any Pacific theater battle except Iwo Jima.
NATIONAL ARCHIVES

The fighting on Makin. The 27th Division had to root die-hard Japanese defenders out of dense foliage and an extensive network of log-reinforced bunkers.
US ARMY

Soldiers of the 27th Infantry Division wait to board landing craft to assault Makin in November 1943. Voyages aboard ship and beach assaults by landing craft were an all too common experience for soldiers in the Pacific theater.
US ARMY

Light tanks bogged down in Makin's thick mud. Armor did provide some much needed support but, by and large, the battle was dominated by small groups of foot soldiers on both sides.
US ARMY

Colonel Gardiner Conroy, commander of the 165th Infantry Regiment, New York lawyer, and part-time soldier, who made the ultimate sacrifice at Makin.
NATIONAL ARCHIVES

Major General Ralph Smith, commander of the 27th Infantry Division. Gentlemanly and scholarly, a combat veteran of World War I, Smith was equal parts intellectual and combat soldier. S. L. A. Marshall once wrote of him, "He is that somewhat rare specimen, a generous Christian gentleman."
NATIONAL ARCHIVES

Major General Holland "Howlin' Mad" Smith (with cigar, looking at watch), USMC and Ralph Smith's nominal superior as commander of the V Amphibious Corps. Volatile and headstrong, Holland Smith felt that Ralph Smith and the 27th Division fought poorly at Makin, sowing the seeds for much future strife between the two men and, in a larger sense, the Army and the Marine Corps.
NATIONAL ARCHIVES

General George Marshall (left), Army chief of staff, and Admiral Ernest King, chief of naval operations. These two strong-willed men learned to work well together, though they never completely resolved the tense Army-Navy struggle for control of operations in the Pacific theater. Instead, they simply split the theater into separate geographic components.
NATIONAL ARCHIVES

General Douglas MacArthur, the Army's master of the Pacific theater. A consummate image maker who cultivated a mythology-laced heroic image among the American public, MacArthur dominated nearly every aspect of the war against Japan. Vainglorious, charismatic, egomaniacal, and honorable—but also power hungry—he ran an underground campaign for the presidency, even as he oversaw vast military operations.
NATIONAL ARCHIVES

8

"My Crime Deserves
More Than Death"

At Rockhampton, the call came on a sleepy Sunday afternoon. The recipient had spent his entire life preparing for this sort of summons. Robert Eichelberger, newly promoted to lieutenant general, was the youngest of five children born to a Southern mother and a prosperous Urbana, Ohio, lawyer who had served in the Union army during the Civil War. The Eichelbergers lived in a beautiful two-story house situated on 235 acres of rich farmland. Though Eichelberger's father, George, dabbled in farming, a successful practice as a railroad lawyer occupied most of his time. Born in 1886 and growing up in the late nineteenth century, Robert had enjoyed a boyhood steeped in tales of the war. His maternal grandfather had been a Confederate surgeon. During the Vicksburg campaign, General John McClernand, one of Grant's commanders, had made his headquarters at the family home. Eichelberger's mother, Emma, regaled the boy with tales of how she had once persuaded McClernand to spare the family cow from the knives of Yankee cooks and how, as a hospital volunteer, she had held a basin to catch severed limbs during amputations. Union veterans often congregated at his father's law office to reminisce. Young Robert—or Bobby as most called him—sat at their collective knee, avidly listening. When he was twelve, his father took him to visit battlefields at Missionary Ridge and Lookout Mountain, further stoking an early interest in the military. The boy read voraciously about the war and numerous other topics he surveyed among the extensive library of books his parents maintained at home.

His childhood was a happy one, rich with athletics, healthy outside play, and the intellectual stimulation of family-dinner-table conversations about current events and politics. But there was a darker side to the Eichelberger home. Though George doted on his kids, he came to think of them as soft

and lazy. He was often absent on business. When he was home, he relentlessly criticized the kids, particularly the four boys, whom he conceptually
pitted against one another in stentorian athletic, social, and academic
competition. Only the eldest, George Jr., a handsome and brilliant lad who,
like his father, graduated from Ohio Wesleyan University, seemed to gar-
ner much respect from George Sr. Because he was the overmatched youngest sibling, no one seemed to take Bobby very seriously. He had a charming,
engaging personality and a wonderful sense of humor, and he was a reasonably good athlete. But he was thin-skinned, overly sensitive to criticism
and personal slights. He was also an average, almost uninterested student.
When he turned seventeen, his father sent him to the poorly regarded Ohio
State University, where he joined the Phi Gamma Delta fraternity and partied much more than he studied. Though he did not flunk out, he left
school and came back home. George Sr. thought the only hope for Bobby
was to earn a law degree and join the family practice, a prospect that held
little appeal for the son. When George Sr.'s law partner was elected to Congress, he offered Bobby an appointment to West Point. "I eagerly accepted,"
Eichelberger later recalled. "I had always been interested in things military." Though Robert struggled academically at the Point and he was
anything but a model cadet, he found in himself a latent talent for soldiering. In 1909, he graduated sixty-eighth in a class of 103 and branched infantry. In the full maturity of manhood, he had grown into a six-foot-one
frame, robust and healthy. He had an expressive, square face that later, in
middle age, tended toward the jowly if he did not watch his weight.

Probably as a result of George Sr.'s severity, all the Eichelberger children, particularly the baby, developed an almost maniacal need for distinction and achievement to win the approval or perhaps just the respect
of their father. Even as Robert's brothers chased greatness in the commercial world, and his sister sought her way in one of the few avenues of social
success available for a woman at the time (namely marrying a rich man),
Robert saw in a military career an opportunity to earn fame and status. In
1913, during a posting to the Panama Canal Zone, he met and married
Emma Gudger, the attractive, convivial daughter of the zone's chief justice
magistrate. North Carolina–born and bright and refined in the manner
demanded of early-twentieth-century officers' wives, Emma proved to
be the perfect soul mate for Bob, as most of his colleagues now called him.
The two were strong Army partners, both totally dedicated to his career.
They had no children, just each other. Their personal bond was soul-deep.

The marriage to "Miss Em," as he came to call her, gave even more urgency to Bob for career success, not only to save face in front of his own family but also with his elitist in-laws as well. As a young officer, he served in a variety of postings, most notably as intelligence chief and key aide to General William Graves, head of the Army's ill-fated Siberian Expedition, from 1918 to 1920, where Bolsheviks, whites, Japanese, French, British, and others battled for supremacy. Eichelberger proved to be brave in combat as well as an able administrator, mediator, and adviser for Graves, who mentored him like a son. Eichelberger earned the Distinguished Service Medal and the Distinguished Service Cross. His Siberian duties afforded him the opportunity to observe the Japanese closely, gaining insights he would put to excellent use two decades later.

In the interwar period, he established an Army-wide reputation as a reliable, commonsense officer with unimpeachable integrity. Polite, considerate, and adept at social networking, he was universally liked. One colleague described him as "an attractive, dynamic guy with great personal charm." Major General Richard Marshall once characterized him as "a big fellow and very smooth . . . an easy-talking conversationalist." Ambitious and intensely focused on upward mobility, the consummate Army insider, Eichelberger graduated from the Army Command and General Staff College at Fort Leavenworth and the National War College in Washington, DC. In the mid-1930s, he transferred to the Adjutant General Corps, which afforded him the opportunity to serve on the US Army general staff, directly working with then Chief of Staff MacArthur and his successor Malin Craig. After Eichelberger spent more than thirty years on active duty, his promotion to brigadier general finally came in October 1940, a happy event that moved Emma to tears of joy. George Patton, an old friend and West Point classmate, and also newly adorned with a general's star, soon thereafter wrote to Bob: "At last they have had sense enough to promote the two best damn officers in the U.S. Army." When the United States entered the war, Eichelberger was serving as the superintendent at West Point, a high-profile job that fulfilled his deep yearning for achievement and one he referred to as "my Number One assignment from the standpoint of desirability." Once, during a visit to his father's grave—George Sr. had died when Robert was a cadet—a friend heard Robert whisper to the tombstone: "You said I wouldn't be appointed to West Point. You said I wouldn't make the grade at West Point, and now I'm running the place."

As much as he loved running West Point, his ultimate goal was to command troops in battle. With the war on, he requested a combat assignment. He commanded the 77th Infantry Division, where he did such a fine job that he was immediately slated for corps command and three-star rank. For a time it appeared he would serve in the North Africa invasion under Eisenhower, another old friend. But the faux pas of another officer plus Eichelberger's excellent reputation soon changed the course of his life and, in that sense, the Pacific War itself. Major General Robert Richardson, an efficient, veteran officer from the War Department, had completed a SWPA inspection tour for MacArthur back in July, pointing out many problems of leadership and inefficiency. With this task completed, the supreme commander planned to appoint him to combat command of the newly forming I Corps. But Richardson had serious concerns about American troops serving under Australian command. Personally, he did not like the idea of reporting to Blamey, whom he thought of as so unfit for his lofty responsibilities that he snidely derided him as "the chief of police of Melbourne." Instead of taking command immediately, Richardson insisted on returning to Washington to discuss his concerns with General George Marshall. With a global war to run, and to a great extent through productive cooperation with allies, the chief of staff had no patience for what he saw as Richardson's narrow-minded, self-centered temerity. "He was so averse to the detail, felt that it depreciated him when his status had been in Australia as my representative on this inspection trip and felt that it was intolerable to serve under Australian command," Marshall later wrote to Lieutenant General Lesley McNair, head of Army Ground Forces. "We haven't the time for this sort of personal business. When you think of full Generals and full Admirals of the British Army and Navy placing themselves subordinate to Eisenhower and working in complete loyalty with him, this business of Richardson does not sit well." Marshall immediately removed him from consideration for command of I Corps. He instead chose Eichelberger, one of several officers he had watched for years and tabbed for significant responsibility in the event of war (contrary to legend, there is still no direct evidence that he ever recorded the names of these men in a black book). MacArthur of course knew Eichelberger well and was pleased to get him. Richardson was shunted instead to the important but obscure job of administering the Army's war in the Pacific. Though he subsequently wrote to MacArthur claiming no "unwillingness or reluctance to go under the present conditions," it was too late. He had unwittingly made an error he could never undo.[1]

After an emotional parting from Emma—"Army wives must be heroines, and they earn no ribbons for it," the general later wrote—Eichelberger arrived in Brisbane on August 25. A couple of weeks later, at the zenith of the Japanese overland advance on Port Moresby, MacArthur had ordered Eichelberger to lead a counterattacking expedition in Papua. But nothing ever came of this. The crisis passed and so, apparently, did MacArthur's enthusiasm for putting Eichelberger in command of US forces in New Guinea. Instead, for several months he consigned him to training troops in northern Australia. Sutherland even forbade Eichelberger from traveling to New Guinea. Itching to get into combat, Eichelberger felt as though he was being treated "more like a lieutenant than a lieutenant general." There was a very simple explanation for this silliness. When Buna seemed like it might be an easy victory, MacArthur did not want to share the credit with anyone, especially a professional equal, and potential rival, like Eichelberger. But now, at the end of November, MacArthur needed Eichelberger to stave off a debacle.

From his headquarters in Rockhampton, Eichelberger had monitored events at Buna. When the call from SWPA headquarters came on that listless Sunday afternoon, he understood exactly what it meant. Before he boarded a plane for Port Moresby, he wrote to Emma. "You may be sure that I shall always be with you in my thoughts. As I think of all the years we have been together, I know you must realize how my admiration, respect and love have increased." It was midafternoon on November 30 by the time Eichelberger and members of his I Corps staff arrived at Government House. Eichelberger and his deeply trusted chief of staff, Brigadier General Clovis Byers, were assigned rooms in the house. The rest of the staff was billeted in tents outside. Even before Eichelberger and Byers could settle into their rooms, they received a summons to meet with MacArthur. On the way they passed Master Sergeant Rogers, the stenographer. He looked up from his work, saw Eichelberger, and thought he looked "concerned and nervous." The two generals were ushered onto the veranda. Sutherland, freshly returned from his meeting with Harding, sat grim-faced at a desk, catching up on paperwork. Kenney sat in a wicker chair. MacArthur stood. Only Kenney, an old friend of Eichelberger's, smiled. Otherwise there were only perfunctory greetings. Eichelberger and Byers took their seats. MacArthur paced around the veranda, holding forth on the dire situation, lecturing rather than conversing, as was typical of his personality. "Bob, I'm putting you in command at Buna. Harding has failed miserably. I want you to relieve Harding, Bob. Send him back to America, or I'll do it for you. Relieve every regimental and battalion commander. If necessary, put sergeants in charge of battalions and corporals in charge of companies. Anyone who will fight. If you don't relieve them, I'll relieve you. Time is of the essence. The Japs may land reinforcements every night." Certainly MacArthur was right to be concerned about the possibility of new Japanese landings. But by this time, he knew this was less likely because of their recent reversals at Guadalcanal. His consternation and impatience stemmed at least partially from personal reasons. He had already lost the Philippines. He had barely hung on to Port Moresby. Now his first offensive in this war was careening toward disaster. How much longer could he maintain the confidence of his superiors in Washington and the veneer of greatness among the American people? He felt enormous pressure to produce a victory and begin his long journey back to the Philippines.

MacArthur continued pacing the veranda. He claimed that 32nd Division troops had ditched their weapons and run away from the enemy, supposedly the first time this had happened in American history, a spurious contention since Americans had run many times, dating all the way back to the Revolution. Warming to his topic and growing more agitated, MacArthur continued grimly: "I can't believe that those troops represent the American fighting man of this war. I would be discouraged if I thought so. They need leadership to galvanize them, to give them back the fighting, aggressive spirit of the American soldier. I know that they are not trained for this type of warfare, that the climate is wearing them down. They are sick, but, Bob, a leader can take those same men and capture Buna." The supreme commander paused, looked at Eichelberger, and then uttered fateful words. "That is the job I'm giving you. Bob, I want you to take Buna or not come back alive." He pointed at Byers. "And that goes for your chief of staff, too, Clovis."

It was a depressing order, one that stemmed from the dreariness and uncertainty of the situation. Eichelberger understood that Buna represented the golden opportunity of his career, the long-awaited chance to distinguish himself as a great battle captain and satisfy his lifelong, genetic yearning for notable achievement. In this personal sense, he and MacArthur were in the same boat—Buna was going to make or break both of their careers.

The mood was lighter the next morning, when the two men enjoyed a nice breakfast of orange juice, bacon, eggs, and fruit. Eichelberger remembered it as "the last good meal I was to have for a long time." He and MacArthur conversed comfortably and joked about their old days working together in Washington. When they finished, MacArthur told the I Corps commander, "If you capture Buna, I'll give you a Distinguished Service Cross and recommend you for a high British decoration. Also I'll release your name for newspaper publication." Eichelberger appreciated this, but he knew what really mattered now for him and his soldiers was survival in the jungle and taking Buna. "We knew we would never get out unless we fought our way out," Eichelberger later wrote.[2]

★

Later that morning, by the time General Eichelberger's plane taxied to a stop at Dobodura, the putrid, moldy stench of Buna's swamps had already assaulted his nostrils. Harding was in his command post tent, dictating a report for Sutherland, when Eichelberger and his staff arrived. Though Harding already knew that Eichelberger was coming to Buna, he was nonetheless troubled by the arrival of Bob and his staff. "Disconcerting rates as a masterly understatement," he later commented in his diary. Harding could not help but wonder if the arrival of the corps commander on a one-division battle front meant that the newcomer would now take control of the battle or even fire him. "I wasn't sure where that left me."

The two commanders had been classmates at West Point. They had known each other for thirty-seven years and shared the strong insider camaraderie that came with all the ups and downs of academy life and Army careerism. In part, this shared sense of duty and professional identity helped gloss over the natural awkwardness that otherwise might have stemmed from a situation in which an equal of yesteryear was now the boss. For well or ill, these kind of relationships constituted the sinews of the service's leadership structure. In spite of MacArthur's instructions, Eichelberger had no intention of firing Harding until he saw the Buna situation for himself. When he greeted his old friend, he told him frankly, "Forrest, I've been ordered by General MacArthur to relieve you, but stick by me and I'll see if I can't keep you here." Harding replied, "I'm glad to hear you say that. I think you'll find that the men are doing a good job under exceedingly difficult conditions." Eichelberger asked if Harding felt that any of his commanders should be relieved. But Forrest, true to form, spoke up loyally in their defense and refused to fire anyone.

On this first day, Eichelberger absorbed the situation as division headquarters saw it. The Japanese perimeter was anchored on their right, or
western, flank at Buna village, and a few thousand yards to the east along
the coast, at the Buna Government Station (mistakenly called "Buna Mission" by American soldiers then and historians ever since). Slivers of land
known as the Government Gardens and the Triangle offered the only terrestrial routes of advance between watery swamps, the overflow of the
Girua River, and an estuary called Entrance Creek. Farther east on the
coast was Giropa Point and a pair of airstrips, one of which was grassy and
overgrown and the other of which was recently built by the Japanese. The
Japanese left, or eastern, flank was firmly in place against the coast, near
Cape Endaiadere, the new airstrip, and the Duropa coconut plantation. The
interior of the perimeter offered enough firm ground for the Japanese to
move troops, weapons, and supplies to meet any threat. "The enemy's brilliant terrain utilization canalized all potential Allied attacks into four narrow fronts," an I Corps report later testified. "1) Through the swamp in
front of Buna Village, 2) against the fork, or so-called 'Triangle,' of the
Soputa-Buna track, 3) across the narrow bridge between the strips, and
4) through the coconut plantation below Cape Endaiadere." The thickness
of the jungle and the instability of the ground made any other route of
advance an impossibility. Maps were generally so inaccurate, they were
worse than useless.

Dictated by this swampy terrain, Harding had divided his command
into two main, noncontinuous regimental-size fronts. The Urbana front,
named in honor of Eichelberger's hometown, was situated on the western
flank in front of the Triangle and Buna village. The Warren front, named
for the county in Ohio where Harding came from, covered the eastern
flank near the new strip and the Duropa Plantation. The trails and swamps
between these two fronts were so treacherous that it took an average soldier
a minimum of two days just to travel on foot between them. There were no
roads, just narrow, muddy unstable trails often made impassable by frequent torrential rains. Only jeeps could hope to operate on these glorified
mudslides. Even with jeeps, travel between Dobodura and either front
could be problematic. Colonel Mott commanded the Urbana front. Colonel J. Tracy Hale, commanding officer of the 128th Infantry Regiment and
a National Guardsman from Milwaukee, controlled the Warren front.
Both continued to attack the tenacious Japanese defenses but with little
progress, though there were reports that Mott's people had closed to within

seventy-five yards of Buna village. At headquarters, Eichelberger heard tales of the difficult conditions and the ferocity of the fighting. That night he got a call from Mott reporting a setback at Buna village due to a powerful Japanese counterattack, which, assisted by the expenditure of several hundred precious artillery shells, his men had held off. Eichelberger spoke with Mott on the phone and promised to decorate him for holding his front. This and the other stories impressed Eichelberger enough for him to write that evening to Sutherland, "The picture . . . is not as bad as I expected." All in all, Eichelberger had "a more favorable impression than I had expected to receive."

Like any good commander, though, Eichelberger was determined to check out the front for himself. "Harding tried in every possible way to keep me from going," he later commented. The corps commander would not relent. Accompanied by Harding, he set off for the Urbana sector the following morning at 0930. Since he could not be everywhere at once, he sent Colonel Gordon Rogers, his intelligence officer, and Colonel Clarence Martin, his operations officer, to inspect the Warren front. What Eichelberger saw in the course of the day stunned and angered him. He found that there really was no actual line, just confused clumps of frightened soldiers scattered around the jungle. While small groups manned forward fighting positions, scores more drifted to the rear.

The few soldiers actually at the front would not go forward. The gap of understanding between a middle-aged, high-ranking newcomer who has dedicated his entire life to careerist Army service and an average young private soldier draftee just hoping to survive the day was vast, especially in a place like Buna. The combat troops did not yet know Eichelberger, nor he them. Almost inevitably, his initial interactions with them were tense and awkward. At one hot spot, Eichelberger offered to decorate anyone willing to investigate a trail with him to pinpoint the location of a Japanese machine gun. For exhausted men so close to death, this was hardly an enticement. No one moved a muscle. In the estimation of one 32nd Division officer who witnessed the scene, medals meant nothing to such soldiers who were "filthy, fever ridden, practically starved, living in a tidal swamp," and seeing their buddies getting killed. Harding later opined drily, "They may have felt that the posthumous award of a piece of ribbon was not such an alluring bait." Leaders were practically invisible. There was seemingly no urgency or organization to anything. Weapons were corroding or unattended in the tropical climate. Patrols were almost nonexistent. Men were even more afraid of the jungle than the Japanese. A sense of lethargy hung over them like a veil.

The poor condition of the troops contributed in a major way to this bad situation. "The men were in sad shape," one of Eichelberger's aides recorded in an historical report that evening. "They were bearded and dirty. They complained of being hungry . . . and rightly, for they were not getting enough food. They were living among their own unburied dead." The stench of these corpses was overwhelming. "You could smell that for twenty-four hours, seven days a week, and you could taste it," Tech 5 Claire Ehle later recalled. Many of the men had beards that made them look, even in Harding's estimation, like members "of the Army of the Potomac." Eichelberger ordered medics to take the temperature of the men in one rifle company. Every single soldier was running a fever. They looked, in the estimation of one doctor "like Christ on the cross." In the memory of one of Eichelberger's staff officers, "their clothing was in rags. Their shoes were uncared for, or worn out. They were receiving far less than adequate rations and there was little discipline or military courtesy." Everyone had diarrhea. Vitamins, quinine pills, and salt tablets were hard to come by. That afternoon, Eichelberger came upon one typical group that, as he later wrote to a friend, "had had nothing to eat since the previous day and had had no hot food in ten days. They were getting two tins of C Ration per man per day." When rations arrived, "they broke into the cans and wolfed the food like starving men."

According to Eichelberger's supply officer, this food allotment amounted to eighteen hundred calories a day, a starvation-level diet. "No rice was going forward to supplement their diet. The men had no cigarettes although there seemed to be no shortage back in the base section. It was evident that a very pallid siege was being waged." Some soldiers had even thrown away their entrenching tools, a sure sign of decay in junior-level leadership. On the Warren front, Rogers and Martin estimated that, at most, 150 soldiers were manning front-line positions, while almost two thousand others drifted aimlessly to their rear, seemingly doing next to nothing. Instead of attacking, as headquarters claimed, "they were washing clothes, cooking and taking it easy," Rogers wrote. Organization was lacking. Units were mixed up. Men looked haggard and exhausted. "The most discouraging thing about the entire situation was the air of depression that hung over the troops." On the other side of the front, the Japanese were growing contemptuous of their American enemies. One training memo called them "inexperienced in controlling large bodies of troops; subordinates are not permitted to use their own initiative, and execute given orders only. By using proper judgment, enemy attacks can be repulsed. American troops are simple minded and easy to deceive." One Japanese soldier sneered to his diary, "The enemy has received almost no training . . . their movements are very slow. It seems they will fire at any sound, due to illusion."

All in all, General Eichelberger was shocked at the mess he observed. "I found conditions far worse than those responsible would have been willing to admit. There was no front line discipline of any kind." Moreover, he soon discovered that, contrary to Mott's claims, there had been no Japanese counterattack the night before. Instead, he was told by several soldiers, according to one witness, "that some of our outposts had heard the Japanese talking and moving around on the island and excitedly reported the situation as a counterattack." This angered him and evaporated his trust in Mott and perhaps even Harding, whom Eichelberger now realized had never even visited his own division's front lines. Seething, Eichelberger grew increasingly curt with his old classmate. When he suggested that troops should be trying to advance by infiltration, Harding snapped back. "They are up against a continuous front, and infiltration tactics are not practical in such a situation."

The growing tension boiled over in a stormy meeting at Mott's shabby command post tent. Eichelberger was displeased over what he had seen on his tour, and he let Harding and Mott know it, in so many caustic words. He even questioned the courage of the troops, something he later regretted doing. Mott had a sharp, sarcastic manner and a talent for antagonizing superiors and subordinates alike. In response to this diatribe from the corps commander against his men, he lost his temper. "I felt constrained to indicate to him that the men were not cowards," he later wrote. They were fighting in terrible conditions, with little food, rest, or support from higher headquarters. Exasperated and irritated by what he perceived as impertinence from a subordinate, Eichelberger bellowed, "You're licked!" a 1940s term for defeat.

For Harding the argument between the two men presented a difficult moment of choice, the sort that defines a career. On one hand, he could side with his superior, tell the colonel to back down, or even relieve him on the spot. But this risked self-preservation at the expense of a subordinate, something anathema to a man as honorable as Harding. On the other

hand, if he stood up for Mott, he risked alienating his new boss and gloss-
ing over the undeniable failures of his command. Loyal to the end, Harding chose the second option. Nonconfrontational by nature, he opted to
communicate his feelings nonverbally. To emphasize his agreement with
Mott, General Harding angrily took an unlit cigarette from his mouth and
flung it on the ground at Eichelberger's feet. The corps commander turned
and left the tent. Later, perhaps as a form of self-therapy, Harding vented
to his diary about Eichelberger. "He showed no appreciation of what the
men had been through or of the spirit shown by most of them in carrying
on despite heavy casualties, the toughest kind of opposition, and the most
trying conditions. I approved of every word [Mott] said and the vehemence
with which he stated the case. It took courage to say it."

Eichelberger was much less impressed. In his opinion, Harding and
Mott were not really looking out for the best interests of their men or else
they would have fed them, cared for their needs properly, and aggressively
led them to attain their objectives. As Eichelberger saw it, the two men
were denying responsibility for the disgraceful condition of their command. "For Colonel Mott to insist that the conditions I described were not
correct," Eichelberger later wrote, "and to insist in an angry manner, placed
him outside the pale." That evening, when Rogers and Martin reported
finding a similar mess on the Warren front, Eichelberger reluctantly concluded that Harding, Mott, and Hale all had to go. "Unfortunately there
was nothing but excuses in the air and sympathy for the soldiers," Eichelberger wrote Sutherland a few days later. "The mission had sort of vanished
into thin air." To MacArthur, the I Corps commander later explained,
"General Harding seemed unable to galvanize his troops into sufficient
aggressiveness to accomplish a successful attack. His desire to protect his
officers caused him to excuse and explain failures. Because of this unwillingness to take remedial action and in spite of a lifelong friendship, I was
forced to request General Harding's relief."

The firing itself was naturally sad and awkward. As night settled over
Dobodura, Harding visited Eichelberger's tent and began to brief him on
new attack plans. Eichelberger was polite but distracted. Instead of com-
menting on the plan, he mentioned the troubling nature of what he had
seen that day. At last Harding blurted, "You were probably sent here to get
heads. Maybe mine is one of them. If so, it is on the block."

Eichelberger sighed and nodded, "You are right." He pointed at Brigadier General Albert "Doc" Waldron, the thin, wiry division artillery com-

mander who had moved heaven and earth just to get a few guns in place to support the push for Buna. "I am putting this man in command of the division."

"I take it I am to return to Moresby," Harding said.

"Yes."

Without a word, Harding left the tent. Waldron followed and expressed his regrets, as did Eichelberger. Harding made no reply. Though the two old classmates ate breakfast together the next day, their relationship was never the same. In fact, it was the last time they ever spoke. Word of the popular Harding's relief spread through the division like a shock wave. "They can't do this to you!" Major Chet Beaver, an aide, roared defiantly. "They can and they did," Harding replied matter-of-factly. Just before the genteel general left, he paid a visit to a group of wounded men and apologized for letting them down. "Hell, no, General, *we* let *you* down!" one of them replied.

Within a few days, Harding, Mott, and Hale were all trundled "over the mountains," back to Moresby. Harding met personally with MacArthur. The SWPA commander acted the very embodiment of disingenuousness. Whereas only a few days earlier he had railed against Harding and called for his immediate relief, he now assured Harding that the division's troubles were normal for troops new to battle and did not really reflect on him as a commander. MacArthur told Harding he just needed a rest and then he would find another job for him. When Harding asked why then he had been relieved, MacArthur replied as if he had played no role in the decision. "I have no idea." Seemingly in hopes of getting his old job back, Harding then wrote an explanatory letter for MacArthur. "No one knows better than I that we haven't performed perfectly. But for troops without . . . experience in the kind of war we have been fighting, we did well with what we had. I know that no one can get more out of *that* division than I can."

In reality, MacArthur did blame Harding for the failure at Buna and he wanted nothing more to do with him. He just did not have the resolve to tell him to his face, a two-faced duplicity unbecoming of a supreme commander. As a result of it, Harding for the rest of his life solely blamed Eichelberger for firing him unfairly. He often ripped Eichelberger privately to fellow classmates and publicly to historians. "You may think my outspoken criticism of Eichelberger displays animus and you may partly be right," he wrote to one Army historian. Predictably, Harding never received another combat command and he held Eichelberger responsible. Eichelberger regretted and resented this, especially because he felt he had bent over backward to give his old comrade leeway, perhaps more than he deserved amid such a terrible situation. "The more I look back on Harding and his relief at Buna," Eichelberger said years later, "I realize I would have tried to save him in spite of General MacArthur's orders to me, had he not . . . lost his temper. He did it openly before other people and left me little choice but to get rid of him."

The whole incident was sad and regrettable. A good man had lost his job, partially because MacArthur's poor planning and intelligence gathering had put him in a terrible situation. But that stood as nothing in contrast to the many other greater tragedies playing out at Buna. Changes had to be made and, difficult situation or not, Harding was ultimately responsible for the lack of results and the rotten condition of his troops. In card parlance, he received a bad hand but made it immeasurably worse. He was especially remiss in failing to visit the front. It revealed a disturbing paucity of commonsense leadership on his part, a theoretician's tendency to shy away from gritty pragmatism. Stilwell, who had served with Harding at the Infantry School and elsewhere, once summed up his opinion of Harding's fitness to lead troops in battle by saying, "Harding is a fine chap, but the man who gave him a combat command should have his head examined."[3]

In the meantime, at Buna, Eichelberger did the best he could to tamp down resentment among the Red Arrow soldiers for axing their popular leader—"There was some talk that I would be shot in the back by some of [Harding's] men," he later wrote to Herring—even as he reorganized the troops for a new offensive. One of the first tasks was to improve the supply situation. The logistical tail was anything but stable. Everything, from bullets to ration cans to bandages, had to be brought in by air from Port Moresby to Dobodura or by sea aboard small luggers from Oro Bay to Hariko. The planes could haul only so much. The boats were vulnerable to Japanese air and sea attacks. Once in place, everything had to be laboriously hauled forward, mainly by Papuan civilians, to the two fronts, either aboard jeeps or by hand. Harding's supply section tried hard to keep their tenuous umbilical cord functioning, but this was problematic. Though they certainly worked hard, for whatever reason, they did not work smart. Organization was especially lacking. Kenney, in his diary, chronicled instances of extreme inefficiency. His aviators flew much food and ammunition to Dobodura, but if the work crews on the ground had enough to eat themselves, they were lax at unloading the planes. "Our crews then unload themselves and the supplies are just thrown on the side of the runway," Kenney told his diary. Petty rivalries also caused trouble. According to Colonel George De Graaf, the I Corps quartermaster, the 32nd Division supply officer was feuding with Mott and "was very bitter and seemed to be more devoted to finding ways to oust Mott than to supervise the supply problem."

Eichelberger quickly discovered that there were huge quantities of food, ammunition, and medicine at Dobodura, as crates had piled up uselessly at the airfield. When De Graaf surveyed and organized this matériel, he found that, in one spot alone, there were twenty thousand D ration chocolate bars and five thousand C ration meals strewn carelessly around. "Some of them had been ruined by improper storage." Eichelberger quickly alleviated this problem, setting up a more efficient supply system. Gone were the days of rotting C rations and eighteen hundred calories per day. On December 3, the troops ate their first hot meal in nearly two weeks. Planes were unloaded with more reliability. Work parties were better organized. Drinking water was fairly plentiful, though it had to be chlorinated by medics or engineers or with purification tablets before consumption.

With front-line manpower scarce, the Allies needed locals to perform the duties of service troops. The bulk of the supplies were hauled forward by Papuan men who were recruited—one might even say coerced—and supervised by the Australians. "Were it not for the availability of natives," De Graaf later wrote, "supply would have fallen down badly." According to I Corps records, more than sixteen hundred Papuans worked on the Buna front. Though the Americans respected these men and treated them well, many still patronizingly thought of them as "natives" or "fuzzy wuzzies," men of a lesser race functioning in a typical menial role. "Always, without overdoing it, be the master," a SWPA pamphlet on New Guinea patronizingly advised servicemen. "The time may come when you want a native to obey you. He won't obey you if you have been in the habit of treating him as an equal." In fact, the success or failure of the battle, in a logistical sense, hinged on their sturdy shoulders. "They were fearsome looking, dressed only in loin clothes, but were really a gentle people," Sergeant Jungwirth assessed perceptively. "Without their help, our task in the jungles of New Guinea would have been much harder." They did not face the same dangers as the soldiers, but they worked tirelessly for not much more than the equivalent of minimum wage, and this, for a fight by outsiders over their homes. The aftertaste of imperialism and the geopolitical struggle of global warfare had indeed made for some strange bedfellows.[4]

For two days, General Eichelberger called a halt to all operations while he installed new leaders, restored unit integrity, planned a new offensive, fed the troops, clothed them properly, got them medical care, and restored their shaken morale. Colonel Eddie Grose, his inspector general, took over the Urbana front. Colonel Martin took command of the Warren front. Both of these men had seen combat as infantrymen in World War I. Eichelberger immediately established more effective ties and coordination with the Australian commanders, especially Herring, with whom he soon forged a strong bond. Indeed, Herring later wrote to Eichelberger that his assumption of command at Buna "was like a very pure breath of fresh air." From this point forward, the two allies began acting more like real partners, rather than backbiting adversaries. This was especially true for the front-line troops, who had already established strong ties of respectful comradeship.

Naturally garrulous, Eichelberger circulated around, giving pep talks, scolding junior leaders when necessary, joking with the men when appropriate, quelling resentment over Harding's firing, trying to present himself as the new leader of an invigorated command. Most of the encounters were pleasant and comradely, especially when Eichelberger took to handing out cigarettes, something that would become a war-long practice for the non-smoking general. He displayed an avuncular, almost swashbuckling persona. Most of the time, he called soldiers "my boy," "lad," or "son." Invariably he referred to members of his staff and his aides by their first names. As he handed out goodies to the men, he often gave them good-natured advice on soldiering or life in general. His geniality and sociability made him difficult to dislike. Like Patton, he was a great believer in the notion of inspirational, up-front leadership, a valorous mask of command. Courageous nearly to a fault, he seemed compulsively drawn to danger. When a front-line sentry advised him to remove his general's stars or risk getting shot by snipers, he replied, "My boy, I would do far more good back in the command post than being shot at up here, unless the men know their commanding general is with them!" When Eichelberger found out one day that Byers had surreptitiously removed the three stars from his collar, he reproved him. "I want the boys to know I'm here with them. Hell, what's the use of my going up front if I go incognito?"

Inevitably, a few of the encounters with the soldiers were awkward, as when he recommended taking daily vitamins to one haggard squad who counted themselves lucky just to have basic food and water, much less such luxuries as vitamin pills. "The men thanked him respectfully for the pre-scription and went on dreaming, as they had for many weeks, about little corners of chocolate bars," one correspondent later wrote of the conversa-tion. More than anything, the fifty-six-year-old general tried to reshape the culture of the command, make it more mission-oriented, even more ruth-less. Taking a cue from the corps commander, Colonel Martin met with his officers and told them there would be no relief for the 32nd Division. They would either leave Buna as victors or dead men. "I was certain that after the shock was over, the troops would fight better than those just hanging on and continually looking over their shoulders for relief to come," Martin later wrote. He ordered that "soldiers would do all they could to better . . . their personal appearance, and their equipment. Beards would come off. Sanitation would be improved."

All of this represented improvement for the Allied situation at Buna, but there was still the little matter of overrunning the Japanese defenders. At 1030 on December 5, Eichelberger launched a new attack on both fronts. Determined to lead from the front and risk his life along with everybody else, he wrote to Emma that morning, "I am doing the work for which I have been trained. You must be a soldier's wife and hope for all good things. Maybe I can do the impossible." There was nothing subtle about the new offensive. Air strikes by nine B-25 medium bombers, plus some artil-lery and mortar fire served as the softening-up bombardment, a paltry mix by the Army's later pre-attack standards. Like the struggle for Buna as a whole, it was really an infantryman's small-unit fight, a frontal assault, but not in masses, since the thick jungle made this impossible. "Our troops could not fight as units," one operations officer later wrote, "but rather as individuals or in twos and threes." At dozens of miserable places, small groups of American infantrymen went forward on the same trails and into the same swamps where previous attacks had failed. "There are Japs up ahead but there also may be Japs behind me and I'm sure as hell there's a couple of them a few yards over to the side," a rifleman at the front told a war correspondent. "We just keep looking for Japs, killing them and push-ing ahead."

The troops still had few weapons beyond grenades and rifles with which to assault the beautifully camouflaged Japanese bunkers. Predictably, they made almost no headway against the maze of pillboxes. "They were practi-cally impenetrable to our fire," Sergeant Gerber recalled. "You could look right into one and it looked like the jungle." In most instances, the Japanese used smokeless gunpowder, making them hard to spot even after they opened fire. Often, the Americans did not see the bunkers until they were enmeshed among them, pinned down by machine gun and rifle fire, trapped like bugs on a spider web. "Realistically we found bunkers by losing men," one survivor said. Another remembered, "The only place we could attack was in their line of fire." Frightened Americans tended to shoot too high, a common problem in combat. On the Warren front, a section of five Australian Bren gun carriers were all knocked out within thirty minutes. "The personnel in the carriers were shot from tree top positions and the carriers themselves lacked sufficient power and weight," according to one Army report.

Japanese riflemen tied themselves to the tops of coconut trees and acted in a dual role as observers for their comrades in nearby bunkers and snipers who picked off men as they tried to advance. Their fire added to the grisly harvest of death. Their exploding bullets scythed through helmets, throats or abdomens. "If there was an opening in the jungle," Sergeant Henry Dearchs, another infantry soldier recalled, "the Japs didn't shoot at the first guy. They'd let you all come in before firing. There was one particular clearing that was extremely dangerous: several guys that stepped into it dropped right there with a bullet in the forehead." Sergeant Dave Richardson, a correspondent for *Yank* magazine, the Army's periodical for soldiers, was so terrified that his hands shook too badly for him to take notes. All around him were "the sounds of war, the bodies, the blood. The Japanese were so close to us and the jungle so thick you could hear [them] talking and hear their mess kits rattling."

Like nearly everyone else, General Eichelberger experienced the horror of the sniper fire. True to form, he was right up front, leading the attack, with all three of his stars displayed on the shoulders of his sweat-soaked fatigues. With him were General Waldron, Colonel Rogers, Colonel De Graaf, and Captain Daniel "Eddie" Edwards, his aide-de-camp, whom he loved like a son (Edwards even signed "Junior" when he wrote letters to the general). Several carried Thompson submachine guns. At the Urbana front, they saw a group of soldiers take some fire within a few yards of their jump-off point and go to ground. With his entourage in tow, Eichelberger strolled over to them and said, "Boys, we are going forward. Come with us." They got up and followed, though undoubtedly some wondered if this old man with the stars was out of his mind. As long as Eichelberger led, the troops were willing to keep going. The same was true when he later encountered members of three attacking rifle companies. While he led and cajoled, they slowly worked forward. Within a few minutes they all became enmeshed in confusing, intimate duels with the unseen snipers. At one point, Eichelberger was pinned down for a quarter of an hour, bullets zipping by about four inches overhead, spattering everywhere around him. "Fifteen minutes, with imminent death blowing coolly on your sweat-wet shirt, can seem like a long time!" Eichelberger later wrote. Everyone pointed their tommy guns at the trees and sprayed them indiscriminately until the enemy fire slackened.

With Buna village only a few hundred yards distant, Eichelberger believed they just needed to keep going and they could take it. "Boys, I'm going forward. Are you with me?" he often asked firmly, almost as an order more than a request. Eichelberger knew soldiers well enough to understand that the question served as an unspoken challenge to their manhood, and perhaps also evoked their sense of shame, powerful motivation indeed. No one of course really wanted to risk his life. But no one wanted to be seen as a coward in front of his comrades. Moreover, no soldier wanted the blame if the crazy old man got killed while he was in a position to fight with him and maybe protect him. "It was the way he said it," one of his staff later wrote of Eichelberger's manner. "He somehow implied that of course they were with him." He also used plenty of humor. When he and a small group of men were stymied in an attempt to overwhelm a pillbox, he quipped, "Boys, I don't know whether or not I'm a good general, but sure as hell I am one fine platoon leader!" When he noticed a pair of war correspondents who were hanging back from the front lines, he approached them, told them about a new attack he had organized, and then said earnestly, "And you, my boys, I am going to ask to lead the charge." The color drained from both their faces until they realized he was not serious. "My God, Colonel," one of them later said to Rogers, "I thought the Old Man meant it!"

Whether through humor, the personal example of risking his own life, or shaming people, more often than not he got troops moving, deeper into danger. Eventually, as he pressed on and shouted instructions to a group of soldiers, he and his entourage ran into more powerfully accurate sniper fire on a trail almost within sight of Buna village. A bullet tore through General Waldron's shoulder. He fell heavily to the ground, badly wounded, though he was able to make it to the rear. Eichelberger decided to replace him as 32nd Division commander with Byers, his own chief of staff. Moments later, a bullet whizzed past Eichelberger and smashed into

Edwards, who was only a couple of feet in front of the general. "As I watched, his knees began to bend under him and he fell forward," Eichelberger said. "He at once told me to keep cover. I dropped when he was hit." Edwards had a well-earned reputation for bravery. A few days earlier, he had personally infiltrated the Japanese lines, reconnoitered Buna village, and brought back valuable information on the strength of Japanese defenses. Now he was hit in the abdomen by an exploding bullet. As he lay bleeding for several long minutes, Colonel De Graaf arrived with a four-man-stretcher team. Accompanied by the general, they manhandled Edwards atop the litter and attempted to carry him to the rear. They were pinned down by machine-gun fire several times as they evacuated Edwards. Witnesses saw tracer rounds zoom past both of Eichelberger's shoulders. Somehow he did not get hit. Colonel Rogers turned and sprayed the trees with his tommy gun. They got Edwards to an aid station. The doctor was not optimistic for his survival. As Rogers recalled, the general was "fuming with rage and stricken with grief," over Edwards. The bullet had missed his spine but exited his back and left a large hole. Sensing that Edwards would die if he did not get immediate surgery, Eichelberger took time out from directing the battle and used his personal jeep to transport the wounded man to the nearest field hospital, where doctors operated on him at once. Returning to the site of Edwards's wounding, Eichelberger and Rogers determined that the sniper had been hunkered down in a deep hole under a tree trunk, probably no more than five yards away. "I doubt if he could see either of us after he fired," Eichelberger said. He later explained to Emma in a letter that "the bird who hurt [Eddie] might have taken me had [Eddie] not been standing a little in front of me. Eddie was armed with a Tommy gun and probably looked more dangerous. One finds a lot of philosophy in life."

Eichelberger's scuffle with the snipers was typical of what was happening all over the Buna perimeter. The Americans were putting pressure on the Japanese, inflicting damage on them, but significant forward movement was negligible. Lieutenant Odell, now in command of F Company, 126th Infantry, received a personal briefing from Eichelberger to take Buna village only a couple hundred yards away, but, because of the Japanese bunkers and the terrain, the close proximity to the objective did not matter as much as it otherwise might have. They had only ten minutes to recon the area. Half the company went on one trail with Odell; the other half on another trail with a replacement lieutenant who was the only other officer in the unit. "Well, off we went, and within minutes our forward rush had definitely and completely halted," Odell wrote. "Of the 40 men who started with me, four had been . . . killed and 18 were laying wounded. We never had a chance and that is all there was to it. Infantry can't advance past pillboxes."

There was one bright spot, though. A platoon from H Company, 126th Infantry, under the command of thirty-three-year-old Staff Sergeant Herman Bottcher, infiltrated past several enemy bunkers and made it to the beach between Buna village and Buna Government Station a few hundred yards farther east along the coast. Bottcher had an unusual background. He was a German-born anti-Nazi who had emigrated to the United States. For several years he worked as a carpenter and went to school in San Francisco. His hatred of fascism was profound enough that, when the Spanish Civil War broke out, he went to Spain and fought for two years on the Loyalist side, an experience he later called "glorious and depressing," though it did make him an ideal small-unit leader in this war. A veteran of the agonizing march over the Owen Stanleys, Bottcher was by now a universally respected combat NCO. When he made it to the beach, he wisely ordered his men to dig in and set fields of fire in either direction. With one machine gun, he and eighteen stalwarts fended off numerous counterattacks, killing many enemy soldiers whose rotting corpses washed in and out with the gentle surf.

For the first time, the Americans had breached the Japanese defensive line and made it within sight of the sea. The narrow salient was dubbed "Bottcher's Corner" by the soldiers of the Urbana front. In that perilous spot Bottcher's platoon remained for nearly a week, periodically joined by other infiltrators, including Eichelberger on one occasion, with Bottcher patrolling back and forth to the American lines to bring up more supplies and reinforcements. He performed like a man possessed, and according to Colonel Rogers, it was partially because Eichelberger had promised him American citizenship in exchange for honorable service. "He was the epitome of the aggressive leader, spurring men and setting a personal example of daring and drive," Rogers wrote. Bottcher not only got his citizenship but also a field commission and the Distinguished Service Cross. Thanks to Bottcher and his men, Buna village was cut off from the Government Station. It wasn't much, but it did signify a more aggressive spirit in the American troops at Buna, and it created a serious wedge in the Japanese perimeter.[5]

There were other salients. Like Bottcher's, they were perilous places to
be. In the jungle maze, small units were cut off, occasionally ambushed.
Survivors got away as best they could; the dead were often left behind. At
one miserable spot a few miles west of Bottcher's Corner, the bodies of
Captain Roger Keast and several others lay rotting. Lieutenant Hershel
Horton, a native of Aurora, Illinois, led a patrol to identify the bodies and
retrieve their dog tags. Keast and Horton were college track athletes who
had once competed against each other—Keast for Michigan State, Horton
for Notre Dame. Horton and three men made their way to the bodies. Just
when Horton turned over Keast's rotting corpse, preparing to clip off his
dog tags, shots rang out. "I was shot two or three times in my right leg and
hip," Horton wrote. He yelled for help, but under intense fire, the other
three soldiers ran for cover. "I dragged myself for a Jap grass shanty about
twelve yards to the rear of where I was shot." One of the men promised to
get him out, but he and the others vanished. Assisted by these men, at least
one patrol tried to get to Horton, but it was suicide because he was lying in
a kill zone.

Isolated and in pain, Horton suffered a terrible ordeal. His hip was shattered. He had a compound fracture in his right leg. "I lay there unattended
in any way without food or water or medical care" for two days. He deliri-
ously called for someone to come and help him. On the third day, medics
got to him, bandaged his wounds, and gave him water. The Japanese
opened up on them and killed one man. The medics left. Horton, meanwhile, battled for his life, all the while in intense pain. Perhaps to distract
from his ordeal, he took out his small prayer book and wrote a stream-of-
consciousness letter to his parents and sister. "Life from then on was a
terrible nightmare. The hot burning sun, the delirious nights. No one came
near me from then on, but I did dig a water hole in four days time, which
was wonderful to me; although it was polluted by all the rotting bodies
within 12 ft. and 14 ft. of me." Day and night, he continued to call for help,
his desperate cries echoing through the eerie jungle. "Each night we could
hear a man yelling in the jungle to the southeast," Tech 4 Springer, a medic,
later wrote. The man was Horton. When Springer and several comrades
lobbied their superiors for permission to go get the lieutenant, it was denied with the warning that "if anyone else got close to the wounded man
they would probably also be shot." By now, the soldiers of the 32nd Division understood all too well that the Japanese pitilessly shot medics, with
no consideration for conceptual laws of war.

Horton tried to crawl to safety, but he was too weak. The Japanese were only fifteen yards away. When Horton succeeded in standing up one day, they shot him in the shoulder and neck. He collapsed to the ground. Panting and sobbing, dehydrated, starving and losing blood, he somehow lingered on. "I . . . lay here in this terrible place, wondering not why God has forsaken me; but rather why He is making me suffer this terrible end?" he asked rhetorically in the letter. "I am not afraid to die although I have nearly lost my faith a couple days here. My life has been good, but I am so young and have so many things undone that a man of 29 should do. I know now how Christ felt on the cross. We may never know God's purpose in striking me down like this, but He *must* have one. God bless you my loved ones. Keep the faith, don't worry. I shall see you all again some day. I prepare to meet My Maker."

A subsequent patrol found the prayer book on Horton's lifeless, decomposing corpse. He lay within fifty feet of Keast, his old friend and rival. As was standard, Horton's possessions were sent to the office of Lieutenant Colonel John Murphy, the effects quartermaster at the Kansas City Quartermaster Depot. With a heavy heart, Murphy personally forwarded it to Horton's father, George. "It will cause you heartache and grief, but at the same time will give you even greater pride in being the father of a son who could face death as he did." Had there been no war, Horton would have graduated with Notre Dame's class of 1943.[6]

★

As the fighting petered out on December 5, Eichelberger decided that he would launch no more general attacks on both fronts. With MacArthur's cries for urgency ringing in his ears, he had hoped victory at Buna might come from one big push, but this had failed. He knew he had hurt the Japanese, but nowhere near enough. In the course of the day, he had lost about 150 men. Though time obviously still mattered, victory could not come quickly through a massive push but rather by relentlessly wearing down the Japanese. Better, he decided, to bring down his opponent by landing hundreds of little punches instead of hoping to score with one haymaker. Given the relatively small size of the Japanese perimeter and the tenacious nature of their soldiers, geographic objectives were only part of the equation for American success. The Buna battle had really boiled down to the stark reality that the Americans now had to annihilate the defenders, bunker by bunker, trench by trench, tree by tree, probably until they were all dead, an extermination duel that was nearly unprecedented in the Army's history. Eichelberger dubbed it "a military nightmare."

Instead of costly all-out attacks on unseen enemy bunkers, Eichelberger emphasized more patrolling to recon and harass the Japanese. He felt these skills had been lacking in the 32nd Division's training. Some of the soldiers had never even experienced a night field exercise. "You will find riding up in front of you, to haunt you, the spectre of all those things you have failed to teach your men," he warned his West Point classmate Major General Fuller, who was in Australia, training his 41st Infantry Division for New Guinea duty. Eichelberger attempted to teach the 32nd Division soldiers more about how to move through the jungle, pinpoint Japanese positions, take them by infiltration rather than frontal assault, or just harass and wear them down. "Our men are climbing trees and becoming snipers," he told Fuller. "Our men creep forward at night."

In truth, the Red Arrow soldiers had already learned a great deal about how to operate in the jungle, though Eichelberger's strong emphasis on patrolling did improve their skills. "Orders were issued that each company, for *TRAINING PURPOSES*, would send out one patrol commanded by an officer each night, the patrol would stay out for two hours!" Colonel Knight, the War Department observer, chronicled. The patrols operated in frighteningly close proximity to the Japanese, so much so that the troops called their officers by their first or last names rather than "sir" or by rank. "The usual mission was to gain information where the Jap was, or what he was doing, and occasionally just to find out where in hell we were," Lieutenant Odell wrote. In most instances, his patrols "were just a matter of lying or crawling in mud or water for hours on end out in the middle of nowhere, wondering if you would ever find your way back, or if there was (or could be) a bit of skin anywhere on your body that ants and mosquitoes hadn't already bitten." Tech 4 Springer, the medic, treated one patroller who spent so much time immersed in the filth of the swamps that his legs and genitals were inundated with small ringworms. "It looked like his body was covered with one complete, uniform tattoo." Springer could do little for him besides apply some antifungal ointment and give him a shot of morphine. When he showed no improvement, he had to be evacuated.

Bit by bit, General Eichelberger's attrition strategy began to work. He launched a series of small, tenacious attacks against the beleaguered enemy garrison at Buna village. These attacks chewed up the remnants of the 2nd Battalion, 126th Infantry—Lieutenant Odell's F Company had only thirty-eight soldiers left—but they inflicted hundreds of casualties on the Japanese. A new battalion from the 127th Infantry—the same people the luckless Harding had lobbied for—relieved the 126th to finish the job.

Spooked by cryptic reports of reinforcement-laden Japanese convoys and impatient for quick results, MacArthur on December 13 prodded Eichelberger, "Time is fleeting and our dangers increase with its passage. However admirable individual acts of courage may be; however splendid and electrical your presence has proven, remember that your mission is to take Buna. All other things are merely subsidiary to this. No alchemy is going to produce this for you; it can only be done in battle and sooner or later this battle must be engaged. Time is working desperately against us." The supreme commander's message contained a significant oversight of one key fact: the mission was no longer limited to physical possession of "Buna," whatever that meant and for whatever value that might provide. The entire perimeter, a heavily fortified coastal strip, could only be taken by exterminating the Japanese garrison in a time-consuming, dangerous process. Unbeknownst to MacArthur, even as he wrote to Eichelberger, the Japanese were actually evacuating Buna village. Spurred on by Eichelberger, troops from the 127th claimed it on the morning of December 14. The place was little more than an odorous mishmash of wrecked huts and shattered coconut trees, strewn with the detritus of discarded clothing, empty food cans, ragged bits of uniform, and bloody bandages. Five days earlier, the Australians had taken Gona, where they buried 638 Japanese corpses. "Everywhere, pervading everything, was the stench of putrescent flesh," one observer wrote.

With Gona and Buna village gone, the Allies had now driven a permanent wedge in the Japanese defensive perimeter. The Japanese defenders were outnumbered, penned into separate areas, cut off from adequate supply and support. At Rabaul, General Adachi was so concerned about their situation that he resolved to go to Buna and lead them in person. The Buna garrison represented his only major combat element and he was loath to see it destroyed. When his staff tried to dissuade him from going to Buna, he said, "If I don't go, who will save the Buna Detachment? I'm not going to look on while my only son is killed in battle." Only a direct order from his superior, General Imamura, kept him in Rabaul.

Throughout the Buna perimeter, in their damp, dank bunkers and muddy trenches, the Japanese soldiers talked incessantly of reinforcements; the daily hope of their arrival helped sustain these beleaguered men. But stocks of medicine and ammunition were dwindling. Twenty Japanese soldiers were dying each day from disease. By the end of December, the number had risen to thirty per day. In the recollection of one officer, the troops spent their days standing "in swamp water up to their armpits suffering from malaria with forty degrees centigrade [104 Fahrenheit] fever." Most of the men were eating half and then quarter rations of sardines, rice, dry vegetables, and coconuts. "The meat is slightly sweet and hard," a young officer, Lieutenant Suganuma, wrote of the coconuts. "It does not fill the stomach very much, but it is tasty." Many now suffered from night blindness brought on by vitamin deficiencies. Hungry and bone-weary, they wondered how much longer they could hold out. "What a discouraging and miserable state of affairs," Sergeant Kiyoshi Wada, a medic, lamented to his diary. "Trees have fallen, limbs have been cracked, and the hospital is in a horrible plight. What is going to happen to us?" Another soldier, anonymous, sadly scrawled in his diary, "Every day my comrades die one by one and our provisions disappear." He and the rest of the garrison were tiring badly. But, as one of his comrades aptly put it, "We are holding out, hoping for a miracle. The victorious army laughs while burning their wills." Unfortunately for the Americans, the growing misery of Buna did nothing to evaporate their determination to keep fighting. "We will hold out to the last," another scribbled menacingly in a notebook. Major General Tsuyuo Yamagata, the highest-ranking Japanese commander in Papua, urged his troops to "recall the words of commendation His Imperial Majesty has been pleased to address to us and determine with one heart to overcome the present crisis and thereby set His Majesty's mind at rest."

When MacArthur found out that Buna village had fallen, he was jubilant. He sent Eichelberger a laudatory telegram. "My heartiest congratulations. Under your magnificent leadership the 32nd Division is coming into its own. Well done, Bob." When MacArthur thereafter realized that the capture of Buna village did not necessarily mean the imminence of final victory, he urged Eichelberger to mass his forces for one final climactic attack against Buna Government Station and the rest of the Japanese defensive perimeter. In his view, only the applied mass of force could achieve the desired results. "Your problem is to apply your full power on your front line rather than limit it to two or three companies. Where you have a company on your firing line, you should have a battalion; and where you have a battalion, you should have a regiment. And your attacks, instead of being made by two or three hundred rifles, should be made by two or three thousand. It will be an eye for an eye and a tooth for a tooth—and a casualty on your side for a casualty on his. I feel convinced that our time is strictly limited and that if results are not achieved shortly, the whole picture may radically change." Eichelberger knew that the mass offensive MacArthur envisioned was an impossibility. "[He] never fully realized the deterioration of the strength of the three infantry regiments," Eichelberger wrote to a friend a few weeks later. "The three rifle companies that did the fighting in all battalions numbered about sixty-five men each."

As Eichelberger sensed, the advice exposed a supreme commander who neither understood Buna's terrain and conditions nor the formidable strength of the Japanese fortifications. Over the course of the war, MacArthur would come to understand jungle warfare fairly well. But at this point, he had almost literally no clue about it. He did not comprehend that swamps, creeks, and dense foliage precluded any possibility of massing infantry formations for World War I–style attacks as he envisioned them. Whether out of oversight or ignorance, he made no mention of the supporting firepower that was so necessary for the "rifles" to destroy bunkers and take ground. He did not grasp that Buna was every bit as much of a battle against the conditions as the Japanese. Beyond the manpower-sapping problems of disease and tropical heat, the fight could be won only by a relentless series of bitter, vulgar, horrifying, close-quarters engagements— small groups of scared men struggling for survival against other small groups of scared men. Had MacArthur personally visited the front, he might have appreciated these realities. Instead, he unwisely chose to rely on questionable reports from Sutherland and Willoughby, both of whom made occasional visits, but never ventured near the actual fighting. To wit, as Sutherland and Eichelberger studied the Triangle through binoculars one day, the chief of staff dismissed the Japanese positions as "nothing but hasty field fortifications." Eichelberger was taken aback at the obtuseness of the statement, one that could only be uttered by someone who had no experience in the actual fighting. "I am only sorry he did not get to look inside one of those bunkers after the fighting," Eichelberger wrote several years later. As an Army insider, Eichelberger was well aware of Sutherland's checkered reputation for byzantine scheming and self-promotion. The I Corps commander had tried to maintain a neutral attitude toward Sutherland, but the experience of dealing with him during the battle had antagonized Eichelberger, especially when Sutherland seemed to shy away from danger. As such, Eichelberger came to mistrust Sutherland and think of him as "just mean," a poor influence on MacArthur, a plotter who seemed intent on becoming the power behind the throne. "He was the type of guy who would enjoy pulling the wings off a fly," Eichelberger summarized later in life, though for most of the war he maintained correct relations with Sutherland, at least on the surface.[7]

Whether MacArthur liked it or not, Eichelberger's deliberate approach was appropriate to the circumstances, and probably the only realistic course of action. Eichelberger knew that, even though victory was now probable, "the fighting was under conditions that are indescribable." The monotonous ninety-degree heat and high humidity sapped energy and made it difficult to stay hydrated. Even with adequate food, men lost weight, in most instances between ten and twenty pounds over the course of a few weeks. One husky 230-pound man lost seventy pounds after a month in the area. Filthy and tired, the men had a shadowy appearance. "They were gaunt and thin, with deep black circles under their sunken eyes," Sergeant Kahn wrote. "They were clothed in tattered, stained jackets and pants. Few of them wore socks or underwear. Often the soles had been sucked off their shoes by the tenacious, stinking mud." Mosquitoes seemed to breed by the second in the moldy swamps. There was never enough insect repellent or enough mosquito nets to ward them off. Leeches preyed on the ankles and legs of anyone who waded through the water. "Our shoes were full of blood, and those sores never went away," one of the afflicted told his diary. Prodigious rains, usually falling in torrents at night, soaked everyone and everything. One-day totals of six to ten inches of rain were not uncommon. "No one could remember when he had been dry," Eichelberger wrote. "The feet, arms, bellies, chests, armpits of my soldiers were hideous with jungle rot." In the recollection of Major David Parker, the observer, "this was especially true of the front line troops, who were forced to sleep in foxholes with no shelter-half or net protection." Clothing and footgear rotted away. Weapons rusted if men did not clean them conscientiously. Engineers made trails usable by day only to see them washed out and inundated with thigh-high mud by nighttime rains. To combat this problem, they cut down saplings, and with substantial assistance from local laborers, built corduroy roads, an improvement but hardly impervious to the ravages of Mother Nature. "Mud was everywhere, deep and difficult to work in, and water stood in every low spot," one engineer wrote. "Ground which when dry was extremely hard and firm transformed into the most impassable of morasses after only short periods of rain." To keep the landing field at Dobodura operating, they constantly mowed the kunai grass and graded the runways.

When the rain ceased, steam rose from the musty green jungle. The intensity of the sun was beyond belief. In the memory of one soldier, it was "almost unbearably hot in the day time as the tropical sun broiled down, the grass shut off all air, and held in the steaming heat. Due to enemy observation any daylight movement among the forward positions had to be by crawling which added to the misery from the heat. There were cases of heat exhaustion daily." Medics worked round the clock tending to the casualties. In a pattern harkening back to an earlier age, disease claimed many more than combat. Soldiers took atabrine, but malaria was nonetheless universal. "[It] would cause the patient to be very debilitated, anemic, and lose all interest in the war and the world in general," said Major Clinton Compere, a surgeon with the 1st Evacuation Hospital.

Of the 10,685 combat soldiers mustered by the 32nd Division's three infantry regiments, some 8,286 men were treated for diseases, primarily malaria, dengue fever, dysentery, and scrub typhus, a figure that outnumbered combat casualties by a factor of more than three to one. Many other cases went unreported, as fever-ridden soldiers refused evacuation or simply kept going, unaware they were sick. On one quiet day, a curious medical officer took the temperature of one hundred men at random and found that sixty were running temperatures two or three degrees above normal. Tech 4 Springer once recorded a temperature of 106.8 in a casualty he treated at one of the roadblocks. All he could do was put wet cloths on his forehead and give him aspirin until he was evacuated. The Australians, with a few thousand more in action, suffered 15,575 cases of infectious disease. Combat-fatigue cases were not yet truly recognized as such by medical authorities, but there were plenty of them. Lieutenant Odell saw several men "collapse from nervous exhaustion—crying like children and shaking head to foot." Compere estimated that between 5 and 10 percent of admissions to the 1st Evacuation Hospital fit this category, but it was difficult to know for sure because they all had malaria and this could have accounted for their altered emotional state. "We couldn't treat them very satisfactorily."

The job of evacuating wounded men from the front was arduous and perilous. Front-line medics braved all manner of enemy fire to retrieve the wounded. "Most of them have a helluva lot more guts than we've got," an appreciative infantryman said. Litter teams prowled the swamps and jungles at night, looking for wounded soldiers, sometimes blundering into the Japanese lines. In almost all instances, casualties were hauled to clearing stations a few hundred yards to the rear, and from there to the threadbare tents of portable surgical hospitals where doctors conducted basic trauma surgery. Behind the lines, Papuan men comprised almost all of the litter carriers. Instead of carrying stretchers low to the ground, like Americans and Australians, they draped them over their shoulders, sometimes hauling wounded soldiers this way for miles on end. Most were barefoot, and yet they never seemed to stumble or fall. They developed a reputation for tenderness that made a deep impression on many of those who occupied the stretchers. "The natives are daubed with mud to the waist and dog-tired, but they lower their burden gently near the operating table," George Moorad, a CBS correspondent related to his listeners on a broadcast.

On average, it took twenty-four to forty-eight hours between the time a man was wounded and the time he got to the doctors. During a typical day of fighting, each hospital, on average, treated fifty patients, stretching available personnel to the limit. Because of the dangerous environment, medical commanders would not allow female nurses to serve at the forward hospitals located near Dobodura and elsewhere close to the lines, exacerbating the shortage of trained caregivers. The most seriously wounded or sick were evacuated by air to a growing network of station hospitals at Port Moresby, where bed capacity grew from 500 to 2,428 in a matter of only a few weeks. As the battle grew more desperate, the standards to qualify for air evacuation were raised. Initially a man was eligible for evacuation if he needed at least seven days of hospitalization, but soon the number was raised to thirty days. In the course of the battle, Kenney's aviators evacuated thirteen thousand American and Australian casualties to Port Moresby and Australia, saving many lives. "I am absolutely sold on air evacuation," Lieutenant Colonel John Lazzari, a surgeon who worked in a portable surgical hospital, later declared.[8]

In the midst of it all, General Eichelberger tried to hold together his fever-ridden army and destroy the Japanese through his attrition plan. Often he wrote to Sutherland, or even MacArthur himself, pleading for forbearance. "I know how anxious General MacArthur must be," he told Sutherland in one typical missive. "Tell him to please be patient." Eichelberger lived in a dingy tent and slept on a cot. The tent contained a small stove on which the general made powdered coffee. Carpet consisted of a shelter half draped over dirt. "I actually have a chair . . . so as things go, I am really quite well off," he cheerfully informed Emma. He hung his clothes and shaving gear on bamboo poles. The nighttime rains often flooded the tent. One morning he awoke to see water within an inch of the bottom of his cot. "Various personal possessions floated around like chips in a millstream," he later wrote. A pair of Papuan craftsmen subsequently installed a bamboo floor that improved his footing but did little to ward off the floods. A passionate advocate of vitamins, he took several tablets every day and made sure that bottles were distributed to the troops. He and the staff ate two meals a day, usually C rations, though they ate the occasional hot breakfast and scrounged for local fruits and vegetables. At midday, Eichelberger indulged in the treat of a D ration chocolate bar. Still the weight melted off him like butter in an oven, more than thirty pounds in a thirty-day period.

Curious about other peoples and cultures, he conversed with Papuans whenever he could. "There was a village with a lot of women in it and they were working along with the men," he wrote to Emma. "They wear calico skirts like the men but of course stick out in front. I have decided long since that the elements of courage or courtesy are not limited to any particular race or creed." Still he was not above sarcastically referring to the locals as "cannibals" in his letters. A natural chronicler and correspondent—almost to the point of obsession—he found time each night to sit down with his stenographer Tech Sergeant Clyde Shuck and dictate expansive letters to Emma, Sutherland, and a raft of friends and colleagues. He drove himself and everyone around him relentlessly, going anywhere regardless of privation or danger. "The conditions . . . are indescribable," he told Sutherland in one report. "For hours I walked through swamps where every step was an effort." He spent most of his daylight hours at the front, leading, cajoling, routinely risking his life in pursuit of victory. "Who wants to go with me today and kill some Japs?" he often asked groups of soldiers. "You can't live forever. Let's go. You and you and you." Other times he told frightened men, either at the front or at his headquarters, "We must not take counsel of our fears." In one typical instance near the Triangle, he came under sniper fire, took cover, looked around, and saw the Japanese rifleman in a nearby tree. He borrowed a Springfield rifle from a soldier, sited on the enemy soldier, and fired. His first shot missed, so he adjusted into "a typical knee firing position, held my breath, aimed low for the rise in trajectory and did all the things taught me on the target range. Naturally, it could not miss and the man plunged downward." Other soldiers added tommy-gun fire, killing several more Japanese. He developed such a reputation for risking his life in front-line action that an admiring Herring wrote personally and pleaded with him not to take so many chances. "We can't afford the possible loss that may result. Would you please look after yourself."

Heedless of such pleas, Eichelberger continued to spend most of his days at or near the forward positions. Casualties among his retinue inevitably piled up. On December 15, General Byers got shot in the right hand by a Japanese sniper and had to be evacuated to Australia, a tremendous loss, since the two were veritable kindred spirits. Days later, Colonel Rogers took bullets in both legs. Eichelberger breathed a sigh of relief when he found out that both would recover. "General Byers is doing splendidly," Captain Robert White, a public affairs officer who was with the I Corps rear detachment in Australia, wrote to Eichelberger. "The doctor said that somehow the force of the bullet had broken the large bone that runs down the base of the little finger to the heel of the palm." Though broken, the bone was already set and blood circulation in his hand was fine. "The General is in great spirits," White enthused. Byers was in a cast and needed several weeks of physical therapy, but he would suffer no more permanent damage than a slightly crooked index finger. Rogers also recuperated well and lobbied hard to return to combat. "What a man!" Eichelberger chortled to Emma. "He thought it a great joke." The general was especially pleased to hear that Edwards had survived his serious wound and, though temporarily bed- and wheelchair-ridden, was on the road to complete recovery. "His doctor reports that Eddie is progressing as well as can be expected," White reported. "Because of the location of Eddie's wound, the time of healing will be longer than that of General Byers. Eddie is in excellent spirits also. He is put on a sun porch every afternoon and has a fair tan . . . for a hospital patient." Captain Edwards added his reassurance that all was well. "Your hospital echelon is anxious to rejoin you in the forward areas," he wrote to Eichelberger. "I am feeling fine. Our greatest concern is that you keep well, avoid mosquitoes and dodge all sniper bullets." With Edwards out of danger, Eichelberger joked to White that it was time to stop worrying about his health and start worrying about his conduct.

Eichelberger was actually under enormous stress, and not just from risking his life and the lives of such close comrades every day. For the general, Buna represented a professional crossroads of sorts. He knew that his entire military career had boiled down to whether he achieved success or failure. For someone with Eichelberger's deep yearning for achievement and distinction, failure was not an option. While he was unwilling to squander lives in pursuit of his military ambitions, there was nonetheless a single-minded ruthlessness about him. Instead of replacing Byers with another division commander, he simply filled the role himself. He continued to fire or reassign commanders without hesitation. He occasionally browbeat officers whom he thought of as weak or ineffective. Though not given to rage, he could, in the absence of results, be quick-tempered and overbearing. His coiled energy bordered on the manic. "When his reputation was at stake, as it was at Buna, and his career hung in the balance, he was like a caged lion," Colonel Grose, who had a love-hate relationship with him, later told an interviewer. Resentful 32nd Division soldiers dubbed him "Eichelbutcher" and called the growing temporary cemetery near Buna village "Eichelberger Square." When he tried one day to motivate Sergeant Jungwirth and his buddies by telling them they were not aggressive enough because they were too afraid to die, they "muttered things under [their] breath that cannot be printed here." Eichelberger knew about and fully understood the resentments of the troops who did the real fighting and dying. He was deeply concerned for their welfare, but he had to focus on the mission as well. "There were advances to be made, and decisions which must not be governed by my own weaknesses or emotions." In other words, someone had to keep driving men where they did not want to go, and keep pushing them beyond what they thought were their limits. "I am convinced that without this kind of personal, determined and resourceful leadership, this particular force would not have been successful," Rogers asserted many years later.[9]

Prodded by Eichelberger, American soldiers day by day attacked and killed tenacious Japanese defenders at such places as the Duropa Plantation, the Triangle, the Government Gardens, and Simemi Creek. Each fight was a struggle to the death. In almost all the small-unit actions, the two sides fought within a couple hundred yards of each other. Often they fought at handshake range. In hopes of luring the Americans into an ambush, Japanese soldiers shouted, "Hey, we give up!" or "Hey, we surrender!" only to gun down anyone who left cover. In response, angry American infantrymen refused to take prisoners. American bunker-busting teams attacked the enemy fortifications, tossing grenades, firing BARs or M1 Garands. Some units were issued flamethrowers, but they did not work.

Fifty-caliber machine guns added some firepower. But most assault troops were poorly armed and supported for their grisly work. They had no demolition-type explosives. Air strikes harassed the Japanese, but the pilots were seldom able to identify and destroy bunkers. Artillery fire was sparse. "Nothing less than 105 howitzers with delayed action fuses could possibly destroy any of those emplacements," Eichelberger wrote. "We had one such weapon on the entire front." Australian twenty-five-pound guns provided most of the other artillery support. At times, 37-millimeter anti-tank guns with canister rounds shredded the defenders, but there were nowhere near enough of these pieces to take the heavy burden off the rifle-men. Eighty-one-millimeter mortars were effective and quite feared by the Japanese, but they could not penetrate most of the bunkers.

Once the attackers identified the location of a bunker, one group sprayed the surrounding trees with fire to eliminate snipers, while the other attempted to get close enough to kill anyone in the bunker. According to one Army report, "The fighting frequently resolved itself into distinct small engagements to capture individual bunkers . . . a very difficult operation . . . flanking movements were almost impossible." Even when the Americans overran a bunker, they had to make sure that Japanese survivors did not infiltrate back into them. "It is important for the attacking force to be certain that all enemy personnel in a 'destroyed' bunker are dead," one junior officer advised. The process was bloody, deliberate, and rudimentary.

As of December 18, the Australian 18th Infantry Brigade under Brigadier George Wootten entered the Warren front. As senior officer, Wootten took command of the front from Colonel Martin, who then reverted to a dual role as his executive officer and a de facto regimental commander. Many of the 18th Brigade soldiers were canny veterans of the fighting in North Africa. They were supported by seven American-made M3 Stuart light tanks crewed by Australians. Equipped with thin armor and only 37-millimeter guns, these tanks would have been outgunned in a European-theater-armored duel, but they were fearsome beasts in this setting. In the space of a few days, the combined armor-infantry force ruptured the Japanese front at the new airstrip, destroyed some two hundred bunkers, advanced through the coconut trees of the Duropa Plantation, and captured almost a mile of front, albeit at the cost of three tanks knocked out and a 35 percent casualty rate among the infantrymen. The Aussie veterans and the lean soldiers of the 128th Infantry fought side by side. "There was much comradely rivalry and friendly recrimination between our battalions," Lieutenant Colonel Alexander MacNab of the 128th wrote fondly of his work with the Diggers. In one instance when a combined group came upon a line of bunkers, an Australian commander shouted, "Let's get the bastards!" In a near frenzy, the Diggers and Yanks attacked. In MacNab's recollection, "We all, Aussies and Yanks, went in on a run. There were not many Japs left. We killed them in the grass with bayonets and with fire when we couldn't reach them."

The prize for each typical advance was usually a couple hundred yards of stinking swamp, jungle, or coastal coconut palms. Companies were down to a few dozen stalwarts. Radios were next to useless for the front-line units in the dense jungle. Signal Corps soldiers strung three hundred miles' worth of communication wire, all of it unspooled by hand, in the wake of any advance. Engineers laid down planks or built footbridges to help the attackers ford the noxious waters that protected the Japanese positions at the island and other similar spots. All too often, the lead troops were shot to pieces as they attempted to advance through such fatal funnels. Still, each day the Japanese-held perimeter slowly shrank as the Americans ate away at them and both sides neared a breaking point. Eichelberger himself was hardly immune to the ravages of attrition. Weary and frustrated at the deliberate pace of operations, he raged in one letter to Sutherland, "I am trying to kill the little devils in any way possible," including blanketing their lines with white phosphorus. "I hope the little devils get their tails burned." When a Christmas Eve attack on the Urbana front failed to eliminate the remnants of Japanese resistance, he admitted the next day to MacArthur, "I think that the all time low of my life occurred yesterday."

What Eichelberger did not know was that the "little devils" were nearly finished. Wasted away from starvation and the exhaustion of fighting so desperately for weeks, many of the Japanese soldiers hardly possessed enough physical endurance to resist as they once had. "Most of the men have been stricken with dysentery," one commander wrote to the 18th Army's chief of staff. "Those who are not ill are without food and are too weak for hand-to-hand fighting." The hope of reinforcement was long gone. For most, only death now beckoned. "All I could do was shed tears of resentment," one wrote bitterly in his diary. "Now we are only waiting for death. The rest of you comrades, get revenge for me. The nature of the enemy is superior and they excel in firing technique." Another who blithely assumed that Imperial Army soldiers would find his body calmly requested that they properly dispose of it. "After my comrades and I are dead, please bury us in your leisure time. I ask this because it is dishonorable to remain unburied." Sergeant Wada consoled himself by staring wistfully at a snapshot of his parents. "I must do my best to the last with the noble spirit of dying for the Emperor," he reminded himself. "Ah, I wonder how things are at home." Another soldier took one last look at a letter from his younger brother back in Japan. "I believe you are conquering heat and doing well," the brother wrote. "Your picture is always looking affectionately at us from the Toko-noma," an alcove where treasured items were placed in a Japanese home.

As death lurked, some took solace in propagandistic idealism. "Repre-senting the Asiatic race we are charged with the important and honorable duty of changing world history," one scribbled in his diary. Another de-clared that the purpose of the Battle of Buna had been "the establishment of the Greater East Asia Co-Prosperity Sphere . . . Exclusion of the White Race from East Asia . . . to extend the light of the Imperial power to the South and give peace to the good people." Infused with the melancholy of impending extinction, most now embraced a kind of defiant fatalism. "Whenever and wherever I die, I will not regret it because I have already given my soul and body to my country, and I have said farewell to my par-ents, wife, brother, and sister," one private scrawled in his diary. Another calmly explained to his wife, in a letter that did not make it out of New Guinea, that he would never see her again. "I would like to write a few lines before I die," he told her. "You have a fine soul, one that is rare in this world. By chance you married unworthy me and you devoted yourself faithfully to me. I will always be grateful. However, your devotion will have been in vain, as I will soon die for our country. There is no greater glory than this for any man. My blood and spirit will be carried on by Kusinuke [their son]. One of your duties is to look after him and teach him." Almost all chose to die fighting or commit suicide rather than dishonor themselves—as they saw it—by surrendering.[10]

At last, on January 3, 1943, Eichelberger's men took Buna Government Station, effectively ending the battle, though isolated groups of enemy sol-diers held out for a few more days. "A systematic combing of the area was carried out by all units to wipe out every trace of the enemy," the opera-tions sergeant of the 127th Infantry recorded in the regimental journal. A couple of hundred beleaguered Japanese managed to escape by sea or by infiltrating through the Allied lines, across the Girua River and westward along the coast to the Sanananda perimeter, where their comrades still held out. The rest died at their posts all over battered Buna. The tired American survivors picked through the ruins of their hard-won objective. "It was a scene of desolation," F. Tillman Durdin of the *New York Times* wrote. "The half dozen buildings were in ruins and some were still burning. Trees were bedraggled. Shells pitted the area. American troops everywhere. Enemy dead littered the beaches; others lay inside the bunkers." Dave Richardson, the *Yank* correspondent, grimly chronicled the ghastly appearance of the Japanese dead. "Some are swollen yellow-green carcasses; others are sun-bleached skeletons with tattered clothes covering their white bones." Burial details policed up these maggot-infested remains and interred them in mass graves. "The smell was almost overwhelming," one of the Americans recalled. Engineers swept for mines and destroyed bunkers. Most everyone else continued the relentless grind of patrolling.

Buna ended in the manner of nearly every subsequent Pacific theater battle, not with any sort of formal surrender or acknowledged conclusion of battle by either side, but mainly by the obvious course of events and a declaration of victory from American commanders. "The Papuan campaign is in its final closing phase," MacArthur's headquarters stated triumphantly. "The Sanananda position has now been completely enveloped. A remnant of the enemy's forces is entrenched there and faces certain destruction." This was true. But it took several more hard weeks of fighting by Australian troops and the 41st Infantry Division's 163rd Infantry Regiment, plus many more agonizing days of front-line-combat command for Eichelberger, before the Allies on January 22 could claim to control Sanananda, thus ending the Papua campaign. General Adachi ordered his remnants to withdraw farther west up the New Guinea coast.

Out of about seventeen thousand Japanese troops in the battle, some thirteen thousand were dead. Allied gravediggers buried seven thousand of them. The rest were either buried by their comrades or simply left to rot anonymously in New Guinea's cruel climate. About four thousand enemy soldiers escaped. Only 350 surrendered. In a disingenuous communiqué, MacArthur claimed that "our losses in the Papuan Campaign . . . are low. The utmost care was taken for the conservation of our forces with the result that probably no campaign in history against a thoroughly prepared and trained army produced such complete and decisive results with a lower expenditure of life and resources." The statement was typical of MacArthur's war-long propensity to portray his command as producing big results with minimum expenditure of lives and matériel in contrast to the supposed profligate waste of other theaters. In truth, the price of victory in Papua was substantial for the Allies. The campaign cost the lives of 2,165 Australians and 930 Americans. Roughly one out of every eleven Americans committed to battle at Buna did not survive. Another twenty-one hundred GIs were wounded. The battle casualty rate was nearly one in four. Eichelberger later estimated that half the riflemen were either killed or wounded. Many thousands more soldiers were, of course, stricken with disease, bringing the overall casualty rates from battle and disease to well over 100 percent. The 32nd Division was shattered and had to be completely rebuilt. The haunted survivors were flown back to Australia for retraining and restoration to health, both physical and mental. It would be another year before the division was ready to go back into combat. As a result, American ground combat capability in SWPA was substantially limited for most of 1943. The Army's official historian quite properly termed the campaign "one of the costliest of the Pacific war."

To what benefit was all this loss? The Papua campaign was anything but pretty. From an intelligence standpoint, it bordered on the disastrous. Training and preparation were amateurish. Combat leadership at the senior-officer level was lacking, at least until Eichelberger's arrival on the scene. Command relationships were unnecessarily complicated, and Allied relations were, initially at least, contentious and counterproductive. Rather than bypassing the strongest pockets of Japanese resistance, MacArthur had, in essence, opted for frontal attacks, presumably because of his preoccupation with achieving a speedy victory. Once the 32nd Division took Buna village on December 14, he might well have left the separate Japanese pockets to starve, rather than take more casualties to clear every enemy position. To his credit, the experience chastened him and made him leery of leading with his chin in future battles. Ugly though it undoubtedly was, Papua marked the first Allied ground victory in the war against Japan. Port Moresby was now secure. Australia would not be invaded. The victory, and Eichelberger's presence in particular, improved relations between the Australians and the Americans. In Papua, MacArthur now had a base from which to continue his Southwest Pacific advance across New Guinea and, someday, to the Philippines. Even in the midst of such a shoestring campaign, with little in the way of air and naval support, the Allies had developed a lethal proficiency in logistics and firepower as well as a nascent competence at aerial and sea operations. "We lost at Buna because we could not retain air superiority, and because our navy and air force could not disrupt the enemy supply line," Major Mitsuo Koiwai, who had led a battalion over the Owen Stanleys and then managed to survive and escape captivity, opined after the war. "Tactically the Allied coordination of fire power and advance was very skillful." What he and other Japanese survivors could not admit was that their enemies had also demonstrated equal, perhaps even superior, fighting spirit, a troubling harbinger for the Imperial Army's future.

MacArthur returned to Brisbane, and his family, on January 9, much later than he had ever expected. "The barber had made his way to Government House four times," Master Sergeant Rogers later wrote in reference to MacArthur's naive initial promise to wait until he returned to Australia to get his hair cut. Eichelberger returned to Rockhampton on January 26, just a few days after the fighting ended at Sanananda. Exhausted, weakened by weight loss and stress, he nonetheless felt enormously proud of what he had accomplished. "It is difficult to convey to the reader the immense relief, the feeling of freedom, the outright joy, that came with victory," he later wrote. "I had been luckier than most of my soldiers." Indeed, as depleted as he was physically, he had never come down with malaria or any other disease. He had not been wounded. He had somehow managed to dodge death many dozens of times. More than anything, he was proud of the combat troops and grateful to them for their valor. "They had proved themselves."

Eichelberger was the first American ground combat commander in World War II to consummate a victory, and he had done it under extraordinarily difficult circumstances. Just as Eichelberger had once looked to his skeptical father for praise and recognition, he now expected grand accolades from MacArthur. Though the SWPA commander did release Eichelberger's name to the media as I Corps commander, and forwarded a personal note of congratulations, he was otherwise oddly cool to the man who had done more than anyone else to salvage victory at Buna. He awarded Eichelberger the Distinguished Service Cross but, in the citation, failed to differentiate his actions from several other recipients who had never even visited the front. When MacArthur relocated his headquarters back to Australia, he did not bother to inform Eichelberger. January communiqués from MacArthur's headquarters described the fighting at Sanananda as mere "mopping up," a dismissive term—soon infamous and offensive to the soldiers who did the fighting—and one that MacArthur would employ often, seemingly to trivialize Eichelberger's efforts to finish off the Japanese in Papua.

The release of Eichelberger's name generated a worldwide wave of favorable stories with headlines like "These Are the Generals—Eichelberger" in the *Saturday Evening Post* and "General Eichelberger Helps Erase Defeat of Bataan" in the *Philadelphia Inquirer*. Although Eichelberger wrote to a friend that "when one faces death as many times as I have in the last month . . . one gets a bit detached on the subject of publicity," this was less than candid. For Eichelberger, the recognition was a dream come true. But his overnight fame did not sit well with his boss. MacArthur was loath to share the limelight with anyone else in SWPA or, for that matter, anywhere else. In a bizarre and awkward meeting, MacArthur made a veiled threat to bust Eichelberger to colonel because of the articles and send him home. Chastened but angry, Eichelberger did all he could to limit his exposure to the media. "I would rather have you slip a rattlesnake in my pocket than to have you give me any publicity," he told his academy classmate and friend Major General Alec Surles, who headed up the War Department's public relations branch.

All of these slights might have comprised nothing more than a mere annoyance to a less sensitive and proud man than Eichelberger. For all his success as a soldier and the unimpeachable nature of his character, he continued to battle his own insecurities and ambitions. Eichelberger believed he had salvaged MacArthur's reputation at Buna. In return, he expected gratitude and proper recognition from a boss he had served loyally in SWPA and also before the war, during his days as chief of staff. To a man of Eichelberger's consideration for others and his correct personal manners, this was just common courtesy. Instead, somewhat stunned at what he perceived as shabby treatment from MacArthur, he grew resentful. Eichelberger was especially angry at a sentence from a communiqué MacArthur released soon after the conclusion of the Papua campaign. "There was no necessity to hurry the attack because the time element in this case was of little importance." For a commander who had repeatedly risked his life and expended the lives of many other good men because he was specifically told by his chief that time was of paramount importance, the statement was hard to take. "I was feeling decidedly hurt," he later admitted. He formed the opinion that MacArthur and those around him were far too detached from the real fighting to understand it in any meaningful way. In a private memo to Emma, he contemptuously referred to

MacArthur as "the great hero [who] went home without seeing Buna before, during[,] or after the fight while permitting press articles from his GHQ [General Headquarters] to say that he was leading troops in battle." The notion that MacArthur personally led the soldiers in action at Buna solidified among the American public (possibly this was why MacArthur became so perturbed by the plethora of stories about Eichelberger's actions in the battle). The myth of MacArthur's presence at Buna bothered Eichelberger on many levels, but especially from the standpoint of personal integrity. More than anything, he felt disappointed in MacArthur and hurt by his actions. "The battle of personalities growing out of Buna was almost as important as the actual fighting," he commented. Indeed, the aftertaste of Buna had become unpleasant. In SWPA, even in the shadow of victory, the seeds of bitterness were now sown.[11]

★

As this climactic drama played out in Papua, the unforgiving probabilities of modern warfare turned, like a fickle lover, on the Japanese at Guadalcanal. The mid-November destruction of the 38th Division convoys had inflicted irreparable damage upon the Japanese. Over the following weeks, US air and sea forces grew progressively stronger while the Japanese grew weaker. The ripple effect of this turnabout inevitably weakened Japanese ground forces, since they could no longer be adequately reinforced and resupplied. Theoretically, Japanese commanders still hoped to go on the offensive, seize Henderson Field, and eject the Americans from the island. But the moment for that had passed. Realistically, as American planes and ships steadily assumed control of the skies above the island and the waters around it, any hope of a new Imperial Army offensive was merely a fantasy.

General Hyakutake still had about twenty-five thousand troops on Guadalcanal. By and large, they were in poor condition. According to an Americal Division intelligence report, "sickness, lack of proper food, and the rigors of jungle fighting under adverse conditions were taking a rather serious toll." Malaria control was almost nonexistent, as were disease-prevention measures as a whole. Dysentery, beriberi, malnutrition, and malaria had claimed the lives of thousands. Food was becoming uncomfortably scarce. Front-line soldiers were subsisting on one-third rations, comprising perhaps a third of a pint of rice per day. They scrounged for coconuts, ferns, roots, bamboo sprouts, wild potatoes, and even grass just to fill their stomachs. Rather than talking about women or family, they conversed, in excruciating detail, about the sumptuous meals of rice dumplings and rice cakes they had once consumed back home. They now routinely called Guadalcanal "Starvation Island." Many, like Private Takeo Kinamoto, were suffering from hunger edema. "My body has swelled up from below the waist, especially my legs," he told his diary. "My testicles swell up and I wonder whether I am alive." One soldier looked around at his comrades and wrote privately, "From the color of their faces, one might wonder whether they were alive or not." Another hungry soldier plaintively asked his diary, "What on earth are we to eat?"

In hopes of finding a way through the tightening American air and sea net, the Japanese used Tokyo Express destroyers to ferry supplies in nocturnal voyages to Guadalcanal. Sanitized fuel drums were packed with rice, powdered miso, powdered soy sauce, matches, candles, and other supplies. They were then bound by ropes into batches of fifty drums and lashed to the decks of the destroyers. When the ships approached a preselected spot on the coast, crewmen dumped the drums overboard. "Then motor boats would tow the drums ashore, where waiting work crews of about two hundred men would pull them up on the beach," wrote General Miyazaki, the 17th Army's chief of staff. The system rarely worked so smoothly. Tow ropes often broke. Drums got hung up and wrecked on coral reefs. Some of the drums simply disappeared at sea. In daylight hours, Allied fliers shot up quite a few. By Miyazaki's estimate, the Imperial Navy disgorged twenty thousand of the containers. At best, only 20 to 30 percent ever made it into friendly hands, nowhere near enough to make a significant impact. A concurrent attempt to resupply Hyakutake's men by submarine also failed.

Japanese logisticians estimated that the troops were getting only between 10 and 25 percent of what they required. While it would be an overstatement to equate their plight with that of the Filipino-American troops on Bataan the previous spring, it nonetheless carried the uneasy, and ironic, whiff of similarity, particularly in relation to hunger, fatigue, and disease. Though not necessarily cut off from the outside world, they were on the wrong side of the logistical tale of the tape. Like Bataan's defenders, though, they enjoyed control of advantageous terrain and they were still full of fight. Hyakutake's front-line units were dug into the many ridges, hilltops, and fingers of high ground that proliferated the island west of Henderson Field.

The Americans on Guadalcanal were hardly in good shape. Malaria infection rates hovered around 100 percent. Disease accounted for nearly two-thirds of Army and Marine casualties. In November alone, nearly eighteen hundred men were so incapacitated by malaria that they were unable to perform their duties. As yet, there were still no malaria-control teams on the island. Men were supposed to take atabrine, but enforcement of the order was lax. After four months of fighting in Guadalcanal's unforgiving tropical environment, the 1st Marine Division was hit especially hard. The division had suffered 10,635 casualties, including 5,749 from malaria.

Though wracked by disease, the Americans had sufficient ammunition, food, and medical care. Their main challenge was how best to unload incoming cargo without the benefit of true port facilities and disseminate it without access to good roads or much in the way of load-bearing vehicles. Given the forbidding terrain and lack of infrastructure, jeeps were the only vehicles that could get anywhere near the front lines. A paucity of service troops also sapped the logistical chain of vitality (a persistent problem throughout the whole Pacific War). Combat troops were sometimes put to work unloading the ships. But this was inefficient and counterproductive— every rifleman who worked in support duties was one less trigger puller who was available to fight. Plus, they resented and disliked being used as dockhands and carriers. As one commander gently put it, combat soldiers were "apathetic toward labor." Unloading operations leaned toward the haphazard. "Supplies of all kinds are piled all over the beaches exposed to weather and hostile shelling or bombing," Major William Tinsley, an ordnance officer, reported to his superiors in late December. Just in from the beaches, clothing, equipment, food, and ammunition often lay in disorganized heaps. Some twenty-five thousand brass shell casings were stacked in rows, sometimes head-high, or strewn randomly along beaches. The unattended bounty proved irresistible for many crafty soldier-thieves, so much so that one newly arrived supply officer joked that his first action upon landing on Guadalcanal "should be the shooting of all friendly troops." As in New Guinea, the Americans turned to local labor for help. At least two thousand men from the Melanesian population that predominated on the island unloaded ships, hauled supplies and fifty-pound loads of water, evacuated wounded soldiers, or served as scouts, usually in exchange for tobacco, food, souvenirs, or money at the rate of about $1.25 per week. The islanders helped alleviate what otherwise might have been a hopeless logistical situation.

In spite of these issues, by comparison to their enemies, the Americans were much better off. Henderson Field's capacity had matured to accommodate about two hundred planes. Many of the runways were now reinforced with steel matting. Pistol Pete was no longer in range to batter the base, and the power of the Tokyo Express was, of course, severely diminished. Occasional enemy air raids comprised the main threat to Henderson; otherwise it had become a secure and growing airfield of considerable potency. By December 8, the entire American Division was ashore and the 25th Infantry Division was on the way from Hawaii. New leadership was in place. Admiral Nimitz had reluctantly decided that Admiral Ghormley was neither aggressive nor dynamic enough to continue serving as theater commander. So he replaced him with Vice Admiral William Halsey, a pugnacious, innovative, larger-than-life naval officer with a flair for combined operations. Halsey had masterminded the mid-November destruction of the Imperial Army's 38th Division convoys in what he viewed as a life-or-death engagement. "If we had lost it, our troops on Guadalcanal would have been trapped as were our troops on Bataan," he later said. "Archie Vandegrift would have been our 'Skinny' Wainwright."

Halsey understood—as did most everyone else—that the 1st Marine Division was near the end of its tether. The leathernecks of the "Old Breed" division had fought their hearts out since invading Guadalcanal in August. They were sapped by months of privation and disease and they badly needed a rest. "A sort of physical depression affected many of us," Private Leckie, the machine gunner, later wrote. The division historian commented, "Every man . . . left a part of himself at Guadalcanal." With Vandegrift's acquiescence, Halsey transitioned control of ground operations from the Marines to the Army. On December 9, with American and much of the 2nd Marine Division in place to guard the perimeter around Henderson Field, the 1st Marine Division began a phased evacuation to Australia that played out over the course of several more days as shipping became available. Vandegrift had proved himself an effective combat leader. He had set the foundation for strong interservice cooperation. "I couldn't tell an Army pilot or mechanic from a Navy or Marine one, nor could I tell a member from the Americal Division from my own men," he told an interviewer shortly after he left Guadalcanal. "It was a homogeneous team."[12]

Halsey's new ground commander was fifty-three-year-old Major General Alexander "Sandy" Patch, a 1913 West Point graduate—and son of an academy alumnus—who had led a machine-gun battalion in World War I. Born to soldiering, Patch had lived his entire life within the Army's orbit, either as a military dependent or an active-duty infantry officer. He had married a general's daughter. His brother, Joseph, was also a professional soldier who attained general officer rank. Sandy's son, Alexander III, known as "Mac" to his West Point classmates, was serving as a young captain with the 79th Infantry Division, training to deploy to Europe.

Good-humored, self-effacing, intensely loyal, and well-liked by his peers, Patch had received command of Task Force 6814 in early 1942. He had led the unit overseas and seen the task force evolve into the Americal Division. With Vandegrift's exit, Patch now assumed control of all Marine and Army ground units on Guadalcanal, including Americal, the 2nd Marine Division, the 147th Infantry Regiment, the 25th Infantry Division upon its arrival over the course of a few weeks from mid-December to early January, plus artillery, engineers, and other supporting units all organized under the umbrella of the XIV Corps. Bald-headed, tan-complected, and medium of build, Patch projected an unusual combination of iron discipline and sensitivity. He was just as prone to offer an enlisted man a ride in his jeep as inspect him. He staunchly believed that character formed the foundation of good leadership. "Soldierly in appearance and deportment, modest to the point of shyness, dignified, quiet, even secretive, he was the equal of any in professional knowledge, human understanding, and decisiveness," Major General Ed Sebree, a close associate who succeeded Patch as commander of Americal, once wrote of him. Patch detested profanity as a sign of character weakness and limited mental acuity. He believed that good leaders were invariably selfless and honest. "An attitude of superiority detracts from the effectiveness of an officer," he once wrote. "The insignia which he wears upon his blouse is not a recognition of accomplishment, but rather an indication of responsibility and of the faith that his country has in him. It will be through his examples to his men, his unselfish concern for those under him, that he will be fulfilling the obligation which he should feel."[13]

Patch's orders from Admiral Halsey and General Harmon were characteristically blunt. He was to "eliminate all Japanese forces" on Guadalcanal. Although the Americans in November had launched a limited offensive to push west from the Matanikau, the perimeter was more or less unchanged from the days of General Maruyama's attempt to take Henderson. The airfield would never be completely secure as long as the Japanese controlled the high ground west of the perimeter. At an elevation of 1,514 feet above sea level, Mount Austen (called Mount Mambulu by locals) anchored the honeycomb bramble of ridges that overlooked the perimeter.

The summit itself was about six miles southwest of Henderson Field. According to one Army report, Mount Austen "rises steeply and erratically from the Lunga plain. Its twisting ridges are generally bare, its deep ravines heavily wooded; but over the summit there is a large cap of jungle. Located three miles south of the seacoast, near the headwaters of the Matanikau, the summit of Mount Austen [provides] a view of the valley of that river, and of the entire Perimeter." Troops from the Imperial Army's 124th, 229th, and 230th Infantry Regiments were dug into bunkers and pillboxes on Mount Austen and its many accompanying ridges and hills. They called the area the Gifu strong point after the town in Japan from which many of them hailed. Patch planned to launch a corps-level offensive to eject the Japanese from all high ground west of Henderson, push them far away from the airfield and then perhaps outflank and destroy them from along the coast. But this ambitious concept had to wait until the 25th Division was fully in place and the logistical moment right.

In the meantime, on December 17, Patch ordered the 132nd Infantry Regiment, newest to Guadalcanal of America's three infantry regiments, to take Mount Austen. Regimental reconnaissance patrols failed to detect the strength of the Japanese presence, because their bunkers were so well concealed and the jungle so dense. Visibility was severely limited and the mere act of movement to Mount Austen greatly impeded by the forbidding junglescape. "The terrain was becoming very difficult, deep draws filled with vegetation, strong spiny vines hampering the advance of the troops," wrote Lieutenant Frank Halsey, a platoon leader.

Not surprising, when two battalions attempted to envelop Mount Austen, they moved with all the grace of a blindfolded man in a dark room. Almost immediately, the assault troops ran into a dizzying maze of mutually supporting, log-reinforced pillboxes that had been designed by highly adept engineer officers on loan from the 8th Area Army. In most instances, the roofs of these fortifications were anchored by three thick logs. The walls were built with more logs, many of which were so covered with moldy moss that they took on a greenish hue. Copious amounts of earth and sandbags fleshed out the body of each bunker. Their silhouettes were low, usually only about three feet above the ground, and they were cleverly concealed by a green hash of jungle foliage. Squad-size groups—armed with at least one, and sometimes two, machine guns—manned each bunker. It hardly mattered that the Japanese were hungry and exhausted. They were determined to fight, usually to the death, and they enjoyed the inherent advantage that comes with concealment, control of high ground, and well-sited fortifications. "The Americans are hateful," one Japanese infantryman wrote venomously in his diary. "I feel as if I would want to kill [many more than] one soldier."

The Americans were raked with accurate machine-gun, knee-mortar, and rifle fire, pinned down in kill zones or forced to take cover in the discomfort of the anonymous jungle. "It seemed as though all the pillboxes were mutually supporting," Lieutenant Halsey wrote. "Well-placed riflemen supported the pillboxes. Movement under these conditions was rugged." In one 1,500-yard span of front, there were seventy-five of these emplacements, arranged in a triangular formation that promised death for anyone who ventured into their broad cones of fire. One of the battalion commanders, Lieutenant Colonel William Wright, was stitched with machine-gun bullets and bled to death before medics could treat him. "He was a great leader or he wouldn't have been there," Private Ralph Cerny said. Wright's body lay in no-man's-land until a patrol led by his intelligence officer managed to get to it and drag it back to friendly territory. Air strikes were ineffective because the aviators had great difficulty spotting their targets. Even copious support from dozens of artillery pieces, ranging in size from 75- to 155-millimeter, could not make much of a difference, unless they happened to score a direct hit on the apertures. "The field of observation was often limited by mammoth trees which towered in front of our lines," commented Captain John Casey, a forward observer. Poor visibility and substandard maps made it chancy to call in fire anywhere near friendly troops. He and other observers took to directing fire onto draws and streambeds in hopes of impeding enemy movement.

Repeated attacks on subsequent days came to nothing. "We tried to gain ground all day but were thrown back," an infantryman wrote of a typical day. The Americans had to content themselves with probing patrols and artillery barrages. "Enemy resistance was stubborn," the unit after-action report commented, with droll understatement. Instead of the quick grab expected by American planners, the battle for Mount Austen morphed into a protracted struggle lasting weeks and involving the entire 132nd Infantry. "I can't tell you how I felt the first time I saw half a man's body lifted off the ground and the other half stayed where it was—cut in two by shrapnel," wrote Sergeant Mack Morriss, a young correspondent with *Yank* magazine, of the fighting. "Men . . . were filthy dirty and from the look of most of them, tired. They were serious and, I think, mad." Occasionally attacking units or patrols got cut off and had to be resupplied by air drop until friendly units could break through to them. At night, the Americans hunkered down in foxholes and kept steady watch for enemy infiltrators who seemed to be everywhere. Their usual tactic was to jump in a foxhole and stab the occupant. Rookie troops, prone to the bogeyman mentality, tended to fire at any shadow or rustling branch. A night or two on the line usually tempered this all-out trigger happiness, if not necessarily the tremendous nervous strain. Still, few were eager to go anywhere in the darkness, since, in the recollection of Lieutenant Henry Ricci, "if you moved, you got shot." The Americans insulated themselves behind barbed wire, firepower, and nightly passwords derived from words the Japanese found hard to pronounce, like "lamentable," "luxury," "Jacksonville," "Lela," "woolly," and "bellow." Instead of responding with their own infiltrators or counter-infiltration teams, the Americans seemed content to cede night mobility to the enemy, a harbinger for much of the rest of this war and the two that followed.

Marine engineers had built a small muddy road that spanned as far as Hill 35, a few thousand yards short of Mount Austen and its environs. America's organic engineers from the 57th Engineer Combat Battalion planned to extend the road wherever the infantry advanced, but torrential rains, steep sixty-degree grades, and a paucity of vehicles and grading equipment made this untenable. Similar to Buna, all supplies had to be jeeped to Hill 35 and then laboriously hauled forward by a combination of soldiers and Melanesian carrying parties, who were impertinently dubbed "the Cannibal Battalion" by the Americans. "At first, trails were so narrow and overgrown that efficient litter evacuation was practically impossible," reported the unit history of the 121st Medical Battalion of the Americal Division. The medics were "put to work cutting away undergrowth, widening and smoothing trails, cutting steps into the sides of steep ridges, and stringing hand ropes along them."

Even with this accomplished, the job of litter evacuation was difficult and labor intensive. On one day alone, it took 175 bearers five hours to evacuate twenty casualties. Litter cases were painstakingly carried away from the lines by medics and locals. When they reached Hill 35 or other suitable spots in the rear, they were loaded aboard specially fitted jeeps that transported them to hospital tents near the beach. The Japanese shot at the medics so routinely, and so accurately, that the Americans soon learned to escort them with a pair of heavily armed guards. The medics also armed themselves; by now none of them wore any medical insignia. The job of moving wounded men on stretchers over brutal terrain and in enervating heat exhausted the carriers quickly. Even the strongest men could only make one or two trips in a day. To save some wear and tear on the carriers, ingenious engineers strung cables across ravines and fitted special litters to be moved across by pulleys. They also modified other litters with skids that allowed the medics to ease them down hills. Not satisfied with these efforts, the engineers dug water wells and even constructed underground shelters, complete with an operating room, for the wounded. "We would treat them in the dark, sometimes by flashlight or lantern," Lieutenant Ricci, a physician, later said of the shelters.

Dead-ended at Mount Austen, the Americans resorted to attacking the surrounding hills. "Japanese centers of resistance were by-passed and isolated," General Sebree wrote. Ferocious battles raged for several high spots, most notably Hill 27, where the 132nd fought for several days to secure a key piece of ground whose capture would allow the Americans to begin encircling the stubborn Japanese and cut them off from their comrades farther to the west. "We were half way up when all hell broke loose," Sergeant Arthur Hodan, a young squad leader, wrote of the Hill 27 fighting in a letter to his parents. "The boys sure were dropping. Platoon Sarg. Greico went out to get one of his boys who was shot in the tummy and while he was carrying him out he was shot in the ass and it came out in front fracturing his pelvis. The boy he was carrying was dead. Marty Jayce was his name. Sarg. Smola was killed and they couldn't get him. Big Boy Richards walked into a machine gun which made a mess of him and his buddy Whity." Hodan was wounded when a mortar shell exploded a couple of feet behind him. "I felt as if I dived off a diving board and landed flat on my back. Boy did it sting."

In one day of fighting for Hill 27, the Americans expended 782 artillery shells; in response the Japanese could muster only thirty 75-millimeter rounds. Though the Japanese, by postwar testimony, were highly impressed with the quantity of US artillery, the imbalance hardly seemed to faze them. As the soldiers of the 132nd tried to consolidate control of Hill 27, they fended off seven separate enemy counterattacks. "Some of the attacks reached the point of hand to hand fighting," the regimental after-action related, with chilling brevity. As this indicated, the fighting was to the death, with no room for sentimentality or introspection. "Once you're an infantryman, you're a trained killer," Private Cerny commented. In addition to the courage of individual soldiers, the assistance of Captain Casey, the artillery forward observer, helped crush the Japanese counterattacks. With each attack, infantry units would report to him, "They are coming again," and he would call down devastatingly accurate fire on them. His sangfroid was such that, during one attack, he found time to trade a closely husbanded can of lobster to a colleague for a jar of caviar. Not until early January could the Americans claim to have any permanent control of Hill 27.

With such maddeningly slow progress, the strain on combatants and commanders was considerable. Colonel Leroy Nelson, who had commanded the 132nd since 1937, was relieved on December 28, either at his own request due to illness or for cause. Many nights, General Patch lay awake in his tent near Henderson Field, listening to marauding Japanese planes, and took solace in thoughts of his wife, Julia. "I know how bravely you are facing the loneliness and emptiness," he wrote in one letter to her, "because *I do too*. My task is to keep the old morale up and it's not easy, Jul—but with a little courage and no end of faith and by constantly reminding myself of the responsibilities and the lifetime of military education which I was subjected to, I will not fail."

In roughly three weeks of bitter fighting, the 132nd Infantry lost 112 killed, 268 wounded, and 3 missing, plus untold hundreds who were battling fever, usually from malaria. Regimental records claimed, with no supporting evidence, that the unit killed five hundred Japanese soldiers and wounded many more. While the surviving Japanese did remain ensconced atop part of Mount Austen, in the fortifications of the Gifu strong point, the 132nd had succeeded in enveloping them, and cutting them off, by controlling the surrounding hills. Day and night, they were pounded by American firepower. In one ninety-minute period, the Americans hurled seventeen hundred artillery shells into the Gifu area. "Enemy bombardment becomes increasingly intense," a young platoon leader, Lieutenant Kiyokuma Okajima, told his diary. "My body is in such condition that I can barely walk. This makes one month that we have been eating just rice gruel. Men are dying one after another, and now the company roster has 20 men, besides the Company Commander. I am very hungry. I wonder if this is how it is when a man is starving. Rice cakes and candies appear in my dreams."[14]

★

The isolation of the Gifu strong point, in tandem with the arrival at the front of the 25th Division—soon to be nicknamed "Tropic Lightning"—allowed Patch to launch his corps-level offensive on January 10. The battered 132nd went into reserve. Two of Tropic Lightning's infantry regiments, the 27th and 35th, went into the line alongside the 8th and 6th Marine Regiments of the 2nd Marine Division. Elements of the Americal's 182nd Infantry Regiment also joined in, as did troops from the 147th Infantry, an independent regiment. Many of the Tropic Lightning soldiers were veterans of the Japanese attack on their base at Schofield Barracks near Pearl Harbor a year earlier. The corps plan was to bulldoze west. Patch knew that the dicey logistical situation, and the forbidding terrain, precluded a rapid advance. He hoped to maintain momentum by avoiding frontal attacks and outflanking the strongest Japanese-controlled hills, similar to the process at Mount Austen. "We intend to move quite slowly, deliberately feeling our way, and encircling small centers of resistance," he wrote to Harmon. "Our supporting weapons will have time to creep up with the advance and furnish adequate support." Predictably, when the offensive began on January 10, the pace was every bit as deliberate as Patch envisioned. The fighting centered around control of the numerous hilltops and finger ridges west of Mount Austen, where mosquitoes swarmed in the moldy tropical heat. Any bypassed group of Japanese merited attention, since they remained dangerous. "The only positive means of being certain that a Jap unit would not bother us was to annihilate it," wrote Major Larsen, a battalion commander. "We were reminded of this lesson constantly throughout . . . World War II." A company commander put it more bluntly, "You have to KILL these Japs before they will leave."

Supported nearly every step of the way by artillery and mortars, infantry battalions moved in long, sweaty columns on narrow jungle trails. Each step was a chore for soldiers laden down with heavy loads of ammunition, food, water, and other gear. At one spot, some GI wit nailed a crude sign to a tree with the words "Rifle Range" and an arrow pointing in the direction of the Japanese lines. The Marines edged along the coast. The 25th Division fought to dislodge or outflank the Japanese among the dizzying green mesh of hills generally known to the Americans as the Snake's Back, the Galloping Horse, and the Sea Horse for the way they looked from the air. In the suffocating jungle, it was difficult to maintain unit integrity and cohesive attacks. "Visual contact could not be maintained at all times and as a result, some of the men would become separated from the others," wrote Corporal Harry Bartlett, a machine gunner with the 35th Infantry. Individuals often felt completely isolated, even though their buddies were no more than fifteen or twenty-five yards away. Canteens ran dry in a matter of hours or even minutes. Overworked carrying parties could not hope to keep up with the insatiable demand. "Water supply was a great problem throughout the whole operation," wrote Major Joseph Ryneska, the supply officer of the 27th Infantry. "In spite of superhuman efforts by all concerned, there was never enough water in the canteens of the forward units." In some instances, soldiers passed out from dehydration and heat exhaustion. "Lack of water soon began to tell on the assault units," wrote Major Robert Bereuter, another staff officer with the 27th. Sergeant Morriss, the *Yank* correspondent, described the supply effort as a "hand-to-mouth affair . . . trails were narrow, one-at-a-time paths hacked . . . out of live vines and rooty, heavy-bodied tropical trees. Soldiers packed everything on their backs. There was no other way."

The combination of the conditions and stubborn Japanese resistance made for an exhausting, pitiless environment. "Men are moving every day in the foulest weather imaginable, working hard to cut trails as they go," Brigadier General John Hodge, the assistant division commander of the 25th, told an interviewer. "They become very uncomfortable, their clothes ringing [*sic*] wet, and at night are faced with the problem of trying to keep warm in one blanket." Commanders had no choice but to push their troops to the limit. "I thought I knew how to handle men, but since I have been here I have revised my ideas," Captain John Gossett of the Americal Division told an Army observer. "I have learned the primitive, rough-and-tumble way. You can't pat all men on the back. You have to be rough with some men in order to get results." Lieutenant Colonel George Bush, whose 3rd Battalion, 27th Infantry tried to secure the Galloping Horse, commented that "as the going became harder, leadership became more important. When things did not run smoothly a forceful leader was essential." For all his geniality, General Patch prowled the lines with a sawed-off shotgun in hand, coaxing and advising, urging the troops to kill "the yellow termites" as he sometimes called the Japanese. "Possessing physical courage, he regarded it as a fixed characteristic, an invariable constant," Sebree once said of Patch. Patch also knew when to delegate authority. He made liberal use of his able chief of staff, Brigadier General Robert "Lil" Spragins to concoct plans and act as his proxy all along the front. "Such *rare* people are the real and silent heroes," Patch wrote of Spragins in a letter to Julia.[15]

The commander of the 25th Division, Major General Joseph Lawton Collins, was also an unusual man, one of the Army's rising stars. "He was a marked man and on the way up," one junior officer in the 25th wrote of him. Clean-cut, trim, and vigorous to the point of freneticism, he looked younger than his forty-six years. The tenth of eleven children fathered by an Irish immigrant who had served as a Union drummer boy during the Civil War, Collins had grown up in New Orleans and graduated from West Point in 1917. Though he did not see action in World War I, Collins developed a reputation, over the following two decades, of exceptional competence and innovative thinking, so much so that General Marshall personally took action to make sure he received combat command in this war. Back in May, when Major General Murray had left the division to assume a training command, Collins had become the commanding general. Cerebral and preternaturally ambitious, Collins thought good leadership stemmed from a mixture of integrity and drive. Inspiration and showmanship were unnecessary. Histrionics smacked of dishonesty. "You just cannot fool the American soldier," he once said, "he'll recognize a phony every time."

As his division fought desperately throughout January, Collins generally led from the front. Even-tempered, friendly, and yet almost always circumspect in his dealings with soldiers, he elicited more respect than outright affection. His persona was that of an imperturbable instructor who instinctively knew what to do. When Lieutenant Floyd Radike's platoon came under persistent sniper fire one day, Collins personally set up a machine gun in a foxhole, sat down alongside Radike, instructed the young officer on how best to suppress the annoying enemy riflemen, and then worked the phones, directing an attack for the day's objective. "No lieutenant in the army ever had a better opportunity to sit next to a masterful leader and soldier while he conducted a battle," Radike later wrote.

Though Collins wore specially made miniature silver stars in an attempt to conceal his rank from enemy snipers, he frequently came under their fire. In one instance, he grabbed an M1 Garand rifle and emptied an eight-round clip in the direction of the offending enemy rifleman. The incident prompted some ribbing from Patch for his subordinate's profligate use of so many bullets to deal with one man. "Such a deplorable state of marksmanship on the part of Major Generals . . . will not be countenanced by this headquarters," Patch wrote Collins, in a joking memo. "Furthermore, it is understood that considerable damage to a coconut tree resulted from [this] firing. This may later develop into a claim against the Government." On another occasion, Collins came upon a unit that was in headlong retreat after being badly mangled while trying to advance in thick jungle. "It's suicide to go down there!" an upset, panicked soldier hollered. Collins knew that this kind of fear was contagious and corrosive. To quell the man's panic, and take the focus away from his understandable fear, he immediately gave him a job to do. "If necessary I would have knocked him down, because somebody had to stop him," Collins later said. Another time, his division artillery commander, who had actually graduated a year ahead of him at West Point, furiously denounced him for ordering fire missions from his artillery units without direct permission. "It's not *your* artillery," Collins replied evenly but pointedly, "it is mine as well. There is only one division commander in this division, and I am it." Soldiers who saw him at the front started referring to him as "J Lightning." The nickname soon evolved into "Lightning Joe." Day after day, he managed crises and directed attacks, usually on the fly. "The Japs were often in position astride very narrow ridges in the deep jungles," he wrote to a colleague. "The only way to drive them from these positions without due loss was to outflank them. Often these flanking movements had to be by way of precipitous hillside slopes that were very tedious and difficult."[16]

In these "tedious" engagements that raged for the rest of January and into February, the two sides mauled each other unrelentingly. The toll of woundings, disease, deaths, and combat fatigue grew by the day. Medics from the 25th Division alone evacuated 832 patients over a two-week period. "I saw men who had fought until they were dead on their feet . . . and so filled with blood and slaughter and horror (and sometimes fear) that they were hardly human," Sergeant Morriss wrote. "They had what we called the 'Guadalcanal stare.' It isn't pretty to see." American combat troops nicknamed the island "the Canal" or simply "the Rock." The sheer brutality of the fighting stripped many to a vulgar core of inhumanity that would have been unthinkable under normal circumstances. Future novelist James Jones, now fighting at the Galloping Horse as a corporal with F Company, 27th Infantry, referred to this emotional point of no return as the "Thin Red Line." Morriss interviewed one young soldier who was lionized as a hero for decapitating a wounded Japanese private and then stabbing another enemy soldier to death and lopping off his head as well. As Morriss spoke to the man, a chaplain approvingly put his arm around the hero, leered at Morriss, and clucked, "My, isn't he bloodthirsty? Nothing the American boy won't do if you get him mad."

One group of soldiers shot a sniper and, before he was even dead, began kicking his teeth out for souvenirs. Another squad passed around a severed

Japanese ear as a trophy of sorts. PFC Willard Dominick, a devout Catholic, sketch artist, and prewar pacifist, was shocked to see a Marine with pincers "jerk two teeth from a skull . . . sending up a sickening stench!" Disgusted and disturbed, Dominick raged to his diary, "The vulture—Are these the virtues we fight for. Is our culture such a thin veneer—Dear God." Major Larsen, whose 2nd Battalion, 35th Infantry had the mission of reducing the Gifu strong point, later claimed that he found the bodies of Americans whom the Japanese had cannibalized. "Their thighs had been cut, meat had been cut off the thighs right down to the bone, and had been eaten." A sensitive and perceptive man, Morriss mused to his diary, "When the bars of civilization come down, they hit with a bang. War in my book is a lot of crap."

The routine of constant attacks, dehydration, and terror was mind-numbing. "Will my ears ever stop ringing with the crys [sic] and prayers of frightened and wounded men?" Sergeant King Cleveland forlornly asked his diary after a particularly stressful evening. "What a horrible sight to see a grown man so overcome with fear that he cries and blubbers like a small baby. I would rather be dead than in the condition some of these men are in." Men could and often did die in the blink of an eye. Corporal Jones was standing near a soldier who took a machine-gun bullet in the throat. As he was hit, he blurted out, "Oh God!" in a gurgling voice. In a matter of moments, he bled to death. "It seemed to me that his yell had been for all of us lying there, and I felt like crying."

Not only were the steadily advancing lead units hard to supply—owing to the forbidding terrain and lack of existing bridges and roads—but as the number of dead American soldiers grew, the problem of removing their bodies for burial was almost insoluble. Lieutenant Radike and his men settled into new positions one afternoon and came upon the remains of an unidentified lieutenant. "His body was in the initial stage of decay; his skin had turned gray and a strong odor was developing." Instead of waiting many hours for an overworked recovery team to arrive, Radike's platoon buried the man in a shallow grave. "Lowering the body in was a traumatic experience. Swelling was advanced and the odor was overpowering." Some units were so eager to spare themselves the terrible sight and smell of their dead buddies that they began to evacuate them ahead of the wounded. "We simply cannot do this," General Collins told his officers. "We all revere our dead, but I am sure that they would want us to bury them where they fell . . . and concentrate on taking care of the wounded." He ordered the troops to bury the dead well off trails to keep their graves from getting disrupted or obscured by vehicles or columns of men. Standard practice was to place one dog tag on the body and another on a marker over the grave. "It kind of made me sick," Private Jerry Martel of the 182nd Infantry later said of the grisly burial task. "But you get used to that—you have to."

The corresponding job of informing the families of the dead was every bit as overwhelming. As the casualties piled up, worried family members who had stopped hearing from their loved ones began to write letters to commanders. In one letter typical of so many others, Helen Maull wrote to General Collins asking for information about her brother, Tech 5 Howard Jordan, a twenty-two-year-old former schoolteacher from Philadelphia who was killed near the Gifu strong point on the first day of the offensive. "My parents are grief stricken, as Howard is an only son. I love my brother dearly, and I refuse to give him up as dead, until I have tried every possible means to locate him," she wrote. Collins found time to check the records, confirm Jordan's death, and write back to his sister. "Of course there is nothing I can say to assuage the grief of your parents and yourself at the loss of an only son and brother. I also have an only boy so I have an inkling of the dread shock it must be to you. But I did not lose my son and I realize . . . your loss is . . . overwhelming."[17]

By January 23, the Americans had secured the village of Kokumbona on the coast about three miles west of the starting line. The Japanese were steadily retreating. Patch continued the advance, funneling an ad hoc interservice force of Marine and Army infantry regiments known as the Composite Army-Marine, or CAM division, west along the coastal high ground. General Sebree commanded this divisional-size unit, whose unique existence served as an encouraging moment of effective interservice cooperation and coordination on the part of the respective commanders. Many Japanese soldiers found themselves bypassed, stranded in isolated positions or wandering in search of friendly lines. The holdouts at the Gifu strong point were now completely surrounded, deep within American-controlled territory, facing impending doom. Exhausted, starving, crazed with thirst, they neared the end of their endurance. A handful were able to slip out and flee west. Most were trapped. "This emaciated body and thin face, my parents could not look at me without crying," one mused in his diary. "This is the end!"

Badly wounded men resorted to suicide. When one junior officer issued a grenade apiece to a group of four wounded soldiers to kill themselves, they requested he allot only one grenade so that the three others could be put to use against the Americans. The four patients clustered closely together around the one grenade, said goodbye, and died together in the blast. Private Soichi Kawai had seen maggots and flies devour the remains of many friends. In his view, cannibalism was preferable to being ignominiously consumed by the parasitical insects. So he told a friend, "Please eat my flesh if I die. Better that than to be eaten by the flies." The 35th Infantry continued to clobber away at Kawai and his comrades. As at Buna, the presence of a lone light tank, commanded by Captain Teddy Deese, made a powerful difference. The tank's 37-millimeter gun destroyed eight emplacements, driving a wedge in the enemy perimeter. In hopes of avoiding needless bloodshed, the Americans appealed to the Gifu defenders to surrender. Captain John Burden, a Japanese-speaking language officer, set up a loudspeaker over which he broadcast a fervent appeal to give up. Burden promised sustenance and medical care. "We have Japanese food and facilities for feeding you. You have fulfilled your obligation to your country and your emperor. Escape is impossible. Further resistance is useless and will only result in your complete annihilation." Cynical Tropic Lightning infantrymen listened to Burden make his entreaties in the unfamiliar language and shook their heads skeptically. "Them little bastards won't give up," one of them predicted. "They're too damn ignorant." As the GIs anticipated, the Japanese responded with nothing but contempt. "I heard one of the enemy talking busily over a loudspeaker," Lieutenant Okajima sniffed. "What fools the enemy are!" With few if any takers, the Americans resumed normal hostilities.

The surrender ultimatum was a tough sell for men who hailed from a culture and an army that viewed capitulation as the ultimate disgrace. "Why should we waste compassion on a crafty enemy who has killed and wounded thousands of our comrades?" asked one Imperial Army memo that argued for the mistreatment of Allied prisoners. The other reality, intuitively understood by many of the Japanese, was the practiced reluctance of that "crafty enemy" to take any prisoners at all. To be sure, Japanese prisoners were treated well if they could survive long enough to make it into captivity, but that was no sure thing. After a few instances of false surrenders earlier in the campaign, most American combat units took on a no-prisoners attitude (cultural and racial hatred was undoubtedly a factor as well). "Seventy-five percent of the blame for this situation can be laid on the officers," Captain Burden wrote. To his immense frustration,

Americans sometimes even shot down potential prisoners when they knew that such actions would only prolong resistance from their surviving comrades. From senior officers on down, no one seemed able or willing to change this mind-set, even with intelligence officers communicating a desperate need for prisoners. "On several occasions word was telephoned in from the front lines that a prisoner had been taken, only to find after hours of waiting that the prisoner had 'died' enroute [sic] to the rear," Burden wrote of his experiences throughout the battle. Even the promise of three days' leave and ice cream failed to move most soldiers and Marines to change their cutthroat ways.

Instead of giving up, the last Japanese at Gifu launched a self-destructive attack on the night of January 22–23 against Major Larsen's 2nd Battalion, 35th Infantry. "Armed with hand grenades, pistols, and rifles, they shouted and charged in true suicidal fashion," said the 35th Infantry Regiment's after-action report. "The skirmish lasted about twenty minutes, but none of our men left his hole until dawn." At sunrise the Americans found eighty-five Japanese bodies, including two majors, eight captains, and fifteen lieutenants. Major Larsen and his men swept the area, captured three prisoners and eliminated all remaining resistance. In the detritus, they found more evidence of cannibalism. On the body of a dead Japanese warrant officer, the major discovered what he thought was a binoculars case. When he opened it, a nauseating odor met his nostrils. "There was meat in there. I took it back to camp, showed it to [a] doctor and he recognized it as a human liver. They were that desperate." Like most Americans, he could not begin to comprehend the Japanese cultural imperative for self-destruction in the face of imminent defeat. "The fanatical sacrifice of more than five hundred Jap soldiers' lives in the final stages of the Gifu defense accomplished absolutely nothing for the Jap high command." General Sebree felt the Japanese were foolish to attempt to hold a line that was so far forward they could not supply it. He believed they would have been better off to set up their main defensive positions "in the vicinity of Kokumbona or father [sic] to the west where . . . supply and evacuation would have been simpler."

The dearth of prisoners led to an inevitable paucity of good intelligence information. With little inkling of Japanese intentions and capabilities, American leaders, especially at theater level, were concerned about the possibility of a strong enemy counteroffensive on Guadalcanal. Reconnaissance flights revealed that the Japanese had reinforced their air, sea, and land strength at Rabaul. Halsey was concerned that a powerful fleet of battleships, aircraft carriers, and transport ships might attempt to land new regiments at Guadalcanal, and he urged Patch to prepare for this possibility. "I had a long series of urgent messages from Higher Command," Patch wrote privately to Julia. The worries about a counteroffensive could not help but rob some momentum from the advance. Patch's leading combat units were, by and large, dispersed on high ground and trails, with problematic flanks, at the end of a shaky logistical tail. They certainly would have been vulnerable to a concentrated offensive by fresh troops.

What the Americans did not know, because as yet their intelligence gathering still left much to be desired, was that the Japanese had no such offensive intentions. In reality, as early as January 4, they had decided to withdraw from Guadalcanal and focus on holding a line farther north in the Solomons (and of course by now they had also lost at Buna-Sanananda and had elected to withdraw in New Guinea as well). The Imperial Navy buildup at Rabaul was designed to cover the evacuation, not a counteroffensive. Aided by the tentative XIV Corps advance, and the failure of the Allied navies to seal off all waterborne escape routes, the Japanese managed on the nights of February 1, 4, and 7 to evacuate 10,655 soldiers from Cape Esperance at the northwest tip of Guadalcanal. Many of the evacuees were so diminished from starvation that sailors had to carry them aboard their ships. "Hardly human beings, they were just skin and bones dressed in military uniform, thin as bamboo sticks," one crewman recalled. "They were so light, it was like carrying infants." Most of the escapees would need many months of recuperation before they were ready to fight again. "The months of bitter fighting and loss of many friends has been agony that is very difficult to wipe away," one Japanese general commented.

Their escape was a small bright spot in an otherwise disastrous and stunning setback for the Japanese. "I never dreamed that we could come all the way down here and lose in a battle," one doomed soldier wrote in a last diary entry. Two-thirds of the thirty-six thousand Imperial Japanese Army soldiers and Special Naval Landing Forces troops who fought on Guadalcanal did not survive. Disease and starvation claimed about nine thousand lives, combat the rest. Some one thousand became prisoners, whether voluntarily or involuntarily, mostly in small groups at the end of the battle. Many of them were immediately put to work burying the bodies of their comrades. The Imperial Navy probably lost at least thirty-five hundred men in surface or air engagements. At Guadalcanal, the Japanese had come out second best in an escalating, combined-arms attrition-centered test of wills. They had spread their combat power far too thin in both the Solomons and New Guinea, a mistake that hastened defeat in both places, and one that created a turnabout of such proportions as to cede the permanent initiative in the Pacific to the Americans. General Miyazaki attributed the American victory to a lethal combination of firepower, proficiency at combined arms, and scientific superiority. He termed this "a logical systematic operation carried out on the basis of qualitative and quantitative superiority." But this explanation—though undoubtedly true—was nonetheless incomplete. In addition to those crucial factors, the Americans proved willing to suffer tremendous hardships and risk many lives in a fight to the death. With the loss of forty-nine hundred sailors and Marines at sea, Guadalcanal was, next to Okinawa, the US Navy's second deadliest battle in the Pacific War. Contrary to most World War II battles, losses in the ground fighting were lower than at sea. About sixty thousand soldiers and Marines participated in the fighting. The Marine Corps lost 1,042 men killed and 2,894 wounded. The Army lost 550 killed and 1,289 wounded, dispersed relatively evenly between the Americal and 25th Divisions. Thousands more, of course, were stricken with disease, but almost all of these men would recover and return to duty. In spite of MacArthur's claims about minimal losses for maximum gain in SWPA, the American ground losses at Guadalcanal were more economical and the victory more decisive.

At the leadership level, the victory at Guadalcanal propelled several careers. Vandegrift received the Medal of Honor and became commandant of the Marine Corps. Collins solidified his prewar reputation as a special soldier who was going places. Though physically diminished by persistent pneumonia, dysentery, and malaria, Patch received much credit from Army decision-makers for the effective performance of XIV Corps. "I've had so much good luck so far," he wrote to Julia. "Am held in good regard by higher authority, that I have a feeling that I'll see you soon." Indeed, General Marshall had taken notice. Concerned for Patch's health, he recalled him home after Guadalcanal and assigned him to a training command. The new job was mainly a way station to get his health back in order and to prepare him for corps- and Army-level command in the European theater. His successor, Major General Griswold, greatly admired Patch's performance in finishing off a determined, potent enemy force to score a landmark Allied victory. "This was a decisive defeat for the Japs," he told his diary. "Sandy Patch did a *fine* job here. He deserves all credit for moral and physical courage and tenacity. Had there been a weak man in command, it is conceivable that Tojo might yet have a foothold here." General Hyakutake, who had tasted defeat in both New Guinea and Guadalcanal, sensed the same thing. He and his staff had escaped to Bougainville aboard a destroyer on the evening of February 4–5. Devastated that he had failed in his mission, and humiliated to have survived the terrible campaign, he intuitively understood that the war had now taken a major turn against Japan. In the aftermath of this catastrophe, he prepared a detailed report for the emperor on the actions of the 17th Army. At the end of the report, he apologized to Hirohito for his failures and declared, with crystalline simplicity, "My crime deserves more than death."[18]

9

Chills

When the United States purchased Alaska from Russia in 1867 for the cool price of 7.2 million dollars, critics derided the transaction as a waste of taxpayer money. The subsequent discovery of gold and oil proved the naysayers wrong, at least from an economic standpoint. From the vantage point of 1940s grand strategical global warfare, the nineteenth-century critics seemed a bit more lucid. Though Alaska had by now matured into territorial status, similar to Puerto Rico, Hawaii, and Guam, it remained underdeveloped and sparsely populated. Geographically huge—Rhode Island could fit inside of it 470 times—Alaska was nearly impossible to defend, so much so that it could well comprise a yawning flank, an entryway of sorts into North America for the Japanese. In hopes of preventing enemy encroachment on the territory, the US government scraped together minor air and sea forces, as well as a smattering of troops, and based them primarily at coastal seaports. By the late spring of 1942, there were about forty thousand Army personnel in Alaska, most of whom were members of Army Air Force squadrons or engineer units assigned to build airfields.

Because of the paucity of roads, initially they were supplied by sea and air, almost as if Alaska were an island. In the apt description of one historian, this was "like feeding an elephant through a straw." To alleviate this untenable logistical situation and make a larger Alaskan military buildup possible, President Roosevelt, with the acquiescence of the Canadian government, ordered the Army to build an overland road to link the continental United States with Alaska. In the space of about nine months, from March to November 1942, some ten thousand engineer troops, about one-third of whom were African-American, labored diligently to construct the Alaska Highway (or the Alcan Highway, for Alaska-Canada Highway), as the route came to be known. Working primarily with bulldozers, graders, and dump trucks, they carved out the road in spite of subzero cold, snow, sleet, torrential spring rains, rivers of mud, clouds of summertime mosquitoes, swollen streams, and a welter of stolid mountains. Surveying on the fly, building wherever the soil permitted, they favored expedience over niceties. One officer commented that the road had "more curves than Hollywood." The road stretched from Dawson Creek, British Columbia, through Yukon and more than sixteen hundred miles to Delta Junction in eastern Alaska. "To our eyes it is a very good road," Colonel Heath Twichell, who commanded one of the African-American units, said shortly after completion. "Although the critical might find fault with it. It is narrow and winding and has piles of trash." Even so, the Alcan Highway was a remarkable achievement. The engineers bridged two hundred streams and eight thousand culverts. One unit alone built twenty-three bridges with a combined length of just under a mile. A concurrent effort, known as Canol, established several pipelines that pumped oil from fields in northern Canada to Alaska. The success of the Alcan Highway and the Canol pipelines demonstrated the incredible know-how, innovation, and efficiency of the Army's Corps of Engineers, regardless of conditions or circumstances, a tremendous advantage for the Allied side (the Navy's remarkable Construction Battalions, or "Seabees," whose role was similar, only redoubled this advantage). By the summer of 1942, the Army was moving, on average, more than two hundred thousand tons of matériel to Alaska each month. A year later, the totals had mushroomed to more than three hundred thousand tons per month.

The completion of the highway made this substantial military buildup in Alaska possible. Japanese actions created the urgency for doing so. In the wake of the stunning Doolittle raid on Japan in April 1942, the Japanese surmised that the offending B-25 bombers had originated from the Aleutians, a long chain of islands that stretched for nearly one thousand miles westward, like a long line of pebbles, from the Alaskan mainland into the North Pacific. Volcanic in origin, barren of resources, forbidding in climate, the Aleutians certainly measured up to the description of one traveler as "the lonesomest spot this side of hell." The Japanese were concerned that the Americans might yet launch more bombing raids from the islands or, far worse, persuade the Soviet Union to join the Pacific/Asia War and use the Aleutians as a vital link to the nearby Soviet far east. From there the two nations might then be in position to stage major air, sea, and ground operations against northern Japan.

Japanese war planners saw an opportunity to prevent these unhappy scenarios by establishing a foothold in the Aleutians from which they might restrict Allied shipping in the North Pacific, sever lines of communication between North America and the Soviet Union, and bomb the Alaskan mainland, perhaps with luck even the West Coast. In June 1942, as part of Admiral Yamamoto's larger plan to provoke a decisive engagement with the US Navy, an Imperial Navy fleet of two light carriers, five cruisers, twelve destroyers, six submarines, and four troop transports, sailed to the Aleutians and probed American naval strength. Even as the Battle of Midway raged far to the south, Japanese planes raided the main American base at Dutch Harbor, located in the middle of the Aleutians, and secured the westernmost islands of Kiska and Attu. At Kiska, they captured a ten-man Navy weather team. On Attu there was no military presence. The entire population consisted of sixty-three-year-old Charles Foster Jones; his wife, Etta—both of whom were teachers—and forty-two Aleuts, the name for the indigenous people who lived among the islands. Japanese soldiers of the 301st Independent Infantry Battalion executed Jones and forced Etta to watch as they decapitated his body. They then took her and the others to Japan as prisoners. She survived the experience, but seventeen others did not. Jones was the only American civilian killed in ground combat against the Japanese on American soil.

The Aleutians proved to be a dead end for the Japanese. Distances were vast, making sea and ground operations highly problematic. The area lacked any semblance of infrastructure, and the Japanese did not have the engineering potency to improvise accordingly. The climate was awful—freezing temperatures, snowstorms, heavy rains, dense fog were all too common. Gale-force winds, known locally as williwaws, made aerial and sea operations difficult. "It was God awful," one American submarine crewman recalled. "Cold. Dreary. Ice glaze. The periscope froze. The decks and lifelines were caked with ice." These sorts of climatic issues, combined with the many demands of more important theaters, steadily weakened the Japanese naval presence, though they did maintain formidable garrisons on both Kiska and Attu, if only to stand in the way of a potential American North Pacific advance.[1]

Still concerned about the Japanese presence on American soil, probably more for reasons of prestige than grand strategy, the Americans built up military strength in Alaska. The Alcan Highway and the pipelines served as vital arteries to the buildup. By January 1943, there were more than one

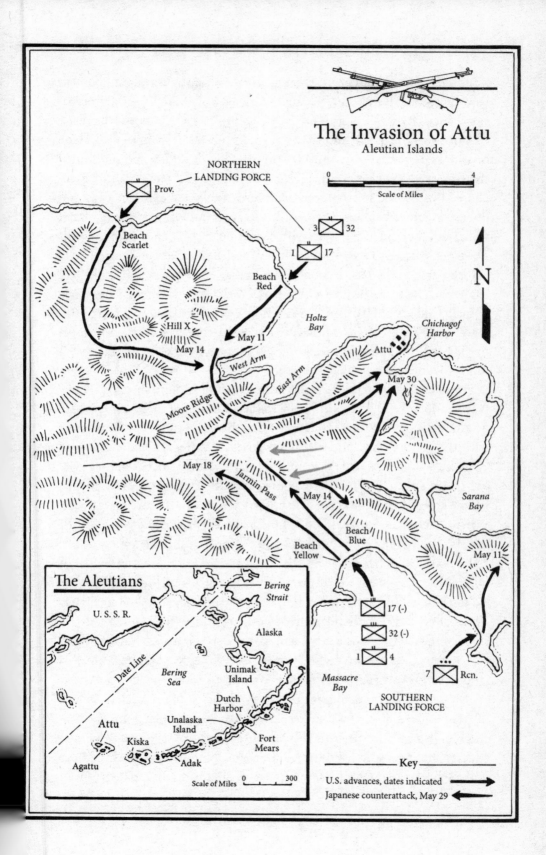

The Invasion of Attu
Aleutian Islands

0   Scale of Miles   4

NORTHERN
LANDING FORCE

Prov.

Beach
Scarlet

3 ☒ 32

1 ☒ 17

Beach
Red

Holtz
Bay

Chichagof
Harbor

Hill X

May 11

Attu

N

May 14

West Arm

May 30

East Arm

Moore Ridge

May 18

Jarmin Pass

Sarana
Bay

May 14

Beach
Blue

May 11

Beach
Yellow

17 (-)

32 (-)

1 ☒ 4

7 ⋮ Rcn.

Massacre
Bay

SOUTHERN
LANDING FORCE

The Aleutians

Bering
Strait

U.S.S.R.

Alaska

Date Line

Bering
Sea

Unimak
Island

Dutch
Harbor

Unalaska
Island

Fort
Mears

Attu

Kiska

Adak

Agattu

Scale of Miles   0   300

Key

⸻ U.S. advances, dates indicated ➡

⸻ Japanese counterattack, May 29 ⬅

hundred thousand troops in theater, with several thousand more on the way, substantial numbers when added to a territory with a prewar population of seventy-two thousand. Few of the troops were happy to be there. "Sailors, soldiers and aviators alike regarded an assignment to this region of almost perpetual mist and snow as little better than penal servitude," the Navy's official historian asserted. Buildings and tents had to be anchored deep in the soil; otherwise blizzards would sweep them away. Engineers burrowed as deep as thirty or forty feet into the earth to tap water wells, and then lined the wells with sturdy boards lest they cave in to the elements. Particles of ashy, volcanic lava soil clung to the brake drums of vehicles and, in the recollection of one soldier, "cut them out just like emery paper." At times bears even fouled power lines and phone wire. Exasperated soldiers often asked one another, "My God, can a man live in this country?" Few answered in the affirmative. A concerned Army observer opined that "in many respects the job of garrisoning these outposts is much tougher than combat."

The isolation of living near the world's ceiling and the absence of creature comforts wore on morale. "The soldiers know that there is no place to go and nothing to do, and doing the same thing day in and day out, along with the bad weather, just gets them down," Lieutenant Colonel Joseph Cannon, a physician, told an Army interviewer. "They can't even get a glass of beer or Coca-Cola." The long hours of winter darkness and the perpetual fog and overcast could not help but wilt the moods of sun-starved men. When Lieutenant Stanley Bent's unit finally experienced a clear day, he joked in a letter home that no one even recognized the sun anymore. "Of course we have all heard of it and read of it and occasionally seen evidences of it in the movies, but we are anxiously awaiting it's [sic] reappearance so we can study it further at first hand." Such luminaries as Bob Hope, Joe E. Brown, Olivia de Havilland, Ingrid Bergman, and Jerry Colonna did visit some of the desolate posts, brightening moods a bit. It was said that Frances Langford was the first white woman ever to set foot on the remote island of Umnak where the Army Air Force had a base.

The scholarly minded spent off-hours participating in archaeological digs supervised by civilian archaeologists. For most, entertainment consisted of listening to the radio or phonograph records. Women were nonexistent. Soldiers who lived in Quonset huts often papered their ceilings with pinup photographs. Courts-martial for homosexuality spiked. Morale was hardly worthy of the term. "I think that a man should not be kept in Alaska very long," Dr. Cannon said. "The boys will crack up." He and others urged higher authorities to implement a rotation system, an impossibility under the circumstances. Marooned in place, soldiers were irritable, argumentative, even resentful. One physician spoke of a theater-wide depression, a kind of surly, melancholic somnolence that sapped the souls of the troops. "Meeting men for the first time, I could pick out the ones who'd been more than six months on the [Aleutians] Chain. They look through things. We called it the Aleutian stare."

American leaders were every bit as anxious to accelerate the pace of operations in the Aleutians as their soldiers were to get out of there. Small task forces seized the undefended islands of Adak, Atka, and Amchitka, all of which were located within a few hundred miles of Attu and Kiska, thus well within range for land-based bombers to attack the Japanese garrisons. Braving the unfriendly elements, 11th Air Force planes soon raided the two Japanese-held islands and menaced enemy shipping. When, on March 26, 1943, a US naval task group under Rear Admiral Charles McMorris intercepted a Japanese resupply convoy and its surface escorts and forced them to retreat back to Japan, the defenders of Kiska and Attu were effectively blockaded. By now, the War Department had decided to retake the two islands in order to remove any semblance of Japanese presence on American soil. After flirting with the idea of invading Kiska first, since it had an airfield and a decent harbor, the planners instead decided on Attu mainly because they believed that the garrison was smaller. Moreover, the capture of Attu, located 190 miles west of Kiska, would isolate and strangle the marooned Japanese soldiers on the latter island.[2]

The American command structure was anything but streamlined, both in coordination and location. As commander in chief of the Pacific Fleet, Admiral Nimitz controlled all naval assets in theater. He was based at Pearl Harbor. His North Pacific Force commander was Vice Admiral Thomas Kinkaid, one of the Navy's leading surface commanders. His headquarters resided on Adak. On the Army side, Lieutenant General John DeWitt, a colorless lifer, who, after Pearl Harbor, had once threatened to unleash club-wielding police on San Francisco city leaders if they did not get serious about homeland defense and control the Western Defense Command and the 4th Army at the Presidio. DeWitt was responsible for defense of the entire west coast of North America, including Alaska. He had spent the

better part of the last year haranguing General Marshall to expand operations in Alaska. Subordinate to DeWitt's headquarters was the Alaska Defense Command at Fort Richardson in Anchorage, under Major General
Simon Bolivar Buckner Jr., son of a Confederate general by the same name.
Athletic and vigorous, Buckner shared DeWitt's vision of fast-moving operations in Alaska lest the Japanese rebound. "About twenty years ago, I
could have knocked out Joe Louis easily, when he was young and weak,"
Buckner once wrote to DeWitt. "Since he has grown up I would hesitate to
meet him in the ring." In Buckner's view, the same principle applied to the
Japanese. As geographic commanders, both men inherently viewed the
war through the myopia of their own areas (rather similar to MacArthur,
actually). Having waited months for a counteroffensive in Alaska, they
were naturally eager to play a significant role in the operation.

DeWitt even hoped to choose the assault division and its key commanders. He had in mind the 35th Infantry Division, an outfit that had
received some amphibious training. For command, he wanted Major General Charles Corlett with Major General Eugene Landrum as his assistant
because both officers had served in Alaska. Instead, General Marshall,
whose enthusiasm for operations in the Aleutians was considerably lower
than DeWitt's, offered him the 7th Infantry Division on a take-it-or-leave-it
basis. Known as the Hourglass Division, the 7th comprised an odd choice.
The unit had just spent months at Camp San Luis Obispo training as a
motorized division for desert warfare in North Africa. But from Marshall's vantage point running an Army engaged in a global war, the 7th was
all he could spare for combat in what he thought of as a tertiary theater. At
the Casablanca Conference in January 1943, he had only vaguely pledged,
in a Joint Chiefs policy memorandum, to "make the Aleutians as secure as
may be."

So regardless of DeWitt's objections, the 7th Division got the job. The
soldiers redeployed to Fort Ord, California, and received some amphibious
training, mainly in the form of practice landings. But the hospitable California coast could not begin to replicate the chilly realities of Attu and its
environs. The island was a largely uninhabitable, craggy volcanic rock,
some thirty-five miles in length and fifteen miles in width. Snowcapped
mountain peaks, stretching as high as three thousand feet, towered over a
vast array of slippery ridges and treeless, soggy valleys. Much of the place
was carpeted with muskeg, a spongy, marshy bog of decomposed sedi-

ment, lichen, and moss, a black muck impassable to wheeled vehicles and sometimes even for men on foot. "The gooiest gumbo you have ever seen," one soldier succinctly commented. There were no roads of any type. The northerly flow of tropical water, generally known as the Black Tide or Japan Current, modified Attu's temperatures in much the same way that the Gulf Stream of the North Atlantic spared Britain and Ireland from icy oblivion. Even in the winter months, low temperatures usually hovered just below freezing on Attu, though snowfall averaged at over seventy inches a year. Heavy downpours were uncommon, but light, misty rain often swept in from the sea, soaking the muskeg valleys and anyone who trod them. Clear days were as rare as proverbial hen's teeth. Fog was endemic, so much so that the island was often draped in it year-round. Invasion planners chose May for the landing primarily because this was the least precipitate, sunniest month of the year. "To the soldiers who had to fight not only the Japanese but the weather and terrain of the island," the Army's official historian wrote, "it must have seemed that the Creator of the universe was an unskilled apprentice when He brought Attu into existence." Corporal Dashiell Hammett, a famous detective novelist in civilian life now turned writer for the Army, observed that "modern armies had never fought before on *any* field that was like the Aleutians. We could borrow no knowledge from the past. We would have to learn, as we went along, how to live and fight and win in this new land."

With the jumbled command hierarchy, and no clear unifying leader, seemingly everyone had a hand in the planning, not unlike a kitchen full of sous-chefs. On the receiving end of the chaos was cigar-smoking Major General Albert "Burfey" Brown, commanding general of the 7th Division. Not only did the fifty-three-year-old West Pointer have to transition his division from preparation for desert warfare to readiness for an amphibious invasion in one of the planet's least hospitable locales, he also had to juggle relations with the naval commanders, DeWitt, Buckner, and their various staffs. DeWitt bluntly informed Brown that he had wanted a different division and a different commander for the invasion, now secretly called "Operation Landcrab" by the planners. DeWitt even tried to place Landrum into a spot as Brown's assistant division commander, ostensibly to share his Alaska experiences, but Brigadier General Joseph Ready was already serving as Brown's second. Instead, DeWitt sent Landrum to Fort Ord as an "adviser" during the planning stage.

At one conference in San Diego, DeWitt contended that a single regiment could take Attu in three days. Somewhat taken aback, Brown replied that, unless Japanese forces were very weak, this was far too optimistic. The terrain alone promised to hold up the advance, much less the possibility of opposition from well-trained soldiers who would have much high ground at their disposal. Brown believed he would need more time to secure Attu, though he did not share any specifics as to an exact timetable. Unimpressed with what he considered to be unjustified pessimism on the part of the 7th Division commander, DeWitt pressed the War Department to replace him, to no avail. Privately, DeWitt told Kinkaid and Buckner that he had little confidence in Brown. Undoubtedly this colored their view of a man they did not know and set the foundation for future trouble.

Naval commanders were understandably concerned about risking their ships for any length of time to possible Japanese surface and submarine attacks. Rear Admiral Francis Rockwell, commander of the amphibious task force, maintained that he could keep his vessels in place for only five days at Attu, lest they be subjected to devastating enemy naval attacks. Brown doubted that a five-day conquest was any more likely than three. This natural tension between the Navy's concerns over risking ships on insecure waters versus the timetable necessary for the Army (or Marine Corps) to secure its land objectives had marked the Guadalcanal campaign, and it would loom as a factor in nearly every subsequent amphibious invasion. As the leading advocate for Landcrab, Dewitt undoubtedly felt pressure from both Marshall and his naval colleagues to produce speedy results. "It is my opinion that [he] sold a reluctant War Department on this operation by assurance of a quick victory," Brown later wrote to Brian Garfield, author of a fine book about the campaign.

The Western Defense commander's views also stemmed from faulty intelligence, the occasional Achilles' heel of the American war in the Pacific, at least before 1944. "Seldom has an operation been planned with less knowledge of the conditions the troops would have to face," Stetson Conn wrote saliently in a history of the campaign. Even though Attu was US territory, information on it was sketchy. The only available map came from a prewar coastal survey by the government's Coast and Geodetic Survey. Commanders knew very little about any terrain more than a thousand yards inland, much less the ubiquitous muskeg. Aerial photographs provided them with nearly all their information. The pictures helped planners prepare sand-table models of the island and estimate Japanese troop strength, but they offered little sense of the weather, the harbor waters around Attu and the nature of the terrain. Nor were the troops properly clothed or equipped for fighting in this North Pacific wilderness. With multiple headquarters involved in planning, and multiple opinions about proper equipage to consider, the requisition process was slow and disorderly. A single supply officer, invested with true authority and reasonable knowledge of Attu's conditions, might well have arranged for the rubber-shoe pac boots, water-repellent trousers, field jackets, sweaters, and insulated sleeping bags necessary to function on the island. Instead, whether due to inertia, ignorance, confusion, or incompetence, most of the troops went into battle wearing inadequate winter field jackets, wool olive-drab trousers, and high-laced leather boots. The inadequacy of the gear was hardly a secret. But since the high-level planners expected only a three-day battle, they supposed that the troops would complete their mission and leave Attu before they experienced any condition-related problems.

At the time that DeWitt made his rosy three-day prediction, he believed there were only five hundred Japanese on Attu, a gross underestimate. By the time the 7th Infantry Division troops boarded their ships in San Francisco on April 24, his intelligence shop had upgraded the number to 1,350. Kinkaid believed the garrison to number somewhere around 1,500. Lieutenant Colonel Robert Fergusson, the 7th Division intelligence officer, estimated, on the basis of reconnaissance photos, enemy strength at 2,200, the most accurate American approximation, but still slightly off. Colonel Yasuyo Yamasaki, the Japanese commander, had at least 2,500 combat troops in place. Referred to by one awestruck American war correspondent as "the shadowy, evil genius of Attu," Yamasaki was an intelligent, experienced infantry commander. He knew precisely how best to fortify Attu's many jags of high ground with perfectly sited, dug-in machine guns, mortars, and antiaircraft guns. Unlike the Americans, his troops were outfitted appropriately in fur-lined uniforms, fur caps, mittens, and moccasins. The rotten climate and the loneliness of living in Spartan isolation on this alien island had degraded most everyone's mood. Except for an occasional submarine foray, they were cut off from the outside world. Food rationing was in effect. Most of the men fully expected an enemy invasion. Their mission, as they understood it, was to hold out until the Imperial Navy could get reinforcements and supplies to them. If necessary, they were all prepared to die.[3]

★

Rockwell possessed enough shipping to carry four reinforced battalions, each of which was packed aboard a troop ship. They were escorted and supported by a potent force of three battleships, four light carriers, three cruisers, nineteen destroyers, plus submarines, destroyer escorts, minesweepers, and other support ships. D-Day was tentatively set for May 7, but problematic weather forced postponement until May 11. The delay was fortuitous because, in early May, Japanese submarines had spotted the convoy and relayed news of its presence to the ground commanders at both Kiska and Attu. For several days the troops went on full alert. By May 9, with no invasion forthcoming, they stood down, no doubt grumbling to themselves about faulty intelligence and false alarms. The Attu defenders were thus in a slightly lowered state of readiness on D-Day.

Aboard the troop ships, the combat soldiers were eager to see land. When they had embarked in San Francisco, few knew their ultimate destination. Many expected they were headed for Hawaii, a welcome and inviting proposition. Instead, the convoy had sailed steadily north. The seas became rougher, the weather colder and gloomier. Low clouds and sheets of rain greeted anyone who ventured on deck. Plaster terrain models of Attu were set up in the officer ward rooms of the various troop ships. Platoon by platoon, men filed in for detailed briefings on their mission. "The limited maps and aerial photos were available for men to study at all times except during mess hours," reported Captain Nelson Drummond, the Army historian who accompanied the invasion force.

The numerous headquarters involved in Operation Landcrab had prepared a dizzying diversity of plans. The final blueprint, insisted upon by General Brown, called for a pincers-style invasion at either end of Chichagof Harbor, on the northeastern side of Attu, one of the few spots with anything like suitable beaches and sea conditions for the landings. The Southern Force, consisting of two battalions from the 17th Infantry Regiment, one from the 32nd Infantry Regiment, plus three batteries of artillery, was scheduled to land at ominously named Massacre Bay where Russian fur trappers had once slaughtered Aleuts. Once off the beach, the Southern Force was to move rapidly through the Massacre Valley and begin to seal off the Japanese at Chichagof. The smaller Northern Force, comprised of the 17th's other infantry battalion and a battery of artillery, was slated to assault from Holtz Bay onto Beach Red—the World War II Army commonly used color-code terms for landing beaches—knife inland and link up with the Southern Force coming from the other direction. Together they would snuff out Japanese resistance in the valleys and all the way to the coast at Chichagof. American commanders also hoped that the pincer landings would force the Japanese to disperse their forces fatally to meet the divergent threats. The rest of the 32nd remained aboard ship as a floating reserve. At General Buckner's insistence, the 1st Battalion of the 4th Infantry Regiment was also added to the order of battle as an operational reserve on Adak. Many of these men had served in theater for months, fighting boredom instead of the Japanese, and they were itching for battle. To wit, when one commander canvassed his unit wondering how many of his men wanted to volunteer for combat on Attu, a staggering 95 percent eagerly raised their hands.

Brown and his colleagues naturally wanted effective eyes and ears for an invasion force venturing into such a mysterious objective, so they decided to augment the two forces with a pair of smaller landings. A battalion-size force of specially trained, heavily armed scouts and reconnaissance troopers under Captain William Willoughby—no relation to MacArthur's intelligence chief—received the mission of landing at 0300 at Austin Cove to confirm that Beach Red was suitable for landing assault troops. With this accomplished, they were then to screen the western flank of the whole invasion and link up with the Northern Force. A platoon from the 7th Division's reconnaissance troop was supposed to land at Alexei Point, east of Massacre Bay, and cover the rear of the Southern Force. The scout units were composed of two hundred wilderness-savvy Alaskans and adventurers trained to a fever pitch by Buckner's intelligence officer, Colonel Lawrence Castner. "Some are Indians, Aleuts, and Eskimos, others are white men," Lieutenant Colonel Keith Ewbank, an Army Ground Forces observer, wrote of them. Brave and ruthless, outfitted appropriately for Attu's conditions, they called themselves "Castner's Cutthroats." The reconnaissance soldiers belonged to the intelligence and recon sections organic to all Army infantry divisions. In contrast to everyone else, these special landing forces were ferried quite uncomfortably aboard the submarines USS *Narwhal* and *Nautilus* and the destroyer USS *Kane*. In all, General Brown had about eleven thousand invasion troops at his disposal. H hour was set for 0740. In hopes of preserving the advantage of surprise, the commanders eschewed a preinvasion bombardment. DeWitt sent Brown a fiery last-minute message. "Make the destruction of the enemy

quick, thorough and complete as punishment for the murder of our comrades and the pollution of our soil."

True to form, heavy fog on May 11 obscured the beaches, necessitating
delays. The assault troops of the Northern and Southern Forces waited in
nervous, cramped discomfort all day aboard their ships. In the meantime,
though, Willoughby went ahead with his mission. The recon troopers had
endured a miserable voyage aboard the *Kane* and they could not wait to
leave. "A large portion of the men were ill throughout the journey," the unit
after-action report chronicled. "The roll and pitch of the vessel threw men
across the deck." Most were soaked to the skin from sea spray. "Men declared they would face a thousand Japs if they could just be put ashore."
Aboard the two submarines, troops outfitted for Attu's chilly climate swel-
tered in full kit and wondered how they would negotiate their way up lad-
ders and squeeze through the narrow passages of the conning tower.
"Army scouts prepare to disembark," the captain of one sub ordered over
the PA system. "The hatches will open in five minutes. The best of luck to
you all." Sailors stood against bulkheads and sadly watched snake-long
lines of soldiers ease their way up. "'Poor suckers,' they seem to say in
unison," Sergeant Jack Werner later wrote in his diary of the moment.

On deck, crewmen and soldiers used air hoses to inflate rubber boats.
The misty night air was cold but invigorating to men who had spent eleven
days submerged inside the cramped subs. When the scouts were safely
tucked aboard their boats, the *Nautilus* and the *Narwhal* slowly submerged
enough for the boats to ease fully into the calm waters. On the way in,
some men caught glimpses of Attu's snow-covered hills and ridges, draped
in an ominous curtain of fog. It took the scouts about an hour to make it
to shore, all the while wondering what they would face there. But they
encountered no opposition. The same was true for the recon troopers from
the *Kane*. "Taut nerves relaxed somewhat," one recalled. "We smiled with
joy at again touching the blessed earth—hostile tho the shore might be."
Though Red Beach was strewn with boulders and only wide enough to accommodate three Higgins boats at a time, Willoughby's unit determined
that it was suitable for the Northern Force landing. He managed to get
word of this to Lieutenant Colonel Albert Hartl, the ranking commander
who in turn, radioed General Brown, "Red play is feasible."[4]

The main landings finally began at 1620. Under less fortunate circumstances, Willoughby's people might have been in some trouble operating

ashore on their own all day, but the Japanese were in a low state of alert-ness. They offered almost no resistance to the Southern Force and North-ern Force landings. By early evening, about thirty-five hundred American soldiers had landed on Attu. Streams of them made their way ashore and stumbled inland. At Red Beach they tramped about one hundred yards across a small spit of ashy low ground and then ascended a steep escarp-ment. "In order to get up the steep slope the men had to dig steps in the side of the hill," Lieutenant Joe Underwood later wrote. At the larger beaches of Massacre Bay, code-named Beaches Blue and Yellow by the Army, men and jeeps landed, moved into Massacre Valley, attempted to ascend the snowy ridges, and soon became enmeshed in the persistent muskeg. "The ground was new to us, the tundra and the snow and the holes gave us a bad time all the way," Lieutenant Charles Paulson, a platoon leader, recalled. Movement through the mushy muskeg was so exhausting, even for well-conditioned young soldiers, that units had to stop to rest every four hundred yards. Fog limited visibility to, at most, a couple hun-dred yards. "The initial attack of the two battalions of the 17th Infantry in the Massacre Valley was greatly hampered by low visibility," wrote Colonel Wayne Zimmerman, the division chief of staff. "The high ground on either side of the attacking forces was in general completely hidden by fog."

Meanwhile, a newly alerted Colonel Yamasaki ordered his men to man a prepared ring of defenses among the boulders and holes of the fog-shrouded knifepoint-high ridges that guarded practically every route of advance. According to one US Army report: "The enemy organized high ground which ordinarily 1) commanded the flanks and rear of inward-pushing forces with plunging fire, 2) was extremely to moderately inacces-sible, 3) was largely secure from our Naval fire and aerial strafing, and 4) offered extreme difficulty for observation and target location from the valley floors." From these well-sited positions, the Japanese unleashed a rain of accurate mortar, machine-gun, and rifle fire on the unsuspecting Americans. The dull *thug-thug* of antiaircraft guns, trained downward to fire into the foggy valleys, only added to the sheets of ordnance. Under normal circumstances, it would have been a real challenge just to climb from the valleys to the high ground; the task of doing this under heavy fire was next to impossible. Soldiers slipped and slid along the ridge lines, got hit and then tumbled or skidded downward. Some were trapped in kill zones, shot to pieces, or hidden from the view of friend and foe alike by the ghostly fog. The dead lay inert, half immersed in snow, mud, or puddles of water. In the chilling recollection of Captain Drummond, the Army historian, accurate enemy fire nailed the Americans from their right and left flanks. "The Japanese . . . had two great advantages—height, which made attack slow, difficult and costly; fog, which hung low down the mountain flanks, to provide them with perfect concealment, yet left the valley floor clear. The Japanese moved up and down with the shifting fog line; our forces moved over a treeless carpet of tundra and snow patches."

Soldiers took terrified cover in shell holes or attempted to dig into the sticky muskeg. Wounded men lay helplessly among the crags and ridgelines, hoping overworked medics could get to them. "When the boys found you lying wounded up here among the crazily crooked gorges, they had to let you down ledges with ropes, carry you across . . . ice-cold creeks and along dizzy cliff brinks," wrote Russell Annabel, a *Saturday Evening Post* war correspondent who accompanied the troops into action. Often wounded men were strapped to litters and perilously hauled by ropes over snowy cliffs. As was the pattern elsewhere, the Japanese shot at the medics mercilessly. Often snipers and machine gunners lured them to wounded men and opened fire. In one instance, a group of litter bearers lay pinned down in a creek bottom for a day and a half, at the mercy of a single machine gun. As Colonel Edward Earle, commander of the Southern Force and the 17th Infantry, checked on the progress of his advance, he took a burst of machine-gun fire that blew off the top of his head, killing him instantly. He went missing for several hours, until a patrol found his body lying alongside a badly wounded scout.

Earle was replaced by Colonel Zimmerman to direct what had become an intimate brawl between ground troops. With the effectiveness of air and naval support largely negated by Attu's conditions, and no tanks to call upon since they simply could not operate in this terrain, American commanders attempted to fill the void with artillery. The Japanese had only a battery of light guns. Within the first couple of days alone, the Americans succeeded in landing four batteries, plus smaller antitank pieces that could be used as artillery. The mushy soil could not accommodate their vehicles— even jeeps bogged down easily. Engineers attempted to smooth out a "quagmire, laughingly called a road," in the recollection of one artilleryman, but with little success. Brigadier General Archibald Arnold, the division artillery officer, ingeniously placed guns and ammo on sleds. Even so, the horrendous terrain made it impossible to move the guns and their supporting equipment very far. Forty percent of tow tractors were bogged down so deeply they had to be abandoned. In one instance, a pair of tractors needed half a day just to tow a battery of 105-millimeter guns six hundred yards. With vehicle movement so problematic, crewmen usually had to haul their guns by hand and dig them in as much as the unfriendly soil allowed. In the appraisal of Captain Warren Hughes, an antitank company commander, the job "was like riding greased pigs in a Roman tandem."

On the first two days of the invasion alone, the Americans fired 5,760 rounds of high-explosive 105-millimeter shells at the Japanese-held hills and ridges. "The 105s were pounding away almost constantly at one target or another while the doughboys got up from behind little knobs in the ground that wouldn't adequately hide a small jackrabbit, and moved in closer," Lieutenant Darwin Krystal, a forward observer, later said. The crew of one gun nicknamed it Betsy in honor of a pinup girl whose photo they had pasted to the recoil mechanism. "Betsy is gonna get a rough ride today!" the crew's gunner exclaimed in the midst of all the firing. The Betsy crew spewed 118 rounds in forty minutes, all the while wiping oil and grime off the image of the pinup girl. Even with cotton or cloth stuffed into their ears, crewmen were deafened by the echo of the steady, mind-numbing muzzle blasts. "It beat on our ears like a hammer," one crewman later said. Guns became so hot that the olive-drab paint on the tubes grew sticky and congealed. Observers had difficulty pinpointing rounds and targets through the fog, so they attempted to saturate the Japanese with an overwhelming shower of firepower. Tractors hauled shells as far forward as they could without getting bogged down. After that, it was up to the crewman to manhandle the fifty-pound shells through the muddy muskeg, up and down hills, all the way to their guns. Every shell that spewed from a gun muzzle was thus the end product of enormous human toil. Still, the fire missions continued, the demand for shells on target remained nearly insatiable, almost in Krystal's estimation, "like food for the ravenous 105s." Mortar crews added to the fireworks. Far too often, the lethality of their shells and those of the artillery was muffled by the spongy ground.[5]

So, even with all this pummeling, the advance was molasses slow. "Day after day we suffered through the same monotonous routine, advancing by inches and fighting frequent small skirmishes," Sergeant James Liccione recalled. As of May 15, with both sides having suffered hundreds of casualties, the disquieting possibility of a stalemate loomed. The Northern and Southern Forces were inching along, but they were several miles apart from each other. A linkup between them in the near future seemed almost impossible. The usual nighttime trigger happiness of troops new to combat wasted untold amounts of ammunition and endangered friend more than foe. Lieutenant Colonel Ewbank, the observer, calculated that the troops had already fired 1,024,000 rounds of small-arms ammunition and 2,442,000 machine-gun bullets. The rotten terrain, the paucity of infrastructure, and inefficient loading plans by the rookie 7th Division staff created a supply snarl. Crates of food, ammunition, and other necessities piled up helter-skelter in the beach areas. With no support troops on hand and no local labor available, since Attu was an empty battlefield, commanders were forced to siphon off combat soldiers to serve on chain gangs to get matériel forward. "After twenty-four hours of this duty, morale among the hand-carrying parties fell so low that men were found dropping their loads a short distance inland and hiding out to catch up on lost sleep," Captain Drummond wrote.

Temperatures hovered between thirty and fifty degrees. Light rain and mist coated the island, especially at night. The chilly, wet weather not only added to the misery of the troops but began to cause casualties among the ill-outfitted Americans. "Our necks were always wet and cold," one platoon leader recalled. "No matter what is done, a soldier will never keep completely dry, but we were too wet, especially our necks and feet." Men lay for days in cold, wet holes, with no opportunity to dry their feet or thaw their extremities, a unique situation for the Army in the Pacific War. "I can think of 1001 things that are more comfortable than curling up to sleep in a water filled mud hole with wet clothes, a freezing temperature, and a piece of wet canvas for a blanket," Captain Hughes later wrote. Immersion or trench foot, a condition caused by perpetual wet, cold feet, proliferated among the rifle companies. In the worst cases, feet turned blue and swelled up twice their size, indicating that frostbite or gangrene had set in. According to one Army report, "Cases of exposure, including frozen feet, some requiring amputation, began to show up at Aid Stations." In fact, more than 40 percent of the 7th Division's casualties were due to exposure. For every soldier who was down with a combat wound, another was evacuated for some form of exposure or sickness. In hopes of combating this problem, General Brown ordered his commanders to rotate companies off the line to spend every third day inside warming tents. This, in addition to the casualties, created the need for reinforcements.

Seeing his manpower sapped by the elements and stubborn enemy opposition, a frustrated Brown kept pummeling the Japanese with relentless attacks from the north and south. The object was always to seize the high ground, a costly, slow, and dirty process. The Northern Force needed several days to effect a linkup between Willoughby's provisional battalion and the main force but did succeed in securing the heights of Moore Ridge, overlooking Holtz Bay. In contrast to this mild progress, the Southern Force made little headway. General Brown personally shuttled back and forth between the beaches and Massacre Valley, trying everything he knew to speed up the advance. "Japanese tactics comprise fighting with machine guns and snipers concealed in rain washes or in holes or trenches dug in each side and at varying heights of hill along narrow passes leading through mountain masses," he wrote in a descriptive memorandum meant for Admiral Rockwell, who was aboard the USS *Pennsylvania*, his command ship. "These positions are difficult to locate and almost impossible to shoot out with artillery. They produce casualties in excess of casualties which can be returned." Too often, flanking attacks were problematic because of impassable terrain. "Progress through passes will, unless we are extremely lucky, be slow and costly, and will require troops in excess of those now available to my command." Brown asked Kinkaid, by way of Rockwell, to send in reinforcements, comprising the floating reserve of two battalions from the 32nd Infantry as well as the 1st Battalion, 4th Infantry on Adak. The 32nd Infantry soldiers arrived on May 13. Since the others had to come from Adak, their arrival would take longer.

At the same time, the patience of Brown's superiors and his naval colleagues was wearing thin. Radio communications between the 7th Division and the Navy were often garbled by atmospheric static or were heavily restricted by security concerns. A PBY plane carrying Brown's dispatches for Rockwell and Kinkaid accidentally dropped them into the sea. For days, neither party had any idea of this. Brown could not understand why the admirals failed to respond to most of his messages. On Adak, a frustrated and worried Kinkaid could not fathom why Brown seemingly refused to provide much information on the Attu battle and assumed he must be failing. Rockwell also questioned why, other than asking for reinforcements, Brown was apparently keeping him in the dark. With little sense of the bitter fighting raging on Attu, the admiral wondered about the necessity of adding the 4th Infantry to Brown's forces. When the *Pennsylvania* narrowly dodged torpedoes from an attacking Japanese submarine, Admiral Rockwell grew especially antsy about the security of his fleet, even after destroyers drove off the enemy vessel. On the afternoon of May 15, he and Brown met for two hours aboard the *Pennsylvania*. Brown explained in depth the difficult situation on Attu and asked for the 4th Infantry. Enlightened about the ferocity of Japanese resistance, Rockwell readily agreed to ask Vice Admiral Kinkaid to send the 4th. But then Rockwell shared the unwelcome news that he intended to withdraw his ships within the next two days. His ammo was running low, and he was deeply concerned that the Imperial Navy might soon counterattack his stationary, vulnerable fleet. Rockwell promised to maintain sufficient landing craft and personnel to continue unloading operations and assured Brown that Kinkaid would probably send some ships to cover Attu.

Brown was crestfallen, but there was little he could do. A World War II division commander engaged in continental operations looked to his Army chain of command for reinforcements, a natural and reasonably straightforward process. In stark contrast, Brown—and every other Army commander engaged in amphibious operations throughout the Pacific—was completely dependent upon the Navy for such assistance, not to mention his logistical support as well. This dependency created an odd dynamic. At Attu and every other amphibious invasion, the ground troops played the starring role. Only they could seize ground and annihilate enemy soldiers. No battle was complete until they gained control of their objectives. And yet, not only did the sea service have to provide for their transportation, reinforcement, and resupply. Naval commanders also had to worry about their own considerable logistical needs in addition to maintaining control over vast swaths of ocean against an enemy who often had powerful air and sea forces at his disposal. The odd coequal and yet mutually dependent relationship between Army and Navy created a natural tension, especially for a generation of senior officers who were not reared in a culture of interservice cooperation. Thus, the perspectives of Brown and Rockwell were naturally quite different. Brown wanted all possible support for the difficult and bloody task of securing Attu. As a soldier whose men were fighting and dying face-to-face with the enemy amid terrible conditions, he expected the Navy to function as an umbilical cord, regardless of any artificial timetable. As a naval officer, Rockwell was trained to protect ships in almost any and all situations. The longer the battle ashore raged, the more vulnerable his ships became. Distant from the bitter vulgarity of ground combat, he found it difficult to grasp its terrible realities. But Rockwell also knew that naval assets comprised mobile firepower, in essence maneuver warfare at sea. Just as most tank commanders loathed a stationary posture, so, too, did maritime warfare experts such as Rockwell dislike the idea of forfeiting their mobility to babysit a landing force.

In spite of these metaphysical differences, Brown and Rockwell got along well at the meeting, especially after they realized what had happened to the general's lost dispatches. They dictated a joint message to Kinkaid updating him on the current situation and requesting the 4th Infantry. At Adak, Kinkaid had remained largely in the dark about events at Attu, and he was anything but happy about it. Whereas Rockwell had established a personal rapport with General Brown, Kinkaid had never actually met him. As yet, the vice admiral knew nothing of the lost dispatches. For all he knew, Brown had simply failed to report updates on his operation to a superior, a military cardinal sin. What's more, the petition for reinforcements included a special request for heavy engineer units and road building equipment, most of which were already loaded aboard freighters at Adak. From the perspective of the commanders on Attu, these construction engineers were badly needed to build inland roads from the landing beaches, not just to alleviate supply issues, but also to facilitate landing of the reinforcements. Kinkaid saw it differently. Because these units were designed for substantial construction jobs and the freighters contained enough gear for two months of work, Kinkaid jumped to the conclusion that Brown's request for these units meant he expected the battle to last at least that long. Perhaps the general even intended to sit and dig in until he received his reinforcements. Conversely, the admiral might just as well have concluded that the presence of the construction units could mean the battle was nearly over, since it made more sense to build permanent bases in a secure environment rather than on a contested battlefield. But this possibility seems never to have occurred to him.

By now DeWitt and Buckner had joined Kinkaid on Adak. DeWitt's prediction of a three-day battle against a few hundred enemy soldiers had obviously proven to be very, very wrong. With every passing day at Attu, DeWitt risked losing face with his War Department superiors and Kinkaid as well. DeWitt blamed not himself, but Brown. Buckner had never wavered from his belief that Landrum was better suited to command at Attu than Brown. To all three men, Brown appeared to be hopelessly bogged down at Attu. DeWitt and Buckner seized on the ignorance of the moment and suggested the general's relief. Instead of visiting Attu himself or taking the trouble to contact Brown personally and hear his side of the story, Kinkaid hastily agreed. With Nimitz's acquiescence, he sacked General Brown on May 16. When Rockwell received the news, he lost his temper, at least according to Commander I. E. McMillian, his gunnery officer. "We . . . were surprised, disgruntled and extremely sorry when you left us," McMillian later wrote to the general. "The Admiral liked and respected you as much as the rest of us did." Brown was at the front when his operations officer breathlessly handed him the sad message. The firing of the widely admired, mild-mannered Brown lowered morale throughout the division. "It is difficult, sir, to tell you of the bitterness in the Division as a result of your relief," Lieutenant Colonel Fergusson later wrote to him. "You'd be the first to denounce such feeling, but it truly exists. No explanation has ever been given to us for the action." Another junior officer later wrote him, "In no other commander have I placed the ultimate final confidence that I have and still do place in you."

Stunned and mystified at the news of his relief, Brown radioed Kinkaid directly, asking him to reconsider, but to no avail. Landrum replaced him the next day. Thus, through a series of miscommunications, misunderstandings, misadventures, and backbiting, along with a healthy dose of detached, ignorant leadership, Brown took the fall. One might even say that he paid the price for being right and his superior wrong about Attu's potency. Though he left Attu immediately, he did not exactly go quietly into the night. He requested an immediate investigation into his relief. When he arrived at Adak, he met with DeWitt and Kinkaid and demanded to know the reason for his firing. Kinkaid indicated that the deciding factor had been Brown's unreasonable request for several months' worth of supplies. "What were you expecting to build there, a stadium or a city?" he needled the general. DeWitt told Brown he had never really wanted him for the job. Brown rejoined that the Western Defense Commander had made him a scapegoat for his ill-advised three-day prediction. Hardly reconciled to what he considered to be a raw deal, Brown left Alaska and took his case all the way to Washington, with a personal appeal to Lieutenant General McNair, head of Army Ground Forces. After investigating the relief, McNair ruled that though Brown's tactics left something to be desired, his superiors acted hastily and out of ignorance. "General Brown's plans and orders were not known and understood thoroughly by Admiral Rockwell, Admiral Kinkaid, General DeWitt and General Buckner when the decision was made to relieve [him]." Truly ambivalent about Brown, McNair assigned him to command of the Infantry Replacement Training Center at Camp Wheeler, Georgia, an important training post where he might demonstrate his worthiness for another combat command. Apparently Brown succeeded. In April 1945, near the tail end of the war in Europe, Brown received command of the 5th Infantry Division.[6]

Ironically for the unlucky Brown, the Attu battle was just beginning to turn at almost the exact moment he lost his job. The capture by the Northern Force of Moore Ridge near Holtz Bay on the evening of May 16–17 created an untenable situation for the Japanese. With a larger American force now on high ground in front of them and another, the Southern Force, slowly advancing behind them in Massacre Valley and the Jarmin Pass—named for a recently fallen American lieutenant—the Japanese risked destruction between these foes. Colonel Yamasaki withdrew his survivors into a new defensive shell dotting the high ground overlooking Chichagof Harbor. The Northern and Southern Forces linked up on May 18 and then turned northeast on the heels of the retreating Japanese. This was the exact outcome anticipated by General Brown's pincers plan. The entire Japanese garrison was now constricted into a hard-pressed perimeter, with an enemy-controlled sea at their backs. "Fog thick, rains every day," one Japanese soldier scribbled in his diary, "only one rice ball. Feet wet and cold, shivering. Disgusting. Better to be dead than alive now." In a double irony, the improved military situation on Attu persuaded Rockwell and the other naval commanders to cancel their plans to withdraw the amphibious task force.

For his part, Colonel Yamasaki still hoped for deliverance from the outside. In response to several messages from his asking for help, his superiors in northern Japan repeatedly indicated that reinforcements were on the way. "The Army in cooperation with the Navy will take all measures to rescue your personnel," Lieutenant General Kiichiro Higuchi, commander of the Northern Area Army, promised in one typical communication. He urged Yamasaki to fight on, if necessary to the death. "I want you to be determined to die gallantly in battle in a manner which will fully display the glory of the Imperial Army." The Imperial Army and Navy flirted with a grandiose plan to send a rescue force of forty-seven hundred soldiers. Then, realizing this was impossible, they concocted multiple schemes to resupply Yamasaki's people, and maybe even evacuate them, by submarine or destroyer. Nothing came to fruition. Yamasaki was trapped.

For nearly ten days, the 7th Division simply plowed north toward Chichagof Bay, battling the Japanese for miserable patches of high ground with unappealing names like Cold Mountain, Black Mountain, Engineer Hill, Fish Hook, Buffalo Ridge, Prendergast Ridge, Sarana Nose, Clevesy Pass, and Point Able. "The Japs were beat up pretty badly and they'd offer only token resistance for quite some time, then suddenly, when we got them cornered, or there were a bunch of them together . . . the fight would flare up and be hot as hell," Sergeant Glenn Swearingen commented. Artillery, antitank guns, air strikes, and naval gunfire battered the Japanese-held hills. In one case, a 37-millimeter gunner spotted a Japanese sniper on the move, manipulated his gun into position, and fired. "The shell streaked . . . and hit the Jap squarely between the hips," Lieutenant John Edrington recalled. "He just disappeared in the explosion." Overworked machine gunners poured water from their canteens onto their weapons lest they overheat. Round the clock, soldiers fought to the death for possession of barren scrub ridges and hills. Nights were short, no more than four or five hours, in the northern hemispheric spring. One artillery forward observer recalled "doughboys sprawled behind rocks [searching] through shifting patches of fog for dim fleeting targets. An attack meant mountain climbing technique, slow careful groping up toward waiting hidden guns."

As American riflemen climbed their way upward among the hills, their Japanese enemies unleashed sheets of machine-gun fire on them or rolled grenades at them. "Most huddled into their holes, sometimes sobbing and screaming as the American doughboys loomed over them," one US officer remembered. Another commander commented, "When the enemy did remain in their position, they would stay in their holes until bayoneted or shot." Browning automatic riflemen emptied magazine after magazine into occupied holes. Rifle companies were down to half or one-third strength. At the start of each attack, terrified soldiers huddled together, as if summoning the courage to keep going. "Their faces were taut, their eyes wide . . . their bodies steeled like springs," war correspondent Robert Sherrod reported in a vivid *Life* magazine article. The monotony of the daily killing was unimaginable. Lieutenant George Thayer, a platoon leader, remembered the fighting as "noise, death, blood, fear, shock, anxiety, rage and resentment for extended periods of time." At Sarana Nose he stumbled upon a three-man Japanese machine-gun crew only a few yards away, close enough to see the expressions on their faces. "I started to fire my carbine from the hip. The carbine held 15 rounds and I emptied it and replaced the magazine and emptied it before I stopped. Fear and excitement kept me firing long after necessary. My impression of these three Japs was that they were young, emaciated and slightly sinister with sparse beards."

Groups ambushed each other amid the hilly blinds, sometimes fighting at handshake distance. "[A] Jap leader . . . tried to gut me with his Samurai sword when I got near him to throw a grenade in a hole," a platoon leader said of one such ambush, to an Army historian a few days after the battle. "I shot him three times in the face with my carbine, and at the same time one of my BAR men let him have about half a magazine. I now have the Samurai sword." Past the point of any pity, American infantrymen left dead enemy bodies where they were killed or used ropes to drag them into shallow graves. One group unceremoniously marked an enemy grave with a crude board that simply read "1 Dead Jap." Almost all the Japanese soldiers refused to surrender. Even had they been inclined to give up, the Americans were hardly willing to risk their lives to take them prisoner. "We get prisoners, but they turn cold too quick," quipped Lieutenant Colonel James Fish, executive officer of the 17th Infantry. Sergeant Werner believed that this self-defeating bloodthirstiness deterred enemy soldiers who might otherwise have been inclined to give up. "They choose death rather than surrender because they are convinced that they would be killed if they surrender," he told his diary. "If we ever convince them to the contrary, we would have a less bloody and easier struggle on our hands." When one highly regarded platoon leader remonstrated his men for refusing to take prisoners, they told him they would obey his every command except one to take live Japanese. Wary infantrymen pitched grenades into occupied holes or emptied their rifles into every prone Japanese soldier they saw, regardless of whether they showed signs of life. Lieutenant Colonel Ewbank, the observer, claimed that the 7th Division was composed of men who carried a special grudge against the Japanese. "Some of them had lost members of their families, or friends, in the Philippines. The general feeling was that their sole mission was to kill Japs."[7]

By May 28, after more than a week of this bloodletting, Colonel Yamasaki had only about eight hundred men who were still in any semblance of condition to fight. Most of them were wracked with diarrhea or suffering from hunger cramps. Another six hundred were incapacitated by wounds. That day, he received a message from Vice Admiral Shiro Kawase, the Japanese naval commander in the North Pacific, to the effect that no Imperial Navy vessels could make it through to him. With no immediate hope of salvation from the outside, he decided to go for broke. Instead of sitting still and awaiting inevitable annihilation in combat or death by starvation, he planned a high-risk attack. By massing his remaining troops, he contrived to break through the American lines, charge down Massacre Valley, and overrun the vulnerable rear areas of the US beachhead, where he could then capture American artillery pieces and fortify his men with the luscious bounty of confiscated enemy supplies. If all went well, he and his force might either hold out until the Imperial Navy was in position to make another try to get through to Attu, or they could go back into the hills with enough food to fight on indefinitely. "We are planning a successful annihilation of the enemy," he told his superiors in a final radio message. A message from Imperial general headquarters in Tokyo, sent through military channels, promised, "We will surely avenge you, devoting ourselves [to] defeating the enemy. We wish you calm sleep as the pillar of the northern defense."

That night, the wounded who were able killed themselves with grenades or pistols. Medics finished off the others with morphine overdoses. Yamasaki prepared detailed written orders, down to the company level, for the attacking force and briefed his men verbally. "Only 35 years of age and I am to die," Lieutenant Paul Nebu Tatsuguchi, a physician, wrote sadly in a final diary entry. Tatsuguchi had graduated from Pacific Union College in California. He spoke fluent English. Before the war he had practiced medicine in California, where he became a Seventh-Day Adventist. He eventually returned to Japan as a medical missionary for the church until he was drafted into the Imperial Army. "Goodbye, Taeke, my beloved wife, who loved me to the end," he wrote just before the attack. "Until we meet again, greet you with Godspeed."

A small American patrol caught a glimpse that evening of the Japanese medics killing their wounded while other enemy soldiers passed around bottles of sake, clear indications either of an enemy attack or mass suicide. The patrol made it back to American lines, but no one could remember the password. Worried about getting shot by their own side, they simply yelled, "Brooklyn Dodgers, New York Yankees, Joe DiMaggio!" It worked. Tech 5

Lee Bartoletti, the patrol leader, reported to his lieutenant what he had seen, but the information failed to arouse any suspicion at higher levels of the coming Japanese attack.

At 0330 Yamasaki's force emerged like apparitions out of the nighttime fog and crashed into the American-held front. They achieved total surprise. By happenstance, they attacked while a confused relief of one company by another had left a gap for them and they poured through it. According to one Army combat historian, "they charged through the disorganized company, reducing it to little pockets of fiercely resisting men who shot down column after column, and still they came." Many Americans were overrun and isolated. "There are very few things that will bring terror . . . to a man's heart faster than a realization that he is all alone on a black night in an area infested by enemy," Captain Hughes wrote sagely. Some who were cut off fought to the end; some played dead; others ran for their lives.

Screaming, shooting, stabbing, grenading, the Japanese attacked with a fury born of total desperation. In English, they hollered such rational phrases as "Lift your fire!" and "Where is that machine gun?" and irrational, chilling phrases like "We die, you die!" and "Kill! Kill!" and "Japanese boys kill American boys!" and "Blood like wine!" among many other imprecations undoubtedly lost to history. "The Japs would come at us yelling like Indians, and our men would shoot them at thirty or forty yards," Captain Ritchie Clark later told a reporter. "Whenever one was wounded, he would grab a grenade and blow himself up." Men fought hand to hand, killing each other with knives and even, in the case of the Japanese, swords. Captain James Pence, a company commander, grabbed one enemy soldier and, in a total frenzy, stabbed him in the back repeatedly until he realized the knife blade had broken inside the dead man.

They swept past the punctured front lines, past Engineer Hill, and into the American rear areas. One group captured a 37-millimeter gun and turned it on the Americans until a particularly courageous soldier got close enough to kill them all with a grenade. They overran medical units, a supply dump, and a headquarters, killing Lieutenant Colonel Fish and his orderly. They slaughtered unsuspecting medics, bayoneted wounded men to death, killed half-awake men in their sleeping bags. In one spot they shot up an aid station tent, instantly killing an exposure casualty. "The top of his head was a mess where a bullet had ripped into his skull, his face was bloody and brain tissue was spattered over the litter," Captain George Buehler grimly recalled. He and the other survivors in the tent successfully played dead for hours, even when Japanese soldiers, on several occasions, entered the tent. When the Japanese approached another tent, someone yelled, "For God's sake, get up and start shooting!" Desperate medics slashed holes in the tent, poked rifles through, and opened fire. When an enemy soldier bayoneted his way through the canvas siding of the tent, slashing one American in the face, another Yank grabbed him, pulled him inside, and beat him to death with the butt of a Thompson submachine gun.

Inevitably, as the attackers rushed around, they became less organized, dispersed into independent, marauding groups with very little overall direction. Plus, with every passing hour, and the advent of daylight, their advantage of surprise diminished as alerted Americans found cover and returned fire with every weapon at their disposal. "They didn't seem to have any fear," Captain Marvin Chernow commented. "They would come straight into gunfire until they were killed or blasted off their feet by the impact of bullets." Near the base of Engineer Hill, not far from the beach, Brigadier General Arnold, the division artillery commander, organized a scratch force of artillerymen, cooks, drivers, engineers, medics, wounded men, and quartermasters who halted Yamasaki's survivors short of their ultimate objective. Yamasaki himself was killed by a bullet while leading an attack at Engineer Hill. American soldiers later found his body in full dress uniform, dead hands still clutching his ceremonial sword.

Understanding that they were doomed, others fought on in small groups, even wrecked any American equipment they could get to, until American patrols cornered and killed them. Hundreds chose suicide. A few blew their brains out with pistols or rifles. Most held grenades to their abdomens or under their chins and blew themselves apart. From a distance, many Americans watched in fascinated horror as the hands, arms, and heads of enemy soldiers flew to and fro. "We had a ringside seat to Hari Kari on the largest scale I've ever seen," Captain Hughes wrote. In the recollection of Sergeant George Gray, a member of Castner's Cutthroats, it was "as strange an experience as anyone could think of. Certainly the most bizarre of my lifetime." Sherrod, the Time Life war correspondent, later examined the terrible remnants, including one mutilated body, "its red and yellow and blue entrails spilling out like yeasty dough." He concluded uncharitably, "The ordinary, unreasoning Jap is ignorant. Perhaps he is human. Nothing on Attu indicates it." One chaplain who surveyed the scene could not suppress a feeling of elation over the dead enemy, an emotion that caused him great guilt. "How can I go back to my church when I've got it in me to be glad men are dead?" he asked rhetorically.

The Americans captured only twenty-nine prisoners and estimated that they had killed at least 2,351 enemy soldiers on Attu. Like nearly every one of Colonel Yamasaki's men, Lieutenant Tatsuguchi did not survive, though he may have attempted to surrender. Major Leonard Wellendorf of the 32nd Infantry recalled encountering a Japanese medical lieutenant who had tied a white rag onto a stick and approached a group led by the major. Everyone covered the man warily. When he slipped and started to fall, someone opened fire, killing him instantly. Wellendorf found a copy of the New Testament on the dead lieutenant and other indications that he had been a Christian. The unit chaplain later gave him a Christian burial.[8]

In Tokyo, Imperial general headquarters issued a face-saving statement, lionizing Yamasaki's men for their final assault. "This added new fuel to the fire of national spirit and stimulated the production of munitions. In short, the Attu suicidal charge was a tremendous stimulant to the fighting spirit of our nation. Never before in the history of Japan had the traditional spirit been stimulated as in this instance." The German military attaché chimed in. "We . . . wish to express our deepest admiration for the heroic deeds carried out by the Attu Garrison Unit, which fought to the last man against great odds."

American casualties bordered on staggering: 549 killed, 1,148 wounded, and 2,132 victims of trench foot, frostbite, exposure, disease, accidents, and combat fatigue, a 25 percent casualty rate for the invasion force. For every Japanese soldier killed or captured, the Americans suffered one and a half casualties, making Attu second in per capita cost only to Iwo Jima among Pacific theater amphibious invasions. Though barren Attu was hardly worth this price, the Americans did learn some lessons about how best to plan amphibious operations, organize an efficient command structure, outfit troops for poor weather, load and unload ships, and coordinate combined arms to succeed in close combat against the Japanese. "Our troops have shown themselves to be more than the equal of the Jap, who, in spite of his tough fighting qualities has many weaknesses which can be taken advantage of," Buckner wrote to a colleague a couple of weeks after the fighting ended on Attu.

Though their intelligence gathering still left something to be desired, Buckner and other commanders attempted to apply these lessons later in the summer when they put together an operation to take Kiska. The 11th Air Force pounded the island with nearly one thousand tons of bombs; naval bombardment added another two hundred tons of ordnance. Expecting a formidable garrison of 10,000 Japanese soldiers, the planners amassed an invasion force of 34,426 properly outfitted assault troops, including 5,300 soldiers from the 13th Royal Canadian Infantry Brigade. The invasion was set for August 15.

By then the Japanese had decided to cut their losses and leave the bleak Aleutians to their enemies. On July 28, Admiral Kawase succeeded in slipping a surface fleet into Kiska to evacuate the garrison of about fifty-two hundred men. By invasion day, reports from aviators indicated that the Japanese might be gone. But Admiral Kinkaid thought it was possible that they were just hiding in Kiska's mountains. He decided to go ahead with the landing. Even if the Japanese were gone, he felt the invasion would make for a good training exercise. So when the troops went ashore, they met no enemy opposition on the empty island, an anticlimactic and yet welcome reprieve, especially for those who had fought on Attu. Even so, the landing force lost twenty-one dead and 121 wounded to mines, booby traps, and nervous friendly fire skirmishes in the island's dense fog. The destroyer USS *Abner Read* struck a mine on August 18, killing seventy sailors and wounding another forty-seven. So the successful Kiska invasion, and the ensuing conclusion of the Aleutians campaign, did come with a cost. Though the North Pacific proved to be a geopolitical and grand strategic dead end, the Americans could take some solace from the fact that the Japanese were permanently gone from North American US soil. Over the months that followed the Kiska invasion, the American military presence in Alaska steadily declined in favor of other places, and so ended the Army's only cold-weather campaign during the war against Japan.[9]

10

The Counsel of Our Fears

Buna and Guadalcanal decisively, and permanently, halted the Japanese advance in the South Pacific and created serious momentum for an Allied counteroffensive. From here on out in the Pacific, the Allies enjoyed the strategic offensive while the Japanese were usually forced to think in terms of defending what they had conquered at such minimal cost during the war's heady early days. Instead of functioning as a springboard into Australia, the South Pacific now amounted to little more than a defensive outpost line for the Japanese. With the naval and aerial balance of power steadily shifting to the Allies, the Japanese no longer thought in terms of a fleet-wide showdown in the open blue waters of the Pacific. Status quo now offered an inviting prospect. If they could stave off any further Allied advance, and thus keep the focus of the war far away from Japan, they might succeed in buying enough time to reap the benefits of controlling Indonesia's immense natural resources, along with major swaths of China, and force the Allies to accept the perpetual existence of this vast Japanese empire. But if they could not prevent the burgeoning Allied war machine from advancing beyond the steamy jungles of the South Pacific, then every mile lost to the Allies brought the war inexorably closer to Japan itself.

The Allies, meanwhile, were still focused on Rabaul. In March 1943, the Joint Chiefs of Staff met in Washington with handpicked representatives of America's Pacific theater commanders. The Joint Chiefs were comprised of Admiral William Leahy, the president's chief of staff; Admiral Ernest King, the chief of naval operations; General Henry "Hap" Arnold, head of the Army Air Forces; and General Marshall. Secretary of War Stimson even attended some of the meetings. Among many other attendees, Generals Sutherland and Kenney represented MacArthur. General Harmon and naval Captain Miles Browning stood in for Halsey. Rear Admiral Raymond Spruance represented Nimitz.

For more than two weeks at this Pacific Military Conference, the group hashed out priorities and strategic planning. At times, the discussions were heated, especially over boundary lines between theater commands. "The bigger your area, the more excuse you had for getting a bigger cut of the manpower, shipping, aircraft, and supplies that were available for assignment to the Pacific," Kenney later wrote. The theater commanders were unanimous, though, in their estimate that, given the strategic priority of resources in favor of the European theater, they could not hope to take Rabaul by the end of 1943. Instead, the conferees decided to envelop it, in effect establishing a sort of institutional momentum for eventually bypassing it altogether. On March 29, twenty-four hours after the final session, the Joint Chiefs issued a simple directive, code-named Operation Cartwheel, to the theater commanders. MacArthur was to continue his westward advance up the New Guinea coast and seize airfields on the islands of Kiriwana and Woodlark, northeast of Buna. Halsey's orders were to take the Solomon Islands as far north as Bougainville. Control of these areas would provide perfectly situated bases from which to pummel Rabaul, outflank it from both the east and the west, and perhaps sever its line of communication with Tokyo.

Rather than risk a potentially bitter debate with his Army colleagues over unified command of these operations, Admiral King acquiesced to the continuation of a murky arrangement in the South Pacific. MacArthur remained the nominal strategic commander and Halsey his tactical subordinate. But, in reality, MacArthur, even though senior in rank, had no real command authority over the feisty admiral, who, as a theater commander, was actually on an equal footing with the SWPA chief. The personal relationship between these two charismatic personalities loomed as an important factor in the potential success or failure of Cartwheel. Immediately after receiving the directive, they both put their staffs to work on joint planning. Like most good commanders, Halsey had an egocentric side, but he was savvy enough to set aside self-importance in his dealings with the vainglorious MacArthur. Nimitz once said of the admiral, "He has that rare combination of intellectual capacity and military audacity, and can calculate to a cat's whisker the risk involved."

In April, when Halsey traveled to Brisbane for a three-day conference with the general, the two professionals immediately established a strong rapport. As second-generation military men, they had a great deal in common. Halsey's father was an 1873 graduate of the Naval Academy, and he had actually known MacArthur's father in the Philippines about forty years earlier. Halsey was impressed with MacArthur's robust physical appearance and his engaging demeanor. "Five minutes after I reported, I felt as if we were lifelong friends," Halsey wrote of his visit. "I have seldom seen a man who makes a quicker, stronger, more favorable impression. The respect I conceived for him that afternoon grew steadily during the war." MacArthur liked Halsey's no-nonsense personality. He struck the SWPA commander as a true fighter and a quick thinker. "I liked him from the moment we met," MacArthur later wrote. "His one thought was to close with the enemy and fight him to the death. The bugaboo of many sailors, the fear of losing ships, was completely alien to his conception of sea action." By the time Halsey left Brisbane, the two senior officers had become bona fide friends. This led to close and productive coordination between the two commands. For MacArthur, the importance of his new friendship with Halsey was profound. Just as his close relationship with Kenney had revolutionized his understanding of airpower, so, too, did his friendship with Halsey rehabilitate the Navy in MacArthur's eyes. After the general's sour experiences in the Philippines, this was an important matter, especially since many of his future operations hinged greatly on the productive use of sea power as well as the minute coordination inherent in amphibious warfare.

The successful conference was just as important for Halsey's well-being. Because of the foggy South Pacific command arrangement, he was in a position of serving two nominal masters. "My original hat was under Nimitz, who controlled my troops, ships, and supplies," he wrote. "Now I had another hat under MacArthur, who controlled my strategy." This could have been a deeply problematic circumstance. But because he enjoyed a strong relationship with both men, he earned himself substantial autonomy and avoided the very real peril of finding himself caught between the often conflicting designs of these two titans.[1]

He succeeded in selling MacArthur on his concept of how best to eject the Japanese from the Solomon Islands. Though the Cartwheel directive mandated only the capture of Bougainville at the northern tip of the island chain, Halsey believed he must first secure New Georgia, located in the heart of the archipelago, about two hundred miles north of Guadalcanal. At Munda, on the northern coast of rambling, jungle-engulfed New

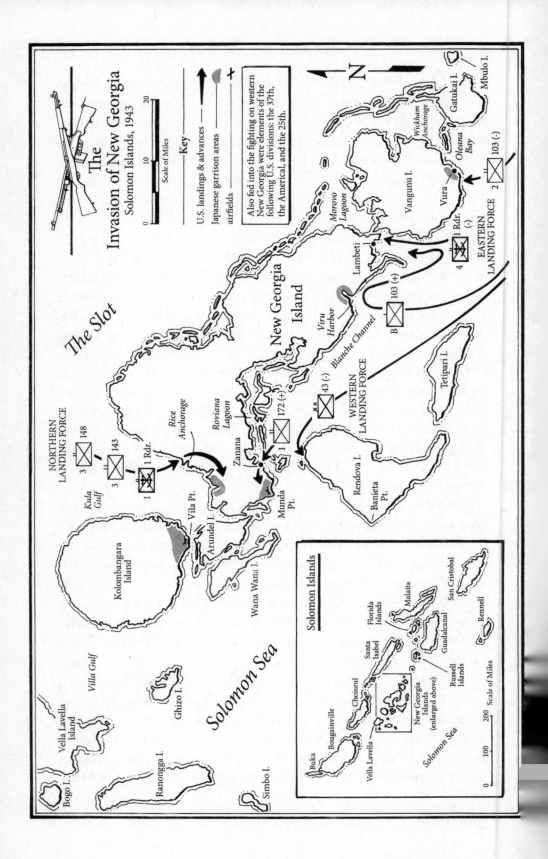

The
Invasion of New Georgia
Solomon Islands, 1943

Key

U.S. landings & advances ———▶

Japanese garrison areas

airfields ✛

Also fed into the fighting on western New Georgia were elements of the following U.S. divisions: the 37th, the Americal, and the 25th.

Scale of Miles

0   10   20

N

Solomon Islands

Buka
Bougainville
Choiseul
Vella Lavella
Santa Isabel
Florida Islands
Malaita
New Georgia Islands (enlarged above)
Russell Islands
Guadalcanal
San Cristobal
Rennell
Solomon Sea

Scale of Miles
0   100   200

The Slot

Solomon Sea

Bogo I.
Vella Lavella Island
Villa Gulf
Ranongga I.
Ghizo I.
Simbo I.

Kolombangara Island

Kula Gulf

NORTHERN LANDING FORCE

3 148
3 143
1 1 Rdr.

Vila Pt.
Arundel I.
Wana Wana I.

Rice Anchorage
Roviana Lagoon
Zanana
1 172 (+)
Munda Pt.

New Georgia Island

xx 43 (-)
WESTERN LANDING FORCE

Rendova I.
Banieta Pt.
Tetipari I.

Blanche Channel
Viru Harbor

Lambeti
B 103 (+)

Morovo Lagoon

1 Rdr. (-)

4 Rdr. EASTERN LANDING FORCE
2 103 (-)
Vura
Oleana Bay

Vangunu I.
Wickham Anchorage
Gatukai I.
Mbulo I.

Georgia Island, the Japanese had built a major airfield at one of the few sites in the chain that could accommodate heavy bombers. Since the latter part of the previous December, Munda-based Japanese aircraft had flown missions against Guadalcanal and numerous other targets along the narrow waters of the Solomon Sea (usually called "the Slot" by Americans). Munda lay 495 miles from Milne Bay, 690 miles from Port Moresby, 150 miles from Bougainville, and 460 miles from Rabaul. In late February, Halsey had used Marine Raiders and elements of the newly arrived 43rd Infantry Division, an Army National Guard unit originally from the New England states—although its roster now included men from nearly every other state—to seize, against no opposition, the Russell Islands, about fifty-five miles northwest of Henderson Field. In the Russells, the Americans built two fighter airfields and edged closer to Munda.

The New Georgia operation entailed complex coordination of air, sea, and ground forces, plus substantial logistical preparations. The geography of the objective was anything but inviting. New Georgia was located in the middle of a tropical cluster that included Vella Lavella, Vangunu, Kolombangara, Rendova, Arundel, and Baanga, among many other smaller islands. New Georgia Island was the sixth largest in the Solomons. With the exception of a few coastal areas like Munda, most of the place was overrun by mountainous rain forest and jungle. According to one contemporary Army report, "its shape describes a chubby numeral seven with a 45 mile shaft northwest by southeast, and a bulbous 20 mile arm pointing south from this shaft's northwest extremity." Whereas Guadalcanal was a stand-alone entity, New Georgia was abutted by Kolombangara and Arundel to the northwest, Rendova to the west, and Vangunu to the southeast. Narrow lagoon waters, pervasive coral reefs, and small barrier islands made much of New Georgia's coastline unsuitable for large-scale amphibious landings. Annual rainfall averaged between one hundred and two hundred inches, much of which descended in torrents. High temperatures ranged into the upper eighties and nineties with enervating humidity. The unchecked tropical climate spawned endemic disease, most notably amoebic dysentery, dengue fever, skin afflictions, and, of course, malaria. A small population of about eighty-seven hundred Melanesians was sprinkled among the coastal areas of New Georgia and its many neighbors. Most were sympathetic to the Allies, in part owing to a Japanese policy of "subjugation by violence," as one Melanesian described the Japanese occupation. The Japanese tendency to confiscate property and loot gardens only solidified their unpopularity, as did a thirty-day forced-labor program they implemented among the islanders ("wages" included a stick of tobacco or a loincloth for a week of toil). "They destroyed everything, kill all the plants, eat all our pigs, destroy our gardens," recalled Jimmy Bennett, a New Georgian scout.

A long-standing British, Australian, and New Zealander presence in the Solomons also aided pro-Allied sentiment. Before the war, the Royal Australian Navy had established a network of observers there and throughout much of the rest of the South Pacific. Comprised primarily of planters, businessmen, and civil servants, they knew the islands and had established relationships with locals. Upon the outbreak of the war, they became known as Coastwatchers. In tandem with the islanders among whom they worked and lived, the Coastwatchers evolved into a remarkable intelligence asset for the Allies and a true thorn in Japanese sides. They rescued downed aviators and marooned sailors. They gathered extensive information on terrain, tides, beach conditions, and Japanese military strength. Some even patrolled extensively in Japanese-held areas and harassed the enemy with hit-and-run warfare. Most all the Coastwatchers maintained clandestine radio communication with Allied intelligence in SWPA and the South Pacific Area, sharing vital information and coordinating closely with Allied war planners. The watchers comprised an extensive fifth column that gave the Allies tremendous local influence and an inherent intelligence advantage that would come to plague the Japanese war effort. On New Georgia the key figure was Major Donald Kennedy, a New Zealander and former civil servant who had elected to stay after the Japanese took over. He organized an effective network of white and Melanesian Coastwatchers who operated on New Georgia and the neighboring islands. In a few instances, they even ambushed and annihilated Japanese patrols.

Thanks to the efforts of Kennedy's men, plus information from people who had lived in the area before the war, Halsey's invasion planners had a good sense of the terrain and landing conditions at New Georgia and the surrounding islands. The exact Japanese order of battle remained a bit more opaque. By June, they had amassed considerable forces in the New Georgia group. In addition to the fighters and medium bombers of Munda and smaller fields on other islands, about 10,500 Imperial Army and Navy troops of the Southeastern Detachment defended the area. Roughly half were on New Georgia and half on the smaller islands, especially Kolom-bangara. The sailors belonged to the 8th Combined Special Naval Landing Force, the Kure 6th Special Naval Landing Force, and the Yokosuka 7th Special Naval Landing Force. The latter two names were inspired by the places in Japan from which many of the troops hailed. Imperial Army soldiers, largely from the 229th and 13th Infantry Regiments, rounded out the garrison. The Imperial Army's Major General Noboru Sasaki, a canny, thoughtful professional, commanded the Southeastern Detachment. Initially the Imperial Army soldiers complained that their naval comrades received better rations. Eventually senior leaders interceded to alleviate this perceived imbalance. The men soon enjoyed ample quantities of soybean sauce, cider, and sake. From Japan came care packages containing letters from schoolchildren, kimonos, soap, toilet paper, and pink packages of toothpaste. In morale lectures, officers spoke of a racial war between whites and Asians and assured their men that New Georgia was destined to become a decisive battleground in that struggle.

Originally the Allies had hoped to invade New Georgia in April or May. But this was too ambitious. Not until the latter part of June would the necessary shipping, supplies, and intelligence data become available. From April to June, opposing air and sea forces continued to battle for supremacy in the central Solomons. Almost every time, the Coastwatchers provided Allied commanders with vital early warning of Japanese movements. The aerial battle climaxed on June 16, when 120 Japanese planes dueled with 104 Army Air Force, Marine, Navy, and Royal New Zealand Air Force fighters in a span of skies stretching from the Russells to Guadalcanal. Though the Japanese sank two ships, crippled another, and inflicted damage on the Guadalcanal base, their own substantial losses negated any positives they might otherwise have reaped.

At the same time, Allied planes and ships repeatedly pounded the New Georgia group, in hopes of softening up the defenders before the invasion. "For about 20 minutes bullets rained as in a squall," one anonymous Japanese soldier wrote in a diary. "Tracers exploded at our eyes and we decided we were about to die. There were about 30 or 40 casualties. It gives you the feeling of having seen life and death before your very eyes." Lieutenant Harumasa Adachi, a young Imperial Army platoon leader, documented several air raids in a diary he kept, including one instance when Allied aircraft suddenly appeared overhead after Adachi had consumed nearly a pint of sake. "As I lay drunk . . . enemy planes flew noisily overhead, but I was not in the least afraid," he noted in his diary. "I must acknowledge the great power of sake." In the latter part of June, as these attacks intensified, many of the soldiers wondered about the whereabouts of their own aviators. "Enemy planes have come over every night and early morning to bomb our unit," Lieutenant Toshihiro Oura told his diary. "Our planes have never come over, leading me to wonder as to whether our air force actually exists. Officers and men have no other alternative other than to wait to be destroyed while doing their very best to the last."[2]

Because Kennedy's Coastwatchers were so effective, the Allies in late June safely landed reconnaissance parties that provided updated information on Japanese troop dispositions, as well as the terrain and conditions. The follow-up invasion force consisted of the reinforced 43rd Infantry Division, about twenty thousand soldiers, plus two Marine Raider battalions and the Marine 9th Defense Battalion. The Raiders were highly trained amphibious shock troops who excelled at scouting and light infantry tactics, quite similar to US Army Rangers. The defense battalion was designed to provide antiaircraft and artillery support to the invasion force. Plus, the battalion's order of battle included a platoon of light tanks. The invasion reserve consisted of two regiments and a field artillery battalion from the 37th Infantry Division, an Ohio National Guard outfit that had defended the Fiji Islands for several months before moving its base to Guadalcanal in April. The 3rd New Zealand Division was available if needed, as was the 25th Infantry Division, though the Tropic Lightning soldiers were still in the process of resting and refitting on Guadalcanal after their recent hard fight to secure the island. Four naval task forces supported the operation— Task Force 33 contained the aviation units, Task Force 72 the submarines, Task Force 36 the surface escorts, and Task Force 31 the troop ships and amphibious landing vessels. In all, the Navy and the Army Air Force provided an umbrella of more than six hundred naval and land-based aircraft. The naval flotilla hinted at the growing strength of Allied sea power. Halsey made available two fleet carriers, three escort carriers, three battleships, nine cruisers, and twenty-nine destroyers.

Munda itself would have been the most desirable, and obvious, place to land this formidable invasion force. However, an extensive barrier reef, and perilously narrow waters, negated this possibility. Instead, the commanders decided on a coordinated series of complementary landings. They would first seize Rendova Island, immediately west of Munda, to use as an artillery base and a staging point for landings on New Georgia. Similar to Attu, the Americans embraced a pincers concept for this main part of the invasion. At Segi Point, on the southeastern tip of New Georgia, they planned to seize a spot on which they could build a fighter strip. The primary landing of the southern pincer was to be at Zanana Beach, less than ten miles from Munda. The northern landing force was to come ashore at Rice Anchorage on the island's north coast, advance inland, and block Japanese reinforcements from reaching Munda. Rear Admiral Richmond Kelly Turner, commander of Task Force 31, was to control these landings until the 43rd Infantry Division (nicknamed "Winged Victory") established a beachhead, after which, theoretically at least, ultimate authority was supposed to pass to the division commander, Major General John Hester, as head of the New Georgia Occupation Force. In effect, this command setup gave Hester the responsibilities of a corps commander but without the necessary authority and staffing, hardly a recipe for success. What's more, the absence of an actual corps commander risked the possibility that Turner might become invested with more authority for the conduct of land operations than would be appropriate for a naval officer. Indeed, the Marines were still chafing over what they saw as Turner's meddling in land matters during the Guadalcanal battle.

All over Halsey's South Pacific Area command, Allied logisticians amassed an incredible bounty of supplies for Operation Toenails, as the landings were now code-named. Inadequate harbor facilities, a shortage of service troops to unload ships, and a tropical storm that destroyed floating quays, bridges, and heavy equipment at Guadalcanal made the task of supplying the invasion a special challenge. By the end of May, the backlog of unloaded freight in the South Pacific Area totaled 160,000 tons, 40 percent of which was earmarked for Toenails. Another problem, as always, was a shortage of service troops. There were just fewer than seventy thousand support soldiers in theater, a shortfall, according to logistical experts, of at least twenty thousand men. In a matter of weeks, understrength work parties managed to unload, store,or reroute the necessary matériel aboard invasion ships, in part by utilizing versatile two-and-a-half-ton, six-wheeled amphibious trucks (known as DUKWs) to ferry supplies to island depots and other destinations. At the Russells alone, the Americans amassed 23,775 drums of fuel and lubricants, 13,085 tons of military equipment, and twenty-eight fully serviced vehicles. Another eighty thousand barrels of gasoline was stored on Guadalcanal. These numbers did not even include the thousands of tons of ammunition, food, spare parts, vehicles, tentage, and other sundry items stored aboard the landing ships. Inside those ships, the troops huddled together as the invasion convoy put to sea on June 29, in the inky blackness of the South Pacific night. Eerie blue-tinged blackout lights bathed everyone in partial darkness, distorting facial features and restricting movement, "lending an atmosphere of unreality," in the recollection of one participant.[3]

★

Following a successful invasion at Segi Point, Turner's task force disgorged some six thousand troops on Rendova throughout the day on June 30. They quickly overwhelmed the tiny Japanese garrison of about 140 men, either annihilating them in small groups or forcing them to flee by water to New Georgia. With control of the island, the Americans unloaded about thirty days' worth of supplies. Soon thereafter, cigar-smoking crewmen from the 192nd Field Artillery Battalion and A Battery of the Marine 9th Defense Battalion landed their powerful 155-millimeter guns. The main enemy opposition came from the air. From Rabaul, Japan's 11th Air Fleet launched three separate maximum effort attacks from morning to late afternoon. For the most part, Allied planes battled them to a standstill, but around 1500, the enemy aircraft did succeed in damaging USS *McCawley*, Admiral Turner's flagship, with a torpedo hit that ripped a truck-size hole in the ship. He transferred his flag to the destroyer USS *Farenholt* and ordered the escorts and landing ships back to Guadalcanal for the evening. That night, American PT boats mistook the *McCawley* for an enemy ship, torpedoed, and sank her, fortunately with no loss of life. The next day, July 1, Japanese planes made it over the Rendova beachhead, unleashed clusters of fragmentation bombs and strafed landing craft with such ferocity that, in the recollection of one infantryman, their bullets were "ricocheting like fire flies in a jar." The heaps of unloaded matériel and parked vehicles scattered just inland from the shore also made for a target-rich environment. Three artillery pieces were damaged, fuel drums exploded, igniting fires and billowing clouds of dense smoke. A medical clearing station lost all its beds and most of its other equipment. Division headquarters saw nearly all its field office equipment wrecked; other bombs destroyed mess stoves. Thirty men were killed and another two hundred wounded. The dead were sealed inside canvas sacks, each of which was then weighed down with a pair of

90-millimeter shells, and buried in Rendova Harbour. The Imperial Navy soon added its own greetings. Under a shroud of darkness, a force of nine destroyers and one cruiser managed to slip into the waters north of Rendova and shell the island. They hit only jungle and did no damage to the beachhead.

The attacks demonstrated that Japanese air and sea forces were still capable of inflicting significant damage, and Allied commanders by necessity remained vigilant against this threat. But the Japanese could not hope to establish the kind of control over the skies and waters around the New Georgia group necessary to halt Toenails in its tracks and defeat the Allies in any other way than a land battle. The same was true to the west at Kiriwana and Woodlark Islands, where the 158th Infantry Regiment and the 112th Cavalry Regiment on June 30 landed unopposed and quickly consolidated American control of these two objectives.

Meanwhile, at Rendova in early July, the invasion force battled the dreadful conditions as much as the Japanese. Torrents of rain and heavy truck traffic soon turned the island's soil "into a morass of red mud," according to one Army South Pacific Area report. Deep, glutinous mud engulfed trucks and jeeps alike. "The mud of the volcanic island seemed bottomless," wrote the Army's historian in a document prepared a few months later. One vital bulldozer sank so deeply that it slipped from sight altogether. Seabees attempted to build corduroy roads. When this failed to keep the mud at bay, they took to winching their trucks just to keep them mobile. Only tractors could hope to negotiate their way through the gobs of reddish muck. Giant, and often unmarked, heaps of medical supplies, fuel, ammunition, barracks bags, and rations were strewn chaotically to and fro. "Mud, rain, heat, insects," Colonel George McHenry, the commander of the 3rd Marine Regiment, 3rd Marine Division, who was attached to the 43rd Division as an observer, jotted in his notes. "Everyone caked with mud to waist . . . clothes never dry. You smell like a goat. Everything rusts." Another Marine observer, Lieutenant Colonel Wilbur McNenny, after viewing the chaotic supply dumps, formed the opinion that the 43rd Division simply brought too much unnecessary gear, a common American tendency in this and all modern wars. "Barracks bags, tentage, and camp equipment of all kinds are useless baggage until the operation is completed," he wrote. "It clutters up the beaches and dumps and losses of such material must be expected if carried to forward areas." In fact, within a few days of the Rendova landing, the division had already lost more than one thousand barracks bags to theft, looting, the conditions, and enemy action. An exasperated Colonel McHenry wrote that "you can get along w/ only an outside suit, spare underwear & sox . . . and if all have a good pair of shoes . . . they should stand at least 1 mo. [of] campaigning. I see no reason to carry anything not necessary to push the firefight vigorously or to sustain life i.e. food & water."

On July 2, Halsey ordered Turner to proceed with the main landings on New Georgia and seize Munda. A battalion from the 43rd Division's 172nd Infantry Regiment led the way for the Southern Landing Force at Zanana. The troops landed under cover of darkness in the early-morning hours of July 3 and encountered no opposition. Under protective cover from artillery batteries at Rendova and smaller outlying islands adjacent to Zanana, they strung barbed wire, fortified a perimeter, and were soon joined by the balance of their regiment, more artillery units, and the 169th Infantry. The Northern Landing Force, consisting of one Marine Raider battalion plus two battalions from the 37th Infantry Division, invaded unopposed at Rice Anchorage on July 5. With no artillery support, their heaviest weapons were light mortars and machine guns. Instead of functioning as an effective blocking force, they soon became enmeshed in hacking their way through thick jungle, manning forlorn roadblocks—quite similar to Buna—and clashing with small groups of Japanese in bitter, intimate firefights. They played only a tangential role in the offensive for Munda. In at least two instances, Japanese reinforcements from Kolombangara sidestepped them and linked up with their comrades at Munda Point (the Allied navies fought multiple engagements with Imperial Navy reinforcement convoys in July, but could not prevent them from getting at least eighteen hundred combat troops through to Sasaki).

The main job of pushing for Munda went to the 169th and 172nd Infantry Regiments. The airfield was less than ten miles from Zanana, but the terrain in between was awful. The Army's official historian described it as "rugged, tangled, and patternless. Rocky hills thrust upward from two to three hundred feet above sea level, with valleys, draws, and stream beds in between. The hills and ridges sprawled and bent in all directions." The soil was muddy and swampy. The green thickness of the jungle limited visibility to no more than a few yards. The languid, almost liquid heat was suffocating. Heavy rains only made the air steamier. A narrow, muddy foot track known as the Munda Trail was all that passed for a road. Photographs and maps provided no information on the contours of the terrain. Even distances remained sketchy. Local scouts and Coastwatchers provided some guidance, but rapid movement was nearly impossible. From July 6 onward, with the 169th on the right and the 172nd on the left, the Americans pressed a couple thousand yards westward out of the Zanana perimeter to the Barike River area, where they soon clashed with Japanese patrols and then ran into General Sasaki's first line of resistance.[4]

Instead of a mobile maneuver battle that would favor the Americans, the battle devolved into a fixed series of individual brawls amid the confusing, disorienting, alien clumps of jungle. The inexperienced 43rd Division was nowhere near prepared to fight in this environment. The soldiers were not conditioned well enough. They had little jungle training. Some of the soldiers, particularly long-serving guardsmen, were too old for combat. Colonel McHenry claimed that the average age of the division was thirty-two. He dubbed the 43rd "an old man's division. The older men could not stand those first few days of hard, back-breaking work . . . and coupled with the mental hazard of combat . . . broke under the strain." They were overly gullible, too. When they were stationed on Guadalcanal, they came into contact with 25th Division soldiers and others who had fought there. In the time-honored tradition of "scaring the rookies," the Guadalcanal veterans had regaled them with tall tales of superhuman Japanese jungle-fighting proficiency. Far too many of the Winged Victory rookies took the veterans at their word. Plus, they had practically no training for night fighting. "Troops to fight the Japanese must be trained and disciplined and led to regard all stories that the Jap is a superman as hokum," declared one anonymously written but penetrating divisional post-battle analysis.

Not surprisingly, when men who were steeped in such "hokum" subsequently encountered serious, resourceful opposition during the Munda offensive, they did not react well, especially at night, when they completely ceded the initiative to the Japanese. In this sense, they were products of their military establishment's vacuous night-fighting doctrine. "Attacks should normally be broken off at least three hours before darkness in order to provide ample time for digging in an all around defense and issuing orders for the night conduct of the defensive plan adopted," wrote Colonel Evans Ames, commander of the Marine 21st Regiment, and an observer during the New Georgia operation. Ames was a typical product of the

American military system, one that seemingly envisioned a tidy nine-to-five war, perhaps reflecting the routinized nature of work patterns in American society as well as a legacy of American frontier history. "We are daytime fighters," Ira Wolfert, a war correspondent, wrote from the Solomons. "And when twilight comes, we revert to our Indian-fighting past and build old-fashioned squares of defense around each separate automatic weapon." Voices like Major General Terry Allen, an innovative and passionate advocate for night operations, were few and far between in the American armed forces. Instead of training soldiers and their commanders to attack and maintain operational initiative at night, the perimeter mentality predominated. Decrying the effectiveness of Japanese harassment against static American fixed positions in the darkness, one 43rd Division commander reported that "our initial plan had been adopted on the advice of other units experienced in jungle warfare. It called for complete immobility at night, with grenades and bayonets as the only defense weapons. Gun crews were directed to fire only in the event of a major attack." By ceding the night to the Japanese, they negated their own advantages of firepower, matériel, and mobility in favor of the sort of intimate hand-to-hand fight preferable to the Japanese.

This hunker-down mentality quickly eroded the psyches of the inexperienced 43rd Division soldiers. Giving in to the natural yearning to be close to others in time of danger, they dug foxholes within a few feet of one another. No one apparently thought to string barbed wire or set up cans or other noise-making items that might tip them off to the approach of Japanese soldiers. In the recollection of one American officer, the sleep-deprived men "knew little of the sounds, smells, noises," of the jungle, "and they knew little of enemy night tactics. The fear of the unknown seized the imagination of these tired men. The phosphorescence of the rotted wood and fox fire became enemy signals used to make future victims. The miasmic odor of the steaming jungle became Japanese-sprayed poison gas." Ceded a near-complete freedom of movement, the Japanese roamed the area, sniping, harassing, tossing grenades, throwing rocks, probing and infiltrating the shaky American lines. Enemy soldiers whistled and shrieked, made bird noises, beat ivory sticks together, set off firecrackers, cried out murderous threats in English, even hollered company code words and the names of real commanders. "The screams are indescribable," PFC Salvatore LaMagna shuddered. To make matters worse, the area teemed with land crabs, whose every movement seemed to indicate an approaching

Japanese predator. "You'd be surprised how noisy a land crab can be when it's pitch black," Private Larry Buckland commented.

The eerie, frightening voices, combined with the creeping land crabs and the alien jungle environment, completely psyched out the passive Americans. Some simply left their foxholes and ran away at the first hint of danger. Few got any semblance of proper sleep. Their exhaustion fed both their fear and their delusions. Hypercharged, imaginative rumors swept through the ranks. Phantom-like Japanese soldiers, supposedly clad in ninja-style robes, were moving through the night with the certainty of ghosts. They were armed with special hooks and ropes designed to drag live Americans from their holes to be gutted like fish or tortured to death. "Sometimes you can imagine you hear them in your sleep," one private wrote of the Japanese in a letter to his sister. Embarrassingly similar to terrified victims in a modern horror movie, many of the crazed soldiers gave in to their fears and lost all rationality. At a battalion aid station, a surgeon stood up in his hole and screamed, "This is the doctor! You people have to leave us alone! We need our rest!" Someone obligingly grabbed the physician and pulled him down into his foxhole before he attracted untold enemy attention. In spite of orders to the contrary, men blindly opened fire or threw grenades at any noise or shadow. "I was as bad as the rest and fired my rifle at something that I later decided was only a bunch of moss," a chagrined Sergeant Franklin Phelps later wrote. He was almost killed one night when a nearsighted rifleman in his platoon spotted him standing near his hole, raised his rifle, and screamed, "There's a Jap right out there." The man's buddy knocked his rifle down, "You fool, that's Sergeant Phelps."

In many instances, grenades struck branches or tree trunks, rolled back and wounded or killed the throwers or men in adjacent foxholes. Friendly fire shootings were rampant. Some of the men were so incapacitated and disoriented by their terror that they mistook their own foxhole mates for Japanese and stabbed them. "A four foot lizard falls into your hole, machetes are flying, next morning you find your buddy bleeding with an arm or leg hanging," PFC LaMagna commented. One man, while screaming at the top of his lungs, ran from foxhole to foxhole, apparently looking for Japanese. His witless comrades stabbed him each time he entered a hole. "Most casualties are from bullets, machetes, and knives," the division surgeon noted in his journal. What was obvious, but left unsaid by the doctor, was the near certainty that most of the casualties were caused by friendly hands. One medical survey of grenade wounds revealed that 50 percent came from US fragments.

PFC LaMagna shared a foxhole with a soldier who was so nervous he could hardly think straight. While LaMagna tried to catch some fitful sleep, the soldier heard land crabs skittering nearby, thought they were enemy soldiers, promptly armed several grenades and, for some reason, propped them on LaMagna's shoulders. LaMagna awakened, saw what was happening, disarmed the grenades and told the soldier to calm down and go to sleep while he stood watch. "About an hour later he stood up in our hole and yelled for the Japs to come on. I yanked him down, he kept on raving. I rapped him across the mouth with my .45 pistol and told him if he didn't stay put, I'd shoot him. That did it. He slumped down in our hole and slept." But the next night, when he shared a hole with someone else, he went completely berserk, grabbed a pistol, and fired wildly at anyone, including his foxhole buddy, whom he wounded in the knee and chest. When his comrades could not get him to cease and desist, they had no choice but to kill him.

The unhappy by-product of this mass hysteria was a disturbing profusion of neuropsychiatric or "war neurosis" casualties. Eventually the Army settled on the term "combat fatigue" to describe the range of mental, emotional, and physical exhaustion that incapacitated otherwise unscathed soldiers. A later generation termed it post-traumatic stress disorder. The symptoms of the worst cases were diverse, generally ranging from shaking or crying uncontrollably to depression to psychosomatic maladies to an inability to connect with reality. "Some have to be bound to keep from doing harm to themselves or others," Colonel McHenry, who witnessed many of the combat-fatigue cases, noted in his journal. "Some . . . are pitiful— shaken mentally and blabbering like infants." Captain Richard Saillant, an engineer company commander whose unit was working to improve the Munda Trail, saw many victims "come fumbling down the trail, usually sobbing or moaning and shaking like men with . . . palsy. Some of these have gone completely blank and have to be led along by the hand. Their eyes are empty of expression and their faces are loose and flabby like an idiot's. It's a heartrending spectacle." Colonel Franklin Hallam, the XIV Corps surgeon who treated many of the lost souls, estimated that "at least 50% . . . were the picture of utter exhaustion, face expressionless, knees sagging, body bent forward, arms slightly flexed and hanging loosely, hands with palms slightly cupped, marked coarse tremor of fingers . . . feet dragging, and an over-all appearance of apathy and physical exhaustion.

About 20% . . . were highly excited, crying, wringing their hands, mumbling incoherently, an expression of utter fright and fear, trembling all over, startled at the least sound or commotion." Only about 15 percent displayed true psychoneuroses or evidence of actual mental illnesses. Almost all these men had a previous history of mental problems. Everyone else had appeared mentally and physically fit before going into New Georgia. And yet that July, they fell victim by the dozens and then the hundreds, overwhelming aid stations and doctors who were trained to treat physical wounds. "They were real men, tired and overworked and short of supplies," Sergeant Phelps raved about the medics. "They did their best and didn't complain." With little understanding of the combat-fatigue problem, and few facilities in which to care for those with physical wounds, much less anyone else, the medics simply processed the afflicted and sent them to Guadalcanal. Hallam estimated that about twenty-five hundred soldiers were evacuated with combat fatigue, almost 80 percent of whom came from the 43rd Division (the 37th and 25th Divisions, once they later joined the battle as reinforcements, accounted for most of the rest). The 169th Infantry alone accounted for seven hundred cases.

In addition to poor physical conditioning, wrongheaded doctrine, and insufficient training, the main culprit for the near epidemic of combat fatigue cases in the 43rd was a paucity of good leadership. Colonel Hallam studied at least one thousand cases to determine the primary cause of evacuation. He discovered that, with telling frequency, when sergeants and officers became combat-fatigue casualties, large numbers of their men did as well. "This gave us the first tangible evidence that incompetent or questionable leadership in small units was an important causative factor." Far too many commanders were not real leaders. Some simply did not understand their responsibilities or had not earned the confidence of their people. Preoccupied with their own personal safety, ignorant of how to operate in the jungle, or perhaps just frightened into inertia, they allowed the understandable fear in their men to metastasize into mass panic and hysteria. "The junior officers or non-commissioned officers were the first to 'break,' and a needless sacrifice of manpower resulted from others becoming 'panicked' at the realization that their leaders were no longer able to direct or lead them," Hallam reported. In one company alone, when a lieutenant, five sergeants, and four corporals were evacuated, thirty-six privates soon joined them in a veritable mass collapse of the unit.[5]

The failure of this junior-level leadership reflected badly on their seniors. This was especially true when the loss of so much manpower to combat fatigue, plus hundreds of regular battle casualties, sapped the strength of the 43rd and, in the face of determined Japanese resistance, stalemated the drive for Munda. The colonel of the 169th and one of his battalion commanders both lost their jobs. As a 1908 graduate of West Point—a year ahead of Eichelberger, Harding, and Patton—General Hester had served as an infantry officer for more than three decades, but with limited command and combat experience. Respected by his peers for his polite demeanor and dedication to duty, he nonetheless struggled to make a positive impact on the division's junior leaders. Howard Brown, a young lieutenant, once described him as "an aloof, superannuated officer who needed to retire long before he got command of the division." Another young commander thought of Hester as "by no means an efficient officer for combat." Two months shy of his fifty-seventh birthday, Hester was suffering from an ulcer so acute that, in hopes of calming his stomach, he was eating baby food. The heat and privation of the jungle only added to his physical misery. The jumbled command and staffing apparatus quickly multiplied his problems. From a threadbare headquarters on Rendova, he and his staff attempted to manage the logistics, administration, and planning of a staff-level headquarters while fighting a brutal division level battle. Even as the division hemorrhaged men from combat fatigue and battle, Hester was forced to divert hundreds of soldiers to unload and haul supplies over three miles, from Zanana Beach to the front. This job alone absorbed better than three companies per regiment, roughly one-quarter of its authorized combat strength. In hopes of alleviating this serious problem, Hester ordered the 172nd to break off its attack and establish another beachhead about a mile to the southwest at Laena, closer to Munda. Although the 172nd succeeded, and cleared the way for a battalion from the division's remaining infantry regiment, the 103rd, to arrive on July 14, the order had the unfortunate effect of diluting Hester's combat power, further stymying the push for Munda. Regardless of the reason, Hester seemed unable to salvage the situation, regain enough momentum to take the airfield and eliminate Japanese resistance.

Monitoring the situation from Guadalcanal, General Harmon worried that continuation of the dysfunctional command arrangement would only worsen the pressure on Hester, which, in turn, might harden the inertia on New Georgia and tempt Admiral Turner to assume direct control of the ground battle. Harmon believed that Major General Griswold, Patch's successor as commander of XIV Corps, should be ordered to New Georgia, along with his staff, and assume control over the entire land battle as head of the New Georgia Occupation Force, thus allowing Hester to focus entirely on his own division. Turner opposed this idea. In his opinion, the introduction of Griswold would somehow comprise a "severe blow to morale." An impatient Harmon promptly hopped on a plane, flew to Halsey's headquarters at New Caledonia, and personally persuaded the admiral to send in Griswold.

The XIV Corps commander had grown up on a cattle ranch in Nevada. He had once attended the University of Nevada, Reno before securing an appointment to the US Military Academy, from which he graduated as an infantry officer in 1910. During World War I, he had fought at Argonne Forest. Between the wars, he had served in a number of intellectually challenging jobs, including as an instructor of tactics at West Point, a student at the Army War College, and a key staffer for the Infantry School at Fort Benning. Mild-mannered, humble, given to introspection, Griswold was one of the Army's leading thinkers on land warfare. "Today is my 33d anniversary of my graduation from West Point," he wrote in his diary on June 15. "Thirty-three years ago I was very confident. I thought then I knew it all. Now I'm not sure of what I know of this military game, so vastly complicated."

When Griswold arrived on New Georgia, he inspected the lines along the Munda Trail and gathered all the information he could on the condition of the 43rd. He came away troubled by what he saw. "Many wounded coming back," he confided to his diary on July 12. "Losses heavy. Men look all fagged out. Bewildered look of horror on many faces. Troops impress me as not having been mentally prepared or well trained." In a letter to Lieutenant General McNair, he opined that "a man who is beside himself with fear is pathetic and dreadful to see, and the thing is like an infectious disease. Officers are not immune." Griswold immediately radioed Harmon. "From an observer point of view things are going badly. Four-three (43) Division about to fold up. My opinion is they will never take Munda." He urged Harmon to arrange for the balance of the 25th and 37th Divisions to reinforce the 43rd. When Harmon passed on this request to Halsey, the admiral agreed straightaway. Plus, he formally invested full control of the land battle to Griswold.

The XIV Corps commander halted operations while he absorbed reinforcements and reorganized his command for a renewed offensive. Though he liked Hester and appreciated the difficulties he faced, he soon formed the opinion that he was out of his depth as a division commander in combat. "I am afraid Hester is too nice for a battle soldier. He is sick and all in." Griswold relieved him, officially for physical incapacity, but in reality for ineffectiveness. Harmon felt badly for Hester, but he concurred. "Most of the blame is mine for not seeing early enough that a Corps Cmdr and staff were *necessary*," a reflective Harmon wrote honestly to a friend. Hester went home to a training command and retired soon after the war ended. To replace Hester, Harmon sent Major General Hodge, a diminutive, occasionally abrasive, tough-minded man who had served as Collins's assistant division commander on Guadalcanal. Hodge's appointment was temporary, only for the New Georgia campaign, because he had recently received command of the Americal Division.[6]

★

Even as fighting continued to rage along the Munda Trail, Griswold cobbled together a new corps-level front, and then paused to rest and reorganize. The 43rd Division, led by the 103rd and 172nd Infantry Regiments, anchored the left part of the line. The battered 169th went into reserve. On the right were elements of the 37th Division's 145th and 148th Infantry Regiments, plus Marine Raiders. In response to an order from Harmon to reinforce the XIV Corps front, General Collins, the commander of the 25th Infantry Division, sent his 161st Infantry Regiment. Griswold sandwiched the 161st between the 145th and the 148th. Unlike Eichelberger at Buna, Griswold enjoyed tremendous artillery resources, an indicator of America's growing firepower advantage over Japan. Each infantry regiment was supported by a battalion of 105-millimeter howitzers, each division by a battalion of 155-millimeter pieces, plus corps artillery assets, and the Marine 9th Defense Battalion. "The maximum rate of fire was limited to one round every 15 seconds, for accuracy by the gun crews," wrote Brigadier General Harold Barker, the 43rd Division's artillery commander. Naval gunfire and air strikes were also available though problematic because of inadequate coordination and questionable accuracy.

With two full divisions in place, Griswold's staff reorganized the logistical pipeline. They located supply dumps on outlying islands—Barabuni for the 37th and Kokorana for the 43rd. Freight was loaded aboard landing craft and shuttled to Laiana, where it was unloaded and prepared for movement to the front. Bulldozer-equipped engineers succeeded in cutting vehicle-worthy trails to the rear areas of the infantry regiments. Medical facilities stabilized. The 17th Field Hospital relocated from Guadalcanal to Rendova and established a 250-bed hospital. Colonel Hallam asked the Navy to provide a larger medical presence aboard LSTs (landing ship, tanks) and other landing craft to foster better casualty evacuation. His sea-service colleagues were only too happy to comply. Collecting points and clearing companies were located closer to the front lines, where they could do the most good in emergencies.

Learning from hard experience, commanders and medics began to deal with the combat-fatigue problem head-on. Instead of simply evacuating anyone who showed symptoms, the doctors now distinguished between bona fide psychoneurotic mental issues and combat exhaustion. The vast majority of cases, probably as much as 80 percent, fit the latter category. "With proper handling, approximately 75 to 80% of these individuals may be returned to duty," Hallam estimated. "To sympathize with or ridicule any of these individuals is definitely inadvisable. The more that can be accomplished in assisting these individuals to be rehabilitated, the more likely they will prove to be better soldiers after they are salvaged." Under Hallam's supervision, medics established rest camps on the barrier islands where exhausted, haunted men could eat a decent meal, sleep on a bed or a cot, change into clean clothes and decompress before transitioning back to their units. The process eased some of the stigma traditionally associated with "cracking up," as many of the soldiers referred to combat fatigue. A standing order in the 37th Division mandated the term "exhaustion" for all cases rather than "psychoneurosis." The division surgeon and the division psychiatrist established clear parameters for diagnosis as well as an extensive examination process to distinguish between combat fatigue and actual neurosis cases. Permanent evacuations now became the exception rather than the rule. "We did salvage many men who were returned to their units, after two or three days rest, a bath and an opportunity to get their feet on the ground," commented Lieutenant Colonel Hobart Mikesell, the division surgeon. "Many of them became useful men in their units." Mikesell and other doctors found that permanently separating a soldier from his unit—and thus his buddies—only made his case worse. "I felt that if they got out of the Division and went back as far as a Field or Station Hospital, they were lost to us." He focused instead on rehabilitating them within the environment of their own division.

General Griswold envisioned a corps-wide offensive to take Munda.

General Sasaki hoped to launch a counterthrust of his own, but the growing American presence on New Georgia, combined with a weakening Japanese grasp of the sea and air, and the fact that he had only about thirty-five hundred soldiers left, forced him to embrace a largely defensive battle. A powerful network of coral and coconut-log pillboxes, numbering well into the hundreds, and fanned out along an oval-shaped perimeter that anchored against the sea, comprised his most potent asset. In the recollection of one Army observer, the pillboxes were "nearly impregnable structures. Ten to twelve feet square, these miniature forts had been formed of three and four layers of logs, banked and covered with as much as six to eight feet of weathered coral. Extending two or three feet above ground but dug ten feet deep, the pillboxes were compartmented by a firing platform and a deeper base for protection against grenades and direct shelling." The dense jungle foliage and the Japanese flair for concealment made them very difficult to see. "They were skillfully camouflaged and the firing slits were very narrow," Lieutenant Colonel Francis McAlister, a Marine observer, wrote. "Against the dark background of the interior plus the fact that the Japanese used a flashless powder made them invisible even after fire was opened." The Japanese even made some of them look like innocuous coconut piles. Rectangular trench systems and machine-gun-laden dugouts protected each pillbox. Crawl trenches, amounting almost to tunnels, allowed Japanese soldiers to maneuver with reasonable protective cover. Front-line soldiers came to believe that smell was a more useful sense than sight to locate the enemy fortifications. "It is true," PFC Arthur Winkle, a machine gunner in the 148th Infantry, wrote home. "You can *smell* a Jap long before you can see him. Something they take."[7]

On July 25, Griswold opened his offensive with a massive bombardment of the Japanese perimeter. At 0609, seven destroyers under Commander Arleigh Burke opened fire on the Lambeti Plantation in the heart of the Japanese perimeter. Burke's ships hurled four thousand five-inch shells, enough to saturate every one hundred yards with seventy shells. Thirty minutes later, 254 bombers and fighters dumped more than half a million pounds of fragmentation and high-explosive bombs on the Japanese. Soon thereafter, artillerymen piled on with 2,150 105-millimeter howitzer shells and 1,182 155-millimeter rounds. An untold number of mortar shells added to the explosive mix. "Are they intending to smash Munda with naval and artillery shelling?" one Japanese diarist asked himself. On the receiving end of this massive pummeling, he and thousands of others simply hun-

kered down inside their stuffy, hot fortifications and endured the maelstrom. An especially heavy concentration of shells exploded just outside of
Lieutenant Oura's dugout. "It is really more than I can bear," he later scribbled in a thoughtful journal entry. "The men were really scared and they
all ran into my dugout. I had to take them out and mercilessly assign them
to other dugouts." The American firepower was so overwhelming that he
compared his circumstance to a "baby's neck in the hands of an adult.
Where have our Air Forces and battleships gone? Are we to lose? We are
standing with rifle and bayonets to meet the enemy's aircraft, battleships,
and medium [artillery]. To be told to win is absolutely beyond reason. The
Japanese Army is still depending on the hand-to-hand fighting of the Meiji
Era while the enemy is using highly developed scientific weapons. If I die,
it will be a spiteful death. My most regretful thought is my grudge towards
the forces in the rear and my increasing hatred toward the operational
staff."

The massive bombardment battered the Japanese and eroded their morale, but it did not come anywhere near destroying the many layers of
pillboxes—an example, among many to follow, that firepower, though potent, was not enough to overcome determined Japanese resistance. This job
could be done only by good tactics, incredible courage, and good coordination. As Griswold's men attacked all along the front, they favored an incremental process to gain ground. Thick coils of jungle limited visibility to
such an extent as to mandate extensive reconnaissance. "The route of advance led into rain forest and jungle that covered a mass of two hundred
foot hills whose summits were usually within two hundred yards of each
other," the Army's campaign historian wrote. "All intervening corridors
were irregular, unpatterned, and confusing."

Commanders first sent out four or five men to locate Japanese positions.
Then they followed with more reconnaissance by a platoon-sized force.
"This often uncovered a portion of the center of resistance but not all of it,"
a 37th Division report explained. "Normally the complete extent of the resistance was not determined until the actual attack developed it." Maps were
inaccurate or incomplete. Hills usually comprised the only distinguishing
terrain features. Before the main body of attackers went forward, artillery
and mortars pounded the routes of advance. Because of the map and terrain
problems, observers had great difficulty calling down accurate fire, thus
enhancing the chances of self-inflicted losses. Throughout the entire campaign, infantry commanders lived in abject fear of friendly ordnance.

By now the Japanese had learned to hold their fire until the Americans were practically right on top of them, sometimes as close as three yards, prompting sharp, close-quarters engagements "by a platoon or company which delivered assault fire to cover close in double or single envelopment by riflemen with grenades," an American commander recalled. Light tanks from the 9th Defense Battalion supported the advance, pouring 37-millimeter fire into any apertures that the crewmen and their accompanying infantry managed to spot. For the first time in the Pacific War, the Americans made extensive use of flamethrowers. When filled to capacity with napalm-infused gasoline, the dual-tank weapon weighed sixty-five pounds. The nozzle could shoot jets of flame to a maximum distance of fifty yards. Operators worked in pairs and coordinated closely with riflemen. For protection against inevitable leaks of the odorous fuel, the men wore gloves. In hopes of camouflaging themselves, many smeared mud on their faces and covered their watches with sheets of black tape. As riflemen disgorged clip after clip on the pillbox apertures, the operators crawled on their bellies to a range of ten or twenty yards, propped up on their knees, and unleashed their long sheets of flame, first to burn away protective foliage and then to target the apertures themselves. The temperature of the fire was as high as twenty-three hundred degrees Fahrenheit.

Lieutenant James Olds, the XIV Corps chemical warfare officer, helped organize the operators into teams and even carried tanks on his own back, contributing to the destruction of thirty bunkers over a five-day period. "The flames leaped through the narrow, eight-inch gun port like a gigantic spark," he wrote of one assault in the 43rd Division's sector. "The job was over in a matter of seconds. There was no outcry, no sound. The sons of Heaven were done for." But the "job" as Olds termed it, was dangerous and exacting, requiring perilous close-quarters encounters and minute coordination at the sharpest end of combat. There were never enough operators to meet the extensive demand, and the layers of interlocking pillboxes were seemingly endless. On a single six-hundred-yard front, the 103rd Infantry identified seventy-four pillboxes. Even when the GIs cleared bunkers, enemy soldiers often reoccupied them. "Intercommunicating tunnels . . . made possible a shifting of strength to meet each assault," wrote Lieutenant Colonel Russell Ramsey, the operations officer of the 37th Division. "It permitted the reoccupation of pillboxes which we had taken but from which we had retired because of inability . . . to occupy the entire resistance area. Unless we were able to accomplish the complete reduction of a center of resistance before nightfall, or to hold a portion during the night at great risk and some cost, the whole job had to be done over again the next day." The difficulty of permanently securing the bunkers, combined with the ubiquity of dense, moldy green jungle, caused regiments to advance unevenly, leaving flanks wide-open, prone to enemy infiltration and local counterattacks. "They would yell like demons sometimes, and other times would be very silent," Sergeant Phelps wrote of the enemy counterpunches. "Several times we hoped they had given up but they'd come back harder than ever." They either fought to the death or withdrew only after they had inflicted damage or consternation upon the Yanks. From their bunkers, the Imperial Army soldiers yelled such pleasantries as "American soldier will die tonight!" or "American cowards!" The GIs responded with an ever popular epithet, "Tōjō eats shit!"

American commanders often had no idea of the location of neighboring units. For several days on Griswold's right flank, the 148th and 161st Infantry Regiments were completely out of touch with each other, in part because Colonel Stuart Baxter, the commander of the 148th, aggressively bulled his regiment forward without keeping contact with the 161st on his left, exposing the latter unit to costly Japanese infiltration. His boss, Major General Robert Beightler, was the only National Guardsman to maintain command of a division in theater. Well regarded by Griswold as a reliable, ethical officer, Beightler became so incensed at Baxter's lone-wolf act that he finally radioed him a sharply worded order to make contact immediately. "At no time have you been in contact on your left although you have repeatedly assured me that this was accomplished. Without fail this must be done. A confirmation of a thorough understanding of this order is directed." Baxter promptly complied, but even so, Beightler felt that his subordinate was attempting "to become the hero for the operation," and never trusted him again. The gap in units evoked uncertainty and occasional resentment among lower-ranking soldiers as well. "It was incomprehensible that a full-strength regiment could be milling around in an area of less than a mile square for three days without finding our flank," sniffed Lieutenant Radike, a sharp-tongued platoon leader in the 161st Infantry.

For obvious reasons, heavy fighting raged for control of any high ground. In one typical instance, soldiers from the 172nd Infantry hurled themselves at Morrison-Johnson Hill, a two-hundred-foot-high clump of jungle, honeycombed with menacing pillboxes. Though covered by several of his men, Lieutenant Robert Scott, a young platoon leader, almost single-handedly took the lead in personally assaulting bunker after bunker, mainly with grenades. At one point, an enemy bullet destroyed his carbine. He found another one and resumed his near-maniacal attack. "The platoon leader, covered by riflemen, proceeded to each successive pill-box on the north slope of the hill, throwing one or two hand grenades into each one," Scott later wrote in a third-person account. "There were twenty-eight dead Japs counted on the hill and no prisoners were taken." In Scott's opinion, the capture of the hill proved that "three or four aggressive men within an enemy fortified position can fix most of the enemy within their emplacements." For his valor, he received the Medal of Honor.

Nine battalions of US artillery were in action now. Some of these guns pounded Bibilo Hill, a neck of high ground immediately northwest of the Munda airfield, with such force that, in the recollection of one commander, "Japs, pillboxes, and guns were flying . . . as much as 15 feet in the air. A lot of them, blown from their holes, would run around in little circles like stunned chickens, to be laid like grass by . . . machine guns."

The fighting raged on with this kind of routine ferocity. The Americans advanced inexorably at a steady, deliberate rate of about eight hundred yards per day. "Having to fight every foot of the way," the 37th Division journal reported with cryptic anguish. Brandishing tommy guns and grenades, small groups of Americans assaulted from hole to hole, pillbox to pillbox, trench line to trench line. Men subsisted on cold C rations and D ration chocolate bars. Some units were cut off and had to be resupplied by air. Others were fortunate to dine on hot soup manhandled forward by sweating cooks. Endurance was stretched to the limit. "Honest and sincere prayers were on the lips of everyone and I cannot deny the fact that I was on the verge of giving up, but somehow just couldn't leave the boys," Captain Robert Howard, a company commander in the 145th, confided to his journal. An impatient Griswold told his own diary. "Fighting is bitter indeed. We are paying a price for every foot of ground taken. The enemy fights until he dies." Harmon told Halsey, "We have a bear by the tail—or perhaps a fighting badger in his hole."

On the Japanese side, companies of 170 men were down to fewer than seventy. The tiny, makeshift hospital facilities were inundated with more wounded soldiers than doctors could treat. Malaria, diarrhea, beriberi, and dengue fever were rife. The concussion of so many shells caused men to stutter uncontrollably and even intruded on the ability of some to speak at all. Burial parties dug unmarked graves with monotonous frequency. Before committing the remains to New Georgia's ruthless soil, they retrieved limbs or locks of hair or fingernails, and burned them in hopes of sending the ashes to family members back home in Japan. Soon the landscape was honeycombed with mangled Japanese bodies. "For a long time the cadavers sprawled all over the hills and streams, stinking and polluting our water," an American platoon leader wrote to one of his old college professors. "Every time I take a drink, I can't help thinking it is Jap juice." When the Americans came upon the maggot-infested bodies, they treated them with brusque, almost predatory disrespect. "Americans bulldozed a lot of them into the sea, or dug a big hole and dumped them in it," recalled Bennett, a New Georgian scout. Staff Sergeant Phelps's unit once counted 102 enemy bodies in front of their positions. The dogfaces often descended upon them like a pack of locusts. "The boys collected a lot of souvenirs," he wrote. "It amounts to almost a mania with some fellows. I've heard that the Japs can't understand why we fight. The Japs of course fight for Tojo and the Emperor, the Germans fight for Hitler. But the Americans of all things seem to fight for 'Souvenirs.'" In one instance, rather than risk destroying a samurai sword by using a grenade to kill a Japanese officer in a bunker, a soldier grabbed a pistol, leaped into the bunker, swiped the sword, and shot the enemy officer. A common sardonic joke claimed that when one GI was about to pitch a grenade into a bunker to kill a Japanese soldier, the man's buddy admonished him to eschew using the grenade: "Shoot him. He's got a watch on."

Unlike on Guadalcanal, food was available in ample quantity for the Japanese, but few had much of an appetite anymore. Standing orders for each soldier mandated killing ten Americans in exchange for his own life.[8]

Medics followed in the wake of the American advance, evacuating casualties along the narrow trails, back to the beaches. More than half the wounded were removed on litters; the rest were ambulatory. The medics cleaned and bandaged wounds, cut away necrotic tissue, and administered medicine. In many cases, they set broken bones and created plaster casts right on the spot. "Plaster was always applied over cleaned, treated, and dressed wounds," wrote Major John Aldes, an orthopedic surgeon. The paucity of Japanese artillery and the close-quarters fighting meant that machine-gun and rifle bullets inflicted about 74 percent of the wounds. Fragmentation wounds from small-caliber artillery pieces and knee mortars accounted for nearly all others. Among the battle injuries, 30 percent were hit in the legs and 35 percent in the arms. Head wounds accounted for 15 percent and neck wounds 8 percent. Chest and abdomen wounds were rare, 2 and 1 percent, respectively. Almost all back and buttocks injuries were caused by bomb and mortar-shell blasts, usually while men lay prone under cover. The medics treated more than four thousand wounded soldiers and Marines in the course of the fighting. Almost three-quarters came from the 37th and 43rd Divisions. Infantrymen comprised about 75 percent of the wounded.

The evacuation route was anything but secure. Japanese patrols sometimes attacked the columns and set upon the helpless, wounded patients. Phelps saw the aftermath of one such ambush. "Those little Jap demons came in during the dark and actually butchered those defenseless unarmed little patients." The mutilated corpses were black with decay, swollen to almost twice their normal size. Only a few escaped, one of whom played dead as the Japanese stabbed him with bayonets. They had dragged one wounded officer several hundred yards away, broken his legs, and inflicted more than two hundred stab wounds before he lost consciousness and died. "Strange creatures these fanatic little men. Sometimes they will stab a dead man as much as fifty times, mutilating him beyond all recognition. It isn't hard to acquire an undying hatred for such a race."

Americans died, usually in ones and twos, sometimes by the half dozen or more amid the endless clovers of deadly pillboxes. Graves-registration units interred them in a temporary cemetery near the beach. "We who had never handled the dead before found it really tough," noted the unit history of the 109th Quartermaster Registration Platoon of burying the many fallen soldiers and Marines. Lieutenant Radike lost his best squad leader and his company commander in the space of a day. He blamed their deaths on the inability of senior officers in different regiments to coordinate their movements effectively. "I had trouble holding the tears back. What a cost for a stupid move into impenetrable jungle." Among the dead was Captain Paul Mellichamp, formerly an aide to General Collins. Mellichamp was killed by a sniper after grabbing a radio from a dead operator and directing witheringly effective 81-millimeter mortar fire, all in the midst of heavy enemy return fire. After learning of Mellichamp's death, Collins, who by now was on the ground in New Georgia, immediately wrote to his widow and shared details of how her husband had been killed. "I had the greatest respect for his character, his personality and his soldierly qualities. His loss has affected me more deeply than that of any other in the division thus far and I still have an empty feeling every time I think we shall not see him again." She later wrote back to convey her appreciation for the general's consolation. "I'm so glad you told me something of the way he was killed. When I'm alone and can do nothing but think, it is impossible to keep questions from entering my head." Mellichamp received the Distinguished Service Cross.[9]

After nine straight days of vicious combat, the unrelenting violence of the American offensive—supported now by a force of ten light tanks from three separate Marine defense battalions—was simply too much for the isolated Japanese garrison. On August 5, the remnants of Japanese resistance collapsed. The Americans reached the beach and captured the airfield. "I shall never forget the thrill of that first view of Munda where we could count approximately two dozen Jap planes which would never fly again," one of the victors later wrote. Brigadier General Leonard Wing, assistant division commander of the 43rd, phoned General Hodge and reported, "Munda is yours at 1410 today." An ebullient Griswold scrawled in his diary, *"We took Munda!"* He cabled Halsey, "Our troops today wrested Munda from the Japs and present it to you . . . as the sole owner." Infantrymen roamed the runways and warily cleared tunnels and bunkers, often more on the lookout for souvenirs than enemy soldiers. They found rice bags, clothing, blankets, and occupation currency. At the Lambeti Plantation, they discovered broken-down American-made trucks, cases of food, candy, cigarettes, tea, fish, dress uniforms, and even white dinner jackets, as if the Japanese had been planning to host a banquet. An American damage-assessment team counted 16,778 destroyed trees throughout the plantation. Around the Munda perimeter, more than 1,060 acres of jungle had been laid waste. Local gardens had been stripped bare by soldiers on both sides or destroyed by shellfire. About half of New Georgian homes were in ruins. General Sasaki had managed to evacuate some of his force, mainly by barge, to the neighboring islands of Kolombangara, Baanga, Arundel, and Vila. Probably the equivalent of about three depleted battalions got away.

The fighting was not over, though. Even with the key objective of the campaign in their hands, it took two more months of operations, euphemistically dubbed "the cleanup" by American commanders, to secure the New Georgia group and permanently eject the Japanese from the central Solomons. The half-strength 169th Infantry, back in action since July 31, invaded Baanga and, assisted by a battalion from the 172nd, took it by August 21. Other troops from the 172nd landed at Arundel on August 27 and needed almost a month to secure it. Reinforced by his 27th Infantry Regiment, Collins pushed north and, alongside troops from the 145th Infantry, cleared out the rest of New Georgia. This unglamorous battle "consumed 20 days, mostly spent in a struggle with mud, jungle, and swamps," according to the theater historian. Collins later described the terrain as "the densest jungle I have yet seen. Incessant rains made road building almost impossible and prevented the emplacement of much artillery." When he asked a soldier about the depth of a nearby swamp, the man replied, "Well, I'll tell you, General. If you slip, you'll go right up to your asshole." Admiral Halsey decided to bypass Kolombangara in favor of a flanking invasion at Vella Lavella. Collins's 35th Infantry Regiment, alongside troops from the 3rd New Zealand Division, captured the island after four weeks of fighting. With Kolombangara bypassed and enveloped, the Japanese decided to pull the plug on the central Solomons. Similar to Guadalcanal, they managed to slip destroyers into Kolombangara and evacuate ninety-four hundred survivors to Bougainville. All the ground fighting was over by early October. A haunted weariness permeated the haggard survivors. "Their eyes were sunk into their sockets and long beards covered their faces," Staff Sergeant John Timmons later wrote of his men. "Their bodies were bent over in a stoop and their clothes were literally hanging on their bones. I never want to see that again!"

Griswold's XIV Corps claimed that 2,483 Japanese troops had been killed in about three months of fighting. The Army's campaign historian put the number at 2,750. In naval and air battles, the Imperial Navy probably suffered between two thousand and three thousand casualties. The US Army lost 972 dead and another 23 missing in action. Not surprisingly, the 43rd suffered the most heavily, with 538 dead; the 37th accounted for 220, and the 25th another 141. All three divisions would need extensive rest and rehabilitation before they were ready for action again. Marine Corps losses totaled 192 killed and 534 wounded.

The operation solidified Griswold as a go-to corps commander and Halsey as an effective theater commander, one who had established a positive, productive relationship with the alpha male of the South Pacific, MacArthur. At the division level, Hodge returned to American and Wing took over the 43rd. Beightler settled in as commanding general of the 37th. Griswold thought of him as perhaps his most reliable subordinate. Collins, effective again in spite of seeing parts of his division parceled out to the control of other commanders, entered a new phase of his career. Even before

Toenails, the ever ambitious general had been exploring the possibility of a transfer to the European theater. He had come to believe that airpower would be the dominant factor in the Pacific War. "The Navy and the ground forces of the Army ought to admit this at once," he had written to General Marshall after the Guadalcanal campaign. "With real airpower, based on these unsinkable islands, we should be able to cripple the powers of Japanese resistance in a reasonably short period of time." Since the war against Germany would undoubtedly require larger ground forces, with more available corps commands, Collins saw this as the place to be. His relationship with Griswold, never particularly close, soured after the corps commander chewed Collins out for the poor appearance of his men. "I tried to explain to him that it was due to the conditions that they were operating under," Collins later said. Griswold understood the terrible conditions as well as anyone, but he saw the Tropic Lightning soldier's mangy appearance as evidence of an undisciplined, dissatisfied division. "Collins is brave, brilliant, aggressive, and has many fine qualities, but he definitely does not have a happy command," Griswold opined in a confidential letter to Lieutenant General McNair. "He is unduly professionally ambitious, professionally selfish as to the work of subordinates, and is without doubt the most egotistical officer I have ever come in contact with. I definitely do not consider him big enough caliber for a Corps Commander, though having learned and being able to discount his personality, I do like him as a good fighting man and as a Division commander." When Harmon afforded Collins the opportunity to spend Christmas at home in Washington, an offer tantamount to a transfer to Europe, Collins leaped at the opportunity. He even packed and left without saying goodbye to his staff, much less his soldiers. Griswold was only too happy to let him go. Collins's successful combat experience was attractive to Eisenhower and Lieutenant General Omar Bradley, his ranking American ground commander for the coming invasion of Normandy. They put him in charge of VII Corps, a post he held for the rest of the war.

The capture of the New Georgia group provided air and naval bases from which the Allies could now push on to Bougainville, thus further progressing the Cartwheel plan to envelop Rabaul. Though the Army had learned many lessons about jungle fighting, combat fatigue, and combined arms the hard way in New Georgia, Toenails demonstrated a burgeoning American maturity in amphibious operations and joint service planning. Moreover, the Japanese had taken yet another backward step in the direction of their home islands.[10]

11

Fighting Two Battles

The same Joint Chiefs Cartwheel directive that unleashed Halsey's New Georgia campaign also mandated the seizure through amphibious and airborne landings of New Guinea's Markham River Valley and Huon Peninsula by MacArthur's forces. Located about one hundred miles northwest of Gona, the Huon and the Markham Valley offered bases from which to continue the relentless advance along New Guinea's north coast and, as MacArthur's strategic concept, known as the Elkton plan, stipulated, begin to envelop Rabaul from the west. For the bombastic SWPA commander, the Huon represented just one of many steps necessary to make his way across the world's second largest island so that he could eventually return to the Philippines. "The immediate objective was the seizure of airfields . . . from which to whittle down the enemy's strength and at the same time provide cover for Allied assaults," he later wrote.

His plans were materially aided by the burgeoning potency of Kenney's 5th Air Force. Over a three-day period in early March, his aviators had savaged Japanese reinforcement convoys in the Bismarck Sea, sinking eight troop transports, four destroyers, and thirty thousand tons of supplies. The sinkings cost the lives of about three thousand Japanese soldiers from the Imperial Army's 51st Division. Many of the thirty-nine hundred survivors were combat-ineffective, separated from their units and their chain of command, or wounded or simply too exhausted to do General Adachi's 18th Army much good. From this point forward, the Japanese were forced to rely on submarines to resupply their New Guinea forces, a totally inadequate practice that could not even hope to satisfy the logistical needs of the 18th Army.

Kenney followed up this coup with another one in August, when his bombers and fighters launched a series of devastating raids on Japanese airfields at Wewak and, in a scenario reminiscent of what had happened to MacArthur's air forces at Clark Field in the Philippines, destroyed dozens

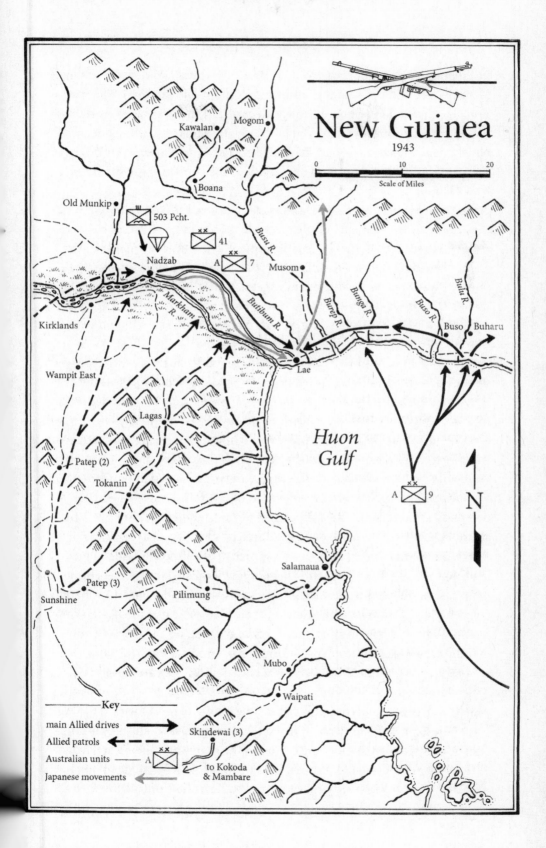

New Guinea
1943

0   10   20

Scale of Miles

Kawalan

Mogom

Boana

Old Munkip

503 Pcht.

41

Busu R.

Musom

A   7

Nadzab

Markham R.

Butibum R.

Burep R.

Bunga R.

Buso R.

Bulu R.

Buso   Buharu

Kirklands

Lae

Wampit East

Lagas

**Huon
Gulf**

Patep (2)

Tokanin

A   9

N

Patep (3)

Pilimung

Salamaua

Sunshine

Mubo

Waipati

Key

main Allied drives

Allied patrols

Australian units   A

Japanese movements

Skindewai (3)

to Kokoda
& Mambare

of Japanese aircraft on the ground. The Americans claimed 175 enemy planes destroyed; the Japanese admitted to about one hundred. The truth probably lay somewhere in between. Regardless, the Wewak raids represented a major Allied victory. The Japanese 4th Air Army, while not completely neutralized, no longer had the ability to prevent or even disrupt Allied amphibious and ground operations (quite similar to the situation at New Georgia).

In tandem with the June invasions at Kiriwana and Woodlark Islands, the Allies landed elements of the Australian 3rd Division, Papuan infantrymen, and the US Army's 162nd Infantry Regiment, 41st Infantry Division, at Nassau Bay, just a few miles southeast of the Huon Peninsula. Their purpose was to pressure the Japanese garrison at the coastal town of Salamaua to distract the enemy from MacArthur's main target, Lae (pronounced *lah-ey*), the second largest port on New Guinea behind only Port Moresby.

From early July to early September, the multinational Allied force steadily advanced northwest and closed in on Salamaua. "In these operations the 162nd encountered fighting on mountain tops, with pillboxes dug into steep hillsides, with little depth to the positions," wrote Colonel Russell Reeder, a War Department observer. "The Allies were favored with air superiority and adequate artillery support." The ridges, mountains, ravines, and gorges were coated with thick jungle, "a mass of under-growths of vines and grasses," in the recollection of Captain Frederic Gehring, a company commander. The suffocating terrain tended to "canalize," the advance—a term dubbed by one commander—along any traversable trails. "It is next to impossible to have flank security patrolling abreast of a moving column," an officer later wrote in an informational pamphlet. As usual, maps and aerial reconnaissance photographs were inadequate. Company commanders improvised by ordering their platoon leaders to sketch the terrain in front of their units. The sketches traveled up the chain of command to the battalion level, providing some semblance of the Salamaua area's geography for field-grade leaders and artillery forward observers.

In the absence of contiguous front lines, squad- or platoon-size patrols, usually moving in long columns, carried the weight of most forward movement. The Papuan infantrymen proved themselves incalculably important. "Their familiarity with the peculiarities of the jungle and their knowledge of this area made them of inestimable value to the Allied conduct of jungle warfare," Captain Gehring wrote admiringly. Recruited and led by Australian officers and NCOs, they routinely functioned as point men for the patrols. In some units, they were aided by specially trained scout dogs who worked closely with their GI handlers. "[They] gave warning of enemy presence within thirty yards under all conditions," one handler commented. "In some instances warnings were given from distances as great as three hundred yards." Other dogs carried messages between forward units and command posts, sometimes ranging as far as three miles through the jungle. Occasionally unlucky soldiers got lost or separated. The fortunate majority made their way back to friendly positions; the few others died in the unforgiving jungle or at the hands of the Japanese. "We searched through the dead soldier's belongings, and found a Bible, a diary and a photo of his mother," a Japanese sergeant wrote in his own diary after he and his squad killed a wayward American. "His mother is a woman with a very kind face. How grieved she would be if she were to hear that her son was killed. Nevertheless this is fate. For many years he has been our enemy, but now that he has become a departed soul, we forgave him for the resentment we held, and buried him."

On patrols, the GIs attempted to travel light, but their loads were nonetheless heavy. The average soldier wore a special jungle pack containing mess equipment, rations, cigarettes, one or two sixty-millimeter mortar rounds, belts of machine gun ammunition, a poncho, a shelter half, a raincoat, a foxhole cover, and a shaving kit. Each man carried a rifle, a machete, an entrenching tool, a cartridge belt with clips, a first aid kit, a pair of canteens, halazone tablets, and quinine or atabrine tablets to combat malaria. Even though the men wore soft fatigue caps, they still carried helmets hooked to the outside of their packs. The average load was about fifty-five pounds. To guard against chilly jungle nights, experienced infantrymen learned to carry an extra pair of wool socks, a jungle sweater, and gloves inside rubberized food containers.

As the forward patrols engaged in an ambush-and-counterambush, cat-and-mouse game of small-unit warfare with the Japanese, commanders found it nearly impossible to keep them adequately supported. "The complexity of supply, communication, and evacuation, which will always remain one of the most difficult problems of jungle warfare, greatly encumbered . . . activities," Captain Gehring later wrote. "Many of the 'niceties' of combat, such as clean clothing, shoes, and food, were excluded in order that indispensable supplies, such as ammunition and water, could be pushed forward." Rain-soaked watches and compasses wore out in a matter of days. Boots might last three or four weeks. Carrying parties often pilfered the most desirable items like canned fruit, coffee, and brand-name cigarettes. Supply officers learned to plan for an additional allowance of 30 percent of these goodies in order to have any hope of getting them to the forward dogfaces.

The Japanese remained almost entirely on the defensive. They dug into ridges and mountains and attempted to bleed the Allies into inertia. "The majority of the infantry combat was along steep, heavily wooded jungle mountains and knife edge ridges averaging from 1,000 to 1,800 ft. in height, the tops of which were thoroughly organized by the defending Japanese," wrote Colonel Archibald MacKechnie, the 162nd's forty-seven-year-old commander, who had once coached the football team at Mississippi State College (now university). Enemy counterattacks consisted mainly of desperate lunges by small, howling, disorganized, self-sacrificial bands. "Corpses lie in the fields as, one by one, by the Emperor's will, we become guardian deities of the fatherland," one Japanese soldier remarked profoundly in a diary entry.[1]

By early September, with the retreating Japanese still fixated on the struggle for Salamaua, General MacArthur was ready to launch his counterstroke. Sallying from Milne Bay, and supported by Kenney's 5th Air Force and the US Army's 2nd Engineer Special Brigade, the Australian 9th Division landed on September 4 at Bulu Plantation about twenty miles east of Lae. Meeting minimal opposition in the beach area, these forces began a relentless westward advance toward the port town. In hopes of further outflanking the Japanese and capturing a key base from which to stage future operations, MacArthur planned to use paratroopers to jump on Nadzab where a prewar grass runway airfield sat astride the Markham River, 18 miles inland from Lae. The job went to the 503rd Parachute Infantry Regiment, the first substantial Allied airborne force in theater. Composed of seventeen hundred paratroopers, the regiment had arrived in Australia late in 1942. In August, they had redeployed to a tent camp at Port Moresby and had begun training in earnest for the Nadzab drop. Thanks to the effectiveness of Allied reconnaissance flights, they knew much about their drop zones. Lieutenant Colonel Kenneth Kinsler, the commander, accompanied by key members of his staff, and his three battalion commanders even hopped aboard a B-17 on August 30 and made a personal reconnaissance of Nadzab. The intelligence section prepared detailed sand tables. Soldiers of all ranks studied them intently. According to the regiment's after-action report, last-minute preparations included "map reading and compass work. An examination was given each man to determine his physical fitness."

Excitement surged through the camp one day when General MacArthur paid a visit, interacting with the soldiers but always maintaining the veneer that made him such a compelling and yet distant figure to the troops. "General MacArthur is very publicity minded and always is accompanied by a corps of photographers," the 2nd Battalion's adjutant noted in the unit journal. Finally, on the morning of September 5, the troopers awoke early, breakfasted on pancakes washed down with coffee, and geared up. Long rows of C-47s sat along a pair of runways. Each airborne stick contained, on average, eighteen jumpers. Like many other leaders, Major Bill Britten, the commander of the 1st Battalion, reflected upon the vast responsibilities of a job in which, as he wrote in a final letter to his wife, "a single decision of a C.O. [commanding officer] meant life and death to an entire unit, and I pray that my decisions will be correct." On an adjacent strip, engines roared to life as fighters and bombers taxied into position, "like gigantic cats slinking behind a fence toward the kill," in the estimation of one trooper. As the sun rose steadily over the eastern horizon, the troopers stood in lines, stick by stick, preparing to board the planes. Once again, General MacArthur materialized, this time with General Kenney in tow. MacArthur circulated from stick to stick shaking hands, greeting the men. "Good luck," he told Lieutenant Colonel Jack Tolson, the 3rd Battalion commander. "Thank you, sir. We're ready," Tolson replied.

When MacArthur learned that Kenney planned to participate in the mission, not as a jumper but as an observer in a B-17 circling overhead, he insisted on tagging along. Kenney tried to dissuade him, to no avail, though he did insist that they ride in different B-17s. "I told him that I didn't like to tempt fate by putting too many eggs in one basket," Kenney later wrote. MacArthur agreed. In his memoirs, the SWPA commander claimed that his decision to go along was inspired by the mood of the 503rd troopers. "I inspected them and found, as was only natural, a sense of nervousness among the ranks. I did not want them to go through their first baptism of fire without such comfort as my presence might bring them." Having disengaged himself so thoroughly from the real fighting at Bataan and Buna, the SWPA commander was seemingly determined to demonstrate his courage anew.

Led by a plane called *Honeymoon Express*, the C-47s began to take off one by one. In all, ninety-six aircraft from the 54th Troop Carrier Wing participated. MacArthur lingered for a few moments to watch them take off and then boarded a B-17 named *Talisman*, piloted by Lieutenant Colonel Harry Hawthorn. Accompanied by Colonel LeGrande "Pick" Diller, his PR man, and Lieutenant Colonel Charles Morhouse, his physician, MacArthur shook hands with each crew member, and then settled in alongside the radio operator for the flight. He had confided in Kenney that getting shot was not his main worry. He was far more concerned about getting airsick "and disgracing myself in front of the kids" as the two middle-aged generals often referred to the young men under their command.

Against the backdrop of a clear tropical morning, the transport planes soon formed three abreast into six plane elements. They were escorted and covered by 206 bombers and fighters that had sallied from eight different fields around Papua New Guinea. Above them all, MacArthur's B-17 flew in formation alongside Kenney's and a third B-17, in what Kenney dubbed a "brass-hat flight." As he watched proudly, the armada approached Nadzab. "This was the picture," he later wrote to General Arnold. "Heading the parade at one thousand feet were six squadrons of B25 strafers with the eight .50 cal. guns in the nose and sixty frag bombs in each bomb bay; immediately behind and about five hundred feet above were six A-20s flying in pairs—three pairs abreast—to lay smoke as the last frag bomb exploded." Behind them were the airborne serials. Above them were fighters and a combination of B-24 and B-17 bombers. To conceal the landings from ground observation, the A-20s shrouded the area in smoke. The follow-up warplanes pasted the airfield and the surrounding drop zones with bombs and bullets. The C-47s descended to altitudes of five hundred feet and under. Aboard them, the paratroopers stood ready, checked their equipment, and, at the signal of each jumpmaster, prepared to jump. "The men are cold and quiet and the attitude is naturally enough and yet strangely too, that of an ordinary jump with full equipment," Lieutenant Jerry Riseley, the 2nd Battalion adjutant, later noted.

Following the lead of their jumpmasters, they disgorged from the planes. Within seconds, hundreds of them leaped into the skies above Nadzab. To Colonel Diller, the PR man riding aboard MacArthur's plane, they looked like "balloons of a carnival, dotted here and there with the colored chutes bearing special equipment." Clouds of smoke from the pre-jump bombing and strafing wafted past them. The jump unfolded with almost lightning quickness. In less than five minutes, seventeen hundred troopers jumped and landed. The only exception was a lone soldier who fainted before he could make it out the door of his plane. Two men fell to their deaths when their chutes failed to open. Another became ensnared in a tree and subsequently fell sixty feet and died. A few others suffered minor bumps and bruises. Otherwise the regiment made it onto the ground unscathed, against no opposition.

Heat, confusion, and tall, sharp-edged kunai grass proved to be more of an impediment than the Japanese. According to the 503rd's after-action report, the grass "was 6 to 10 feet high and so entangled that it was difficult to make much headway against it." Machete-wielding troopers hacked their way through it as best they could. Company C's historian remembered that the length of the grass tended to magnify the already stifling heat and restrict mobility. "One man could not break trail over fifteen minutes. Many of the men passed out from the heat." Visibility was of course limited. Like many other troopers, Private Louis Aiken landed alone, with no other friendly faces in sight. For all he knew, Japanese soldiers could be only a few feet away in the confusing maw. When he heard rustling in the grass, "I immediately prepared for hand to hand combat." Instead, he found himself literally face-to-face with a machine gunner from another company. "We peered at each other and burst out laughing."

Within a few hours, Major Britten's 1st Battalion consolidated control of the airfield while the other two battalions spread out, patrolled, and established a perimeter. Australian artillerymen from 2nd Battalion, 4th Field Artillery Regiment—trained to parachute by the 503rd—jumped in with two of their disassembled twenty-five-pound pieces. B-17s dropped fifteen tons of supplies to help sustain the regiment in the short term. The long-term plan was to fly in American engineers and a brigade from the Australian 7th Division. The next morning, C-47s began landing on the airfield. Over the course of four days, they carried in thirty-seven hundred troops along with jeeps and other equipment. At the height of the airlift, a C-47 landed every twenty-seven seconds. Also, a battalion of Australian engineers and a Papuan infantry battalion advanced from the west, crossed the Markham River, reached the airfield, and joined the effort to improve the airstrip. The paratroopers focused on patrolling. "The mission of the regiment was defensive," the unit after-action report stated. "Large patrols were sent out in all directions. Several encountered enemy patrols, but very little action was met as the Japs always withdrew."

The combination of the successful landings near Lae, the pressure on Salamaua, and the nearly bloodless seizure of a rapidly maturing airfield at Nadzab unhinged the Japanese position in the Markham Valley and, to a great extent, in the Huon Peninsula as a whole. General Adachi elected to withdraw as many troops as he could, abandoning both Lae and Salamaua by September 12. Exhausted Japanese survivors filtered west along the New Guinea coastline, away from the relentless Allied advance. "You won't find many smiling faces among the men in the ranks in New Guinea," one Japanese infantry officer wrote sadly. "They are always hungry; every other word has something to do with eating." A subsequent invasion, on September 22, near Finschhafen, at the eastern tip of the peninsula, by the Australian 20th Brigade and the American 2nd Engineer Special Brigade, only compromised the Japanese that much more, and led to complete defeat for them in Huon. Within ten days, the Allies captured Finschhafen. By that time, engineers had completed six functioning airstrips at Nadzab. With elements of three Australian divisions, plus engineers and Papuan infantry, in action, MacArthur ordered the withdrawal of the 503rd on September 17. In this sense, he utilized the airborne unit exactly in the role for which it was designed—rapid seizure of an objective instead of protracted infantry combat. In addition to the three jump fatalities, the regiment lost eight men killed and twenty-six wounded in patrol actions. The 162nd Infantry paid a far heavier price for its contribution to Allied victory at the Huon Peninsula. Over the course of nearly three months of fighting, Colonel MacKechnie's outfit lost 102 men killed, 447 wounded, and 242 sick. For the rest of 1943, the Australian divisions played the lead role for the Allies, ushering the Japanese relentlessly west.[2]

★

After visiting New Guinea and other tropical locales in the South Pacific, Lieutenant General Brehon Somervell, head of Army Service Forces, laconically wrote, "The Army is really fighting two battles: one against the enemy, and the other against the jungle." At times the second battle seemed even more challenging than the first. The vivid colors of the green jungle, the azure sea, and the kaleidoscopic wildlife did create scenes of breathtaking beauty. But beneath the seemingly idyllic, languid backdrop lay a ruthless, adventive environment, one whose every purpose appeared to be dedicated to the harassment and destruction of human beings. "This seemingly beautiful island held torture," one engineer marveled. The extreme tropical climate was alien to anything the average soldier had experienced back home. Over much of New Guinea, annual rainfall averaged between 100 and 150 inches. Some places even recorded totals over 200. "There is no misery existable as to arrive in the damn jungle during the rainy season," an engineer wrote to his wife. "Everything becomes wet . . . a steady drip falls from the back of [your] helmet and rolls down your itchy skin." Streams and rivers became impassable. Bridges were swept away. The job of building or maintaining roads amounted to a daily struggle to manage mud. "We got so used to working in the pouring rain, the men stopped complaining about it," PFC Douglas, an engineer, later wrote. Clothes, equipment, foxholes, and tents were inundated. "One night when we had a heavy rain, the water was coming through our tent about three or four inches deep and I woke up just in time to catch my shoes going by," Tech 4 Dale Venter told his family in a letter.

Soaked with musty water, canvas tents and leather items were so infused with mildew that they often rotted away altogether. In grassy, plateau areas near the coast, temperatures could climb as high as 135 degrees with humidity over 80 percent. With highs in the mid to upper nineties, temperatures were usually lower in the rain forests that coated much of the island, but humidity was higher. "It is the humidity that runs you down," Major Compere, a physician, commented. "You perspire profusely." Sweat and filth were the noxious currency of the realm. Whether on the front lines or in rear area bases, soldiers found it nearly impossible to stay dry, cool, or clean for any length of time. "I am sweating, stinking, smelling like a dead Jap," Sergeant Mike Bredice told a buddy in a colorful letter. "Socks and clothes glued to my body and smelling awful rotten!" Lieutenant John Harrod, a young ordnance officer, vividly wrote to his mother "of seeing wet, sweaty jungles, and crossing streams with our packs on, and wet, sticky clothes. Soldiers in chow line and lying around dirty, dishevelled and young, and somehow, innocent-looking. Men swimming in the sea—the harbor native craft slipping about, the refreshing coolness of evening—the sudden come and go of tropical storms . . . native wild pigs scuttling through the underbrush . . . birds chattering in the jungle." Latrines usually consisted of crude wooden outhouses with makeshift seats over malodorous pits or drums. Units stationed in coastal areas often built pier-type latrines, hanging over the ocean water, a kind of natural sewage system. Almost all drinking water came from wells. With concrete in short supply, even the sturdiest prefabricated wooden buildings often had dirt or gravel floors. Garbage was burned or heaped into vast pits and plowed over with mud by bulldozers. In some cases, units stacked their waste onto barges, floated them out to sea and dumped the whole mess overboard "where they would be caught by down-shore currents," according to one base's after action report.

Skin rashes and lesions, diarrhea, and intestinal worms were ever present problems. Insects practically ruled the landscape, prompting a persistent interspecies struggle for supremacy against these tiny adversaries. "There were more different types of bugs in this place than I, or anyone else, had ever seen," wrote PFC Douglas. Tiny chiggers, invisible to the naked eye, clung to razor-sharp blades of kunai grass, spreading scrub typhus among soldiers who moved through the grass with exposed arms and necks. The disease could be deadly. One physician estimated a 5 percent mortality rate from scrub typhus, "running higher than the combined mortality of all medical diseases in this area." Ants and flies were constant companions for any GI who hoped to consume a meal in peace. Leeches infested the jungle foliage and practically any water source, to the point where it was almost impossible to avoid them. "They will probably get in through to your skin no matter what you wear," advised a pocket guide disseminated among the soldiers. Men learned never to tear them off, lest their heads remain embedded and cause skin infections. Instead, the soldiers burned them with cigarettes or lighters or sprayed them with soapy water or insect repellent. Waves of termites ate away at huts, sometimes collapsing them. At times, they even weakened the wooden frames of American hospital buildings. In the swamps, the jungles, the river valleys, the ditches, the rutted mud roads, the coastal basins, mosquitoes bred in the billions, a suffocating, constant presence, every single one of them a threat to GI health because of their propensity to spread malaria. "At night they are unbearable," Captain Talcott Wainwright, a physician, related in a report about subsisting in New Guinea's jungle environment. Mosquito bars and nets offered some protection, but they were impractical to deal with and by no means available in anything like sufficient quantities, especially as the population of Allied soldiers grew. Insect repellent was common and useful, but a soldier could go through an entire bottle in just a day or two. "The problem was that you could smell it," Captain Cecil Helena noted. "At night that was not the best thing, as you could be detected . . . by the Japanese."[3]

Throughout 1943, even as the Allies gained the upper hand against the Japanese, the mosquitoes remained unsubdued, so much so that they almost threatened to unravel the momentum of MacArthur's battlefield victories. Malaria infection rates skyrocketed to a staggering 251 cases per 1,000 soldiers per annum. If anything, this was probably an underestimate, since soldiers with mild cases seldom sought medical treatment. In some units, the infection rate was 100 percent. For every casualty inflicted by the Japanese, malaria claimed five. One SWPA analyst estimated that as many as 54 percent of all theater hospital admissions were due to the disease. Many of the victims were in very poor condition, fortunate even to survive. "Malaria would cause the patient to be very debilitated, anemic and lose all interest in the war and the world in general," Major Compere commented. In one typical case, PFC Douglas suddenly felt hot and feverish, so much so that he removed most of his clothes and staggered into a hospital. "They wrapped me in a blanket, put a tag around my neck and made me lie down on a stretcher." His temperature registered at 105.7. He passed out and spent several days alternating between a state of unconsciousness and delirium. He hallucinated and carried on mock conversations with his wife—some of them sexual—and railed against General MacArthur, whom he did not like. It was many days before he had the strength to eat normally and walk again, much less return to his unit.

Though the disease was seldom life-threatening—one death per 650 hospital admissions—it was nonetheless debilitating. When a soldier was hospitalized for malaria, his stay lasted, on average, twenty-five days. In 1943, the SWPA theater lost nearly one million man days to malaria. At Milne Bay alone, the Americans were losing 12,000 man-days per month to the disease. "Malaria represents at least 80% of our unhealthiness," Major Roger Egeberg, the command surgeon, reported to Colonel Percy Carroll, chief surgeon of SWPA's Services of Supply. In turn, Carroll wrote to his superiors in the Surgeon General's office in Washington that "with the contemplated increase in the number of our forces occupying areas where malaria is very prevalent, it will be necessary to increase our malaria control measures." By September 1943, there were seventeen fully or partially equipped, twelve-man malaria-control units in New Guinea. The typical unit was commanded by a captain with a lieutenant as his executive officer. Most of the officers, and many of the enlisted men, were trained biologists, entomologists, or epidemiologists. In their constant struggle to subdue the mosquitoes, they took to spraying clouds of aerosol insecticide from steel containers known as "bug bombs." The bug bombs could eliminate the insect population within a 150,000 cubic foot area. In many instances, Allied malariologists hired locals to don tanks full of insecticide and circulate around on foot, spraying likely breeding areas. The units even set diesel fires in known breeding areas, roasting the mosquitoes and their larvae in similar fashion to the way infantrymen utilized flamethrowers to torch enemy soldiers. "At the beginning of the observations, 212 . . . of the 362 potential larval sites had *Anopheles* [mosquito] larvae present," the 17th Malaria Survey Unit reported of one typical fire operation. "All were negative when oiling was completed."

But, since it was nearly impossible to eliminate all mosquitoes by spraying, oiling, or draining swamps or other inundated spots, the most prevalent malaria prevention method was pharmaceutical. Atabrine was the most common antimalarial drug in theater. To be sure, atabrine did not prevent malaria; it just suppressed the debilitating symptoms of high fever and delirium. If a soldier took it regularly, he stood a very high chance of warding off the worst effects of malaria and remaining healthy enough to stay on duty. The drug had some unappealing side effects. If taken in excessive dosages, it caused nausea and vomiting. Even with the proper dosage, atabrine tended to cause an odd yellowing of the skin, at least among white soldiers. In exceptional cases—maybe one or two people in one thousand—it could induce psychoses. Soon an erroneous rumor swept through SWPA that the drug led to impotence, a far more troubling side effect to the average soldier than any other. Given this belief, the very real unpleasant side effects, and the fact that some soldiers actually wanted to contract malaria so they could be evacuated out of New Guinea, the main challenge for commanders was in getting their troops to take the drug on a regular basis. "Nothing of importance can be left to the individual inclination of the soldier," General Eichelberger asserted. Indeed, if left to their own devices, most men would probably slack off on taking the drug. In the estimation of one malariologist, far too many soldiers had a "devil may care" attitude. Nor, in the sweltering tropical heat, would they tend to embrace other commonsense, but less comfortable, measures to suppress the incidence of malaria, such as rolling down their sleeves or wearing long trousers, caps or helmets. It was up to leaders, from the squad level all the way up to theater level, to enforce anti-malaria discipline. For sergeants, lieutenants, and captains, this meant making sure each man actually took his daily atabrine tablets and covered himself up enough to ward off mosquitoes. For General MacArthur, who fully understood the threat posed by malaria, it meant maintaining constant pressure on his subordinates. When he met with Colonel Paul Russell, a visiting malaria expert, he told him, "Doctor, this will be a long war if for every division I have facing the enemy, I must count on a second division in hospital with malaria and a third division convalescing from this debilitating disease." Russell came away from the meeting convinced that the general was "not at all worried about defeating the Japanese, but he was greatly concerned about the failure up to that time to defeat the Anopheles mosquito." The SWPA commander made a point of prioritizing the effort to eradicate malaria, primarily by making it clear to all of his subordinate commanders that they themselves were responsible for malaria prevention among their troops, and that he planned to evaluate them accordingly. When one of MacArthur's generals expressed a decided lack of enthusiasm to Colonel Carroll about enforcing malaria control measures, the colonel asked, "Now, do you want me to go back and tell General MacArthur that you told me that you didn't want to do that?" The chagrined general quickly changed his tune and promised to do everything possible to keep his men from contracting malaria.

The same mind-set gradually took hold throughout much of New Guinea. "Enforcement of the measures for the prevention of Malaria is a command responsibility and will be pursued with vigor by commanders of all grades," one unit commander wrote in a formal order that typified many others circulated throughout SWPA. "The success of Malaria prevention will be given weight in determining the efficiency of commanders of units." In addition to maintaining atabrine and clothing discipline, officers empowered their medics and attached malaria control units to enforce proper prevention standards. They also invested great amounts of time and effort to educate their soldiers on the perils of malaria. "Informal types of lectures were given in which the disease of malaria was explained, the methods of acquiring it . . . and the problems of transmission met with in New Guinea," Major Donald Patterson, a malariologist, commented in a contemporary oral history. "Roadside signs were used to keep the men aware of the malaria hazard and problems." Often the experts gave lectures to groups large and small or just circulated relevant literature. Other times, they briefed the commanders, "who in turn lectured to their men," according to Major John Swartzwelder, commanding officer of the 2nd Malaria Survey Unit. Atabrine discipline improved enough to create an occasional shortage of the drug. "The supply barely equals the demand," Lieutenant Colonel George Littell, a medical officer with SWPA headquarters, reported to his superiors late in 1943. Thirty million tablets per month were necessary just to meet the Army's minimum needs in New Guinea.

The vast effort did bear some fruit. Though the malaria problem never completely went away, it did diminish. By the end of 1943, infection rates in SWPA declined to 179 cases per 1,000. At Milne Bay, they plummeted to 31 cases per 1,000. The average hospital stay shrunk from twenty-five days to fifteen and then six, freeing up some ten thousand hospital beds throughout the theater. This "battle involving science and discipline," as MacArthur's headquarters termed it, would never altogether cease in the tropics, but malaria would not plague the Army so badly as it had in the initial stages of the campaign in New Guinea.[4]

The same could not quite be said for soldier morale in such a remote, forlorn, jungle environment that offered little in the way of natural diversions or comforts. "There are only four things that will keep soldiers happy," one battalion commander wrote to his wife. "1) Fighting 2) Drinking 3) Gambling, and 4) Women." In New Guinea, few of the four were available in anything like the quantities the troops desired. Nor were many consumer items accessible. Though mail service was generally good, units north of the Owen Stanleys did not even have access to post exchanges until the middle of 1943. Even then, there were chronic shortages of razor blades, lighters, matches, watches, stationery, alarm clocks, pocketknives, fountain pens, and magazines. Letter writing relieved some of the chronic boredom and want. A survey of enlisted men revealed that most wrote two or more per day. Sergeant Bredice penned scores, including bizarre missives to Bing Crosby, Betty Grable, and Lana Turner, asking them to make him godfather to their kids. "Please send me a picture of your baby," he beseeched Turner. "I always admired you for your beauty and acting. I'd give anything to be a godfather to your child."

Opportunities for female companionship were almost nil. For one thing, the few local women whom GIs encountered were strictly off-limits, owing to cultural taboos on both sides. For another, almost all of these dark-skinned women were unappealing to the typical American soldier, no matter white or black. "All they talk of is women . . . until I am almost out of my wits listening to them," one soldier wrote of his sex-starved comrades. Not surprisingly, the Army's venereal disease rates declined to virtual nonexistence. As the Allies gained New Guinea ground and began to establish secure bases and medical installations, a trickle of female nurses arrived. Bowing to gender customs of the time, and probably out of the prevailing cultural obsession with protecting them from defilement by the Japanese, operational and medical commanders shielded the nurses from danger like precious relics. When medical units deployed to forward areas, they routinely left their nurses in Australia until conditions were safe. Enlisted male orderlies who stood in for the officer nurses during combat resented being ordered around by them once the danger abated. "Thus, when the nurses move in, the morale of the enlisted element hits bottom," said one theater-wide report. To make matters worse, the enlisted men were forbidden to date the nurses, even as male officers could do so at will.

Sexual tension in theater was such that command authorities felt compelled to place round-the-clock armed guards around nurses' quarters lest they be accosted by lovesick GIs. "They were escorted to and from the hospital and could not leave their quarters during their free time unless they were part of a supervised group activity," wrote the Army's official Nurse Corps historian. A pair of armed guards escorted any nurse who left her unit's area, no matter the reason. Army authorities claimed this was to protect them from Japanese guerrilla patrols, but in reality it was "to discourage incidents of sexual harassment and fraternization." Captain Peggy Carbaugh, chief nurse of the 2nd Station Hospital at Nadzab, told an Army historian that "at times a few prowlers . . . have been around our area but no one was hurt seriously." The "prowlers" might well have been only curiosity-seeking gawkers. Even though the nurses were clad just like the men in coveralls or shirts and trousers, most of the harmless gawkers just hoped for a glimpse of anything feminine. But in a different unit, a knife-wielding soldier snuck into the nurse's quarters and lay down next to one of their cots, apparently intending to rape or assault someone. A nurse spotted him and struggled for the knife, suffering a nasty cut in the process. The soldier escaped only to get captured the next day. The guarding was especially zealous whenever an African-American unit happened to be nearby. "Nurses dislike being under guard at all times, although most of them realize that this is done mainly because of colored troops in our area," Captain Marian Grimes, another chief nurse, breezily told a 1944 interviewer, reflecting the casual contemporary racist assumption that black soldiers posed some sort of special menace to white nurses.

Even as some Army authorities labored to prevent interracial encounters, others were more concerned with stamping out homosexuality, a persistent and yet highly taboo subculture among the many thousands of men stationed on the island. "From time to time crusades have been made against homosexuals in the theater," Major Henry Gwynn, a medical officer who witnessed many such inquisitions, said in early 1944. "This is mainly due to the interest of line officers in this subject. It seems doubtful in my mind whether all this furore is either necessary or desirable." Indeed, the provost marshal spent untold man-hours hunting for gay men. The more "offenders" they tracked down, the more they interrogated these suspects who, in turn, revealed the identities of their lovers. This, in turn, led the investigators onto the trail of still other individuals, in a kind of never-ending web. The discriminatory search even led to the resignation of one chaplain and the official suspicion of one unnamed general.

The barrenness and isolation of New Guinea seemed to exacerbate all the usual human foibles. Admissions to hospitals for emotional and psychological problems were high, probably affecting between 5 and 10 percent of soldiers. In the view of Colonel S. A. Challman, a neuropsychiatrist, this rate was "the highest in the world. There was no relaxation or leisure. There were no amenities. The men lived in a rainy, muddy atmosphere, full of insects. There was no place to go for any change. There just wasn't any such thing as a cool drink, or a candy bar, or anything at all except ordinary GI diet, and the men were just plain uncomfortable. Worst of all, the men felt that they were stuck there, that they were there for life possibly." Many lobbied fiercely for some sort of rotation policy, but given the paucity of shipping and manpower in theater, this was little more than a pipe dream. The vast majority really were "stuck there" in New Guinea for the indefinite future.

★

A dark underbelly of depression, problem drinking, resentments, stealing, fighting, and suicide festered among the troops, especially those who were used for hard labor. "We are unloading boats with supplies and everything," one military policemen wrote angrily to his mother, "and it is really work. It rains almost every day . . . and the heat is terrible. We work in the rain just like we work in the sun." The work parties witnessed firsthand just how much better sailors ate and drank than soldiers. Some of the troops were even put to work unloading beer earmarked only for naval personnel. In the dispassionate tone of one observer report, this "makes many a soldier dissatisfied with his lot." The parties regularly stole all the beer they could. For most other soldiers, though, beer was a rarity. Instead, they fashioned their own stills and made moonshine out of a noxious blend of fruit juice, coconut juice, raisins, sugar, potato peelings, and other sundries. The "jungle juice," as the men called it, had a very high alcohol content, so it packed a fierce wallop. "We had to ration it because ninety-five percent alcohol can be deadly," one officer remembered. But few officers were able to police jungle juice consumption with any semblance of order. In some units, men drank so much home brew that, when called upon for guard duty, at least one in three could not even stand up, much less walk straight. "That goes on all the time in this outfit," one major wrote to his wife. Another soldier, an enlisted man, related to his family the typical sight around him of a "poor devil . . . shot to hell and drinking heavily to keep up his nerve. Others are out laying around like dead men." The heavy drinking occasionally led to arguments and fights. PFC Paul MacDonald, a member of an antiaircraft battalion, saw two men in his outfit get drunk one night and wander into the latrine to have sex when a third man, apparently a spurned lover in a triangle, interrupted them. The couple turned on the interloper. "[They] fell on the poor queer and started beating hell out of him . . . the guy takes off and runs through our barracks screaming bloody murder." Supply shortages and bare-bones circumstances, combined with a typically obstructive Army bureaucracy, led to scrounging and thievery, sometimes on a grand scale. "I have told falsehoods galore, deceived people, organized bands to steal lumber and nails at night, stolen trucks, cursed superior officers, disobeyed Army regulations, and forged names," Major Britten reported to his wife of the midnight requisition mentality prevailing in the 503rd alone. "All this to secure a few small items that will keep our men physically fit."[5]

In some outfits, tension simmered between officers and enlisted men, usually over excessive discipline, rotten conditions, poor food, or noticeably different living arrangements. "I just can't stand our officers," Staff Sergeant Frank Pawlikoski raged to a friend in a typical letter. "They're all for themselves. They walk around all dressed up, giving orders here and there, have stooges to do their laundry and take care of their quarters and personal things. This is a hell of a way for overseas officers to act. Fresh out of school, don't know nothing about handling men at all. They ride the men like a bunch of slaves." Private Roland Dettler grew so fed up with what he considered to be deficient leadership that he wrote an expository letter that he mailed through a base censor's office rather than his unit commanders. "It's beyond human belief of the stupidity, meanness, and rottenness of these officers. God, how I could write a book." In one anti-aircraft unit, an officer allegedly beat a private with a rifle butt, withheld food from him, and forced him to dig a hole when he was sick and wounded. "This case is worse than General Patton's," wrote Private Joseph Klimaszeski in a reference to the famous general's Sicily slapping incidents. The aggrieved soldier subsequently attempted suicide. "He cut himself about 20 times all over . . . he lost a lot of lot of blood," but somehow lived. The Army considered the case serious enough to warrant an investigation by the inspector general.

As the 503rd Parachute Infantry Regiment languished uneasily after the anticlimactic Nadzab jump, morale issues and dissatisfaction with Colonel Kinsler's leadership also led to a full-blown inspector general investigation. "Just one big happy family," Lieutenant Riseley wrote sarcastically in his journal. "Everyone loves everyone." In reality, officers were bickering among themselves. Few respected Kinsler, whom they thought of as effete and cowardly, out of his depth as an airborne commander. Some had even written to higher authorities asking to be transferred to a better-led parachute unit. The investigator questioned men of all ranks, looking for information "like a monkey searching for fleas," in Riseley's colorful phrase. After the exhaustive questioning, the inspector general came to believe that "Colonel Kinsler has not shown the qualities of leadership which might have been expected of an officer of his rank and experience; the officers of this regiment almost unanimously lack confidence in his leadership and the men as a whole share that feeling."

Instead of facing the outcome of an investigation that was clearly not trending his way, Kinsler chose another option. On the afternoon of October 21, he invited his battalion commanders to his tent and shared a bottle of whiskey with them. Later that evening, he went out on a date with an Australian nurse. During the date, as the nurse watched helplessly, he pulled out his .45-caliber pistol and shot himself through the heart. "Boy, what a foul individual he was," Major Britten later commented in a letter to his wife. "His escapades with the women and his drunken orgies was known by every soldier in the Regiment. Furthermore, his inefficient handling of the Regiment was pathetic. The investigation revealed so many startling things that Kinsler could not face it, so he chose to die as he lived, by shooting himself . . . after enjoying himself with . . . [a] nurse, and a bottle of gin at a lonely road." Lieutenant Colonel George Jones, a battalion commander who was universally respected, ascended to command of the regiment. Jones's explanation for the colonel's suicide was more charitable than Britten's. "I personally believe that Kinsler was out of his mind because of the amount of Atebrin [*sic*] he had taken. He was as yellow as a scratch pad." Another senior officer shared the view that Kinsler's actions "could not have been those of a man in his normal senses."

To prevent such tragedies and provide for the mental and emotional welfare of the troops, the Army slowly increased access to entertainment and recreation, especially after a 1943 survey revealed that 19 percent wanted more books, 40 percent more magazines, 53 percent more phonograph records, and 60 percent more movies. Reading material of all kinds became much more common in theater. The growing logistical bases even published their own newspapers. At Finschhafen, the *Foxhole Observer* boasted a circulation of better than ten thousand by early 1944. A radio station came into service, broadcasting news, stateside programs, popular music, sporting events, and church services up to eight hours a day. "Night Riders," an evening request program, grew popular enough to generate calls and letters from as far away as Australia. In October, Armed Forces Radio broadcast the World Series between the New York Yankees and the Saint Louis Cardinals, in which the New Yorkers avenged their defeat of the previous year. Humble chapels soon sprung up all over Allied-held New Guinea, ministering to the spiritual needs of Jewish, Protestant, and Catholic soldiers alike. A sprinkling of Hollywood stars, including John Wayne, Gary Cooper, Una Merkel, and Phyllis Brooks, visited New Guinea, performing variety shows or just visiting with troops, especially in hospitals. Theater-minded soldiers staged their own productions for their buddies. Some built their own stages out of discarded lumber or simply performed from the back of a truck. Musically talented soldiers scrounged for instruments, formed bands, and played concerts. At one supply base, there were more than 130 performances on twenty-three different stages in a two-month period alone.

Athletics were a natural diversion for men who were themselves products of a sports-crazy nation. From Port Moresby to Oro Bay, Lae and many smaller spots, playing fields soon dotted the tropical landscape. GIs began competing in softball leagues, baseball leagues, football leagues, boxing matches, and volleyball tournaments. A few played Ping-Pong or competed in informal swim meets. At Finschhafen, the predominantly African-American 870th Engineer Aviation Battalion bested eleven teams from other units to win the base's first softball tournament. The games provided a healthy and energy-consuming diversion, a perfect antidote to an island-wide malaise of boredom that might otherwise have led many into trouble. Gambling on the contests was common. So was card playing. Poker games, most of the penny-ante variety, went on round the clock. "The number of players who participated was approximately 15 to 20 but only seven could play at one time," Captain John McKinney, an officer in the SWPA signals section, later wrote of the poker sessions that absorbed many off-duty hours for his buddies and him. "When one dropped out, another took his place. The game continued for several nights, usually three or four." By far movies were the most common, and popular, diversion. Almost all the theaters were outdoors, usually just a projector and a makeshift screen. Even the prospect of frequent downpours and occasional enemy air raids failed to dampen the enthusiasm for this staple of American entertainment. Over a three-month period at one base, soldiers at forty-three different theaters took in 453 shows. For obvious reasons, combat films were not popular. The troops favored musicals, westerns, comedies, and romance adventures or pretty much any movie that featured an attractive female star. Major Britten found himself "spellbound" by *Keeper of the Flame* starring Spencer Tracy and *Reunion in France* with Joan Crawford, John Wayne, and Philip Dorn. "The story and the acting in each were superb," he opined.[6]

The morale-oriented diversions became possible, in part, because of the remarkable ability of Allied logisticians to turn one of the world's most primitive areas into a workable base by the end of 1943. Somervell had noted the previous year, "The facilities that are normally available to an army in its advance and supply are missing: there are no roads; no buildings to take over; no water supply; no docks or other port facilities." New Guinea had not one mile of railroad. As of May 1943, the island contained only six hundred miles of surfaced road. The harbors were small, sparsely equipped, and ill-suited to handle the large cargoes necessary to support modern operations. With troop strength edging toward six figures, and the war moving ever north and west, away from the original Australian bases, the Army in New Guinea required some 340,000 tons of matériel per month just to subsist, and yet Milne Bay could handle only twenty-five hundred tons per day, Port Moresby just fifteen hundred; Buna and Salamaua between them could eke out eleven hundred.

Once landed, the cargo was anything but secure from the elements—everything from food to medicine to uniforms to bridging equipment could spoil or degrade in the island's moldy, mildew-laden environment. Metal might rust in a matter of days; rodents burrowed into crates, gnawing malevolently at any contents; blotches of fungus spread like cobwebs over tent flaps, trousers, and open cans of food. Harassed all the while by occasional Japanese air raids, engineers, port battalions, quartermasters, transportation units, and Navy Seabees toiled diligently to establish a series of coastal logistical bases at Port Moresby, Milne Bay, Buna, and other preexisting ports, plus new bases at Lae, Oro Bay, and Finschhafen, as well as scores of inland airfields, unit camps, and smaller supply bases. Crews sometimes worked twenty-hour days. In the recollection of one unit history, they often braved "dangerous swamps, sliced their way through thick, ugly jungles, stumbled awkwardly along muddy trails, fought off the germs of malarial mosquitoes, and endured the great loneliness of a primitive island."

Bulldozers and other construction vehicles were precious as gold. The commander of one aviation engineering battalion estimated that eight hundred properly equipped men could accomplish as much as fifty thousand men working only with hand tools. Almost overnight, docks, jetties, piers, storehouses, troop quarters, hospitals, airstrips, sawmills, mess halls, post exchanges, repair depots, roads, bridges, and a slew of prefabricated, corrugated metal, or wooden buildings, housing everything from administrative headquarters to hospital wards, came into being. By the end of the year, the engineers had built 750,000 square feet of storage space, a remarkable achievement, though the Army still required another quarter million just to properly store and process the masses of incoming matériel. Milne Bay soon teemed with cargo barges, caterpillar cranes, a half-dozen cold-storage boxes, each of which contained six thousand cubic feet of refrigeration space, and a special plant to reassemble vehicles that had been shipped in parts (to save limited shipping space).

Crews labored round the clock to service and unload cargo ships. Oro Bay alone transitioned from "merely an indentation in the New Guinea coastline," in the description of one unit history to a major logistical hub where fifty thousand troops staged for future operations. Eight runways were operational, as were eight docks, four of which could accommodate Liberty ships. Engineers had completed 125 miles of road, including a vital route to Dobodura, thirty-five bridges, as well as several hospital and headquarters installations. At Lae, they needed only two days to complete a workable airfield. By mid-December they had finished a first-class road link between Lae and Nadzab. A slew of pipelines, docks, signals, and ord-nance dumps soon followed. According to the history of the Lae base com-mand, the maturing infrastructure "made possible construction of the facilities for . . . four aerodromes at Nadzab from which the Fifth Air Force operated." At Milne Bay, in the space of just a few months, the 339th Engi-neer Construction Battalion completed 12 docks, 37 bridges, 130 culverts, 10 jetties, 20,000 feet of pipeline, 3 hospitals, plus scores of administrative buildings.

In the course of the war, the Army alone in the SWPA theater received more than 2.1 million measurement tons of matériel, almost all of which originated from San Francisco and Los Angeles. For obvious reasons, more than 95 percent of matériel and troop movement was made by water. The Australian and American navies and the US Coast Guard—collectively fighting a global oceanic war together—had nowhere near enough ship-ping to handle the demand of SWPA and other theaters. Moreover, New Guinea's coral- and shoal-laden north coast was perilous for large ships. The Army filled the shipping gap by commissioning its own multinational mishmash flotilla, dubbed "MacArthur's Navy," consisting of barges, tug-boats, cargo vessels, privateers, and the like under the loose jurisdiction of the Transportation Corps. "The vessels of the fleet were derived from three sources," wrote the corps historian, "the Army's prewar fleet, the purchase or charter of ships and craft from private owners, and the construction of new shipping." Their existence represented a triumph of pragmatism and improvisation as well as a mutual back-scratching arrangement between the Army and the Navy. The New Guinea buildup owed much to their efforts.[7]

★

Even as General MacArthur attempted to bend the unforgiving realities of logistics to his grand strategical concepts, he was also spinning a complex political web. On the surface, his relations with the Australians remained cordial. He and Prime Minister Curtin enjoyed a productive, mutually respectful relationship. The general treated Blamey and his other Austra-lian military colleagues with courtesy and exchanged hardly a cross word with any of them. Though he remained a distant, almost Olympian figure to the Australian people, he continued to live in Brisbane with Jean, where they maintained a positive, friendly reputation among the population. But, after the Buna-Gona campaign, MacArthur increasingly began looking to an operational future beyond British New Guinea, a future that he knew would be dominated by American military forces. He began to distance himself from the Aussies, and he quietly urged his subordinates to do the same. "[He] told me to meet the Australian high command, pay my respects, and then have nothing further to do with them," Eichelberger recalled of some advice he got from MacArthur. The SWPA commander envisioned no major Australian role in most future operations, particularly the massive campaign he hoped to mastermind to liberate the Philippines. Nor did he want American soldiers serving under Australian command any longer than was necessary. So he began working behind the scenes to sidestep General Blamey and establish an army-level American ground-combat formation under MacArthur's personal control. Instead of terming it as an army and thus theoretically subject to Blamey's control as commander of Allied land forces in New Guinea, MacArthur called it the "Alamo Force," a moniker that hinted at a minor task force of some kind. He chose sixty-two-year-old Lieutenant General Walter Krueger, a self-made military professional with more than four decades of Army service, to command. Not only did MacArthur think highly of Krueger, a man who had originally joined the Army as a private, but MacArthur also knew that Krueger had enough seniority to establish clear sovereignty from any possible senior-level Australian authority. In this manner, the first army-level formation in SWPA came into being from February through May, 1943. Many months later, it would assume the title of 6th Army, but for the time being, it was officially termed the Alamo Force and tucked, with an open secret type of unobtrusiveness, into the SWPA order of battle under the direct control of MacArthur's headquarters. "Whether the procedure—or lack of it—was right or wrong, the new arrangement was probably the only one that, in the circumstances that had developed, would have been politically acceptable in Washington," the Australian official historian later wrote evenly and probably accurately.

Under less Machiavellian circumstances, Eichelberger would have been the natural choice to command Alamo Force. However, not only was he too junior, but the publicity he had engendered after Buna probably made MacArthur leery of affording him such a prominent upward step. Instead, MacArthur, throughout all of 1943, consigned Eichelberger and I Corps to training duties in Australia, a vexing and unexpected turn of events for the sensitive victor of Buna. As the commander who had earned America's first ground-combat victory in World War II, he felt he deserved better treatment. Now relegated to the bench, Eichelberger took to calling himself "the mayor of Rockhampton," after the town where his headquarters was located. He grew antsy and struggled with dark moods. His chief of staff, Clovis Byers, freshly recuperated from the finger wound he had suffered at Buna, wrote to Emma that there was now "little for Bob to do but plan. The result is that his tremendous mental energy keeps him thinking constantly about what might be happening and causes him to be restless."

The inactivity reinforced the thoughtful, reflective Eichelberger's penchant for overanalyzing his situation. Already resentful of MacArthur for his self-promoting, disingenuous communiqués and his failure to visit the front at Buna, Eichelberger began to develop animosity against the SWPA commander for holding him back. To be sure, Eichelberger admired MacArthur's intellect, respected his authority, and was savvy enough to remain on good interpersonal terms with him. But as the year unfolded and Eichelberger's frustrations deepened, he privately nurtured real anger against his boss. Confidentially with Byers, and in letters to Emma, he contemptuously referred to MacArthur as "Sarah," after the notoriously vain French actress Sarah Bernhardt. When Eichelberger realized he was under serious consideration by General Marshall for other army-level commands—the 1st and the 9th Armies—he got his hopes up that this might come to fruition. Eichelberger yearned for a return to the less byzantine world of combat command. "All of us are anxious to go into action again," he told a friend in one letter. To Emma, he professed a special grudge against the Japanese. "Personally I am willing to fight them any time or at any place. The happiest time I have had since I left you was when I was in a plane headed into action against them." But, in truth, he pined away for action anywhere against any Axis adversary, preferably out from under MacArthur's thumb (and Krueger's) and in a high-profile theater. Eichelberger was not an egomaniac in the MacArthur mold. Nor was he animated by the self-serving lust for military glory that so characterized his friend and classmate George Patton. Nonetheless, he did share their love of the limelight and their need for the powerful narcotic of public adulation. At heart, Eichelberger wanted his own military show and his own special place in history. He knew that as long as he remained in SWPA, he would always operate in MacArthur's shadow. A transfer to the high-profile European theater offered the possibility of liberation from this version of posterity's doghouse. During an awkward conversation in mid-May at MacArthur's Brisbane residence, MacArthur informed Eichelberger of the War Department's interest and indicated he would not stand in his way. Though Eichelberger did not say he definitely wanted the transfer, he hardly needed to, since it would have represented a major promotion. "I felt very much elated, naturally, since it looked like a grand chance for me," he later commented. To make his intentions clear to Washington, he wrote directly to Lieutenant General McNair about the Army command. "I do not intend to abandon a lifelong policy of never asking for favors. I merely want you to know that if the question of my personal desire ever arises I shall be delighted to take the . . . detail or any other detail deemed suitable by you if the offer is ever communicated to me."

Expectant weeks and then months passed. Nothing happened, even though Eichelberger came to find out, through mutual friends, that Eisenhower wanted him to command 1st Army in the impending invasion of France, *the* plum job for any American senior officer in this war, and probably any other. In late September, MacArthur revisited the transfer subject with Eichelberger, this time indicating that 9th Army would be his if he wanted it. The following day MacArthur did an about-face. He said if he released Eichelberger for the command, it would reflect badly on the I Corps commander because, in Eichelberger's recollection, "people back there would always feel that he had gotten rid of me in the same way he had done in the case of [George] Brett." Instead of speaking up and arguing against this specious contention, Eichelberger made the mistake of assenting, probably because he felt the ultimate decision would likely be out of MacArthur's hands. If so, he was wrong. Neither Marshall nor Eisenhower was willing to cross swords with MacArthur over Eichelberger's reassignment. Weeks before the September meeting with Eichelberger, MacArthur had actually told Marshall very clearly that he had no intention of letting Eichelberger leave SWPA. "I hold [him] in highest esteem both professionally and personally," he cabled. "He is entirely happy in his present command and I am very desirous of keeping him. His services are of more value here than they could be in any assignment."

MacArthur's outlook tended toward the myopic and the self-interested. He seldom thought in terms of what was best for the global Allied war effort as a whole. Convinced as he always was that Washington did not provide SWPA with anything like adequate support, MacArthur was loath to give up a valuable field commander, especially to Eisenhower, whom he disliked and thought of as a disloyal traitor for leaving the Philippines years earlier. Instead, MacArthur maintained the outward appearance to

Eichelberger of watching out for his best interests while privately he did all he could to restrict his options. Basically, MacArthur wanted to put Eichelberger in storage until he needed him again. The needs of others in the global war mattered little to MacArthur. Eichelberger was his and he would not let him go.

Gradually, in the waning weeks of 1943, as Lieutenant General Bradley assumed command of 1st Army and Lieutenant General William Simpson took command of the 4th Army as an obvious prelude to control of the 9th, Eichelberger realized what had happened. "He did everything he could to hold me back," Eichelberger later summarized of his boss's devious actions. At almost the same time, Eichelberger found out that Byers and Colonel Rogers, his intelligence officer during the Buna campaign, had compiled an extensive dossier, supported by copious eyewitness accounts, to nominate the general for the Medal of Honor for his actions at Buna. Though nomination for the medal typically and properly came from one's superiors rather than subordinates, in Eichelberger's case, he had had no immediate superior on-site to observe his actions, and yet he had clearly demonstrated remarkable valor in a manner rare for a modern lieutenant general. Marshall understood this and so was poised to approve the decoration. As a courtesy to MacArthur, he consulted him on the matter. In a moment of breathtaking hypocrisy and self-serving vitriol, MacArthur personally torpedoed the nomination. "I . . . not only do not . . . approve the award but urgently recommend against it. Nothing is so injurious to morale as a belief that favoritism and privilege are exercised by high authority in such matters." He further recommended that the "War Department discourage such action as being subversive of military discipline." MacArthur might just as well have been describing the circumstances behind his own Medal of Honor award, though he seemed oblivious to this unsavory reality. As yet, he had not faced one fragment of enemy fire in New Guinea. But for whatever reason, he still felt compelled to derail the Medal of Honor nomination of a senior leader who had survived daily danger, sometimes of the most extreme variety, and engineered a crucial victory.

When Eichelberger found out about MacArthur's role in denying him the medal and the various army commands, his irritation with MacArthur solidified into a tremulous, self-righteous, and occasionally self-pitying wave of anger that would last a lifetime. In his view, MacArthur had denied him not only the just deserts his Buna valor had earned; he had also denied him the immortality that would have ensued from commanding troops in the invasion of Europe. And all this while sidelining him from combat in SWPA. The rage boiled over in a secret memo for Emma when he sarcastically referred to MacArthur as "the great hero who willingly sent me to my death or the great daily risk thereof. All this from our hero of Bataan and Buna." In a subsequent letter to her he said that "if I thought that having kept me from commanding three armies as well as the Medal of Honor would be all that would be done to me, I would feel better." Reflecting years later, he explained. "I resented these facts because there is a great difference between commanding a corps of 50,000 to 65,000 men and an army of . . . one-half to one million men. It would be equivalent to . . . a chairman of the board refusing to permit a vice-president to be promoted president of a big corporation." Chastened and yet resigned now to staying under MacArthur's command for the rest of the war, he had enough self-control to conceal and suppress his resentments and stay outwardly loyal to his boss. Eichelberger focused primarily on staying ready for whenever the SWPA commander might call on him again to lead troops in action. "I shall do my duty towards my country," he wrote to Emma, "but I shall not do it with quite the same elan [sic] and enthusiasm."[8]

At the same time, MacArthur's attention was hardly focused on Eichelberger. Even as he crafted grand strategy and directed the limited operations to secure control of the Huon Peninsula, he began to maneuver, quite secretly, for a promotion of his own. Behind the scenes, he was plotting to attain the Republican presidential nomination for the 1944 election. He utilized key members of his military staff, most notably Sutherland and Willoughby, in this effort. Dating back to his days as chief of staff, MacArthur had always been cozy with the political right, and he had nursed presidential ambitions for at least that long. He was especially popular with isolationists—who seemed oddly indifferent to the general's moderate internationalist views—and Midwestern conservatives. Beyond the cult of personality hero-worship of MacArthur that had swept through the country during the Philippines campaign, MacArthur had become a powerful symbol to many anti-Roosevelt voters, politicians, and editorialists who came to see him as more competent than the president on military matters and more devoted to America's true best interests. Pro-China politicians, always a force in the Republican party, liked his commitment to an Asia-first strategy. In their view, the Europe-first policy had ensnared the United States into a war fought primarily to benefit the enhancement of British and Soviet power, "colonial despotism or revolutionary terror," in the words of one commentator, while American interests lay elsewhere. Ever since the general's escape from the Philippines, they had lobbied the administration to put him in charge of all American military operations on a global scale, or at least the entire war effort against Japan. Some, like Joseph Harsch of the *Christian Science Monitor*, even hinted that the Roosevelt administration had deliberately divided the theater command and starved MacArthur of resources "partly because of jealousy of MacArthur's great popularity and partly because the conservative opposition press launched a MacArthur-for-President campaign." The general's SWPA headquarters did little to discourage this viewpoint.

The first rumblings of MacArthur's under-the-radar campaign began in the spring of 1943 while Sutherland was in the United States for the Cartwheel talks. He met with Clare Boothe Luce, who had just been elected to the House of Representatives as an anti-Roosevelt Republican. She was, of course, the wife of Henry Luce, who controlled the pro-Chinese, conservative Time Life empire. She invited powerful Michigan senator Arthur Vandenberg, the very soul of Midwestern isolationism, to the gathering at Luce's Washington apartment (Kenney was also present). Though no record exists of what the group discussed, the meeting seemed to ignite everyone's excitement for a MacArthur candidacy, including the general himself. A couple of weeks later, MacArthur ordered an aide to travel from Australia to Washington to hand-deliver a secret message to Senator Vandenberg. "I am most grateful to you for your complete attitude of friendship. I only hope that I can some day reciprocate. There is much that I would like to say to you which circumstances prevent. In the meanwhile I want you to know the absolute confidence I would feel in your experienced and wise mentorship."

The canny Vandenberg understood what the communication meant—MacArthur was keenly interested in becoming president, though, as an active-duty soldier, he could never publicly declare these intentions or openly run, unless he was drafted as a candidate by others. Perhaps with MacArthur in mind, the War Department had recently decreed that no service member could seek or be elected to public office while in uniform. Vandenberg and other Republicans had promptly accused the administration of a ham-fisted attempt to negate potential military challengers like MacArthur. "I do not know whether General MacArthur would even consider the nomination . . . but I am quite sure that the Executive Department of the government has no power whatever to dictate to the free people of America whom they should nominate and elect as president," New York Republican Hamilton Fish said. Secretary Stimson hastily retorted that the provision did not apply to the general—for what reason he did not really explain.

Regardless, throughout 1943 and early 1944, Vandenberg took the lead in establishing an underground campaign to secure the nomination for MacArthur. General Robert Wood, the wealthy head of the America-first isolationist movement, agreed to underwrite the campaign. Vandenberg lined up what he called a "cabinet" of several key supporters that included John Hamilton, the former Republican National Committee head, as campaign chair, and conservative publishers Frank Gannett, Roy Howard, and Colonel Robert McCormick, a longtime friend of MacArthur's, to set the stage for publicity. In spite of MacArthur's popularity with average Americans, the two leading contenders for the Republican nomination were Wendell Willkie, who had represented the party in 1940, and Thomas Dewey, the liberal internationalist governor from New York. Vandenberg hoped that their supporters might deadlock the delegate vote and lead to a successful draft for MacArthur as a "finish the war" candidate who enjoyed universal respect and tremendous military prestige. The senator's strategy depended on deftly handled behind-the-scenes groundwork and manipulation. "I feel that his nomination must be essentially a spontaneous draft, certainly without the appearance of any connivance on his part," Vandenberg told his diary. "It seems to me more important than ever that we should give our own 'commander-in-chief' no possible excuse upon which to hang his own political reprisals. I cling to the thought that if MacArthur can be nominated it will be as the result of a ground swell and not as the result of any ordinary pre-convention political activities."

But there was connivance on MacArthur's part, and quite a bit of it. He designated Willoughby to act as his intermediary with Vandenberg. The two corresponded regularly. Willoughby communicated MacArthur's satisfaction with the effort to secure the nomination. Vandenberg forwarded updates on the progress of his labor. "I am consulting with 'our cabinet' regarding the permanent employment of one appropriate man to take over the details of this entire undercover movement. The difficulty is in finding the *right* man who will fully understand the necessity for operating under 'our rules.'" During another trip to Washington, Sutherland spoke with former president Herbert Hoover to discuss MacArthur's presidential hopes. Hoover predicted that Dewey would probably get the nomination, but suggested the vice presidency for MacArthur, with full powers to run the war effort. Sutherland thought his boss would be amenable to the arrangement (exactly why any newly elected president in his right mind would ever yield such powers to his number two was apparently not discussed).

Back in SWPA, MacArthur on several occasions discussed his presidential ambitions with subordinates. During a June 1943 meeting with Eichelberger, he mentioned his hopes for the Republican nomination. "I can see that he expects to get it, and I sort of think so, too," Eichelberger commented in his diary. Years later, Eichelberger described MacArthur as having an "intense desire" to be president and added that "before the 1944 election, he talked to me a number of times about the presidency, but would usually confine his desires by saying that if not for his hatred, or rather the extent to which he despised FDR, he would not want it." In Brisbane one day, MacArthur walked into Sutherland's office and said, "Dick, when I get elected we will go back to Washington. I will take you with me. You will be my chief of staff. We will move in the War [Department] building and we will run the war. I will let Congress run the country." Another time, he reminded Sutherland that "old Zach Taylor made it to the White House and so can I." MacArthur routinely argued with Colonel Lloyd Lehrbas, a former newspaperman and member of his public relations staff, who felt that the general should not run for president. "After valiant debate, he usually came red-faced out of MacArthur's office," Master Sergeant Rogers, the stenographer, later wrote. The general corresponded with politicians and politically active friends who supported his candidacy. Most of the correspondents were well-meaning admirers of MacArthur or opponents of the New Deal. A few, like retired Major General George Van Horn Moseley, were venomous extremists. A vicious and paranoid anti-Semite whose views bordered on the fascist, Moseley had once served with MacArthur. He was convinced that the New Deal was leading to the establishment of a left-wing dictatorship in America. Now, in hopes of staving off the takeover, he urged the SWPA commander to return home to campaign. In Moseley's opinion, "the Jews and the un-Americans" were invested in another Roosevelt victory that MacArthur's candidacy might prevent. "I beg of you to be careful as to what you say or do until you have been put in touch with the tragic situation at home."

When Eleanor Roosevelt visited SWPA from late August through mid-

September 1943, MacArthur studiously avoided her, probably for fear that being photographed with her would anger potential anti–New Deal supporters. To wit, even as he welcomed five US senators from both parties to his Port Moresby headquarters and hosted them for three days during the Nadzab operation, he forbade Eleanor from visiting New Guinea on the grounds that it was too dangerous for her. "We were old friends and she took my refusal in good part," he later wrote disingenuously. Even when Jean hosted a large dinner for Mrs. Roosevelt at Lennon's Hotel, MacArthur refused to come back from Moresby to attend. "General MacArthur was too busy to bother with a lady," Eleanor later wrote to a friend.

Instead of dealing directly with the First Lady, he designated Eichelberger to host her and serve as the equivalent of a three-star babysitter during a whirlwind tour of Australia and New Zealand. With tongue firmly in cheek, Eichelberger later referred to the job as "the most hazardous assignment of my career. It is one thing to have fortitude on a battlefield, but quite another to face the booby traps and land mines of international diplomacy." The assignment caused no shortage of sympathetic chuckles among Eichelberger's many friends around the senior ranks of the Army. One of them, Brigadier General Floyd Parks, jibed, "I am convinced now that General MacArthur really knows his men when he selected super-diplomat Eichelberger for the job." Kidding aside, Parks was actually right. The job suited Eichelberger's engaging and extroverted temperament nicely and the visit went well. He came away impressed with the warmth of the First Lady's personality and her knack for talking to soldiers as she made the rounds of bases and hospitals. "She was indifferent to personal hardship, and always gracious. She could not be kept out of wards where wounds smelled evilly and agony was a commonplace. These were the men, she said, who needed comfort the most. Her simplicity . . . endeared her to the troops; her graciousness endeared her to the Australians; and her visit stored up a reserve of goodwill that was like a family bank account."

In spite of the machinations of MacArthur, his handpicked staffers, Vandenberg, and the others, the general's candidacy eventually came to nothing. Dewey proved to be too strong and Willkie too weak for any sort of delegate deadlock. Vandenberg's strategy depended on perfect timing and a groundswell of near universal support at the convention—based primarily on emotion—for the general, a political Hail Mary of sorts. He had no control over the amateurish MacArthur for President clubs that insisted upon placing their man on primary ballots where he could not hope to compete effectively. Plus, he was surprised, and vexed, by a decided lack of excitement for MacArthur among returning soldiers who had served in SWPA. "I am disturbed about one thing which to me is quite inexplicable," he wrote to Wood. "I am constantly hearing reports that veterans returning from the South Pacific are not enthusiastic about our friend." He wondered if somehow only anti-MacArthur veterans were getting furloughs home, so he asked a constituent who was serving in the South Pacific to canvas his fellow soldiers for their opinions. The result was the same, "growing unpopularity for our friend." One soldier, writing to his mother late in 1943, expressed a fairly typical sentiment. "I guess everyone back home thinks MacArthur is some swell fellow. But the boys in the Southwest Pacific have another idea. He doesn't do anything but ride around in his big car and live in a Hotel. He doesn't know how it is up here in the jungle."

Ironically, Senator Vandenberg also found out that he could not control the grandiose and poor political instincts of his candidate. MacArthur had corresponded with Representative Arthur Miller of Nebraska, a rabid anti–New Dealer who supported the general's campaign for the presidency. "Unless this New Deal can be stopped our American way of life is forever doomed," Miller told MacArthur. Instead of dodging such a specific domestic political issue, the general wrote back and told Miller, "I do unreservedly agree with the complete wisdom and statesmanship of your comments." In April 1944, Miller inexplicably released the contents of this private correspondence to the press. Vandenberg was furious at Miller for making the letters public. But he was taken aback at MacArthur's imprudence. For MacArthur, the humiliation and controversy that ensued from the publication of this correspondence killed any slim hopes he might have had of a convention upset and forced him to issue a mortifying, unequivocal statement disavowing any political aspirations. As a political amateur, he had hoped, in vain, to be carried into office by wave of indignant, enthusiastic support and, as with so many other areas of life, he had assumed that rules did not apply to him. *New York Times* correspondent Turner Catledge, who spoke to him often about politics, "far more than other generals," later said, "I believe that he was hoping for a popular avalanche of support . . . but I do not think he had the stomach for campaigning. When the avalanche did not come, he backed out of the political picture reluctantly."

MacArthur's troubling run for the presidency while serving in uniform and commanding troops in an active theater has no precedent before or since in American history. It was true that Washington, Jackson, Taylor, Grant, Theodore Roosevelt, and other part-time soldiers had all made the transition from general (or colonel, in Roosevelt's case) to president. McClellan had tried and failed. The difference was that none of them ran while on active duty in a combat zone. MacArthur did, thus violating his soldier's duty of apolitical obedience to civilian, constitutional authority. Not only was it disloyal and insubordinate, it could have set a dangerous precedent for high-level military intrusion into domestic politics and civilian authority. Fortunately for him, the vast majority of the American people, and the soldiers who were serving under his command, knew little of his behind-the-scenes scheming for political power. In the light of posterity, though, his actions revealed the dangerously megalomaniacal character of the man.[9]

12

Surviving

Lieutenant General Jonathan "Skinny" Wainwright, the proud cavalryman who had once commanded Allied forces in the Philippines, now felt powerless, humiliated, anguished. Late in the summer of 1942, the Japanese had moved him and other colonels and generals from Tarlac on Luzon to Formosa (or Taiwan). The journey aboard ship was cramped and uncomfortable—he shared a tiny stateroom with Major General Ned King, who had surrendered at Bataan—but the conditions were downright luxurious compared to the shipboard experiences many other prisoners endured then and later in the war. In hopes of confusing Allied intelligence as to his whereabouts, the Japanese shuttled Wainwright among three Formosa prison camps—Karenko, Tamazato and Muksaq— over the next two years. His treatment varied from reasonable to abysmal, with a strong dose of the latter. Like almost everyone else, he endured multiple beatings at the hands of Japanese guards. In the most humiliating instance, a guard stood Wainwright in place while he repeatedly slapped and punched him, apparently in retribution for the internment of Japanese-Americans. The beating was violent enough to knock the general off his feet. Stunned and angry, he kept thinking, "A private should never strike a lieutenant general!"

Another time, as he prepared his room for inspection, a guard suddenly entered and screamed at him in Japanese. Wainwright was so startled that he knocked his porcelain food bowl onto the floor and broke it. The Japanese soldier responded by slapping the general several times in the face. During the beating, the man accidently jabbed Wainwright in the left wrist with his bayonet. The enlisted prisoners endured even worse. "Some . . . were slugged as many as three times every day, and it became a rare sight to find one whose eyes were not blacked, nose mashed, or head and body full of lumps," Wainwright recalled.

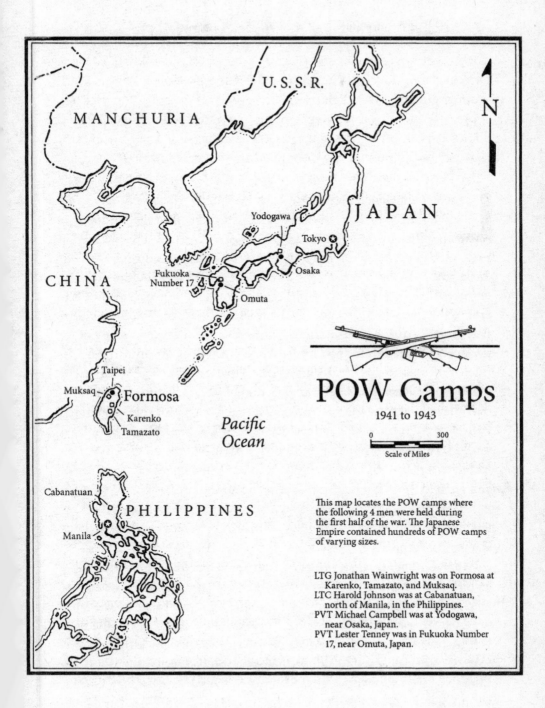

MANCHURIA

U.S.S.R.

JAPAN

Yodogawa

Tokyo ✪

CHINA

Fukuoka
Number 17

Osaka

Omuta

N

Taipei

Muksaq

Formosa

Karenko

Tamazato

*Pacific
Ocean*

POW Camps

1941 to 1943

0 ——— 300

Scale of Miles

Cabanatuan

PHILIPPINES

Manila

This map locates the POW camps where
the following 4 men were held during
the first half of the war. The Japanese
Empire contained hundreds of POW camps
of varying sizes.

LTG Jonathan Wainwright was on Formosa at
   Karenko, Tamazato, and Muksaq.
LTC Harold Johnson was at Cabanatuan,
   north of Manila, in the Philippines.
PVT Michael Campbell was at Yodogawa,
   near Osaka, Japan.
PVT Lester Tenney was in Fukuoka Number
   17, near Omuta, Japan.

For months, the Japanese fed Wainwright and the others starvation-level rations, consisting mainly of boiled rice three times a day. Round the clock, the prisoner's thoughts centered around food. "The skin of our buttocks just hung down the backs of our skeletonized legs like deep pockets," Wainwright later wrote. "But we were beyond all mortification over our appearance. There was nothing in our minds except food." Their starving bodies had consumed fat and muscle tissue to the point where men nearly took on the appearance of skeletons. Hunger pangs constantly plagued them. "During the starvation process, one is *always* hungry," wrote Brigadier General Beebe, who had served as Wainwright's chief of staff. "The first thought on waking in the morning is food. The last thought at night . . . is one of hunger." Their inadequate meals served only to intensify their craving for more food. Often their rice was laced with dozens of inch-long, slimy-white, black-headed worms. Initially the prisoners carefully removed the worms from the rice. But as their hunger grew worse, "we closed our eyes and simply ate, telling ourselves that there might even be protein in a worm," Wainwright wrote.

The hungry men took to augmenting their rice with snails, weevils, and the viscera of slaughtered Japanese farm animals. Almost everyone had the vitamin-deficiency disease beriberi, at least to some degree. As nutrient-deprived bodies consumed their own protein, the victims experienced the terrible symptoms of the disease, either in a dry or wet form. Dry beriberi ate away the protein sheaths around the afflicted man's nerve endings, "sort of like insulation on an electrical wire," in the recollection of Sergeant Knox. The feet grew especially sensitive, even to the light touch of a fly, much less any serious walking in the ill-fitting, awkward wooden clogs the Japanese made most of the prisoners wear in lieu of their Army-issue footgear. The pain was intense, like an electrical current. Feet grew so sensitive and painful that men lost control of their muscles. The afflicted developed a distinctive slapping shuffle step that was readily audible to their similarly affected peers. In some cases, prisoners experienced a degeneration of their optic nerves to the point where ordinary sunlight could cause flash burns to their eyes. Wet beriberi was even worse. It led to hunger edema, a painful swelling throughout the body, as the system, in essence, flooded itself. Wet beriberi usually started in the lower extremities and worked upward. "It would build up in the legs and genitals," one prisoner recalled. "When the water got up around the heart, the patient died." At this advanced stage of the disease, the victims took on a ghastly appearance. One witness recalled seeing men "so puffed up with water that their legs were the size of elephant legs. Their scrotum was the size of a basketball." Robust Colonel Bunker, once an all-American football player at West Point, and mentor to generations of Coast Artillerymen, developed just this sort of terrible wet beriberi. By the time the disease had reached its final stages, he had swollen to twice his normal size. Wainwright visited him on his deathbed. The colonel was so wracked with the disease that he no longer even recognized his old commander. "He must have suffered beyond belief from the constant pain of hunger," Wainwright later commented.

At the three camps, the general lived in unheated, rickety, wooden barracks buildings. After living in the tropics, the winter cold was particularly hard to take for him and others, too. "We had nothing but khaki uniforms, we were starved and couldn't generate sufficient body heat to keep warm," Beebe wrote. Wainwright slept on a metal or bamboo bunk cushioned only by a flimsy straw mattress and pillow. At Karenko, he shared a small room with King while most everyone else slept in open bays. At Muksaq, he rated his own eight-and-a-half-by-ten-foot room. King still deeply regretted having to surrender at Bataan. He was so depressed that, in the privacy of their room, he often sat slumped for hours on end, head in hands, wisps of reddish-gray hair poking through the openings between his fingers. Wainwright found King's protracted bouts of melancholy slightly annoying, as did Skinny's aide, Captain Thomas Dooley. "Gen. King, as usual, throws cold water on every good outlook we have," Dooley sniffed in a secret diary he kept throughout his captivity. Publicly, Wainwright maintained an even, professional demeanor. When arguments broke out among the prisoners, he stepped in and proclaimed, "That's enough." When men complained too much, he would say, "Cut out your bitching."

But in truth, Wainwright, too, had difficulty warding off his own melancholy. The sense of sadness and shame over his surrender festered in his soul like a wound. He worried that, even if he survived and the United States won the war, he would end up reviled in his home country, perhaps even court-martialed for his actions. Actually, unbeknownst to him, General Marshall had nominated him for the Medal of Honor. As with Eichelberger's nomination, General MacArthur did everything he could to derail Wainwright's. When Marshall asked for the SWPA commander's thoughts on the potential award, he replied unequivocally, "I do not . . . recommend him for the Medal of Honor. It would be a grave mistake which later on might well lead to embarrassing repercussions to make this award." He hinted darkly and vaguely at unspecified deficiencies on Wainwright's part. In reality, he was loath to share the Medal of Honor limelight with a man he still unfairly held responsible for the loss of the Philippines. For the time being, Marshall relented and shelved the nomination, though he was determined to revisit it at a more opportune time in the future.

Tōjō's no-work, no-food order applied to Wainwright and the other senior officers. Initially Skinny protested the order as a violation of the Geneva Convention and refused to let his men comply. But facing the very real possibility of mass starvation, he relented. At the Taiwan camps and throughout their empire, the Japanese assigned the prisoners to hard agricultural labor, tending farms and gardens, in exchange for small amounts of money and food, including their own homegrown crops. The prisoners cleared brush and rocks, felled trees, dug deep into the hard soil to plant seeds, and tended the crops. The labor was backbreaking for the starving captives, and especially so for the sixty-year-old Wainwright. Eventually he and the other older men were reassigned to goat-herding duty. "The work of herding them made a man of age and rank feel foolish," he later said. Perhaps that was the point.

Gradually, by the second half of 1943, the treatment grew better, particularly at Muksaq, where the Japanese fed the prisoners a survivable diet of rice, vegetables, and fruit, augmented with occasional meat and the diverse contents of Red Cross packages. He and the others were allowed to meet, albeit only under constant guard supervision, with a Japanese representative from the International Red Cross. Wainwright's room included a small table and a chair. The beatings stopped. He was permitted to write postcard-size letters each month to his wife, Adele, back in Skaneateles, New York. The contents were generally of the innocuous "I am fine how are you?" variety. In turn, she wrote him three hundred letters, care of the Red Cross, throughout his captivity, though only six were ever delivered to him (and the first not until May 1944).

Like thousands of other POW relatives, Adele Wainwright struggled to stave off despair. "Each day of my life seems worse than the last as I look into the future," she wrote to General Marshall at one point. In some cases, the Japanese, for propaganda purposes, allowed prisoners to broadcast short messages intended for their families. Shortwave radio operators throughout North America picked up these broadcasts and routinely relayed the contents to family members. In one typical instance, the mother of Colonel Donovan Swanton, a long-serving soldier who had commanded an infantry regiment in the Philippine Army, received a message from him to the effect of "I am in good health and spirits. The authorities are doing what they can to make us comfortable. I would like chocolate bars, edam cheese, canned meat, and any concentrated foods. The last letter from you is a year old." The radio operator, William Lathrop of Chatham, New Jersey, added his own well-wishes. "I can share with you the joy that comes from knowing that your son is alive and well as I have a cousin who is in . . . prison camp on Formosa." Wainwright recorded a similar, censored short broadcast for Adele. "Am well and cared for. Have written to you regularly, try to write me," he said.

Consumed with worry for Skinny, she threw herself into war-related work as an airplane spotter and Red Cross volunteer. Her living room was filled to bursting with surgical dressings and wool. Day after day, she and the other volunteers rolled the dressings and sewed the wool. "My days are filled with work and so they pass," she wrote to other POW families in a communal newsletter called *Philippine Postscripts*. As the commander's wife, she received hundreds of letters and long-distance calls from "frantic relatives." She could offer them little besides vague reassurances. At a Syracuse radio station, she recorded a broadcast of her own, in hopes that Skinny might somehow hear it. "Everything at home is fine," she assured him. "I keep very busy." She traveled to Panama City, Florida, where a shipyard was named for her husband. Around the country, plazas, streets, schoolyards, and parks were named for him as well. She attended special General Wainwright honorary days in Hartford, Connecticut, and Governors Island, New York. In Hartford, the governor of Connecticut read a resolution passed by the state assembly expressing to Skinny, "heartfelt gratitude and deep admiration for the heroic defense of Bataan and Corregidor Island." Adele was nearly speechless with emotion. Somehow news of this moving ceremony made it into the *Nippon Times*, an English-language propaganda newspaper published by the Japanese government. When one of Wainwright's officers smuggled a copy of the article to show him, he read it carefully and surmised that it was all just a Japanese trick. He still could not imagine that Americans on the home front saw him as a hero instead of a goat.[1]

All over the Japanese empire, from Formosa to Manchuria to the Philippines to the Japanese home islands, thousands of other American POWs who had once served under Wainwright struggled just as mightily, or even more so than their commander, to survive. In the home islands, some were working in war industries where the Japanese armed forces had contracted with private firms to use them as veritable slaves. With Japan mobilizing for a protracted total war, and millions of young men transitioning from civilian industries to the military, the country badly needed cheap labor. Allied POWs provided an easily manipulated resource. On Honshu, at Yodogawa, near Osaka, Private Campbell and about four hundred other Americans toiled in a steel mill. The young private had once served as a rifleman in the 31st Infantry Regiment. He had escaped Bataan only to be captured at Corregidor. The Japanese worked the prisoners as carriers, foundry hands, and loaders. Campbell's job was to assist in the making of fifty-gallon barrels. He and the others worked backbreaking eight-to-ten-hour days with only three days off per month. At work, they were under the charge of the private company that owned the mill. During off-duty hours, the Imperial Army was responsible for them. They lived in thread-bare, rat-infested barracks with only a potbelly stove to help them ward off the winter cold. They slept on wooden boards covered only by thin blankets. The barracks had indoor plumbing and bathing facilities, albeit with no hot water. The prisoners wore flimsy factory-issued uniforms made out of paperlike synthetic materials. Campbell was fortunate to have an overcoat to keep him warm. The Japanese issued him and the other prisoners canvas shoes that were four or five sizes too big. Only by folding the toes backward could he even keep them on his feet. The Japanese paid the men low wages, maybe enough to buy a little extra tobacco or food. Here, as at every other camp, cigarettes comprised a kind of gold-standard currency among the prisoners. Cigarettes could buy food, clothing, medicine, and services, mainly because many of the prisoners were consumed by the hunger for tobacco. "For a great majority of men it was a far more urgent need than food," Campbell commented. Starving smokers traded food for a few cigarettes or maybe even just a few puffs from a butt. As a nonsmoker whose father had raised him to avoid all tobacco usage, Campbell found himself in an advantageous bargaining position, though he initially recoiled at the idea of procuring extra food at the expense of his fellow prisoners. "I tried to talk them out of it, telling them the need for nourishment, but they were past caring." Most expected to die anyway, so they figured they would indulge their habit. As a result, Campbell ate many extra bowls of rice. Another prisoner even contended that "many men have no change of clothes because of trading clothes for cigarettes."

Rations were, at best, subsistence level, though there were some varia-

tions. The more a man worked, the more food he received. The most arduous jobs rated eight hundred grams of rice per day; the lightest warranted
four hundred grams. The sick received even less than four hundred grams.
Medics were under constant pressure to return them to duty. Three times
a day, the prisoners sat down to a meal of rice with a side of watery soup or
a little fish. Occasionally the soup was spiced with a few radishes or sweet
potato tops. At times, they received delicacies that, under other circumstances, would have provoked little besides revulsion. The POW cooks
baked cookies one day and issued two per man. Campbell gobbled them
down only to find out later that ground silkworms comprised the main
ingredient. Another time the Japanese gave the prisoners some sort of
chocolate-covered "candy" that turned out to be ants. "My stomach suddenly churned and I retched," he later wrote. For the sake of survival, he
learned to eat baked grasshoppers, raw seaweed, and a noxious powder
made from the gills, heads, and entrails of fish. One of his buddies even
baked an improvised pie, made out of rice dough and rat meat. He had
found a rat's nest over his bunk, chased the mother away, smothered her
six babies, and turned them into a meal. "I asked him why he did this
strange thing. He said that it was not as strange as it seemed. The rats made
his life miserable and he decided to get even with them by devouring their
young."

Indeed, the rats were more than just a nuisance. They grew to the size
of small cats and chewed through anything, from bunks to leather goods.
They carried fleas that spread to the men, burrowed under their skin,
sucked their blood, and caused terrible rashes and fevers. The rats were
such a menace that they even feasted on the bodies of those who died. "The
rats . . . tore their stomachs open," Campbell wrote. "They dragged their
intestines out and scattered them all over the floor. They chewed their
faces, toes and fingers off." The prisoners learned to post a guard with the
bodies just to ward off the aggressive rats. By the middle of 1943, four or
five prisoners were dying each week. One-quarter of the camp population
had perished of starvation, disease, or simply a broken spirit. Still, the
nightmarish routine of onerous factory labor and bare-bones survival continued, a merciless, darkly nihilistic world. "Our very souls were laid bare,"
Campbell later reflected. "We saw each other in a true light. Our weaknesses stood out, the selfishness, the greed, the cunning, the stealth, the
crookedness, and all other human frailties. It soon became a matter of
survival of the fittest. Rarely did I see an act of kindness or of compassion."

To the south, on Kyushu, Private Tenney, the young tank crewman who had managed to survive the Bataan Death March and Cabanatuan POW camp, now worked in a coal mine owned by the Mitsui conglomerate. Because he had attempted to escape from Cabanatuan, he believed the Japanese on Luzon viewed him as a troublemaker and had earmarked him for relocation to Japan. He and about eight hundred other Americans, plus Dutch, Javanese, British, and Australian prisoners lived at Fukuoka Number 17, a prison camp located near the coastal city of Omuta, on the island's west coast. The prison compound was small but adequate. An eight-foot-high wooden fence with a triple layer of electronic barbed wire enclosed a three-hundred-yard square of eleven wooden buildings. The barracks were roomy, equipped with latrines, hot-water bathing facilities, and even closets. Tenney and the others slept on reasonably comfortable tatami mats. As at Yodogawa, the more strenuous a man's work, the more food he received. Those who extracted the coal, shoveled it into cars, and pushed those unwieldy cars out of the mines, received about 750 grams of rice per day compared with 550 grams for the sick and those with less-taxing camp jobs. A small peppering of onions, potatoes, radishes, squash, tomatoes, cucumbers, cabbage, fish, octopus, mussels, clams, pork, beef, horse, dog, and cat meat augmented the prisoner's diet. On one glorious occasion, prisoners hijacked a wagon full of mandarin oranges and ate many of them whole without the Japanese finding out. Slapping and beatings were common. The Japanese allowed a smattering of mail into the camp and permitted the prisoners to send home one small postcard every three months. Some of the men recorded radio messages for their loved ones, though most were never aired. The camp hospital was reasonably well stocked with medicine. The ranking doctor, Captain Thomas Hewlett, earned a reputation for tireless, selfless service, and undoubtedly saved many lives. The mines operated round the clock. Prisoners received only three days off per month. Supervised by Japanese civilian laborers, the prisoners worked in fifty-man sections that focused on preparation, extraction, or exploration. Shifts generally lasted between ten and twelve hours. At the beginning of each shift, supervisors usually assigned a required quota of coal to be extracted, though prisoners routinely defied the quota or simply fudged their totals.

When the blackened, exhausted laborers emerged from the half-mile-deep mine shaft, they could immediately wash the layers of filthy dust from their skin or bathe after a three-mile trek back to the barracks. Privates earned ten yen a day; sergeants got fifteen; officers either supervised the sections or worked non-mining jobs, though they were usually paid more. "Working conditions in the Coal Mine were not good," wrote Major John Mamerow, Fukuoka 17's POW commander, in an official postwar report. "Clothing was not adequate and there was a great shortage of shoes. The men were required to work in water soaked tunnels and in many cases in running water. There were many tunnel cave-ins."

As a Chicago native, Tenney knew nothing about coal mines, but he and his comrades learned quickly how to make it through their nightmarish days. "Many of us were virtually able to fall asleep while shoveling coal," he recalled. "Our bodies were so totally exhausted and our energy so sapped that we were able to do the shoveling as an action of our subconscious, sort of from rote memory." Like many other survivors, he learned how to pace himself and game the system. On one occasion when he felt he could not last another day in the mine, he inflicted a wound on his left hand, but made it look like he had suffered it in a mining accident, thus earning several precious days in the infirmary while still drawing full rations. Other times he got out of work as a result of self-inflicted leg ulcers he created by cutting himself and rubbing lye soap into his wounds. In one memorable instance, he and his buddies sabotaged the conveyor-belt machine that slowly moved newly extracted coal up the various levels of the mine, shutting down operations for hours. Clever and resourceful, he became a consummate trader, earning a reputation as a man who could acquire anything for a price, sometimes for fellow prisoners, other times for Japanese supervisors or guards. "I got a kick out of it, and I always insisted that each trade include some kind of writing paper as part of my payment." Quite unconsciously, he developed a survival strategy: maintain a positive attitude, never yield to pessimism, establish the long-term goal of reuniting with loved ones, stay physically and mentally active, and, most important, develop a feel for each and every situation. For Tenney, this meant "paying attention to a wide variety of telltale events and individual traits to gauge how to act. I learned that life has great value. No single day can be wasted or thrown away."[2]

★

At this stage of the war, the Japanese still held the majority of their American prisoners in the Philippines where they had originally captured them. Because the Japanese still could not fathom the notion of females in military service, they considered the Army nurses to be civilian internees rather than prisoners of war. So instead of imprisoning the nurses in a military camp, they sent them to venerable University of Santo Tomas, in the heart of Manila, where they had previously established an internment camp for Allied civilians. Surrounded by high masonry walls and an iron fence, the grounds and buildings of the three-hundred-year-old university comprised a ready-made incarceration center. In addition to the sixty-nine nurses, more than thirty-five hundred men, women, and children were shoehorned into a campus the size of about ten city blocks. With only one hundred toilets on the campus, and constant water-pressure issues, the internees had to work together to maintain basic sanitation. The nurses labored in the camp hospital and lived dormitory-style in converted class-rooms on the second floor of the campus's main building. Privacy was nonexistent. The living quarters were subject to Japanese searches at any hour of the day. Each nurse had only six feet of cot space. They stowed all personal items under their beds. A few of the women built shelves or stacked boxes over the foot of their beds. Essentially, they lived right on top of one another. "I don't believe there was any person who was used to that type of thing," Lieutenant Alice Hahn later reflected. "Generally speak-ing . . . everybody needs a little space." Like most of the others, Lieutenant Eunice Young deeply missed the freedom that came with the privacy of having one's own room or home. "Until you've tried to live out of half a suitcase year in, year out, parking all you own on the bed by day, and under the bed when you are asleep, you have no conception of the priceless value of liberty."

The imperial authorities who ran the camp provided adequate food. In an illicit diary, Lieutenant Mueller recorded typical daily meals of "cracked wheat for breakfast, coffee, bananas. For lunch we had noodles, some meat stock and cocoa. Sometimes beans or rice or meat. Evening meal we had stew, bananas, tea, always rice. Sometimes we had chicken, duck eggs & hamburgers, limes & pudding." Internees also organized their own gar-dens. In addition, they bought or traded with locals for more food. Well-heeled Manila residents from nonbelligerent countries contributed even more food. They were led by Ida Hube, a Swiss citizen who had once served in the Army Nurse Corps with senior nurses Captain Davison and First Lieutenant Nesbit. Working closely with Davison and Nesbit, Hube per-sonally arranged for delivery of sweet cakes, canned milk, Ovaltine, nuts, candy, fruit, vegetables, bread, sugar, sewing kits, purses, and sanitary napkins to the nurses. Throughout 1943, with enough to eat and drink for the time being, the nurses fought boredom more than any other privation.[3]

Ninety-five miles to the north, at Cabanatuan, life had improved somewhat for the thirty-five hundred prisoners at the largest single camp for American POWs of the Japanese. The camp now had a working power system maintained by a prisoner who had been an electrical engineer in civilian life. A trickle of mail made it into and out of the camp. In the wake of the arrival of Red Cross packages at the end of 1942, the quantity and quality of the daily rations got slightly better. Food consumption rose from starvation to subsistence levels. Death and disease rates declined. The average prisoner received between two thousand and twenty-six hundred calories per day. "The year 1943—the first half at least—proved to the best, so far as food is concerned, of all the three years at Cabanatuan," a postwar Army provost marshal study contended. Meals consisted mainly of steamed rice, beans, scrawny sweet potatoes, or onions or squash, augmented with a little carabao meat, maybe an ear of corn or a tomato. "It's usually made into a hash with greens or mongoe [sic] beans and it all helps to put the rice down," Captain Forquer noted in his diary. In some cases, prisoners carried on illicit food trades with Japanese guards or enterprising Filipinos who filtered items through sparsely monitored sections of Cabanatuan's surrounding barbed wire.

As at other camps, the Japanese put the prisoners to work in exchange for small wages. At Cabanatuan, the work requirement also generated a new source of food because most able-bodied prisoners labored on a thirteen-hundred-acre camp farm and got to keep some of their produce. These workers received more rations than those who did not. "Life . . . revolved around the farm and the different work details," Sergeant Knox later recalled. All day long they toiled under the tropical sun or in pouring rain, moving rocks, tilling soil with primitive pick-mattocks and hoes, under the gaze of quick-tempered guards who often communicated with rifle butts and fists. "Practically every man who worked on the farm detail was beaten up at least once," Sergeant Raymond Castor wrote in a postwar report for the Army's Provost Marshal. The Americans delighted in assigning lampoonish nicknames to the guards, like Sailor, Fish Eyes, Pygmy, Air Raid, Five O'Clock Shadow, Charlie Chaplin, Big Sonofabitch, and Donald Duck. When the latter learned of his nickname, he asked the Americans where it came from. They told him it was the name of a famous American movie star whom he resembled. This pleased him greatly, at least for a while. "In Manila one day he happened to catch a Disney cartoon," Corporal Chick Saunders recalled. "When he got back to camp, he beat the hell out of everybody for weeks."

Lieutenant Colonel Harold Johnson's expertly run commissary enhanced the camp's supply of food and other consumer items. Not only had he succeeded in cooking the financial books to maximize every last GI peso, fool the Japanese, and acquire more supplies, but he had also become an expert negotiator, regardless of whether he was dealing with his Japanese adversaries or Filipino merchants. "All of our prices are lower than they are in the market at Cabanatuan which helps us a lot with the limited amount of money we receive," he wrote in a secret diary. Because of the commissary, substantial quantities of eggs, bananas, peanuts, mongo beans, panocha, and cigarettes circulated around the camp. Though prices steadily rose throughout 1943, they remained reasonable for the average prisoner. By the fall, bananas still cost less than a peso per kilo. An egg cost twenty centavos. Peanut prices inflated from about two pesos for three quarts to three pesos. "Nearly every afternoon for a long time, we shelled about a cupful of these and fried them in Primco [oil] and then ate them while still warm," Captain Fendall fondly wrote.

The general fund that Johnson had organized to make sure the poorest and the sickest prisoners received access to their fair share of commissary items was so well established that, in Johnson's recollection, carefully chosen officers now vetted applicants "to determine whether the income requirement was met and then they were screened by the medics." Another source of sustenance came from clandestine networks of friendly Filipinos who risked their lives to provide prisoners with food, clothing, money, medicine, and news of the outside world. "There is in Manila an 'Invisible Committee' for the purpose of extending aid to American prisoners of war," a December 1943 State Department memo affirmed. The Americans dubbed these aid networks "the Underground Railroad." Johnson worked closely with the "Miss U" undercover group run by Ramon and Lorenza Amusategui, a socially prominent, extraordinarily courageous, local couple. Johnson and other prisoners communicated with them via secret notes smuggled in and out of the camp. They addressed one another by pseudonyms. Ramon was Sparkplug or Noel because he had been born on Christmas Day, or sometimes just Sparky. Lorenza went by the eccentric moniker Screwball Number 3. "My pseudonym was always a source of merriment among the recipients of my screwy letters," Lorenza later wrote, "but then, to make these boys laugh, was the best medicine." One of her POW correspondents once ribbed her, "I do hope for you the war ends pretty soon so you can be relieved of that [alias]." Johnson was known by the less colorful name CJ.

The Amusateguis were not content just to risk their lives for the prisoners. They also expended their own personal wealth. They sold their car, rings, watches, diamonds, and a valuable bracelet for thousands of pesos, which they then donated to the prisoners. Lorenza solicited a ten-thousand-peso donation from her father, a prominent local physician. She and Ramon spent many days hitting up well-to-do friends and acquaintances for money. "We here in Manila never laxed in our seeking for funds, and a day's work consisted of Ramon and I going to persons likely to come forth with some form of donation, and meeting at an appointed time, tired and feet aching from the amount of walking, done to achieve what was foremost in our hearts," she wrote. They entrusted the smuggled money to the care of Johnson and Captain Frank Tiffany, alias Everlasting, a chaplain. Together Johnson and Tiffany saw to it that the funds did the most good for as many prisoners as possible. "Operations for the welfare of the whole will always have my wholehearted support," Johnson told Ramon in one secret letter. Though Johnson did once persuade the Japanese to send him under heavy guard to Manila on commissary business, there is no evidence that he ever actually met the Amusateguis or any other members of the Miss U network. On the Manila trip, he did encounter a young boy who whistled "God Bless America" and flashed him the V-for-victory sign. With the guards alongside, Johnson could not acknowledge the boy, but the encounter bolstered his morale for weeks.

Inside Cabanatuan, Johnson and the other prisoners lived—emotionally at least—on rumors and war news. Filipinos and other friends from the outside passed along information and the prisoners had access to the occasional newspaper including the ubiquitous *Nippon Times*. This and other Japanese media sources usually teemed with far-fetched stories of grand imperial victories, but sometimes they did admit reversals, such as the loss of Attu. At times, operatives spirited in Manila papers, but the Americans now had access to an even better source of information. The prisoners operated a highly secret shortwave radio that a clever engineer had built from spare parts. The radio was small enough to hide inside of a canteen. "I was responsible for procuring some of the material that was used in it," Johnson later said of the radio. "We had to make our own batteries." At night, a trusted group clustered around the radio and heard broadcasts from as far away as San Francisco and Tokyo. They heard of German defeats in the Soviet Union, the victorious Allied invasions of North Africa and Sicily, as well as Guadalcanal, Midway, New Guinea, and New Georgia. The listeners then spread the news among their comrades. "We knew things were going our way and it was just a matter of time," Johnson said. Even with factual news circulating around Cabanatuan, rumors still abounded. Spain had supposedly joined the war on the Allied side. Germany would surrender by the end of 1943. The Allies had opened a road from Calcutta to China capable of accommodating ten thousand trucks. General Krueger had taken over as SWPA commander after General MacArthur retired to become General Marshall's personal aide. A Baptist preacher even claimed that the Pope had converted to his faith. "A deluge of wild rumors swept over us," marveled Captain Bumgarner, the physician. "There had been a devastating earthquake in Japan with tens of thousands killed . . . Roosevelt announced that the war would be over by Christmas. The skeptics among us wanted to know *which* Christmas." The moods of some prisoners rose and plummeted with each rumor. As circumspect, seasoned professionals, Bumgarner and Johnson were inclined to take them with a large grain of salt. Johnson developed a quiet determination to hold on long enough for the inevitable liberation and a day when he could see his wife, Dorothy, again.

The improvement of camp conditions made possible a diverse array of morale-boosting diversions that alleviated some of the monotony, stress, and melancholy of prison life. Chaplains conducted regular religious services. With an average of 125 services per week, Catholic chaplains were especially prolific. Learned men offered lectures on history, philosophy, theology, languages, anatomy, geography, wine, food, and a slew of other topics. Prisoners dubbed the lectures the "University of Cabanatuan." Some men wrote poetry or music. Many kept secret diaries. Others had enough energy to play a little volleyball or baseball. A small group of golden-voiced men formed a glee club. Other artistically inclined prisoners staged theater productions. Led by Lieutenant Colonel Ovid Wilson, "a tall, gaunt, bald-headed officer with a delightfully dry sense of humor," as one colleague remembered him, the actors organized a theater group. They wrote scripts, built props and a stage, and made costumes, usually after a long, hard day working on the farm. Some focused on comedy, others on drama. Corporal Eddie McIntyre earned great popularity, and more than a few jeering whistles, by donning a turban and evening gown to portray a female character.

Every other Saturday evening, Wilson's thespians put on a play, usually in front of a full house. The offerings included original productions and such famous shows as *Journey's End*, *Gone with the Wind*, *Uncle Tom's Cabin*, *What Price Glory?*, *Frankenstein*, and *A Christmas Carol*. Every now and again, the prisoners got to see a movie, usually some variety of absurdist Japanese propaganda—in one instance, prisoners were even pressed into duty as extras in a movie that portrayed the American surrender at Bataan—but they did get to see some Marx Brothers films. A POW band provided a constant and popular source of entertainment. The band had evolved since the previous summer, as musically talented prisoners entered the camp or became healthy enough to play. Some had brought their instruments with them. Others acquired instruments that had been smuggled in. By the fall of 1943, the orchestra had fifteen members, including a conductor, two arrangers, two singers, two trumpet players, a trombonist, a sax player, three guitarists, two piano players, and a drummer. They performed background music for the Saturday-evening plays. Every Wednesday evening they gave a one-hour concert. "In addition the Orchestra played at the Camp Hospital, in the kitchens at evening meals and occasionally special numbers were played at Japanese celebrations," wrote Lieutenant Colonel Barr in a POW diary. According to Barr, the band performed at least one thousand different pieces of music, from popular tunes to original POW compositions.

At the height of Cabanatuan's rejuvenation, a camp library prospered. "A few of the first prisoners to come to Cabanatuan had been fortunate enough to bring with them some reading matter, mostly a few works of fiction, some technical books, and a few scattered magazines," an Army report chronicled. Local donations, smuggling, and trading added to these original holdings. By the summer of 1943, the library occupied its own spacious building and boasted thirty-five hundred books, six hundred magazines, and fifty games. The building featured reference, information, membership, and reservation desks, plus a reading room, and of course an area for the stacks. Among the volumes were atlases, almanacs, and maps that afforded prisoners the opportunity to follow the course of operations. Anyone could arrange to become a member with borrowing privileges. The vast majority of the prisoners made some use of the library. The volunteer librarians implemented a reserve and lending system. Books could be checked out for five to seven days, magazines for five. "The penalty for overdue books was two days['] loss of library privileges for each overdue day," Major Cecil Sanders wrote in a comprehensive history of the library. Extreme offenders lost their membership privileges altogether, a true deterrent. Because the reading material tended to deteriorate with such heavy circulation, the librarians created a binding section whose members lovingly repaired or maintained the books and magazines.

Lieutenant Colonel Johnson, by nature a thoughtful, studious man, gravitated toward theological reading material. He spent hours contemplating doctrine of the various Christian denominations. He read the Bible and anything else he could arrange to borrow from the library. "I could endure this incarceration . . . with plenty of reading material at hand," he told his diary. He found that he could finish an entire novel in one day if he did not have many duties or distractions. In spite of the opportunity to read and enjoy a nominally better living standard than the horrendous first few months of captivity the year before, a heavy, almost leaden tension hung over Johnson and his fellow prisoners. They were pawns of the Japanese, largely dependent on them for any continued decent treatment. The decency could end any day. Everyone knew this, and each man probably worried about it privately, in the back of his mind, as a sort of uneasy, queasy reality. "The monotony of camp life grows with each passing day," Johnson scribbled plaintively in his diary. "Freedom looks ever more precious." No one could say when, or if, they would ever again enjoy that precious freedom.[4]

13

Toils

Mei-ling Soong, known to nearly all Americans as Madame Chiang Kai-shek, understood power and image. She also keenly understood the United States and its political pulse, certainly more so than the average American and probably even better than most American politicians. Wellesley-educated, forty-four years old, blessed with tremendous intelligence and a regal beauty, she mixed easily with Westerners. She spoke perfect finishing-school English, with a tendency toward expansive, rolling r's. She was equally at ease in literary and political circles. She seemed to embody the quintessential American fantasy of a westernized China—clever, defiant, steely, Christian, and politically progressive, an indomitable Asian partner.

When she toured the United States in the winter of 1942–1943, a brilliant casting agent could not have chosen a more perfect individual to represent the face of Chiang's troubled regime. She spent nearly three months in seclusion at the Presbyterian Hospital in New York City and the Roosevelt family home in Hyde Park, recuperating from an undisclosed illness. Like a pop star who arrives onstage fashionably late in order to prime audience anticipation, her mysterious health sabbatical seemed to stoke all the more public interest in her. In February 1943 she began making public appearances, sparking something of a national frenzy of pro-Chinese adulation. When she arrived in Washington and took up residence in the White House, crowds lined the streets to cheer her motorcade. On the eighteenth of that month, she became the first woman ever to address the House of Representatives. When she entered the chamber, she received a four-minute standing ovation. Introduced by Speaker of the House Sam Rayburn as "one of the outstanding women of all the earth," she stood on the House rostrum, with multiple microphones perched in front of her and an oversize American flag draped behind her. Trim and petite, clad in a black one-piece dress with a high mandarin collar, she presented the very picture of Chinese elegance. The gallery was packed. For every fortunate person who had received a ticket, ten others had been turned away.

She held forth on the importance of the war in Asia and the sacrifices China had made. She even took a jab at the Europe-first policy. "The prevailing opinion seems to consider the defeat of the Japanese as of relative unimportance and that Hitler is our first concern. This is not borne out by actual facts, nor is it to the interests of the United Nations as a whole to allow Japan to continue not only as a vital potential threat but as a waiting sword of Damocles, ready to descend at a moment's notice. Let us not forget that Japan in her occupied areas today has greater resources at her command than Germany. Each passing day takes more toll in lives of both Americans and Chinese." Playing to her audience, she lauded American servicemen and described the United States as "not only the cauldron of democracy but the incubator of democratic principles. Basically and fundamentally we are fighting for the same cause."

The reaction to her speech was enthusiasm tinged with adoration, especially among Republicans, many of whom were pro-MacArthur, pro-China, Asia-firsters (a political bloc generally called the "China lobby"). Several times she was interrupted by applause. When she finished, she received a rousing standing ovation. "I never saw anything like it," one veteran congressman later exclaimed. "Madame Chiang had me on the verge of bursting into tears." Mei-ling shook Rayburn's hand warmly, worked the crowd, and then went to a Senate committee room, where she joined Eleanor Roosevelt and other dignitaries for a lunch of grapefruit cocktail, salad, chicken à la king, green peas, muffins, cherry pie, and coffee.

Seemingly not hungry, she ate little and picked at her food, "dainty as a canary," in the estimation of one journalist. "Congressmen were wholly captivated by her personality, amazed by her presence, dizzied by her oratorical ability," gushed Frank McNaughton of Henry Luce's *Life* magazine, the figurative bible of the China lobby. She appeared on the cover of *Time*, the other pillar of Luce's publishing empire. The magazine described her as giving "the U.S. something it had lacked, a clear look into the eyes and face of China." At a White House press conference the next day, she sat between the Roosevelts, conveying an unspoken image of proprietary friendship between two great nations. "All the time Mrs. Roosevelt let her left hand rest reassuringly on the right arm of Mme. Chiang's chair," wrote Nancy MacLennan in the *New York Times*. The only hint of dissension was when a reporter asked FDR how fast the American government could get more planes and supplies to China. When the president indicated as fast as the Lord would let them, Mei-ling interjected pointedly, "The Lord helps those who help themselves." Roosevelt's face reddened, either from wrath or embarrassment.

She took that message far and wide, speaking at venues all over America, collecting money for the United China Relief fund, urging more aid for her country. She visited Wellesley, walking the snow-covered campus in pants and a winter coat, accepting honors as the institution's most distinguished alumna. At Madison Square Garden in New York, she shared the stage with Willkie, who described her as "an avenging angel" to an adoring audience of twenty thousand people. In Los Angeles, a parade was staged in her honor. She addressed thirty thousand admirers at the Hollywood Bowl. Her speech was tinged with moving, but less than truthful, vignettes from the war in China. "The heartbreaking fight of the young Chinese air cadets who had unlimited courage and almost no acceptable equipment," a *Life* magazine reporter chronicled. "Madame's frequent trips to the front with the Generalissimo . . . the intense loyalty of the people to their leaders despite gravest adversity." The tales provoked a reverential silence and tears among many in her audience. As part of the proceedings, the Los Angeles Philharmonic unveiled a new composition called "The Madame Chiang Kai-shek March." Edward G. Robinson and Walter Huston read a prepared script lionizing China. Mei-ling rubbed elbows with a legion of stars, including Spencer Tracy, Henry Fonda, Bob Hope, Gary Cooper, Shirley Temple, Ginger Rogers, Ingrid Bergman, and Rita Hayworth.

Americans responded to Mei-ling with overwhelming adulation, bordering on hero-worship. She received hundreds of letters and telegrams a day. Some Americans sent her gifts by mail or tried to give them to her in person at speaking appearances. A New Jersey housewife mailed her a three-dollar money order, care of the White House. At one early-morning train stop, a stationmaster insisted on presenting her with a batch of homemade cookies baked by his wife. Writer Basil Miller hustled into publication an infomercial-style book entitled *Generalissimo and Madame Chiang Kai-shek: Christian Liberators of China*. Reflecting public opinion, media coverage of her was almost universally favorable. "What she wants, she wants for the Family of Man over the entire earth," Carl Sandburg opined dreamily in the *Washington Post*. The outpouring of coast-to-coast affection for her was so striking that, for a time, some in the War Department and the White House worried that the president might actually be forced by overwhelming public pressure to eschew the Europe-first policy.

Secret Service agents and Chinese attendants accompanied Mei-ling everywhere she went during her seven-month visit. Snow White, as the State Department code-named her, lived in the sort of resplendent luxury that might have made Marie Antoinette blush. She slept on satin sheets and insisted they be changed every day or even more often if she decided to take a nap. In New York, she stayed at the finest suite in the Waldorf. In Washington, she lived in the White House. Behind the scenes, she was considerably less appealing than the public persona on display in adrenaline-charged speaking appearances and laudatory magazine articles. Her habit of clapping her hands for service, rather than ringing a more dignified bell, quickly alienated the White House staff. She smoked constantly. She insisted that the US government fly a special cargo of English cigarettes from New York to Washington just for her. She allegedly refused an interview with a black reporter because of his race. Instead of greeting a crowd that had gathered at a Utah train stop to see her, she sent one of her maids out to pose as the real Madame Chiang. She had a tendency to change her schedule at a whim, presenting security issues for her Secret Service detail. When the chief of the detail asked her to keep more regular hours or make more firm arrangements with him, she demanded his relief. She buttonholed staffers and policy makers alike, constantly and almost ferociously lobbying for Chinese aid.

Secretary of War Stimson patronizingly referred to her as "a most attractive and beguiling little lady." She made no secret of her dislike for Lieutenant General Stilwell, ripping him routinely. One of his aides once referred to her as "that scheming bitch. Honesty and ethics meant nothing to her." To the moralistic Stilwell, she merely represented "a gang of thugs with the one idea of perpetuating themselves and their machine. Money, influence, and position the only considerations of the leaders. Intrigue, double-crossing, lying reports. Hands out for anything they can get; their only idea to let someone else do the fighting . . . indifference of 'leaders' to their men . . . continued oppression of masses. And we are maneuvered into the position of having to support this rotten regime and glorify its figurehead, the all-wise great patriot and soldier—Peanut. My God." At dinner in the White House one night, when the conversation turned to a strike called by the labor leader John L. Lewis, Roosevelt asked Mei-ling how her government would treat him. She ostentatiously drew a finger across her throat. In spite of himself, the pro-union Roosevelt laughed, though others were hardly amused. Before the Madison Square Garden rally, she stood up 270 VIPs, including nine governors, who waited in vain for her to attend a dinner in her honor. According to Secretary of the Treasury Henry Morgenthau, the president, after all the weeks of dealing with Mei-ling, was "just crazy to get her out of the country," not necessarily because of any personal disliking for her, but because he was concerned that stories of her diva tendencies would leak out and erode popular support for Chiang's regime.[1]

Mei-ling's duality paralleled that of the Nationalist government. On an epidermal surface tattooed with political advocacy and distorted media coverage, it seemed an ideal ally, a bulwark against Japanese expansionism, and a great hope for a postcolonial Asian future. The corrupt, incompetent, and repressive dermal layers of the regime's skin—largely unseen by the average American—were less appealing. Mei-ling and her husband often made the point, and they were absolutely correct, that China had experienced destruction and suffering on a scale unimaginable to Western minds (a historical truth that is still relatively overlooked outside of Asia). In spite of all their flaws, the Chinese were tying down significant Japanese resources and manpower. But the Nationalist regime hardly represented democracy as Americans understood the term.

Throughout 1943, the uneasy alliance partners continued to spar over Operation Anakim, Stilwell's ambitious plan to retake Burma and reestablish a land link between China and its Western allies. Everyone brought their distinct political baggage to the cluttered alliance table. Chiang still saw little purpose in risking major engagements against the Japanese, especially with the communists lurking as a shadow government in northern China and Wang's accommodationist government still going strong in Japanese-occupied areas. The British continued to play a deft game of assurance and retreat, at first agreeing to the use of Royal Navy amphibious assets to take Rangoon, Royal Air Force squadrons to provide air cover, and a British-Indian Army to fight in Burma until the inevitable demands of the European theater prompted them to backpedal. In truth, they had little other cohesive strategic objective than maintaining their imperial presence, primarily in India. Churchill remained mystified at the American preoccupation with China, and he had no intention of expending scarce British resources in the jungles of Burma. The Americans played a double game of their own. In their words, they described China as a great power and assured Chiang of his nation's overarching importance. In their deeds, they assigned the Generalissimo's country the lowest priority in resources, and this in spite of Mei-ling's successful public relations campaign. At one point, she thought she had secured agreement from the War Department to have an American infantry corps sent to the theater. In truth, there was no possibility of this ever coming to fruition, a brutal reality that spoke volumes about American priorities.

Not surprisingly, Major General Chennault's plan to win the war through an air campaign offered a magic bullet sort of appeal to these uneasy, irregular partners. Unlike Stilwell, the courageous and charismatic airman had established a good relationship with the Chiang couple, stretching back to 1937, when he had retired from the Army, left his home in Texas, and gone to work for them as a consultant. Ever since his first meeting with Mei-ling, he had been enthralled by her. "She will always be a princess to me," he wrote in his diary that evening. The ensuing years had done nothing to dampen his enthusiasm. "To this day I remain completely captivated," he wrote several years after the war. In Mei-ling's opinion, Chennault had "won the affection and admiration of the Chinese by his deeds, which had proved him to be a true friend of China." His plan to unleash a war-winning strategic bombing campaign with a maximum force of five hundred aircraft held an irresistible appeal for Chiang and his wife. It offered the tantalizing prospect of subduing Japan without suffering the sort of casualties inherent in ground combat and without having to implement meaningful reforms to the Nationalist Army or the government as a whole. Chiang could potentially defeat Wang, reoccupy the lost provinces that had suffered under Japanese occupation, and amass substantial resources to deal with the Communists. Best of all, most of the heavy lifting would be done by foreign airmen. The concept appealed to Roosevelt, too, especially as the costly fighting in the South Pacific intensified. Stilwell's plan for a grim, plodding ground campaign through some of Asia's worst terrain seemed to pale by comparison.

In late April 1943, with Churchill and his entourage scheduled to arrive in Washington for the Trident conference, the president summoned Stilwell and Chennault to the capital to argue for their respective plans. The relationship between the two men was correct in person, stormy at distance. They saw warfare through different lenses—Chennault as an air-power zealot; Stilwell as a pragmatic ground pounder. Their personalities were poles apart, with Chennault playing the cavalier to Stilwell's round-head. One Chiang biographer described them as "chalk and cheese—a Confederate versus a Yankee, a Good Ole Boy who recognized human foibles against a puritan who prized moral courage." Swashbuckling and colorful, beloved by his aviators, the craggy-faced Chennault was the aerial version of a grizzled sea dog. "He looks as if he'd been holding his face out of a cockpit into a storm for years," one of his pilots once affectionately said of him. Captain Billy McDonald, who flew with him for years, and served as a close aide and confidant, revered him. "He is a great man," McDonald wrote in a letter to his father, "and will go down in history as one of the outstanding men of the age." But, in the higher reaches of Army leadership, Chennault enjoyed anything but a good reputation. Generals Marshall and Arnold thought of him as courageous but strategically inept, disloyal to his superiors and possibly corrupt, owing to his possible association with some shady but obscure gold deals in China. Marshall told him to his face that he did not trust him. "For all his combat ability and ability to inspire the men of his own command," one colleague said of him, "[he] was a man utterly without principle." Stilwell believed that Chennault was using his air plan to undercut him, perhaps even scheme with the Chiangs to replace him as theater commander. Awkwardly, the two generals traveled home on the same C-87 transport plane. Chennault worked feverishly to update the plan he had presented to Willkie back in October, while Stilwell occasionally glowered at him, but otherwise maintained his distance.

At the White House, both had the opportunity to sell their ideas to Roosevelt over the course of several meetings between April 30 and May 2. Glib and energetic, Chennault was a more effective speaker than the dour Stilwell. Like many airmen of the time, he oversold a potent asset, offering victory primarily through airpower. In the original plan he had written up for Willkie, he had claimed, "Given real authority . . . I can cause the collapse of Japan. I can do it in such a manner that the lives of hundreds of thousands of American soldiers and sailors will be saved, and that the cost to the country will be relatively small." He was savvy enough not to utilize such cheap sales lingo with this audience. Instead, he spoke in terms of material support. With sufficient aircraft and proper priority of supply tonnage over the Hump, he envisioned a progressive strategic air campaign to roll back Japanese power in China and bring the enemy to his knees. He told the president that with ten thousand tons of supplies per month, his aviators would sink or severely damage one million tons of enemy shipping.

"If you can sink a million tons, we'll break their backs," an excited Roosevelt replied, with a giddy slap of his hand on the table.

In contrast to Chennault's gospel of airpower, Stilwell could offer only the old testament fundamentals of lines of communication, main supply routes, economics, logistics, and ground combat. He certainly agreed that Chennault's China-based planes could inflict serious damage upon the Japanese. However, the Japanese were bound to realize this and, in response to the aerial campaign, use their considerable advantage in ground power to overrun Chennault's poorly defended airfields. In the process, they might even collapse Chiang's shaky army. The Generalissimo had given the American government his assurances that his army could prevent this from happening, but Stilwell—and anyone else who understood the real state of Chinese ground forces—knew this was a hollow promise, little more than a cultural formality to save face. As Stilwell saw it, only a truly proficient Nationalist Army could protect the air bases and make any sort of sustained aerial campaign viable. The army could be improved only by reforms, proper training, modern weaponry, modern matériel, and the rejuvenation of the nearly ruined Chinese economy, all of which could not happen in the absence of a supply route linking China with the outside world. Chennault's planes "would do the Japs some damage but at the same time will so weaken the ground effort that it may fail," he wrote. "Then what the hell use is it to knock down a few Jap planes." He continued to argue for Anakim. With control of Burma, the Allies could complete their plan—already under way—to build a road link to China, thus fueling a long-term effort to resuscitate Chiang's army into a well-led force of 120 divisions, maybe eventually augmented by one or two American divisions. Then, and only then, could the Allies use China as a platform for a devastating strategic bombing campaign. "Air coverage over nothing is in my opinion of little value," Stilwell commented bitingly in a memo for Marshall. Basically, Stilwell was arguing that, on the Asian continent, airpower must follow ground power, and Chennault precisely the opposite.

Unfortunately for Stilwell, his subdued, glum demeanor undercut the fundamental logic of his arguments. In the key meetings with Roosevelt, he sat slumped over, head down, muttering ineffectively of Chinese weakness, disappointing his patron Marshall. Stilwell was such a drip that the president later asked Marshall if he might be sick and no longer up to doing his job. The chief of staff assured Roosevelt that Stilwell was fine. Vinegar Joe also proved to be distressingly incapable of modifying his tart honesty into a productive direction. When Roosevelt asked both Stilwell and Chennault what they thought of Chiang, Stilwell immediately replied. "He's a vacillating, tricky undependable old scoundrel who never keeps his word." Chennault of course enjoyed a much better relationship with Chiang than did Stilwell. But he also had a stronger appreciation for the prevailing pro-Nationalist political winds in Washington. "Sir, I think the Generalissimo is one of the two or three greatest military and political leaders in the world today," the aviator said. "He has never broken a commitment or promise made to me."

Chennault was offering a strategic get-rich-quick scheme, a military equivalent to getting in shape by taking a pill or going on a red-meat diet instead of exercising and eating balanced meals. Just as the easy wrong is always more appealing than the more difficult right, so, too, was the case with Chennault's plan. Barbara Tuchman wrote of him perceptively, "His interest was not China per se but airpower." He could never explain exactly how he planned to protect his Chinese airfields from the Japanese offensive that would surely result from his aerial attacks. "He did not think it was necessary to use ground troops to defend air bases," Colonel Dorn, Stilwell's close aide, later claimed. To any fair-minded planner, Chiang's promises that the Chinese Army would somehow keep the enemy at bay were hardly reassuring.

Not surprisingly, considering the tantalizing nature of Chennault's offering and the weakness of Stilwell's interpersonal skills, the president decided in favor of Chennault. Anakim did remain on the books and the road-building campaign would continue. But priority of supplies over the Hump now went toward Chennault's air effort, instead of to build up the Chinese Army. The president even took the remarkable step of ordering Chennault to report directly to him, bypassing his nominal superior Stilwell and higher military authorities, something that did not sit well with Marshall, who held Chennault in great contempt for agreeing to such a disloyal arrangement. "For this alleged breach of military protocol, General Marshall has never forgiven me," Chennault later wrote. Stilwell had never thought highly of Roosevelt. The president's decision only solidified his sub-rosa contempt for him. In a memo to Marshall, Stilwell groused that Roosevelt had a "total misapprehension of the character, intentions, authority and ability of Chiang Kai-Shek." Privately, in his diary, he claimed that the president had never given him a fair chance to speak his piece. "So everything was thrown to the air offensive," he raged before jabbing a literary pen at Chennault. "What's the use when the World's Greatest Strategist is against you."[2]

Stilwell's defeat at the Trident Conference indicated a clear lack of confidence in him within the Roosevelt administration, and seemed to augur the end of his time in command. Indeed, even as the strategic debate played out in the White House meetings, others actually were conspiring for the beleaguered Stilwell's relief. T. V. Soong, the Western-savvy Chinese foreign minister and Mei-ling's older brother, conceived of a way to ease Stilwell out by establishing a new command hierarchy with a Chinese officer in charge. T.V.'s agenda went way deeper than simply getting rid of Stilwell. Harvard-educated, financially adept, an able administrator, he saw himself as the natural person to lead China. Relegated to the back bench when Mei-ling took America by storm, he was troubled by her growing power as the public face of the Nationalist regime. By maneuvering Stilwell out and placing a military ally in command, he hoped to undercut his sister, assume greater influence over lend-lease operations, and marginalize his brother-in-law Chiang, with whom he had never gotten along particularly well.

At an August 21 meeting with Roosevelt, T.V. told the president that if Stilwell continued in his job, there would be "cause for concern about Sino-American cooperation." Roosevelt saw no need to imperil the important relationship over a commander in whom he had little confidence. He agreed to Stilwell's removal if this suited the Chinese. From Chungking, Chiang indicated a willingness to make a change. Marshall and Stimson even began exploring other jobs for Stilwell. Marshall contemplated tapping competent, low-key Lieutenant General Somervell, the current head of Army Service Forces, to replace him. Somervell was even traveling in theater. Meanwhile, T.V. produced a scathing, and somewhat ignorant, anti-Stilwell memo for Harry Hopkins, the president's key aide. In the memo, T.V. outlined Stilwell's many instances of rudeness or poor judgment, especially in relation to his oversight of the lend-lease effort, and concluded, "Stilwell does not smoke, drink, or chew. He would make a typical highly regarded Boy Scout leader in any country . . . there can be no doubt that [he] . . . is completely unfitted to be a major military leader." Actually, Stilwell was not a teetotaler, and he did smoke cigarettes, but T.V. was at least right that he did not chew tobacco. Back in China by now, Stilwell had an inkling that somebody was scheming for his removal, but he did not know who. "With me out can't they get the Br[itish] to agree to postponement [of Anakim]?" he mused to his diary. "Is that the reason or . . . the Chennault build-up? Or spite? Or fear of me? No way to tell."

Ironically, his erstwhile antagonist Mei-ling, along with her sisters, took action to save him. Catching wind of her brother's machinations, Mei-ling quickly ascertained that if he succeeded, then her power and influence, as well as her husband's, would inevitably wane. In this light, saving Stilwell equated to thwarting her brother. Throughout September and October, in a series of clandestine meetings with Stilwell, she and her sisters counter-plotted to thwart T.V.'s plans, mainly by rehabilitating the general's image with Chiang. "[She] keeps letting it out that he is very hard to handle, that you have to catch him at the proper moment, that he forms opinions on little evidence, that 'they' are telling him all sorts of stuff about me," Stil-well noted in his diary, "[She] let out that she has a hell of a life with the Peanut: no one else will tell him the truth so she is constantly at him with . . . disagreeable news. It can't be easy to live with the crabbed little bastard. They are working on Peanut."

The power struggle climaxed in mid-October when, contrary to T.V.'s expectations, he returned home to find that Stilwell's fate was anything but decided. Somervell, for one, had no intention of playing any part in the sacking of his colleague. "Though I had asked General Marshall for an overseas command twice before, I had no desire to relieve Stilwell," he later wrote. "Under such circumstances, any action which I might take in the matter would be tinged with self-interest. This made me all the more deter-mined to see that Stilwell was not removed." He apprised Stilwell of what was in the wind. "Well, well, it was T.V.," Stilwell marveled to his diary about the identity of the plotter. In a meeting with Chiang, Stilwell admit-ted to mistakes and promised, somewhat disingenuously, to amend his prickly ways and work more cooperatively. Chiang merely asked that Stil-well understand his subordinate place as chief of staff and avoid a superior-ity complex. "This was all balderdash but I listened politely," Stilwell later opined. In a top secret, deeply analytical personal memo, he poured out his true, unreconstructed feelings about Chiang. "I am satisfied that he will never undertake a thorough purge of incompetents and crooks in the army until it is too late. He has no friends at all, only servants who are without exception ill at ease in his presence. He has for years been surrounded by yes-men who invariably dress matters up as they think will please him. He has no patience with anyone who disagrees with him and flares up angrily at any opposition. What he cannot explain away to his own satisfaction he simply ignores or brushes aside somewhat contemptuously. He has no sound education. His conception of strategy and tactics is ghastly. That China is still in the ring is more despite, than on account of him."

Among themselves, the Soongs volcanically argued their respective cases before Chiang. He decided to keep Stilwell in place (perhaps no surprise, since a wife's influence over a husband tends to be stronger than that of a brother-in-law). In a stormy meeting with Chiang, T.V. asked, "Are you the chief of an African tribe that you should change your mind so capriciously?" Deeply insulted, the Generalissimo slammed his fist onto a breakfast table so hard that the dishes cascaded to the ground. Emotionally wrung out, humiliated, foiled in his designs, T.V. went home and burst into tears. For many months thereafter, Chiang consigned him to virtual house arrest due to a manufactured illness. Meanwhile, as if to symbolize a joyous new beginning, the Chiangs invited Stilwell, Somervell, and Chennault to their home for tea. Stilwell cynically dubbed it "the grand reconciliation scene." In Somerville's recollection, "the meeting developed into a love feast during which Stilwell and the Generalissimo swore eternal friendship, Chennault promised to be a good boy, and the way was cleared for cooperation and progress." Chiang came away from the pleasant meeting optimistic for his future with the Americans. "Stilwell has expressed his regrets, and I am glad to retain his services and once again to put my confidence in him. This represents a turning point in Sino-American relations." An emotionally exhausted Stilwell wrote to his wife, Win, "It has been a nasty damn experience and I was on the point of telling them to go to hell, but now it's all smoothed over." To his diary, he aptly summarized, "Christ, but this has been a mess." His job was safe—for now.[3]

★

Many miles away from the scheming of generals and politicians in Chungking and Washington, the force of seventy-five thousand American servicemen and women stationed around the China-Burma-India (CBI) theater labored assiduously to implement their commander in chief's war policies. With no substantial American ground-combat forces in place, the flavor of the American presence leaned decidedly toward the logistical and the aerial. While Chennault's newly activated, China-based 14th Air Force attempted to fulfill his grand vision of crippling the Japanese war machine by air, the aviators of the Air Transport Command (ATC) redoubled their efforts to move war matériel from their bases in eastern India to western

China. The fighter and medium-bomber groups of the India-based 10th Air Force occasionally protected the transport planes, but largely focused on tactical strike missions against Japanese targets in Burma and elsewhere.

The lend-lease freight meandered on a long journey even before it reached the ATC fields in northeastern India. Following the voyage by ship from the United States, it was unloaded in Karachi, Calcutta, or Bombay and then moved for days or weeks along substandard Indian roads, railroads, and waterways. The typical ATC mission spanned about five hundred miles, from Dinjan in India's Assam province, over the menacing Patkais, the edges of the Himalayas, and onward to Kunming. The young crewmen called this treacherous air corridor "the Hump." Though the ATC men were derided in some Army Air Force circles as the "Army of Terrified Copilots," their job was daunting and perilous, more as a result of conditions than enemy opposition. With peaks spanning well over ten thousand feet along the route, minimum cruising altitude was fifteen thousand feet. Cloud formations were dense, weather unpredictable, winds ferocious, at nearly 150 miles per hour. Ground crewmen had to perform maintenance at night "because shade temperatures of from 100 to 130 degrees Fahrenheit render all metal exposed to the sun so hot that it cannot be touched by the human hand without causing second degree burns," noted Colonel Edward Alexander, the ATC commander. One of their key aircraft, the C-46 Commando, had so many bugs that it was a veritable death trap. Because of fuel leaks and a venting problem, the aircraft had a terrifying tendency to catch fire and explode. At one point, one in five exploded in flight over the Hump. An early batch of Commandos was found to have seven hundred glitches that required fixing.

The pressure to carry out Roosevelt's strategic vision and get tonnage into China was such that commanders routinely sent crews aloft in any kind of weather, aboard planes that were hardly airworthy. The delivery of tonnage steadily rose—about 4,500 in August, 6,500 in November, and an encouraging 12,641 in December. Chennault called the massive airlift effort "one of the great epics of the war." Even with the delivery of extra tonnage, though, the logistics of the airlift were still problematic because the planes consumed a gallon of fuel for every gallon they delivered, and much of the matériel went to sustain the 14th Air Force rather than Chiang's army. Mishaps rose as well. Between June and December, there were 155 accidents, costing the lives of 168 crewmen. "We are paying for it in men and airplanes," Colonel Thomas Hardin, commander of the Hump operations, wrote to a colleague mournfully of the costly results. "The kids here are flying over their head—at night and in daytime. We are asking boys to do what would be most difficult for men to accomplish. With the men available, there is nothing else to do."[4]

For the fliers and nearly every other American deployed to what most thought of as a culturally exotic, low-priority theater, the challenge of maintaining good morale and a sense of importance to the larger war effort was profound. Army survey teams were troubled to find that 51 percent of the soldiers had no clear idea as to why the Allies were even fighting in this theater. Only 43 percent felt that their jobs had any importance. About a third worked only hard enough "just to get by." A solid 41 percent had no interest in their work. Soldiers complained of poor food, a sense of alienation in a strange locale, and the harsh climate. "It's either too hot, too cold, too wet or too dry, wotta country," one wrote of India. Another told a survey taker, "I feel that twelve months' service in this theater is enough to drive any high-strung person insane. I say end the war as soon as possible regardless of [the] cost in lives." The scarcity of Allied shipping meant that British, Indian, and Chinese hosts were largely responsible for feeding the visiting GIs (a substantial undertaking for two famine-wracked countries). With their bodies unattuned to local food, and indigenous water anything but potable, most of the Americans endured gut-clenching bouts of diarrhea so notorious that they were soon dubbed "Delhi Belly," the "Karachi Crud," or the "Chinese Crud." "I do not think a diet of locally produced Chinese foods is sufficient," one master sergeant complained. "No soldier should be made to subsist on the present diet for two years."

Though movies were common, the remoteness of the theater made it difficult for entertainers to visit. "Celebrities and show people seem scarce," a Bihar-based corporal commented. The troops learned to make their own entertainment. Medics of the 159th Station Hospital in Karachi built a recreation hall and managed to get their hands on a piano and a record player. The 181st General Hospital, also in Karachi, maintained a recreation center. Plus, the unit regularly sent its nurses and other personnel to a mountain rest camp where temperatures were much cooler and the troops could see USO shows and go horseback riding. The recreation room of another Karachi-based unit featured Ping-Pong tables, a horseshoe set, and board games. Soldiers based in Delhi had access to four movie theaters and, in the recollection of one officer, "ice cream parlors with fairly good ice cream and milk, dances, and parties."

Prevailing cultural taboos among white soldiers against mixing with nonwhite women inhibited some from seeking liaisons and only added to the feeling of desolation. But thousands either ignored the taboos or rejected them. Serious relationships were rare; sexual encounters were not. In many cases, the timeless soldier search for feminine companionship led off-duty men into the arms of Chinese and Indian prostitutes, mainly in the cities, though some Chinese hookers were so eager for GI business that they followed American units into remote areas. "The Chinese do not like their women to mix with us for two reasons," commented Major A. R. Gallo, a surgeon. "First, because we are a strange race and second, because we have too much money. Once our men start patronizing a house of prostitution, paying the girls the way our boys usually pay, the girls don't want to go back to the Chinese." Not surprising, venereal diseases soon spread among the Americans. After spending just one night's leave in Bombay (now called Mumbai), a unit of 1,400 soldiers immediately reported 127 cases. Theater-wide, the doctors identified 2,600 new cases. Attempts to punish the afflicted produced no good results. "Court-martials don't lower venereal rates and it is a damned injustice to any soldier," a sergeant in China complained. As was true elsewhere, medical authorities largely blamed the problem on African-American soldiers, since their infection rates were noticeably higher than those of whites. "I have found that colored troops just will not take venereal disease very seriously," Captain Malcolm Bouton, a VD control officer, complained to an interviewer from the Army's Surgeon General office. "You can lecture to them, talk to them privately, use discipline, and still they won't use prophylaxis intelligently." It was true that African-American soldiers recognized fewer racial barriers in relation to sex with Asian women, leading to more sexual contact and better chances of contracting disease. But regardless of race, commanders who enforced the discipline of proper prevention measures—usually in the form of medical inspections, rigorously enforced prophylaxis measures, and monitored recreational activities—generally succeeded in controlling sexually transmitted diseases. The obvious reality was that forestalling infection was far less costly than expending the necessary resources to treat an afflicted soldier. In this sense, the old bromide about the superiority of an ounce of prevention over a pound of cure held remarkably true.

The average American soldier was almost entirely ignorant of the linguistic, religious, and cultural nuances of Asia. "You could never dream of the complexities that combine to make this fabulous country," PFC Louis

Marsili marveled of India in a letter to a friend. "So many different races and religions—wealth and poverty—beauty and ugliness—ancient customs and ceremonies, all these combine to make this land the most amazing spot on the face of the globe." Marsili and thousands of other Americans were taken aback at the poor hygiene, filth, and poverty they witnessed. "Sanitation is nonexistent in the Far East," Lieutenant Ray Chesley, a medic, commented. "The streets are used as sewers and garbage dumps." People frequently relieved themselves in public streets, streams, or rivers from which they drew water for cooking and washing. Ninety percent of the Chinese population were rural farmers who had little access to a modern standard of living that Americans took for granted. "You may be shocked, at first, to see how desperately poor most Chinese are," a guidebook warned the soldiers. "Their houses and clothing seem dirty and unkempt. Take this all as a matter of course as the Chinese do, and do not offend their sense of good taste by even seeming to even notice it." The guidebook to India advised the GIs, "You will see more beggars with more pitiful faces and misshapen bodies than you have ever seen before." In a letter to friends, Lieutenant William Hughes, a Signal Corps officer stationed in India, described "bodies lying uncared for on the streets, the hundreds of hideously deformed people, the poverty and filth, elephants walking down the middle of a road, the oxen, cows and water buffalo everywhere on the streets, beggars haunting your every footstep, the millions of insects and birds . . . elephantiasis victims, lepers, Hindus worshipping ivory statues. It's a jolt to wake up and find that only a small percentage of the world's population enjoy anything approaching the economic, social and religious standards of America."

Most of the Americans tended to look down on their allies racially or at least view them as backward. One soldier described the Chinese, whom he disparagingly called "Chinks," as "dirty as you can get without washing. Their hair is long and matted and they have on just enough dirty rags to cover themselves." Another man, in a letter to his parents, disparaged the Chinese as "such a dumb ignorant people . . . and they are our allies. They haven't changed in the past thousand years, just doing things the same old way their fathers did." When one brash lieutenant colonel arrived in theater, he immediately announced that he hated all Chinese, considered them racially inferior and simply would not work with them. Even when his commander threatened to court-martial him, he would not relent. "His attitude was violent, belligerent and insubordinate," the commander later wrote. In the end, the colonel actually accepted a demotion to captain in exchange for a transfer.[5]

With the objective of improving the training and overall quality of the Nationalist Army, Stilwell implemented a liaison program of embedding American officers with Chinese units. The job required tremendous diplomatic skills, cultural savvy, and patience. The Americans, after all, were advisers, not commanders. As such, their authority was limited, usually dependent upon their effectiveness and, all too often, the willingness of Chinese commanders to listen to them. "You must at all times conduct yourself and maintain personal appearance creditable to an officer of the United States Army," their instructions commanded. "The influence you are able to exert will depend largely on the amount of confidence the Chinese have in you, both from a personal standpoint, and from your professional knowledge. Your methods must be flexible, depending on conditions and personalities. The job of a liaison officer calls for exercise of tact and common sense."

Their frustrations were legion. Training standards were low, weapons sometimes scarce. Rifle marksmanship was poor. Staff work was negligible, as was supply administration. Chinese officers ruled with nearly unlimited power. The NCO corps hardly existed. Enlisted men mattered little to the authorities. Troops were often in poor physical condition. Some bordered on starvation. Sanitation and personal courtesy, as Americans understood these concepts, could be nonexistent. "The sum total effect of their disregard for privacy, their table manners, and the smell of their latrines at times becomes almost unbearable," wrote one medical officer. Chinese notions of stealing were far too permissive for American tastes. Liaison men learned to keep all valuables on their persons or under hidden lock and key. Otherwise they might as well expect their belongings to become communal property. Corruption, known colloquially in China as "the squeeze," pervaded seemingly everything and everyone. Commanders stole their soldier's pay or sold food and equipment earmarked for their men. A black market in stolen goods and weapons, much of it American, flourished (sometimes with the aid and abetment of crooked American supply soldiers). The constant Chinese preoccupation with saving face, too often at the expense of truth and efficiency, tested the patience of all but the most understanding Americans. Not many Chinese spoke English, and few of the Americans were conversant in any Chinese dialect, ceding much power and influence to interpreters who were usually themselves of mixed quality and commitment. Often interpreters or individual commanders appeared to take advice perfectly, telling Americans what they wanted to hear, while doing something else entirely, either to help the American save face or because they simply disagreed. In the recollection of one liaison officer, they would only comply "if the American officer is present, and likely to report on failures."

The Americans were especially appalled at the poor state of Chinese medical care and the incredible callousness of their hosts toward the sick and the wounded. "The value of human life is not considered of the greatest importance as in many other nations," the history of an American medical liaison group stated. "The usual attitude toward the wounded soldier is one of [indifference] because, in the first place, as a soldier, he's not worth much, and second if he does die, there will be that much more food and equipment for the others." Major Gallo, who worked closely with Chinese medical units, formed the opinion that "to them, human life is cheap. The important thing in the Chinese Army is the rifle. There is only one rifle to every four or five soldiers, so that if a man is wounded, there are always plenty of others to pick up his weapon and carry on." The majority of Chinese medical officers and enlisted men had no professional training. Most had simply failed in other jobs and were shunted into medical duties, a clear sign of the low priority afforded by the Chiang regime to the health of its soldiers. American doctors who trained their Chinese charges soon learned that they must certify all participants in their programs as bona fide medics or else consign those who did not measure up to the humiliation of losing face in front of their peers.

In general, the Americans came to respect the toughness and resilience of the average Chinese soldier, if not always his commanders and political masters. "The Chinese soldier has all of the capabilities which go towards making an effective combat army," Brigadier General Dorn, who oversaw the advisory effort for the Yunnan-based divisions (known as the Y Force) that Chiang and Stilwell planned to use in northern Burma as part of Operation Anakim, wrote in an early 1944 analysis. One adviser wrote in an evaluation of his unit, "The Chinese soldier . . . is a hard worker, uncomplaining, puts in very long hours, does what he is told without asking questions . . . even though he gets very little food or clothing and practically no medical attention."

Focused as ever on the tactical mission of fighting the Japanese Army, many of the liaison officers grew frustrated with what they perceived as a

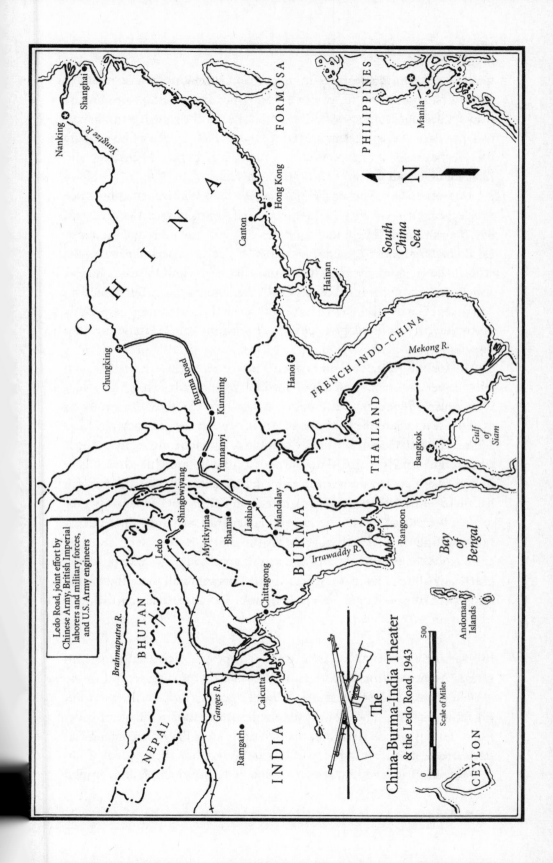

Ledo Road, joint effort by Chinese Army, British Imperial laborers and military forces, and U.S. Army engineers

The China-Burma-India Theater & the Ledo Road, 1943

Scale of Miles

500

0

N

CHINA

FORMOSA

PHILIPPINES

Nanking

Shanghai

Yangtze R.

Hong Kong

Canton

South China Sea

Hainan

Manila

Chungking

Burma Road

Kunming

Yunnanyi

Hanoi

FRENCH INDO-CHINA

Mekong R.

THAILAND

Bangkok

Gulf of Siam

Shingbwiyang

Myitkyina

Bhamo

Lashio

Mandalay

BURMA

Irrawaddy R.

Rangoon

Bay of Bengal

Ledo

Chittagong

Brahmaputra R.

BHUTAN

NEPAL

Ganges R.

Calcutta

Ramgarh

INDIA

Andoman Islands

CEYLON

Chinese reluctance to engage in much combat. Naturally distrustful of foreigners, especially after years of Open Door imperialism, the Chinese wondered about American motives and chafed at the smug cultural arrogance of their Western friends. Many of the Chinese soldiers who actually had fought on and off for years were loath to listen to the advice of inexperienced, unblooded Americans. "The Americans cannot fight!" Graham Peck, an American who worked for the Office of War Information, once overheard a Chinese officer tell another. "The Americans just dance, drink, and make money. They understand nothing but machines and are interested only in comfort." As one liaison officer wrote in a secret memo of the attitude he encountered with the Nationalist Army unit to which he was attached, "These people could not understand how a few Americans, who had never been engaged in combat, could teach them anything—especially when they, the Chinese, had been fighting against the Japanese invasion force for years."

Though the Americans undoubtedly improved the health, welfare, and fighting readiness of the Chinese formations they advised, a furrowed-brow sense of concerned exasperation—eerily reminiscent of emotions experienced by later generations of American advisers in such places as Vietnam, Afghanistan, and Iraq—eventually set in among many of those who worked closely with Chiang's army. "It is my opinion that the Chinese Army today is an inefficient, uninterested, incapable and selfish mob which has no national interests at heart whatever and does not desire to fight for its people or its country," thundered Lieutenant Colonel Charles Lutz, a liaison officer, in a secret report for his superiors. "It has been marked by an overpublicized, self seeking and selfish group who . . . have procured practically all the national assets of China. In spite of all these things, the armies of China will fight if and when the proper incentive is furnished."[6]

★

In hopes of providing, at least in part, that proper incentive, American soldiers were working hard to build the road that was so central to the welfare of the Chinese Army and Stilwell's designs as a whole. The work began in mid-December 1942 at the small eastern Indian village of Ledo, where a small railroad terminus marked the limit of British colonial infrastructure. The concept of the road was ambitious and unprecedented—in the skeptical British view, it was futile, doomed to inevitable failure by mud and disease. The British had all they could handle just to construct and maintain airfields in India, build up the Indian Army, and keep a lid on local independence efforts. The ambitious road project held little appeal for the imperial representatives of John Bull. Stilwell and his cohorts planned to construct a modern road from Ledo, some 103 miles to Shingbwiyang in Burma, and from there another 172 miles to the key crossroads Burmese town of Myitkyina, where an existing one-lane track stretched northeastward to Bhamo, where a one-lane blacktop highway—confusingly called the Burma Road—ran all the way to Nationalist-controlled western China. The distance between Ledo and Kunming, the ultimate destination in China, was 1,080 miles. Nor was the daunting job confined just to road building. From Ledo onward, Stilwell's troops had to construct supply and air bases out of whole cloth and somehow get matériel forward, all with limited manpower.

By far, though, the most difficult task was to establish the gravel road, essentially from scratch, between Ledo and Shingbwiyang, through some of the most forbidding terrain on earth, where scientists had classified 1,500 species of jungle vegetation, 40 different kinds of poisonous snakes, untold thousand variations of mites, leeches, mosquitoes, ticks, flies, spiders, and scorpions. "The jungle . . . is tall and dark and silent as death," an Army pamphlet warned GIs. "It is an ageless confusion of tangle, matted undergrowth which confines progress to dim, narrow trails. It is almost as if Mother Nature uses this country as a proving ground to try out new models of pests with which to plague mankind." One American engineer referred to the country as "probably the most difficult ever encountered in any military campaign in this war . . . mountainous terrain, canyon sections, and narrow terraces along torrential streams . . . vegetation cover constituting some of the impenetrable jungle growth on the face of the earth." At the Indian-Burmese frontier, the five ranges of the Patkai mountains presented a dizzying array of peaks, steep grades, sheer drops, and rocky slopes. Some of the peaks rose as high as six thousand feet. Annual rainfall averaged 150 inches, primarily during the monsoon season, from May to September. In some instances, storms dumped as much as fourteen inches of rain during a twenty-four-hour period. Unruly rivers and rain-swollen creeks abounded. Fault planes honeycombed the mushy clay soil. "In the foot hills and mountains, the side hills were so steep that a piece of equipment could not be moved forward until a trail had been carved in the precipitous side," recalled Brigadier General John Arrowsmith, the American engineer commander. "Bulldozers could not be leap-frogged so that the road could be pushed at several points at the same time. No dozer could pass another without becoming the leading piece of equipment itself. Nothing, except a person on foot could pass."

Led by the African-American 45th Engineer Regiment and 823rd Engineer Aviation Battalion, a remarkably diverse force labored shoulder to shoulder, clearing thick jungle, carving the road out of thick mud and bramble. There were Royal Engineer survey teams; British-supervised Indian laborers from the Indian Army, local tea companies, and state labor units; and Chinese troops from the Nationalist Army's 10th Engineer Regiment, as well as advance units from the two infantry divisions the Americans were training at Ramgarh. The infantrymen provided security against occasional harassment from Japanese patrols. Chinese engineers focused on logging, clearing brush, and building culverts and temporary bridges. Carrying parties of Indian porters hauled provisions and equipment through mud and jungle, over ever longer distances as the work progressed. Allied transport planes dropped supplies to engineers who had advanced too far forward to be sustained by land. Most of the necessary equipment—such as graders, rollers, rockcrushers, and air compressors—was American manufactured, intended for Chiang Kai-shek's army. In a case of reverse lend-lease, he gave much of it back to the Americans to assist their efforts.

Through it all, the American engineers worked at the advanced point of the whole effort in a counterintuitive instance of logistical troops preceding combat soldiers. Maps were inaccurate at best, completely useless at worst. The survey teams scouted ahead and plotted the course of the road. The lead bulldozer then began tearing into the jungle. "Then came groups blasting and dynamiting giant trees and jungle growth," an engineer's report chronicled. "The ground was next levelled and graded, ditches, drains and culverts were installed, and finally the gravel from the streams was dumped to form a surface." American medical units followed in the wake of the laborers, treating the odd casualty and attempting to ward off the usual assault on soldier constitutions by tropical diseases. According to one unit after-action report, the medics "fought the mud, rain and jungle pestilence to render aid to the sick and ailing."

As was the case for nearly all segregated units in the World War II army, the black soldiers of the 45th and the 823rd were largely led by white

officers, a blatantly prejudicial custom that reflected the ugliness of unre-
solved American racial issues. In spite of the inequality, the morale and
efficiency of the engineers troops remained high. They worked round the
clock, in difficult conditions, often with great ingenuity. Only the 823rd
possessed D7 bulldozers heavy enough to clear the jungle adequately, but
they had a problem. Because of shipping irregularities, their own complement of seven dozers had arrived bladeless. So they borrowed one from the
British engineers and affixed it to the lead vehicle. When this dozer needed
repair and maintenance, they transferred the blade to a different vehicle.
Brigadier General Arrowsmith managed to locate a couple more blades in
India, meaning that three dozers could function at any given time. Not
until the spring of 1943 did the unit's organic blades finally arrive.

Shelter consisted of small tents pitched in makeshift camps that occasionally were subject to Japanese air raids. The men subsisted on rice and
corned beef, slivers of local bread, and golf-ball-size potatoes collectively
washed down with stale coffee. "We have to serve corned beef every day
and, lots of times, twice a day," one cook complained. "The boys HATE it,
and give us poor cooks hell as if it were our fault." In general, the 823rd
cleared foliage and carved the outline of the road while the 45th trailed
behind, grading the surface and applying gravel. At the same time, D4
bulldozers hacked away at stubborn stands of bamboo and tree stumps like
"a puppy dog might nip at the heels of a five-hundred-pound boar," in the
recollection of one soldier.

The crews averaged three-quarters of a mile per day. For every mile of
completed road, they moved fifty thousand cubic yards of earth. Every
three miles of road, on average, required one bridge—either prefabricated,
pontoon or wooden—and an untold number of culverts. Rockcrushers
could not keep up with the insatiable demand for gravel. Crewmen regularly collected rocky, gravel-like soil from riverbeds and hauled it twenty-
five or thirty miles to spread over the road. The Americans denoted the
progress from Ledo with mile markers, similar to highways back home.
Mile marker 10 meant ten miles away; 20 meant twenty miles away, and so
on. The first thirty miles to the east of Ledo were relatively flat and amenable to construction. At mile marker 34.5, dubbed "Hellgate" by the GIs,
the terrain grew steeper and led into the Patkais, where the going got
tougher.

On February 28, 1943, at marker number 43.3, they crossed into Burma.
They marked the occasion by stretching a line of red, white, and blue tape

at the border. Lieutenant Colonel Ferdinand Tate, commander of the 823rd, fired his pistol in the direction of Burma as the lead dozer plunged forward and snapped the tape. The men stood at attention while a bugler sounded "To the Colors." An artistically inclined soldier painted a sign that read, "Welcome to Burma. This Way to Tokyo!" The two original units were soon joined by another African-American outfit, the 382nd Engineer Construction Battalion, as well as the all-white 330th Engineer General Service Regiment, and, eventually, more white engineer and bridging units. In some places, the path of the new road intersected with escape routes used by the Burma refugees during the desperate retreat in the spring of 1942, when tens of thousands had perished. According to a theater-level history of the project, "ample evidence of this tragedy was . . . seen by the engineering crews engaged in the construction work. They found the path littered with human skeletons and their pitiful belongings."

The farther east the road builders progressed, the more profound were the vestiges of this monumental—and still historically anonymous— human calamity. Stick and brush lean-tos, or bustees, honeycombed the area. Tatters of clothing clung to these shelters or fluttered in the wind. Along the muddy paths was strewn the flotsam and jetsam of life— crockery, bowls, blankets, suitcases, shoes, boots, bayonets, saddles, sandals, mugs and drinking glasses, even phonograph records. In one spot lay the skeleton of a grizzled soldier, rifle at his side, British World War I–era medals from the Palestine and Waziristan campaigns lying in his thorax. His arms were wrapped around a female skeleton wearing the soiled remains of a sari, mute proof that clothing weathered the elements better than flesh. The skeleton of a little girl in a pink dress lay near the tiny bones of an infant still wrapped in a blanket. The hills, valleys, and riverbanks were almost dense with such human remains. "After a year and a half in the open, the skeletons had been picked and weathered clean, and most of the clothing had rotted away," Major Walter Jones, an American physician attached as a liaison officer to the Chinese 10th Engineers, recorded somberly in his diary. "The little family tragedies and the large group tragedies could easily be reconstructed. In isolated bustees, would be the skeleton of one or two adults and two or three children. All down the south face of Kabkye Bum [a prominent hill] were hundreds of bustees containing remains of bodies. I have no idea how many thousands of skeletons I saw . . . or how many more could be found in the brush a few yards off the trail. This picture of the useless starvation, exhaustion, and weary death of so many fathers, women, and children is something that cannot easily be forgotten."[7]

The combination of a temporary Japanese thrust into the nearby Hukawng Valley, supply problems, and the onset of torrential monsoon rains ground the effort to an almost total halt about forty-seven miles east of Ledo, only a few miles into Burma. From May through September, the crews made little headway. "Our handful of troops was fighting a losing battle with the monsoons," one officer later summarized in a report on the progress of the road. "As fast as a trail would be opened up the freshly cut bank would slide down on us, often covering both men and machines," wrote Major William Savage, the engineering officer for the 330th. "If we started sloping the banks far enough back to prevent sliding, it meant moving thousands of yards of dirt on the steep hillsides and even then we had no assurance that the shelf itself wouldn't drop out from under us." The sheer volume of rain bordered on the unbelievable. One unit recorded eight and a half inches in a four-hour period and then fifteen inches over a three-day span. Hospitals along the road were so inundated with rainwater that they could not keep their patients dry. "Rains come right through the roof, wet the patient and the floor, and there is ankle-deep mud down the center of each ward," Colonel Isidor Ravdin, a physician, told an interviewer. Rainwater created disastrous mud- and rockslides. Gravel disintegrated or dispersed. Swollen rivers swept bridges and culverts away. It was impossible to control drainage to any effective degree. Torrents of water cascaded down mountainsides and collected in swollen gullies. A precious D7 bulldozer slid off the road, into a ditch, and became so engulfed in a sea of rancid mud that only its exhaust pipe remained visible.

The crews spent most of their working hours repairing and maintaining existing tracts of highway rather than building new sections. "Lots of times we would lose five or six miles because the road would be washed out by rain," recalled Captain Richard Johnston, a company commander in the 382nd. "Then we would have to rebuild it." Chinese units used mules to haul supplies. Their hooves tore up the road, created rivulets of mud the consistency of viscous yellow soup, and only added to the road's general state of degradation. The men found it nearly impossible to stay dry for any length of time. Clothing and equipment was inundated with moisture and mold. Shoes wore out in a matter of two or three weeks. Ravenous purple-hewed leeches thrived in the watery conditions. "They clung to the leaves of the brush, and to every piece of vegetation on the ground and would

grab on to a man wherever he happened to come within reach of their waving head," one officer recalled. Rare was the man who was not nursing
multiple sores from the bloody bites of these nauseating pests. Ravenous
termites bred exponentially in these conditions, eating through bamboo
structures like tiny saws. The medics of one hospital were astonished to see
six of their wards collapse from termite damage in a single night. Almost
half the 330th's manpower was needed just to keep the outfit's camp from
washing away. "In two or three days mud was shoe-top to knee deep
inside . . . tents and the company street was a bottomless river of mud,"
Savage later wrote.

To avoid mudslides, they learned to anchor all tents on timber or bamboo floors. Supply became an issue because the carrying parties had great
difficulty negotiating their way through the unruly seas of mud, not to
mention the heavy downpours. Vehicle convoys could hardly traverse any
substantial distance. Individual planes dropped whatever cargo they could,
but at best, the forward-most units lived a hand-to-mouth kind of existence. "The picture was that of more and more men moving in, with less
and less supply, over a road that was getting worse and worse, for the enlightened purpose of felling more and more trees across that road," Major
Walter Jones, the physician, quipped to his diary.

The monsoons even exacerbated cultural tensions. As a group of American soldiers watched a Chinese-built bridge wash away one day, they
laughed to themselves sardonically, as Americans are often wont to do in the
face of such uncontrollable adversity. The Chinese, though, believed the
Americans were laughing at them, a direct insult and loss of face in their
culture. When the American commander discovered that the Chinese were
upset, he hastened to explain to the Chinese commander that it was the
American way to respond to cruel fortune with cynical laughter. Tropical
diseases like malaria sapped the vitality of the effort all the more. As yet,
there were few malariologists in theater and no standing orders to take atabrine regularly. Almost all of the Indian laborers and porters were infected,
at least half the Chinese soldiers, and some 20 percent of the Americans. The
disease was occasionally fatal among the Chinese and Indians, rarely for the
Americans. The 20th General Hospital recorded two thousand Americans
cases with two fatalities. Many of the Chinese troops were underweight,
vitamin-deficient, and weakened by multiple bouts with malaria. "Most of
them harbor intestinal parasites, especially hookworm," Lieutenant Colonel
Thomas Fitz-Hugh, a physician with the 20th General Hospital, asserted.

The poor weather and the resultant minimal progress eroded morale like floodwaters grooving a low country field. Among many men, a sense of hopelessness set in. "The opinion of most people you talk to out in the jungle (including some Engineers) is that this road will not be completed and in shape in time to be significant in the war here," Captain George Bonnyman, a staff officer, wrote at midsummer to Brigadier General Boatner, commander of Stilwell's forward headquarters at Ledo. Vinegar Joe himself understood the myriad challenges inherent in the task, so he was not especially surprised with the slow going. "It is obvious you have a tremendous job here, not only in construction, but also in shaking down a lot of very raw units," he wrote in early April to Major General Raymond Wheeler, his able Services of Supply chief who preceded Boatner as master of the Ledo headquarters. "There has been so much done here, and everybody is so willing and interested that I have no business to criticise anything. So I won't."

By late summer, though, after months with little progress, Stilwell's mood was far less pliable. Anxious to get to Shingbwiyang so that his northern Burma offensive could go forward, and eager to prove the British wrong about the viability of the road, his patience thinned by the day. After reading a damning status report from Colonel Merrill, his operations officer, and then flying from China aboard his DC3 "Uncle Joe's Chariot" and making several on-site visits himself, he fixed blame for the inertia—probably unfairly—on Arrowsmith, the engineer commander, whom he thought of as a contemptible château general type. In one diary entry, Stilwell even referred to him as "that insect." In another he ripped him as a "sulky, indifferent bird, who can't see that this is the chance of a lifetime. You wouldn't catch him out in the mud, pushing. No, he's the Big Shot at the base, directing." In truth, Arrowsmith was probably doing everything humanly possible to get the project back on track amid a terrible weather situation. But he was not the sort of hands-on leader that Stilwell could relate to or admire. Fair or not, Stilwell held Arrowsmith responsible for the debacle, so his days were numbered. On August 23, Stilwell fired him.

To replace the luckless man, the War Department sent Brigadier General Lewis Pick, a seasoned engineer whose service dated back to World War I. Pick had the good fortune to take over just as the monsoon rains abated and just as more troops, including the 209th Engineer Combat Battalion, became available for road duty. His can-do attitude mirrored that of Stilwell. "I've heard the same story all the way from the States," he lectured his new staff. "It's always the same—the Ledo Road can't be built. Too much mud, too much rain, too much malaria. From now on we're forgetting this defeatist spirit. The Ledo Road is going to be built, mud and malaria be damned!" He personally assured Stilwell that he would reach Shingbwiyang by the end of 1943. He made sure to place his personal headquarters at the most advanced point of the roadhead. During the rains, the work pace had slowed to one shift per day. With better weather, he resumed a round-the-clock schedule. To provide illumination at night, he rounded up extra lighting equipment, stripping rear areas of generators, and then showed his men how to create even more light by burning flares in buckets of oil. He sent work parties ahead of the vanguard to establish forward supply depots to sustain momentum once the road reached each depot. He implemented a rotation system that provided the troops with occasional light duty in the rear or R and R in Calcutta (though some were impressed into the job of unloading ships during their supposed vacation). He began parallel work on a fuel pipeline designed to stretch all the way to China.

Personal visibility was important to him. He often circulated among the lead construction crews. During his rounds, he liked to cut a branch from a jungle tree and carry it around. The men began calling him "Pick, the man with the stick." They referred to the road they were building as "Pick's Pike," and spoke among themselves of the "Race for Shing." By the middle of November, progress resumed to three-quarters of a mile per day. The 330th reached mile marker 71. A couple of weeks later, the crews were completing a mile of highway per day. On December 27, after two and a half months of almost continuous work, the leading bulldozer reached Shingbwiyang at miler marker 114.5, establishing a continuous road all the way back over the Patkais to Ledo. "A hoarse cheer went up from the throats of a few hundred bearded US Army engineers gathered on a mountainside as the last stump was dynamited into the ravine and the lead bulldozer pounded aside the few remaining stumps of bamboo," wrote Albert Ravenholt, a war correspondent.

From Ledo to Shingbwiyang, the engineers had cleared 1,875 acres of jungle and mountain while moving 11,220,000 cubic yards of earth. Along the route, Signal Corps units had installed five hundred telephones with fifteen exchanges and laid some twelve hundred miles of field wire. Pick led an exhilarated column of jeeps and trucks into Shingbwiyang and presided over an exuberant celebration. A convoy trucked in ninety-six hundred cans of beer, along with doughnuts, coffee, and candy. The 18th

Special Service Unit played a concert and staged a variety show. A fresh column of fifty-five trucks, loaded with newly trained troops from the Chinese 38th Infantry Division, added to the party. Pick later said that much of the credit for completion of this stretch of road belonged to the African-American engineers, "who had done most of the grueling work." He also singled out the 330th for special praise. "Yours is a remarkable record and deserves the highest commendation," he told them.

In the wake of the celebration, the engineers turned the small town of Shingbwiyang into a bona fide staging base, constructing an airstrip and a sixteen-hundred-bed hospital. Behind them was a road that stretched for more than one hundred miles to Ledo. Its completion, against little enemy opposition, represented only the first stage of the larger goal of linking India to China by land—"the first lap of the race" in the words of one officer—but it was the toughest part of that job, mainly because of the Patkais and the particular ferociousness of the jungle terrain along the India-Burma border. "Our pioneering days were finished," a relieved Savage nimbly summarized. With a usable supply route into northern Burma, Stilwell could now move on Myitkyina and thus launch an entirely new ground phase of his effort to reestablish a permanent link between Chiang's China and its allies. The establishment of the Ledo-Shingbwiyang road meant that Anakim could now go forward. After a year and a half of frustrating planning and politicking, Stilwell's golden moment was finally at hand.[8]

14

Makin

The same Trident Conference in which Stilwell and Chennault had battled for the strategic soul of the China-Burma-India theater also set the course for future operations in the Pacific. Admiral Ernest King, the chief of naval operations, had always seen the Central Pacific as the most direct route to Japan. The scattered island groups of Micronesia offered the opportunity for quick-hitting amphibious invasions to secure bases from which to continue the westward advance and isolate the garrisons of bypassed islands. At the same time, the expansive blue waters of the open sea afforded the opportunity for the Americans to take advantage of their growing naval and air strength in maneuver warfare. To the hard-nosed naval officer—a prickly man who suffered incompetents only at their extreme peril and whose daughter once described him as "even-tempered, he's just mad all the time"—MacArthur's push to regain the Philippines and sever Japan's links to its southern empire was wrongheaded. Far better to go for Tokyo itself than to deal with the worthless immensity of New Guinea and the South Pacific, much less the political and amphibious complexity of liberating the Philippines archipelago. Moreover, a powerful Central Pacific drive under Admiral Nimitz could outflank the Japanese at Rabaul and New Guinea, rendering them superfluous at little cost. The obvious by-product of King's Central Pacific strategy was US Navy domination of the nation's war against Japan, something King thought wholly appropriate given the vast oceanic geography of the theater and the potency of the Imperial Navy. So he argued tirelessly for the strategic priority to fulfill his vision, even as MacArthur advocated for his more Army-centric concept.

At the Trident Conference, Roosevelt and the other policy makers forged a compromise that equated to a truce of sorts between the Navy and the Army. They formalized the previously established, two-pronged, divided command approach, with MacArthur continuing his ongoing

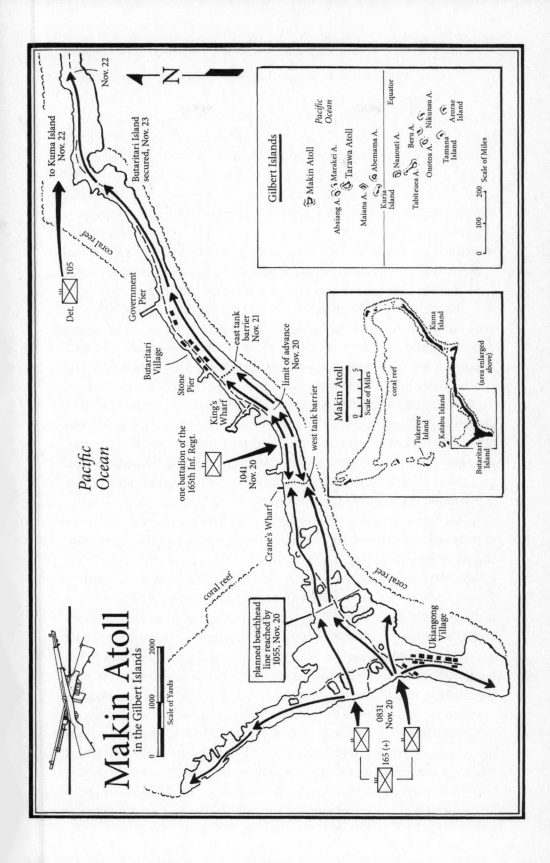

Makin Atoll
in the Gilbert Islands

Pacific
Ocean

Scale of Yards
0   1000   2000

to Kuma Island
Nov. 22

Nov. 22

Butaritari Island
secured, Nov. 23

Det. | 105 |

coral reef

Government
Pier

Butaritari
Village

Stone
Pier

east tank
barrier Nov. 21

King's Wharf

limit of advance
Nov. 20

one battalion of the
165th Inf. Regt.

| 1041 |
Nov. 20

west tank barrier

Crane's Wharf

coral reef

planned beachhead
line reached by
1055, Nov. 20

coral reef

Ukiangong
Village

| 165 (+) |

| | 0831
Nov. 20

Gilbert Islands

Makin Atoll

Abaiang A.   Marakei A.   Tarawa Atoll

Maiana A.   Abemama A.

Kuria
Island

Nanouti A.

Tabiteuea A.   Beru A.   Nikunau A.

Onotoa A.   Tamana
Island

Arorae
Island

Pacific
Ocean

Equator

Scale of Miles
0   100   200

Makin Atoll

Scale of Miles
0   5

coral reef

Kuma
Island

(area enlarged
above)

Tukerere
Island

Katabu Island

Butaritari
Island

operations in SWPA while Nimitz led the advance through the mid-Pacific. They thought of Nimitz's prong as the main effort and authorized the seizure of the Marshall Islands, a collection of atolls located about twenty-three hundred miles southwest of the Hawaiian Islands and twenty-eight hundred miles from Japan. But, as yet, Nimitz did not have enough shipping and troops to invade the Marshalls, especially without first securing the Gilberts, some two hundred miles to the southeast. In August 1943 he and the Joint Chiefs agreed to focus first on the Gilberts. The obvious main target was the Tarawa atoll, home to the only finished Japanese airfield in the island chain. From here, Japanese planes remained in position to launch raids on the Solomons and perhaps hinder shipping between the United States and Australia. Initially the planners intended to invade Nauru, about four hundred miles west of the Gilberts and home to three enemy airfields. But perilous terrain, and the strength of the Japanese defenses, persuaded them by late September to choose the Makin atoll instead. Control of Tarawa and Makin amounted to control of the Gilberts and a nice stepping-stone to the Marshalls.

To the Japanese, the Gilberts represented an outpost line at the eastern extreme of their empire. Shortly after Pearl Harbor, they had seized, against almost no opposition, Tarawa and Makin, where they established small garrisons and minor air bases intended mainly for reconnaissance. On August 17, 1942, 221 Marines under the command of Lieutenant Colonel Evans Carlson raided the Makin atoll. Their purpose was to divert Japanese attention from Guadalcanal, gather intelligence on the Japanese presence in the Gilberts, and capture prisoners. Though the raid bolstered home-front morale and demonstrated the impressive valor of Marine combat troops, it was largely a failure. The Marines snuffed out the small defending force, killing about forty-eight Japanese, but captured no prisoners and gained very little usable intelligence. The American evacuation was chaotic, carried out with little of the ethos that defines the Corps. The Americans lost eighteen killed in action, all of whose remains were, by the necessity of circumstances, left behind. Another twelve were missing—nine of whom had actually been separated and abandoned. These unfortunate men were later captured and executed when the Japanese returned to the island. Worse, at least from a bigger-picture point of view, was the fact that the raid awakened the Japanese to the weakness of their Gilberts outposts. Over the course of the next year, they sent reinforcements and strengthened their defenses, especially at Tarawa, where they constructed concrete and log emplacements impervious even to the largest of naval guns, and stationed several thousand quality troops of the Kure 6th Special Naval Landing Force.[1]

Nimitz had two substantial ground-combat elements at his disposal for the job of taking Tarawa and Makin. Major General Julian Smith's 2nd Marine Division, based in New Zealand, drew the mission of invading Tarawa, while the Army's 27th Infantry Division was to assault Makin. The 27th was a New York National Guard unit. Nicknamed the Orion Division as a sort of double entendre to pay homage to Major General John O'Ryan, the original commander, as well as the constellation Orion, the unit enjoyed a proud World War I lineage as a gritty, dependable, fighting force. O'Ryan was actually the only National Guard commander who held on to his job through the entire war, a notable achievement considering General Pershing's penchant for firing general officers, especially guardsmen. Mobilized anew for federal service in October 1940, the division deployed to the Hawaiian Islands in the spring of 1942, where after a stint defending the island of Hawaii, most of the unit eventually ended up on Oahu.

Initially the men spent most of their time guarding against a possible Japanese invasion. The troops manned and developed beach defenses. To maintain clear fields of fire, they spent many thousands of man-hours hacking kiawe plants with cane knives and brush hooks. At Schofield Barracks and other billets they dealt with a bedbug problem. "We would be interested in methods of control regarding these insects," Captain DeWitt Smith, a physician serving with the division, laconically told a fact-finding interviewer from the Army Surgeon General's office. Throughout the spring and summer of 1943, the troops engaged primarily in jungle training, physical conditioning, and weapons familiarization. In mid-August, once tapped for the invasion, they transitioned to intensive amphibious training. Relentlessly they practiced embarking and debarking from mock boats, negotiating their way down cargo nets attached to walls, organizing themselves into boat teams, getting used to the feel of life belts, and equipping themselves appropriately for amphibious warfare. Some soldiers had to learn to swim. As a finisher, they were made to don full combat gear and tread water effectively. Eventually they practiced climbing in and out of real Higgins boats and other landing craft, often at night. A cadre of officers traveled to Camp Elliot on the West Coast, where they took a rigorous two-month amphibious warfare course. Staff officers learned the rudiments of load planning and worked with their naval colleagues on such tasks as troop billeting and landing schedules.

For obvious reasons, everything needed for the operation, from bullets to tractors, had to be carried over vast ocean distances and thus planned and accounted for by naval and ground staffers. Lieutenant Colonel Charles Ferris, the division supply (G4) officer, devised an ingenious pallet system that greatly reduced matériel losses and made the job of unloading easier and more efficient (not to mention safer). The Navy opposed the pallet idea because it was wasteful of shipping space, a cardinal sin in the nautical world. By one estimate, pallet loading left 46 percent of a typical ship's cargo space unused. Ferris worked closely with a naval quartermaster officer to synchronize the system with the Navy's cargo requirements as much as possible. "The use of pallets consumes eight (8) to twelve (12) percent additional space than that which normally be required for combat loading," he conceded in a preinvasion memo. "However . . . it is the general consensus of opinion that pallet loading is most essential for a successful landing operation as it reduces the following: 1) The exposure of personnel to hostile fire. 2) It permits clearing the beach expeditiously. 3) It reduces breakage and wastage tremendously. 4) It permits the establishment of dumps by simply dragging pallets of the same type to the same general vicinity." Under Ferris's direction, 1,850 toboggan- and sled-style pallets, each four by six feet in size, were packed for the operation.

The logistics of amphibious movement were indeed daunting. One attack transport troop ship, or APA, could carry, at most, a battalion-size unit of twelve hundred soldiers. For every soldier aboard ship over a one-month period, it took one ton, or seventy cubic feet, of shipping space to carry, feed, transport, and provision him. To carry out the invasion, each soldier was equipped with a field pack, multiple bandoliers of small-arms ammunition, four grenades, two K ration meals, and a gallon of water. For Operation Galvanic, as the Gilberts invasions were code-named, Navy store ships amassed 1,483 tons of fresh food and 1,273 tons of chilled and frozen victuals. In addition to a full complement of troops, one cargo ship alone was scheduled to haul a twenty-four-day supply of rations, 3,000 five-gallon cans of water, 18,570 gallons of gasoline, 70,000 gallons of diesel oil, 28,200 gallons of special high-octane gasoline for landing craft, 7,684 gallons of motor oil, 3,655 pounds of grease, plus artillery and machine-gun ammunition, medical supplies, signals equipment, and spare parts. In addition, there were such various and sundries as bazookas, binoculars, machetes, TNT explosives, Bangalore torpedoes, mortars, freshly printed maps, construction material for improving the airfields, jeeps, trucks,

Barco hammers, bulldozers, special distillation devices to provide troops with fresh drinking water once ashore, and bridging equipment.

By October, the rifle battalions began to carry out full dress-rehearsal mock landings with the Navy. "The practice cruises are conducted almost exactly as if they were in operation against the enemy," wrote one officer. This meant loading and unloading pallets and other cargo as if for the real thing, a taxing, tedious process. The assault troops typically spent several days aboard ship, getting used to life at sea before gearing up, climbing into landing craft and hitting Hawaiian beaches, often in pitch-darkness. "We have had good training on the cargo nets and the boats in calm and heavy sea," Lieutenant Colonel Gerard Kelley, a battalion commander, scrawled in his diary. "The men rapidly became accustomed to the motion of the ship. They go over the nets (in a relaxed manner) without fear or hesitation."[2]

Major General Ralph Smith, the division commander, strongly believed that the repetitious, challenging training would save lives in combat. He had assumed command in the fall of 1942, while the division defended the beaches of Hawaii. Visible and gregarious, and yet exacting as a trainer, he had quickly become a popular figure among the soldiers, only a minority of whom were actually prewar guardsmen. He was a stickler for physical fitness. "No matter how much a man may know or what skills he may have, if he hasn't the stamina to stand up under pressure, he won't be able to use his knowledge and skills," he once told an interviewer.

By the eve of the Makin invasion, Smith had more than a quarter century of Army service under his belt. He came from a Midwestern farming family. As a young man, he taught school, ran a 160-acre farm, and earned college credit in his extra hours. He joined the Army as a National Guard private before World War I and earned a Regular Army commission because of his competence and education. He served on the Western Front with two distinguished divisions, the 1st and the 4th, and was wounded in the fall of 1918. Every bit as much an intellectual as a soldier, he became fluent in the French language and developed a unique expertise on the country and its culture. He became proficient enough to teach French at West Point during MacArthur's superintendency, and he later earned a posting at the prestigious L'Ecole de Guerre in Paris, where he matured into one of the Army's leading experts on European armies and economies. At first blush, this intellectual armament made him a better fit for the war against Germany, but the circumstances of global warfare dictated differently. By World War II, after years of professional schooling, staff work, and occasional command duties, he had carved out a reputation as a first-rate field soldier and scholar, a man of even temperament and genteel character. "His extreme consideration for other mortals would keep him from being rated among the great captains," S. L. A. Marshall, who knew him well, once wrote. "He is that somewhat rare specimen, a generous Christian gentleman."

Smith and his staff learned on September 28 of the change in objective from Nauru to Makin. With D-Day set for November 20, they had fewer than two months to plan the myriad details and ready their soldiers. Fortunately they had access to a nice cross section of useful intelligence information about the objective. Army Air Force planes, staging from such threadbare island bases as Canton, Funafuti, and Baker, flew photo reconnaissance missions over the Gilberts, as did Navy carrier- and land-based aircraft. The submarine USS *Nautilus* prowled the waters around Tarawa and Makin, taking nearly two thousand panoramic photographs with a specially fitted periscope camera. Their work was nerve-racking. For fear of discovery, the periscope could remain only two feet above the water and only for one minute at a time. The sub had ferried and extracted part of Carlson's raiding force the previous year, so the crew was already familiar with the area. The 27th's assistant intelligence officer, Captain Donald Neuman, also rode along. Upon *Nautilus*'s safe return to Hawaii, he regaled his colleagues with spine-tingling tales of evading a Japanese destroyer, including several hours resting at the bottom of the sea while the enemy vessel dropped depth charges.

The photographs themselves were very useful to the assault commanders. In one preinvasion diary entry, Lieutenant Colonel Kelley described them as "a great help as they were taken at the same elevation that we'll get from the landing boats." Veterans of the Makin raid—including the president's son Lieutenant Colonel James Roosevelt, who had served as Carlson's executive officer—related good information on beach conditions, terrain, and Japanese tactics. Lieutenant Commander Gerhard Heyen, an Australian naval officer who had lived on Makin, and Private Fred Narruhn, of the 1st Fiji Infantry Regiment, who had grown up there, shared an insider's knowledge of tidal conditions, weather, soil, foliage, and local culture.

Thanks to all this excellent information, the 27th's planners developed a good understanding of their objective. They learned that Makin atoll consisted of a triangular ring of coral reef and small islands about ten to twelve feet above sea level. The only two islands of any size or significance were Butaritari, the main objective, and Kuma, located a few hundred yards to the north and, at low tide, accessible on foot by reef. Together, the two skinny islands stretched like elongated rubber bands for about thirteen miles, with an average of no more than five hundred yards in width. Butaritari was crutch shaped, "with the armrest facing generally West and the leg of the crutch pointing East and slightly North," according to the description of a divisional intelligence digest. The northern coast was bordered by a lagoon, the southern by the open sea. Coconut groves, swamps, jungle bramble, and muddy bobai pits characterized much of the terrain. The population of seventeen hundred Melanesians and Polynesians used the pits to grow nutrient-rich taro leaves, their staple food. A single unpaved road ran from west to east across the island. Beaches on the western and lagoon side of the island were studded with jagged coral ridges and boulders but still feasible for landings.

The Americans sometimes incorrectly referred to the island as Makin, a moniker more properly affixed to the entire atoll. The invasion planners identified a Japanese seaplane base on Butaritari and estimated enemy strength at somewhere between five hundred to eight hundred troops. The garrison actually consisted of 798 men of varying fighting quality. The core combat soldiers were 284 troops of the Imperial Navy's 3rd Special Base Force Makin Detachment, along with 100 ground crewmen and aviators. Another 414 construction laborers, half of whom hailed from Korea and had little military training, rounded out the force. Though the Japanese did have an eight-inch coastal defense gun and a trio of 37-millimeter antitank guns, they were mainly armed with machine guns and rifles. Their main advantage lay in the challenging terrain and an extensive network of log-reinforced bunkers, trenches, and rifle pits located in the central part of the island between two major moatlike tank barriers, both of which were more than five feet deep and thirteen feet wide. Japanese naval forces from Truk and other bases might well have posed a threat to the invaders except for one major factor: Japanese losses in the aerial battles over New Georgia and New Guinea had deprived their surface vessels of adequate air support, in effect immobilizing them.

The American invasion fleet, meanwhile, consisted of some two hundred ships carrying about 35,000 assault and garrison troops and 117,000 tons of cargo. "Pearl Harbor is jammed with the world's largest battleships, light and heavy cruisers and aircraft carriers," Kelley enthused. "Passing amongst them you experience a tremendous sense of power and security and delight in being fortunate [enough] to be born American." In spite of the burgeoning American naval power, there were only enough available attack transports to earmark one reinforced regimental combat team of 6,470 soldiers from the 27th Division for the Makin mission and over 18,000 troops from the 2nd Marine Division to attack the more heavily defended Tarawa.

The invasion armada was divided into two major components. Task Force 52, or Northern Attack Force, carried the Makin force aboard the USSes *Leonard Wood, Neville, Pierce, Calvert,* and *Alcyone,* plus a few smaller vessels. They were supported by four battleships, four cruisers, three escort carriers, and five destroyers. Task Force 53, or Southern Attack Force, under Rear Admiral Harry Hill, consisted of sixteen transports supported by three battleships, five cruisers, five escort carriers, and twenty-one destroyers. A powerful fast carrier fleet, referred to by the eminent naval historian Samuel Eliot Morison as "the greatest carrier force hitherto assembled anywhere," provided mobile air support. This fleet included four new Essex-class carriers, five light carriers, and the venerable war-horses USS *Enterprise* and USS *Saratoga*. Rear Admiral Turner, of Guadal-canal and New Georgia fame, was the commander of the Northern Attack Force and the senior tactical naval commander.

The 27th Division and the 2nd Marine Division were organized into the V Amphibious Corps under the nominal command of Marine Major General Holland Smith, whom the Corps thought of as one of its premier amphibious warfare experts. But, outside of influence over planning and training, Holland Smith had no actual command authority because the respective division commanders were to control their own land battles (and the naval-attack-force commanders enjoyed authority over practically every other aspect of the mission). Historian Harry Gailey correctly referred to Holland Smith's role as tantamount to "a supernumerary during the Gilberts operation." Smith even had to talk his way into going along on the operation, a frustrating circumstance for a man whose notoriously short fuse had earned him the nickname of "Howlin' Mad."

Ralph Smith chose the 165th Infantry Regiment, home to many of his longest-serving soldiers, for the mission of securing Butaritari. Over Holland Smith's objections, he chose a pincers invasion concept. The 1st and 3rd Battalions, commanded respectively by Kelley and Lieutenant Colonel Joseph Hart, were scheduled to land first at Red Beaches 1 and 2 on the western coast of the island. Lieutenant Colonel John McDonough's 2nd Battalion would act as a follow-on force, landing on the northern coast, code-named Yellow Beach, located between a pair of wharves and the tank barriers. Both groups were supported by Lee medium tanks of the 193rd Tank Battalion. The 27th's commander hoped to trap the Japanese defenders in a vise grip between the two invasion forces.

On November 10, Task Force 52 left Pearl Harbor and sailed west. The soldiers were crammed together aboard the troop ships. Bunks were stacked four and five high. "There was space aboard for a battalion-plus, if we all held our breath," quipped Lieutenant Colonel S. L. A. Marshall of riding aboard the USS *Calvert*. Assigned to the 27th as a historical observer, he was in the process of devising new methods of writing battle history. He was especially intrigued by the notion of interviewing the men who did the real fighting. Conscientious and good-humored, but given to self-serving hyperbole, he entertained his fellow officers with an apocryphal story of how a failed English test had once kept him from attending West Point and yet now, Marshall claimed, two of his books were required reading in the academy's English department.

At this stage, most of Marshall's potential soldier-subjects were at least acclimated enough to life at sea as to avoid seasickness and disorientation. They spent much of the voyage talking, sleeping, reading, playing cards, checking equipment or weapons, engaging in calisthenics, or attending religious services topside. Initially they were tense—as rookies headed into combat are wont to be—but the mood lightened greatly when the convoy passed the equator, prompting lighthearted line-crossing ceremonies, a long maritime tradition in which King Neptune initiated pollywogs into shellbacks who now understood the mysteries of the deep. No one was immune, regardless of rank. As part of the ceremony, they crawled through tubs of garbage, recited poetry, sang, danced, and dressed in colorful costumes. Lieutenant Colonel Kelley donned a sailor's dress-white uniform, complete with blue cap, and toted a swab. "The men got a kick out of seeing me dressed up and many funny cracks were passed, including one, 'Hey, Popeye!' We had a lot of fun."

The ceremonies broke the monotony of the voyage and defused some of the natural tension that permeated among soldiers waiting to go into action. The same was true for the intelligence briefings that occupied many otherwise idle hours. Commanding officers and squad leaders discussed unit missions in exhaustive detail with their troops. "The men have been lectured daily on the plan for the forthcoming operation," Marshall wrote in notes he kept during the voyage. "These lectures have initiated them into practically everything that it is to be known about Makin atoll, the enemy strength, the details of the attack, their own roles and functions of all co-operating units. Every man knows the spot where [he] is to land almost as well as if he had tried it in rehearsal. Even the squad leaders have discussed with their men what they are to do in detail after they hit the beach. The morale seems to get higher as the men get nearer to the scene. The men are so calm that the whole experience becomes unreal." Soldiers studied re-connaissance photographs and perused remarkably accurate, colorful sand-table scale models of landing beaches and the interior of Butaritari. "We had some colored sketches made of all phases of [the] plan of attack down to include the tactics of the squads," one commander later wrote. "These when shown on a large screen were worth more than a million words."[3]

On the afternoon of November 19, the Northern and Southern Attack Forces spotted each other and then separated to make their final ap-proaches to their assigned objectives. Some 105 miles of ocean separated Makin from Tarawa to the south. Aboard the warships, nervous reports of approaching enemy planes kept crewmen at their battle stations. In reality, the Japanese air reaction to the Gilberts invasions amounted to only a couple of ineffectual individual attacks on LSTs. Aboard the Calvert, Lieu-tenant Colonel Kelley had posted on the ship's bulletin board a final pre-battle message to the troops that harkened to the Irish heritage many of them shared. "As we land on the beach I will be crying 'Faugh ah Ballagh' which means in Gaelic 'Clear the Way!'" Lieutenant Commander John Hughes, Calvert's executive officer, presented Kelley with an American flag to take ashore. The two officers and several other men signed their names alongside an inscription that noted the time, place, and unit. Captain Ste-phen Meany, a Catholic priest and regimental chaplain, blessed the flag and said mass in the mess hall. On deck, Lieutenant Joe Giltner, the Prot-estant chaplain (in a regiment dominated by Catholics), held a final prein-vasion service a few hours before the troops were scheduled to hit the beach. A full moon lit the young faces of the soldiers as they sang and whistled along. Some took turns giving solos. Finally, Giltner asked, "Will you do one last thing for me? Will you sing 'The Old Rugged Cross'?" As one, they sang the popular hymn together.

A couple of hours later, as halting streaks of sunlight glazed the eastern horizon, most were packed into landing craft, tensely waiting to head into Butaritari. Previous to D-Day, B-24 Liberators from the 7th Air Force and Navy carrier aircraft had pounded Makin targets (and Tarawa as well). Now a thunderous preinvasion bombardment preceded the landings. At 0610, carrier planes strafed and dive-bombed, dropping one-ton "daisy cutter" bombs designed to shred all foliage and flesh within one hundred yards of detonation. Once the aviators had dropped their deadly eggs, they settled into prearranged sectors overhead to act as gunnery spotters or keep a sharp eye out for enemy submarines and planes. The fleet then unleashed a massive wall of firepower. The combined might of the battleships *Pennsylvania*, *New Mexico*, and *Mississippi*, plus the accompanying cruisers and destroyers, hurled ordnance at Butaritari, pummeling the beaches and the bunkers between the tank barriers with 1,990 fourteen-inch shells, 1,645 eight-inch rounds, 7,490 five-inch shells, half of which were fitted with delayed fuses to foster greater penetration before their explosions. Coconut trees shattered and flew in every direction. A trench near the West Tank Barrier, a substantial antitank ditch, was torn apart. In total, more than seventeen hundred tons of projectiles hammered the island. A final flight of planes buzzed in ahead of the lead landing craft and strafed Butaritari one more time. Hazy plumes of smoke and dust wafted overhead, a seeming funeral cortege to the defenders, at least in the estimation of the hopeful assault troops. But, in truth, the damage to the Japanese defenders was minimal. Though traumatized and concussed, most of them succeeded in weathering the steel storm safely inside bunkers and dugouts. "This fire, though effective, left a surprisingly large number of positions intact, several of which were dummy positions," Major General Ralph Smith, the division commander, later wrote. "The actual destructive effect of the bombardment was less than had been hoped for." Admiral Turner, from his more distant vantage point, assessed the supporting fire more favorably. "The effect of naval and air bombardment was highly satisfactory . . . and contributed materially in the reduction of hostile resistance." This divergence of opinion between Army and Navy about the effectiveness of preinvasion bombardment was not unique to Makin. It would become fairly common in the many operations to come. Ironically, and tragically, the Makin bombardment might actually have proved deadlier to the Americans than the Japanese. During the shooting, one of the *Mississippi*'s gun turrets exploded, killing forty-three sailors and wounding another nineteen.

The leading troops rode aboard unarmored landing vehicle tracked (LVT) amphibious craft that were generally known as amtracs or alligators. Wonderfully versatile, the vehicles could traverse substantial distances in choppy seas, negotiate their way over coral reefs, and run on land. With a crew of two or three men, each LVT could carry about a dozen soldiers. "They were worth their weight in gold," one commander opined. Sergeant Adrain Romero, an LVT commander, called them "the answer to amphibious operations." At General Ralph Smith's request, about fifty of them had been assigned to the division two weeks earlier. They were crewed by soldiers from the 193rd Tank Battalion, most of whom had only had enough training time to establish a basic familiarity with their vehicles. In the view of one naval observer, the LVTs looked like "prehistoric monsters foraging for game." They carried assault troops from an attached battalion of the 105th Infantry Regiment, whose job was to get ashore, establish a foothold, and clear the way for the main waves of the 165th that rode aboard Higgins boats.

The alligators disgorged rockets and .50-caliber machine-gun fire, even as they made their way over reefs and boulders to begin depositing the troops on Red Beaches 1 and 2 at about 0830. "We carried out the landing, holding our formation well in spite of rough water," Lieutenant Carl Delashmet, an LVT platoon leader, later testified. "One vehicle bellied on a large rock as it hit the shore, halting it for only a few minutes." Opposition was negligible to nonexistent. "I jumped down from my boat and stood straight up for two or three minutes, waiting for somebody to shoot at me," said Major Edward Bradt, one of the first men to land on Red Beach 2. "Nobody shot. I saw many other soldiers do the same thing."

Nature proved to be a greater impediment to the landings than the Japanese. According to the 193rd's after-action report, Red Beach 1 and its approaches were honeycombed with "broken lava boulders on the beach and coral heads under the water surface." The boulders damaged tracks, tore gashes in the underbellies of LVTs, and immobilized Higgins boats from follow-up waves. Nine alligators were damaged badly enough to require subsequent repairs. The corridors to the beach were so narrow that, at most, only three landing craft could make it into the beach at any given time. Most of the assault troops were forced to hop off their boats well before the beach and splash their way through deep water. "Men were going into water up to their waists, slipping on coral rocks, stumbling into holes in the reef," Lieutenant Colonel Kelley later told his diary of the 1st

Battalion's landings. "The footing was terrible. We slipped and stumbled in. I looked back and saw wave after wave joining the general scramble off boats. We all got ashore but only because the Japs were too dumb to have that beach defended." Actually the lack of opposition was due to the low state of Japanese capabilities rather than any particular mistake on their part. Undoubtedly, though, Red Beach 1 could have been a bloodbath if the Americans had faced any kind of formidable defenses and determined opposition.[4]

As it was, the bulk of the 1st and 3rd Battalions made it ashore unhindered by the enemy. Within a couple of hours, they made contact with each other, established a beachhead, and began advancing east against minimal opposition. Shortly thereafter, antiaircraft batteries from the 93rd Coast Artillery Battalion and a dozen 105-millimeter howitzers from the 105th Field Artillery Battalion were ashore and in position to provide fire support. At about 1030, the LVTs and Higgins boats of the 2nd Battalion, comprising the eastern half of Smith's pincers, zigzagged into Yellow Beach under a curtain of protective naval bombardment and last-minute strafing runs by carrier planes. Japanese fuel dumps exploded, belching clouds of oily smoke into the air, periodically obscuring the intense late-morning sun. The noise of the shelling, the planes, the explosions, and the roaring of landing craft engines all made it difficult to hear. Incongruously, a lighthearted, almost carnival atmosphere prevailed on some of the boats. Some men read magazines; others hastily ate meals, exchanged playful barbs, or slept. "One man, upon seeing the hundreds of fish that had been killed by the explosion of shells in the water, remarked that after the fight, "he would pick up enough fish to feed the detachment," Lieutenant Edward Kalina later wrote. Lieutenant Joseph Kiley's soldiers serenaded him with an enthusiastically loud, though slightly off-key, version of "Happy Birthday to You!"

Coral reefs, boulders and shell holes impeded the approaching landing craft, though not as seriously as at Red Beach. When the boats were about five hundred yards from shore, enemy machine-gun and rifle fire began spewing from the general direction of the two wharves that bracketed Yellow Beach. In spite of the natural obstacles and the fire, the LVTs managed to make it to the muddy shore, where soldiers proceeded to jump over the sides, spread out, and take cover. "That's when the men began to pull themselves forward on their stomachs and toss hand grenades at everything that moved," wrote Lieutenant Willard Marlowe, whose platoon was among the first units to land. "We had gone through this assault maneuver so many times in training that now we were going through it automatically. We knew just what to expect of every man. Nothing is more important in combat. The sharp coral ripped our combat suits and tore into our flesh as we crawled forward, taking what cover we could behind rocks, trees, and fallen timbers from wrecked buildings in Butaritari village." With the help of covering fire from his men, he personally killed a three-man machine-gun crew.

Because of the coral and the shallowness of the water even now at high tide, most of the thirty-five Higgins boats and other craft carrying the medium tanks of A Company, 193rd Tank Battalion could not make it all the way in to the beach. Two of the tanks got bogged down in the deep water of shell holes; others had to mush forward out of the water and into the imperfect beachside terrain. "They were held up on land by shell holes, taro pits, and the burning fuel dump," reported Lieutenant Colonel Harmon Edmondson, commander of the 193rd. Sergeant Henry Knetter's tank fell into a taro pit and got stuck in a tree stump. "I fired about 100 rounds with the .30 [machine gun] at a bunch of Japs running west on the ocean side," he later recalled in an official report. "Hung up as we were, no other gun could be brought to bear. We were pulled out by 2 other tanks but soon got hung up on another stump." Aboard one Higgins boat, Lieutenant Aloysius Rolfes, a young rifle platoon leader, saw bullets spattering the water and told his men to get down as low as they could. A few moments later, the boat, like so many others in the follow-up waves, ground to a halt on a patch of coral. The coxswain dropped the ramp, looked at Rolfes, and said, "Lieutenant, you're on your own!" Rolfes and hundreds of other infantrymen were deposited into waist-high water, dodging the bullets that almost seemed to be skipping off the surface as they steadily made their way on to the beach. According to Lieutenant Colonel McDonough, they had to "wade through . . . water for a distance of approximately 300 yards to the beach. They presented a perfect target for enemy fire from the flanks but suffered only a few casualties." His battalion lost three men killed, a few others wounded, and secured the beach in a matter of minutes against only scattered, disorganized groups of Japanese. Like the other two battalions at Red Beaches 1 and 2, they were fortunate that Japanese resistance was slight.

By nightfall, McDonough's outfit had crossed the road and reached the ocean coast. Firmly ashore on the west and east sides of Butaritari, the

American pincers steadily advanced toward the tank barriers and each other. Though the doomed Japanese were outnumbered and outclassed in every way, they did have the advantage of defending favorable terrain. "In defensive combat, positions will be constructed to employ the principle of sudden fire at opportune moments," stated a Japanese doctrinal memo on island defensive warfare. "Sudden fire and sniping will be especially stressed at close range." The heavy foliage provided great concealment for the Japanese and the unsteady ground impeded any kind of rapid advance on foot or by vehicle. "Smoking-out the snipers that were in the trees was the worst part of it," First Sergeant Pasquale Fusco of G Company, 165th Infantry commented. "We could not spot them even with glasses and it made our advance very slow. When we moved forward, it was as a skirmish line, with each man being covered as he rushed from cover to cover. That meant that every man spent a large part of his time on the ground."

Soon the struggle for the island centered mainly around the perimeter of Japanese bunkers and trenches between the tank barriers. From east and west, the Americans battered their way forward against enemy defenders who usually preferred to fight to the end rather than surrender. Tanks had difficulty operating on the marshy ground. Coordination between tank crewmen and infantrymen was problematic. Command arrangements were ambiguous. "Individual tank commanders refused to carry out my orders even after I had made myself known to them," Lieutenant Colonel McDonough complained in a post-battle report. "This happened with other infantry leaders also." Moreover, there was no efficient way for the two to communicate directly. All too often, infantrymen had to resort to the frustrating and dangerous practice of banging with the butts of their rifles on a tank turret to get the attention of their armored colleagues. "It took the better part of the first day to make them understand just how we wanted them to work," one infantry commander later commented. Gains were measured in the hundreds of yards.[5]

To the west, Lieutenant Colonel Kelley's 1st Battalion soldiers advanced slowly that afternoon along the slippery, chewed-up island road, steadily harassed by sniper fire and machine-gun nests that posed just enough of a threat to mandate caution among the advance troops. About 250 yards away from the West Tank Barrier, at a bend in the road that comprised an ideal ambush spot, a Japanese machine-gun team and accompanying rifle-men raked the leading platoon with sheets of accurate fire, pinning down the Americans. "This position proved to be one of the toughest nettles found at Makin," Marshall later reported. "An extensive covert [sic] of thick vegetation, including coconut palms, mangrove trunks, tenambe, etc. screened the interior of this bulge."

Bobai pits and gullies further restricted the mobility of the attackers and provided potential hiding places for the Japanese. On the lagoon side of the road, Lieutenant Daniel Nunnery, the platoon leader, personally killed a Japanese soldier with his M1 carbine, took cover behind a tree trunk, and attempted to see where the fire came from. Soon thereafter, Lieutenant Colonel Kelley, the battalion commander, approached from behind and asked Nunnery what was holding him up. "He pointed in the direction of [a] bobai pit," Kelley wrote. Moments later, a burst of fire caught Nunnery and blew his head apart. The native of Queens in New York City was killed instantly. According to one eyewitness, "his brains were lying back over his skull." A wounded soldier whose left arm was mangled and bloody lay on the other side of the road, closer to the pit. Kelley took cover, tried to ascertain the strength of the Japanese position and how he might destroy it. As he did this, he saw the regimental chaplain, Father Meany, dash across the road and hit the dirt right in the kill zone, alongside the wounded man. The priest as turning slightly left to retrieve something from his prayer case when shots rang out and bullets tore into his right arm and shoulder. "He put his hand up to his right shoulder and sank down," Kelley recalled. "I prayed he was only wounded and not dead . . . as I feared from the way he slumped down." Private Jean Berthiaume, a bespectacled, French-speaking soldier from Vermont, rushed to the aid of Father Meany. He knelt over the wounded priest, administering first aid. As he did so, a bullet smashed into his back. Berthiaume slumped over and began to cry softly. In French, the young private began saying confession, "Bless me, Father, for I have sinned." Meany understood enough French to hear him out and provide a little comfort. Another bullet ripped into Berthiaume's back and then another penetrated his helmet and missiled through his head, tearing a large hole above his eyes. Berthiaume immediately fell dead over the priest.

Fifty-four-year-old Colonel J. Gardiner Conroy, commander of the 165th Infantry, had been present at this scene a few minutes earlier but had gone back several hundred yards to enlist the support of a light tank platoon. So he had not witnessed the casualties piling up at the road bend, and he was of the opinion that his regiment's advance had been halted by nothing more threatening than a lone rifleman. A descendant of Thomas Fitzsimons, a signer of the Declaration of Independence, Conroy was a National Guard officer from a prominent Brooklyn Irish-American family. He had more than thirty years of part-time military experience under his belt, including combat service with the 27th Division in World War I. In civilian life, he practiced law as the counsel for a Brooklyn department store and donated many hours to a wide array of Catholic charitable endeavors. Like many Guard officers, he resented and vaguely feared the predomination of West Pointers in the Army. He worried that his superiors might someday replace him with a ring knocker, and he sometimes even wondered if he would survive the war at all.

Convinced as he was that nothing more than a random rifleman was holding up the advance, Colonel Conroy saw no need to exercise any particular caution when he returned to the scene of the ambush. At 1455 hours, he strode forward, upright—almost as if walking in a park in civil life—and shouted for Nunnery's platoon to get moving. Lieutenant Colonel Kelley, still lying under cover, turned to his right and saw Conroy about a hundred feet away, walking straight in the direction of the road and the prone figures of Meany and Berthiaume, right at the enemy line. Kelley frantically waved his arms and yelled at Conroy to take cover. "He didn't seem to grasp the situation," Kelley later jotted in his diary. "I pleaded with him to get down." As Conroy reached a clearing, the realization seemed to hit him. He halted, bent over slightly, and began to turn in Kelley's direction. "Before he could utter a word, he was hit in the forehead and was dead before he hit the ground."

Under more fortunate circumstances, Conroy's actions could have been inspirational. The military lore of World War II is filled with tales of commanders like Eichelberger or Patton who spurned or dismissed desultory enemy fire to motivate their troops into action. Unlike the stars of those stories, Conroy was not lucky. Enshrouded in the fog of war that concealed the mortal threat posed by the enemy before him, he paid with his life for valorous ignorance. His actions revealed a courageous, committed commander, albeit one who could have benefited from a bit more circumspection and some unglamorous information gathering. "He was leading his men like the gallant soldier he was," General Ralph Smith later said of him, "and he died a soldier's death." In the end, though, all that separated him from the Eichelbergers of the world was ill fortune. Moreover, Conroy might have sensed that he would not live through the Makin battle. Back in Hawaii, he had occasionally hinted to Lieutenant Colonel Kelley that he would one day succeed him. "You'll have to watch that when you get the regiment," he would say. Kelley never knew for certain if Conroy said this because he felt he would be relieved or killed. In a condolence letter to Conroy's widow, Marie, he made no mention of her husband's possible premonition. "I hope you'll find a measure of comfort in the knowledge that he didn't suffer any appreciable time and that the manner in which the end came to him was as a soldier would wish it. I feel terribly humble in any attempt to console you and your daughters who have loved him more than we could."

Regardless, Kelley had little time to mourn his dead colonel. He immediately ascended to command of the 165th. Bombarded with requests to retrieve Conroy's body and go to the aid of Father Meany, Kelley gave the difficult order to leave them in place, at least until he could organize a new attack or darkness could provide some chance of getting to them undetected. Otherwise, he figured he would simply lose more men in the kill zone. He even had to issue a direct order to Lieutenant Colonel Lafayette Yarwood, the division chaplain and another Catholic priest, to keep him from going after Father Meany. For all Kelley knew, Meany was dead. If Yarwood also got killed, the unit would be without a priest, thus putting at risk, in Kelley's estimation, "the spiritual comfort he could give to hundreds of men." That night, Lieutenant Warren Lindquist, commander of the regimental Intelligence and Reconnaissance platoon, led a patrol that successfully recovered Meany and got him to the unit aid station. Though the young priest was badly wounded, he was alive and would recover, probably thanks to the first aid efforts of the courageous Private Berthiaume. "As you probably know, your son Jean was killed while kneeling beside me, after he had been wounded," Father Meany later wrote to Private Berthiaume's mother.

Shortly before dawn on November 21, another party retrieved the body of Colonel Conroy and took it to the aid station, where medics gently placed a blanket over their dead colonel. That afternoon, Father Yarwood conducted a heartfelt burial service for Conroy, Nunnery, and several other dead soldiers, in a small enclosure designated for a division cemetery called "Gate of Heaven."[6]

No more than a mile or two away, fighting raged in the heart of the Japanese defensive network between the tank barriers. "The Japanese . . . were living in terrible conditions," Lieutenant Rolfes later recalled. "They were living in mud holes. They were [masters] at using whatever they had

in hand to make a fortification . . . and they fought feverishly." Pressured
on two sides, they concealed themselves and ambushed any Americans
who entered into their line of fire or, even more commonly, let one group
pass behind them and then opened fire on the next group, in hopes of cutting off the first. In the recollection of one American small-unit commander, their fortifications were "about fifty feet long, made of sturdy 12 to
15 inch logs, covered first with sand bags and then with plenty of loose
sand. The japs lived through a terrific bombardment in them and were still
fit to fight." Even when tanks pumped 75-millimeter shells into the bunkers at the point-blank range of twenty feet, they seldom collapsed.

The Americans quickly learned to assault the enemy works methodically, with every possible means of fire support. Tankers maneuvered as
close as possible and raked apertures with machine-gun fire. Squads of
infantrymen stood alongside, firing their rifles or pitching grenades into
trench lines, rifle pits and bunkers. Engineers dashed in and hurled nine-
pound TNT charges in between the logs of bunkers. "Generally there was
an open pit for an mg [machine gun], a covered shelter, and a communication trench," Sergeant Fusco later told an interviewer. "The walls of the pits
were from three to five feet in thickness and the trenches were about four
feet deep. The pit was usually connected with a very strong dugout revetted
with sandbags and logs and on the opposite end was another entrance
somewhat below the surface of the earth. To knock out these emplacements, an eight-man squad would crawl to within about fifteen yards of it
and then take up station around it according to available cover. The BAR
man and his assistant would cover the main entrance. Two men armed
with grenades would make ready on both flanks of the shelter. They would
rush the pit and heave grenades into it, then without stopping, dash to the
other side and blast the entrance with several more grenades." Eventually
after all this preparation, they physically assaulted the shelter, usually with
fixed bayonets.

Among the Japanese, the naval troops were generally more committed
to fighting to the death than were the ground crewmen and the laborers
(many of whom were Korean and anything but enthusiastic about laying
down their lives for their Japanese imperial overseers). "If the enemy cannot be driven off, the fight will be continued to the death," they and the
troops of other island garrisons were ordered by their superiors in an official document. "But a glorious end will not be sought too quickly. Every
added day of resistance and every extra one of the enemy killed or wounded

is important." Even family members back home often conveyed the expectation of total self sacrifice for the nation. "You are my son and yet you are not my son," one mother wrote to her soldier son. "You are the son of the Emperor. Your body is not yours—it belongs to the Emperor." The varying shades of commitment among the enemy troops to such self-sacrificial ideals were lost on the Americans, not just for cultural reasons, but because so many Japanese seemed more than willing to fight to the death. "A Japanese soldier will go to almost any length to kill one American soldier," Lieutenant Marlowe advised his fellow infantrymen in a post-battle article about his experiences on Butaritari. "It doesn't seem to matter to him that he himself has no chance of escape." When Lieutenant John Campbell, a young platoon leader, and his men attempted to take a pair of enemy soldiers prisoner, one of them held his hands up as if to surrender and then, once he drew close enough to Campbell, brandished a saber and slashed the lieutenant on the wrist and ankle before he was cut down by Campbell's men. Another squad came upon a group of dead enemies sitting in a semicircle, each of whom had put a bullet in his own brain rather than risk capture.

The Japanese soldier's propensity to hunker down and sell his life dear contributed to an understandable caution among the American attackers, especially with their visibility and mobility limited amid Butaritari's bramble. Ground had to be secured repeatedly lest individual snipers stay behind or infiltrate the American lines to inflict casualties. A mild paranoia infused the men about the perceived ubiquity of the Japanese. For instance, rumors soon spread that Japanese snipers had taken shelter inside a pair of sunken old ships—or hulks, in American parlance—that lay in the lagoon at Yellow Beach. Reports of enemy fire, from machine-gun tracer rounds to individual rifle shots, infused American units from the squad level ashore to the ships offshore. Eventually commanders diverted resources to silence the hulks for good. Ships bombarded them. Tanks shelled them, so inaccurately as to pose a danger to LVTs and other craft that were ferrying equipment and supplies to the beachhead. Some of the landing craft returned the perceived fire. In many instances, their bullets pinned down troops from the rifle companies that were fighting between the tank barriers. An air strike of carrier planes even skip-bombed the hulks, and with tragic consequences. One of the planes experienced a hung bomb. Instead of dropping on the hulk, the plane disgorged its deadly cargo on three light tanks and a group of American infantrymen who were sniper hunting. All three tanks were put out of action. A large fragment tore through Private John Costello's head, killing him instantly. Another killed Corporal Elmer Conway as he took cover in a shell hole. The company executive officer, Lieutenant Ed Gallagher, had been standing on one of the tanks, directing fire. A fragment smashed into his abdomen and knocked him off the tank. He died shortly thereafter. "Ed mounted one of the . . . tanks and effectively manned its machine gun against the enemy," Lieutenant Colonel Kelley later wrote to Gallagher's mother, either unable or unwilling to share the awful truth that her son had actually been killed by American ordnance. "During the firing Ed was hit and seriously wounded. Ed did not rally from his serious wounds and he passed away. His initiative, courage, and leadership were an inspiration to all his men." After the bombing and shelling of the hulks ended, a squad-size patrol clambered aboard a pair of LVTs and investigated them directly. They found no evidence of any Japanese presence, not even one spent cartridge.[7]

By now, Major General Ralph Smith and his nominal V Amphibious Corps superior Major General Holland Smith were both ashore. The latter Smith was functioning as little more than a frustrated observer, so his mood was anything but bright. He knew the Marines at Tarawa had already suffered heavy casualties and were fighting desperately to annihilate the stubborn Japanese defenders. As a lifelong Marine with thirty-eight years of service to his credit, he yearned to be there with them. Holland Smith's devotion to and affection for his Marines knew no bounds. But tethered to the Northern Attack Force by Admiral Turner, Smith knew he could not go to Tarawa until the 27th Division took Butaritari, thus freeing the Northern Attack Force to head south in support of the Marines. Based on what he knew of the horrific Tarawa fighting, he even pondered the necessity of redeploying a battalion from the 165th to help out the 2nd Marine Division. Headstrong, impatient, erratic, prone to ill-considered emotional outbursts, parochial in outlook, Holland Smith had little actual combat experience. In World War I, he had served as a staff officer. During the interwar period, he had focused on the study of amphibious operations, evolving into a passionate advocate for offensive invasions, a mission uniquely suited to his service. The Marine Corps meant everything to Holland Smith. According to his biographer, to him, "there was no greater distinction, no higher honor," than serving as a Marine. Certainly this was laudable. But he was the sort of Marine whose rightful pride in the Corps nonetheless seemed dependent upon a dysfunctional contempt for the

Army. It is hard to imagine that the Corps could have chosen an officer more ill-suited by outlook and temperament for joint-service duty.

Not surprisingly, he did not mesh well with the cerebral, circumspect Ralph Smith. Eager to finish the Butaritari battle and move on to Tarawa, Holland Smith soon began badgering his Army colleagues to speed up their operations. The notion of urgency was, of course, anything but unreasonable. The longer the battle raged on Butaritari, the longer that Admiral Turner had to stay in place and risk his ships to potential Japanese air and sea attacks. Plus, every soldier who fought at Makin remained unavailable to help the Marines, if need be, at Tarawa. The question, then, was not so much the desirability of urgency—a concept with which Ralph Smith and his commanders all agreed—but the question of what urgency really meant in the context of real combat. Did urgency mean frontal attacks to take objectives, regardless of the cost? Did it mandate embracing the danger of bypassing individual Japanese who might still pose a mortal threat? The Army commanders thought not. Holland Smith disagreed. Like most Marines, he favored rapid operations, even at the risk of heavy casualties, on the theory that the quick seizure of any objective eventually proved less costly than protracted, drawn-out battles. Certainly, under the right circumstances, the viewpoint held some merit. But in Holland Smith's case, it led to a tendency to dismiss enemy resistance altogether and disparage the differing operational views of his Army colleagues as reflective of lesser military merit and competence. He later described the 27th's battle at Butaritari as "infuriatingly slow . . . an operation the Marines could have completed in a few hours."

As the troops methodically rooted the Japanese out of seemingly every bunker and every tree, Smith's patience wore ever thinner. He took to roaming around, haranguing small unit leaders about the weakness of the Japanese opposition, often demonstrating an embarrassing ignorance of the tactical situation. Once he walked to where he thought the front lines were and saw only a few inactive troops and no evidence of any enemy resistance. "It was as quiet as Wall Street on Sunday," he later wrote. He chewed the soldiers out for their lack of drive. Angry at what he believed was yet another example of the Army's passive stolidity, he later told Kelley, "There's no enemy. I've been out in front of our front lines and can't find a Jap." When Kelley and several other officers later investigated the spot where General Smith had visited, they found that it was actually well behind the lines. The men he had scolded were from the regimental service company whose job was to carry supplies, not fight on the front lines. When he witnessed soldiers spraying treetops with rifle fire as a precaution to neutralize potential snipers, he remonstrated them for poor fire discipline. In one case, he even threatened to confiscate the weapons of a supposedly trigger-happy patrol. "During the completion of the patrol, two snipers were located and killed within two hundred yards of the spot where General Smith was encountered," Captain Charles Coates, the commander, later testified. Though Smith's concerns for the dangers of profligate fire in the presence of other friendly units were hardly illogical, he tended to lace his scolding sessions with counterproductive, unprofessional public denunciations of the Army and its leaders. "He said the Army sits on its ass and are afraid to move, got a bunch of dumb lieutenants and sundry other things," Lieutenant Bernard Ryan recalled of one dressing-down he received at the hands of the general.

Inevitably, the volatile Marine general focused his frustration on Ralph Smith. "I was furious with [him]," Holland Smith later wrote. "I was anxious to go to Tarawa and here he was fiddling around with an operation that should have been ended long before in my opinion." One time, as they sat together in Ralph Smith's command tent several hundred yards inland from Red Beach, Holland Smith chided his Army counterpart, "Get your troops going; there's not another goddamned Jap left on this island." Taken aback, Ralph Smith replied, "General, that plain isn't so." S. L. A. Marshall, who personally witnessed the bizarre exchange, formed an irretrievably poor opinion of the Marine general. "This man acted like a sadist and tyrant all the time he was ashore at Makin. He is not only a bully but he is also a jughead when it comes to fighting."

A veritable cauldron of bad blood began to boil between Holland Smith and his Army colleagues, a brew that would grow only more noxious, more toxic over time. Apparently in an attempt to impugn the honor of the 27th and buttress his arguments about the Army's inefficiency, Holland Smith asserted in a postwar memoir that Colonel Conroy's body had lain unattended for two days, decomposing in the tropical heat. "No attempt had been made by either his officers or his men to recover the body and give it a Christian burial. The body lay a few yards from the main road traversed by troops, jeeps, and trucks, in full sight of men and only a short distance from the beach. It was inconceivable to me that soldiers of a regiment, whose loyalty is centered on the man directly in command . . . could permit his body to lie uncovered for two days. To me this callous disregard of a soldier's common duty to his commanding officer was an ominous commentary on the morale of the regiment. I ordered Ralph Smith to recover the body immediately and bury it. In that order I used emphatic language."

The claim was as erroneous as it was scurrilous. Contemporary records and multiple eyewitness accounts of participants prove beyond a shadow of a doubt that Conroy's body was recovered the morning after he was killed, that it was buried in the ceremony officiated by Father Yarwood on the afternoon of November 21, that Holland Smith even attended the service, and that he gave no vociferous burial order to Ralph Smith. Knowing the pain and uncertainty that Holland Smith's irresponsible allegations might cause Marie Conroy, an indignant Kelley eventually wrote to her and shared much of this evidence, with the assurance that her husband had, in fact, received a proper burial. "I regret very much that this man, Holland Smith, has seen fit to publish the story he did. I am at a complete loss to understand even a bad reason for his story which had never been heard by me before and which has absolutely no substance in fact. I hope that what I have written . . . may in some measure reduce the distress caused you by the lie that Holland Smith has written." Though the dysfunctional relationship between the two Generals Smith had little effect on the Makin campaign, it did lay the unhappy foundation for serious future problems.[8]

Though Holland Smith's attempts to curtail instances of irresponsible, unfocused shooting were clumsy and counterproductive—mainly because of his dense, brusque personality—his concern for the problem held much validity. On Butaritari, as practically elsewhere in the Pacific War, the Americans basically ceded the night to the Japanese. Commanders ordered their men to dig foxholes and stay in them until dawn. Lieutenant Colonel McDonough, according to one report, issued instructions "that there shall be no movement within his perimeter during the night." New to combat, plagued each night by swarms of mosquitoes, and very nervous about the threat posed by enemy soldiers whom they imagined lurking behind nearly every shadow, the 27th Division soldiers tended to fire away at any perceived threat. In one infamous instance, an engineer soldier shouted, "There's a hundred and fifty Japs in the trees!" prompting a massive outpouring of firepower at little more than phantoms. The Japanese propensity to call out the individual names of soldiers or commanders or to shout requests such as "We need medics out here," or "Hey, Charlie, where's my buddy?" only added to the anxiety. Seemingly with every gust of wind or rustling of foliage, soldiers unleashed machine gun and rifle fire, sometimes also grenades, into the night. Tracers stabbed, whippet-like, through the darkness. "No one could talk to anybody until the sun came up," an observer recalled. "They fought shadows."

Because of their jumpiness and poor fire discipline, the Americans probably did more damage to themselves than the Japanese. Friendly fire killings were all too common and might have accounted for as many as a third or more of American casualties. A sergeant was shot to death one night when he failed to give a password as quickly as his interrogators wanted. "'Trigger happiness' (and panic at night) caused most of our . . . casualties," Captain Thew Wright, a company commander, contended. S. L. A. Marshall, the historian, witnessed a great deal of self-destructive nocturnal shooting and almost died from it himself. "There was seldom a moment free of gunfire within our own positions. We took casualties be-cause of it. A man sleeping 5 feet from me . . . was shot by a sentry and killed in mistake for a Japanese. When the man sleeping next [to] him jumped up to protest, he almost was winged. I did not say a word or move a muscle except to crouch lower in my foxhole. Had I moved, I would have been shot. Here was stark panic fear, and there was no sensible way to contend with it except to await the sentry's relief in dead quiet." Ralph Smith was fully cognizant of the problem. In an official post-battle report, he admitted, "promiscuous firing by 'trigger happy' individuals is a serious danger to our own troops. It is a great temptation for men in battle for the first time to fire and ask questions later. Strict discipline for offenders is necessary." He later commented that rookie soldiers "don't know what's going on and they piss in their pants. That's the kind of thing that always happens."

Though undoubtedly this was true and certainly the 27th's soldiers be-gan to calm down as they gained more experience, the profligate shooting reflected a major oversight in American doctrine and training. The reign-ing custom of dawn-to-dusk fighting squelched most any initiative for pur-suing nighttime offensive operations. In the darkness a bunker mentality prevailed. Firepower was merely the crutch upon which frightened soldiers leaned. Too often they had little grasp of actual Japanese capabilities and were allowed by their leaders to let their imaginations run wild. "Troops must be thoroughly familiar with night tactics and ruses of the enemy," Lieutenant Kalina wrote in a reflective paper several years after the war. But they seldom were. He and other commanders tried to tamp down the trigger happiness, but since they largely eschewed night operations that might have built the confidence of their soldiers to take the fight to the enemy in spite of darkness—or perhaps just better recognize real from imagined threats—they instead simply waited until experience calmed the men and began to limit their self destructive shooting. In this sense, the 27th Division was not much different from the overwrought divisions at New Georgia and New Guinea and even the Marines in the early stages of the Guadalcanal campaign.[9]

By the evening of November 22, the Americans had captured both tank barriers, cleared out the Japanese bunker system within them, and had overrun all but about five thousand yards on the eastern extreme of Butaritari. That afternoon, a small force under Major Bradt had boarded LVTs and seized Kuma Island, cutting off a potential route of Japanese escape and making contact with many Gilbertese who had taken shelter there to escape the fighting on Butaritari. Ralph Smith addressed the locals and conversed with several French missionary priests, in their own language, from whom he learned much about the Japanese garrison and occupation as well as the executions of the Makin-raid prisoners.

On Butaritari, Lieutenant Colonel Hart's battalion manned the forward positions. The unit had spent the day slogging through swampy terrain, hunting snipers, under an intense tropical sun. The men were exhausted and dehydrated. "It seemed a miracle to me that they could keep going on," S. L. A. Marshall, who was with them, later wrote. "Their jaws were down and seemed to be sunken almost to their chests. There was a yellowish spittle around the lips which is always seen in fighting men when they are not only parched but in a state of extreme exhaustion." Few had the energy to dig substantial foxholes, nor would the thin, root-peppered soil permit such excavations. Most stacked coconut logs in front of themselves, cleared fields of fire for their weapons, and settled down for the night. On either side of the road, a pair of 37-millimeter antitank guns anchored the battalion perimeter.

The surviving Japanese were now penned into the last sliver of Butaritari and cut off from any route of escape. Most felt duty- or honor-bound to fight to the end rather than surrender. "When . . . enveloped by the enemy, there is no alternative but to charge unto death," they had been told in a common training notebook. "Suicide is the ultimate step in the spirit of attack." That night they fortified themselves with sake. They sang, beat drums, and clinked glasses or bottles. They screamed "Blood for the emperor!" "Heil Hitler!" and even the names of individual American soldiers.

Throughout the night, they emerged from a thick stand of trees and launched a series of haphazard attacks against the 3rd Battalion perimeter. Violent sheets of American return fire bracketed much of the area. Japanese knee-mortar and machine-gun fire barked in response. The fighting was mano a mano; artillery played no role, only the two antitank guns. At one of the 37-millimeter guns, Corporal Louis Lula, a Chicagoan, saw a group of Japanese bearing down on him from only about twenty or thirty yards away. In seconds they were in and around the gun position. Both sides flung grenades back and forth. PFC George Porter hurled a grenade and screamed, "That's for Tōjō, you sons of bitches!" The gun crewmen blazed away with their M1 carbines. "We didn't think we had a chance to live until daylight and we felt that the necessary thing was to sell our lives as dearly as possible," Lula later said.

He managed to kick a live Japanese grenade aside, make it to his gun, snap the breech shut, and fire a canister round into a group of enemy soldiers, decimating them. A few of the mangled survivors crawled back to their original positions, guzzled more sake, and bled to death. An unseen enemy soldier screamed, "Come on in, you Yankee bastards, and we will treat you right!" In some spots, the fighting was intimate, hand to hand. At one foxhole, PFC George Antolak, PFC Carl Samuels, and Corporal Charles Steadman found themselves in a fight to the death with a trio of enemy soldiers at such close quarters that neither side could shoot. Antolak wrenched a saber from one Japanese and stabbed him to death with it. Samuels removed his own helmet and smashed another over the head with it. Steadman beat the third to death with the stock of his rifle. Elsewhere a sword-wielding Japanese officer lunged into PFC Elio Bizzari's foxhole with a scream, "I've got you, Joe!" With horrifying speed, he plunged his sword all the way through Bizzari. The blade entered just above the American's heart but somehow missed any vital organs. Private Gerard Heck emerged from a neighboring foxhole and shot the enemy officer but did not kill him. Somehow PFC Bizzari managed to remove the sword from his body, draw his trench knife, and slash the man to death. By dawn, the fighting had mercifully petered out. The American perimeter remained intact. The majority of the Japanese participants were dead. In front of and around the lines, the Americans counted fifty-one rotting enemy bodies. "Not one wounded Jap was found along the front," S. L. A. Marshall, who examined many of the enemy bodies, later wrote. "Many of the dead had been mangled by the canister [fire], losing limbs or having their stomachs torn out or their jaws shot away." Patrols found more bloated corpses in the woods. Some of the Japanese soldiers had killed themselves by holding grenades to their heads or abdomens. In the nighttime defensive battle, the Americans lost three killed and twenty-five wounded.

Supported by tanks, Hart resumed his advance and, within a few hours, eliminated the few remaining Japanese and secured the rest of the island. Patrols continued to hunt down individual Japanese, but the battle was over. At midday on November 23, Ralph Smith radioed a pithy report to Admiral Turner, "Makin taken!" The 27th Division soldiers re-embarked aboard ships that took them back to Hawaii while a garrison force under Colonel Clesen Tenney occupied the atoll. Engineers subsequently built an airstrip that was home to two fighter squadrons and a medium-bomber squadron. At Butaritari, the Japanese lost at least four hundred killed, of whom three hundred were combat troops from the 3rd Special Base Force. The Americans captured 105 prisoners, all but one of whom were laborers. The 27th lost sixty-six dead and 152 wounded, many to friendly fire. The Navy paid a higher price. In addition to the sailors killed aboard the *Mississippi*, Turner lost the escort carrier USS *Liscome Bay* to a Japanese submarine on the morning of November 24. A total of 644 sailors lost their lives in the sinking; only 272 survived. Among the dead was Rear Admiral Henry Mullinix, Turner's carrier commander, and Ship's Cook Third-Class Doris Miller, an African-American sailor whose standout bravery during the Pearl Harbor attack had earned him a Navy Cross and subsequent coast-to-coast fame. The loss of *Liscome Bay* highlighted the Navy's legitimate concerns for its stationary ships during amphibious invasions, though subsequent notions that a quicker battle at Makin would have prevented the loss of the carrier are specious because the ship would still have remained in Gilberts waters and hence similarly vulnerable to the enemy submarine. American fatalities at Makin were thus almost twice those of the overmatched Japanese. Even worse, the Marines lost 1,085 dead, plus thirty attached naval corpsmen, to take Tarawa in three and a half days of ferocious fighting. Another 2,292 Marines and corpsmen were wounded. At Tarawa, the formidable garrison of 4,836 Japanese naval troops and Korean laborers largely fought to the death. The Marines captured 146 prisoners, only seventeen of whom were Japanese.

Immediately after Makin, Ralph Smith described the operation to a reporter as "phenomenally successful." This was hyperbole. In reality, Makin was a costly victory, a learning experience for everyone involved. With overwhelming advantages in firepower, sea power, airpower, and manpower, his soldiers had performed reasonably well, and yet they had also betrayed gaps in their training and their lack of battle experience. The unit's casualties, though low, probably would have been significantly lighter with better fire discipline and night indoctrination. At Tarawa, the Marines had incurred shocking losses and had experienced the full fury of Japanese suicidal resolve, a troubling but instructive harbinger for the future. Among the services involved in Operation Galvanic, the Army had suffered by far the least. In a larger sense, the Americans had paid dearly for the Gilberts, but the returns were valuable. No longer could Japanese ships and planes menace sea lanes between North America and Australia or New Zealand. The Gilberts, provided four major air bases, including Tarawa and Makin, from which the Army Air Force would launch raids hundreds of miles in every direction against enemy shipping and island bases. Galvanic opened the way for larger operations in the Marshall Islands, deeper within the Japanese defensive perimeter and closer to the home islands. From the Gilberts to the Marshalls, Nimitz's Central Pacific prong slowly outflanked Rabaul and other Japanese bases in the Solomons even as MacArthur's Southwest Pacific drive through New Guinea and the western Solomons gradually strangled the Japanese from a different direction.[10]

This titanic war, stretching from the Asian landmass to the northern Pacific, from Australia to Makin, had now turned decidedly in favor of the Allies. At the same time, the United States had evolved from an underprepared, inward-looking regional power to an internationalist military and economic superpower. Its army was now on the cusp of full maturity, slowly, steadily growing into a mortal adversary for its Japanese counterpart.

Now was the end of the beginning and, in retrospect, perhaps even the beginning of the end.

Acknowledgments

A great many people made this first book of the victory in the Pacific Series possible. So many, in fact, that for every one I mention here, two or three others could probably lay claim to some role, especially because my research and writing occupied the better part of a decade. For those whom I have not mentioned, usually out of consideration for brevity, I offer my deep apologies and assurances that I have greatly appreciated your assistance. The input of so many knowledgeable, helpful people does not, of course, change the fact that I am solely responsible for any errors of commission or omission.

The dedicated military archivists at the National Archives and Records Administration embody professionalism and expertise, none more so than the dean of them all, Tim Nenninger, who was kind enough to lead me to an incredibly rich vein of primary-source material during my months in residence. The same was true for the remarkable staff at the United States Military History Institute, the leading repository of Army history and one of my favorite places on earth. Shannon Schwaller expertly processed my massive list of requests and, in the process, saved me a tremendous amount of time and consternation. Steve Dye always took the lead to access whatever I needed in a timely and efficient manner. During my visit to the Hoover Institution Archives at Stanford University, Carol Leadenham helped me find a fascinating array of firsthand material from among dozens of individual papers collections. This book is much the richer for her assistance. Elizabeth Dunn and the staff at the David M. Rubenstein Rare Book and Manuscript Library on the campus of Duke University made General Eichelberger's vast collection of correspondence, dictations, reports, musings, and photographs available to me in full. There is no way to overstate the importance of the Eichelberger papers, in bringing not only the general himself to life but also the story of the war as a whole.

In spite of many bureaucratic challenges, Susan Lintelmann and

Suzanne Christoff of the United States Military Academy Library helped me access the library's vast array of individual papers collections, much of it from graduates who became prisoners of the Japanese. Genoa Stanford at the Donovan Research Library, Fort Benning, Georgia, made an extensive assemblage of Infantry School papers from Pacific War veterans available to me. Laura Farley at the Wisconsin Veterans Museum in Madison provided me with a fascinating group of letters and other firsthand accounts that greatly enhanced the Pearl Harbor and Buna chapters. Mary Hope, senior archivist at the Army's Office of Medical History, Fort Sam Houston, Texas, and Carlos Alvarado, her assistant, made sure I had access to a rich trove of oral histories and interviews from Army nurses who served in the Pacific. Reagan Grau at the National Pacific War Museum in Fredericksburg, Texas, took the time and trouble to give me digital versions of many dozens of original oral histories from Army and Marine veterans. The stewards of the extensive oral history archive at the University of North Texas, J. Todd Moye and Amy Hedrick, worked hard to make a vast collection of individual accounts available to me in digital format.

The almost limitless collection of letters, diaries, interviews, and other primary-source material at the National World War II Museum in New Orleans is a relatively underutilized archive. Lindsay Barnes and Nathan Huegen helped me tap into this remarkable resource both on-site during my visit and at a distance as well. Frank Shirer at the US Army Center of Military History (CMH) in Washington, DC, went the extra mile to compile for me in electronic format much of the American and Japanese institutional history of the war, from command reports to special studies to Japanese monographs and postwar interviews as well as vivid, underutilized theater and battle histories, allowing me to bring a vividness and immediacy to the chapters that otherwise might not have been possible. I do not know that mere words can convey my appreciation to Frank. During my visit to CMH, Siobhan Blevins kindly helped me access even more of this insider's Pacific War.

At first glance, the Eisenhower Presidential Library in Abilene, Kansas, seems an odd place to look for revealing source material from the American war with Japan. However, a great many Army veterans of the war, from generals on down, donated their fascinating papers to this library, as did many units that fought in theater. In addition, Eisenhower's letters and writings from his purgatorial days as an aide to MacArthur offer a rich portrait of the SWPA commander and his proclivities. I am grateful to

Kevin Bailey and Tim Rives for making my visit to Abilene so productive. The mecca for all things MacArthur is, not surprisingly, the MacArthur Memorial Archives and Museum in Norfolk, Virginia. Chris Kolakowski, the director, and Jim Zobel, the archivist, set new records for cordiality and helpfulness during my extensive visit. I was absolutely blown away by the richness of the MacArthur Memorial's Pacific War collections and especially Chris's and Jim's unique levels of expertise on the Army in the war.

At the Association of the United States Army, the redoubtable Roger Cirillo, the muse of all modern Army historians, was kind enough to share, over the course of some long conversations, much knowledge and many productive suggestions. My good friend Kevin Hymel, another sage on the World War II Army, conducted the photo research and shared much good advice over the many years since I first shared my vision for the series with him over dinner at a restaurant in Portland, Maine. During the course of many conversations, Robert von Maier, the savvy editor of *Global War Studies*, helped shape my focus and enhance my understanding of the vast and diverse assortment of topics covered by this series. The National Endowment for the Humanities (NEH) awarded this project a prestigious, and much needed, Public Scholar Grant, and I am deeply appreciative. The vital support and partnership of the NEH made possible a level of depth and complexity to the research that I otherwise could not have attempted.

Closer to home, the staff at the State Historical Society of Missouri worked hard to provide me with individual access to a fascinating archive of several thousand letters written by servicemen and -women during the war. At Missouri University of Science and Technology, where I am privileged to work, the library and interlibrary loan staffs tirelessly fulfilled my dizzying range of requests for rare and not-so-rare books, articles, and dissertations. My colleagues in the Department of History and Political Science remain a daily source of inspiration and excellence: Diana Ahmad, Michael Bruening, Petra DeWitt, Larry "Legend" Gragg, Patrick Huber, Tseggai Isaac, Alanna Krolikowski, Michael Meagher, Justin Pope, Jeff Schramm, Kate Sheppard, all of our distinguished emeriti, particularly my old friend and mentor, Russ Buhite, and especially our outstanding department chair, Shannon Fogg. Another thank-you—of so many over the years—goes to Robin Collier, our world-class department secretary and guiding light.

I would like to thank my dear friend Rick Britton, a cartographer of singular talent, for once again producing an absorbing set of original maps that—in my view at least—have done much to illuminate my prose. Many thanks go to Brent Howard, executive editor at Dutton, whose keen insight into good storytelling and good scholarship sets him apart from his peers. I greatly appreciate his belief in my work and the innumerable ways he continues to improve it with his relentlessly good judgment and unfailing professional eye. Michael Congdon, my sagacious agent and friend, helped guide and shape this work, so much so that, if not for his efforts, I do not believe it would have come to fruition. I greatly appreciate his wise counsel and also his willingness to listen to my pessimistic diatribes about the remote chances for a Cardinal championship each upcoming baseball season.

I am especially grateful to friends and family, all of whom seem inexplicably resolved to put up with me, and all of whom have helped sustain me during the long gestation process for this book: Pat O'Donnell, Paul Clifford, Sean Roarty, Michael Roarty, Mike Chopp, Steve Loher, Steve Kutheis, Steve Vincent, John Villier, Jon Krone, Professor Dave Cohen, James Gavin McManus, the late Tom Fleming, Dick Hyde, Charlie Schneider, Doug Kuberski, Don Patton, Chris Ketcherside, Curtis Fears, Joe Ferraro, Don Rebman, Bob Kaemmerlen, Ron Kurtz, Joe Carcagno, all of my 7th Infantry Regiment Cottonbaler buddies, and many other friends than I have space to mention.

I'm extremely blessed to be part of a loving and supportive family. On the Woody side, I am very grateful to Nancy, Charlie, Doug, Tonya, David, Angee, and my nephews and nieces for many acts of kindness and a lot of laughs over the years. Ruth and Nelson, my mother and father-in-law, are like bonus parents. I cannot ever repay them for all their love and support, though I can certainly continue to commend Nelson for his impeccable taste in baseball teams. A special thank-you to my elder siblings, Mike and Nancy, for a lifetime of support and friendship. My nieces Kelly and Erin are grown women now, and far smarter and more focused than I was at their age (or, let's be honest, even at my present age!). My teenaged nephew Michael is already taller than I am—which admittedly might not be saying much—but he is making us all proud with his intelligence and athleticism. Thank you, all, for many moments of affection and warmth. I have been blessed with incredible and supportive parents. Michael and Mary Jane McManus have given me such a great life that I could never possibly repay them, though I do try, probably ineffectively. Perhaps a simple and sincere thank-you will suffice. As always, my wife and soul mate, Nancy, has borne the greatest cross, enduring long absences and an author's deep absorption in a new project. Naturally to her goes my deepest and most heartfelt thanks, not just for her enduring and true love, but for indulging my life-long passion for words on paper. . . .

John C. McManus
Saint Louis, Missouri

Selected Bibliography

Archives and Manuscript Collections

Abilene, Kansas. Dwight D. Eisenhower Presidential Library (EPL).
Carlisle, Pennsylvania. United States Army Military History Institute (USAMHI).
College Park, Maryland. National Archives and Records Administration, II (NA).
Columbia, Missouri. State Historical Society of Missouri Research Center (SHSM).
Denton, Texas. University of North Texas Oral History Collection (UNT).
Durham, North Carolina. David M. Rubenstein Rare Book and Manuscript Library, Duke University (DU).
Fort Benning, Georgia. Maneuver Center of Excellence HQ Donovan Research Library (DRL).
Fort Leavenworth, Kansas. Ike Skelton Combined Arms Research Library (CARL).
Fort Sam Houston, Texas. Army Nurse Corps Collection, Army Medical Department Center of History and Heritage Museum (AMEDD).
Fredericksburg, Texas. Nimitz Education and Research Center, National Museum of the Pacific War (NMPW).
Knoxville, Tennessee. University of Tennessee Special Collections Library, Repository of the Center for the Study of War and Society (SCUTK).
Madison, Wisconsin. Wisconsin Veterans Museum (WVM).
New Orleans, Louisiana. National World War II Museum (WWIIM).
Norfolk, Virginia. Douglas MacArthur Memorial Library and Archives (DMM).
Palo Alto, California. Hoover Institution Library and Archives, Stanford University (HILA).
San Diego, California. Special Collections Library and University Archives, San Diego State University (SDSU).
Washington, DC. Library of Congress, Veterans History Project (LOC).
Washington, DC. US Army Center of Military History (CMH).
West Point, New York. United States Military Academy Library Archives (USMA).

Books

Age, Hayrack. *The Reluctant Admiral: Yamamoto and the Imperial Navy.* Tokyo: Kondansha International, 1979.
Agoncillo, Teodoro. *The Fateful Years: Japan's Adventure in the Philippines, 1941–1945, Volume One.* Quezon City, Philippines: R. P. Garcia, 1965.
Alexander, Joseph. *Utmost Savagery: The Three Days at Tarawa.* New York: Ivy Books, 1995.
Anders, Leslie. *The Ledo Road: General Joseph W. Stilwell's Highway to China.* Norman: University of Oklahoma Press, 1965.
———. *Gentle Knight: The Life and Times of Major General Edwin Forrest Harding.* Kent, OH: Kent University Press, 1985.

543

Astor, Gerald. *Crisis in the Pacific: The Battles for the Philippine Islands by the Men Who Fought Them*. New York: Dell, 1996.

Barker, Anthony, and Lisa Jackson. *Fleeting Attraction: A Social History of American Servicemen in Western Australia During the Second World War*. Nedlands: University of Western Australia Press, 1996.

Bartsch, William. *Victory Fever on Guadalcanal: Japan's First Land Defeat of World War II*. College Station: Texas A&M University Press, 2014.

Beck, John Jacob. *MacArthur and Wainwright: Sacrifice of the Philippines*. Albuquerque: University of New Mexico Press, 1974.

Beebe, John, ed. *Prisoner of the Rising Sun: The Lost Diary of Brigadier General Lewis Beebe*. College Station: Texas A&M University Press, 2006.

Belden, Jack. *Retreat with Stilwell*. New York: Alfred A. Knopf, 1943.

Belote, James, and William Belote. *Corregidor: Saga of a Fortress*. New York: Harper & Row, 1967.

Bergerud, Eric. *Touched with Fire: The Land War in the South Pacific*. New York: Penguin Books, 1996.

Blazich, Frank, ed. *Bataan Survivor: A POW's Account of Japanese Captivity in World War II*. Columbia: University of Missouri Press, 2016.

Borneman, Walter. *MacArthur at War: World War II in the Pacific*. New York: Little, Brown, 2016.

Brady, Tim. *His Father's Son: The Life of Ted Roosevelt, Jr*. New York: New American Library, 2017.

Braly, William. *The Hard Way Home: From Corregidor to Manchuria, Three Years a Prisoner of the Japanese in World War II*. Washington, DC: Infantry Journal Press, 1947, reprint.

Brands, H. W. *Bound to Empire: The United States and the Philippines*. New York: Oxford University Press, 1992.

Bumgarner, John. *Parade of the Dead: A U.S. Army Physician's Memoir of Imprisonment by the Japanese, 1942–1945*. Jefferson, NC: McFarland, 1995.

Bywater, Hector. *Seapower in the Pacific: A Study of the American-Japanese Naval Problem*. New York: Houghton Mifflin, 1921.

Campbell, James. *The Ghost Mountain Boys: Their Epic March and the Terrifying Battle for New Guinea—the Forgotten War of the South Pacific*. New York: Crown, 2007.

Caraccilo, Dominic, ed. *Surviving Bataan and Beyond: Colonel Irvin Alexander's Odyssey as a Japanese Prisoner of War*. Mechanicsburg, PA: Stackpole Books, 1999.

Chennault, Claire. *Way of a Fighter: The Memoirs of Claire Lee Chennault*. New York: G. P. Putnam's Sons, 1949.

Chwialkowski, Paul. *In Caesar's Shadow: The Life of General Robert Eichelberger*. Westport, CT: Greenwood, 1993.

Collie, Craig, and Hajima Marutani. *The Path of Infinite Sorrow: The Japanese on the Kokoda Track*. Crows News, Australia: Allen & Unwin, 2009.

Collins, J. Lawton. *Lighting Joe: An Autobiography*. Baton Rouge and London: Louisiana State University Press, 1979.

Condon-Rall, Mary Ellen, and Albert Cowdrey. *The U.S. Army in World War II: The Technical Services, The Medical Department: Medical Service in the War Against Japan*. Washington, DC: Center of Military History, United States Army, 1998.

Conn, Stetson, Rose Engelman, and Byron Fairchild. *United States Army in World War II: The Western Hemisphere, Guarding the United States and Its Outposts*. Washington, DC: Center of Military History, United States Army, 2000.

Cooper, Jerry, ed. *To Bataan and Back: The World War II Diary of Major Thomas Dooley*. College Station: Texas A&M University Press, 2016.

Cooper, Norman. *A Fighting General: The Biography of Gen. Holland M. "Howlin' Mad" Smith*. Quantico, VA: Marine Corps Association, 1987.

Craven, Wesley, and James Cate, eds. *The Army Air Forces in World War II, Volume IV, The Pacific: Guadalcanal to Saipan, August 1942 to July 1944*. Washington, DC: Office of Air Force History, United States Air Force, 1983.

———. *The Army Air Forces in World War II: Volume VII, Services Around the World*. Washington, DC: Office of Air Force History, United States Air Force, 1983.

Crowl, Philip, and Edmund Love. *United States Army in World War II: The War in the Pacific: Seizure of the Gilberts and Marshalls*. Washington, DC: Office of the Chief of Military History, Department of the Army, 1955.

Daugherty, Leo. *The Allied Resupply Effort in the China-Burma-India Theater During World War II*. Jefferson, NC: McFarland, 2008.

Day, John III, ed. *An Officer in MacArthur's Court: The Memoir of the First Headquarters Commandant for General Douglas MacArthur in Australia*. Fremont, CA: Robertson, 2014.

Day, Ronnie, ed. *Mack Morriss: South Pacific Diary, 1942–1943*. Lexington: University Press of Kentucky, 1996.

———. *New Georgia: The Second Battle for the Solomons*. Bloomington and Indianapolis: Indiana University Press, 2016.

Dexter, David. *Australia in the War of 1939–1945: Volume VI, the New Guinea Offensives*. Canberra: Australian War Memorial, 1961.

Dod, Karl. *United States Army in World War II: The Technical Services, The Corps of Engineers in the War Against Japan*. Washington, DC: Office of the Chief of Military History, Department of the Army, 1966.

Dorn, Frank. *Walkout: With Stilwell in Burma*. New York: Thomas Y. Crowell, 1971.

Drea, Edward. *MacArthur's Ultra: Codebreaking and the War Against Japan, 1942–1945*. Lawrence: University Press of Kansas, 1992.

Duffy, James. *War at the End of the World: Douglas MacArthur and the Forgotten Fight for New Guinea, 1942–1945*. New York: NAL/Penguin, 2016.

Eastman, Lloyd. *Seeds of Destruction: Nationalist China in War and Revolution, 1937–1949*. Stanford, CA: Stanford University Press, 1984.

Eichelberger, Robert. *Our Jungle Road to Tokyo*. New York: Viking, 1950.

Eisenhower, Dwight. *Crusade in Europe*. New York: Doubleday, 1948.

———. *At Ease: Stories I Tell to Friends*. Garden City, NY: Doubleday, 1967.

Encel, Vivien, and Alan Sharpe. *Murder! 25 True Australian Crimes*. Sydney, Australia: Kingclear Books, 1997.

Falk, Stanley. *Bataan: The March of Death*. New York: W. W. Norton, 1962.

Fenby, Jonathan. *Chiang Kai Shek: China's Generalissimo and the Nation He Lost*. New York: Carroll and Graf, 2003.

Ferrell, Robert, ed. *The Eisenhower Diaries*. New York: W. W. Norton, 1981.

———. *The Question of MacArthur's Reputation: Côte de Châtillon, October 14–16, 1918*, Columbia: University of Missouri Press, 2008.

Frank, Richard. *Guadalcanal: The Definitive Account of the Landmark Battle*. New York: Random House, 1990.

Fussell, Paul. *Wartime: Understanding and Behavior in the Second World War*. New York: Oxford University Press, 1989.

Gailey, Harry. *Howlin' Mad vs. the Army: Conflict in Command, Saipan 1944*. Novato, CA: Presidio Press, 1986.

———. *MacArthur Strikes Back: Decision at Buna: New Guinea, 1942–1943*. Novato, CA: Presidio Press, 2000.

———. *MacArthur's Victory: The War in New Guinea, 1943–1944*. New York: Ballantine Books, 2004.

Garfield, Brian. *The Thousand-Mile War: World War II in Alaska*. New York: Ballantine Books, 1969.

Gibney, Frank, ed. *Senso: The Japanese Remember the Pacific War*. Armonk, NY: M. E. Sharpe, 1995.

Hall, Gwendolyn, ed. *Love, War, and the 96th Engineers (Colored): The World War II New Guinea Diaries of Captain Hyman Samuelson*. Urbana and Chicago: University of Illinois Press, 1995.

Halsey, William, and Bryan J. Halsey. *Admiral Halsey's Story*. New York: McGraw-Hill, 1947.

Hammel, Eric. *Munda Trail*. New York: Avon Books, 1989.

Herman, Arthur. *Douglas MacArthur: American Warrior*. New York: Random House, 2016.

Holzimmer, Kevin. *General Walter Krueger: Unsung Hero of the Pacific War*. Lawrence: University Press of Kansas, 2007.

Horton, D. C. *New Georgia: Pattern for Victory*. New York: Ballantine Books, 1971.

Hough, Frank, Merle Ludwig, and Henry Shaw. *History of U.S. Marine Corps Operations in World War II, Volume I: Pearl Harbor to Guadalcanal*. Washington, DC: Historical Branch, G3 Division, Headquarters, US Marine Corps, 1958.

Hubbard, Preston. *Apocalypse Undone: My Survival of Japanese Imprisonment During World War II*. Nashville, TN: Vanderbilt University Press, 1990.

Huff, Sid. *My Fifteen Years with MacArthur*. New York: Paperback Library, 1964.

James, D. Clayton. *The Years of MacArthur, Volume II*. Boston: Houghton Mifflin, 1975.

Jenkins, Burris Jr. *Father Meany and "The Fighting 69th."* New York: Frederick Fell, 1944.

Johnston, George. *The Toughest Fighting in the World*. New York: Duell, Sloane and Pearce, 1943.

Jones, James. *From Here to Eternity*. New York: Charles Scribner's Sons, 1951.

———. *WWII: A Chronicle of Soldiering*. New York: Ballantine, 1975.

Kahn, E. J. *G.I. Jungle: An American Soldier in Australia and New Guinea*. New York: Simon & Schuster, 1943.

Kenney, George. *General Kenney Reports: A Personal History of the Pacific War*. Washington, DC: Office of Air Force History, United States Air Force, 1987, reprint.

Kerr, E. Bartlett. *Surrender and Survival: The Experience of American POWs in the Pacific, 1941–1945*. New York: William Morrow, 1985.

Knox, Donald. *Death March: The Survivors of Bataan*. New York and London: Harcourt Brace Jovanovich, 1981.

Kolakowski, Christopher. *Last Stand on Bataan: The Defense of the Philippines, December 1941–May 1942*. Jefferson, NC: McFarland, 2016.

Krueger, Walter. *From Down Under to Nippon: The Story of the Sixth Army in World War II*. Washington, DC: Combat Forces, 1953.

Lardner, John. *Southwest Passage: The Yanks in the Pacific*. Philadelphia: J. B. Lippincott, 1943.

Leckie, Robert. *Helmet for My Pillow*. New York: Bantam Books, 1979.

Lee, Clark. *They Call It Pacific: An Eye-Witness Story of Our War Against Japan from Bataan to the Solomons*. New York: Viking, 1943.

Lee, Ulysses. *United States Army in World War II: The Employment of Negro Troops*. Washington, DC: Center of Military History, United States Army, 1963.

Leighton, Richard, and Robert Coakley. *United States Army in World War II: Global Logistics and Strategy, 1940–1943*. Washington, DC: Center of Military History, United States Army, 1995.

Leutze, James. *A Different Kind of Victory: A Biography of Admiral Thomas C. Hart*. Annapolis, MD: Naval Institute Press, 1981.

Lord, Walter. *Day of Infamy*. New York: Henry Holt, 1957.

Luvaas, Jay, ed. *Dear Miss Em: General Eichelberger's War in the Pacific, 1942–1945*. Westport, CT: Greenwood, 1972.

MacArthur, Douglas. *Reminiscences*. New York: Da Capo, 1964.

———. *Reports of General MacArthur: The Campaigns of MacArthur in the Pacific, Volume I*. Washington, DC: Department of the Army, 1994.

Manchester, William. *American Caesar: Douglas MacArthur, 1880–1964*. New York: Dell, 1978.

Marshall, S. L. A. *Battle at Best: Electrifying Accounts of Action at the Front Line–As It Really Was*. New York: Jove Books, 1963.

———. *Bringing Up the Rear: A Memoir*. Novato, CA: Presidio Press, 1979.

Martin, Adrian. *Brothers from Bataan: POWs, 1942–1945*. Manhattan, KS: Sunflower University Press, 1992.

Maurer, Maurer, ed. *Air Force Combat Units of World War II*. Washington, DC: Office of Air Force History, United States Air Force, 1983.

Mayo, Lida. *Bloody Buna*. Garden City, NY: Doubleday, 1974.

McCarthy, Dudley. *Australia in the War of 1939–1945: Volume V, South-West Pacific Area, First Year: Kokoda to Wau*. Canberra: Australian War Memorial, 1959.

McDonald, William, III, and Barbara Evenson. *The Shadow Tiger: Billy McDonald, Wingman to Chennault*. Birmingham, AL: Shadow Tiger, 2016.

McManus, John. *Grunts: Inside the American Infantry Combat Experience, World War II Through Iraq*. New York: NAL/Caliber, 2010.

———. *September Hope: The American Side of a Bridge Too Far*. New York: NAL/Caliber, 2012.

McMillan, George. *The Old Breed: A History of the First Marine Division in World War II*. Washington, DC: Infantry Journal Press, 1949.

Miller, Basil. *Generalissimo and Madame Chiang Kai-shek: Christian Liberators of China*. New York: Zondervan, 1943.

Miller, Ernest. *Bataan Uncensored*. Long Prairie, MN: Hart, 1949.

Miller, John. *United States Army in World War II: The War in the Pacific: Guadalcanal: the First Offensive*. Washington, DC: Historical Division, Department of the Army, 1949.

———. *United States Army in World War II: The War in the Pacific: Cartwheel: the Reduction of Rabaul*. Washington, DC: Office of the Chief of Military History, Department of the Army, 1959.

Millett, Allan. *Semper Fidelis: The History of the United States Marine Corps*. New York: Free Press, 1991.

Milner, Samuel. *United States Army in World War II: The War in the Pacific: Victory in Papua*. Washington, DC: Center of Military History, United States Army, 2003.

Mitchell, Lieutenant Robert, with Sewell Tyng and Captain Nelson Drummond Jr. *The Capture of Attu: A World War II Battle as Told by the Men Who Fought There*. Lincoln: University of Nebraska Press, 2000.

Mitter, Rana. *Forgotten Ally: China's World War II, 1937–1945*. Boston: Houghton Mifflin Harcourt, 2013.

Monahan, Evelyn, and Rosemary Neidel-Greenlee. *All This Hell: U.S. Nurses Imprisoned by the Japanese*. Lexington: University Press of Kentucky, 2000.

Moore, John. *Over-Sexed, Over-Paid, and Over-Here: Americans in Australia, 1941–1945*. St. Lucia, Australia: University of Queensland Press, 1981.

Morison, Samuel Eliot. *History of United States Naval Operations in World War II, the Rising Sun in the Pacific, Volume III*. Boston: Little, Brown, 1948.

———. *History of United States Naval Operations in World War II, Volume VII: Aleutians, Gilberts and Marshalls, June 1942–April 1944*. Boston: Little, Brown, 1951.

———. *The Two-Ocean War: A Short History of the United States Navy in the Second World War*. New York: Galahad Books, 1997.

Morton, Louis. *The United States Army in World War II: The War in the Pacific: The Fall of the Philippines*. Washington, DC: Office of the Chief of Military History, Department of the Army, 1953.

——. *The United States Army in World War II: War in the Pacific: Strategy and Command: The First Two Years*. Washington, DC: Center of Military History, United States Army, 2000.

Moser, Don. *Time-Life World War II Series: China-Burma-India*. Alexandria, VA: Time-Life Books, 1978.

Murphy, Edward. *Heroes of World War II*. New York: Ballantine Books, 1990.

Norman, Elizabeth. *We Band of Angels: The Untold Story of the American Women Trapped on Bataan*. New York: Random House, 1999.

Olson, John. *O'Donnell: Andersonville of the Pacific*. Self-published, 1985.

Peck, Graham. *Two Kinds of Time: A Personal Story of China's Crash into Revolution*. Boston: Houghton Mifflin, 1950.

Perrett, Geoffrey. *There's a War to Be Won: The United States Army in World War II*. New York: Random House, 1991.

Potts, E. Daniel, and Annette Potts. *Yanks Down Under, 1941–1945: The American Impact on Australia*. Melbourne, Australia: Oxford University Press, 1985.

Prange, Gordon. *At Dawn We Slept: The Untold Story of Pearl Harbor*. New York: Penguin Books, 1981.

Radike, Floyd. *Across the Dark Islands: The War in the Pacific*. New York: Ballantine Books, 2003.

Redmond, Juanita. *I Served on Bataan*. Philadelphia and New York: J. B. Lippincott, 1943.

Rogers, Paul. *The Good Years: MacArthur and Sutherland*. New York: Praeger, 1990.

——. *The Bitter Years: MacArthur and Sutherland*. New York: Praeger, 1990.

Romanus, Charles, and Riley Sunderland. *The United States Army in World War II: China-Burma-India Theater, Stilwell's Mission to China*. Washington, DC: Office of the Chief of Military History, Department of the Army, 1953.

——. *United States Army in World War II: China-Burma-India Theater, Stilwell's Command Problems*. Washington, DC: Center of Military History, United States Army, 1987.

Romulo, Carlos. *I Saw the Fall of the Philippines*. Garden City, NY: Doubleday, Doran, 1942.

Salecker, Gene. *Blossoming Silk Against the Rising Sun: U.S. and Japanese Paratroopers at War in the Pacific in World War II*. Mechanicsburg, PA: Stackpole Books, 2010.

Sandler, Stanley, ed. *World War II in the Pacific: An Encyclopedia*. New York: Free Press, 1991.

——, editor. *Ground Warfare: An International Encyclopedia, Volume Two*. Santa Barbara, CA: ABC-Clio, 2002.

Schaller, Michael. *Douglas MacArthur: Far Eastern General*. New York: Oxford University Press, 1989.

Schrijvers, Peter. *Bloody Pacific: American Soldiers at War with Japan*, 2nd ed. New York: Palgrave Macmillan, 2010.

Schultz, Duane. *Hero of Bataan: The Story of General Jonathan M. Wainwright*. New York: St. Martin's, 1981.

Scott, Robert. *God Is My Co-Pilot*. New York: Charles Scribner's Sons, 1944.

Shaw, Henry, Bernard Nalty, and Edwin Turnbladh. *History of United States Marine Corps Operations in World War II: Central Pacific Drive*. Washington, DC: Historical Branch, G3 Division, Headquarters, US Marine Corps, 1966.

Shortal, John. *Forged by Fire: Robert L. Eichelberger and the Pacific War*. Columbia: University of South Carolina Press, 1987.

Slackman, Michael. *Target Pearl Harbor*. Honolulu: University of Hawaii Press, 1990.

Slim, William. *Defeat Into Victory*. London: Cassell, 1956.

Smith, Holland, and Percy Finch. *Coral and Brass*. New York: Charles Scribner's Sons, 1949.

Smith, Rex Alan, and Gerald Meehl, eds. *Pacific War Stories in the Words of Those Who Survived.* New York and London: Abbeville Press, 2004.

Smith, S. E., ed. *The United States Marine Corps in World War II, Volume I.* New York: Ace Books, 1969.

Snedeker, Edward. *Hell's Islands: The Untold Story of Guadalcanal.* College Station: Texas A&M University Press, 2007.

Sorley, Lewis. *Honorable Warrior: General Harold K. Johnson and the Ethics of Command.* Lawrence: University Press of Kansas, 1998.

Spector, Ronald. *Eagle Against the Sun: The American War with Japan.* New York: Vintage Books, 1985.

Stauffer, Alvin. *The United States Army in World War II: The Quartermaster Corps: Operations in the War Against Japan.* Washington, DC: Center of Military History, United States Army, 2004.

Stilwell, Joseph, and Theodore White, ed. *The Stilwell Papers.* New York: William Sloane, 1948.

Stone, James, ed. *Crisis Fleeting: Original Reports on Military Medicine in India and Burma during the Second World War.* Washington, DC: Office of the Surgeon General, Department of the Army, 1969.

Taylor, Jay. *The Generalissimo: Chiang Kai-shek and the Struggle for Modern China.* Cambridge, MA: Belknap Press of Harvard University Press, 2009.

Tenney, Lester. *My Hitch in Hell: The Bataan Death March.* Washington, DC: Potomac Books, 1995.

Toland, John. *But Not in Shame: The Six Months After Pearl Harbor.* New York: Random House, 1961.

Tuchman, Barbara. *Stilwell and the American Experience in China, 1911–1945.* New York: Macmillan, 1970.

United States Army. *The Capture of Makin, 20–24 November, 1943.* Washington, DC: Center of Military History, United States Army, 1990.

United States Navy. *United States Navy Combat Narrative: The Aleutians Campaign, June 1942–August 1943.* Washington, DC: Naval Historical Center, Department of the Navy, 1993.

Vandenberg, Arthur Jr. *The Papers of Senator Vandenberg.* Boston: Houghton Mifflin, 1952.

Wainwright, Jonathan. *General Wainwright's Story.* Garden City, NY: Doubleday, 1946.

Walker, Charles. *Combat Officer: A Memoir of War in the South Pacific.* New York: Ballantine Books, 2004.

Waterford, Van. *Prisoners of the Japanese in World War II.* Jefferson, NC: McFarland, 1994.

Weinstein, Alfred. *Barbed Wire Surgeon.* New York: Macmillan, 1948.

Whitman, John. *Bataan: Our Last Ditch.* New York: Hippocrene Books, 1990.

Wolfert, Ira. *Battle for the Solomons.* Boston: Houghton Mifflin, 1943.

Woolfe, Raymond. *The Doomed Horse Soldiers of Bataan.* Lanham, MD: Rowman & Littlefield, 2016.

Wyant, William. *Sandy Patch: A Biography of Lt. Gen. Alexander M. Patch.* Westport, CT: Praeger, 1991.

Zimmer, Joseph. *The History of the 43rd Infantry Division, 1941–1945.* Baton Rouge, LA: Army and Navy Publishing, 1946.

Notes

Prologue

1. 81st Infantry Division, Operation Report, the Capture of Angaur Island, 17 September–22 October 1944, Record Group 407, Entry 427, Box 10334, Folder 381–0.3; First Lieutenant Burnie Rye, Survey of the Death of Sergeant John H. Weathers, in 322nd Infantry Regiment, Casualty Report, Angaur Island, Fall 1944, Record Group 407, Entry 427, Box 10387, Folder 381-INF-322–1.16, both at National Archives (NA), College Park, MD; MG Paul Mueller, Address at Dedication of 81st Infantry Division Cemetery and Post Chapel, Angaur Island, 1500, 25 November 1944, Rex Beasley Papers, Vertical Files, Box 59, Folder 10; 81st Infantry Division, correspondence regarding KIA soldiers and their burial, 1944–1945, Paul Mueller Papers, Box 2, both at the US Army Military History Institute (USAMHI), Carlisle, PA. The mileage numbers are approximate and based on map study.
2. Cole Kingseed, "The Pacific War: The U.S. Army's Forgotten Theater of World War II," *Army* 63, no. 4 (April 2013): 50–56.
3. Major General Oscar Griswold, letter to Lieutenant General Lesley McNair, November 30, 1943, Record Group 337, Entry 58A, Box 9, NA; Lieutenant General Robert Eichelberger, letter to Miss Em (his wife), April 3, 1945, Robert Eichelberger Papers, Box 9, David M. Rubenstein Rare Book and Manuscript Library, Duke University (hereafter DU), Durham, NC; Censorship Intercepts from Mail of the 27th Infantry Division, 1944–1945, Robert Richardson Papers, Box 73, Hoover Institution Archives (HILA), Stanford University, Palo Alto, CA; Stanley Sandler, ed., *World War II in the Pacific: An Encyclopedia* (New York and London: Garland, 2001), 82; Allan Millett, *Semper Fidelis: The History of the United States Marine Corps* (New York: Free Press, 1991), 438–39; Robert Eichelberger in collaboration with Milton Mackaye, *Our Jungle Road to Tokyo* (New York: Viking, 1950), 200; Paul Fussell, *Wartime: Understanding and Behavior in the Second World War* (New York: Oxford University Press, 1989), 155. The 2010 HBO miniseries *The Pacific*, though a fine piece of work about the combat experience, focused entirely on the Marines and thus unfortunately reinforced the mistaken notion that the Corps fought the ground war against Japan.
4. Major General Stanley Larsen, letter to Brigadier General Everett E. Brown, December 18, 1965, Everett E. Brown Papers, Box 1, USAMHI; John McManus, *Grunts: Inside the American Infantry Combat Experience, World War II Through Iraq* (New York: NAL/Caliber, 2010), 9–10. Updated data on American wartime casualties can be accessed at www.fas.org under "American War and Military Operations Casualties: Lists and Statistics."
5. Ronald Spector, *Eagle Against the Sun: The American War with Japan* (New York: Vintage Books, 1985), 560.

Chapter 1. Stunned

1. Robert Greenwood, interview with Dr. Ronald Marcello, July 7, 1974, #230; Martin Rodgers, interview with Dr. Ronald Marcello, June 22, 1988, #752, both at University of North Texas Oral History Program (UNT), Denton, TX; Gordon Prange, *At Dawn We Slept: The Untold Story of Pearl Harbor* (New York: Penguin Books, 1981), 97; James Jones, *From Here to Eternity* (New York: Charles Scribner's Sons, 1951); Stanley Falk, "The U.S. Army and 7 December, 1941," *Army* (December 1991): 21–22; A. P. Hyde, "Pearl Harbor: Then and Now," *After the Battle*, no. 38, (1982): 2–3. Information on the ethnic makeup of Hawaii in 1940 can be accessed at www.ohadatabook.com.

2. James Nasser, interview with Dr. Ronald Marcello, November 13, 1987, #736; Kenneth Nine, interview with Dr. Ronald Marcello, April 28, 1990, #798; Leon Sell, interview with Dr. Ronald Marcello, June 13, 1976, #337; Greenwood interview, all at UNT.

3. William Coughlin, interview with Dr. Ronald Marcello, September 17, 1988, #771; William Moore, interview with Ms. Lisa Meisch, March 4, 1998, #1221; Pamela Bradbury, interview with Dr. Ronald Marcello, April 28, 1990, #791; Nine, Greenwood interviews, all at UNT; Private Harold Kennedy, letter to his mother, September 16, 1941, Harold Kennedy Papers, Box 1, USAMHI; Walter Lord, *Day of Infamy* (New York: Henry Holt, 1957), 9–10. Navy military policemen were often called Shore Patrol.

4. Monica Conter Benning, interview with Ms. Patricia Sloane, May 26, 1982, Army Nurse Corps Oral History Collection, Army Medical Department Center of History and Heritage (AMEDD), Fort Sam Houston, TX; Bradbury, Greenwood interviews, UNT; Samuel Eliot Morison, *History of United States Naval Operations in World War II, The Rising Sun in the Pacific, Volume III* (Boston: Little, Brown, 1948), 100; Prange, *At Dawn We Slept*, 481–82; Lord, *Day of Infamy*, 4–10; Monica Conter Benning, obituary, *News-Press* (Fort Myers, FL), July 22, 2012.

5. Morison, *Rising Sun in the Pacific*, 83–98; Prange, *At Dawn We Slept*, 494–501; the biography of Yamamoto is by Hiroyuki Agawa, *The Reluctant Admiral: Yamamoto and the Imperial Navy* (Tokyo: Kondansha International, 1979); Steve Twomey, "First Shots," *World War II*, November/December 2016: 40–47; Donald Young, interviewer, "Missed Opportunity at Pearl Harbor," *World War II*, November 2000: 50–56, this is an interview with Kermit Tyler; Blake Clark, "Remember Pearl Harbor! Part I," *Infantry Journal*, April 1942: 14; Hyde, "Pearl Harbor Then and Now," *After the Battle*, 12–19; Falk, "US Army and 7 December," *Army*, 21–22.

6. Stephen A. Kallis, "Experience of War: Pearl Harbor Survivor's Story," *MHQ*, Winter 2001: 18–20; Greenwood, Coughlin interviews, UNT; Morison, *Rising Sun in the Pacific*, 94–95; 98–113; Prange, *At Dawn We Slept*, 503–504; Hyde, "Pearl Harbor Then and Now," *After the Battle*, 33–37; Falk, "US Army and 7 December," *Army*, 22.

7. Greenwood interview, UNT; Clark, "Remember Pearl Harbor! Part I," *Infantry Journal*, 19–20; "Seeing Red at Pearl Harbor," *World War II*, November/December 2016: 25; Hyde, "Pearl Harbor Then and Now," *After the Battle*, 36–37; Falk, "US Army and 7 December," *Army*, 22; Prange, *At Dawn We Slept*, 521–27; Lord, *Day of Infamy*, 79–80.

8. 25th Infantry Division, History, 1941–1945, Record Group 407, Entry 427, Box 6929, Folder 325–0, NA; Eunice Yeo, unpublished memoir, 1, Stewart Yeo Papers, Box 1; Hollis Peacock, unpublished memoir, 10–18, WWII Veterans Survey, #3444, both at USAMHI; Nine, Sell interviews, UNT; Aubrey Newman, "The Forward Edge," *Army*, December 1967, 8–9; Hyde, "Pearl Harbor Then and Now," *After the Battle*, 38–42; Falk, "US Army and 7 December," *Army*, 22–23; James Jones, *WWII: A Chronicle of Soldiering* (New York: Ballantine, 1975), 7–8; Lord, *Day of Infamy*, 80–83; Prange, *At Dawn We Slept*, 526–27.

9. Ruth Lawson, unpublished memoir, 2–3, Record Group 15, Box 33, Folder 7, Contri-

butions from the Public Collection, Douglas MacArthur Memorial Archives (DMM), Norfolk, VA; Peacock, unpublished memoir, 19–23; Major Stewart Yeo, letter to his father, December 15, 1941, Stewart Yeo Papers, Box 1; Yeo, unpublished memoir, 2–4, all at USAMHI; Bess M. Tittle, "Experience of War: 'Take Care of the Baby,'" *MHQ*, Autumn 1991: 112; Falk, "US Army and 7 December," *Army*, 23–25; Clark, "Remember Pearl Harbor," *Infantry Journal*, 14; Lord, *Day of Infamy*, 171–73, 190–91; Jones, *From Here to Eternity*, 716–20. The information about liaisons with local girls comes from Jones. Though this is a work of fiction, the fact that he personally experienced the construction of the pillboxes, plus the level of detail he provided in his account carries with it the strong whiff of truth.

10. Lieutenant Colonel Herbert Blackwell, letters to Eloise, December 1941, Box 1, Folder 9, World War II Document Collection, USAMHI; Sell interview, UNT; Newman, "The Forward Edge," *Army*, 8–9; Falk, "US Army and 7 December," *Army*, 25–26; Kallis, "Pearl Harbor Survivor's Story," *MHQ*, 20; Rex Alan Smith and Gerald Meehl, eds., *Pacific War Stories in the Words of Those Who Survived* (New York and London: Abbeville, 2004), 56–57; Lord, *Day of Infamy*, 168–74; Prange, *At Dawn We Slept*, 566. Another parallel for the phenomenon of shock rumors is September 11, 2001. On that terrible day, I heard that the president and Congress had declared war, that gas prices had immediately quadrupled, and, at the government's behest, that the prices would remain at this level or higher. I also heard from one acquaintance that the government would soon round up all Arab-Americans and place them in camps. Obviously there was not a shred of truth in any of these rumors.

11. Bertha Gilmore Martin, oral history, May 23, 1982, Army Nurse Corps Collection, Series III, Oral Histories, Box 46, Folder 14, USAMHI; Joseph Pomerance, interview with Dr. Ronald Marcello, December 6, 1980, #534; Ada Olsson, interview with Dr. Ronald Marcello, December 7, 1978, #461; Hedwige Kaczanowski Gray, interview with Dr. Ronald Marcello, July 5, 1974, #222, all at UNT; Lieutenant Rhoda Ziesler, diary, December 7, 1941, MSS 1914, Box 2, Folder 1, Wisconsin Veterans Museum (WVM), Madison; Monica Conter Benning interview; AMEDD; "Letters from Readers," *American Journal of Nursing*, April 1942: 425–26 (includes two anonymous letters from nurses who served at Hickam); I. S. Radvin and Perrin Long, "The Treatment of Army Casualties in Hawaii," *Army Medical Bulletin*, April 1942, 2–3.

12. Elizabeth Elmer Murphy, interview with Dr. Ronald Marcello, March 30, 1977, #373; Revella Guest, interview with Dr. Ronald Marcello, December 8, 1978, #471; Gelane Barron, interview with Dr. Ronald Marcello, July 7, 1974, #235; William Havel, interview with Dr. Ronald Marcello, April 22, 1994, #1026; Sell interview, all at UNT; Elizabeth Elmer Murphy, oral history, May 23, 1982; Mildred Van Protz, oral history, May 23, 1982, Army Nurse Corps, Series III, Oral Histories, Box 46, Folders 15 and 6, USAMHI; John Moorhead, "Surgical Experience at Pearl Harbor," *Journal of the American Medical Association* 118, no. 9 (February 28, 1942): 712–14; Blake Clark, "Remember Pearl Harbor!" Part Two, *Infantry Journal*, May 1942: 35–36; Radvin and Long, "Treatment of Army Casualties in Hawaii," *Army Medical Bulletin*, 2–8; Lieutenant Mary Slaughter, letter to his family, December 1941, copy in author's possession; Michael Slackman, *Target: Pearl Harbor* (Honolulu: University of Hawaii Press, 1990), 185–87; Lord, *Day of Infamy*, 192–94.

13. Nine, Murphy, Olsson interviews, UNT; Slaughter letter; Newman, "The Forward Edge," *Army*, 9; Kallis, "Pearl Harbor Survivor's Story," *MHQ*, 21; Hyde, "Pearl Harbor Then and Now," *After the Battle*, 42–43; Morison, *Rising Sun in the Pacific*, 123–27; Lord, *Day of Infamy*, 204–7, 219–20.

14. Company F, 163rd Infantry Regiment, History, 1940–1943, Record Group 407, Entry 427, Box 9084, Folder 341-INF-163-0; Anonymous, diary, Imperial Japanese Army soldier, December 1941, #713, Record Group 165, Entry 79, Box 273, ADVATIS, Cur-

rent Translations, #62–64, both at NA; Major General Joseph Stilwell, diary, December 7–8, 1941, HIA, accessible at www.hoover.org; Slaughter letter; Theodore Cook Jr., "Tokyo, December 8, 1941," *MHQ*, Autumn 1991: 30–35; Rana Mitter, *Forgotten Ally: China's World War II, 1937–1945* (Boston: Houghton Mifflin Harcourt, 2013), 236; Walter Borneman, *MacArthur at War: World War II in the Pacific* (New York: Little, Brown, 2016), 3; Douglas MacArthur, *Reminiscences* (New York: Da Capo, 1964), 117; Frank Dorn, *Walkout: With Stilwell in Burma* (New York: Thomas Y. Crowell, 1971), 3–4; Donald Knox, *Death March: The Survivors of Bataan* (New York and London: Harcourt Brace Jovanovich, 1981), 8–10.

Chapter 2. Hostages to Fortune

1. Louis Morton, *The United States Army in World War II: The War in the Pacific: The Fall of the Philippines* (Washington, DC: Office of the Chief of Military History, 1953), 3–8; Hector Bywater, *Seapower in the Pacific: A Study of the American-Japanese Naval Problem* (Boston and New York: Houghton Mifflin, 1921), 254; H. W. Brands, *Bound to Empire: The United States and the Philippines* (New York: Oxford University Press, 1992) 25–26.

2. American War Leader Series, "General Douglas MacArthur," circa 1944, World War II Participants and Contemporaries Collection, John Pumphrey Folder, Dwight D. Eisenhower Library (EL), Abilene, KS; Albert Reid, Eminent Americans, Box 7, Charles Willoughby Papers, USAMHI; Robert Eichelberger, Dictations, 1954–1955, Box 73, Robert Eichelberger Papers, David M. Rubenstein Rare Book and Manuscript Library, Duke University (DU), Durham, NC; Clare Boothe Luce, "MacArthur of the Far East," *Life*, December 8, 1941; Bill Hogan, "The Battle of Anacostia Flats," *MHQ*, Winter 2017: 66–75; D. Clayton James, *The Years of MacArthur, Volume I, 1880–1941* (Boston: Houghton Mifflin, 1970), 73–75, 170–71, 234–42, 303–5; William Manchester, *American Caesar: Douglas MacArthur, 1880–1964* (New York: Dell, 1978), 43–44, 98–125, 158–59; Arthur Herman, *Douglas MacArthur: American Warrior* (New York: Random House, 2016), 142–48, 237–42; Gerald Astor, *Crisis in the Pacific: The Battles for the Philippine Islands by the Men Who Fought Them* (New York: Dell, 1996), 21–25; Robert Ferrell, *The Question of MacArthur's Reputation: Côte de Châtillon, October 14–16, 1918* (Columbia: University of Missouri Press, 2008); Dwight Eisenhower, *At Ease: Stories I Tell to Friends* (Garden City, NY: Doubleday, 1967), 216–17; MacArthur, *Reminiscences*, 29; Morton, *Fall of the Philippines*, 8–10. In the Eichelberger dictations, he related a story told to him by Brigadier General Henry Reilly, an artillery commander who served in the 42nd with MacArthur. Reilly claimed that MacArthur's war reputation was overblown and that he was in a position to award himself decorations.

3. Dwight Eisenhower, interview with Dr. D. Clayton James, August 29, 1967, Record Group 32, Oral History #5; General Douglas MacArthur, letter to General Malin Craig, September 16, 1937, Record Group 15, Box 23, Contributions from the Public Collection; William Manchester, oral history, October 6, 1982, Record Group 32, Oral History #33, all at DMMA; Lieutenant Colonel Dwight Eisenhower, letter to General Douglas MacArthur, August 23, 1938, DDE Pre-Presidential Papers, 1916–1952, Box 74, EL; Michael Schaller, *Douglas MacArthur: The Far Eastern General* (New York: Oxford University Press, 1989), 37–40; Morton, *Fall of the Philippines*, 10–13; James, *Years of MacArthur, Volume I*, 536–56; Manchester, *American Caesar*, 188–96; Herman, *Douglas MacArthur*, 278–86; MacArthur, *Reminiscences*, 103–8; Eisenhower, *At Ease*, 225–31. For insight into Eisenhower's day-to-day experiences while working for MacArthur in the Philippines, see Robert Ferrell, ed., *The Eisenhower Diaries* (New York: W. W. Norton, 1981), 7–36.

4. General George Marshall, cables to Lieutenant General Douglas MacArthur, July

1941, Record Group 2, Personal Files, Box 1, Folder 1; Lieutenant General Douglas MacArthur, Administrative Diary, July 1941, Box 3, Folder 4, both in Records of HQ, USAFFE, 1941–1942; Brigadier General Charles Willoughby, interview with Dr. D. Clayton James, August 28, 1967, Record Group 49, Box 4, D. Clayton James Collection, all at DMMA; Brigadier General Clifford Bluemel, interview with Dr. D. Clayton James, July 8, 1971, Clifford Bluemel Papers, Box 4, United States Military Academy Library Archives (USMA), West Point, NY; Morton, *Fall of the Philippines*, 15–17; Manchester, *American Caesar*, 209–11.

5. Colonel Malcolm Fortier, letter to Dr. Louis Morton, January 10, 1952; Colonel Richard Mallonee, notes, both in Louis Morton Papers, Box 17; Colonel Glen Townsend, "Defense of the Philippines," speech, no date, Louis Morton Papers, Box 9; Brigadier General Charles Drake, Operations of the Quartermaster Corps, Philippine Islands, July 27, 1941–May 6, 1942, Eugene Mitchell Papers, Box 1, all at USAMHI; Colonel James D. Carter, interview with Dr. D. Clayton James, August 23, 1971, Record Group 49, Box 2, D. Clayton James Collection, DMMA; Major Alfredo Santos, "The 1st Regular Division in the Battle of the Philippines," June 7, 1947, 51–52, School of Logistics, located at Combined Arms Research Library (CARL), Fort Leavenworth, KS; Major Beverly Skarden, "The Operations of Company A, 92nd Infantry, Philippine Army, 3 January 1942–24 March 1942, Personal Experience of a Company Commander," 1946–1947, 4, Advanced Officers Course, Donovan Research Library (DRL), Fort Benning, GA; Major W. J. Lage, "The Operation of 3d Battalion, 11th Infantry (11th Division PA) at Zaracosa, Philippines, 28 December–29 December 1941, Personal Experience of a Regimental Machine Gun Officer and Commander of the Covering Forces in the Withdrawal," 1947–1948, 4–5, Advanced Infantry Officers Class No 2, DRL; Charles H. Bogart, "A Doctor's Perspective on the Philippines, 1941–1942," *Council on America's Military Past*, July 1989: 44–46; John Whitman, *Bataan: Our Last Ditch* (New York: Hippocrene Books, 1990), 27–29; Morton, *Fall of the Philippines*, 26–30; James, *Years of MacArthur, Volume I*, 616.

6. Staff and Plan of Induction of Philippine Army Units, Record Group 407, Entry 427, Box 1157, Folder 98. USFI-0.3, NA; Morton, *Fall of the Philippines*, 32–50; Morison, *Rising Sun in the Pacific*, 157–59.

7. Michael Campbell, questionnaire, WWII Veterans Survey #9728; Michael Campbell, unpublished memoir, 67–77, Box 12, John Olson Papers, both at USAMHI; Madeline Ullom, interview with Colonel James Hunn, April 9, 1983, AMEDD; Lieutenant Alexander "Sandy" Nininger, letter to his family, November 30, 1944, Box 1, Alexander Nininger Papers, USMA; *Reports of General MacArthur: The Campaigns of MacArthur in the Pacific, Volume I* (Washington, DC: Department of the Army, 1994 edition), 7; Jonathan Wainwright, *General Wainwright's Story* (Garden City, NJ: Doubleday & Company, 1946), pp. 9–10; Astor, *Crisis in the Pacific*, pp. 10–17, 34–35. The comments about MacArthur's failure to evacuate his own family are mine alone and not from any of these sources.

8. Lieutenant General Richard Sutherland, interview with Dr. D. Clayton James, November 12, 1946, Box 2, Louis Morton Papers, USAMHI; General Douglas MacArthur, answers to questions submitted by Dr. Louis Morton, February 8, 1954, Record Group 10, Box 119, Folder 11, General Douglas MacArthur Private Correspondence, DMMA; Ronald Spector, *Eagle Against the Sun: The American War with Japan* (New York: Vintage Books, 1985), pp. 54–59, 72–75; Morton, *Fall of the Philippines*, pp. 64–70; Manchester, *American Caesar*, p. 184; Astor, *Crisis in the Pacific*, p. 26.

9. Japanese Monograph No. 1, Philippines Operations Record, Phase I, 6 November, 1941–June 1942, 8–5.1 AC1, U.S. Army Center of Military History (CMH), Washington, D.C., copy in author's possession courtesy of Frank Shirer; Imperial Japanese Army, "To Win the War You Need Only Read This," Pamphlet, Record Group 2,

Personal Files, Box 5, Folder 4; Sergeant Nakamura, diary, December 8, 1941; Captain Hidaka, diary, November 19, 1941, both in Box 5, Folder 3, Records of Headquarters, USAFFE, 1941–1942, all at DMMA; Morton, *Fall of the Philippines*, pp. 52–61. Japan did not have an independent air force in World War II. Similar to the United States, the Japanese had an Army Air Force and naval aviation.

10. Japanese Monograph No. 1, CMH; Faubion Bowers, interview with Dr. D. Clayton James, July 18, 1971; Major General Richard Marshall, interview with Dr. D. Clayton James, July 27, 1971, both in Record Group 49, Boxes 1 and 3 respectively, D. Clayton James Collection; Willoughby interview; MacArthur answers to questions, all at DMMA; Sutherland's contentions about running Eisenhower out of the Philippines were discussed by Lieutenant General Robert Eichelberger in his Dictations, 1957, Box 73, Robert Eichelberger Papers, DU; D. Clayton James, "The Other Pearl Harbor," *MHQ*, Winter 1994: 23–26; Paul Rogers, *The Good Years: MacArthur and Sutherland* (New York: Praeger, 1990), 36–40; Morton, *Fall of the Philippines*, 78–84; background information on Brereton can be found at www.af.mil and in John McManus, *September Hope: The American Side of a Bridge Too Far* (New York: NAL/Caliber, 2012), 26–27. MacArthur later denied any knowledge that Brereton had requested authorization for a Formosa raid. See his press release in the *New York Times* on September 28, 1946. For the record, MacArthur said that, had he known, he would have denied permission because of his belief that the mission "would have had no chance of success."

11. Lieutenant General Lewis Brereton, letter to Albert Simpson, April 3, 1952; Lieutenant General Lewis Brereton, diary, December 8, 1941, Lewis Brereton Papers, Box 1, EL; Lieutenant General Lewis Brereton, statement, January 30, 1946, Louis Morton Papers, Box 19; Lieutenant General Lewis Brereton, notes from conversation with Clare Boothe Luce, April 1942, Charles Willoughby Papers, Box 7; Lieutenant General Richard Sutherland, letter to General Douglas MacArthur, August 1, 1951, William Jenna Papers, Box 1, all at USAMHI; USAFFE, chief of staff journal, December 8, 12, 1941, Record Group 2, Personal Files, Box 2, Folder 5, Records of the HQ, USAFFE, 1941–1942; MacArthur, diary, December 8, 1941; answers to questions, all at DMMA; Lieutenant Randall Keator, Statement, June 27, 1942; "Kate," letter to folks regarding Randall Keator's odyssey; Lieutenant Randall Keator, Distinguished Service Cross Citation, December 21, 1941, all in Randall Keator Collection, #2000.203.008, National World War II Museum (WWIIM), New Orleans; Walter Edmonds, "What Happened at Clark Field," *The Atlantic*, July 1951, 19–31; Ernest Miller, "Bataan Uncensored, Part II," *The National Guardsman*, April 1949, 2; James, "The Other Pearl Harbor," *MHQ*, 24–26; D. Clayton James, *The Years of MacArthur, Volume II* (Boston: Houghton Mifflin, 1975), 3–7; Christopher Kolakowski, *Last Stand on Bataan: The Defense of the Philippines, December 1941–May 1942* (Jefferson, NC: McFarland, 2016), 18–23; Lester Tenney, *My Hitch in Hell: The Bataan Death March* (Washington, DC: Potomac Books, 1995), 1–2; Mary Ellen Condon-Rall and Albert Cowdrey, *The U.S. Army in World War II: The Technical Services, The Medical Department: Medical Service in the War Against Japan* (Washington, DC: Center of Military History, United States Army, 1998), 25; Knox, *Death March*, 13–14; MacArthur, *Reminiscences*, 117–120; Astor, *Crisis in the Pacific*, 59–66; Morton, *Fall of the Philippines*, 84–88.

12. Albert Simpson, USAF Historical Section, letter to Lieutenant General Lewis Brereton, 1952; Brereton letter to Simpson, diary, all in Lewis Brereton Papers, Box 1, EL; Brigadier General William Brougher, comments, Louis Morton Papers, Box 3; Brereton statement, notes from conversation with Clare Boothe Luce; Sutherland letter to MacArthur, interview with James, all at USAMHI; MacArthur, diary, DMMA; James, "The Other Pearl Harbor," *MHQ*, 28–29; Claire Chennault, edited by Robert

Hotz, *Way of a Fighter: The Memoirs of Claire Lee Chennault* (New York: G. P. Putnam's Sons, 1949), 124; MacArthur, *Reminiscences*, 120–21; James, *Years of MacArthur, Volume II*, 8–15; Rogers, *The Good Years*, 94–99; Kolakowski, *Last Stand on Bataan*, 21–23; Astor, *Crisis in the Pacific*, 66–67; Captain Chihaya Takahashi, Interrogation Nav No. 15, USSBS No. 74, located at www.ww2db.com. Chennault had many titles during the war. For the sake of simplicity, I have chosen to call him the "air commander."

13. Captain Godfrey Ames, diary, December 1941, Record Group 407, Philippine Archives Collection, Box 125, Folder 1, NA; Brigadier General Donald Blackburn, senior officer oral history, 1982–1983, Donald Blackburn Papers, Box 1, USAMHI; Major Carlos J. Herrera, "The Philippine Constabulary in the Battle of the Philippines," 23–24, School of Combined Arms, Regular Course, 1946–1947, CARL; Charles Van Landingham, "I Saw Manila Die," *Saturday Evening Post*, September 26, 1942, 12–13; Joseph Connor, "Imaginary Invasion," *World War II*, November/December 2015: 62–67; Captain John Gordon, "The Best Arm We Had," *Field Artillery Journal*, November–December 1984: 27–28; Teodoro Agoncillo, *The Fateful Years: Japan's Adventure in the Philippines, 1941–1945, Volume One* (Quezon City, Philippines: R. P. Garcia, 1965, 69–75; Clark Lee, *They Call It Pacific: An Eyewitness Story of Our War from Bataan to the Solomons* (New York: Viking, 1943), 40–41, 45–47, 69; *Campaigns of MacArthur, Volume I*, 8–9; MacArthur, *Reminiscences*, 123; Morton, *Fall of the Philippines*, 115–19.

14. Carlos Romulo, *I Saw the Fall of the Philippines* (Garden City, NY: Doubleday, Doran, 1942), 30–32; Sid Huff with Joe Morris, *My Fifteen Years with MacArthur* (New York: Paperback Library, 1964), 34; James Leutze, *A Different Kind of Victory: A Biography of Admiral Thomas C. Hart* (Annapolis, MD: Naval Institute Press, 1981), 163–64, 233–51; Morison, *Rising Sun in the Pacific*, 171–83; Borneman, *MacArthur at War*, 68–70, 96–99; James, *Years of MacArthur, Volume II*, 20–23; MacArthur, *Reminiscences*, 102, 128; Kolakowski, *Last Stand on Bataan*, 23–27. Hart lived in a suite just below MacArthur's in the Manila Hotel. The admiral had several informal conversations with MacArthur, usually when the general was clad only in a bathrobe. The discussions were generally one-sided. MacArthur would pace about and pontificate while Hart listened.

15. Report of Operations of North Luzon Force and I Philippine Corps in the Defense of North Luzon and Bataan from 8 December 1941–9 April 1942; Report of Major General George Parker, formerly commanding the South Luzon Force and the II Philippine Corps, from 8 December 1941–9 April 1942, both in Record Group 407, Entry 427, Box 1157, Folder 98-USFI-0.3; 11th Infantry Division, Historical Data, Record Group 407, Entry 1113, Philippine Archives Collection, Box 1478, all at NA; Headquarters, Hawaiian Department, Observer Notes on Japanese Landings, July 1, 1942; Colonel Glen Townsend, "Defense of the Philippines," speech, Louis Morton Papers, Boxes 8 and 9, respectively; Brougher comments, all at USAMHI; Japanese Monograph No. 1, CMH; Hidaka, diary, December 12, 1941, DMMA; Kolakowski, *Last Stand on Bataan*, 26–27; Morton, *Fall of the Philippines*, 98–112; *Campaigns of MacArthur, Volume I*, 6–9. Townsend was a regimental commander in the 11th Infantry Division.

16. Operations of the Provisional Tank Group, USAFFE, 1941–1942, Record Group 407, Entry 427, Box 1158, Folder 98-USFI-0.3; Operations of North Luzon Force; both at NA; History of 26th Cavalry Regiment Experiences in the Luzon Campaign, Clinton Pierce Papers, Box 2; Colonel William Chandler, "A Combat History of the U.S. 26th Cavalry," Chester L. Johnson Papers, Box 1, Folder 1946, both at USAMHI; Japanese Monograph No. 1, CMH; Benjamin Morin, unpublished memoir, 1–3, Roger Mansell Papers, Box 9, Folder 1, HIA; David Sears, "The U.S. Cavalry's Last Charge," *World*

War II, March/April 2015: 48–52; Raymond Woolfe, *The Doomed Horse Soldiers of Bataan* (Lanham, MD: Rowman & Littlefield, 2016), 136–94; Lee, *They Call It Pacific*, 82–83; Wainwright, *General Wainwright's Story*, 32–35, 39; Tenney, *My Hitch in Hell*, 22–24; Kolakowski, *Last Stand on Bataan*, 37–41.

17. 16th Division, Luzon Campaign, 24 December 1941–3 January 1942, Record Group 407, Philippine Archives Collection, Box 17, NA; General Douglas MacArthur, Radiogram to the War Department, December 22, 1941, Record Group 2, Personal Files, Box 2, Folder 2, Records of Headquarters, USAFFE, 1941–1942, DMMA; Japanese Monograph No. 1, CMH; Bluemel interview, USMA; Sutherland interview, USAMHI; Santos, "1st Regular Division in the Battle of the Philippines," 29–32, CARL; *MacArthur Campaigns of MacArthur, Volume I*, 10–14; MacArthur, *Reminiscences*, 123–24; Kolakowski, *Last Stand on Bataan*, 45–47; Morton, *Fall of the Philippines*, 138–44. Santos was a highly decorated soldier who eventually became chief of staff of the postwar Republic of the Philippines armed forces.

18. Lieutenant General Richard Sutherland, letter to Dr. Louis Morton, May 29, 1951, Louis Morton Papers, Box 2, USAMHI; Major General Richard Marshall, Speech to the American Society, no date, Record Group 29b, Richard J. Marshall Papers, Box 1, Folder 2, DMMA; Van Landingham, "I Saw Manila Die," *Saturday Evening Post*, 13, 70; Morton, *Fall of the Philippines*, 232–35; Lee, *They Call It Pacific*, 125–27; Romulo, *I Saw the Fall of the Philippines*, 73–79.

19. MacArthur, diary, December 24, 1941, DMMA; Lewis Beebe, unpublished memoir, 6, Lewis Beebe Papers, Vertical Files, Box 29, Folder 445; Lieutenant General Masaharu Homma, interview with Colonel Walter Buchly, March 1946, Louis Morton Papers, Box 8; Sutherland letter to Morton, interview, all at USAMHI; Romulo, *I Saw the Fall of the Philippines*, 60–63; Huff, *My Fifteen Years with MacArthur*, 37–40; Rogers, *MacArthur and Sutherland: The Good Years*, 118–20; Leutze, *Different Kind of Victory*, 245–47; Manchester, *American Caesar*, pp. 249–52; Borneman, *MacArthur at War*, pp. 103–4.

20. Army Transportation Service, Report of Activities in the Philippine Islands, 8 December 1941–6 May 1942, Record Group 407, Philippine Archives Collection, Box 10; Operations of North Luzon Force, both at NA; Brigadier General Charles Drake, "Operations of the Quartermaster Corps, Philippine Islands, July 27, 1941–May 6, 1942," Eugene Mitchell Papers, Box 1; Brigadier General Charles Drake, letter to Major General Orlando Ward, 1952, Louis Morton Papers, Box 2; Beebe memoir, 8–9; Marshall speech, all at USAMHI; Major Clarence Bess, "Operations of Service Company, 31st Infantry (Philippine Division), 5 January–9 April 1942, Philippine Island Campaign, Personal Experiences of a Service Company Commander," Advanced Infantry Officers Course, 1947–1948, 12–13, DRL; Alvin Stauffer, *The United States Army in World War II: The Quartermaster Corps: Operations in the War Against Japan* (Washington, DC: Center of Military History, United States Army, 2004), 8–15; Ernest Miller *Bataan Uncensored* (Long Prairie, MN: Hart, 1949), 75; James, *Years of MacArthur, Volume II*, 30–37.

Chapter 3. Doomed

1. Operations of North Luzon Force; Operations of the Provisional Tank Group, both at NA; Colonel Harry Skerry, letter to Major General Orlando Ward, January 16, 1952; Colonel William Maher, letter to Dr. Louis Morton, November 11, 1949, Louis Morton Papers, Boxes 2 and 12, USAMHI; Major William VandenBergh, "Executing the Double Retrograde Delay: The 194th Tank Battalion in Action During the Luzon Defensive Campaign, 1941–1942," *Armor*, November–December 2002, 28–29; Duane Schultz, *Hero of Bataan: The Story of General Jonathan M. Wainwright* (New York: St. Martin's, 1981), 118–20; John Toland, *But Not in Shame: The Six Months After Pearl*

Harbor (New York: Random House, 1961), 141–43; Wainwright, *General Wainwright's Story*, 43–45; Morton, *Fall of the Philippines*, 205–10; Knox, *Death March*, 43–46; Kolakowski, *Last Stand on Bataan*, 65–66.

2. Colonel William Doyle, interview with Captain Perry Miller, July 29, 1942, Louis Morton Papers, Box 16; Drake, "Operations of the Quartermaster Corps"; Campbell, unpublished memoir, 80, all at USAMHI; MacArthur, answers to questions, DMMA; Lieutenant Colonel Adrianus van Oosten, "The Operations of the 1st Battalion, 45th Infantry (PS Philippine Division) in the Battle of the Tuol Pocket, Bataan, 29 January–19 February, Philippine Island Campaign, Personal Experiences of a Battalion Executive Officer," Advanced Infantry Officers Course, 1947–1948, 7, DRL; Gordon, "The Best Arm We Had," *Field Artillery Journal*, 29–30; Stauffer, *The Quartermaster Corps*, 13–17; MacArthur, *Reminiscences*, 126–27; *Campaigns of MacArthur, Volume I*, 15 and endnote 29; Kolakowski, *Last Stand on Bataan*, 71–74.

3. 65th Brigade, Combat in the Mount Natib Area, Bataan, 1942, Record Group 407, Philippine Archives Collection, Box 17; 16th Division, Luzon Campaign, both at NA; 57th Infantry Regiment, Report of Operations, 8 December 1941–9 April 1942, Louis Morton Papers, Box 16; Lieutenant Colonel George Clarke, interviews with Captain Percy Miller, August 14–15, 1942, Louis Morton Papers, Boxes 2 and 16; Lieutenant Colonel Philip Fry, journal, January 1942, Philip T. Fry Papers, Box 1; Homma interview, all at USAMHI; Japanese Monograph No. 1, CMH; Nakamura, diary, January 10, 1942, DMMA; Major John Olson, "The Operations of the 57th Infantry (PS) Regimental Combat Team (Philippine Division) at Abucay, Bataan, Philippines, 10 January–23 January 1942, Personal Experiences of a Regimental Adjutant," Advanced Infantry Officers Course, 1947–1948, 9–20; Major Ernest L. Brown, "The Operations of the 57th Infantry (P.S.) Philippine Div., Abucay, January 1942, Personal Experiences of a Company Commander," Advanced Officers Course, 1946–1947, both at DRL; Lieutenant Colonel H. K. Johnson, "Defense Along the Abucay Line," *Military Review*, February 1949, 50–52; Gordon, "The Best Arm We Had," *Field Artillery Journal*, 29–30; Miller, *Bataan Uncensored*, 145; Knox, *Death March*, 63; Kolakowski, *Last Stand on Bataan*, 83–85.

4. General Harold K. Johnson, letter to Mrs. Pauline Kresge (sister of Sandy Nininger), July 19, 1966; Major Royal Reynolds, letter to Mr. James F. Cook, March 4, 1946; Ruth Patterson Spang, letter to John Patterson (nephew of Sandy Nininger), March 10, 1984; John Patterson, letter to Mrs. Carl F. Spang, March 30, 1984; Cadet Alexander "Sandy" Nininger, letters to family, April 13, 1940, May 21, 1941; Alexander Nininger Sr., letter to Alexander Nininger Jr., December 24, 1941; Ms. Betty McGough, letter to Mrs. Myrtle Willard (biological mother of Sandy Nininger), April 13, 1943; "Some Memories of Sandy Nininger [*sic*] as Recalled by his Mother"; Second Lieutenant Alexander Nininger Jr., Medal of Honor citation; Lieutenant Alexander "Sandy" Nininger, commemorative album; multiple contemporary newspaper accounts, all material located in the Alexander Nininger Papers, Boxes 1 and 2, USMA; Lieutenant Colonel Austin Montgomery, Transportation Officer, interview with Dr. Louis Morton, January 23, 1948, Louis Morton Papers, Box 2; 57th Infantry Regiment, Report of Operations; Clarke interviews, all at USAMHI; Olson, "Operations of the 57th Infantry Regimental Combat Team at Abucay," 15; Brown, "Operations of the 57th Infantry, Personal Experiences of a Company Commander," 14, both at DRL; Earl Holden, "The Little Crucifix in the War Hero's Life," *Atlanta Journal and Constitution Magazine*, March 19, 1961, no pagination; Mike Clary, "Fort Lauderdale WWII Hero to be Honored in Arlington," *Sun Sentinel* (Fort Lauderdale), March 17, 2010; Edward Murphy, *Heroes of World War II* (New York: Ballantine Books, 1990), 22–23; Astor, *Crisis in the Pacific*, 115–16. The only significant Japanese submachine gun of the war was the Type 100. It was relatively rare and probably not in service during

the 1941–1942 campaign. Lieutenant Colonel Montgomery recovered Nininger's body and transported it to the churchyard. There have been many postwar tributes to Nininger. Two transport ships were named in his honor, as was a Veterans Nursing Home in the Fort Lauderdale area and a rifle range at Fort Benning. The Key Club International, of which he was a member, gives out the annual Sandy Nininger Award to high school seniors who exemplify his character. The West Point Association of Graduates each year confers the Alexander R. Nininger Award for Valor at Arms to the active-duty graduate who most closely mirrors his character and courage. In 1994, a statue in downtown Fort Lauderdale was dedicated to his memory. A specially embossed headstone has also been placed in his honor at Arlington National Cemetery. The First Division cadet barracks at West Point is currently named for him. His nephew has made three separate trips to Bataan in an effort to locate his remains, but to no avail.

5. Captain Elbridge Fendall, unpublished memoir, 4, Record Group 407, Philippine Archives Collection, Box 129, Folder 13, NA; Major/Lieutenant Colonel Harold K. Johnson, diary, 1941–1942, Record Group 407, Philippine Archives Collection, Box 135, Folder 1, NA; Lieutenant Colonel Harold K. Johnson, letter to Colonel Edmund Lilly, January 3, 1946, Edmund Lilly Papers, Box 1; Major/Lieutenant Colonel Harold K. Johnson, diary, 1941–1942, Harold K. Johnson Papers, Series I, Personal Correspondence, Box 89; General Harold K. Johnson, interview with Dr. D. Clayton James, July 7, 1971, Harold K. Johnson Papers, Series VI, Oral Histories, Box 201, Folder 1; General Harold K. Johnson, senior officer oral history, January 27, 1972, Harold K. Johnson Papers, Series VI, Oral Histories, Box 201, Folder 2; Clarke interviews; Fry, journal, January 1942, all at USAMHI; Lewis Sorley, *Honorable Warrior: General Harold K. Johnson and the Ethics of Command* (Lawrence: University Press of Kansas, 1998), 44–50; Whitman, *Bataan: Our Last Ditch*, 134–35, 139–40, 147–48, 152–53; Kolakowski, *Last Stand on Bataan*, 88. The Johnson diary is written in the format of long letters to his wife, Dorothy; a partial typewritten version of the Johnson diary is available in the Louis Morton Papers, Box 7 at the USAMHI. Not surprisingly, in his interview, Clarke never mentioned his incapacitation and relief.

6. Captain Archie McMaster, memoir of the Tuol Pocket, 16–24, Louis Morton Papers, Box 13; Colonel Glen Townsend, 11th Infantry Regiment, "The Toul Pocket," Louis Morton Papers, Box 15; Townsend speech; Commander John Bulkeley, letter to Dr. Louis Morton, March 5, 1948, Louis Morton Papers, Box 2; 57th Infantry Regiment, Report of Operations; General Douglas MacArthur, Training Memorandum No. 10, February 1, 1942, Louis Morton Papers, Box 12; Johnson, diary, 1942; oral histories, all at USAMHI; Hidaka, diary, January 23–25, 1942, DMMA; anonymous Imperial Japanese Army medical officer, diary, January 21–25, 1942, Record Group 165, Entry 79, Box 411, Captured Documents; Lieutenant John Wright, diary, circa 1942, Record Group 407, Philippine Archives Collection, Box 125, Folder 2; Operations of the Provisional Tank Group, both at NA; Van Oosten, "Operations of the 1st Battalion, 45th Infantry," 10–25, DRL; Santos, "1st Regular Division in the Battle of the Philippines," 39–40, CARL; Japanese Monograph No. 1, CMH; John Lukacs, "Triumph on Bataan," *World War II*, September/October 2010): 50–57; Gordon, "The Best Arm We Had," *Field Artillery Journal*, 30–31; Morton, *Fall of the Philippines*, 296–346; Knox, *Death March*, 77–79; Wainwright, *General Wainwright's Story*, 61–62; Murphy, *Heroes of World War II*, 24–25; Whitman, *Bataan: Our Last Ditch*, 358–59. For an especially detailed and well-researched description of these battles, see Chapters 13–17 of Whitman's outstanding book.

7. USAFFE, Communiqués, December 1941–March 1942, Record Group 200, Entry 19810 (A1) Richard Sutherland Papers, Box 15; General Douglas MacArthur, Message to All Unit Commanders, January 15, 1942, Record Group 407, Philippine Archives

Collection, Box 10; General Dwight D. Eisenhower, letter to Major General Orlando Ward, March 28, 1950, Record Group 319, Entry 75, Box 16, Records of the Office of the Chief of Military History, Stilwell's Mission to China, all at NA; Brigadier General LeGrande "Pick" Diller, interview with Dr. D. Clayton James, May 31, 1977, Record Group 49, Box 5, D. Clayton James Collection; Brigadier General LeGrande "Pick" Diller, oral history, September 26, 1982, Record Group 32, Oral History #23; Eisenhower interview; most of the MacArthur–Marshall correspondence can be found in Record Group 2, Personal Files, Records of HQ, USAFFE, 1941–1942, all at DMMA; Robert Eichelberger, dictations, 1959, Robert Eichelberger Papers, Box 73, DU; Sutherland interview, USAMHI; Cecil Forinash, interview with Mr. Stan Tinsley, August 17, 1991, Oral History Collection, Center for the Study of War and Society, Special Collections, University of Tennessee-Knoxville (SCUTK); Matthew Klimow, "Lying to the Troops: American Leaders and the Defense of Bataan," *Parameters*, December 1990: 48–60; Louis Morton, *The United States Army in World War II: War in the Pacific: Strategy and Command, the First Two Years* (Washington, DC: Center of Military History, United States Army, 2000), 186–92; John Jacob Beck, *MacArthur and Wainwright: Sacrifice of the Philippines* (Albuquerque: University of New Mexico Press, 1974), 69; Dwight Eisenhower, *Crusade in Europe*, (New York: Doubleday, 1948), 21–23; James, *Years of MacArthur, Volume I*, 435–37; Toland, *But Not in Shame*, 186; Rogers, *The Good Years*, 137; Manchester, *American Caesar*, 171, 260–61; Morton, *Fall of the Philippines*, 390–404; Ferrell, *The Eisenhower Diaries*, 44. Diller was MacArthur's main publicity officer throughout the war. Eisenhower, in his excusing failure but not abandonment statement, was also referring to the people of China and Malaysia. Robert Eichelberger, who served as a key aide to MacArthur during his tenure as chief of staff, claimed that MacArthur once told him, "George Catlett Marshall is the most overrated officer in the United States Army. He'll never be a general officer as long as I'm chief of staff."

8. Dean Sherry, letter to Dr. William Belote, October 16, 1963, William and James Belote Papers, Box 2, USAMHI; Lieutenant General John "Jack" Wright, interview with Dr. D. Clayton James, June 28, 1971, Record Group 49, Miscellaneous Files, Part II; Mrs. Jean MacArthur, oral history, September 28, 1984, Record Group 32, Oral Histories #51 and 78, both at DMMA; William Sanchez, oral history, June 24, 2011, Nimitz Education and Research Center, National Museum of the Pacific War (NMPW), Fredericksburg, TX; Ames, diary, January 1942, NA; "Corregidor," *After the Battle*, no. 23 (1979): 2–4; James Belote and William Belote, *Corregidor: The Saga of a Fortress* (New York: Harper & Row, 1967), 54–55; Miller, *Bataan Uncensored*, 193–94; Borneman, *MacArthur at War*, 118–20; Lee, *They Call It Pacific*, 234; Huff, *My Fifteen Years with MacArthur*, 41–42; Manchester, *American Caesar*, 253–25. I would like to pass along a special thanks to Mr. Reagan Grau at the National Museum of the Pacific War for making a huge collection of the museum's oral histories available to me in digital format.

9. President Manuel Quezon and General Douglas MacArthur, correspondence, January–February 1942; General Douglas MacArthur, Estimate of Situation, February 5, 1942, Record Group 2, Personal Files, Box 2, Folders 3 and 4, Records of the HQ, USAFFE, 1941–1942; General Carlos Romulo, oral history, October 7, 1982, Record Group 32, Oral History #39; Madeline Ullom, questionnaire, Record Group 15, Box 41, Folder 6, Contributions from the Public Collection; Jean MacArthur, oral history, all at DMMA; President Franklin Roosevelt, radiogram to President Manuel Quezon, January 30, 1942; President Manuel Quezon, radiogram to President Franklin Roosevelt, February 8, 1942; General Douglas MacArthur, radiogram to War Department, February 11, 1942; President Franklin Roosevelt, radiogram to President Manuel Quezon, February 11, 1942; General Douglas MacArthur, radiogram to

General George Marshall, February 16, 1942, all at Record Group 200, Entry 19810 (A1) Richard Sutherland Papers, Box 34, NA; Huff, *My Fifteen Years with General MacArthur*, 45–50; Manchester, *American Caesar*, 256–64; Schaller, *The Far Eastern General*, 59–60. Ullom was a nurse in the Malinta hospital. She saw Jean visit the wounded every day. During the Revolution, George Washington's wife, Martha, joined her husband each winter when fighting was at a standstill and the Army was hunkered down, secure in camp. At times during the Civil War, Ulysses Grant's wife, Julia, stayed with him, but never while he was directing combat operations. His adolescent son Fred occasionally accompanied him during the Vicksburg campaign until Grant decided the danger was too great and sent him home.

10. General George Marshall, radiogram to General Douglas MacArthur, February 24, 1942; Summary of Developments in MacArthur's Case, February 1942; Major General Richard Sutherland, letter to Secretary of War, March 16, 1942, all in Record Group 15, Box 23, Folder 23, Contributions from the Public Collection; Major Carlos Romulo, Dispatches Relating to MacArthur, 1942, Record Group 2, Personal Files, Box 2, Folder 4, Records of HQ, USAFFE, 1941–1942, all at DMMA; General Douglas MacArthur, radiogram to General George Marshall, February 24, 1942; General George Marshall, radiogram to General Douglas MacArthur, February 25, 1942; James, *Years of MacArthur, Volume II*, 129–38; MacArthur, *Reminiscences*, 139–41; Schaller, *Far Eastern General*, 61–63; the full medal citation is reproduced in MacArthur, *Reminiscences*, 147. MacArthur and his father, Arthur, became one of only two father-son Medal of Honor recipients in American history. The other duo is Theodore Roosevelt, for San Juan Hill, and his son Theodore Jr. for Utah Beach. After the war, Eisenhower said that he was offered the Medal of Honor following the successful North Africa campaign. He thought the award would be inappropriate for a senior officer who faced little danger. He pointedly said that he refused to accept it, "because I knew a man who had received one for sitting in a hole." See General Robert Eichelberger Dictations, 1955, Robert Eichelberger Papers, Box 73, DU.

11. President Manuel Quezon, Executive Order #1, January 3, 1942, Record Group 200, Entry 19810 (A1), Richard Sutherland Papers, Box 57, NA; Private First Class Paul Rogers, notes, diary, February 13, 1942, Record Group 46, Box 1, Folder 8, Paul Rogers Papers, DMMA; Paul Rogers and Carol Petillo, "An Exchange of Opinion: MacArthur, Quezon, and Executive Order Number One—Another View," *Pacific Historical Review*, 1983, 93–102; Carol Petillo, "Douglas MacArthur and Manuel Quezon: A Note on an Imperial Bond," *Pacific Historical Review*, 1979): 107–17; Schaller, *Far Eastern General*, 59–64; Rogers, *The Good Years*, 165–69; Ferrell, *Eisenhower Diaries*, 63; conversion from 1942 to twenty-first-century money can be accessed at www.dollartimes.com. Though Rogers seemed discomfited by the payments as he typed up the paperwork in 1942, he defended his former chief decades later, lamely pointing to special British government payments to Field Marshal Douglas Haig as a precedent for such bonuses.

12. 16th Naval District, Plans for Torpedo Boat Squadron Three, March 10, 1942, John Bulkeley Papers, Box 1, EL; Vice Admiral John Bulkeley, interview with Dr. D. Clayton James, July 2, 1971, Record Group 49, Miscellaneous File, Part I; Diller, Jean MacArthur oral histories, all at DMMA; James, *Years of MacArthur, Volume II*, 100–10; Rogers, *The Good Years*, 187–94; MacArthur, *Reminiscences*, 140–45; Huff, *My Fifteen Years with MacArthur*, 51–75; Manchester, *American Caesar*, 289–312; Borneman, *MacArthur at War*, 143–59. On MacArthur's recommendation, Bulkeley received the Medal of Honor for this mission and his many other brave exploits during the campaign. He escaped and returned home a war hero, the central character of a book and movie entitled *They Were Expendable*. He retired in 1975 as a vice admiral. Chris Kolakowski, the sagacious director of the MacArthur Memorial in Norfolk,

Virginia, argues that MacArthur, out of a deep-seated psychological need to justify his exit from the Philippines, honestly convinced himself that there were major rescue forces waiting for him in Australia. Thus, Chris sees the general's "surprise" as real. While I agree that MacArthur's emphasis on the existence of a rescue force did stem from a need to justify his exit, I believe he was far too savvy and calculating to convince himself of such a tall tale.

13. Joseph Chabot, interview with Dr. D. Clayton James, July 2, 1971, Record Group 49, Miscellaneous File, Part I, DMMA; Colonel Milton Hill, interview with Colonel J. K. Evans, Far Eastern Branch, July 4, 1942; Richard Marshall, interview with Louis Morton, April 7, 1948, both in Louis Morton Papers, Box 2; Johnson, interview with James, all at USAMHI; John Taylor, "'I Have Taken a Dreadful Step,'" *MHQ*, Summer 2005: 25; Morton, *Fall of the Philippines*, 361–66; Wainwright, *General Wainwright's Story*, 3–5; Schultz, *Hero of Bataan*, 199 and, for Wainwright's background, see chapters 1–3; also see www.arlingtoncemetery.net and www.historylink.org for more information on Wainwright's career and his distinguished military family.

14. Lieutenant Clara Mueller, diary, 1942, Record Group 407, Philippine Archive Collection, Box 137, Folder 4; Fendall, unpublished memoir, 12–13, both at NA, Lieutenant Colonel Walter Waterous, statement of experiences and observations concerning the Bataan campaign and subsequent imprisonment, 52, Louis Morton Papers, Box 6; Lieutenant Eugene Conrad, "The Operations of the 31st Infantry (Philippine Division) Defense of Bataan, 8 December 1941–9 April 1942," Infantry School Monograph, 1946–1947, 18–19, World War II Veterans Survey #2260201 and Louis Morton Papers, Box 15; Richard Mallonee, unpublished memoir, 245–49, Richard Mallonee Papers, Box 1; Drake, "Operations of the Quartermaster Corps"; Campbell, unpublished memoir, 84; Skerry, letter to Ward, all at USAMHI; Brigadier General Hugh Casey, inspection of MLR, Bataan, March 8, 1942, Record Group 2, Box 8, Folder 4, Records of HQ, USAFFE, 1941–1942; Master Sergeant James Peter Bennett, letter to Master Sergeant William Troynosky, March 18, 1942, Record Group 2, Box 14, Folder 3, Records of HQ, USAFFE, 1941–1942, both at DMMA; Sergeant R. Miguel, 45th Infantry Regiment, diary, March 1942, World War II Participants and Contemporaries Collection, Vera Stromquist Folder, EL; Major Everett Mead, "The Operations and Movements of the 31st Infantry Regiment (Philippine Division) 7 December 1941–9 April 1942 (Philippine Islands Campaign) Personal Experiences of a Regimental S-4," Advanced Infantry Officers Course, 1947–1948, 24–25, DRL; Major Louis Morton, "The Glory and Tragedy of Bataan," *The Army Combat Forces Journal*, (December 1955): 35–37; Woolfe, *Doomed Horse Soldiers of Bataan*, 310–11; Knox, *Death March*, 91–92; Schultz, *Hero of Bataan*, 194–95; Morton, *Fall of the Philippines*, 366–79; Stauffer, *The Quartermaster Corps*, 26–30; Colonel Wibb Cooper, Medical Corps, "Medical Department Activities in the Philippines from 1941 to 6 May 1942 and Including Medical Activities in Japanese Prisoner of War Camps," located at www.mansell.com.

15. General Hospital Number 1, Official History; General Hospital Number 2, Official History, both in Record Group 407, Philippine Archives Collection, Box 12; Sergeant Thomas Houston, diary, January 26, 1942, Record Group 407, Philippine Archives Collection, Box 133, Folder 2; Lieutenant Clara Mueller, diary, January–March, 1942, Philippine Archives Collection, Box 137, Folder 4, all at NA; Waterous, statement of experiences, 39–53, USAMHI; Hattie Brantley, interview with Ms. Judith Petsetski, April 9, 1983; Lieutenant Juanita Redmond and Eunice Hatchitt, interview with Colonel Albert G. Love, July 6, 1942, both at AMEDD; Michele Manning, "Angels of Mercy: The Army Nurse Corps on Bataan and Corregidor," *Parameters*, Spring 1992: 86–91; Elizabeth Norman, *We Band of Angels: The Untold Story of the American Women Trapped on Bataan* (New York: Random House, 1999), 39–81;

Alfred Weinstein, *Barbed Wire Surgeon* (New York: Macmillan, 1948), 20; John Bumgarner, *Parade of the Dead: A U.S. Army Physician's Memoir of Imprisonment by the Japanese, 1942–1945* (Jefferson, NC: McFarland 1995), 69–73; Juanita Redmond, *I Served on Bataan* (Philadelphia and New York: J. B. Lippincott, 1943) 61–63, 116–17; Dominic Caraccilo, ed., *Surviving Bataan and Beyond: Colonel Irvin Alexander's Odyssey as a Japanese Prisoner of War* (Mechanicsburg, PA; Stackpole Books, 1999), 81–82; Knox, *Death March*, 82–89; Morton, *Fall of the Philippines*, 376–84; Condon-Rall and Cowdrey, *Medical Service in the War Against Japan*, 30–37; Cooper, "Medical Department Activities," www.mansell.com.

16. Captain Achille Tisdelle, diary, February 16, 1942, Louis Morton Papers, Box 5; Ted Ince, interview with Dr. William Belote, June 25, 1964, William and James Belote Papers, Box 2, both at USAMHI; *Morrison Hill Gazette*, February 1942, Record Group 407, Philippine Archives Collection, Box 125, Folder 1; Houston, diary, January 31, 1942, both at NA; E. L. "Jim" Horton, interview with Dr. Charles W. Johnson, August 16, 1993, Oral History Collection, SCUTK; Lieutenant Henry Lee, letter to his family, February 12, 1942, Folder 1735, Accession #1368, World War II Letters Collection 68, State Historical Society of Missouri (SHSM), Columbia; Morton, *Fall of the Philippines*, 384–89; Romulo, *I Saw the Fall of the Philippines*, 105–17; for more information on C Battery, see www.corregidor.org. Lee died in captivity. He wrote a small book of poems that was later published in the United States and made him famous. The capitalized passages are in the original *Morrison Hill Gazette*.

17. Combat History Division, G1 Section HQ, AFWESPAC, 1946, "Triumph in the Philippines, Part I," 176–81, 189–94, Record Group 407, Entry 1113, Philippine Archives Collection, Box 1480; Anonymous Signal Corps Soldier, Imperial Japanese Army, diary, April 1942, Record Group 165, Entry 79, Box 281, ADVATIS, Current Translations, #121; General Hospital Number 1, Official History, all at NA; Tisdelle, diary, April 3–4, 1942; Fry, journal, April 1942; Conrad, "Operations of the 31st Infantry," 20–21, all at USAMHI; Mead, "Operations and Movements of the 31st Infantry Regiment," 26, DRL; Miguel, diary, April 5–6, 1942, EL; Brigadier General Clifford Bluemel, letter to Major General Ned King, May 24, 1951, USMA; Japanese Monograph No. 1, CMH; Louis Morton, "The American Surrender in the Philippines, April–May 1942," *Military Review*, August 1949: 5–6; Thaddeus Holt, "King of Bataan," *MHQ*, Winter 1994: 38; Morton, *Fall of the Philippines*, 411–41; Knox, *Death March*, 94–108; Tenney, *My Hitch in Hell*, 31; Norman, *We Band of Angels*, 84–92; Wainwright, *General Wainwright's Story*, 78–83.

18. Major General Edward King, memo of instructions for Colonel E. C. Williams, April 8, 1942, Record Group 407, Philippine Archives Collection, Box 128, Folder 8; "Triumph in the Philippines, Part I," 192–201; General Hospital Number 1, Official History, all at NA; Major General Edward King, interview with Dr. Louis Morton, February 12, 1947, Louis Morton Papers, Box 12; Colonel Halstead "Chick" Fowler, letter to Dr. Louis Morton, March 22, 1949, Louis Morton Papers, Box 12; Tisdelle, diary, April 8, 1942, all at USAMHI; Achille Tisdelle, oral history, no date, Record Group 32, Oral History #47, DMMA; Thaddeus Holt, "King of Bataan," *MHQ*, Winter 1994: 32–41; Morton, "The American Surrender in the Philippines," *Military Review*, 6–7; Major General Edward King, diary, April 9, 1942, reproduced at www.philippine-defenders.lib.wv.us.

19. Major Marshall Hurt, surrender notes, Record Group 407, Philippine Archives Collection, Box 128, Folder 8; "Triumph in the Philippines, Part I," 202–06; Colonel James Collier, interview with Dr. Louis Morton, November 20, 1946, Louis Morton Papers, Box 2; Achille Tisdelle, unpublished memoir, 8–12; Major Achille Tisdelle, interview with Lieutenant Colonel J. C. Bateman, January 22, 1946; Tisdelle, diary, April 9, 1942, all in Louis Morton Papers, Box 5; King interview, all at USAMHI;

Colonel James Collier, interview with Dr. D. Clayton James, August 30, 1971, Record Group 49, Box 2, D. Clayton James Collection; Tisdelle, oral history, both at DMMA; Holt, "King of Bataan," *MHQ*, 40–41; Morton, "The American Surrender in the Philippines," *Military Review*, 7; Stanley Falk, *Bataan: The March of Death* (New York: W. W. Norton, 1962), 21–25; Morton, *Fall of the Philippines*, 463–67.

20. Office of the Provost Marshal General, Report on American Prisoners of War in the Philippines, November 19, 1945; Military Intelligence Division, Prisoners of War in the Philippine Islands, September 20, 1944, both in Record Group 389, Entry 460A, Provost Marshal Records, Box 2135; General Hospitals Number 1 and 2, Official Histories, all at NA; Japanese Monograph Number 1, CMH; Brigadier General Clifford Bluemel, postwar statement, no date, Clifford Bluemel Papers, Box 4, USMA; Falk, *Bataan: The March of Death*, 45–101, 131; E. Bartlett Kerr, *Surrender and Survival: The Experience of American POWs in the Pacific, 1941–1945* (New York: William Morrow, 1985), 51–59; Knox, *Death March*, 118–19; Tenney, *My Hitch in Hell*, 42–53.

21. Captain Pedro Felix and Major Eduardo Vargas, witness statements, *United States of America v. Masaharu Homma*, January 10, 1946, Record Group 407, Philippine Archives Collection, Box 148; anonymous Imperial Japanese Army Signal Corps soldier, diary, April 12, 1942; Fendall, unpublished memoir, 20–25; Provost Marshal, Report on American Prisoners of War in the Philippines; Military Intelligence Division, Prisoners of War in the Philippine Islands, all at NA; Bataan to O'Donnell March, Statements by American Soldiers, March 18, 1943, Hugo Neuhaus Papers, Box 1; Johnson, oral history, February 7, 1972; Mallonee, unpublished memoir, 427, all at USAMHI; Miguel, diary, April 12–21, 1942, EL; Arthur Thomas, interview with Roger Mansell, May 15, 2000, Roger Mansell Papers, Box 22, Folder 19, HIA; Donald Young, "The Bataan Poet," *World War II*, April 2004, 24; Martin Blumenson, "Harold K. Johnson: 'A Most Remarkable Man,'" *Army*, August 1968: 19–26; John Olson, *O'Donnell: Andersonville of the Pacific*, self-published, 1985, 18–19; Falk, *March of Death*, 102–200; 227–229; Kerr, *Surrender and Survival*, 51–59; Tenney, *My Hitch in Hell*, 48–64; Sorley, *Honorable Warrior*, 56–64; Knox, *Death March*, 150–52; Toland, *But Not in Shame*, 310–29. For more insight on the capability of innocuous, otherwise morally upright people to commit terrible atrocities under certain circumstances, see Christopher Browning's classic study, *Ordinary Men: Reserve Police Battalion 101 and the Final Solution in Poland.*

22. Lieutenant Colonel Louis Bowler, diary, April 1942, Record Group 59, Box 1, Folder 16, Louis Bowler Papers, DMMA; Lieutenant Colonel Elvin Barr, diary, April 1942, Record Group 407, Philippine Archives Collection, Box 125, Folder 7; C Battery, 60th Coast Artillery Regiment, unit diary, April–May 1942, Record Group 407, Philippine Archives Collection, Box 123, Folder 3; Combat History Division, G1 Section, HQ, AFWESPAC, 1946, "Triumph in the Philippines, Volume II," 66–69, Record Group 407, Philippine Archives Collection, Box 1481, all at NA; Colonel Stephen Mellnik, "How the Japs Took Corregidor," *The Coast Artillery Journal,* March/April 1945: 7–10, 17; *After the Battle,* "Corregidor," 2–4; Morton, *Fall of the Philippines,* 491–92, 536–41; Wainwright, *General Wainwright's Story,* 86–88, 98–99.

23. Lieutenant Ruby Motley, oral history, April 26, 1945, Record Group 112, Entry 302, Surgeon General, Inspections Branch, Box 221, Interview No. 149; Barr, diary, April 1942; C Battery, 60th Coast Artillery Regiment, diary, April–May 1942; Lieutenant Clara Mueller, diary, April 1942, all at NA; Edith Shacklette, oral history, April 9, 1983, Army Nurse Corps Collection, Series III, Oral Histories, Box 46, Folder 7; Campbell, unpublished memoir, 91, both at USAMHI; Brantley interview, AMEDD; Jack McClure, "Besieged on the Rock," *MHQ,* Summer 2002: 21; Manning, "Angels of Mercy," *Parameters,* 93–95; *After the Battle,* "Corregidor," 11; Condon-Rall and Cowdrey, *Medical Service in the War Against Japan,* 40–42; Wainwright, *General*

Wainwright's Story, 96–97; Redmond, *I Served on Bataan*, 144–47; Norman, *We Band of Angels*, pp. 100–2; Morton, *Fall of the Philippines*, 544–46; Balete and Balete, *Corregidor, Saga of a Fortress*, 128–30; Major General George Moore, "The Moore Report, Part C, Conduct of the Campaign," April 25, 1942, and May 2, 1942, located at www.corregidor.org; Cooper, "Medical Department Activities, www.mansell.com.

24. E. Carl Engelhardt, unpublished memoir, 42, E. Carl Engelhardt Papers, Box 1; Beebe memoir, p. 17; N. B. Sauve, unpublished memoir, p. 32, N. B. Sauve Papers, Box 1, all at USAMHI; General Jonathan Wainwright, letter to Dr. Louis Morton, January 14, 1949, Jonathan Wainwright Papers, Personal Correspondence, Letters K-O, USMA; Lucy Wilson Jopling, unpublished memoir, 1–6, Record Group 15, Box 40, Folder 14, Contributions from the Public Collection, DMMA; Helen Cassiani Nestor, interview with Major Thomas Beeman, April 9, 1983, AMEDD; Manning, "Angels of Mercy," *Parameters*, 95–97; Schultz, *Hero of Bataan*, 264–71; Wainwright, *General Wainwright's Story*, 96–107; Beck, *MacArthur and Wainwright*, 209–12; Redmond, *I Served on Bataan*, 149–59; Norman, *We Band of Angels*, 104–13. Many of the nurses who became POWs carried their resentment of Redmond and several other evacuees for years. Redmond had dated Major Thomas Dooley, Wainwright's aide-de-camp, but they were not in a relationship, by any definition of that word. See Jerry Cooper, ed., *To Bataan and Back: The World War II Diary of Major Thomas Dooley* (College Station: Texas A&M University Press, 2016), 52–53, 57, 67–69. Unbeknownst to Wainwright, his chief of staff, Brigadier General Lewis Beebe, cabled Sutherland in Australia and asked him to get MacArthur to order Wainwright out of Corregidor, either to Mindanao or Australia. The reply was negative. In spite of the fact that MacArthur had ordered several individuals out of Corregidor, Sutherland claimed that the general had no jurisdiction to do so with Wainwright.

25. Imperial Japanese Army, Letters of commendation, heroism, and devotion to duty during capture of Corregidor, 1942, Record Group 165, Entry 79, Box 271, ADVATIS, Current Translations, #27–29; "Triumph in the Philippines, Part II," 69–72; Battery C, 60th Coast Artillery Regiment, diary, May 1942, all at NA; Kazumaro "Buddy" Uno, "Corregidor: Isle of Delusion," Imperial Japanese Army Press Bureau, 1942, 29–31, 34–38, Louis Morton Papers, Box 8; Beebe memoir, 20–21, both at USAMHI; Japanese Monograph Numbers 1 and 2, 8–5.1 AC2, CMH; Bill Sloan, "Hard Time on the Rock," *World War II*, May/June 2012: 54; McClure, "Besieged on the Rock," *MHQ*, 22–25; Wainwright, *General Wainwright's Story*, 114–19; Morton, *Fall of the Philippines*, 553–61; Belote and Belote, *Corregidor: Saga of a Fortress*, 145–70; Ray Lawrence, letter to Dr. Belote, October 3, 1963; J. Michael Miller, "From Shanghai to Corregidor: Marines in the Defense of the Philippines," both located at www.corregidor.org.

26. Lieutenant General Jonathan Wainwright, radiogram to General George Marshall, May 5, 1942; cable to President Franklin Roosevelt, May 6, 1942; surrender message to Major General William Sharp, May 7, 1942; General Douglas MacArthur, radiogram to Major General William Sharp, May 11, 1942, all in Record Group 200, Entry 19810 (A1) Richard Sutherland Papers, Box 34; "Triumph in the Philippines, Volume II," 72–91, all at NA; Tech 5 Irving Strobing, last messages, May 6, 1942, Harry P. Ball Papers, Box 1 and Louis Morton Papers, Box 11; Beebe, unpublished memoir, 22–37; Uno, "Corregidor: Isle of Delusion," 23–28, all at USAMHI; Irving Strobing, oral history, July 7, 1985, NMPW; Wainwright, letter to Morton, USMA; Brigadier General Bradford Chynoweth, interview with Dr. D. Clayton James, August 22, 1971, Record Group 49, Box 2, D. Clayton James Collection, DMMA; MacArthur's derogatory comments about Wainwright's decision to surrender were made to Lieutenant General Robert Eichelberger during a lunch on March 23, 1945, and are recorded in Eichelberger's diary for that date, Box 1, Robert Eichelberger Papers, DU; Taylor, "'I Have Taken a Dreadful Step,'" *MHQ*, 30; Morton, "The American Surrender in

the Philippines," *Military Review*, 9–14; Belote and Belote, *Corregidor: Saga of a Fortress*, 168–80; Beck, *MacArthur and Wainwright*, 217–30; Morton, *Fall of the Philippines*, 562–84; Wainwright, *General Wainwright's Story*, 123–46; Schultz, *Hero of Bataan*, 295–14; Borneman, *MacArthur at War*, 206–7; James, *Years of MacArthur, Volume II*, 148–51; Ferrell, *Eisenhower Diaries*, 54. The story of Wainwright's tortuous surrender negotiations could almost fill a book. For the sake of brevity, I covered only the highlights. All of these published sources include detailed accounts of the surrender.

Chapter 4. Allies of a Kind

1. Historical Section, China-Burma-India Theater, "History of the China-Burma-India Theater, 21 May 1942–25 October 1944," 8–6.1 AA4, CMH; Barbara Tuchman, *Stilwell and the American Experience in China, 1911–1945* (New York: Macmillan, 1970), 237.

2. Brigadier General Thomas Hearn, Comments on Joseph Stilwell, no date, Record Group 319, Entry 75, Box 9, Records of the Office of the Chief of Military History, Stilwell's Mission to China, NA; Frank McCarthy, letter to John Hart, February 4, 1964; Brigadier General Frank Dorn, letter to John Hart, July 4, 1960; Colonel David Barrett, letter to John Hart, February 17, 1960; General Joseph Stilwell, West Point records, all in John Hart Papers, Box 1; Colonel Frank Dorn, letter to Ms. Lilian E. Kirby, December 6, 1948, Frank Dorn Papers, Box 1; Brigadier General Frank Dorn, thoughts on Stilwell, no date, Frank Dorn Papers, Box 4, Folder 15, all at HIA; Arcadia Conference Proceedings, CCS Conference Proceedings, 1941–1945, Box 1, EL; Major General Joseph Stilwell, diary, December 1941–January 1942, www.hoover .org; Joseph Stilwell, edited by Theodore White, *The Stilwell Papers* (New York: William Sloane, 1948), ix–xi, 13–27, 33; Tuchman, *Stilwell and the American Experience in China*, 3–4, 125–30; Dorn, *Walkout*, 8–10.

3. Brigadier General Haydon Boatner, "Our Lend Lease Activities in China, May through October 1941," June 14, 1974, Haydon Boatner Papers, Box 2, HIA; General Dwight Eisenhower, letter to Major General Orlando Ward, March 28, 1950, Record Group 319, Entry 75, Box 6, Records of the Office of the Chief of Military History, Stilwell's Mission to China, NA; Arcadia Conference Proceedings, EL; Major General Joseph Stilwell, diary, January 1942, www.hoover.org; Michael Haith, " 'I'll Go Where I'm Sent': 'Vinegar Joe' Stilwell in the CBI," *Military Review,* May 1992: 73–76; Charles Canella, "Study in Combined Command," *Military Review,* July 1965: 55–60; Lloyd Eastman, *Seeds of Destruction: Nationalist China in War and Revolution 1937–1949* (Stanford, CA: Stanford University Press, 1984), 136; Charles Romanus and Riley Sunderland, *The United States Army in World War II: China-Burma-India Theater, Stilwell's Mission to China* (Washington, DC: Office of the Chief of Military History, Department of the Army, 1953), 61–73; Mitter, *Forgotten Ally*, 242–45; Tuchman, *Stilwell and the American Experience in China*, 234–45; Stilwell and White, *The Stilwell Papers*, 20–34. Eisenhower worked very closely with Marshall during this time. In the letter to Ward, Ike explained the chief of staff's thinking in relation to China. "Part of his idea—at least as he expressed it to me—in sending a very high ranking officer to China was to provide a symbol of American intent." The underline was in the original.

4. Lieutenant Ray Chesley, oral history, June 19, 1944, Record Group 112, Entry 302, Surgeon General, Inspections Branch, Box 219, Interview Number 53, NA; General George Marshall, Memo to Lieutenant Joseph Stilwell, instructions as United States Army representative in China, February 2, 1942, Joseph Stilwell file; Historical Section, "History of the China-Burma-India Theater," both at CMH; Stilwell, diary, February–March, 1942, www.hoover.org; Stilwell and White, *Stilwell Papers*, 39–54; Dorn, *Walkout*, 17–31; Mitter, *Forgotten Ally*, 243–49; Tuchman, *Stilwell and the*

American Experience in China, 252–60. Romanus and Sunderland, *Stilwell's Mission to China*, 73–74.

5. Mei-ling Soong, aka Madame Chiang Kai-shek, interview with Mr. Charles Romanus and Mr. Riley Sunderland, June 21, 1949, Record Group 319, Entry 75, Box 9, Records of the Office of the Chief of Military History, Stilwell's Mission to China, NA; Dorn, letter to Kirby, thoughts on Stilwell, both at HIA; Colonel Haydon Boatner, memo on Anglo-Chinese Relations at Lashio, March 21–April 25, 1942, dated May 13, 1942, Haydon Boatner Papers, Box 1, USAMHI; Japanese Monograph Number 133, Burma Operations Record, Outline of Burma Area Line of Communications, 1941–1945, 8–5.1 AC133; Historical Section, "History of the China-Burma-India Theater," both at CMH; Stilwell, diary, March 1942, www.hoover.org; Gordon Browne, "'We Took a Hell of a Beating': General 'Vinegar Joe' Stilwell in Burma," *Infantry*, May–August 2000: 21–22; Stilwell and White, *Stilwell Papers*, 59–69, 85; Dorn, *Walkout*, 72–73; Mitter, *Forgotten Ally*, 255–58; Tuckman, *Stilwell and the American Experience in China*, 283–86.

6. Brigadier General Haydon Boatner, Comments on "Crisis Fleeting" by James Stone, Haydon Boatner Papers, Box 1, HIA; Historical Section, "History of the China-Burma-India Theater," CMH; Alan Lathrop, "The Employment of Chinese Nationalist Troops in the First Burma Campaign," *Journal of Southeast Asian Studies* 12, no. 2 (September 1981): 403–32; George Rodger, "Flight From Burma," *Life*, June 8, 1942; William Slim, *Defeat into Victory* (London: Cassell, 1956), 109–10; Don Moser, *Time-Life World War II Series: China-Burma-India* (Alexandria, VA: Time-Life Books, 1978), 27–28; Jack Belden, *Retreat with Stilwell* (New York: Alfred A. Knopf, 1943), 197–99, 225–27; Mitter, *Forgotten Ally*, 259; Dorn, *Walkout*, 102, 146–48; Romanus and Sunderland, *Stilwell's Mission to China*, 141–42; Tuchman, *Stilwell and the American Experience in China*, 199–200; Dorn, *Walkout*, 101–02. Dorn claimed that he found out after leaving Burma that only one hundred thousand out of nine hundred thousand refugees survived.

7. Captain Ray Chesley, letter to Brigadier General Haydon Boatner, April 30, 1945, Haydon Boatner Papers, Box 1; Colonel Robert Williams, diary, May 1942, Robert Parvin Williams Papers, Box 1, Folder 3; Colonel Robert Williams, unpublished memoir, no pagination, Robert Parvin Williams Papers, Box 1, Folder 8, all at HIA; Major Felix Nowakowski, letter to Mr. Riley Sunderland, February 13, 1950, Record Group 319, Entry 75, Box 7, Records of the Office of the Chief of Military History, Stilwell's Mission to China, NA; Historical Section, "History of China-Burma-India Theater," CMH; Stilwell, diary, May 7–8, 1942, www.hoover.org; Colonel Paul Jones, "The Withdrawal from Burma and the Stilwell Walkout," at www.cbi-theater.com; Clare Boothe Luce, "Burma Mission, Parts I and II," *Life*, June 15 and 22, 1942; "Stilwell's Flight from Burma," no byline, *Life*, August 10, 1942; Browne, "'We Took a Hell of a Beating,'" *Infantry*, 25–26; Haith, "'Vinegar Joe' Stilwell in Burma," *Military Review*, 76–77; Robert Scott, *God Is My Co-Pilot* (New York: Charles Scribner's Sons, 1944), 104–06; Jonathan Fenby, *Chiang Kai Shek: China's Generalissimo and the Nation He Lost* (New York: Carroll and Graf, 2003), 377–78; Jay Taylor, *The Generalissimo: Chiang Kai-shek and the Struggle for Modern China* (Cambridge, MA: Belknap Press of Harvard University Press, 2009), 207–08; Belden, *Retreat with Stilwell*, 311; Stilwell and White, *The Stilwell Papers*, 98–104; Dorn, *Walkout*, 98–100, 234; Tuchman, *Stilwell and the American Experience in China*, 291–300; Mitter, *Forgotten Ally*, 258–62. Nowakowski was one of the officers who endured a physical collapse.

8. Lieutenant Colonel Charles Lutz, Report on Combat Efficiency of the Chinese Army, February 27, 1944, Record Group 319, Entry 76, Box 3, Records of the Office of the Chief of Military History, Stilwell's Command Problems, NA; Stilwell, diary, June 1942, www.hoover.org; Theodore White, "Chiang Kai-Shek," *Life*, March 2, 1942;

James Ehrman, "Ways of War and the American Experience in the China-Burma-India Theater, 1942–1945," 298–302, dissertation, Kansas State University, 2006; Stilwell and White, *Stilwell Papers*, 111–17; Taylor, *The Generalissimo*, 209–10; Tuchman, *Stilwell and the American Experience in China*; 304–07; Moser, *China-Burma-India*, 61; Romanus and Sunderland, *Stilwell's Mission to China*, 152–57.

9. Dorn, letter to Kirby, HIA; Mei-ling Soong, interview, NA; Stilwell, diary, June 25–28, 1942, www.hoover.org; Stilwell and White, *Stilwell Papers*, 119–26; Taylor, *The Generalissimo*, 211–13; Romanus and Sunderland, *Stilwell's Mission to China*, 169–73; Tuchman, *Stilwell and the American Experience in China*, 311–15; Moser, *China-Burma-India*, 61–62; Mitter, *Forgotten Ally*, 60; Dorn, *Walkout*, 23–24, 72–73. By late June, Chiang was already quite put out with his American allies. In April, without consulting him or coordinating with him, they had launched the Doolittle raid against Japan. The bombers were to land on fields in east Zhejiang. Chiang knew this would provoke a major reaction from the Japanese, and he was correct. After most of the planes ditched or crash-landed in China, the Japanese launched a major operation by a quarter million soldiers to take the fields and exact reprisals against the population for helping shelter the downed American fliers. The Chinese suffered the loss of the airfields, thirty thousand military casualties and many thousands more among the civilian population. "The Japanese slaughtered every man, woman, and child in these areas, let me repeat, every man, woman, and child," Chiang wrote angrily to General Marshall. Thus, what was a low-cost morale raid for the Americans was, for the Chinese, a devastating, costly bloodbath.

10. Patrick Hurley, letter to Major General Orlando Ward, January 11, 1952, Record 319, Entry 76, Box 11, Records of the Office of the Chief of Military History, Stilwell's Command Problems; Mei-ling Soong, interview, both at NA; Historical Section, "History of the China Burma India Theater," CMH; Stilwell, diary, October 1942, www.hoover.org; White, "Chiang Kai Shek," *Life*, March 2, 1942; Romanus and Sunderland, *Stilwell's Mission to China*, 180–314; Stilwell and White, *Stilwell Papers*, 134–38, 156–61; Taylor, *The Generalissimo*, 214–20; Tuchman, *Stilwell and the American Experience in China*, 331–40; Chennault, *Way of a Fighter*, 212–16. Chiang was not the only person working behind the scenes to have Stilwell fired. Lauchlin Currie, a presidential envoy who visited China around this same time, formed the opinion that Stilwell could not work well with Chiang and should be recalled. Upon returning home, he reported this recommendation to Roosevelt, who, in turn, asked for General Marshall's views. The general strongly dissented and, in tandem with Secretary Stimson, persuaded the president to keep Stilwell in place.

Chapter 5. Partners

1. Allen Douglas, unpublished memoir, 273, World War II Participants and Contemporaries Collection, Allen Douglas Folder, EL; William Dunn, CBS News, broadcast transcript, March 27, 1942, Record Group 52, Box 1, Folder 11, William Dunn Papers, DMMA; Company F, 163rd Infantry, History, NA; Louis Morton, "Command in the Pacific, 1941–1945," *Military Review*, December 1961, 76–81; John Moore, *Over-Sexed, Over-Paid, and Over-Here: Americans in Australia, 1941–1945* (St. Lucia, Australia: University of Queensland Press, 1981), 94; John Lardner, *Southwest Passage: The Yanks in the Pacific* (Philadelphia: J. B. Lippincott, 1943), 63.

2. Brigadier General Stephen Chamberlin, memo, "Special Arrangements for General MacArthur's Arrival," March 20, 1942; Brigadier General Stephen Chamberlin, memo to General [George] Brett, "Steps for General MacArthur's Arrival," March 19, 1942, both in Stephen Chamberlin Papers, Box 1, 1942 Folder, USAMHI; Faubion Bowers, interview with Dr. D. Clayton James, July 18, 1971, Record Group 49, Box 1, D. Clayton James Collection, DMMA; Morton, "Command in the Pacific," *Military*

Review, December 1961, 60–62; James, *Years of MacArthur, Volume II*, 108–10; 171; Manchester, *American Caesar*, 313–15; Lardner, *Southwest Passage*, 76, 81; Borneman, *MacArthur at War*, 160–62, 192; Huff, *My Fifteen Years with MacArthur*, 76–79.

3. Brigadier General Stephen Chamberlin, letter to Brigadier General Brehon Somervell, February 26, 1942, Record Group 319, Entry 48, Box 7, Records of the Office of the Chief of Military History, Global Logistics and Strategy, 1940–1943; Major General Robert Richardson, Memorandum for General Douglas MacArthur, July 4, 1942, Record Group 200, Entry 19810 (A1) Richard Sutherland Papers, Box 39, both at NA; US Army Forces in Australia, G1 History and Diary, February 24, 1942, Richard J. Marshall Papers, Box 3, USAMHI; Dr. James Masterson, "United States Army Transportation in the Southwest Pacific Area, 1941–1947," 1949, 497–510, 2–3.7 AZ C1 and 2–3.7 AZ C3: "Military History of the United States Army Services of Supply in the Southwest Pacific Area," 8–5.8 AA vl, 12–20; "History of the United States Army Service of Supply, Southwest Pacific and Army Forces Western Pacific, Base Section 4," 8–5.8 AA v13, no pagination; "History of the United States Army Services of Supply, Southwest Pacific and Army Forces Western Pacific, Base Section 6," no pagination, 8–5.8 AA v15; "History of the United States Army Services of Supply, Southwest Pacific and Army Forces Western Pacific, Base Section 7," 10, 21, 8–5.8 AA v16, all at CMH; Lieutenant General George Brett with Jack Kofoed, "The MacArthur I Knew," *True*, October 1947, 27; Edward Drea, " 'Great Patience Is Needed': America Encounters Australia, 1942," *War & Society*, May 1993, 21–27; E. Daniel Potts and Annette Potts, *Yanks Down Under, 1941–1945: The American Impact on Australia* (Melbourne, Australia: Oxford University Press, 1985), 16–17; John Day III, ed. *An Officer in MacArthur's Court: The Memoir of the First Headquarters Commandant for General Douglas MacArthur in Australia* (Fremont, CA: Robertson, 2014), 217; Morton, *Strategy and Command*, 252; Manchester, *American Caesar*, 324–27; James, *Years of MacArthur, Volume II*, 171–77; Moore, *Over-Sexed, Over-Paid, and Over-Here*, 52–54; Potts and Potts, *Yanks Down Under*, 18–21; Stauffer, *The Quartermaster Corps*, 50–58. US Army Forces in Australia became SWPA in April 1942. Another copy of the Chamberlin letter to Somervell is in Box 1, 1942 Folder of the Chamberlin Papers at USAMHI. The Richardson memo can also be accessed in Box 1 of the Richard J. Marshall Papers at USAMHI.

4. Company A, 163rd Infantry Regiment, History, 1940–1944, Record Group 407, Entry 427, Box 9084, Folder 341-INF-163–0; Richardson memo, both at NA; Captain Frederic Cramer, diary, September 19, 1942, Frederic Cramer Papers, Box 1, USAMHI; History of US Army Services of Supply Southwest Pacific and Army Forces in Western Pacific, 1941–1946, Base Section 3 at Brisbane, no pagination, 8–5.8 AA V12, CMH; Kathryn Ast Hatch, interview with Ed Metzler, March 12, 2006, NMPW; Douglas, unpublished memoir, 275–76, EL; Special Service Division, Services of Supply, United States Army, "Pocket Guide to Australia," 1; E. J. Kahn, *G.I. Jungle: An American Soldier in Australia and New Guinea* (New York: Simon & Schuster, 1943), 27; Moore, *Over-Sexed, Over-Paid, and Over-Here*, 93; Stauffer, *The Quartermaster Corps*, 102–25; Potts and Potts, *Yanks Down Under*, 35, 88–89, 196.

5. 118th General Hospital, History, September–December 1942, Record Group 112, Entry UD1012, Surgeon General, HUMEDS, Box 30; Company F, 163rd Infantry Regiment, History, both at NA; William Dunn, CBS News Broadcast Transcript, May 24, 1942, Record Group 52, Box 1, Folder 14, William J. Dunn Papers, DMMA; Gwendolyn Hall, ed., *Love, War, and the 96th Engineers (Colored): The World War II New Guinea Diaries of Captain Hyman Samuelson* (Urbana and Chicago: University of Illinois Press, 1995), 131–33; Moore, *Over-Sexed, Over-Paid, and Over-Here*, 107; Lardner, *Southwest Passage*, 148–49; Rogers, *The Good Years: MacArthur and Sutherland*, 207–08; Potts and Potts, *Yanks Down Under*, 133–42, 151–52.

6. Company F, 163rd Infantry Regiment, History, NA; Douglas, unpublished memoir, 302–03, EL; Smith and Meehl, eds., *Pacific War Stories*, 174; Potts and Potts, *Yanks Down Under*, 142–45.

7. Company E, 163rd Infantry Regiment, History, Record Group 407, Entry 427, Box 9084, Folder 341-INF-163-0, NA; Clarence Jungwirth, unpublished memoir, 74, WWIIM; Frank Kunz, unpublished memoir, 26, Record Group 15, Box 59, Folder 7, Contributions from the Public Collection; Paul Rogers, letter to Weldon "Dusty" Rhoades, October 16, 1981, Record Group 46, Box 1, Folder 7, Paul Rogers Papers, both at DMMA; PFC L.K. Peacock, letter to Fran and Joyce Garvey, December 8, 1943, Folder 2289, Accession #2179; Sergeant Paul Kinder, letters to Ruth and Sam, April 30 and 21, 1943, Folder 1632, Accession #1711, all at SHSM; Moore, *Over-Sexed, Over-Paid, and Over-Here*, 159–61; Potts and Potts, *Yanks Down Under*, 336–48; Lardner, *Southwest Passage*, 148; Rogers, *MacArthur and Sutherland: The Good Years*, 208–10.

8. US Army Forces in Australia, G1 History and Diary, May 1942, Marshall Papers; Sauve, unpublished memoir, pp. 36–37, both at USAMHI; "History of SOS SWPA, Base Section 4," no pagination, CMH; Monique Hole, "Edward Leonski Hanged by US Military on Australian Soil," *Sydney Herald Sun*, June 6, 2012; Vivien Encel and Alan Sharpe, *Murder! 25 True Australian Crimes* (Sydney, Australia: Kingclear Books, 1997), 50–60; Potts and Potts, *Yanks Down Under*, 148–51, 233–35, 322–24, 396; Moore, *Over-Sexed, Over-Paid, and Over-Here*, 131–33, 192–95. The Australians nicknamed Edward Leonski "The Brownout Strangler." His heinous actions are well remembered in the country and were portrayed in a 1986 movie called *Death of a Soldier*. The internet contains plenty of information on him as well. See, for instance, www.murderpedia.org and www.adb.anu.edu.au.

9. Southwest Pacific Area, Annual Venereal Disease Report, January–December 1944, Record Group 112, Entry 31, Surgeon General, Administrative Records, Box 209; Major James Joelson, Chief of Urological Section, 4th General Hospital, oral history, September 27, 1943, Record Group 112, Entry 302, Surgeon General, Inspections Branch, Box 218, Interview Number 6; 118th General Hospital, History, September–December 1942, all at NA; Southwest Pacific Area, Annual Report of Chief Surgeon, 1942 with Supplement for January–February 1943, Richard J. Marshall Papers, Box 3, USAMHI; "History of U.S. Army SOS, SWPA, Base Section 7," 36–37, CMH; Potts and Potts, *Yanks Down Under*, 148, 322–24; Condon-Rall and Cowdrey, *Medical Service in the War Against Japan*, 57–59, 63–64; Moore, *Over-Sexed, Over-Paid, and Over-Here*, 213; Stauffer, *The Quartermaster Corps*, 249–50.

10. War Department, "Command of Negro Troops," February 29, 1944, 10–14, Leonard Russell Boyd Papers, Box 1, HIA; Soldier Attitude Surveys, Negro Study, 1942–1943, Record Group 330, Entry 92, Records of the Secretary of Defense, Box 4, S32; Mr. H. B. Chandler, letter to Honorable Frank Forde, Minister for the Army, May 21, 1942 (the letter was addressed to Forde but forwarded to MacArthur); General Douglas MacArthur, letter to Mr. H. B. Chandler, May 28, 1942, Record Group 200, Entry 19810 (A1), Richard Sutherland Papers, Box 42, all at NA; Douglas, unpublished memoir, 296, EL; Kay Saunders, "Conflict Between the American and Australian Governments over the Introduction of Black American Servicemen into Australia during World War II," *Australian Journal of Politics and History* 33, no. 2 (1987): 39–46; E. Daniel Potts and Annette Potts, "The Deployment of Black American Servicemen Abroad during World War Two," *Australian Journal of Politics and History* 35 (1989): 92–96; Drea, "'Great Patience Is Needed,'" *War & Society*, 25–26; Ulysses Lee, *The United States Army in World War II: The Employment of Negro Troops* (Washington, DC: Center of Military History, 1963), 432–36, 591–98; Anthony Barker and Lisa Jackson, *Fleeting Attraction: A Social History of American Servicemen in*

Western Australia During the Second World War, (Nedlands: University of Western Australia Press, 1996), 177–88; Hall, *Love, War, and the 96th Engineers (Colored)*, 46–47, 233; Moore, *Over-Paid, Over-Sexed, and Over-Here*, 209–15; Potts and Potts, *Yanks Down Under*, 187–94. There is more information on the Townsville mutiny at www.ozatwar.com. Per capita, black soldiers were significantly more likely to be court-martialed for serious crimes such as rape than white soldiers. From this great distance of many decades later, there is no way to know if this tendency to run afoul of military justice was because black soldiers were really committing more crimes per capita or whether they were simply more likely to be caught, charged, and court-martialed.

11. Warrant Officer O. W. Kummerlow, letter to his family, April 9, 1944; Sergeant John Montero, letter to Noah, April 19, 1944, both in Record Group 496, Entry 74, Box 456, Records of the General Headquarters, SWPA/USAFP, Personal Letters Held by Censor, NA; "History of USOS, SWPA, Base Section 3 at Brisbane," no pagination, 8–5.8 AA V12, CMH; Lieutenant General Sir Iven Mackay, Speech to Officers of 9th Australian Infantry Brigade, December 9, 1942, Richard J. Marshall Papers, Box 1, USAMHI; Douglas, unpublished memoir, 299, EL; Peacock letter, SHSM; Lieutenant General George Kenney, diary, December 7, 1942, Record Group 54, Box 2, George Kenney Papers, DMMA; Moore, *Over-Sexed, Over-Paid, and Over-Here*, 217–24; Potts and Potts, *Yanks Down Under*, 281, 294–97, 302–15. The clip from *Australia Is Like This* can be accessed at www.youtube.com, as can video excerpts about the so-called Battle of Brisbane. Also, there is information on the Brisbane violence at www.ozatwar.com. Private Grant was charged with manslaughter, tried in a general court-martial, and acquitted. To this day, some Australians believe this verdict was a travesty of justice and that the US Army should formally apologize.

Chapter 6. Hell

1. Provost Marshal, Report on Prisoners of War in the Philippines, NA; Lieutenant Colonel Arthur Shreve, diary, April 1942, Louis Morton Papers, Box 4; Mallonee, unpublished memoir, 441, both at USAMHI; Archie McMaster, unpublished memoir, 105, Archie McMaster Papers, Volume 1, USMA; Michael A. (Buffone) Zarate, "American Prisoners of Japan: Did Rank Have Its Privilege?" master's thesis, US Army Command and General Staff College, Fort Leavenworth, KS, 1991, 70–72, CARL; Olson, *O'Donnell: Andersonville of the Pacific*, 32–47; Miller, *Bataan Uncensored*, 232–33; Tenney, *My Hitch in Hell*, 66–67; Knox, *Death March*, 157–58; Kerr, *Surrender and Survival*, 60–61; Headquarters, 8th Army, Office of the Staff Judge Advocate, *United States of America v. Yoshio Tsuneyoshi*, May 24, 1949, accessible at www.mansell.com. After the war, Tsuneyoshi was tried for war crimes and sentenced to life in prison.

2. Colonel Charles Lawrence, POW Report, November 28, 1945, Record Group 389, Entry 460A, Provost Marshal Records, Box 2122, Taiwan Camps Folder, NA; Lieutenant Colonel Alfred C. Oliver, Statement on Camp O'Donnell, no date, John Olson Papers, Box 12; Colonel Michael Quinn, diary, April 1942, Jonathan Wainwright Papers, Box 5; Mallonee, unpublished memoir, 442–43; Tisdelle, unpublished memoir, p. 13, all at USAMHI; Zarate, "American Prisoners of Japan: Did Rank Have Its Privileges?" 73–76, CARL; Olson, *O'Donnell: Andersonville of the Pacific*, 85–106; Knox, *Death March*, 159; Weinstein, *Barbed-Wire Surgeon*, 74; Kerr, *Surrender and Survival*, 62–63; Miller, *Bataan Uncensored*, 234; *United States of America v. Yoshio Tsuneyoshi*, www.mansell.com.

3. Provost Marshal, Camp Conditions Report, Philippine Islands, Record Group 389, Entry 460A, Provost Marshal Records, Box 2135, Japanese Camps Folder, NA; Thomas interview, HIA; Lieutenant Colonel Chester Johnson, letter to Ila, Janet, and

Happy, March 31, 1947, Chester L. Johnson Papers, Box 1, 1946–1947 Folder; Mallonee, unpublished memoir, 443; Tisdelle, unpublished memoir, 13, all at USAMHI; Knox, *Death March*, 161–62; Miller, *Bataan Uncensored*, 236–37; Olson, *O'Donnell: Andersonville of the Pacific*, 109–19; Cooper, "Medical Department Activities in the Philippines," www.mansell.com.

4. Provost Marshal, Report on Prisoners of War in the Philippines; Provost Marshal, Camp Conditions Report, Philippine Islands, both at NA; Zarate, "American Prisoners of Japan: Did Rank Have Its Privilege?" 68–70, 79–85, CARL; Basil Dulin, letter to John Olson, no date; Major Richard Gordon, letter to John Olson, no date; Zoeth Skinner, letter to John Olson, April 18, 1984 and November 14, 1985, John Olson Papers, Box 9; Mallonee, unpublished memoir, 443–45; General Harold K. Johnson, oral history, February 7, 1972, all at USAMHI; McMaster, unpublished memoir, 106–09, USMA; Miguel, diary, May 1942, EL; Frank Blazich, ed., *Bataan Survivor: A POW's Account of Japanese Captivity in World War II* (Columbia: University of Missouri Press, 2016), 76–78; Preston Hubbard, *Apocalypse Undone: My Survival of Japanese Imprisonment During World War II* (Nashville: Vanderbilt University Press, 1990), 95–97; Tenney, *My Hitch in Hell*, 70–72; Olson, *O'Donnell: Andersonville of the Pacific*, 111–19, 129–57; Knox, *Death March*, 163–70; Kerr, *Surrender and Survival*, 64–65; Weinstein, *Barbed Wire Surgeon*, 78. During the Civil War, the Union side similarly dishonored itself by treating Confederate prisoners abysmally at such hellholes as Elmira. Since Olson used Andersonville as the analogous camp to O'Donnell, I have confined my discussion to the infamous Confederate camp, but with full recognition that both sides mistreated POWs during the Civil War.

5. Special Division, Department of State, Memorandum on Conditions at Manila, December 18, 1943, Record Group 389, Entry 460A, Provost Marshal Records, Box 2135, Philippine Report, Miscellaneous; Major Stephen Mellnik, POW account, April 4, 1943, Record Group 200, Entry 19810 (A1) Richard Sutherland Papers, Box 54; PFC Darrell Kadolph, 59th Coast Artillery Regiment, POW Affidavit, February 4, 1945, Philippine Archives Collection, Box 148; First Lieutenant Ruby Motley, oral history, April 26, 1945, Record Group 112, Entry 302, Surgeon General, Inspections Branch, Box 221, Interview Number 149; Provost Marshal, Report on Prisoners of War in the Philippines, all at NA; Engelhardt, unpublished memoir, 58–59; Campbell, unpublished memoir, 99–112; Uno, "Corregidor: Isle of Delusion," 58–60, all at USAMHI; PFC Robert Spielman, notes, Record Group 133, Box 1, Folder 11, Paul H. Marshall Papers; Bishop McKendree, questionnaire, Record Group 15, Box 41, Folder 1, Contributions from the Public Collection; Lieutenant Colonel Louis Bowler, diary, May 1942, all at DMMA; Armand Hopkins, unpublished memoir, 25–26, Armand Hopkins Papers, Box 1, USMA; William Braly, *The Hard Way Home: From Corregidor to Manchuria, Three Years a Prisoner of the Japanese in World War II* (Washington, DC: Infantry Journal, 1947, reprint), 8–15; Evelyn Monahan and Rosemary Neidel-Greenlee, *All This Hell: U.S. Nurses Imprisoned by the Japanese* (Lexington: University Press of Kentucky, 2000), 90–94; Norman, *We Band of Angels*, 132–41; Belote and Belote, *Corregidor: Saga of a Fortress*, 178–83; Cooper, "Medical Department Activities in the Philippines from 1941 to 6 May 1942 and Including Medical Activities in Japanese Prisoner of War Camps," located at www.mansell.com. The garrisons of smaller Manila Bay islands, most notably Fort Drum, surrendered at the same time as the Corregidor command. Uno, the American-educated Japanese correspondent, claimed to interview numerous prisoners on Corregidor who made anti-American and anti-Semitic statements.

6. Military Intelligence Division, Prisoners of War in Taiwan, October 20, 1944, Record Group 389, Entry 460A, Provost Marshal Records, Box 2122, Taiwan Prisoner of War Camp Folder; Provost Marshal, Report on Prisoners of War in the Philippines, both

at NA; Beebe, unpublished memoir, 35–40; Mallonee, unpublished memoir, 451–52, both at USAMHI; Kerr, *Surrender and Survival*, 102–03; Wainwright, *General Wainwright's Story*, 142–75; Schultz, *Hero of Bataan*, 314–40; Braly, *Hard Way Home*, 30–42.

7. Notes on the Feeding of American Military Personnel Interned in Cabanatuan Prison Compound #1, Record Group 112, Entry 31, Surgeon General, Administrative Records, Box 213; Major James Bruce, oral history, May 15, 1945, Record Group 112, Entry 302, Surgeon General, Inspections Branch, Box 222, Interview No. 151; Hospital at Cabanatuan Prison Camp and Japanese Atrocities from a Medical Standpoint, Record Group 389, Entry 460A, Provost Marshal Records, Box 2135, Cabanatuan Folder; Camp Conditions Report; Provost Marshal, Report on Prisoners of War in the Philippines, all at NA; Staff Sergeant Bernard Hopkins, diary, October 28, 1942, Louis Morton Papers, Box 4, USAMHI; Zarate, "American Prisoners of Japan: Did Rank Have Its Privilege?" 93–102, CARL; Private Gerald Reeves, letter to his mother, May 4, 1941; Major General J. A. Ulio, adjutant general, telegram, February 1, 1943; War Department telegram, June 21, 1943; Major General Edward Witsell, acting adjutant general, letter to Mrs. Ellen Reeves, September 19, 1945; Major R. E. Campbell, Assistant Adjutant General, letter to Mrs. Ellen Reeves, October 15, 1945, all in Melba Mitchell Collection, #2009.030, WWIIM; Knox, *Death March*, 201–02; Bumgarner, *Parade of the Dead*, 93–94; Kerr, *Surrender and Survival*, 96.

8. Captain Godfrey "Roly" Ames, POW, diary, undated, circa summer 1942, Record Group 407, Philippine Archives Collection, Box 123, NA; Zarate, "American Prisoners of Japan: Did Rank Have Its Privilege?" 105–13, CARL; Stewart Wolf and Herbert Ripley, "Reactions Among Allied Prisoners of War Subjected to Three Years of Imprisonment and Torture by the Japanese," *American Journal of Psychiatry* 104, no. 3 (September 1947), 181–82; Hubbard, *Apocalypse Undone*, 95; Knox, *Death March*, 203–16; Tenney, *My Hitch in Hell*, 109–10.

9. Military Intelligence Division, Prisoners of War in the Philippine Islands, 11; Notes on the Feeding of American Military Personnel Interned in Cabanatuan Prison; Camp Conditions Report, Philippine Islands, Provost Marshal Report on Prisoners of War in the Philippines; Lieutenant Colonel Harold K. Johnson, statement, June 29, 1946; letter to Larry, October 16, 1945, both in Record Group 407, Philippine Archives Collection, Box 143A, Folder 8; Lieutenant Colonel Harold K. Johnson, diary, January 10, 1943, Record Group 407, Philippine Archives Collection, Box 135, Folder 2, all at NA; Zarate, "American Prisoners of Japan: Did Rank Have Its Privilege?" 105–13, CARL; Johnson oral histories, January 27, 1972 and February 7, 1972, USAMHI; Martin Blumenson, "Harold K. Johnson: 'Most Remarkable Man,'" *Army*, August 1968: 22–23; Sorley, *Honorable Warrior*, 62–69; Kerr, *Surrender and Survival*, 125–28; Tenney, *My Hitch in Hell*, 110–11.

Chapter 7. Possibilities

1. Lieutenant General Haruyoshi Hyakutake, Report to the Throne: War Situation in Southeast Area, no date, located in Translation of Japanese Documents, Volume IV, 8–5.1 AD1 V4, CY1; Japanese Monograph Number 37, Southeast Area Operations Record, Volume 1, January 1942–June 1943, 1–13, both at CMH; General Douglas MacArthur, radiogram to General George Marshall, Record Group 200, Entry 19810 (A1), Richard Sutherland Papers, Box 56, NA; Louis Morton, "Command in the Pacific, 1941–1945," *Military Review*, December 1961, 80–84; Samuel Milner, *The United States Army in World War II: Victory in Papua* (Washington, DC: Center of Military History, US Army, 2003 version), 33–55; John Miller, *The United States Army in World War II: Guadalcanal, the First Offensive* (Washington, DC: Historical Division, Department of the Army, 1949), 1–21; Richard Frank, *Guadalcanal: The Definitive Account of the Landmark Battle* (New York: Random House, 1990), 29–45; Harry

Gailey, *MacArthur Strikes Back: Decision at Buna: New Guinea, 1942–1943* (Novato, CA: Presidio Press, 2000), 35–43; Morton, *Strategy and Command*, 301–23; James, *Years of MacArthur, Volume II*, 193, 344; Borneman, *MacArthur at War*, 211–21.

2. South Seas Detachment, Operational Orders for the Invasion of Port Moresby, August 10, 1942, #281, Record Group 165, Entry 79, Box 271, ADVATIS, Current Translations, #18–23; Private Jiro Takamura, diary, August 21, September 21, 1942, #862, Record Group 165, Entry 79, Box 274, ADVATIS, Current Translations, #77–78; Lieutenant Kogoro Hirano, diary, August 9, September 23, 1942, #218, Record Group 165, Entry 79, ADVATIS, Current Translations, #9–22; anonymous Japanese officer, diary, September 1942, #358, Record Group 165, Entry 79, ADVATIS, Current Translations, #27–29, all at NA; Hyakutake, Report to the Throne; Japanese Monograph Number 37, 13–25, both at CMH; Alison Pilger, "Courage, Endurance and Initiative: Medical Evacuation from the Kokoda Track, August–October 1942," *War & Society*, May 1993: 54; Philip Bradley, "The Kokoda Trail," *After the Battle* no. 137 (2007): 2–21; George Raudzens, "Testing the Air Power Expectations of the Kokoda Campaign, July to September 1942," *Journal of the Australian War Memorial* (October 1992); Samuel Milner, "The Battle of Milne Bay," *Military Review*, April 1950, 18–29; Dudley McCarthy, *Australia in the War of 1939–1945: Volume V, South-West Pacific Area, First Year: Kokoda to Wau* (Canberra: Australian War Memorial, 1959), 108–335, specific quotes and figures from pages 142, 195, 334–35; Craig Collie and Hajima Marutani, *The Path of Infinite Sorrow: The Japanese on the Kokoda Track* (Crows Nest, Australia: Allen & Unwin, 2009), 1–2, 55–57, 63, 121–27, 139–45, 187–91; Stanley Sandler, ed., *Ground Warfare: An International Encyclopedia, Volume Two* (Santa Barbara, CA: ABC-Clio, 2002), 468; Lida Mayo, *Bloody Buna* (Garden City, NY: Doubleday, 1974), 15–65, 80–84; Eric Bergerud, *Touched with Fire: The Land War in the South Pacific* (New York: Penguin Books, 1996), 252–53; Milner, *Victory in Papua*, 56–100; *Campaigns of MacArthur, Volume I*, 73 and endnote 9 provides the logistical information on Australian operations. Though I have cited specific dates for the Japanese diaries, I also drew from many other entries to illustrate the overall experience of Kokoda for Japanese soldiers.

3. Natalie Sutherland Carney, letter to Dr. Paul Rogers, no date, Record Group 46, Box 1, Folder 3, Paul Rogers Papers, DMMA; Kahn, *G.I. Jungle*, 47–49; Day, *An Officer in MacArthur's Court*, 283–94, 329–29; James, *Years of MacArthur, Volume II*, 245–46; Huff, *My Fifteen Years with General MacArthur*, 84–86; Manchester, *American Caesar*, 361–67; Rogers, *The Good Years: MacArthur and Sutherland*, 207. Elaine was a frequent subject of Australian society and gossip columns even well before her tryst with Sutherland. Her wedding to Bessemer-Clark was a particularly well-covered event. See, for instance, "The Week in Melbourne: Brookes-Clark Wedding—Many Delightful Presents" in the January 9, 1936, edition of the *Sydney Morning Herald*.

4. Major General George Kenney, diary, August–September 1942, Record Group 54, Box 1, George Kenney Papers; General George Kenney, interview with Dr. D. Clayton James, July 16, 1971, Record Group 49, Box 3, D. Clayton James Collection; Richard Marshall interview with James, all at DMMA; George Kenney, *General Kenney Reports: A Personal History of the Pacific War* (Washington, DC: Office of Air Force History, United States Air Force, 1987, reprint), 28–30, 52–53; Wesley Craven and James Cate, eds., *The Army Air Forces in World War II, Volume IV, The Pacific: Guadalcanal to Saipan, August 1942 to July 1944* (Washington, DC: Office of Air Force History, United States Air Force, 1983, reprint), 97–109; Milner, *Victory in Papua*, 101–07; James, *Years of MacArthur, Volume II*, 200–01; Manchester, *American Caesar*, 346–51; MacArthur, *Reminiscences*, 157–67; Rogers, *The Good Years: MacArthur and Sutherland*, 277–79.

5. I Corps, "History of the Buna Campaign," 1–8; US Army Center of Military History,

"Papuan Campaign: The Buna-Sanananda Operation, 16 November 1942–23 January 1943," 4–5, both at CARL; Sergeant Paul Kinder, letter to Ruth and Sam, November 9, 1942, Folder 1632, Accession #1711, SHSM; Kenneth Springer, unpublished memoir, 4, 9–13, World War II Veterans Survey, #157011; Major Alfred Medendorp, "The March and Operations of Antitank and Cannon Companies, 126th Infantry, 32nd Infantry Division, in the Attack on Wairopi, 4 October–28 November 1942, Papuan Campaign, Personal Experiences of a Patrol Commander," The Ground General School, 1949, 3–9, both at USAMHI; Lieutenant Robert Odell, personal notes, hospital statement and diary, December 1942, letter to Lieutenant Colonel John Kemper, July 18, 1944, Record Group 319, Entry P41, Box 3, Records of the Office of the Chief of Military History, Victory in Papua and Record Group 319, Entry P41, Box 1, Records of the Office of the Chief of Military History, American Forces in Action: the Papuan Campaign; Lieutenant Colonel Herbert M. Smith, letter to Major General Orlando Ward, March 9, 1951, Record Group 319, Entry 53, Box 5, Records of the Office of the Chief of Military History, Victory in Papua, all at NA; Major General Hugh "Pat" Casey, letter to Major General Anderson, July 18, 1974, Record Group 15, Box 23, Folder 3, Contributions from the Public Collection, DMMA; Herbert M. Smith, interview with James McIntosh, circa 1999, WVM; E. J. Kahn, "The Terrible Days of Company E, Part One," *Saturday Evening Post*, January 8, 1944, 10–11, 42–44; Leslie Anders, *Gentle Knight: The Life and Times of Major General Edwin Forrest Harding* (Kent, OH: Kent University Press, 1985), 228–236; James Campbell, *The Ghost Mountain Boys: Their Epic March and the Terrifying Battle for New Guinea— the Forgotten War of the South Pacific* (New York: Crown, 2007), 81–89, 130–42; Milner, *Victory in Papua*, 110–15. "Papuan Campaign" is also available in booklet format from the US Army Center of Military History. Because it was impossible to move self-propelled artillery pieces and antitank guns over the Kapa Kapa Trail, General Harding converted the soldiers from these two companies into light infantry and used them as the point element over the trail ahead of the 2nd Battalion. Medendorp was their senior officer and patrol leader.

6. Interrogations on Japanese Operations on Guadalcanal; Major General Shuichi Miyazaki, Personal Account, Guadalcanal, both in 383.4, CMH; 1st Battalion, 8th Marine Regiment, History of Enemy Action on Guadalcanal, August 4, 1943, Record Group 127, William Bartsch Papers, Victory Fever Boxes, unprocessed, DMMA. For excellent background on the August–September phase of Guadalcanal, see Frank Hough, Merle Ludwig, and Henry Shaw, *History of U.S. Marine Corps Operations in World War II, Volume I: Pearl Harbor to Guadalcanal* (Washington, DC: Historical Branch, G3 Division, Headquarters, US Marine Corps, 1958); William Bartsch, *Victory Fever on Guadalcanal: Japan's First Land Defeat of World War II* (College Station: Texas A&M University Press, 2014); Frank, *Guadalcanal*; and William Bartsch, "Victory Fever at the Tenaru," *World War II*, November–December 2014.

7. History of United States Army Forces in the South Pacific Area During World War II, 30 March 1942–1 August 1944, 78–116, 8–5.7 BA; Historical Section, South Pacific Base Command, Guadalcanal Campaign, 7 August 1942–21 February 1943, Volume I, pp. 38–55, 8–5.7 BC vl; Interrogations on Japanese Operations on Guadalcanal; Miyazaki, Personal Account, all at CMH; Narrative History of Task Force 6814 and Americal Division, January 23, 1942, to June 30, 1943, CARL; XIV Corps, Japanese Ground Activities on Guadalcanal, April 1943, Record Group 127, Box 39, World War II Geographic Files, Folder A6.5–1; Americal Division, Narrative of Operations on Guadalcanal, May 28, 1943, Record Group 407, Entry 427, Box 4802, Folder 300–0.3; Major Donald Dickson, oral history, May 24, 1943, Record Group 38, Entry P11, Box 7, Records of the Chief of Naval Operations, World War II Oral Histories and Interviews, 1942–1945, all at NA; Sergeant Mack Morriss, *Yank* magazine, letter to Major

Hartzell Spence, February 12, 1943, George Burns Collection, Box 3, USAMHI; 1st Battalion, 8th Marines, History of Enemy Action on Guadalcanal, DMMA; Karel Magry, "Guadalcanal," *After the Battle* no. 108 (2000): 7–12; Colonel Conrad Lanza, "The Solomon Islands," *Field Artillery Journal* (February 1943): 107; Lieutenant Colonel Samuel Baglien, "The Second Battle of Henderson Field," *Infantry Journal*, May 1944, 24–25; Stanley Jersey, "Hell's Island," *World War II*, January–February 2008: 44–46; R. R. Kean, "'Pistol Pete': Akio Tani, the 'Mantis' Sent Marines Scrambling," *Leatherneck*, October 1992; Robert Leckie, *Helmet for My Pillow* (New York: Bantam Books, 1979), 99–101; Charles Walker, *Combat Officer: A Memoir of War in the South Pacific* (New York: Ballantine Books, 2004), 9–14; Craven and Cate, *The Army Air Forces in World War II, Volume IV*, 51–57; Miller, *Guadalcanal: The First Offensive*, 125–51; Hough et al., *Pearl Harbor to Guadalcanal*, 322–29; Frank, *Guadalcanal*, 312–39; Bergerud, *Touched with Fire*, 391–93.

8. Interrogation of Major General Harukazu Tamaki, former chief of staff, 2nd (Sendai) Division, September 12, 1946; interrogation of Colonel Shigetaka Obara, former CO, 29th Infantry Regiment, September 16, 1946, both at Record Group 319, Entry 87, Box 2, Records of the Office of the Chief of Military History, Guadalcanal, the First Offensive, NA; History of the United States Army Forces in the South Pacific, 125–32; interrogations on Japanese operations on Guadalcanal; Miyazaki, personal account, all at CMH; Brigadier General Kiyotake Kawaguchi, memo, circa September 1942, John A. Burden Papers, Box 1, HIA; Brigadier General Kiyotake Kawaguchi, diary, October 1942; Colonel Masajiro Komiya, personal notes, October 1942; Captain Jiro Katsumata, recollections and diary, October 1942; Sergeant Hisachiki Hara, diary, October 1942; Lieutenant Kenji Masumoto, diary, October 1942, all in Record Group 127, William Bartsch Papers, Victory Fever Boxes, unprocessed, DMMA; Jersey, "Hell's Island," *World War II*, 46–50; Miller, *Guadalcanal: The First Offensive*, 152–59; Hough et al., *Pearl Harbor to Guadalcanal*, 329–35; Frank, *Guadalcanal*, 338–51.

9. 164th Infantry Regiment, Report of Battle for Henderson Field, October 24–31, 1942, Record Group 407, Entry 427, Box 4973, Folder 300-INF-164-0.3.0; XIV Corps, Narrative of Japanese Operations on Guadalcanal; Americal Division, Narrative of Operations on Guadalcanal; 1st Marine Division, Division Commander's Final Report on the Guadalcanal Operation, 19 September–5 December 1942, Record Group 127, Box 39, World War II Area Geographic Files, Folder A7-4; Major General Alexander Vandegrift, oral history, February 4, 1943, Record Group 38, Entry P11, Box 29, Records of the Chief of Naval Operations, World War II Oral Histories and Interviews, 1942–1945; Tamaki, Obara interrogations, all at NA; History of the United States Army Forces in the South Pacific, 132–35; Interrogations on Japanese Operations on Guadalcanal; Miyazaki, personal account, all at CMH; Lieutenant Kenji Matsumoto, diary, October 1942; Private Ichiro Takizawa, diary, October 1942; Komiya, personal notes, October 1942; Katsumata, diary, October 1942, all in Record Group 127, William Bartsch Papers, Victory Fever boxes, unprocessed at DMMA; 182nd Infantry Regiment, Historical Record, Guadalcanal, Jayjock Collection, #2009.366, WWIIM; "Fighting on Guadalcanal," Department of the Army pamphlet, 1943, 65–66; James Murphy, "Sinking a Jap Transport," *Coast Artillery Journal*, September–October 1944: 24–25; Margry, "Guadalcanal," *After the Battle*, 12–17; Baglien, "Second Battle of Henderson Field," *Infantry Journal*, 25–28; Jersey, "Hells' Island," *World War II*, 48–51; Stanley Jersey and Edward Snedeker, *Hell's Islands: The Untold Story of Guadalcanal* (College Station: Texas A&M University Press, 2007), 280–93; Samuel Eliot Morison, *The Two-Ocean War: A Short History of the United States Navy in the Second World War* (New York: Galahad Books, 1997), 196–208; Miller, *Guadalcanal: The First Offensive*, 156–89; Craven and Cate, *The Army Air Forces in World War II, Volume IV*, 53–60; Hough et al., *Pearl Harbor to Guadalcanal*, 330–45; Frank,

Guadalcanal, 346–67; Bergerud, *Touched with Fire*, 313–17; Walker, *Combat Officer*, 18–25. Another Marine, Sergeant John Basilone, received the Medal of Honor for his actions to defeat the abortive Japanese attack at the Matanikau. This was portrayed in the 2010 HBO miniseries *The Pacific*. In 2017, on the seventy-fifth anniversary of the battle, the Solomon Islands government declared Edson's Ridge a national park.

10. Major General Edwin "Forrest" Harding, letter to Lieutenant General Robert Eichelberger, October 27, 1942, Robert Eichelberger Papers, Box 7, DU; SWPA, G2 Information Bulletin, Enemy Ground Dispositions, September 15, October 1, 1942, Record Group 3, Box 15, Folders 5 and 6, Records of HQ, SWPA, 1942–1945; Bowers, Marshall, interviews, all at DMMA; I Corps, "History of the Buna Campaign," 6; "Papuan Campaign," 14–16, both at CARL; Edward Drea, *MacArthur's Ultra: Codebreaking and the War Against Japan, 1942–1945* (Lawrence: University Press of Kansas, 1992), 16–18, 49–53; Rogers, *The Good Years*, 265; James, *Years of MacArthur, Volume II*, 79–80; Borneman, *MacArthur at War*, 525; Milner, *Victory in Papua*, 135–46; Anders, *Gentle Knight*, 228–45; Campbell, *Ghost Mountain Boys*, 165–69; Mayo, *Bloody Buna*, 88–101. For more information on Willoughby's background and career, see his entry at www.arlingtoncemetery.net.

11. Sergeant G. J. Caling, 2/2 Infantry Battalion, personal account, Record Group 319, Entry 53, Box 5; Colonel H. F. Handy, "Report of Military Observer in the Southwest Pacific, September 26–December 23, 1942"; Major David B. Parker, SWPA liaison to 1st Australian Army, "Notes on Engineer Operations in Buna Area," January 12, 1943, all located in Records of the Office of the Chief of Military History, Victory in Papua; Colonel Harry Knight, "Observations of the Battle of Buna," also titled as "Observer Report on SWPA Operations, October–December 1942," 3–4, Record Group 337, Entry 15A, Box 51, Folder 6; Odell, personal notes, all at NA; Medendorp, "March and Operations of Antitank and Cannon Companies," 13, USAMHI; The "invisible green men" reference is in General Robert Eichelberger, letter to Mr. H. J. Manning, March 13, 1961, Box 23, Robert Eichelberger Papers, DU; "Papuan Campaign," 27–33, CARL; Japanese Monograph, Number 37, 20–31, CMH; McCarthy, *Kokoda to Wau*, 384–402; Milner, *Victory in Papua*, 153–88; Anders, *Gentle Knight*, 246–52; Mayo, *Bloody Buna*, 88–93; Bergerud, *Touched with Fire*, 216–17.

12. Major Richard Boerem, letter to Dr. Samuel Milner, November 2, 1951; Major General Edwin "Forrest" Harding, letter to Dr. Samuel Milner, July 24, 1951, both in Record Group 319, Entry 53, Box 4, Records of the Office of the Chief of Military History, Victory in Papua; Lieutenant Colonel Herbert A. Smith, letter to Dr. Samuel Milner, January 20, 1950; Major General Edwin "Forrest" Harding, diary, November 27–30, 1942, both in Record Group 319, Entry 53, Box 3, Records of the Office of the Chief of Military History, Victory in Papua; SWPA, Communiqués #225–228, November 23–27, 1942, Record Group 200, Entry 19810 (A1) Richard Sutherland Papers, Box 15; Colonel Lief "Jack" Sverdrup, Report from Inspection of Buna-Dobodura, January 23, 1943, Record Group 319, Entry 53, Box 5, Records of the Office of the Chief of Military History, Victory in Papua; Knight, "Observer Report on SWPA Operations," 5; Odell, letter to Kemper, all at NA; Major General Edwin "Forrest" Harding, letters to Colonel Edward Lauer, April 5, 1953, February 27, 1954, Leslie Anders Papers, Box 1, WWII Folder, USAMHI; Kenney, diary, November 1942, DMMA; E. J. Kahn, "The Terrible Days of Company E, Part Two," *Saturday Evening Post*, January 15, 1944, 78; George Johnston, *The Toughest Fighting in the World* (New York: Duell, Sloane and Pearce, 1943), 177; Rogers, *The Good Years*, 326–30, 336; Kenney, *General Kenney Reports*, 135–36, 150–51; Milner, *Victory in Papua*, 200–03; Anders, *Gentle Knight*, 250–60; James, *Years of MacArthur, Volume II*, 208–09, 236–37; Bergerud, *Touched with Fire*, 248–49; Mayo, *Bloody Buna*, 102–12.

Chapter 8. "My Crime Deserves More Than Death"

1. General Robert Eichelberger, dictations, 1961, Box 74, Robert Eichelberger Papers, DU; Lieutenant General Robert Eichelberger, letter to Coach Earl "Red" Blaik, August 6, 1945, Record Group 41, Box 3, Folder 2, Robert Eichelberger Papers; Colonel John Kemper, Historical Division, interview with Dr. D. Clayton James, July 13, 1971, Record Group 49, Box 3, D. Clayton James Collection; Marshall, interview, all at DMMA; Major General Robert Richardson, letter to General Douglas MacArthur, no date, Record Group 200, Entry 19810 (A1), Richard Sutherland Papers, Box 39; Richardson, memo for MacArthur; General George Marshall, letter to Lieutenant General Lesley McNair, October 6, 1942, Record Group 337, Entry 58A, Box 9, all at NA; General Robert Eichelberger, dictations, 1961, Robert Eichelberger Papers, Box 1, Folder 6, USAMHI; Matthew Fath, "Intrepidity, Iron Will, and Intellect: General Robert L. Eichelberger and Military Genius," master's thesis, US Army Command and General Staff College, Fort Leavenworth, KS, 35–48; Paul Chwialkowski, *In Caesar's Shadow: The Life of General Robert Eichelberger* (Westport, CT: Greenwood, 1993), 1–56; Robert Eichelberger, *Our Jungle Road to Tokyo* (New York: Viking, 1950), ix–xxvi; John Shortal, *Forged by Fire: Robert L. Eichelberger and the Pacific War* (Columbia: University of South Carolina Press, 1987), 1–31. Emma was also frequently known as Emmaline and Emmalina.

2. Lieutenant General Robert Eichelberger, diary, November 29–December 1, 1942, Robert Eichelberger Papers, Box 2, Folder 6; General Robert Eichelberger, Dictations, 1961, 9, Robert Eichelberger Papers, Box 1, Folder 11, both at USAMHI; Lieutenant General Robert Eichelberger, letter to Colonel Chauncy Fenton, October 20, 1943, Box 8, Robert Eichelberger Papers; Lieutenant General Robert Eichelberger, unsent letter to Major General Virgil Peterson, January 19, 1943, Box 7, Robert Eichelberger Papers; General Robert Eichelberger, Memorandum on Victory in Papua, 1957, Box 73, Robert Eichelberger Papers; Lieutenant General Robert Eichelberger, dictations, 1948, 5–7, Box 33, Robert Eichelberger Papers, all at DU; Lieutenant General Clovis Byers, interview with Dr. D. Clayton James, June 24, 1971, Record Group 49, Box 2, D. Clayton James Collection; Kenney, diary, November 30–December 1, 1942, both at DMMA; Lieutenant General Clovis Byers, "A Lesson in Leadership," *Military Review*, December 1963, 12–13; Rod Paschall, "MacArthur's Ace of Spades," *MHQ*, Spring 2006: 71–72; Jay Luvaas, ed., *Dear Miss Em: General Eichelberger's War in the Pacific, 1942–1945* (Westport, CT: Greenwood, 1972), 32–33; Eichelberger, *Our Jungle Road to Tokyo*, 4, 20–23; Rogers, *The Good Years*, 336; Shortal, *Forged by Fire*, 46–48; Chwialkowski, *In Caesar's Shadow*, 57–59; Kenney, *General Kenney Reports*, 157–58; Milner, *Victory in Papua*, 203–4. MacArthur's stark imprecation to take Buna or not come back alive has solidified in historical memory as symbolic of the battle. Reflecting years later on the moment, Byers remembered it a little differently than the other participants. In his recollection, the supreme commander told Eichelberger, "I want one of two messages from you: that you have taken Buna or your body lies there. And that goes for you, too, Clovis." Such are the vagaries of memory.

3. Report of the Commanding General, Buna Forces, on the Buna Campaign, December 1, 1942–January 25, 1943, 10, Collections of 20th Century Military Records, 1918–1959, Series II, Reference Publications, Box 21, EL; Lieutenant General Robert Eichelberger, letters to Major General Richard Sutherland, December 1, 9, 1942, Record Group 319, Entry 53, Box 3, Records of the Office of the Chief of Military History, Victory in Papua; Major General Edwin "Forrest" Harding, letter to General Douglas MacArthur, December 7, 1942, Colonel John Mott, Statement, December 10, 1942; Major General Edwin "Forrest" Harding, letter to Dr. Samuel Milner, July 24, 1951, all in Record Group 319, Entry 53, Box 4, Records of the Office of the Chief of

Military History, Victory in Papua; Harding, diary, December 1–4, 1942; Notes on Characteristics and Fighting Ability of American and Australian Forces, December 20, 1942, #189, Record Group 165, Entry 79, Box 271, ADVATIS, Current Translations, #9–22, all at NA; Lieutenant General Robert Eichelberger, letter to Colonel Edward Lauer, October 17, 1953, Leslie Anders Papers, Box 1, WWII Folder; Lieutenant General Robert Eichelberger, diary, December 1–3, 1942; Dictations, 1961, all at USAMHI; I Corps, Buna Campaign Daily History, December 1–3, 1942, Box 33, Robert Eichelberger Papers; Lieutenant General Robert Eichelberger, Report on Relief of Major General E. F. Harding, February 19, 1943, Box 16, Robert Eichelberger Papers; General Robert Eichelberger, letter to Dr. Samuel Milner, July 4, 1957, Box 20, Robert Eichelberger Papers; 1948 Dictations, 4; Memo on Victory in Papua; unsent letter to Peterson, all at DU; Claire Ehle, Interview with Mik Derks, November 25, 2002, WVM; Byers interview, DMMA; Byers, "Lesson in Leadership," *Military Review*, 13; Anders, *Gentle Knight*, 261–68, 296–97, 305, 313; Milner, *Victory in Papua*, 204–12; Eichelberger, *Our Jungle Road to Tokyo*, 24–26; Chwialkowski, *In Caesar's Shadow*, 58–60; Shortal, *Forged by Fire*, 48–52. As a last resort, Eichelberger asked his staff for their views on whether to fire Harding. They unanimously recommended his relief. The logical person to replace Harding would have been the assistant division commander, Brigadier General Prayne Baker, but he was in Port Moresby, handling the division's rear echelon and administration. One by-product of the fictional Japanese counterattack was a longtime controversy over the actions of Sergeant David Rubitsky, a well-regarded 128th Infantry Regiment combat soldier who was said to have manned a machine gun all night and mowed down at least five hundred enemy soldiers. He later claimed he was denied the Medal of Honor because of anti-Semitism on the part of Mott and other unnamed senior officers. This prompted a latter-year Army investigation in which he was again denied the medal. The main problem with the stories of his exploits was that there was no attack and, according to Japanese records, they did not even have five hundred soldiers in that sector. For more information on the controversy, see Rubitsky's 1999 oral history, plus the affidavits and correspondence in the David Rubitsky Papers, all at the Wisconsin Veterans Museum. Also see Richard Halloran, "Army Cites Strong Evidence in Barring Medal," *New York Times*, December 16, 1989.

4. Colonel Joseph Sladen Bradley, letter to Dr. Samuel Milner, January 26, 1950, Record Group 319, Entry 53, Box 3, Records of the Office of the Chief of Military History, Victory in Papua, NA; General Robert Eichelberger, letter to General Sir Edmund Herring, August 26, 1959, Box 73, Robert Eichelberger Papers, DU; Colonel George De Graaf, Notes on the Buna Campaign, Lessons Learned, February 1, 1943, Record Group 29c, Box 1, Folder 3, Richard J. Marshall Papers; Colonel George De Graaf, letter to Lieutenant General Robert Eichelberger, March 1948, Record Group 15, Box 13, Folder 17, Contributions from the Public Collection; Kenney, diary, November 30, 1942, all at DMMA; Report of the Commanding General, Buna Forces, 77–85, EL; Allied Geographical Section, SWPA, "You and the Native: Notes for the Guidance of Members of the Forces in their Relations with New Guinea Natives," 4, Charles Trent Papers, Box 1, USAMHI; Jungwirth, unpublished memoir, 51, WWIIM; Eichelberger, *Our Jungle Road to Tokyo*, 25–26; Kenney, *General Kenney Reports*, 156–57; Milner, *Victory in Papua*, 198–201, 228–29. Even with a more efficient logistical system in place, the Americans during the Buna battle still never had more than sixteen days' worth of provisions on hand at Dobodura and elsewhere.

5. Colonel Gordon Rogers, comments on manuscript, June 26, 1950; Colonel John "Eddie" Grose, interview notes, November 15, 1950, both in Record Group 319, Entry 53, Box 3, Records of the Office of the Chief of Military History, Victory in Papua; Colonel Clarence Martin, Comments on Manuscript, 1952, Record Group 319, Entry

53, Box 5, Records of the Office of the Chief of Military History, Victory in Papua;
Eichelberger letter to Sutherland, December 5, 1942; Odell, personal notes, all at NA;
Report of the Commanding General, Buna Forces, 21–23, 64–67, EL; Colonel Fred
Brown, Anecdotes about Robert Eichelberger, 1961, Robert Eichelberger Papers, Box
1; Eichelberger, diary, December 3–5, 1942, both at USAMHI; Captain Robert White,
letter to Mr. Thom Yates, March 1943, Record Group 41, Box 1, Folder 3, Robert
Eichelberger Papers, DMMA; Dave Richardson, oral history, May 4, 1993, NMPW;
Ehle interview, WVM; Colonel Gordon Rogers, Colonel Merle Howe, Personal State-
ments on Bravery of Lieutenant General Robert Eichelberger at Buna, April 16 and
20, 1943, Box 33, Robert Eichelberger Papers; Lieutenant General Edward Herring,
letter to Lieutenant General Robert Eichelberger, January 27, 1943, Box 7, Robert
Eichelberger Papers; Lieutenant General Robert Eichelberger, letters to Emma
Eichelberger, December 5, 1942, April 11, 1943, Box 7, Robert Eichelberger Papers;
Lieutenant General Robert Eichelberger, letter to Mr. Fred Cretin, August 23, 1954
re: Herman Bottcher, Box 19, Robert Eichelberger Papers; Lieutenant General Robert
Eichelberger, Dictations, September 27, 1948, Box 68, Robert Eichelberger Papers;
Eichelberger letter to Herring; I Corps Buna Campaign Daily History, December 5,
1942, all at DU; Dave Richardson, "There's No Front Line in New Guinea," *Yank*,
March 12, 1943, 3; George Moorad, "Fire and Blood in the Jungle: The Story of Our
Toughest Jungle Fighter–German-born Herman Bottcher," *Liberty*, July 7, 1943, 18–
19, 38–40; Edward Drea, "A Very Savage Operation," *World War II*, September 2002,
51–52; Kahn, "Terrible Days of Company E, Part Two," *Saturday Evening Post*; Paschall, "MacArthur's Ace of Spades," *MHQ*, 72–73; Eichelberger, *Our Jungle Road to
Tokyo*, 28–32; Bergerud, *Touched with Fire*, 217–20; Johnston, *Toughest Fighting in
the World*, 222–24; Campbell, *Ghost Mountain Boys*, 234–47; Milner, *Victory in
Papua*, 234–45; Luvaas, *Dear Miss Em*, 39–40. For excellent primary sources on the
life of Herman Bottcher, see www.hermanbottcher.org.
6. Captain Pete Dal Ponte, comments on manuscript, July 12, 1950, Record Group 319,
Entry 53, Box 5, Records of the Office of the Chief of Military History, Victory in
Papua, NA; Lieutenant Hershel Horton, letter to his family, December 11, 1942,
Folder 1380, Accession #2155; Lieutenant Colonel John Murphy, letter to Mr. George
Horton, October 30, 1943, Folder 2058, Accession #2155, both at SHSM; Springer,
unpublished memoir, 16, USAMHI; "Administration News, Lieutenant H.G. Horton
Killed in New Guinea," *Notre Dame Scholastic*, February 5, 1943, 9; "Hershel Hor-
ton's Last Letter," *The Notre Dame Alumnus*, April 1944, 6; Campbell, *Ghost Mountain Boys*, 105–06, 183–91, 252, 257. "126th Infantry in the Australian Zone during the
Battle of Buna," at www.32nd-division.org; For information on Roger Keast's college
athletic career, see his synopsis page at www.onthebanks.msu.edu; Hershel Horton
is buried at Spring Lake Cemetery in Aurora, Illinois. For more information see
www.findagrave.com. Some of the salients were called roadblocks by the Americans.
The most notable was maintained on the Sanananda track by a group under the
command of Captain Meredith Huggins.
7. 127th Infantry Regiment, History of the Buna Campaign, 16 November 1942–1 February 1943, Record Group 407, Entry 427, Box 8014, Folder 332-INF-127-0.1, 1599;
First Lieutenant Suganuma, diary, December 1942, #347, Record Group 165, Entry
79, Box 271, ADVATIS, Current Translations, #9–22; Sergeant Kiyoshi Wada, diary,
December 1942, #348, Record Group 165, Entry 79, Box 271, ADVATIS, Current
Translations, #27–29; ATIS Interrogation Report, Serial 95, 12 in ATIS Information
Bulletin, Ration Supply System and Ration Scale of Japanese Land Forces in SWPA,
February 6, 1944, Record Group 165, Entry 79, Box 313, Bulletin #6; anonymous
Imperial Japanese Army soldier, diary, December 1942, #713, Record Group 165, En-
try 79, Box 273, ADVATIS, Current Translations, #62–64; Major General Tsuyuo

Yamagata, Message to the Troops in Buna, Girua, December 1942, #494, Record Group 165, Entry 79, Box 272, ADVATIS, Current Translations, #46–48; General Douglas MacArthur, letter to Lieutenant General Robert Eichelberger, December 25, 1942, Record Group 319, Entry 53, Box 3, Records of the Office of the Chief of Military History, Victory in Papua; Eichelberger, letter to Sutherland, December 5, 1942; Knight, Observer Report on SWPA Operations, 12; Odell, personal notes, all at NA; Lieutenant General Robert Eichelberger, letter to Brigadier General Floyd Parks, February 1, 1943, Floyd Parks Papers, Box 5; Report of the Commanding General, Buna Forces, 59–60, both at EL; General Robert Eichelberger, letter to Dr. Samuel Milner, June 14, 1957, Robert Eichelberger Papers, Box 1, Folder 5; Springer, unpublished memoir, 16, both at USAMHI; Lieutenant General Robert Eichelberger, letter to Major General Horace Fuller, December 14, 1942, Box 7, Robert Eichelberger Papers; Lieutenant General Robert Eichelberger, dictations, "After My Return from Buna-Sanananda," April 18, 1948, Box 68, Robert Eichelberger Papers; Eichelberger unsent letter to Peterson, all at DU; Japanese Monograph Number 37, 38–40, CMH; Eichelberger, *Our Jungle Road to Tokyo*, 42–43; Mayo, *Bloody Buna*, 142–45; Milner, *Victory in Papua*, 217; Chwialkowski, *In Caesar's Shadow*, 61; Shortal, *Forged by Fire*, 55–57. The Japanese attempted unsuccessfully to retake Gona. MacArthur's concerns about reinforcements were not idle. Imperial Navy convoys did land some troops in the Buna-Gona area, but not enough to make a positive difference in the battle. Almost ten years after the battle, Sutherland tried to get even with Eichelberger in a letter to the Army's chief of military history. "General Eichelberger displayed fine qualities of leadership in the Papuan campaign, and equal leadership and greater skill in later operations," Sutherland conceded, "but his writing has established the fact that he is not particularly modest in recording his own activities." See Sutherland, letter to Major General Orlando Ward, April 6, 1951, Record Group 319, Entry 53, Box 5, Records of the Office of the Chief of Military History, Victory in Papua, NA.

8. 2nd Field Hospital, Quarterly Report, 1942, Record Group 112, Entry UD1012, Surgeon General, HUMEDS, Box 62; Major Clinton Compere, oral history, November 19, 1943, Record Group 112, Entry 302, Surgeon General, Inspections Branch, Box 218, Interview Number 21; Lieutenant Colonel John Lazzari, oral history, July 5, 1945, Record Group 112, Entry 302, Surgeon General, Inspections Branch, Box 222, Interview Number 168; Parker, Notes on Operations Near Buna; Odell, personal notes, all at NA; Eichelberger, letter to Parks; Report of the Commanding General, Buna Forces, 104–106, both at EL; Springer, unpublished memoir, 16, USAMHI; George Moorad, CBS, broadcast transcript, Record Group 52, Box 1, Folder 20, William J. Dunn Papers, DMMA; Frank Hostnik and John Rury, "Michigan Medics in Action: The 107th Medical Battalion in World War II," *Michigan History*, January/February 1988: 15–17; Dave Richardson, "Medics Are Tough in New Guinea," *Yank*, June 18, 1943, 3; Kahn, *G.I. Jungle*, 121; Milner, *Victory in Papua*, 247, 371–72; Condon-Rall and Cowdrey, *Medical Service in the War Against Japan*, 142–45; Bergerud, *Touched with Fire*, 111–12; Eichelberger, *Jungle Road to Tokyo*, 39–40; Dod, *Engineers in the War Against Japan*, 197–200.

9. Lieutenant General Robert Eichelberger, letter to Major General Richard Sutherland, December 9, 1942, Record Group 319, Entry 53, Box 3, Records of the Office of the Chief of Military History, Victory in Papua; Grose, interview notes; Rogers, Comments on Manuscript, all at NA; Lieutenant General Robert Eichelberger, letters to Emma Eichelberger, December 6, 30, 1942, Box 7; Lieutenant General Edmund Herring, letter to Lieutenant General Robert Eichelberger, December 6, 1942, Box 7, Robert Eichelberger Papers; Captain Robert White, letter to Lieutenant General Robert Eichelberger, Box 7; Robert Eichelberger Papers; I Corps Campaign History, December 6–20, 1942; Eichelberger dictations, 1948; Lieutenant General Robert

Eichelberger, diary, December 1942, all at DU; General Robert Eichelberger, Dictations, 1955, 121, Robert Eichelberger Papers, Box 1, Folder 12; Brown, Anecdotes, 1961; Jungwirth, unpublished memoir, 55, all at USAMHI; Brigadier General Clovis Byers, letter to Brigadier General Floyd Parks, March 7, 1943, Floyd Parks Papers, Box 5, EL; Byers, "Lesson in Leadership," *Military Review*, 13–14; Eichelberger, *Jungle Road to Tokyo*, 68–69; Luvaas, editor, *Dear Miss Em*, 41–49; Chwialkowski, *In Caesar's Shadow*, 60–62.

10. 128th Infantry Regiment History, October 15, 1940–February 28, 1943, Record Group 407, Entry 427, Box 8038, Folder 332-INF-128–0.1; Lieutenant General Robert Eichelberger, letter to Major General Richard Sutherland, December 19, 1942, letter to General Douglas MacArthur, December 25, 1942; 18th Infantry Brigade, Lessons Learned, Buna-Sanananda Campaign; Lieutenant Colonel Alexander MacNab, letter to Dr. Samuel Milner, April 18, 1950, all in Record Group 319, Entry 53, Box 3, Records of the Office of the Chief of Military History, Victory in Papua; Captain Robert White II, "Bunker Busting," rough draft for *Infantry Journal*, October 1943, Record Group 319, Entry 53, Box 4, Records of the Office of the Chief of Military History, Victory in Papua; Corporal Tanaka, Notebook, 1942, #203, Record Group 165, Entry 79, Box 271, ADVATIS, Current Translations, #9–22; anonymous Imperial Japanese Army soldier, diary, December, 1942, Current Translations #62–64; Wada, diary, December 1942; Martin, comments on manuscript, 1952; Knight, Observer Report on SWPA Operations, 13–16; Parker, Notes on Operations Near Buna; Odell, personal notes, all at NA; Report of the Commanding General, Buna Forces, 66–69, 102–04, EL; I Corps, Campaign History, December 16–25, 1942, including anonymous Imperial Japanese Army soldier, diary, December 1942; Eichelberger, unsent letter to Peterson, both at DU; Japanese Monograph Number 37, 44–46; Colonel Samuel Auchincloss, Signals Section, Lessons Learned in the Buna Campaign, April 22, 1943, Record Group 68, Box 1, Folder 1, Samuel Sloan Auchincloss Papers, DMMA; Karl Dod, *United States Army in World War II: The Technical Services, The Corps of Engineers in the War Against Japan* (Washington, DC: Office of the Chief of Military History, United States Army, 1966), 199–205; Milner, *Victory in Papua*, 246–303; Mayo, *Bloody Buna*, 144–58.

11. 41st Infantry Division, Report on New Guinea Campaign, 21 December 1942–21 January 1943, Record Group 407, Entry 427, Box 9001A, Folder 341–0.3; F. Tillman Durden, Dispatches, 1943, Record Group 319, Entry 53, Box 4, Records of the Office of the Chief of Military History, Victory in Papua; 127th Infantry Regiment, History of the Buna Campaign; 128th Infantry Regiment, History; GHQ, SWPA, Communiqué #291, January 28, 1943, all at NA; Master Sergeant Walter Schauppner, 127th Infantry Regiment, Journal, January 2–3, 1943, MSS 572, Box MSS 211, Folder 14, WVM; Jungwirth, unpublished memoir, 57, USAMHI; Lieutenant General Robert Eichelberger, Memo for Emmalina, October 22, 1943, Record Group 41, Box 2, Folder 9, Robert Eichelberger Papers, DMMA; Report of the Commanding General, Buna Forces, 36–41, 104–06, EL; I Corps Campaign History, December 26–29, 1942; Eichelberger, unsent letter to Peterson; Eichelberger, Memo on Victory in Papua, 1957; dictations, 1948, After My Return from Buna-Sanananda, all at DU; Japanese Monograph Number 37, 47–62, CMH; David Wittels, "These Are the Generals—Eichelberger," *Saturday Evening Post*, February 20, 1943; John McCullough, "Eichelberger Erases the Defeat of Bataan," *Philadelphia Inquirer*, January 24, 1943; Dave Richardson, "Mess of Destruction Is Left in War's Wake on New Guinea's Tropical Shores," *Yank*, May 21, 1943, 5; Paschall, "MacArthur's Ace of Spades," *MHQ*, 74–75; Milner, *Victory in Papua*, 332–41, 364–74; Rogers, *MacArthur and Sutherland: The Good Years*, 347; Eichelberger, *Our Jungle Road to Tokyo*, 38–49; Shortal, *Forged by Fire*, 55–60; Luvaas, *Dear Miss Em*, 64–65; James, *Years of MacArthur, Volume II*, 271–77.

12. Japanese Monograph Number 35, Southeast Area Operations Record, Volume II, February 1943–August 1945, no pagination, 8–5/1 AC35; Historical Section, South Pacific Base Command, Guadalcanal Campaign, 7 August 1942–21 February 1943, Volume II, pp. A1-A25, 8–5.7 BC v2; History of US Army Forces in SPA, 631–32; Interrogations on Japanese Operations on Guadalcanal; Miyazaki, Personal Account; Hyakutake, Report to the Throne, all at CMH; Lieutenant Colonel John Homewood, G4, Letters to General Breene, November 23, 30, 1942, Record Group 494, Entry 398, US Army Forces, Middle Pacific, Box 68, Folder 1; Major William Tinsley, Observations on Unloading and Supply Dumps on Guadalcanal, December 30, 1942, Record Group 494, Entry 398, US Army Forces, Middle Pacific, Box 67, Folder 4; American Division, Narrative of Operations on Guadalcanal, Enemy Operations Affecting American Division; Vandegrift, oral history, all at NA; Private Takeo Kinamoto, diary, November 27, 1942, John A. Burden Papers, Box 1, HIA; anonymous Imperial Japanese Army soldier, diary, December 13, 1942, Record Group 127, William Bartsch Papers, Victory Fever Boxes, unprocessed, DMMA; George McMillan, *The Old Breed: A History of the First Marine Division in World War II* (Washington, DC: Infantry Journal Press, 1949), 127–28, 134–40; Frank Gibney, ed., *Senso: The Japanese Remember the Pacific War* (Armonk, NY: M. E. Sharpe, 1995), 132; Jersey and Snedeker, *Hell's Islands*, 343; Leckie, *Helmet for My Pillow*, 113; Miller, *Guadalcanal: The First Offensive*, 220–31; Condon-Rall and Cowdrey, *Medical Service in the War Against Japan*, pp. 117–22.

13. Biographical Papers, background articles on Lieutenant General Alexander "Sandy" Patch, Box 1; Résumé of General Patch's trip from New York to New Caledonia as Commanding General of Task Force 6814, Box 5; Major General Alexander Patch, letter to Brigadier General Ed Sebree, March 26, 1943, Box 2, all in Alexander Patch Papers, USMA; Otto Petr, letter to Brigadier General Everett Brown, April 7, 1963, Everett Brown Papers, Box 1, USAMHI; Major General Alexander M. Patch, "Some Thoughts on Leadership," *Military Review*, December 1943, 7; Uzal Ent, "Alexander Patch's Wartime Service Spanned Both the Pacific and European Theaters of Operations," *World War II*, May 2002: 76–80; Major General Edmund Sebree, "Leadership at Higher Levels of Command as Viewed by Senior and Experienced Combat Commanders," US Army Leadership Human Research Unit, 1961, 21; William Wyant, *Sandy Patch: A Biography of Lt. Gen. Alexander M. Patch* (Westport, CT: Praeger, 1991), 12–47. Also see Patch's entry at www.ww2gravestone.com. Petr served as a private in the American Division. On several occasions, Patch gave him a ride in his jeep. The two men apparently shared a mutual interest in seashells.

14. 132nd Infantry Regiment, Overseas History, January 1942–June 1943, Record Group 407, Entry 427, Box 4961, Folder 300-INF-132–0.1; 132nd Infantry Regiment, the Battle of Mount Austen, Record Group 407, Entry 427, Box 4962, Folder 300-INF-132–0.1; 121st Medical Battalion, Unit History, January 1942–June 1943, Record Group 407, Entry 427, Box 4998, Folder 300-MED-0.1; Brigadier General Edmund Sebree, Informal Report on Combat Operations, April 16, 1943, Record Group 407, Entry 427, Box 4805, Folder 300–0.4; Colonel Snigetaka Obara, interview with Lieutenant James Wickel, September 16, 1946, Record Group 319, Entry 87, Box 2, Records of the Office of the Chief of Military History, Guadalcanal, the First Offensive; American Division, Narrative of Operations at Guadalcanal, Enemy Operations; XIV Corps, Japanese Ground Activities on Guadalcanal, all at NA; Narrative History of Task Force 6814, CARL; Japanese Monograph Number 35; Historical Section, Guadalcanal Campaign, Volume 1, 101–06; Interrogations on Japanese Operations on Guadalcanal, all at CMH; Major General Alexander "Sandy" Patch, letter to Mrs. Julia Patch, December 23, 1942, Box 2, Alexander Patch Papers, USMA; Major Frank Halsey, "The Operations of the 132nd Infantry Regiment (American Divi-

sion) at Mount Austen, Guadalcanal Island, Solomon Islands, 15 December 1942–9 January 1943, Personal Experience of an Anti-tank Platoon Leader," Advanced Infantry Officers Course, 1947–1948, 8–16, DRL; anonymous Imperial Japanese Army soldier, diary, December 14, 1942, Box 1, John A. Burden Papers, HIA; Ralph Cerny, interview with Dr. Peter Lane, September 18, 2000, #1384, UNT; Henry Ricci, oral history; William Trubiano, interview with Mr. Richard Misenhimer, December 30, 2003, both at NMPW; Lieutenant Okajima, diary, January 10, 14, 1943, Kenneth Pryts, World War II Veterans Survey, #5472; Morriss letter, both at USAMHI; Karel Magry, "Guadalcanal," *After the Battle* no. 108 (2000): 20–22; Captain John Casey, "An Artillery Forward Observer on Guadalcanal," *The Field Artillery Journal*, August 1943: 563–67; Andrew Carroll, "Words of Reassurance from a Brutal Front," *World War II*, June/July 2008: 23–24; Ronnie Day, ed., *Mack Morriss: South Pacific Diary, 1942–1943* (Lexington: University Press of Kentucky, 1996), 53–54; Dod, *Engineers in the War Against Japan*, 207–09; Jersey and Snedekder, *Hell's Islands*, 354–69; Miller, *Guadalcanal, The First Offensive*, 233–52. Sergeant Hodan's complete letter is reproduced in the Carroll article.

15. Operations of the 25th Infantry Division on Guadalcanal, 17 December 1942–5 February 1943, Record Group 407, Entry 427, Box 6932, Folder 325–0.3, pp. 36–47 (note: this is a detailed post-battle debriefing and series of reports compiled by the officers and sergeants of the division); 27th Infantry Regiment, Report on Combat Operations, Record Group 407, Entry 427, Box 7040, Folder 325-INF-27–0.3; Brigadier General John Hodge, interview notes, Record Group 407, Entry 427, Box 6934, Folder 325–0.4; Americal Division, Narrative of Operations at Guadalcanal, all at NA; 182nd Infantry Regiment, Historical Record, Guadalcanal, WWIIM; Historical Section, Guadalcanal Campaign, Volume 1, 110–14; History of US Army Forces in SPA, 150–152, both at CMH; 25th Infantry Division, Informal Report on Combat Operations, Guadalcanal, March 27, 1943, J. Lawton Collins Papers, Box 2, EL; Colonel S. R. Larsen, "The Operations of the 2nd Battalion, 35th Infantry (25th Division), on Mount Austen, Guadalcanal, 8–24 January 1943, Personal Experiences of a Battalion Commander," School of Combined Arms Regular Course, 1946–1947, 13, CARL; Lieutenant Harry Bartlett, "The Operations of the 35th Infantry Regiment (25th Infantry Division) on Guadalcanal in the Attack and Reduction of the Gifu Strong Point, 10–25 January 1943, Personal Experience of a Machine Gun Platoon Instrument Corporal," Advanced Infantry Officers Course, 1948–1949, 24; Major Robert Bereuter, "The Operations of the 27th Infantry (25th Infantry Division) on Guadalcanal, Solomon Islands 10 January 1943–26 January 1943, Personal Experience of a Regimental S2," Advanced Infantry Officers Course, 1947–1948, 14–15, both at DRL; Major General Alexander "Sandy" Patch, letter to Mrs. Julia Patch, March 28, 1943, Box 2, Alexander Patch Papers, USMA; "Fighting on Guadalcanal," War Department Pamphlet, 53; Sebree, "Leadership at Higher Levels of Command," 21; Gary Bousman, "But You Don't Look Like a Minister," unpublished article, copy in author's possession; Mack Morriss, "C Company at Kokumbona," *Yank*, April 23, 1943, 8–9; Miller, *Guadalcanal, the First Offensive*, 253–78; Wyant, *Sandy Patch*, 58–69. The anecdote about the "Rifle Range" sign is from the Bousman account. Spragins performed so well that he was promoted and given command of the 44th Infantry Division in the European theater.

16. General Joseph Lawton Collins, Elements of Command, speech, August 30, 1971, J. Lawton Collins Papers, Box 6, Folder 9; General Joseph Lawton Collins, Oral History, January 25, 1972, J. Lawton Collins Papers, Box 1, both at USAMHI; Major General Alexander Patch and Brigadier General A. J. Barnett, Memo for Major General Joseph Collins, January 26, 1943; Major General Joseph Lawton Collins, letter to Major General Ralph Smith, March 1, 1943, both in J. Lawton Collins Papers, Box

2, EL; Operations of the 25th Infantry Division on Guadalcanal, 123–24, NA; Lieutenant Colonel Theo Moore, "'The Crux of the Fight': General Joseph Lawton Collins' Command Style," Monograph, School of Advanced Military Studies, United States Army Command and General Staff College, 2001, 1–33, CARL; Geoffrey Perret, *There's a War to Be Won: The United States Army in World War II* (New York: Random House, 1991), 242; J. Lawton Collins, *Lightning Joe: An Autobiography* (Baton Rouge and London: Louisiana State University Press, 1979), 1–6, 148–59; Floyd Radike, *Across the Dark Islands: The War in the Pacific* (New York: Ballantine Books, 2003), 65–70; General Joseph Lawton Collins entry at www.arlingtoncemetery.net; Collins's brother James Lawton Collins was also a general. James's son Michael served in the Air Force as a pilot and became famous as one of the three astronauts on the 1969 Apollo 11 moon landing mission.

17. Operations of the 25th Infantry Division on Guadalcanal, 120–21, 162, NA; Sergeant King Cleveland, 97th Field Artillery Battalion, diary, January 24, 1943, Marsha Taylor Collection, #2009.421, WWIIM; Lieutenant General Stanley "Swede" Larsen, oral history, August 1976, Stanley Larsen Papers, Box 1; Morriss letter, both at USAMHI; Mrs. Helen Maull, letters to Major General Joseph Lawton Collins, March 15, May 9, 1943; Major General Joseph Lawton Collins, letter to Mrs. Helen Maull, April 25, 1943, J. Lawton Collins Papers, Box 2; 25th Infantry Division, Informal Report on Combat Operations, all at EL; Jerry Martel, Oral History, May 3, 1993, NMPW; Paul Maggioni, "Art Education," *World War II*, June 2017: 50; Paul Maggioni, "The Thin Line Between Fact and Fiction," *World War II*, January/February 2017: 46–47; Day, *South Pacific Diary*, 62–67; Jones, *WWII*, 41; Radike, *Across the Dark Islands*, 52–54.

18. Notes on Operations on Guadalcanal, Tulagi, Buna-Rabi Areas, November 27, 1942, #210–215, Record Group 165, Entry 79, Box 271, ADVATIS, Current Translations, #9–22; Americal Division, Narrative of Operations on Guadalcanal; Hodge, interview notes; Sebree, Informal Report on Combat Operations; Operations of the 25th Infantry Division on Guadalcanal, 85–86; XIV Corps Japanese Ground Activities on Guadalcanal, all at NA; Private Sochi Kawai, Recollections; anonymous Imperial Japanese Army soldier, diary, January 1943, both in Record Group 127, William Bartsch Papers, Victory Fever boxes, unprocessed, DMMA; Major General Oscar Griswold, diary, April 25, 1943, Oscar Griswold Papers, Box 1; Larsen, oral history; Okajima, diary, January 1943, all at USAMHI; 25th Infantry Division, Informal Report on Combat Operations, EL; Captain John Burden, "The Work of the Language Section . . . in the South Pacific Area," and "Conduct of an Interrogation," both in John A. Burden Papers, Box 1, HIA; Larsen, "Operations of the 2d Battalion, 35th Infantry on Mount Austen, Guadalcanal," 18, CARL; Historical Section, Guadalcanal Campaign, Volume 1, 115–36; History of US Army Forces in SPA, 150–52; Interrogations on Japanese Operations on Guadalcanal; Miyazaki, Personal Account; Hyakutake, Report to the Throne, all at CMH; 182nd Infantry Regiment, Historical Record, Guadalcanal, WWIIM; Major General Alexander "Sandy" Patch, letter to Mrs. Julia Patch, December 24, 1942, Alexander Patch Papers, Box 2, USMA; Mack Morriss, "Jap Trap," *Yank*, March 5, 1943, 3–4; Clayton Laurie, "The Ultimate Dilemma of Psychological Warfare in the Pacific: Enemies Who Don't Surrender and GIs Who Don't Take Prisoners," *War and Society*, May 1996; Miller, *Guadalcanal, the First Offensive*, 306–09, 325–50; Frank, *Guadalcanal*, 595–96, 613–14; Gibney, *Senso*, p. 132; Collins, *Lightning Joe*, 159–67; Morison, *The Two-Ocean War*, 212–14; Wyant, *Sandy Patch*, 70–80.

Chapter 9. Chills

1. Japanese Monograph Number 46, Aleutians Operations Record, June 1942–July 1943, 8–5.1 AC46, CMH; Major David Huntoon, "The Aleutians: Lessons from a Forgotten

Campaign," School of Advanced Military Studies, US Army Command and General Staff College, Fort Leavenworth, KS, 1988, 8–22; Major Matthew Metcalf, "The Battle of Attu and the Aleutians Campaign," School of Advanced Military Studies, US Army Command and General Staff College, Fort Leavenworth, KS, 2014, 2–18; Lieutenant Commander Carol Wilder, "Weather as the Decisive Factor of the Aleutian Campaign, June 1942–August 1943," master's thesis, Fort Leavenworth, KS, 1993, 44–49; Major Shawn Umbrell, "First on the Line: The 35th Engineer Battalion in World War Two and the Evolution of a High Performance Combat Unit," master's thesis, Fort Leavenworth, KS, 2009, 56–75, all at CARL; Samantha Seiple, "Cutthroat Business," *World War II,* March/April 2012: 50; Mike Dunham, "The Lone Civilian: One Alaska War Hero's Unique Place in History," *Alaska Dispatch News,* May 23, 2014; Cornelia Dean, "In Road-Building, Black Soldiers Defied Prejudice," *New York Times,* July 23, 2012; "The U.S. Army Campaigns of World War II: Aleutian Islands," US Army Center of Military History Pamphlet, 3–12; Stetson Conn, Rose Engelman, and Byron Fairchild, *United States Army in World War II: The Western Hemisphere, Guarding the United States and Its Outposts* (Washington, DC: United States Army, Center of Military History, 2000), 223–70; Richard Leighton and Robert Coakley, *United States Army in World War II: Global Logistics and Strategy, 1940–1943* (Washington, DC: Center of Military History, United States Army, 1995), 732–33; Brian Garfield, *The Thousand-Mile War: World War II in Alaska* (New York: Ballantine Books, 1969), 171–76; Lieutenant Robert Mitchell with Sewell Tyng and Captain Nelson Drummond, *The Capture of Attu: A World War II Battle as Told by the Men Who Fought There* (Lincoln: University of Nebraska Press, 2000), xiii, 1; Morton, *Strategy and Command,* 419–25; Dod, *Engineers in the War Against Japan,* 284–319; Perret, *There's a War to Be Won,* 269. The Alaska-Canada Highway is still a major route connecting the Lower 48 with Alaska. For more information see www.bellsalaska.com. Information on Alaska and its history can be accessed at www.alaska.gov and www.alaskafacts.co.

2. Lieutenant Colonel Joseph Cannon, oral history, December 22, 1943, Record Group 112, Entry 302, Surgeon General, Inspections Branch, Box 218, Interview Number 35; Lieutenant Colonel W. B. Moore, Report on Overseas Observations, September 7, 1945, Record Group 337, Entry 15A, Box 75, Folder 599, both at NA; Major Robert Johnson, "Aleutian Campaign, World War II: A Historical Study and Current Perspective," master's thesis, Fort Leavenworth, KS, 1992, 82–101; Lieutenant Colonel J. G. Bennett, "Two Years in the Aleutian Area: Personal Experience of a Battalion Commander," School of Combined Arms, Regular Course, 1946–1947, Command and General Staff College, Fort Leavenworth, KS, 9–12; Huntoon, "Lessons from a Forgotten Campaign," 20–22; Metcalf, "Attu and the Aleutians Campaign," 13–15, all at CARL; Lieutenant Stanley Bent, letter to his parents, May 29, 1943, Folder 203, Accession #2822, SHSM; Conn et al., *Guarding the United States and Its Outposts,* 268–75; Leighton and Coakley, *Global Logistics and Strategy,* 732; Mitchell et al., *Capture of Attu,* 2–6; Morison, *The Two-Ocean War,* 265–71; Garfield, *The Thousand-Mile War,* 217–19.

3. Combined Chiefs of Staff, Memo of Proceedings, Casablanca, January 22, 1943, CCS Conference Proceedings, 1941–1945, Box 1, EL; Captain Nelson Drummond, 1st Information and Historical Service, HQ, United States Army Force, Pacific Ocean Areas, "The Attu Operation, Volume 1," 13–24, 40–55, 68–76; 8-5.3 EA V1; 1st Information and Historical Service, G-2 Historical Subsection, "The Attu Operations," 8-5.3 EA Miscellaneous Material Bulky Files, 2–9; Japanese Monograph Number 46, all at CMH; Major Jeremy Easley, "The Aleutian Islands Campaign: The Strengths and Weaknesses of Its Planning and Execution," School of Advanced Military Studies, US Army Command and General Staff College, Fort Leavenworth, KS, 2014, 20–23; Johnson, "Aleutian Campaign, World War II," 104–24; Wilder, "Weather

as the Decisive Factor of the Aleutian Campaign," 70–75; Major General Albert Brown, Comments on "The Capture of Attu," letter to Mr. Brian Garfield, December 27, 1967, Colonel H. K. Howell, letter to Dr. Jesse Remington, December 5, 1960, all in Albert E. Brown Papers, Box 2; 7th Infantry Division, G2 Estimate of Enemy Situation, April 26, 1943, Robert Fergusson Collection, Box 1; Warren Hughes, unpublished memoir, 4, World War II Veterans Survey, #1240104, all at USAMHI; Russell Annabel, "Mad Dog Hunt on Attu," *Saturday Evening Post*, August 14, 1943, 24; Bill Yenne, "Fear Itself," *World War II*, August 2017, 30–35; Dashiell Hammett, Intelligence Section, Field Forces Headquarters, "The Battle of the Aleutians," *Military Review*, April 1945, 28–31; Dashiell Hammett, "Showdown in the Aleutians," *MHQ*, Spring 2017: 54–60; No Author, *United States Navy Combat Narrative: The Aleutians Campaign, June 1942–August 1943* (Washington, DC: Naval Historical Center, Department of the Navy, 1993) 78–85; Conn et al., *Guarding the United States and its Outposts*, pp. 277–280; Morton, *Strategy and Command*, 428–31; Garfield, *The Thousand-Mile War*, 63, 224–27. Information on Attu's climate is derived from the Western Regional Climate Center. Sources are mixed on the spelling of the Japanese commander's name. Some list him as Yamazaki and others as Yamasaki. I believe the latter is correct.

4. Lieutenant Colonel Keith Ewbank, Observer Report on the Attu Action, August 14, 1943, 5, Record Group 337, Entry 15A, Box 51, Folder 4, NA; 7th Cavalry Reconnaissance Troop, After Action Report, Robert Fergusson Collection, Box 1; Sergeant Jack Werner, diary, May 11, 1943, World War II Veterans Survey, no number; Brown, Comments on "Capture of Attu," all at USAMHI; Lieutenant Colonel Lynn Davis Smith, Preliminary Report on Attu Landing, May 30, 1943; Johnson, "Aleutian Campaign, World War II," 126–30; Easley, "Aleutian Islands Campaign, Strengths and Weaknesses," 23–30; Bennett, "Two Years in the Aleutians Area," 9, all at CARL; "Attu Operations," Bulky Files, 10–21; Drummond, "The Attu Operation, Volume 1," 97–132, both at CMH; Lee Bartoletti, "Amphibious Assault on Attu," *World War II*, November 2003: 44–47; Robert Burks, "Logistics Problems on Attu," *Army Logistician*, May–June 2003: 34–36; Robert Anderson, "Attu: WWII's Bloody Sideshow," *Army*, May 1983, 38–43; *Navy Combat Narrative: The Aleutians Campaign*, 84–100; Mitchell et al., *Capture of Attu*, 6–9.

5. Battle Report of Company B, 17th Infantry Regiment, Attu, June 17, 1943, Record Group 407, Entry 427, Box 6202, Folder 307-INF-17-7-0.3; 17th Infantry Regiment, Initial Landing and Assault of Massacre Bay-Holtz Pass (Attu), 11–31 May 1943, Record Group 407, Entry 427, Box 6187, Folder 307-INF-17-0.3; Major Charles Drummond, Report of Overseas Observations, September 4, 1945, 1, Record Group 337, Entry 15A, Box 74, Folder 580; Ewbank, Observer Report on Attu Action, 4–7, 10, all at NA; "Action on Attu: Know Your Enemy," 9, Harold Rosenthal Papers, Box 1, USMA; Hughes, unpublished memoir, 4–5; Lieutenant Darwin Krystal, Sergeant Benjamin Wolfington, personal accounts in "Stories of and by Veterans of the Attu Campaign," compiled by Lieutenant Robert Mitchell, 1943, Robert Fergusson Collection, Box 1, both at USAMHI; Captain Joe Underwood, "The Operations of Company 'I' 32nd Infantry (7th Infantry Division) on Attu Island, 13–30 May 1943, Personal Experience of a Company Executive Officer," Advanced Infantry Officers Course, 1947–1948, Fort Benning, GA, 7, DRL; Smith, Preliminary Report on Attu Landing, CARL; "Attu Operations," Bulky Files, 12–24; Drummond, "The Attu Operation, Volume 1," 210–25, both at CMH; Annabel, "Mad Dog Hunt on Attu," *Saturday Evening Post*, 25; Conn et al., *Guarding the United States and Its Outposts*, 281–91; Mitchell et al., *Capture of Attu*, 27; Garfield, *The Thousand-Mile War*, 231–53. Lieutenant Robert Mitchell fought in the Battle of Attu and then immediately after served as a combat historian interviewing the survivors. He organized this material

into a three-hundred-plus-page document entitled "Stories of and by Veterans of the Attu Campaign." Excerpts from these interviews formed the basis for the book *Capture of Attu,* published with his name as lead author. However, the entire unedited bulk material is in the Robert Fergusson collection at the USAMHI. Quite simply, it is a remarkable, honest treasure trove of contemporary firsthand accounts, unfiltered by latter-year temporizing or self-censorship.

6. Lieutenant General Lesley McNair, Memorandum for the Deputy Chief of Staff, US Army, Regarding Major General A. E. Brown, June 5, 1943; Memorandum for the Chief of Staff US Army, Regarding Major General A. E. Brown, May 24, 1943; Major General Albert Brown, letter to Lieutenant General Lesley McNair, June 1, 1943, all in Record Group 337, Entry 58A, Box 9; Ewbank, Observer Report on Attu Action, 7, Appendix, all at NA; Memorandum for the Chief of Staff, Regarding Relief of Major General Albert E. Brown as Commanding General Landing Force Attu, Aleutian Island Operation, 16 May 1943; Commander I. E. McMillian, letter to Major General Albert Brown, April 11, 1944; Lieutenant Colonel Robert Fergusson, letters to Major General Albert Brown, March 10, 1943, and March 14, 1946; Captain Hubert Long, letter to Major General Albert Brown, November 17, 1943; Major General J. E. Moore, letter to Major General Albert Brown, April 16, 1946; Major General Albert Brown, letters to Mr. Brian Garfield, December 27, 1967, January 9, 1968; Mr. Brian Garfield, letter to Major General Albert Brown, December 29, 1967, all in Albert E. Brown Papers, Box 2; Hughes, unpublished memoir, 7, all at USAMHI; Wilder, "Weather as the Decisive Factor of the Aleutian Campaign," 80; Johnson, "Aleutian Campaign, World War II," 137–41, both at CARL; "Attu Operation," Bulky Files, 28–46, Annex 5; Drummond, "The Attu Operation, Volume 1, 75–76, 170–71, both at CMH; James A. Liccione, "One Man's War," *World War II,* October 2004: 14. Also see his personal entry at the National World War II Museum website, www.nww2m .com; "Aleutians Islands," CMH Pamphlet, 21; *Navy Combat Narrative: The Aleutians Campaign,* 106–09; Conn et al., *Guarding the United States and Its Outposts,* 292–94; Garfield, *The Thousand-Mile War,* 256–72. During the planning process, Buckner's staff officers urged Brown to recon Attu by air. For whatever reason, he never made any reconnaissance flights. This oversight probably put him in a vulnerable position when he did not produce rapid results. Even after he received a combat command in 1945, Brown continued to do whatever he could to clear his name. At his insistence, the Army conducted a postwar investigation of his relief as well as the veracity of unfavorable remarks by DeWitt on his fitness report. At last, in 1948, the Army expunged all negative information from his record, an obvious admission that his relief was not justified. Even so, to his dying day he resented what had happened to him.

7. Ewbank, Observer Report on Attu Action, 8, Appendix B, 3–4; 17th Infantry Regiment, Initial Landing and Assault, both at NA; Smith, Preliminary Report on Attu Landing; Johnson, "Aleutian Campaign, World War II," 141–47, both at CARL; Captain Nelson Drummond, 1st Information and Historical Service, HQ, United States Army Force, Pacific Ocean Areas, "The Attu Operation, Volume 2," 307–08, 8-5.3 EA V2; Drummond, "The Attu Operation, Volume 1," 244–45; Japanese Monograph Number 46, 141–42, all at CMH; First Lieutenant Darwin Krystal, letter to his mother, May 25, 1943, Folder 1685, Accession Number 1292, SHSM; George Thayer, unpublished memoir, 1–3, World War II Veterans Survey #8059; Sergeant Glenn Swearingen, Sergeant Earl Marks, Lieutenant John Edrington, and Corporal Tony Pinnelli, personal accounts in "Stories of and by Veterans of the Attu Campaign," compiled by Mitchell; Werner, diary, May 19, 1943, all at USAMHI; "Action on Attu: Know Your Enemy," 13, USMA; Captain N. L. Drummond, "Your Own Forward Observer," *Infantry Journal,* July 1944, 24–26; Robert Sherrod, "Company X on Attu," *Life,* June 21, 1943, 30–32; Bartoletti, "Amphibious Assault on Attu," *World*

War II, 47–48; Anderson, "WWII's Bloody Sideshow," *Army*, 45; Conn et al., *Guarding the United States and Its Outposts*, 294–95.

8. Colonel Yasuyo Yamasaki, final field orders, May 1943, plus explanatory comments by Lieutenant Colonel Robert Fergusson, Yasuyo Yamasaki Papers, Folder 1; Lieutenant Paul Nebu Tatsuguchi, diary, May 28–29, 1943, Harold Rosenthal Papers, Box 1, both at USMA; copy of diary is also in Ruth B. Harris Collection, MS1230, Box 1, Folder 21, SCUTK; 17th Infantry Regiment, Initial Landing and Assault, NA; Captain Albert Pence, Sergeant Robert Gonzales, PFC Anthony Krsinic, Captain George Buehler, Major Leonard Wellendorf, personal accounts in "Stories of and by Veterans of the Attu Campaign," compiled by Mitchell; Hughes, unpublished memoir, 11–13, both at USAMHI; Japanese Monograph, Number 46, 146–56; Drummond, "The Attu Operation, Volume 2," 499–525, both at CMH; Johnson, "Aleutian Campaign, World War II," 148–51, CARL; Robert Sherrod, "Perhaps He Is Human," *Time*, July 5, 1943; "Battle of Attu: The Japanese Side of It," *Journal of America's Military Past* 13, no. 4 (December 1985): 3–8; Bartoletti, "Amphibious Assault on Attu," *World War II*, 49, 74; Annabel, "Mad Dog Hunt on Attu," *Saturday Evening Post*, 67, 70; Anderson, "Attu: WWII's Bloody Sideshow," *Army*, 45–46; Seiple, "Cutthroat Business," *World War II*, 49–50, 54–55; Mitchell et al., *Capture of Attu*, 104–29; Garfield, *The Thousand-Mile War*, 292–300. According to Fergusson, the 7th Division gave Colonel Yamasaki's sword to West Point.

9. Lieutenant General Simon Bolivar Buckner Jr., letter to Major General Charles Corlett, June 12, 1943, Record Group 337, Entry 58A, Box 9, NA; Japanese Monograph Number 46, 178–79; also see Japanese Monograph Number 47, Northern Area Monthly Reports, January–May 1943, 8-5.1 AC47 and Translation of Japanese Documents, Volume VII, 8-5.1 AD1v7, all at CMH; Johnson, "Aleutian Campaign, World War II," 150–69, CARL; Rex Knight, "Until the 'Battle of the Pips' confused the Americans, any escape from Kiska looked hopeless," *World War II*, January 1992, pp. 8, 64–67; Brendan Coyle, "Ghosts of Kiska," *World War II*, March/April 2015, pp. 40–47; Anderson, "Attu: WWII's Bloody Sideshow," *Army*, pp. 45–46; "Aleutian Islands," CMH Pamphlet, pp. 23–26; *Navy Combat Narrative: The Aleutians Campaign*, pp. 117–128; Conn et al., *Guarding the United States and Its Outposts*, pp. 295–300; Garfield, *Thousand-Mile War*, pp. 297–300, 327–337. For more information on the invasion of Kiska, see The Infantry School papers by Lieutenant Colonel Kenneth Ward, who served as a reconnaissance troop commander, and Major James Low, who was an assistant operations officer for an assault element. Both papers are available in digital and hard copy format at DRL.

Chapter 10. The Counsel of Our Fears

1. Elkton Plan, Copy Number 5, February 12, 1943, USAMHI; Historical Section, South Pacific Base Command, History of the New Georgia Campaign, Part I, 8-5.7 BF v1, pp. 3–10; Japanese Monograph Number 35, Southeast Area Operations Record, Volume II, February 1943–August 1945, 8-5.1 AC35; History of United States Army Forces in the South Pacific Area During World War II, pp. 164–169, all at CMH; Brigadier General Stephen Chamberlin, Dictations, The Plan to Isolate Rabaul, October 8, 1948, Box 68, Robert Eichelberger Papers, DU; Kenney diary, March 1943, DMMA; John Miller, *United States Army in World War II: The War in the Pacific, Cartwheel, the Reduction of Rabaul* (Washington, D.C.: Office of the Chief of Military History, Department of the Army, 1959), pp. 9–19; Ronnie Day, *New Georgia: The Second Battle for the Solomons* (Bloomington and Indianapolis: Indiana University Press, 2016), pp. 17–21; Eric Hammel, *Munda Trail* (New York: Avon Books, 1989), pp. 3–20; William Halsey and J. Bryan III, *Admiral Halsey's Story* (New York: McGraw-Hill Book Company, 1947), pp. 129, 153–155; MacArthur, *Reminis-*

cences, pp. 173–174; Kenney, *General Kenney Reports,* pp. 213–218; Morton, *Strategy and Command,* pp. 387–399; Borneman, *MacArthur at War,* pp. 288–294; James, *Years of MacArthur, Volume II,* pp. 314–318.

2. Colonel G. R. Carpenter, Summary of Occupation of Russell Islands, May 24, 1943, Record Group 337, Entry 15A, Box 51, Folder 12; United States Army Forces in the South Pacific Area, Service of Supply, Final Closeout Report on the Russell Islands, October 15, 1945, Record Group 494, Entry 398, U.S. Army Forces, Middle Pacific, Box 76, Folder 3; Observer Reports of the Landing of the 43rd Division (less 172nd Infantry) plus 3rd Marine Raider Battalion on the Russell Islands, February 1943, RG407, Entry 427, Box 9151, Folder 343–0.3.0; Lieutenant Harumasa Adachi, diary, February 11, 1943, Record Group 127, Box 243, World War II Geographic Files, Captured Japanese Document; 43rd Infantry Division, History, July–September 1943, Record Group 407, Entry 427, Box 9150, Folder 343–0.3, all at NA; Probationary Officer Toshihiro Oura, diary, June 28, 1943, John A. Burden Papers, Box 1, HIA; Jimmy Bennett, interview with Mr. Richard Misenhimer, August 13, 2002, NMPW; Japanese Monograph Number 35; History of New Georgia Campaign, Part I, 11–26; History of United States Army Forces in the South Pacific Area During World War II, 170–82, all at CMH; D. C. Horton, *New Georgia: Pattern for Victory* (New York: Ballantine Books, 1971), 8–27; Craven and Cate, *The Army Air Forces in World War II, Volume IV,* 217–18; Miller, *Cartwheel,* 26–55; Day, *New Georgia,* 55–72; Hammel, *Munda Trail,* 21–28. Although the Americans clearly won the contest for the skies over New Georgia, their estimates of Japanese losses were exaggerated. Admiral Halsey, for instance, claimed that the Americans destroyed 106 Japanese aircraft for the loss of only six friendly planes. See page 158 of *Admiral Halsey's Story* and also page 29 of History of New Georgia Campaign, Part I.

3. 43rd Infantry Division, History, July–September, 1943, NA; History of New Georgia Campaign, Part I, 43–61; History of United States Army in the South Pacific Area, 172, 176–78, 182–84, both at CMH; Major K. Graham Fuschak, "The 43rd Infantry Division: Unit Cohesion and Neuropsychiatric Casualties," master's thesis, US Army Command and General Staff College, Fort Leavenworth, KS, 1999, 34–37; Joseph Zimmer, *The History of the 43rd Infantry Division, 1941–1945* (Baton Rouge, LA: Army and Navy Publishing, 1946), 14–22; Miller, *Cartwheel,* 72–84; Hammel, *Munda Trail,* 45–61. The Allies also used infantry-trained Fijian scouts.

4. Colonel George McHenry, diary, July 1943, Record Group 127, Box 242, World War II Area Geographic Files, agenda and conference notes; Colonel George McHenry and Lieutenant Colonel Gabbert, Notes and Comments on Rendova and Munda, July 23, 1943, Record Group 127, Box 241, World War II Area Geographic Files, Folder B3–2; Lieutenant Colonel Wilbur McNenny, Observer Report, New Georgia Operation, Record Group 127, Box 241, World War II Area Geographic Files, Folder A1–2; 43rd Infantry Division, History, July–September, 1943, all at NA; Salvatore LaMagna, questionnaire, unpublished memoir, 4, World War II Veterans Survey, no number, USAMHI; History of New Georgia Campaign, Part I, Chapter 2, 1–37; History of United States Army in the South Pacific Area, 187–89, both at CMH; Joseph Lieberman, "Road Construction on New Georgia," *The Military Engineer,* March 1944, 75–78; Miller, *Cartwheel,* 55–62, 85–96; Day, *New Georgia,* 89–106.

5. 103rd Infantry Regiment, Analysis, New Georgia Campaign, Record Group 407, Entry 427, Box 9184, Folder 343-INF-103–0.3.0; 169 Infantry Regiment, History, New Georgia Campaign, Record Group 407, Entry 427, Box 9195, Folder 343-INF-169–0.1; Major General Oscar Griswold, Informal Report on Combat Operations in New Georgia Campaign, January 18, 1944, Record Group 407, Entry 427, Box 4014, Folder 214–0; Sergeant Franklin Phelps, Memories of Munda, 8–20, Record Group 407, Entry 427, Box 9196, Folder 343-INF-169–0.6; Colonel Evans Ames, Notes on Visit to

Munda Area, August 18–23, 1943, Record Group 127, Box 241, World War II Area Geographic Files, Folder A5.7–1; Colonel Franklin Hallam, XIV Corps, Headquarters, Medical Service, New Georgia Campaign, October 31, 1943, 31–38, Record Group 494, Entry 398, US Army Forces, Middle Pacific, Box 79, Folder 4; Lieutenant Colonel James Fox, Chief of Medical Service, 39th General Hospital, Oral History, December 6, 1944, Record Group 112, Entry 302, Surgeon General, Inspections Branch, Box 220, Interview Number 112; McHenry, diary, July, August 10, 1943, notes, all at NA; "C.J.," letter to Mrs. Jessie Lucas, July 23, 1944, Folder 1812, Accession Number 1383, SHSM (the letter was incorrectly dated 1944 instead of 1943); Combat Lessons, Number 1: Rank and File in Combat, 19; Fuschak, "43rd Infantry Division: Unit Cohesion," 41–46, both at CARL; History of the New Georgia Campaign, Part I, Chapter 3, 14–17, 25–32, CMH; Captain Richard Saillant, journal, July 10, 1943, World War II Veterans Survey, no number, Joe Carey Box; LaMagna, unpublished memoir, pp. 5–6, 5A, both at USAMHI; Ira Wolfert, *Battle for the Solomons* (Boston: Houghton Mifflin, 1943), 138; Miller, *Cartwheel*, 120–22. A copy of Griswold's report can also be found in Box 2 of the William Howard Arnold Papers at USAMHI. Fortunately for the Americans, disease was not as big of a problem at New Georgia as it had been at Buna and Guadalcanal. To be sure, many were still affected by dysentery, skin ailments, and malaria, but these afflictions accounted for few evacuations.

6. Major General Oscar Griswold, letter to Lieutenant General Lesley McNair, August 29, 1943, Record Group 337, Entry 58A, Box 9, NA; Major General John Hodge, letters to Major General J. Lawton Collins, June 3, 23, 1943, J. Lawton Collins Papers, Box 2, EL; General J. Lawton Collins, conversations, 1983, J. Lawton Collins Papers, Box 1; Griswold, diary, June 15, July 12, 25, 1943, both at USAMHI; Fuschak, "43rd Infantry Division: Unit Cohesion," 17–19, 48–53; History of the New Georgia Campaign, Part I, chapter 3, pages 38–42, chapter 4, page 34, both at CMH; Miller, *Cartwheel*, 123–36; Hammel, *Munda Trail*, 150–54. For background on both Hester and Griswold, see www.westpointaog.org/memorials.

7. Lieutenant Colonel Francis McAlister, USMC, Observer Report, New Georgia Operation, August 7, 1943, Record Group 127, Box 241, World War II Area Geographic Files, Folder A1–1, 6; Lieutenant Colonel Hobart Mikesell, oral history, December 7, 1943, Record Group 112, Entry 302, Surgeon General, Inspections Branch, Box 218, Interview Number 22; Lieutenant Colonel Edward Grass and Lieutenant Colonel M. R. Kaufman, Neuropsychiatric Experiences with the 37th Infantry Division, December 18, 1943, Record Group 112, Entry 31, Surgeon General, Administrative Records, Box 240; Hallam, Medical Service, New Georgia Campaign, 38–53; Griswold, Informal Report on Combat Operations in New Georgia Campaign, all at NA; Japanese Monograph Number 35; History of the New Georgia Campaign, part I, chapter 3, pages 55–56, both at CMH; PFC Arthur Winkle, letter to friends, August 16, 1943, Folder 3264, Accession Number 1948, SHSM; Harold Barker, "Artillery Operations of the New Georgia Campaign," *The Field Artillery Journal,* August 1944: 530–36; Miller, *Cartwheel*, 137–42; Hammel, *Munda Trail*, 153–61.

8. 103rd Infantry Regiment, History, 1941–1944, Record Group 407, Entry 427, Box 9183, Folder 343-INF-103–0.1; 37th Infantry Division, Miscellaneous Historical Data on New Georgia, Record Group 407, Entry 427, Box 8608, Folder 337–0.20; Lieutenant Colonel Russell Ramsay, Report of Operations, Munda–New Georgia, August 25, 1943, Record Group 127, Box 241, World War II Area Geographic Files, Folder B3–5–1; Colonel Stuart Baxter, Personal Memoir, 1–30, Record Group 127, Box 243, World War II Area Geographic Files, New Georgia Research: Griswold, Informal Report on Combat Operations in the New Georgia Campaign; 43rd Infantry Division History; Phelps, Memories of Munda, 29–34, all at NA; Bennett interview,

NMPW; the Infantry School, "Infantry Combat, Part Eight: New Georgia," 13, Charles Ryder Papers, Box 9, EL; Captain Robert Howard, journal, July 25, 1943, World War II Veterans Survey #4816, USAMHI; Oura, diary, July 1943, HIA; Captain Robert Scott, "The Operations of the 3rd Platoon, Company 'C,' 172nd Infantry (43rd Infantry Division) at Morrison-Johnson Hill, Approaching the Munda Airstrip, New Georgia Island, British Solomon Islands, 28 July 1943, Personal Experiences of a Platoon Leader," Advanced Infantry Officers Course, 1948–1949, 13–24, DRL; Lieutenant "Some Ching," letter to Dr. L. C. Post, Special Collections Library, San Diego State University; History of the New Georgia Campaign, part I, chapter 4, pages 17–46, CMH; Eric Hammel, "Mauled Before Munda," *World War II*, April 2004, 33–40; James Olds, "Front and Center," *Chemical Warfare Bulletin*, June–July 1944, 5–8; Barker, "Artillery Operations of the New Georgia Campaign," *The Field Artillery Journal*, pp. 533–36; John Kennedy Ohl, *Minuteman: The Military Career of General Robert S. Beightler* (Boulder, CO: Lynne Rienner, 2001), 106–20; Miller, *Cartwheel*, 143–63; Hammel, *Munda Trail*, 203; Radike, *Across the Dark Islands*, 138.

9. Major John Aldes, Orthopedic Surgery, South Pacific Area, 9, Record Group 112, Entry 31, Surgeon General, Administrative Records, Box 239; Hallam, Medical Service, New Georgia Campaign, 43–44; 37th Infantry Division Miscellaneous Historical Data on New Georgia; Phelps, Memories of Munda, 35, all at NA; Major General J. Lawton Collins, letter to Colonel Clarence Orndorff, October 12, 1943; letter to Mrs. Sallie Mellichamp, August 31, 1943; Mrs. Sallie Mellichamp, letter to Major General J. Lawton Collins, September 22, 1943, all in J. Lawton Collins Papers, Box 2, EL; Miller, *Cartwheel*, 152; Condon-Rall and Cowdrey, *Medical Service in the War Against Japan*, 184–90; Radike, *Across the Dark Islands*, 137.

10. 148th Infantry Regiment, History, New Georgia, August 9, 1943, Record Group 407, Entry 427, Box 8741, Folder 337-INF-145–0.2; Narrative Report on Combat Activities of 1st Battalion, 148th Infantry, September 13, 1943, Record Group 127, Box 243, World War II Geographic Files, New Georgia Research; 27th Infantry Regiment, Combat Reports, New Georgia Campaign, Record Group 407, Entry 427, Box 7040, Folder 325-INF-27–0.3; United States Army Forces in South Pacific Area, Service of Supply, Summary of Damages Caused in the Occupation of the New Georgia Islands, Record Group 494, Entry 398, US Army Forces, Middle Pacific, Box 76, Folder 3; Major General Oscar Griswold, Lessons Learned from Joint Operations, January 21, 1944, Record Group 494, Entry 398, US Army Forces, Middle Pacific, Box 68, Folder 2; Major General Oscar Griswold, letter to Lieutenant General Lesley McNair, November 30, 1943, Record Group 337, Entry 58A, Box 9; Admiral William Halsey, letter to Major General Orlando Ward, August 27, 1952, and Lieutenant General W. E. Riley, letter to Admiral William Halsey, August 13, 1952, both in Record Group 319, Entry 49, Box 3, Records of the Office of the Chief of Military History, Cartwheel, the Reduction of Rabaul; 43rd Infantry Division History; 169th History, New Georgia Campaign; Ramsey, Report of Operations; Griswold, Informal Report on Combat Operations in the New Georgia Campaign, all at NA; Operations of the 25th Infantry Division in the Central Solomons, New Georgia–Arundel–Vella Lavella, 16 August to 12 October 1943, J. Lawton Collins Papers, Box 3; Major General J. Lawton Collins, letter to General George Marshall, January 26, 1943; letter to Brigadier General Robert McClure, September 3, 1943; letter to Major General Charles "CL" Bolte, Adjutant General's Office, May 28, 1943, all in J. Lawton Collins Papers, Box 2; the Infantry School, "Infantry Combat Part Eight," 9, all at EL; John Timmons, World War II Veterans Survey, no number; 109th Quartermaster Graves Registration Platoon, unit history, the Guadalcanal Campaign and the Solomons, Harold P. Henry Papers, Box 1; Griswold, diary, August 1943; Collins, oral history, 1972, all at USAMHI; History of United States Army Forces in the South Pacific Area

During World War II, 195–208; History of the New Georgia Campaign, Part I, chapter 4, pages 48, 54, chapter 8, page 18, both at CMH; Mack Morriss, "Infantry Battle in New Georgia," *Yank*, October 15, 1943, 3–5; Collins, *Lightning Joe*, 171–81; Halsey, *Admiral Halsey's Story*, 170–72; Ohl, *Minuteman*, 120–21; Miller, *Cartwheel*, 163–88; Hammel, *Munda Trail*, 265–79; Day, *New Georgia*, 285–86.

Chapter 11. Fighting Two Battles

1. Colonel Archibald MacKechnie, Notes on the 162nd Infantry in New Guinea, June–September 1943, Record Group 200, Entry 19810 (A1) Richard Sutherland Papers, Box 58 and also Record Group 407, Entry 427, Box 9083, Folder 343-INF-162–0.6; Colonel Russell "Red" Reeder, Notes on Campaign in New Guinea, November 3, 1943, Record Group 407, Entry 427, Box 9083, Folder 341-INF-162–0.3.0; Anonymous Imperial Japanese Army NCO, diary, 1943, #1032, Record Group 165, Entry 79, Box 277, ADVATIS, Current Translations, #94–96; Corporal Tanaka, statement, November 1943, #1230, Record Group 165, Entry 79, Box 279, ADVATIS, Current Translations, #111–112, all at NA; Combat Lessons, Number 3: Rank and File in Combat, 64–65, 69–70; Combat Lessons, Number 4: Rank and File in Combat, 51–52, CARL; Japanese Monograph Number 38, Southeast Area Operations Record, 18th Army Operations, Volume II, June 1943–February 1944, no pagination, 8-5.1 AC38, CMH; Major John George, "A Night Assault Landing," Armor School Monograph, 1948, Fort Knox, KY, 2–12, USAMHI; Captain Frederick Gehring, "The Operations of Company K, 162nd Infantry (41st Infantry Division) in the Salamaua Operation 20 July–12 September 1943, Personal Experiences of a Company Commander," 7–13, 28–31, DL; John George, "Three Nights on George Ridge," *Infantry Journal*, April 1944: 21–24; Anonymous, "Dogs in the Jungle," *Infantry Journal*, January 1945; Tim Brady, *His Father's Son: The Life of Ted Roosevelt, Jr.* (New York: New American Library, 2017), 220–21; Harry Gailey, *MacArthur's Victory: The War in New Guinea, 1943–1944* (New York: Ballantine, 2004), 48–60; *Reports of General MacArthur, Volume I*, 118–22; MacArthur, *Reminiscences*, 176; Miller, *Cartwheel*, 189–202; Craven and Cate, *The Army Air Forces in World War II, Volume IV*, 129–99; Kenney, *General Kenney Reports*, 197–206, 251–79. For the 162nd Infantry, the sharpest fight of the Salamaua campaign took place at Roosevelt Ridge, a key piece of high ground near Tambu Bay. The ridge was named for Lieutenant Colonel Archibald Roosevelt, who commanded the regiment's 2nd Battalion. He was the son of President Theodore Roosevelt and the brother of Brigadier General Ted Roosevelt, both recipients of the Medal of Honor. Archibald had been wounded in combat in World War I. At Roosevelt Ridge, he was badly wounded again and sent home. He became the only soldier to be 100 percent disabled from wounds in both world wars.

2. Major Bill Britten, letters to his wife, September 5, 6, 1943, John W. Britten Papers, Box 1; GHQ, Southwest Pacific Area, Communiqué, September 5, 1943, both at USAMHI; 503rd Parachute Infantry Regiment, Report on "Outlook" Operation, October 31, 1943; C Company, 503rd Parachute Infantry Regiment, History, both in 503rd Parachute Infantry Regiment Records, Box 1533, EL; Lieutenant Jerry Riseley, adjutant's journal, August–September 1943; Louis Aiken Personal Account, both in Jerry Riseley Papers, Box 1, HIA; anonymous Imperial Japanese Army officer, diary, September, 1943, #1225, Record Group 165, Entry 79, Box 279, ADVATIS, Current Translations, #111–112; Allied Translator and Interpreter Service, Information Bulletin, Japanese Reaction to Allied Paratroops, December 31, 1943 Record Group 165, Entry 79, Box 313, Bulletin #3A, both at NA; Japanese Monograph Number 38, CMH; Major Matthew Sweeney, "American Airborne Operations in the Pacific Theater: Extending Operational Reach and Creating Operational Shock," School of Advanced Military Studies, US Army Command and General Staff College, Fort Leavenworth,

KS, 2014, 8–18; Major Channing Greene, "Canopies of Blue: The American Airborne Experience in the Pacific in the Second World War as a Case Study in Operational Art and Multi-role Flexibility," School of Advanced Military Studies, US Army Command and General Staff College, Fort Leavenworth, KS, 2008, 30–39, both at CARL; James Duffy, *War at the End of the World: Douglas MacArthur and the Forgotten Fight for New Guinea, 1942–1945* (New York: NAL/Penguin, 2016), 230–42; Gene Salecker, *Blossoming Silk Against the Rising Sun: U.S. and Japanese Paratroopers at War in the Pacific in World War II* (Mechanicsburg, PA: Stackpole Books, 2010), 112–37; Miller, *Cartwheel*, 207–21; Kenney, *General Kenney Reports*, 287–96; Borneman, *MacArthur at War*, 306–11; MacArthur, *Reminiscences*, 179–80; James, *Years of MacArthur, Volume II*, 325–30; Craven and Cate, *The Army Air Forces in World War II, Volume IV*, 180–87.

3. United States Army Forces in the South Pacific Area, Services of Supply, History of the South Pacific Base Command, Record Group 494, Entry 398, US Army Forces, Middle Pacific, Box 69, Folder 3; Sergeant Mike Bredice, letter to Pal Guido Morengo, April 9, 1944, Record 496, Entry 74, Box 456, Records of the General Headquarters, SWPA/USAFP, Personal Letters held by Theater Censor; Captain T. B. Magath, USNR, oral history, July 3, 1943, Record Group 38, Entry P11, Box 18, Records of the Chief of Naval Operations, World War II Oral Histories and Interviews; Colonel William Parson, oral history, August 19, 1944, Record Group 112, Entry 303, Surgeon General, Inspections Branch, Box 219, Interview Number 87; Captain Talcott Wainwright, Report on Jungle Travel in New Guinea, November 16, 1942, Record Group 112, Entry 31, Surgeon General, Administrative Records, Box 75; Compere oral history, all at NA; History of US Army Services of Supply, Southwest Pacific and Army Forces Western Pacific, 1941–30 June 1946, History of Base B at Oro Bay, New Guinea from December 1942 until March 1944, 112–113, 8–5.8 AA V17, CMH; 339th Engineer Combat Battalion, "This Is an Engineer's War," 4, 6, Greg Myers Collection, WWIIM; Cecil Helena, oral history, circa 1990, Cecil Helena Papers, Vertical Files, Box 35, Folder 11, USAMHI; Tech 4 Dale Venter, letter to his family, September 22, 1944, Folder 3083, Accession Number 1893; Lieutenant John Harrod, letter to his mother, April 1944, Folder 1238, Accession Number 2435, both at SHSM; Douglas, unpublished memoir, 402, EL; War and Navy Departments, "A Pocket Guide to New Guinea and the Solomons," 1943, 31–32; Condon-Rall and Cowdrey, *Medical Service in the War Against Japan*, 140–41.

4. Major Donald Patterson, Assistant Malariologist, SWPA Services of Supply, oral history, December 14, 1944, Record Group 112, Entry 302, Surgeon General, Inspections Branch, Box 220, Interview Number 116; Lieutenant Colonel George Littell, Report of Medical Department Activities, December 3, 1943, 5–8, Record Group 112, Entry 302, Surgeon General, Inspections Branch, Box 218, Interview Number 26; Major Roger Egeberg, Monthly Informal Report of Activities, December 12, 1942, Record Group 112, Entry 31, Surgeon General, Administrative Records, Box 209; Major Whitman Newell and Major Theodore Lidz, "The Toxicity of Atabrine to the Central Nervous System"; Colonel George Decker, Chief of Staff, 6th Army/Alamo Force, order issued on behalf of Lieutenant General Walter Krueger, Control of Malaria, May 31, 1943, both in Record Group 112, Entry 31, Surgeon General, Administrative Records, Box 210; 17th Malaria Survey Unit, Residual Effect of Diesel Oil on Incidence of Adult Malaria Mosquitoes, Base B, August 3, 1944, Record Group 112, Entry 31, Surgeon General, Administrative Records, Box 212; Major John Swartzwelder, oral history, September 11, 1944, Record Group 112, Entry 302, Surgeon General, Inspections Branch, Box 220, Interview Number 95; Compere oral history, all at NA; Denton W. Crocker, "Malaria Survey and Malaria Control Detachments in the SWPA in World War II," unpublished paper, Denton W. Crocker Papers, Vertical Files, Box 61, Folder

1, USAMHI; Douglas, unpublished memoir, 402–14; Report of the Commanding General, Buna Forces, 72, both at EL; Robert Joy, "Malaria in the American Troops in the South and Southwest Pacific in World War II," *Medical History*, 1999, Number 43, 192–207; John Greenwood, "The Fight Against Malaria in the Papua New Guinea Campaigns," accessed at www.history.amedd.army.mil/bookdocs/wwii/Malaria2; Condon-Rall and Cowdrey, *Medical Service in the War Against Japan*, 123–27, 139–41.

5. Colonel Willis Tack and Lieutenant Colonel Frank Lawrence, "Observations of in the Southwest Pacific Theaters, April–July, 1943," Record Group 337, Entry 15A, Box 51, folder 10; Sergeant Mike Bredice, letters to Bing Crosby, Lana Turner, and Betty Grable, April 1944, Richard Lambert, letter to wife, no date, PFC Paul MacDonald, letter to Ethel, March 22, 1944, Major Ellis Huey, letter to his wife, November 28, 1943, and "Bub," letter to his mother, December 5, 1943, all in Record Group 496, Entry 74, Box 456, Records of the General Headquarters, SWPA/USAFP, Personal letters held by Theater Censor; Colonel S. A. Challman, oral history, September 13, 1945, Record Group 112, Entry 31, Surgeon General, Administrative Records, Box 240; Captain Peggy Carbaugh, oral history, September 13, 1944, Record Group 112, Entry 302, Surgeon General, Inspections Branch, Box 220, Interview Number 97; Captain Marian Grimes, oral history, September 11, 1944, Record Group 112, Entry 302, Surgeon General, Inspections Branch, Box 220, Interview Number 94; Major Henry Gwynn, Oral History, May 23, 1944, Record Group 112, Entry 302, Surgeon General, Inspections Branch, Box 219, Interview Number 73, all at NA; Major Bill Britten, letters to wife, November 28, 1943, January 14, 1944, John W. Britten Papers, Boxes 1 and 2; Robert Jackson, unpublished memoir, 27, World War II Survey #3849, both at USAMHI; "The Army Nurse Corps," Center of Military History, 26, located at www.history.army.mil/books; Peter Schrijvers, *Bloody Pacific: American Soldiers at War with Japan* (New York: Palgrave Macmillan, 2010), 109; Condon-Rall and Cowdrey, *Medical Service in the War Against Japan*, 268–70.

6. Staff Sergeant Frank Pawlikoski, letter to Steffie, no date, Private Joseph Klimaszeski, letter to Mrs. Ruby Cartis, January 4, 1944; Private Roland Dettler, letter to his parents, January 13, 1944, all in Record Group 496, Entry 74, Boxes 456 and 457, Records of the General Headquarters, SWPA/USAFP, personal letters held by Theater Censor; Tack and Lawrence, "Observations of the Southwest Pacific Theaters," all at NA; History of US Army Services of Supply Southwest Pacific and Army Forces Western Pacific, 1941–30 June 1946, Finschhafen, New Guinea Since Activation 1943 until April 1944, no pagination, 8–5.8 AA V20, CMH; Riseley, adjutant journal, October 8, 1943, HIA; Brigadier General George Jones, letters to Lieutenant General Edward Flanagan, 1985–1986, Record Group 43, Box 9, Folder 20, Weldon B. Hester Papers; Lieutenant General Walter Krueger, letter to General Douglas MacArthur, November 5, 1943, Walter Krueger Papers, Box 9, USMA; John McKinney, unpublished memoir, no pagination, Record Group 15, Box 29, Folder 13, Contributions from the Public Collection, both at DMMA; Britten letter, November 28, 1943; Lieutenant Colonel Bill Britten, letter to his wife, February 28, 1945, at www.thedropzone.org; Schrijvers, *Bloody Pacific*, 109. The inspector general quote is from Krueger's letter to MacArthur.

7. United States Army Forces in the Pacific, History of the South Pacific Base Command, NA; History of US Army Services of Supply Southwest Pacific and Army Forces Western Pacific, 1941–30 June 1946, History of Base B at Oro Bay, New Guinea from December 1942 until March 1944, 31–35, 8–5.8 AA V17; History of US Army Services of Supply Southwest Pacific and Army Forces Western Pacific, 1941–30 June 1946, Base at Lae until March 1944, no pagination, 8–5.8 AA V19; History of US Army Services of Supply, Finschhafen; Masterson, "United States Army Transportation in the Southwest Pacific," 80–88, 260–64, 317–18, 433–44, all at CMH; 339th

Engineer Construction Battalion, "This Is an Engineer's War," 5, WWIIM; Kay Larson, "MacArthur's Navy," *Coast Guard*, December 1999, 32–35; Ed Dennis, "MacArthur's Navy," recollections, Record Group 62, Box 1, Folder 3, Ed Dennis Papers, DMMA; Stauffer, *Quartermaster Corps: Operations in the War Against Japan*, 84–89; Dod, *The Corps of Engineers: The War Against Japan*, 257–67. As the New Guinea bases grew, MacArthur's headquarters devised a lettering system to identify each one. Oro Bay, for instance, was known as "Base B."

8. Lieutenant General Robert Eichelberger, letter to Lieutenant General Lesley McNair, May 28, 1943, Record Group 337, Entry 58A, Box 9, NA; Robert Eichelberger, dictations, 1953, Robert Eichelberger Papers, Box 1, Folder 1; Dictations, March 28, 1955, Robert Eichelberger Papers, Box 1, Folder 2, both at USAMHI; Lieutenant General Robert Eichelberger, letter to Colonel Chauncy Fenton, October 22, 1943; letters to Emma, April 13, 1943, and December 30, 1943; Brigadier General Clovis Byers, letter to Emma, December 17, 1942, March 31, 1943, December 23, 1943; Lieutenant General Robert Eichelberger, letter to Lieutenant General Walter Krueger, September 30, 1943, Boxes 7 and 8; Lieutenant General Robert Eichelberger, letters to General Malin Craig, July 25, 1943, and October 11, 1943, Box 16; Robert Eichelberger, dictations, April 18, 1948, Box 68; Robert Eichelberger, letter to Lieutenant General Clovis Byers, October 23, 1959, Box 22, all in Robert Eichelberger Papers, DU; Brigadier General Clovis Byers, letter to Brigadier General Clarence Martin, January 14, 1944, letter to Colonel Rex Chandler, January 4, 1944, both in Clovis Byers Papers, Box 3, Folder 3–1, HIA; Lieutenant General Robert Eichelberger, letter to Brigadier General Floyd Parks, December 6, 1943, Floyd Parks Papers, Box 5, EL; General Douglas MacArthur, telegrams to General George Marshall, August 1943, Record Group 46, Box 2, Folder 14, Paul Rogers Papers; Eichelberger, Memorandum for Emmalina, all at DMMA; David Dexter, *Australia in the War of 1939–1945: Volume VI, the New Guinea Offensives* (Canberra: Australian War Memorial, 1961), 222; Walter Krueger, *From Down Under to Nippon: The Story of the Sixth Army in World War II* (Washington, DC: Combat Forces, 1953), 10–11; Kevin Holzimmer, *General Walter Krueger: Unsung Hero of the Pacific War* (Lawrence: University Press of Kansas, 2007), 104–05; Luvaas, *Dear Miss Em*, 66–70; Chwialkowski, *In Caesar's Shadow*, 81–89; James, *Years of MacArthur, Volume II*, 312–13. Though Eichelberger had no evidence, he also blamed Sutherland for persuading MacArthur to deny him command of 1st Army.

9. President Franklin Roosevelt, letter to General Douglas MacArthur, August 15, 1943, Box 9, Folder 61; Senator Arthur Vandenberg, letter to Brigadier General Charles Willoughby, August 17, 1943 Box 11, Folder 45; Major General George Van Horn Moseley, letters to General Douglas MacArthur, December 14, 19, 1943, Box 8, Folder 24; Lieutenant General Robert Eichelberger, letters to General Douglas MacArthur, circa 1943, Box 4, Folder 8, all in Record Group 10, General Douglas MacArthur, private correspondence; Generals George Marshall, Douglas MacArthur, Robert Eichelberger, messages regarding Eleanor Roosevelt visit to SWPA, August–September, 1943, Record Group 46, Box 2, Folder 10, Paul Rogers Papers, DMMA; "Bub," letter to his mother, NA; Philip Briggs, "Wartime Politics: General MacArthur and the Presidential Election of 1944," unpublished paper, 1983; Eichelberger, dictations, November 12, 1953, both at USAMHI; Brigadier General Floyd Parks, letter to Lieutenant General Robert Eichelberger, November 3, 1943; Lieutenant General Robert Eichelberger, letter to Brigadier General Floyd Parks, no date, both in Floyd Parks Papers, Box 5, EL; Robert Eichelberger, dictations, 1948, 1953, Boxes 68 and 73, Robert Eichelberger Papers, DU; Lieutenant General Robert Eichelberger, letter to Lieutenant General Walter Krueger, September 23, 1943, Walter Krueger Papers, Box 9, USMA; John McCarten, "General MacArthur: Fact and Legend," *The American*

Mercury, January 1944, 7–18; *Time*, May 8, 1944, 8; Arthur Vandenberg Jr., *The Private Papers of Senator Vandenberg* (Boston: Houghton Mifflin, 1952), 76–89; Paul Rogers, *The Bitter Years: MacArthur and Sutherland* (New York: Praeger, 1990), 23–24; James, *Years of MacArthur, Volume II*, 403–40; Borneman, *MacArthur at War*, 380–93; Schaller, *Far Eastern General*, 78–84; MacArthur, *Reminiscences*, 178–79; Eichelberger, *Jungle Road to Tokyo*, 78–88.

Chapter 12. Surviving

1. Military Intelligence Division, "Prisoners of War in Taiwan (Formosa)," October 20, 1944, Record Group 389, Entry 460A, Provost Marshal Records, Box 2122, Taiwan Prisoner of War Camp Folder, NA; Mr. William Lathrop, letter to Mrs. James Swanton, February 28, 1943, Donovan Swanton Papers, Box 1; McMaster, unpublished memoir, 117, both at USMA; Beebe, unpublished memoir, 44–48, 53; Campbell, unpublished memoir, 121, both at USAMHI; *Prisoner of War Bulletin*, September 1943, Ivor William Collection, #2009.153.021, WWIIM; Adele Wainwright, letter, *Philippine Postscripts*, March 1, 1944; Zarate, "American Prisoners of Japan: Did Rank Have Its Privilege?" 159–69, both at CARL; Van Waterford, *Prisoners of the Japanese in World War II* (Jefferson, NC: McFarland, 1994), 215; John Beebe, ed., *Prisoner of the Rising Sun: The Lost Diary of Brigadier General Lewis Beebe* (College Station, TX: Texas A&M University Press, 2006), 142–44; Kerr, *Surrender and Survival*, 170–71; Knox, *Death March*, 221–22; Dooley, *To Bataan and Back*, 105, 135; Wainwright, *General Wainwright's Story*, 190–212; Schultz, *Hero of Bataan*, 333–40, 344–72. Unbeknownst to Wainwright, he was featured on the cover of the May 8, 1944, issue of *Time* magazine. The issue included a brief biography and a laudatory account of his actions before and during the surrender at Corregidor.

2. Major John Mamerow, POW Report on Fukuoka #17, April 12, 1946, Record Group 389, Entry 460A, Provost Marshal Records, Box 2125, Fukuoka #17 Folder, NA; Captain John Olson, letter to Mr. Simon Nash, April 23, 1947, John Olson Papers, Box 6; Thomas Hewlett account in "The Japanese Story," American Ex POW Inc., Packet Number 10, National Medical Research Commission, 1980, 74–78, John Olson Papers, Box 1; Campbell, unpublished memoir, 109–26, both at USAMHI; Zarate, "American Prisoners of Japan: Did Rank Have Its Privilege?" 179–90, CARL; Peter Maas, " 'They Should Have Their Day in Court,' " *Parade*, June 17, 2001, 4–6; Kerr, *Surrender and Survival*, 175–87; Waterford, *Prisoners of the Japanese in World War II*, 201–03; Knox, *Death March*, 385, 391–97; Tenney, *My Hitch in Hell*, 122–48, 197, 205–06. Olson was at Yodogawa the same time as Campbell. The two men became lifelong friends. Tenney is featured in the *Parade* article. The Japanese held a few hundred American prisoners in Burma and other South Asian sites. To access a wealth of information about the various POW camps, individual prisoners and their experiences, as well as official reports, see www.mansell.com.

3. Special Division, Department of State, Memorandum on Conditions in Manila; Military Intelligence Division, Prisoners of War in the Philippine Islands; Mueller, diary, circa 1943, all at NA; Zarate, "American Prisoners of Japan: Did Rank Have its Privilege?" 155–58, CARL; Alice Hahn Powers, oral history, April 9, 1983, Army Nurse Corps Collection, Series III, Oral Histories, Box 48, Folder 7; "The Japanese Story," 26, both at USAMHI; "The Army Nurse Corps," 30–31; Monahan and Neidel-Greenlee, *All This Hell*, 98–122; Norman, *We Band of Angels*, 142–68.

4. Major Cecil Sanders, History of Cabanatuan Camp Library, Record Group 407, Philippine Archives Collection, Box 143, Folder 4; Lieutenant Colonel Elvin Barr, the Band at Cabanatuan, Record Group 407, Philippine Archives Collection, Box 125, Folder 8; Lieutenant Philip Meier, diary, July 20, 1943, Record Group 407, Philippine Archives Collection, Box 136, Folder 13; Lorenza Vazquez de Amusategui, "Personal

Narrative in Re 'Miss U' Undercover Group," 1–19, Lieutenant Colonel Harold Johnson, letter to "Sparkie," February 8, 1944, letter to Larry, October 16, 1945, Johnson statement, Captain Frank Tiffany, letter to "Screwball," September 14, 1943, all in Record Group 407, Philippine Archives Collection, Box 143A, Folder 8; Sergeant Raymond Castor, POW Report, Record Group 389, Entry 460A, Provost Marshal Records, Box 2133, Hitachi 8B Camp Folder; Johnson diary, June 14, August 22, November 15, 1943; Fendall, unpublished memoir, 106; Provost Marshal Report on Prisoners of War in the Philippines; Forquer's diary is quoted in Camp Conditions Report, Philippine Islands; Hospital at Cabanatuan Prison Camp; Notes on the Feeding of American Military Personnel Interned in Cabanatuan; Special Division, Department of State, Memorandum on Conditions in Manila; Military Intelligence Division, Prisoners of War in the Philippine Islands, all at NA; Major General Chester Johnson, West Point's Tragic Loss Honored by Memorials at Cabanatuan, Armand Hopkins Papers, Box 2; Hopkins, unpublished memoir, 47, 61, both at USMA; Johnson, oral history, January 27, 1972; Johnson, interview with James, both at USAMHI; Blumenson, "Harold K. Johnson: 'Most Remarkable Man,'" *Army*, 22–23; Adrian Martin, *Brothers from Bataan: POWs, 1942–1945* (Manhattan, KS: Sunflower University Press, 1992), 98–108; Knox, *Death March*, 229–35, 243–45; Kerr, *Surrender and Survival*, 151–55; Sorley, *Honorable Warrior*, 69–71; Hardee, *Bataan Survivor*, 94–95; Bumgarner, *Parade of the Dead*, 123–33; Weinstein, *Barbed Wire Surgeon*, 162–67.

Chapter 13. Toils

1. Brigadier General Frank Dorn, letter to Mr. John Hart, August 3, 1960, John Hart Papers, Box 1, HIA; W. H. Lawrence, "Mme. Chiang Asks Defeat of Japan, and House Cheers," *New York Times*, February 19, 1943; W. H. Lawrence, "President Tells Mme. Chiang More Arms Will Be Rushed," *New York Times*, February 20, 1943; Nancy MacLennan, "Mme. Chiang Poises as if for Flight," *New York Times*, February 20, 1943; "Editorial: Speech to Congress, Madame Chiang Kai-Shek Calls Upon the U.S. to Join China—In War and Peace," *Life*, March 1, 1943; Frank McNaughton, "Mme. Chiang in the U.S. Capitol," *Life*, March 8, 1943; "Mass Tribute to Mme. Chiang," *Life*, March 15, 1943; "Mme. Chiang in Hollywood," *Life*, April 19, 1943; "Madame," *Time*, March 1, 1943; Basil Miller, *Generalissimo and Madame Chiang Kai-shek: Christian Liberators of China* (New York: Zondervan Publishing House, 1943); Stilwell and White, *The Stilwell Papers*, 190–91; Taylor, *The Generalissimo*, 229–30; Fenby, *Chiang Kai-Shek*, 393–97; Tuchman, *Stilwell and the American Experience in China*, 349–53; Mitter, *Forgotten Ally*, 296–97.
2. Proceedings, Trident Conference, Combined Chiefs of Staff Conference Proceedings, 1941–1945, Box 2, EL; Brigadier General Thomas Hearn, interview with Mr. Charles Romanus, May 17, 1950, Record Group 319, Entry 75, Box 9, Records of the Office of the Chief of Military History, Stilwell's Mission to China; Major General Claire Chennault, letter to Major General A. C. Smith, and comments on manuscript, March 30, 1954, Record Group 319, Entry 77, Box 8, Time Runs Out in CBI; Madame Chiang Kai-shek, interview with Romanus and Sunderland, all at NA; Historical Section, "History of the China Burma India Theater," CMH; Brigadier General Haydon Boatner, letter to Mr. John Hart, April 20, 1960, John Hart Papers, Box 1; Brigadier General Haydon Boatner, notes, May 14, 1974, Haydon Boatner Papers, Box 4; Brigadier General Frank Dorn, letter to Mr. John Hart, July 20, 1960, John Hart Papers, Box 1; Dorn, letter to Kirby, all at HIA; Stilwell, diary, April 29–May 22, 1943, www.hoover.org; John Hersey, "Claire Chennault," *Life*, May 29, 1944; Haith, "I'll Go Where I'm Sent,'" *Military Review*, 77–80; William McDonald III and Barbara Evenson, *The Shadow Tiger: Billy McDonald, Wingman to Chennault*

(Birmingham, AL: Shadow Tiger, 2016), 234; Stilwell and White, *The Stilwell Papers*, 204–06; Taylor, *The Generalissimo*, 230–35; Fenby, *Chiang Kai-Shek*, 383; Chennault, *Way of a Fighter*, 34–35, 213–26; Tuchman, *Stilwell and the American Experience in China*, 217, 366–73; Romanus and Sunderland, *Stilwell's Mission to China*, 317–33. One positive aspect of Stilwell's trip to America was that he got to spend some time at home in Carmel with his wife, Win. I would like to thank William McDonald III for sending me a complimentary copy of his fine book about his father, Captain Billy McDonald.

3. Lieutenant General Brehon Somervell, letter to Major General Orlando Ward, May 1, 1950; Lieutenant General Joseph Stilwell, Comments on the Chiang Couple, October 12, 1943, both in Record Group 319, Entry 75, Boxes 7 and 9, respectively, Records of the Office of the Chief of Military History, Stilwell's Mission to China, NA; Boatner letter to Hart, HIA; Stilwell, diary, September 28–October 21, 1943, www.hoover.org; Tuchman, *Stilwell and the American Experience in China*, 381–95; Stilwell and White, *The Stilwell Papers*, 228–35; Romanus and Sunderland, *Stilwell's Mission to China*, 374–79; Fenby, *Chiang Kai-Shek*, 403–07; Taylor, *The Generalissimo*, 234–40.

4. Stephan Wilkinson, "Over the Hump," *MHQ*, Autumn 2016: 44–51; Theodore White, "The Hump: The Historic Airway to China Was Created by U.S. Heroes," *Life*, September 11, 1944; James Ehrman, "Ways of War and the American Experience in the China-Burma-India Theater, 1942–1945," doctoral dissertation, Kansas State University, 2006, 169–97; Maurer Maurer, ed., *Air Force Combat Units of World War II* (Washington, DC: Office of Air Force History, United States Air Force, 1983), 465–66, 469; Wesley Craven and James Cate, eds., *The Army Air Forces in World War II: Volume VII, Services Around the World* (Washington, DC: Office of Air Force History, United States Air Force, 1983), 114–32; Chennault, *Way of a Fighter*, 233–36; Romanus and Sunderland, *Stilwell's Mission to China*, 314–17.

5. "A History of Soldier Morale in the CBI and IB Theaters," 1–7, Record Group 319, Entry 77, Box 3, Records of the Office of the Chief of Military History, Time Runs Out in CBI; Lieutenant Dorothy Sykes, 159th Station Hospital, oral history, October 4, 1943, Record Group 112, Entry 302, Surgeon General Inspections Branch, Box 218, Number 11; Lieutenant Eleanor Bradley, 181st General Hospital, oral history, December 30, 1944, Record Group 112, Entry 302, Surgeon General Inspections Branch, Box 221, Interview Number 121; Lieutenant Lucy Wainwright, 97th Station Hospital, oral history, October 25, 1943, Record Group 112, Entry 302, Surgeon General Inspections Branch, Box 218, Interview Number 18; Lieutenant Colonel Thomas Fitz-Hugh Jr., 20th General Hospital, oral history, January 11, 1944, Record Group 112, Entry 302, Surgeon General Inspections Branch, Box 218, Interview Number 31; Major A. R. Gallo, oral history, May 23, 1945, Record Group 112, Entry 302, Surgeon General Inspections Branch, Box 222, Interview Number 154; Captain Malcolm Bouton, Venereal Disease Control Officer, oral history, April 4, 1945, Record Group 112, Entry 302, Surgeon General Inspections Branch, Box 221, Interview Number 143; Chesley, oral history, all at NA; Brigadier General Haydon Boatner, "U.S. Command of Chinese Troops in World War II," Haydon Boatner Papers, Box 4, HIA; PFC Louis Marsili, letter to Mrs. Rowland, September–October 1944, Folder 1886, Accession Number 2987; "Rich," letter to his family, no date, Folder 14, Accession Number 699; Lieutenant Howard Longhead, letter to his parents, April 4, 1945, Folder 1797, all at SHSM; Lieutenant William Hughes, letter to Betty and Lyman, February 7, 1944, William Hughes Collection, #2010.101.001, WWIIM; War and Navy Departments, "Pocket Guide to China" and "Pocket Guide to India," both at www.cbi-theater.com; Schrijvers, *Bloody Pacific*, 153–54; Condon-Rall and Cowdrey, *Medical Service in the War Against Japan*, 292–94.

6. Lieutenant Colonel Charles Lutz, liaison officer, Report on Combat Efficiency of the

Chinese Army, February 29, 1944; "A Brief History of the Medical Department of Y-Force Operations Staff,"April 1943–October 1944, Record Group 319, Entry 76, Boxes 3 and 5, respectively, Records of the Office of the Chief of Military History, Stilwell's Command Problems; Major Walter Jones, medical liaison officer, Chinese 10th Engineer Regiment, diary, 1943, Record Group 112, Entry 31, Surgeon General Administrative Records, Box 12; Colonel James McDonough, History of the Medical Service in the CBI, December 1, 1944, Record Group 112, Entry 31, Surgeon General Administrative Records, Box 12; Major John Grindlay, 20th General Hospital, oral history, April 29, 1944, Record Group 112, Entry 302, Surgeon General Inspections Branch, Box 219, Interview Number 58; Lieutenant Colonel Irvine Marshall, Assistant Surgeon, Services of Supply, oral history, January 19, 1945, Record Group 112, Entry 302, Surgeon General Inspections Branch, Box 221, Interview Number 124; Gallo, oral history, all at NA; Brigadier General Haydon Boatner, Instructions for Liaison Officers from this Headquarters to Chinese Units; postwar notes on liaison officers, Haydon Boatner Papers, Box 1, USAMHI; Lieutenant General Joseph Stilwell, Memo for Chiang on Liaison Officers, September 27, 1943; Brigadier General Haydon Boatner, Memo on Chinese Commanders, September 24, 1943, both in Haydon Boatner Papers, Box 4; Boatner, comments on "Crisis Fleeting"; US Command of Chinese Troops in World War II; Brigadier General Frank Dorn, memo for Lieutenant General Joseph Stilwell, "Will the Chinese Fight?"; Colonel Reynolds Condon, liaison officer, Opinions of the Chinese Army, March 21, 1944, both in Frank Dorn Papers, Box 1, Folder 30, all at HIA; Graham Peck, *Two Kinds of Time: A Personal Story of China's Crash into Revolution* (Boston: Houghton Mifflin Company, 1950), 378–379; James Stone, ed., *Crisis Fleeting: Original Reports on Military Medicine in India and Burma During the Second World War* (Washington, DC: Office of the Surgeon General, Department of the Army, 1969), 89–93; Charles Romanus and Riley Sunderland, *United States Army in World War II: China-Burma-India Theater, Stilwell's Command Problems* (Washington, DC: Center of Military History, United States Army, 1987), 33–34, 348.

7. History of Services of Supply, China-Burma-India, 11 June 1942–24 October 1944, Headquarters, SOS, Advance Section Number 3, 4–6, 22–25, 8–6.1 AB V8; Brigadier General Lewis Pick, Report on the Stilwell Road Overland Line of Communications, 5–10, 8–6.1 AC; Historical Section, "History of China-Burma-India Theater," all at CMH; "A History of Soldier Morale," 6; Jones, diary, 1943, both at NA; Nancy Broadbank, "The Context of Heroism: The African American Experience on the Ledo Road," master's thesis, Eastern Michigan University, 1998, 67–80; Ehrman, "Ways of War," 114–17; 330th Engineer Regiment, "Unit History, China-Burma-India Theater of World War II"; "The Ledo Road: General Joseph W. Stilwell's Highway to China," Army pamphlet; "Stilwell Road: The Story of the Ledo Lifeline," Army pamphlet, all at www.cbi-theater.com; Leslie Anders, *The Ledo Road: General Joseph W. Stilwell's Highway to China* (Norman: University of Oklahoma Press, 1965), 34–48; Leo Daugherty, *The Allied Resupply Effort in the China-Burma-India Theater During World War II* (Jefferson, NC: McFarland, 2008), 184–92; Dod, *The Corps of Engineers in the War Against Japan*, 406–12; Lee, *Employment of Negro Troops*, 610–15; Romanus and Sunderland, *Stilwell's Command Problems*, 13–14; Stone, *Crisis Fleeting*, 114–19.

8. History of the Services of Supply, China-Burma-India Theater, 11 June 1942–24 October 1944, Headquarters, Medical Section, 20–42, 8–6.1 AV V18; History of Services of Supply, Advance Section Number 3, 6–18, 14–15, 22–25; Pick, Stilwell Road Overland Line of Communications, 5–16, 23–27, all at CMH; Lieutenant General Joseph Stilwell, memo for Major General Raymond Wheeler, April 6, 1943, Record Group 319, Entry 75, Box 6, Records of the Office of the Chief of Military History, Stilwell's Mission to China; Colonel Isidor Ravdin, 20th General Hospital, oral history,

January 23, 1945, Record Group 112, Entry 302, Surgeon General Inspections Branch, Box 221, Interview Number 127; Fitz-Hugh, oral history; Jones, diary, 1943; McDonough, History of the Medical Service in the CBI, all at NA; Richard Johnston, interview with William Alexander, February 17, 1999, #1351, UNT; Stilwell, diary, August 20, 1943, at www.hoover.org; "The Story of Pick's Pike," Army pamphlet; 330th Engineer Regiment, "Unit History"; "Ledo Lifeline," all at www.cbi-theater .com; Ehrman, "Ways of War," 118–35; Broadbank, "Context of Heroism," 2–3; William Savage, "Experiences in Building the Stilwell (Ledo) Road," *The Missouri Engineer,* January 1946: 5–7, 13–14; Dod, *The Corps of Engineers in the War Against Japan,* 432–39; Lee, *Employment of Negro Troops,* 610–15; Anders, *The Ledo Road,* 59–103; Stone, *Crisis Fleeting,* 108; Stilwell and White, *Stilwell Papers,* 218.

Chapter 14. Makin

1. William Allmon, "Gilbert Islands Campaign: Takin' Makin," *World War II,* November 1998: 58–59; Stanley Sandler, ed., *World War II in the Pacific: An Encyclopedia* (New York & London: Garland, 2001), 301; Philip Crowl and Edmund Love, *United States Army in World War II: Seizure of the Gilberts and Marshalls* (Washington, DC: Office of the Chief of Military History, Department of the Army, 1955), 12–25, 61–62; Henry Shaw, Bernard Nalty, and Edwin Turnbladh, *History of United States Marine Corps Operations in World War II: Central Pacific Drive* (Washington, DC: Historical Branch, G3 Division, Headquarters, US Marine Corps, 1966), 23–28, 49; S. E. Smith, ed., *The United States Marine Corps in World War II, Volume I* (New York: Ace Books, 1969), 272–82; Joseph Alexander, *Utmost Savagery: The Three Days at Tarawa* (New York: Ivy Books, 1995), 13–19, 31–32; Harry Gailey, *Howlin' Mad vs. the Army: Conflict in Command, Saipan 1944* (Novato, CA: Presidio Press, 1986), 53–58; *The Capture of Makin, 20–24 November 1943* (Washington, DC: US Army Center of Military History, 1990), 3–5; Morton, *Strategy and Command,* 522–27; "The U.S. Army Campaigns of World War II: The Central Pacific," pamphlet, 10–14; good information on the Makin raid can be accessed at www.pacificwrecks.com.

2. United States Army Forces in the Central Pacific Area, Participation in Galvanic Operation, 370.2; Lieutenant Colonel S. L. A. Marshall, "Notes on the Makin Operation (20–25 November 1943)," Volume I, 3–5, 9–14, 182–84, 2–3.7 BJ, both at CMH; Colonel S. L. A. Marshall, Supplementary Notes on the Makin Operation, June 2, 1944, 6; Lieutenant Colonel Charles Ferris, memo and letter to Lieutenant Colonel S. L. A. Marshall, November 7, 1943, both in Record Group 319, Entry P56, Box 1, Records of the Office of the Chief of Military History, American Forces in Action, the Capture of Makin; Lieutenant General Robert Richardson, comments on the manuscript of the Gilberts-Marshalls Campaign, January 31, 1949, Record Group 319, Entry 62, Box 4, Records of the Office of the Chief of Military History, Seizure of the Gilberts and the Marshalls; Captain DeWitt Smith, oral history, September 29, 1943, Record Group 112, Entry 302, Surgeon General, Inspections Branch, Box 218, Interview Number 10, all at NA; Lieutenant Colonel Gerard Kelley, diary, October 7–10, 1943, Gerard Kelley Papers, Box 1, HIA; Allmon, "Takin' Makin," *World War II,* 59–60; Samuel Eliot Morison, *History of United States Naval Operations in World War II, Volume VII: Aleutians, Gilberts and Marshalls, June 1942–April 1944* (Boston: Little, Brown, 1951), 110–11; Crowl and Love, *Seizure of the Gilberts and the Marshalls,* 51–56; *Makin,* 26–28; For more information on the 27th Division's background before and during World War II, see www.dmna.gov. Marshall estimated the gross shipping weight per soldier as 1,850 pounds, slightly less than the Navy's estimate of one ton.

3. Observations and Recommendations from the Makin Operation, 5, Record Group 319, Entry P56, Box 1, Records of the Office of the Chief of Military History, the

Capture of Makin; Marshall Supplementary Notes, both at NA; Lieutenant Colonel S. L. A. Marshall, "Makin Operation, Volume II," 1–4, 2–3.7 BJ; Marshall, "Notes on the Makin Operation, Volume I," 4–9, 20, 27–30, both at CMH; Major General Ralph Smith, interview with Mr. Owen Cunningham, Oahu radio station, December 8, 1943, and Major General Ralph Smith, diary, September–November 1943, Ralph Smith Papers, Boxes 1 and 3, respectively; Kelley, diary, October 16 and November 14, 1943, all at HIA; Allmon, "Takin' Makin," 60; Holland Smith and Percy Finch, *Coral and Brass* (New York: Charles Scribner's Sons, 1949), 113–17; S. L. A. Marshall, *Bringing Up the Rear: A Memoir* (Novato, CA: Presidio Press, 1979), 62–63; Gailey, *Howlin' Mad vs. the Army*, 35–48; Morison, *Aleutians, Gilberts and Marshalls*, 97–98, 114–18, 336–41; Crowl and Love, *Seizure of the Gilberts and the Marshalls*, 44–49, 70–74.

4. Major General Ralph Smith, "Participation of Task Force 52.6, 27th Infantry Division in Galvanic (Makin) Operation," December 11, 1943, Record Group 337, Entry 15A, Box 52, Folder 63; Marshall, supplementary notes; Observations and Recommendations from the Makin Operations, 2, all at NA; Marshall, "Notes on the Makin Operation, Volume I," 40–44, CMH; Major General Ralph Smith, letter to Lieutenant General Robert Richardson, December 2, 1943, Ralph Smith Papers, Box 1; Sergeant Adrain Romero, Statement, January 6, 1944, Lieutenant Carl Delashmet, Statement, no date, 193rd Tank Battalion, After Action Report, all in Ralph Smith Papers, Box 12; Kelley, diary, November 19–20, 1943, all at HIA; Allmon, "Takin' Makin," *World War II*, 60–62; Burris Jenkins, *Father Meany and the Fighting 69th* (New York: Frederick Fell, 1944), 15–18; *Capture of Makin*, 17–21, 35–41; Marshall, *Bringing Up the Rear*, 63–64; Crowl and Love, *Seizure of the Gilberts and Marshalls*, 75–82; Morison, *Aleutians, Gilberts and Marshalls*, 120–26. The Marines had a small presence at the Makin landing. A platoon from the V Amphibious Corps Reconnaissance Company landed with the leading LVTs. Father Meany said that Chaplain Giltner's service was conducted in the officers' lounge. Marshall, who attended the service, indicated that it was on deck. Because Marshall was a participant, I employed his version.

5. ATIS, Enemy Publications, Combat Regulations for Island Garrison Forces (Shubi) Provisional Study of Island Defense, December 25, 1943, 12, Record Group 165, Entry 79, Box 213, #415; Observations and Recommendations from the Makin Operations, 3, both at NA; Captain Edwin Kalina, "The Operations of Company M, 105th Infantry (27th Inf. Div.) Battle of Makin Island, 30 Oct-25 Nov 1943 (Personal Experiences of a Company Executive Officer)," Advanced Officers Course, 1946–1947, 13, DRL; Marshall, "Notes on the Makin Operation, Volume I," 43–47, 96–97, 161–64, 185–88, CMH; Aloysius Rolfes, interview with Christopher Jansen, no date, AFC/2001/001/55273, Veterans History Project, Library of Congress, Washington, DC (LOC); Lieutenant Colonel John McDonough, Makin Landing Operation, December 9, 1943, Ralph Smith Papers, Box 12; 193rd Tank Battalion AAR, both at HIA; Lieutenant Willard Marlowe as told to Lieutenant L. R. Barnill, "Taking Makin," *Infantry Journal*, June 1944: 28–29; Allmon, "Takin' Makin," *World War II*, 63–64; *Capture of Makin*, 51–63; Crowl and Love, *Seizure of the Gilberts and Marshalls*, 82–88.

6. Lieutenant Colonel Lafayette Yarwood, letter to Major General Ralph Smith, February 17, 1949; Captain Warren Lindquist, letter to Major General Ralph Smith, February 10, 1949; Father Stephen Meany, letter to Major General Ralph Smith, March 17, 1949, and letter to Colonel Gerard Kelley, March 1, 1949; Smith interview with Cunningham, all in Box 1, Ralph Smith Papers; Lieutenant Colonel Gerard Kelley, letter to Mrs. Marie Conroy, January 9, 1944, letter to Mr. Benjamin Conroy, January 18, 1944; Colonel Gerard Kelley, letter to Major General Ralph Smith, February 9, 1949,

all in Box 1, Gerard Kelley Papers; Kelley, diary, October 16, November 20, 1943, all
at HIA; Marshall, "Notes on the Makin Operation, Volume I," 74–81, CMH; "Colonel
J.G. Conroy Killed in Battle for Makin Island," *Brooklyn Eagle*, November 24, 1943;
Colonel James Gardiner Conroy, obituary, *Brooklyn Eagle*, October 23, 1947; Father
Stephen Meany, letter to Mrs. Agatha Berthiaume, August 9, 1946, this and other
information about Berthiaume at "A Short Story of Private Jean Paul Berthiaume,"
www.sutori.com; Jenkins, *Father Meany and the Fighting 69th*, 29–52; Marshall,
Bringing Up the Rear, 64; Crowl and Love, *Seizure of the Gilberts and Marshalls*, 96–
97. In late December 1943, Father Meany actually helped officiate a requiem funeral
mass for Berthiaume. After the war, Meany arranged for a regular mass to be said
for Berthiaume at a New Jersey parish.

7. Colonel Gerard Kelley, letter to Major General Harry Maloney, January 31, 1949,
Record Group 319, Entry 62, Box 4, Records of the Office of the Chief of Military
History, Seizure of the Gilberts and the Marshalls; Colonel S. L. A. Marshall, letter
to Dr. Kent Roberts Greenfield, April 2, 1952, Record Group 319, Entry 62, Box 6,
Records of the Office of the Chief of Military History, Seizure of the Gilberts and the
Marshalls; ATIS, Information Bulletin, Self-Immolation as a Factor in Japanese
Military Psychology, April 4, 1944, Record Group 165, Entry 79, Box 314, Bulletin #14,
6; Combat Regulations for Island Garrison Forces, 25; Observations and Recom-
mendations from the Makin Operations, 4, all at NA; Marshall, "Notes on the Makin
Operation, Volume I," 44, 97–100, 106–08, 117–21, CMH; Rolfes, interview, LOC; Ka-
lina, "Operations of Company M," 16–17, DRL; Lieutenant Colonel Gerard Kelley,
letter to Mrs. Agnes Farr (mother of Lieutenant Edward Gallagher), April 6, 1944;
Mrs. Agnes Farr, letter to Colonel Gerard Kelley, March 31, 1944, both in Box 2, Gerard Kelley Papers, HIA; Marlow, "Taking Makin," *Infantry Journal*, 30; *Capture of
Makin*, 70–75, 98–99; Crowl and Love, *Seizure of the Gilberts and Marshalls*, 108–11.

8. Marshall letter to Greenfield; Marshall Supplementary Notes; Conroy letter to Maloney, all at NA; Major General Ralph Smith, letter to Captain Ernest Flemig, March
21, 1949; Lieutenant Colonel William Van Antwerp, letter to Major General Ralph
Smith, March 24, 1949; Captain Warner McCabe, aide-de-camp, letter to Major General Ralph Smith, February 22, 1949; Captain Ernest Flemig, letter to Major General
Ralph Smith, March 27, 1949; Major Jacob Herzog, letter to Colonel William Van
Antwerp, March 28, 1949; Colonel Gerard Kelley, letter to Mrs. Marie Conroy, February 14, 1949; letter to Major General Ralph Smith, August 15, 1949; Meany, letters
to Kelley and Smith; Yarwood, letter to Smith; Lindquist, letter to Smith, all in Box
1, Ralph Smith Papers, HIA; Norman Cooper, "The Military Career of General Holland M. Smith, USMC," dissertation, University of Alabama, 1974, 1, and chapters
1–10; Captain Charles Coates, Statement on Makin Battle, published within Robert
Sherrod, "An Answer and Rebuttal to 'Smith Versus Smith': The Saipan Controversy," *Infantry Journal*, January 1949: 25; Norman Cooper, *A Fighting General: The
Biography of Gen Holland M. "Howlin' Mad" Smith* (Quantico, VA: Marine Corps
Association, 1987), 113–19; Alexander, *Utmost Savagery*, 225–26; Marshall, *Bringing
Up the Rear*, 69, 74, 77–78; Holland Smith and Finch, *Coral and Brass*, 123–129; Gailey, *Howlin' Mad vs. the Army*, 20–34, 60–61, 71–82. Flemig was in charge of the
burial detail for Conroy's body. In 1949, when Holland Smith published excerpts of
his memoir in the *Saturday Evening Post*, his attacks on the Army's proficiency and
claims about Conroy's body set off a firestorm of angry rejoinders from his Army
counterparts. This prompted Ralph Smith to compile a mass of evidence that Conroy's body had been recovered and had received a proper burial. Knowing the pain
that Holland Smith's unfounded accusations had caused for the Conroy family,
Colonel Kelley immediately wrote to the colonel's widow and shared the evidence of
his proper burial. By that time, Conroy's remains had been brought home and in-

terred in Brooklyn's Holy Cross Cemetery, where they still lie today alongside his beloved Marie, who died in 1957. The second volume of this series will cover the ultimate showdown between Holland Smith and his Army colleagues, particularly in relation to the Battle of Saipan.

9. Marshall letter to Greenfield; Smith, Participation of Task Force 52.6, 27th Infantry Division in Galvanic, 7, both at NA; Marshall, "Notes on the Makin Operation, Volume I," 100, 120–24; Marshall, "Makin Operation, Volume II," 23, both at CMH; Captain Thew Wright, Observations on Makin Operation, 2, Ralph Smith Papers, Box 3; McDonough, Makin Landing Operation, both at HIA; Kalina, "Operations of Company M," 25, DRL; Cooper, "The Military Career of General Holland M. Smith," dissertation, 228; Marshall, *Bringing Up the Rear*, 70; Gailey, *Howlin' Mad vs. the Army*, 76–77; Crowl and Love, *Seizure of the Gilberts and Marshalls*, 108.

10. Marshall, letter to Greenfield; Smith, Participation of Task Force 52.6, 27th Infantry Division in Galvanic; ATIS, Self-Immolation as a Factor in Japanese Military Psychology, 16, all at NA; Harold Smith, *Chicago Tribune*, dispatch, December 4, 1943, Gerard Kelley Papers, Box 1, HIA; Marshall, "Notes on the Makin Operations, Volume I," 127–58, CMH; Lieutenant Colonel S. L. A. Marshall, "The Fight on Saki Night," *Infantry Journal*, April 1944: 8–15; S. L. A. Marshall, *Battle at Best: Electrifying Accounts of Action at the Front Line—As It Really Was* (New York: Jove Books, 1963), 143–169; Morison, *Aleutians, Gilberts and Marshalls*, 139–41; Crowl and Love, *Seizure of the Gilberts and Marshalls*, 122–26; Alexander, *Utmost Savagery*, 250; Cooper, *A Fighting General*, 119; Shaw, Nalty, and Turnbladh, *Central Pacific Drive*, 90, 638. For information on the sinking of *Liscome Bay* and the deaths of Mullinix and Miller, see www.navalmuseum.org.

Index

Note: Page numbers in *italics* indicate maps and illustrations.